Visual Basic 6: The Complete Reference

Visual Basic 6: The Complete Reference

Noel Jerke

Osborne/**McGraw-Hill**
Berkeley New York St. Louis San Francisco
Auckland Bogotá Hamburg London Madrid
Mexico City Milan Montreal New Delhi Panama City
Paris São Paulo Singapore Sydney
Tokyo Toronto

Osborne/**McGraw-Hill**
2600 Tenth Street
Berkeley, California 94710
U.S.A.

For information on translations or book distributors outside the U.S.A., or to arrange bulk purchase discounts for sales promotions, premiums, or fund-raisers, please contact Osborne/**McGraw-Hill** at the above address.

Visual Basic 6: The Complete Reference

34567890 AGM AGM   019876543210

ISBN 0-07-211855-5

Publisher
Brandon A. Nordin

Editor-in-Chief
Scott Rogers

Acquisitions Editor
Wendy Rinaldi

Project Editor
Madhu Prasher

Editorial Assistant
Monika Faltiss

Technical Editor
Rima Regas

Copy Editor
Judith Brown

Proofreader
Karen Mead

Indexer
Valerie Robbins

Computer Designers
Ann Sellers
Jani Beckwith

Illustrator
Brian Wells
Beth Young

Series Design
Peter Hancik

Cover Design
Regan Honda

This book is dedicated to my daughter Gabrielle Nicole Jerke. May God bless you and be with you little one!

About the Author

Noel is the Senior Vice President of Operations for Judd's OnLine, Inc. in Winchester, VA. He manages their daily operations, which provides a wide range of businesses with Internet solutions. Noted customers include Martha Stewart, Reba McEntire, and the Air Force. Noel received a B.S. degree in Computer Science and Economics from Trinity University, San Antonio, TX. Noel is an experienced technology manager and has a strong background in corporate development, e-commerce, and Internet technologies. He is currently a technical editor for Security Advisor and is a contributing writer for Office/Access/Visual Basic Advisor. The focus of his writing involves a wide variety of popular technology topics such as client/server programming, Internet programming, e-commerce, and developing and building Web sites. Noel has also authored Waite Group Press' *Visual Basic Multimedia How-To, Visual Basic API How-To, Visual Basic Script Interactive Course,* and *Visual Basic Client Server How-To.* Noel can be reached at noelj@juddsonline.com or you can visit his Web site at http://www.activepubs.com.

Contents at a Glance

Part V
Appendixes

Contents

Part II

Working with Windows

Part III
Client/Server Development

Part IV

Internet Application Development

Part V

Appendixes

Acknowledgments

As always, I thank my wonderful wife for supporting me in this effort. It was a big push to get this book done before we became parents.

Also, I would like to thank Osborne/McGraw-Hill and especially Wendy Rinaldi for giving me the opportunity to write this book. Visual Basic is a powerful tool that all developers should have in their programming tool set.

Last, but not least, I would like to thank the Lord for the many blessings on our family. May it be to your ultimate glory.

Introduction

Visual Basic is one of the most popular programming languages on the market today. Microsoft has positioned it to fit multiple purposes in development. The language ranges from lightweight Visual Basic Script programming, to application-specific programming with Visual Basic for Applications, and finally, full-fledged enterprise development with Visual Basic 6.0.

Visual Basic 6.0 is designed to deploy applications across the enterprise and to scale to nearly any size needed. The ability to develop object models, database integration, server components, and Internet/intranet applications provides an extensive range of capabilities and tools for the developer.

This book offers the reader a thorough review of all the key concepts and capabilities to be found in Visual Basic 6.0. An introduction is provided to the program's many new features, including the exciting new Internet capabilities. You will find good descriptions of the key capabilities followed by code examples. This book seeks to provide very clear and straightforward implementations of key features with detailed explanations of how each works. The reader should walk away with an in-depth understanding of how to utilize all of VB's capabilities for building industrial-strength enterprise applications.

In Chapter 1, "What Is New in Visual Basic 6.0," we review the many new features of Visual Basic. Topics include the new CoolBar control, building Internet/intranet applications, and data access.

Chapter 2, "Working with the Visual Basic Development Environment," explains one of Visual Basic's many strengths is the development environment. In this chapter we review the menu structure, toolbars, and coding tools. Also, we create sample projects to review the process for building an application from scratch.

In Chapter 3, "Building Objects in Visual Basic," you'll read that one of the most important features of Visual Basic is the ability to create and utilize objects. This chapter reviews the class object as well as how to build a sample object model with classes. The fundamentals of an object's properties, methods, and relations are reviewed in the context of Visual Basic.

Chapter 4, "Connecting to Databases" shows that building data-driven applications is another key feature of Visual Basic. Version 6.0 adds a powerful new capability—ActiveX Data Objects (ADO). This is the replacement technology for Remote Data Objects (RDO). The new data environment add-in will be utilized for adding data capabilities to our applications. And Visual Basic has added powerful new data reporting capabilities.

An exciting new feature of Visual Basic is the ability to build server-side and client-side Internet applications. Chapter 5, "Introduction to Building Internet Applications," reviews the creation of IIS applications and DHTML applications.

They didn't put the "Visual" in Visual Basic for nothing. In Chapter 6, "Designing User Interfaces," we explore user interface design with Visual Basic forms. Topics include menus, toolbars, tab strips, ActiveX controls, and much more.

Visual Basic applications run in the Windows environment. This rich environment provides many tools for working in your application. Topics in Chapter 7, "Building Programs in the Windows Environment," include working with printers, building common dialog boxes, and working with drives, files, folders, and graphics.

In Chapter 8, "Working with the Windows API," you'll read that the Windows environment provides a rich application programming interface (API) for building applications. Visual Basic does a good job of hiding many of these complex API calls. But, when we need to, we can dip into the rich set of functions, structures, and constants to enhance our applications. This chapter reviews utilizing the API within Visual Basic.

Now that you have built the foundation of your application, what do you do? In Chapter 9, "Error Handling, Debugging, and Deploying Applications," we review techniques for debugging your application, building solid error handling, and utilizing the Package and Deployment wizard to deploy your application.

One of the most powerful features of enterprise development with Visual Basic is the ability to build multitier applications. In Chapter 10, "Building Multitier Applications," we lay out the multitier foundation of a project tracking system. The chapter discusses how this application will be implemented in Visual Basic.

In Chapter 11, "Building the User Interface," we begin working on the user interface tier of our project tracking system. The interface will be designed for efficiency and ease of use. Appropriate considerations will be given for interfacing with the other tiers of the application.

Once we have the design and user interface in place, we are ready to build the business logic tier behind our project tracking system. In Chapter 12, "Building the Business Logic," a class structure will be implemented for handling the project tracking business logic.

Once we have the application built, we are ready to break it up into the different tier applications and deploy them. In Chapter 13, "Deploying the Tracking System," a review of ActiveX EXEs, ActiveX DLLs, and the different deployment methods is done.

In Chapter 14, "Building IIS Applications," we jump into the new world of Internet development in Visual Basic 6. We review how to build IIS applications that integrate with a database and are supported by multiple browsers.

Dynamic HTML is an excellent way of building highly interactive applications for Web pages. With Internet Explorer 4.x you can build applications that are data driven and live in a Web browser. In Chapter 15, "Building Data-Driven DHTML Applications," we explore building a data-driven application.

ActiveX documents are forms that can appear within Internet browser windows but take on their normal appearance. In Chapter 16, "Building ActiveX Documents," we explore turning a Visual Basic application into an ActiveX document.

One of the hottest topics on the Internet today is e-commerce. With Visual Basic's new Internet capabilities, we can build our own e-commerce shopping basket system. In Chapter 17, "Designing an E-Commerce System," we lay out the object model and database structure.

The design built in Chapter 17 is implemented in Chapter 18, "Building an E-Commerce System," into an e-commerce shopping basket system utilizing an IIS application.

In the appendixes we review the different application types available in Visual Basic, the Active Server Pages object model, and the ActiveX controls provided with Visual Basic.

Conventions

Throughout this book, you will find several conventions to help guide you. The first is the use of notes and tips. These give extra guidance and insight into the particular topic being discussed.

For the programming projects, you will find a CD icon to indicate when the sample code can be found on the CD. For the projects that have form controls and properties, you will find a table outlining the form/object and the appropriate properties. Note that not all properties are shown—typically when the defaults are the settings.

*All IIS Applications will need to be copied to your local system before they can be run since the files require updating. Also, in general you will want to copy files off of the CD to your local system. **You will need to set the read/write properties to allow for writing to the files**.*

The code in chapters is clearly explained in step-by-step descriptions in the text as well as comments in the code itself. Some of the exercises in the chapter will require at least the Professional Edition of Visual Basic. It is highly recommended that the Enterprise Edition be used to take advantage of the full benefits of Visual Basic 6.0.

The Complete Reference

Visual Basic 6

Part I

Visual Basic 6.0 Overview

In Part I we will review the new features in Visual Basic and summarize the core features in the tool. The first chapter introduces you to the many new features in Visual Basic. Chapter 2 reviews working with the Visual Basic development environment, including the interface, toolbars, and additional features. Chapter 3 summarizes the important concept of building and working with objects in Visual Basic. This key concept is the foundation for any type of enterprise-level development.

In Chapter 4 we will review the data access features of Visual Basic, including the new ActiveX Data Object. Finally, in Chapter 5 Visual Basic 6.0's new powerful Internet features are introduced.

Many of the concepts laid down in the first part will be expanded in the rest of the book. If you are new to Visual Basic, Part I should give you a good overview of the core features of the product. If you are an advanced Visual Basic programmer, you will learn about the new features in Visual Basic.

Chapter 1

What Is New in Visual Basic 6.0?

V isual Basic 5.0 made several leaps forward in its ability to build and deploy corporate applications. The addition of classes for object-oriented development, creation of controls, and COM objects all made Visual Basic 5.0 a powerhouse for client/server development. Visual Basic 6.0 takes the next steps in moving the language forward to the Internet and building on the robust foundation developed in Visual Basic 5.0. In this chapter we will review some of the additions and enhancements to the language and development environment.

Before you launch into serious Visual Basic 6.0 development, you are encouraged to review the MSDN (Microsoft Developer Network) CD that comes with Visual Basic. The CD contains extensive documentation on the new features and capabilities of Visual Basic 6.0. These new features will be covered in this book, but MSDN is always a good resource.

If you are new to the world of Visual Basic, you may be confused about what the differences are between version 6.0, Visual Basic for Applications (VBA), and Visual Basic Script (VBScript). The easiest way to differentiate among them is by complexity and richness of the Visual Basic language and development environment. VBScript is a lightweight scripting language for use in Web page development. Specifically, VBScript is used in creating Active Server Pages on an Internet Information Server (IIS) and in client-side programming of browsers. VBA is used for programming in applications such as Microsoft Office and is supported in different flavors by Microsoft Excel and PowerPoint. In fact, third-party tools such as Visio are supporting VBA as an application development tool. Finally, Visual Basic 6.0 is used in creating applications of all types, including standard client applications, server applications, and Internet applications.

Visual Basic 6.0 itself has three versions. The basic version, Learning Edition, is built primarily for creation of stand-alone applications and basic programming. The Professional Edition provides developers with a full set of tools for developing solutions, including ActiveX controls, the Internet Information Server application designer, integrated visual database tools and data environment, ActiveX Data Objects (ADO), and the Dynamic HTML page designer. The Enterprise Edition includes all the features of the Professional Edition plus SQL Server, Transaction Server, IIS, SourceSafe, SNA Server, and much more.

Microsoft has added significant functionality in several core areas. They are outlined as follows:

- **Data access:** A key addition for helping programmers build database applications is support for ActiveX Data Objects, Microsoft's new data access technology. Development tools include a SQL editor, data environment for developing data objects, and data report designer.

- **Internet features:** What may be the most significant new functionality is the ability to create both server- and client-side Internet applications. Visual Basic finally comes to the Internet.

- **New and updated controls:** Microsoft continues its legacy of creating and enhancing controls for supporting rapid application development.

- **Component creation:** Visual Basic continues to emerge as a world-class development tool for creating and working with components ranging from ActiveX controls to integration with Microsoft's Transaction Server.

- **Language features:** True to the long tradition of Visual Basic, there have been many language enhancements that make working with strings, numbers, and objects even easier and more powerful.

- **Wizards:** Wizards and more wizards have been added to the tool set to support rapid application development of enterprise-level applications.

We will review many of these new features in this chapter and will explore their use throughout the rest of the book.

Data Access

The ability to connect to databases is crucial for any type of corporate Visual Basic development. Typically, the developer is either accessing a local Microsoft Access MDB file or connecting to a back-end Microsoft SQL Server or Oracle Server database. In Visual Basic 5.0, the big change was the use of Remote Data Objects (RDO) for data access. In Visual Basic 6.0, we have yet one more type of data object; you guessed it—ActiveX Data Objects (ADO).

Note *Those of you who have been doing Active Server Pages Internet development over the last year are probably familiar with the use of ADO 1.0/1.5. It has been a key part of building database connectivity for Web applications with Internet Information Server and Visual InterDev. Version 2.0 of ADO is included with Visual Basic 6.0.*

When Microsoft designed ADO, they wanted to make it simple and widely accessible by utilizing the OLE DB technology (see the MSDN) and making it callable through COM (component object model). Compared to Remote Data Objects (RDO) and the Data Access Object (DAO), ADO is much simpler to understand and implement. The following diagram shows the ADO object model:

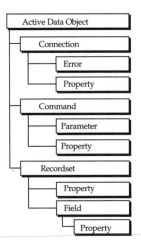

Table 1-1 summarizes the primary objects in ADO. Chapter 4 will delve deeper into the ADO object model and its use in database development in your applications.

Microsoft makes it very clear that ADO is their "premier data access technology." Certainly RDO and DAO are still supported for backward compatibility, but for all new development, ADO should be strongly considered. However, if you have existing applications built in DAO or RDO, you do not have to plan migration to ADO immediately. DAO and RDO continue with robust support and some improvements.

ADO Object	Description
Connection	Maintains connection information such as cursor type, connect string, query time-out, connection time-out, and default database.
Command	Maintains information about a command, such as a query string, parameter definitions, etc. Note that you can execute a command string on a Connection object of a query string as part of opening a Recordset object *without* defining a Command object. The Command object is particularly useful when you want to define query parameters or execute a stored procedure that returns output parameters. The Command object supports a number of properties to describe the type and purpose of the query and support ADO optimization.

Table 1-1. *ADO Object Definitions*

ADO Object	Description
Error	Contains extended error information about error conditions raised by the data provider. Since multiple errors can be returned by the data provider, the error collection can have multiple error objects defined.
Field	Contains information about a single column of data within a recordset. The Recordset object uses the Fields collection to contain all of its Field objects. This Field information includes data type, precision, numeric scale, defined size, actual size, and much more. The Field object is useful for evaluating the type of data returned. Two key methods, AppendChuck and GetChuck, are supported for working with large binary data.
Parameter	Contains a single parameter associated with a command. The Command object uses the Parameters collection to contain all of its Parameter objects. ADO Parameter objects can be created automatically by sending queries to the database. Most often this feature is used with stored procedures for passing and returning parameters.
Property	Contains a provider-defined characteristic of an ADO object. ADO objects have two types of properties: built-in and dynamic. Built-in properties are those properties implemented in ADO and available to any new ADO object. Dynamic properties are defined by the underlying data provider and appear in the Properties collection for the appropriate ADO object. For example, a property may indicate whether a Recordset object supports transactions or updating.
Recordset	Contains a set of rows returned from a query, including a cursor into those rows. You can open a Recordset object (that is, execute a query) without explicitly opening a Connection object. However, if you do first create a Connection object, you can open multiple Recordset objects on the same connection. This is the object you use to retrieve the results of your query (for example, rs("chrName")).

Table 1-1.   *ADO Object Definitions* (continued)

Developing for the Internet

Who can deny the rapid rise of Internet technology? Where a business is deploying intranets, extranets, or Internet sites, Internet applications have become pervasive and crucial to corporate development. With Visual Basic 5.0, you were primarily limited to using either an Internet Explorer Web browser embedded in your application or the Internet controls for initiating FTP and HTTP transfers. The other option was to do Active Server Pages scripting and call COM objects built into Visual Basic. That has all changed with Visual Basic 6.0. In fact, the enhancements to Internet capabilities are among the most exciting aspects of Visual Basic 6.0.

Internet Information Server (IIS) Applications

As you would suspect from the title, Microsoft has integrated Windows NT's Web Server, Internet Information Server (IIS), with Visual Basic 6.0. An IIS application is a Visual Basic application that uses a combination of client-side HTML and server-side Visual Basic code to build a browser-based application. The IIS application code resides on the server, where it receives requests from a browser, runs code associated with the requests, and returns responses to the browser in HTML format. For those of you familiar with Active Server Pages development, there is some similarity. In fact, the ASP object model is available within the IIS application. Before you can build and run IIS applications, you will need to be running Internet Information Server 3.x or higher (preferably version 4.x) on your Windows NT Server.

IIS applications are best thought of in the same light as three-tier client/server development. The first tier is the data layer that makes up the database. The second tier is the business logic. And the third tier traditionally is the Visual Basic forms-based user interface. With IIS applications, you can replace the third-tier user interface with a Web browser that is running anywhere on your intranet or on the Internet. And you have complete control from your Visual Basic application as to how that user interface responds to user actions.

IIS applications simply intercept a user request and return an HTML page to the browser. Of course, you have the full power of Visual Basic behind that process. For example, you can query databases, replace complete sections of the page based on the user response, create pages on the fly, or access any preexisting business objects you may have on your internal network.

IIS applications replace traditional functionality found in CGI/PERL development and can replace or enhance existing Active Server Pages applications. The beauty of using Visual Basic is that you get a full-featured programming language behind your Web pages instead of a limited scripting environment. But, to the user, you are sending out standard HTML Web pages. It is important to note that IIS applications do *not* require the use of Internet Explorer. It is up to you as the application developer to decide which browser(s) specification you will build your pages to support.

Note *Internet programming has gone through several phases of development. The first applications were typically Common Gateway Interface (CGI) based with supporting languages such as PERL for working with text. The second generation was database-focused scripting environments such as Microsoft's Internet Information Server and Visual Basic Script or JScript. Now we are beginning to see the next generation of Internet development tools with Visual Basic 6.0 and its powerful new features.*

For the developer, an IIS application is made up of a special type of object called a *web class*, which in turn contains a series of resources called *web items*. The web class acts as the central functional unit of the application (similar to the traditional form), processing data from the browser and sending information to the users. You define a series of procedures that determine how the web class responds to these requests. The web items are the HTML pages and other data the web class can send to the browser in response to a request. You can of course use traditional Visual Basic class modules for encapsulation of business logic, and make references to existing COM objects.

Note *The component object model (COM) is a platform-independent, distributed, object-oriented system for creating binary software components that can interact. Whew .... Basically that means the objects expose their methods for getting basic information passed back and forth between each other. That "communication" is irrespective of operating system (platform independence) and distribution (location and/or machine). As we will see throughout this book, the use of objects that can interact and encapsulate functionality is crucial to building applications.*

Active Server Pages applications are somewhat similar to IIS applications. Both allow the developer to create dynamic Web sites that perform their processing on the server rather than in the client browser. Active Server Pages are for script developers interested in authoring Web pages with limited business logic functionality. ASP offers the powerful capability of intermingling script code with HTML code on the same page. IIS applications are for Visual Basic developers building complete Web-based applications, rather than Web pages. IIS applications allow for complicated business processing in the traditional client/server sense. The benefit to both is that the client can access the application from any type of platform and any type of browser.

DHTML Applications

You have probably heard of Dynamic HTML (DHTML) programming for both Internet Explorer 4.x and Netscape 4.x. DHTML programming resides in the client browser on the client machine. It traditionally consists of manipulating the browser interface using client-side script code such as JavaScript or VBScript. Microsoft has added one more powerful method for building DHTML applications using Visual Basic 6.0.

A DHTML application is a Visual Basic application that uses a combination of the Internet Explorer 4.x DHTML object model and compiled Visual Basic code on the client machine in a Web browser. A DHTML application resides on the browser machine, where it interprets and responds to actions that the end user performs in the browser (sounds like a Visual Basic form!). The DHTML application is essentially a Web page on the client machine that uses Visual Basic code to react to users' actions on the page. Such actions include clicking on a hyperlink, a mouse movement, or responses to browser events.

The chief benefit of using DHTML applications on the client side is that it does not require a trip back to the server to change the page makeup. For example, if the user is using a calculator that needs to dynamically update the user interface based on the user's input, the page could calculate and update the interface in the browser with no trips to the server. The difference, of course, with Visual Basic is that you have the full power of the Visual Basic programming language at your disposal. You are not limited to a scripting environment.

A DHTML application is a group of HTML pages that work together to perform a process. You write Visual Basic code to handle events that occur when these pages are viewed in the browser. You can respond to events that occur on any element on the page—from clicking a button, to loading an image, to passing the mouse over a certain part of the page. If this sounds similar to Visual Basic's forms programming, you are correct. The only limitation is that the Visual Basic application cannot extend back over the Internet to touch business logic or databases on the server. That would require the user to submit the page back to the server. Of course, on the back end, there could be an IIS application just waiting to respond.

DHTML applications are designed to work best on intranets. An *intranet* is a Web site or series of Web sites that belong to an organization and can be accessed only by the organization's members. Many corporations use an intranet, rather than the Internet, to offer their employees easy access to corporate information, such as customer order information, sales data, or vacation hours, while preventing outside access to that data. Within this controlled environment, you can be assured of the browser population, bandwidth needs, and so on.

In addition to writing Visual Basic code to hook up to a Web page, you can use a special page designer in Visual Basic to create DHTML Web pages that act as the user interface of your application. You can also pull an existing Web page into Visual Basic and modify it. This allows you to tailor the process to your preferences—if you are familiar with HTML and want to create your own pages, you can do so without using the DHTML page designer. The DHTML page designer does not natively support features such as cascading style sheets (CSS) and other extended HTML coding. But, of course, you can develop your Web pages in your favorite Web programming tool and import them into your DHTML application.

In the last section of this book we will take an in-depth look at Microsoft's new Internet features for Visual Basic 6.0. Don't discount the possibilities of improving existing forms-based client/server applications by extending them to the Internet or building a robust Web interface.

New Controls and Application Design Capabilities

What would ADO be without a data control to go with it? Of course, for DAO and RDO there were corresponding controls to make integrating data into your user interface easy to accomplish. The ADO data control uses ADO to quickly create connections between data bound controls and your database. *Data bound controls* are any controls that feature a DataSource property.

As with RDO and DAO, you can use the ActiveX Data Objects directly in your applications. The ADO data control has the advantage of being a graphic control and an easy-to-use interface that allows you to create database applications with a minimum of code. But, if you want to abstract your data away into a business logic tier, giving the user direct access to the data with the ADO control (see Figure 1-1) breaks some of the rules.

Several of the controls found in Visual Basic's toolbox can be data bound, including the CheckBox, ComboBox, Image, Label, ListBox, PictureBox, and TextBox controls. Additionally, Visual Basic includes several data bound ActiveX controls, such as DataGrid, DataCombo, Chart, and DataList. You can also create your own data bound ActiveX controls or purchase controls from other third-party developers.

Now that most people know about the new coolbar that came out with Internet Explorer 3.0 and has become a mainstay for Windows interface design (even for Netscape), how could Microsoft leave that out of Visual Basic 6.0? Well, indeed they

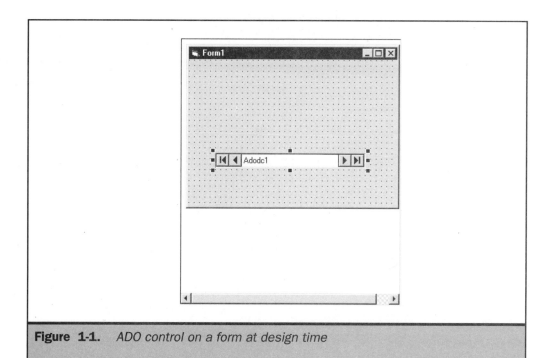

Figure 1-1. *ADO control on a form at design time*

didn't. The CoolBar control contains a collection of Band objects used to create a configurable toolbar that is associated with a form. On that coolbar you can place other controls on each band and associate them with the band. To get started with a little programming for the book, let's take a look at SampleProj1 on the CD for Chapter 1.

Go ahead and create a new Standard EXE project. In order to use the coolbar, go to the Project menu and select Components. The coolbar is found in the Microsoft Windows Common Controls-3 6.0 component. And the flat scroll bar is found in the Microsoft Windows Common Controls-2 6.0 component. Once these two are added to your project, you can drag and drop one coolbar and one flat scroll bar to your form. To build our demonstration, we will draw a text box, a progress bar, and a command button on the coolbar.

The next step is to tie each of these three controls to one of the bands on the coolbar. Follow these steps:

1. Right-click on the coolbar and bring up the properties.

2. Go to the Bands tab, as shown in Figure 1-2.

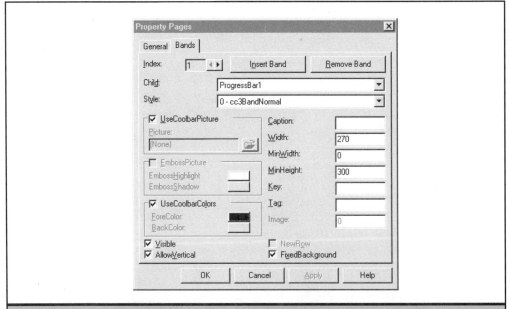

Figure 1-2. *Bands tab setting for the CoolBar control*

3. For each Band index, select a child control to display on that band. When you do that, it ties one of the controls to be placed on the coolbar to that band.

4. Add the flat scroll bar to the page as well, to see its new design style for your applications.

5. Set the key properties of all the controls as outlined in Table 1-2.

Component/Property	Setting
Form	Sample1
Caption	"Chapter 1 - Sample 1"
CoolBar	CoolBar1
Child1	ProgressBar1
Child2	Command1
Child3	Text1
Text Box	Text1
Text	Text1
Command Button	Command1
Caption	"Click!"
ProgressBar	ProgressBar1
Appearance	1
Flat Scroll Bar	ScrbDemo
LargeChange	25
Max	500
Small Change	10

Table 1-2.   *Components and Properties for the Form*

Now we are ready to place some code behind our user interface. Add the following to the click event of our Command button:

```
Private Sub Command1_Click()
'   Check the value of the progress bar control
'   If the value is 0 then set it to 10.  Otherwise
'   add on half of the remaining value.
If ProgressBar1.Value = 0 Then
    '   Set the value to 10 for starters
    ProgressBar1.Value = 10
Else
    '   Increase the value by half of the percentage left to go
    ProgressBar1.Value = ProgressBar1.Value + ((100 - _
    ProgressBar1.Value) / 2)
End If

End Sub
```

Once you have the controls set up on the page, add the code above to the click event of the Command button. This code increases the value of the progress bar but ensures it never exceeds 100 percent by adding half of the remaining percentage.

Now we are ready to run the application. Upon launch, the page is loaded with the coolbar configured with our three controls. Figure 1-3 shows the form at run time. Go ahead and click on the button a few times and move the coolbar bands around. Notice how the size of each of the controls changes with the size of the band. Also click a few times on the scroll bar to see its effect as well. Figure 1-4 shows the project with the coolbar and scroll bar changed.

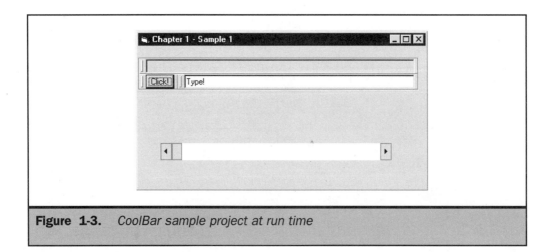

Figure 1-3. *CoolBar sample project at run time*

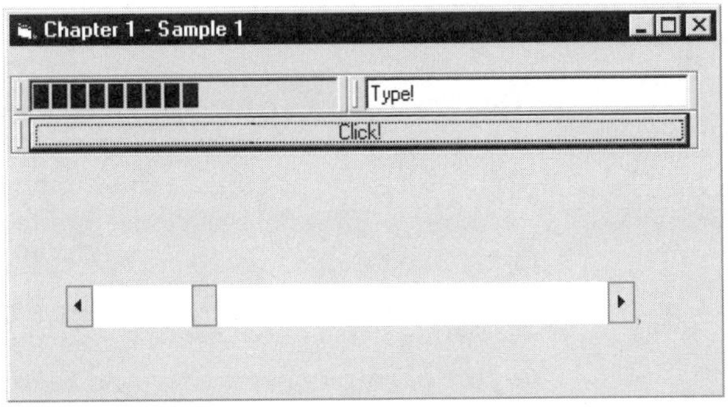

Figure 1-4. *CoolBar sample project with the coolbar and scroll bar changed*

New and Improved: VB's Control Set
Gets Bigger and Better

Besides the coolbar and ADO data control, a host of new controls have been added to VB. And many of the existing controls have been updated. If you are new to programming in Visual Basic, the use of controls in your applications is crucial to building superior user interfaces and adding encapsulated functionality. For example, instead of having to write a complete set of data access tools, you can use a control such as DBGrid for displaying and updating data. Complete functionality right out of the box (or control) has always been one of the hallmark benefits of Visual Basic. It is this ability to buy functionality for your applications right off the shelf that makes Visual Basic one of the best rapid application development (RAD) tools on the market. Table 1-3 outlines some of the more notable additions and changes. You can find a reference in Appendix C.

Control or Enhancement	Description
DataGrid	An OLE DB-aware version of DBGrid, this control allows you to quickly build an application for viewing and editing recordsets. The key is that it supports the new ADO data control.
DataList, DataCombo	These controls are OLE DB versions of the DBList and DBCombo controls. They also support the new ADO data control.

Table 1-3. *New Controls and Enhancements*

Control or Enhancement	Description
DataRepeater	This great addition to your database tool set lets you build a custom control that has data bound controls on it. The control can then be placed on a form in your application with the data repeater and have it repeat the user control. For example, you can build one control that can be used to build reporting lists easily. An example would be a report of employees that would repeat a series of controls showing the report data.
DateTimePicker	This control provides a drop-down calendar for quick entry of dates and times.
Hierarchical FlexGrid	This updated version of the FlexGrid control, in addition to supporting all the functionality of FlexGrid, can display a hierarchy of ADO recordsets. Each recordset returned is displayed as a separate band within the grid and can be formatted independently. Note that none of the data is editable.
ImageCombo	This control behaves like the standard ComboBox control with one addition: you can now add images to the list of items.
MonthView	The end user can use this control to pick dates and contiguous ranges of dates from a graphic representation of a calendar.
ImageList–Enhancements	Support for .gif, .jpg, and .cur files has been added.
Dynamic controls	A key new feature is programmatically adding and removing controls to or from a form at run time.

Table 1-3. *New Controls and Enhancements* (continued)

Tip *Check out MSDN to find a detailed listing of the new controls, their properties, methods, and events.*

Microsoft continues to enhance the standard controls that come with Visual Basic. Many of the enhancements relate to data access and data binding. The DataRepeater control, new grid control, and additional features will aid in the development of client/server applications.

What's New in Syntax

There have been some additions to the basic language features of Visual Basic. One is a new Dictionary object to replace the Collection object. The Dictionary object overcomes some of the Collection object's limitations and is easier to use because it generates fewer run-time errors for common operations and is more flexible. As with the Collection object, you can store unstructured data associated with a unique key. The Collection object in many instances would generate run-time errors.

Another new feature is the ability to access properties or methods by specifying a string containing the name. That provides the ability to dynamically manipulate an object at run time without explicitly coding the property or method name during development.

Continuing in the long tradition of Visual Basic, version 6.0 adds numerous string and number manipulation features. Table 1-4 outlines the new functions.

Function	Description
Filter	Returns a zero-based array containing a subset of a string array based on a specified filter criteria.
FormatCurrency	Returns an expression formatted as a currency value using the currency symbol defined in the system control panel.
FormatDateTime	Returns an expression formatted as a date or time.
FormatNumber	Returns an expression formatted as a number.
FormatPercent	Returns an expression formatted as a percentage (multiplied by 100) with a trailing % character.
Join	Returns a string created by joining a number of substrings contained in an array.
MonthName	Returns a string indicating the specified month.
Replace	Returns a string in which a specified substring has been replaced with another substring a specified number of times.

Table 1-4. *New String and Number Functions*

Function	Description
Round	Returns a number rounded to a specified number of decimal places.
Split	Returns a zero-based, one-dimensional array containing a specified number of substrings.
StrReverse	Returns a string in which the character order of a specified string is reversed.
WeekdayName	Returns a string indicating the specified day of the week.

Table 1-4. *New String and Number Functions* (continued)

Especially powerful are the functions that provide data formatting and validation for easy manipulation of data entered by the user. For example, the Replace function makes it easy to search for a particular set of characters in a string and replace them with a second set of characters. Before, this would have been a series of loops and InStr search code.

Many of the functions new to version 6.0 have been available in Visual Basic Script for some time.

Building Controls in Visual Basic

One of the new advances in Visual Basic is the ability to create *lightweight* controls (windowless controls). These controls don't have the window handle (hWnd property). This means they use fewer system resources, making them ideal for Internet applications, distributed applications, or any application where system resources may be a limiting factor. Traditional examples of lightweight controls include the Label control and the Image control.

Your first choice should always be to build lightweight controls, since they are smaller and require fewer resources. But it is important to keep in mind that a lightweight control cannot contain a standard control (requiring a windows handle). So, if you are going to place any standard controls that have a hWnd property onto a control you are designing, it cannot be a lightweight control.

If you need to add a windows handle to your control for manipulation by another program, you will not want a lightweight control.

You create a lightweight user control by setting the Windowless property to True at design time when creating the control. Not all containers support lightweight controls. When your lightweight user control runs in a host that doesn't support it, it will automatically run in windowed mode. The system will assign it an hWnd on the fly. Hosts that are known to support lightweight controls include Visual Basic 4.0 or later, Internet Explorer 4.0 or later, and Visual Basic for Applications.

Advancing the Integrated Development Environment with Wizards

Can you say wizards? Visual Basic 6.0 brings many new wizards to the table to ease and aid development. One of the biggest changes is with the Setup wizard. In fact, it has been renamed the Package and Deployment wizard. The new wizard lets you deploy your .cab to a Web server, network share, or other folder. The new wizard incorporates data access support for ADO, OLE DB, RDO, ODBC, and DAO as well as support for the new IIS and DHTML applications. It also features better control over Start menu groups and icons for your setup program.

With Visual Basic moving into the deployment of applications on business object servers, client machines in both DHTML and Forms format and IIS Web servers, this wizard continues to meet the needs for application deployment.

Table 1-5 outlines the new wizards in version 6.0.

Wizard or Enhancement	Description
Data Object	Automates the creation of middle-tier objects bound to the data environment or UserControls.
Data Form—enhancements	Builds code-only forms where controls are not bound to a data control and uses ADO code. The wizard is integrated with the Application, Chart, and FlexGrid wizards.
Application—enhancements	Lets you save your settings as profiles for later use, allowing you to create multiple applications with the same format. You can also launch the Data Form wizard and the Toolbar wizard from the Application wizard to create dataforms and toolbars. Menus are now completely customizable.

Table 1-5.   *New and Enhanced Wizards*

Wizard or Enhancement	Description
Add-in designer	Allows you to begin development by easily specifying your add-in's default load behavior, name, target application, version, and other properties if desired.
Toolbar	Opens automatically when you add a toolbar to a form so that you can create customized toolbars (you must have the Application wizard loaded).

Table 1-5.   *New and Enhanced Wizards* (continued)

Data Environment Designer

One more feature, the data environment designer, can be added to the IDE to provide powerful database tools for your application. The data environment designer provides an interactive environment for creating programmatic run-time data access. At design time, you set property values for Connection and Command objects, write code to respond to ADO events, execute commands, and create aggregates and hierarchies. You can also drag data environment objects onto forms or reports to create data bound controls. Figure 1-5 shows the designer launched in the Visual Basic IDE.

At run time, the data environment creates ADO Command and Connection objects for each Command and Connection object defined in the data environment designer. If the Command object is marked as "Recordset Returning," an ADO Recordset object is also created. The ADO Command object is added as a method from the data environment run-time object, and the ADO Connection and Recordset objects are added as properties.

Design environments can be used not only as direct data sources for data binding to controls on a form but also to programmatically create an instance of the data environment and execute its Command objects. With design environments, you can create data relationships and model data. If you have been using Visual InterDev, you will find this somewhat familiar. In the next chapter, we will create a sample data environment program.

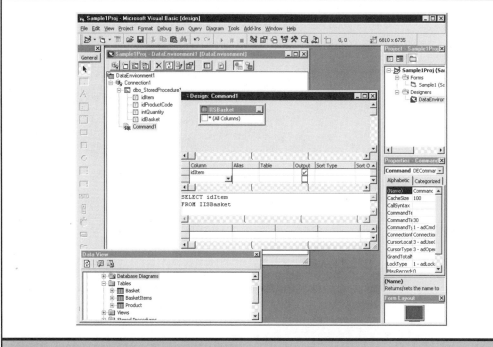

Figure 1-5.   *Data environment designer*

Summary

Visual Basic is a powerful programming environment that has been enhanced with
version 6.0. Microsoft has expanded and developed its platform for client/server
development with new and extended wizards, new and enhanced controls, Internet
development and integration, and much more. As you launch into this new version of
Visual Basic, look deep into the development environment for tools and capabilities to
help aid in your development.

What's Next

In the next chapter we will look at the IDE in more depth and review event-driven
programming. The rest of Part I will focus on introducing building components,
connecting to databases, and building your first Internet applications.

The
Complete
Reference

Visual
Basic 6

Chapter 2

Working with the Visual Basic Development Environment

Programming in Visual Basic has always been about building Windows programs. Windows has been one of the most popular graphical user interface (GUI) operating systems, and Microsoft revolutionized Windows development with the advent of Visual Basic. Windows works in an *event-driven* environment, meaning the user is in control, and programs need to create and respond to events (such as a mouse click). Visual Basic became one of the first "visual" tools to provide an elegant interface for working in this environment. And the sixth iteration adds the ability to work in a different type of visual environment—the Internet.

In this chapter we are going to explore the basics of the VB Integrated Development Environment (IDE), work with event-driven programming, and get an introduction to using objects in our applications. Visual Basic has always been popular for one other kind of development—databases. Version 6 gives us even more tools in the IDE to work with databases, and this chapter introduces you to a powerful new IDE tool, the data environment. So hold on to your hats; let's get started!

The Development Interface

If you are familiar with Visual Basic (also known as VB), one of the first things you will notice is several new windows in the startup Integrated Development Environment (or IDE) for VB. If you are just getting started with Visual Basic, you will find many powerful tools in the IDE ready to help you build your applications. Visual Basic 6.0 changes the default development interface at startup from Visual Basic 5.0. Figure 2-1 shows Visual Basic at startup with a new project.

Development Windows

The tools found standard in the IDE at startup are your palettes for creating your application. Each provides a specific function for working with your application. The one that will be most familiar to the Visual Basic programmer is the Component Toolbox. In Figure 2-1, this is found on the left side of the image. The toolbox provides a set of tools that you use at design time to place controls on a form. In addition to the default toolbox layout, you can create your own custom layouts by selecting the Add tab when you right-click on the toolbox. These multiple tabs allow you to logically organize your components. This can be a big help if you are working on a large project with many components.

The center window in our IDE is the form designer. This is where you will build the interface to your application. You add components, graphics, and pictures to a form to create the look you want. Each form in your application has its own form designer window. We will explore using the form designer later in this chapter.

 Tip *You can have multiple forms in your application to break up discrete sections of your application.*

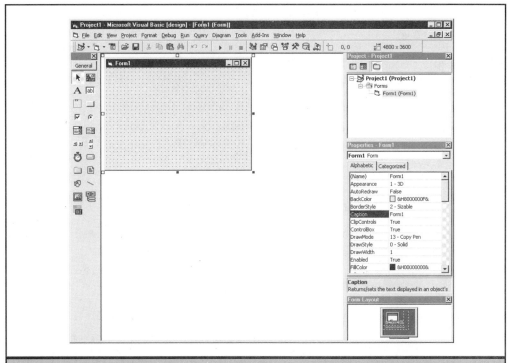

Figure 2-1. *Visual Basic 6.0 Integrated Development Environment*

Note Until Visual Basic 6.0, the only interface option was the standard form designer. Now Microsoft has added the web class designer and the DHTML designer. In effect, you can now build browser interfaces for your applications. This will be explored further in Chapter 5 and the last part of the book.

The window on the upper right of the IDE in Figure 2-1 is the Project Explorer, which lists the forms and modules in your current project. A *project* is the collection of all the files you have created to build your application. From this window you can add and delete files in your project.

The Properties window is directly below the Project Explorer. This is where you will set properties for your forms and components. A *property* is a characteristic of an object, such as size, caption, or color. For example, we might want to put a text box in our application and set the text typed in to be red, bold, and the Arial font. You would use the Properties window to set these characteristics. Note the help window that is part of the Properties window. If you select a property, help is displayed regarding that property.

The last window in Figure 2-1 is the Form Layout window, directly below the Properties window. The form layout allows you to position the forms in your application using a small graphical representation of your form on the screen. This way, you can define where on the screen your form will be launched when you run your program.

Menus

Thirteen menus are available to you, each focusing on a specific purpose. Table 2-1 provides an overview of each.

Menu	Description
File	Provides basic project management such as starting projects, saving projects, compiling projects, and printing project code.
Edit	Provides the standard cut, copy, and paste options; but, depending on context, also provides searching, database editing, and much more.
View	Controls the interface of the IDE. You can show and hide all of the development windows, debugging windows, database tools, and various toolbars.
Project	Lets you manage your project. You can add forms, modules, controls, references, designers, and set your project properties such as name, compile settings, etc.
Format	Provides tools for formatting your user interfaces. Alignment options for controls, ordering of controls, and spacing are provided.
Debug	Provides different debug mode settings and tools for debugging your project code.
Run	Gives you the options for running, breaking, and stopping your application.
Query	Lets you work with database queries in your application. Microsoft has worked hard to provide a lot more database integration within Visual Basic to make it into a robust client/server development tool.

Table 2-1. *Visual Basic's Menus*

Menu	Description
Diagram	Goes along with the query menu. It is used for creating database diagrams of data you are working with in your project. You can include annotations and show relationships.
Tools	Provides code creation tools, SourceSafe management tools, and options for customizing the IDE.
Add-Ins	Provides functionality you can add to your application via custom-built add-ins. Examples include source control, Windows API Viewer, tools for building classes, and much more.
Window	Provides window management tools for the IDE.
Help	Links to MSDN for providing Visual Basic documentation and help.

Table 2-1. *Visual Basic's Menus* (continued)

Microsoft continues to provide extensive functionality in the IDE, and the new menu options for data management provide even more capabilities. As we work through projects in the book, we will use many of the menu options. MSDN can also be used as a reference for any of the menu features.

Toolbars

True to the visual development environment, there are many toolbar options in Visual Basic. You can extensively customize your toolbar options by selecting the Toolbars options on the View menu. There are six basic toolbars, including the menu, standard, edit, debug, form editor, and shortcut menus. In most cases the toolbar buttons provide direct links to the menu options. Feel free to play with different options for customizing and floating your toolbars. Many of the buttons provide drop-down menus and extensive context-sensitive help. And Microsoft has moved the toolbars to the new coolbar format.

Debugging

Three key windows are used in debugging applications. Figure 2-2 shows the Visual Basic IDE with the Immediate window, Locals window, and Watches window.

The Immediate window automatically opens when your application is in break mode. You can then type or paste a line of code and press ENTER to run it. This allows you to test different code options and see the results easily.

The Watches window allows you to watch the value of variables in your application that you place in the window. You can update the values of the variables at run time during a break to see the effect. The Locals window automatically displays all the declared variables in the current procedure and their values. This includes properties for any components, forms, and so on.

Document Interface Modes

Two different run-time visual styles, or modes, are available for the Visual Basic IDE. With the Single Document Interface (SDI), all of the IDE windows are free to be moved anywhere on screen. As long as Visual Basic is the current application, they will remain on top of any other applications. With the Multiple Document Interface (MDI) option, all of the IDE windows are contained within a single resizable parent window. You can easily switch between the two modes. To do so, follow these steps:

1. Select Options from the Tools menu.

2. Select the Advanced tab.

3. Check or uncheck the SDI Development Environment check box.

The IDE will start in the selected mode the next time you start Visual Basic.

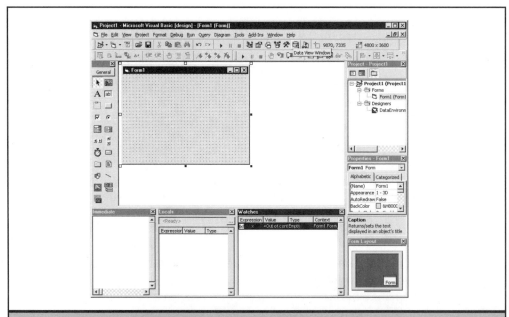

Figure 2-2.   *The Visual Basic IDE with the Immediate window, Locals window, and Watches window*

Tip   *Run Visual Basic from the command line with a /sdi or /mdi parameter to start it automatically in one mode or the other.*

Coding Environment

That covers the basics for the visual side of things, but what about the coding side? To work with placing code in your application, double-click on any form or module in your application. When you do so, the form designer window is replaced with the Code window. Figure 2-3 shows the Visual Basic IDE with the Code window.

The Code Editor is a window where you write most of your code. It is a highly specialized word processor with a number of features that make writing Visual Basic code a lot easier than using something like Notepad. Included are color coding for keywords and automatic syntax checking to notify you when you might have accidentally written some incorrect code (never happens—right!).

Some of the more useful features are AutoList and Auto Quick Info. AutoList is shown in Figure 2-4. When you type the name of a form or control you are working with in the editor, it will automatically list all properties and methods you can access. That way you don't have to try and remember or reference all the different properties and methods to ensure you have the right spelling, for example.

Auto Quick Info is a related feature that provides syntax for functions. In Figure 2-5 the Code Editor shows the syntax for the msgbox function. This provides an excellent reference for different arguments to subroutines and functions as well as methods you may call. All of these features are targeted at ease of use and rapid application development for the developer.

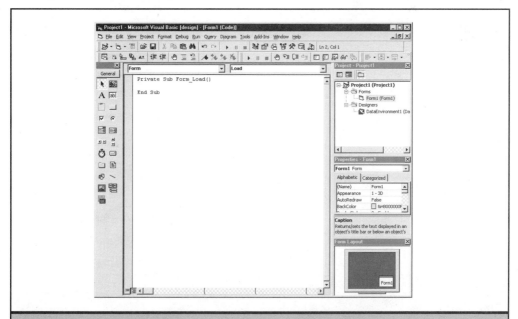

Figure 2-3.   *The Code Editor shown in the Visual Basic IDE*

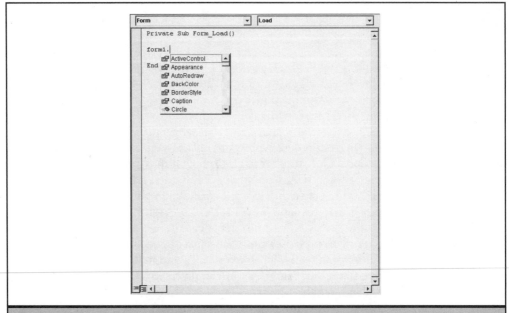

Figure 2-4. *The Code Editor with AutoList showing properties and methods*

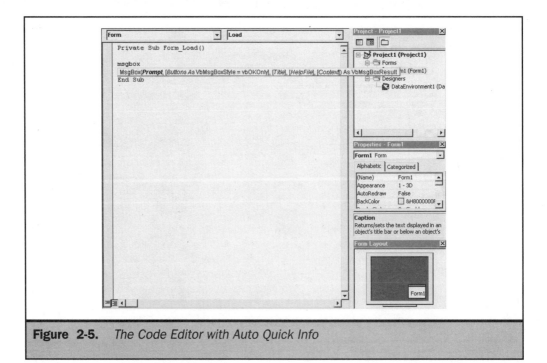

Figure 2-5. *The Code Editor with Auto Quick Info*

Code within the editor is subdivided into separate sections for each object contained in the module you are working with. Switching between sections is accomplished using the object list box. In a form module, the list includes a general section, a section for the form itself, and a section for each control you have placed on the form.

Each section of code can contain several different procedures, accessed using the procedure list box (next to the object list box). The procedure list for a form module contains a separate section for each event procedure for the form or control. For example, the click event of a form can be readily accessed in this list.

Two different views of your code are available in the Code Editor window. You can choose to view a single procedure at a time or to view all of the procedures in the module, with each procedure separated from the next by a line. To switch between the two views, use the view selection buttons in the lower-left corner of the editor window.

Compiling Your Project

Although we will discuss compile options in more detail throughout the book, an overview here will give you an idea of how you can compile all that code you have written into an executable program.

On the Project menu, select the Properties options. The Properties dialog box is shown. The Compile tab, as shown in Figure 2-6, contains a list of Visual Basic's compile options. Table 2-2 outlines the main options. Two of the options for native compile can affect performance and debugging. The Favor Pentium Pro setting

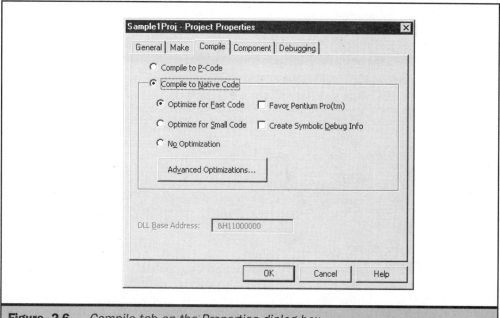

Figure 2-6. *Compile tab on the Properties dialog box*

Option	Description
Compile to P-Code	Compiles a project using pseudocode (p-code). P-code is an intermediate step between the high-level instructions in your VB program and the low-level machine code your computer's processor executes. At run time, Visual Basic translates each p-code statement into native code. By compiling directly to native code format, you eliminate the intermediate p-code step when the program is run. In almost every situation, you are going to want to avoid the use of p-code. In general, native code compilation is much faster at execution time.
Compile to Native Code– Optimize for Fast Code	Maximizes the speed of the .exe and .dll files by instructing the compiler to favor speed over size. The compiler can reduce many constructs to functionally similar sequences of machine code. In some cases, the differences offer a trade-off of size versus speed. If you are delivering a client/server application of any robustness, given the low cost of hard drive space, this may be important for your end user's use of the program.
Compile to Native Code– Optimize for Small Code	Minimizes the size of the .exe and .dll files by instructing the compiler to favor size over speed. The compiler can reduce many constructs to functionally similar sequences of machine code. If you do not select this option, you may have code that is larger in size but faster. This option can be crucial for delivering code over the Internet. The smaller the program, the faster the download time. But you will need to consider the ultimate impact on performance for the end user.
Compile to Native Code– No Optimization	Compiles without optimizations.

Table 2-2.   *Compile Settings for VB Code*

optimizes the code to run on an Intel Pentium Pro processor. The code still runs on all processors but will not perform as well. The second option is to include the Symbolic Debug Info in your executable. That allows your program to be debugged by tools such as Visual C++. An additional file, .pdb, will be included with your project.

More information on the ins and outs of compilation options can be found on the MSDN CD provided with Visual Basic.

What Is Event-Driven Programming Anyway?

Visual Basic's user interface programming is all about responding to events and user actions. It is the users' actions that drive the event responses in your application. Based on the event response, you can choose the code in your application that is appropriate to respond to the event. For example, suppose your form has a button that a user can click on. When the user clicks on it, you want to pop up a message box and thank the user for clicking on the button.

In this scenario, the user's *action* initiates an *event* in your application. Specifically, that event is the click event for the button. Then, as the programmer, you decide what to do in response to the action that caused the click event. In this case, you want to show a message box to the user. This is called event-*driven* programming because the code that is executed is driven by events that happen to your program. Thus, the msgbox code that is executed is driven by the action of the user to click on the button.

In a formal sense, an event is an action recognized by a form or control in your application. Event-driven applications execute VB code in response to an event. Each form and control in Visual Basic has a predefined set of events. If one of these events occurs and there is code in the associated event procedure, Visual Basic invokes that code. You will find that Visual Basic forms and controls are rich in events. Take a text box for example. You can control your responses to a user's action all the way down to the pressing of a key! If you don't want the user typing the Q key because you hate words with Q in them, by golly you can provide a message box response telling them so!

Are you wondering how your application ever gets started? There are events that don't necessarily have to be user driven. For example, when a form is loaded for display, certain events are automatically fired off (such as Form_Load). In that load event you might decide to open a connection to a database and load data into text boxes on the form. Or an event might be fired off after a connection is made to a database.

If you remember in our earlier review of the IDE, the Code Editor window provides a list of objects on your form as well as a list of events. It is in the code view that you can select an object and review its events to decide where to place your code. Figure 2-7 shows the Code Editor with the events list visible for the form.

Event-driven programming isn't too hard to get the hang of. Just remember that you will need to respond to user events that take place on the user interface you provide for your application. You even need to think about such things as events to end the application. A classic example is prompting users to save some data they have entered before the application closes. Throughout this book we will be working with event-driven programming, and a couple of examples later in the chapter will help get you started.

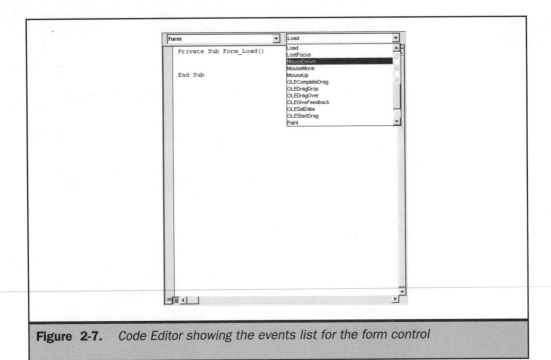

Figure 2-7.   *Code Editor showing the events list for the form control*

Working with Objects and Controls

Everything hinges on the use of objects and controls in your application. In fact, just about everything in Visual Basic is an object of some kind. The form interface you use in development is an object. The custom controls are types of objects. And, of course, you can create your own objects with classes.

The Toolbox—Controls Galore

Unarguably one of the most powerful and popular features of Visual Basic is the use of controls for building user interfaces. The ability to encapsulate complete functionality in an easy-to-use interface lends itself to rapid application development and code reuse. The marketplace for custom controls has grown extensively since Visual Basic was launched.

Custom controls are what allow you to build the user interface on your form. They are the building blocks of your application. There are certainly the standard controls that we have all become familiar with, such as the label, text box, command button, and so on. But there are myriad other controls on the market, and Microsoft has provided a solid set with Visual Basic.

Note *Speaking of custom controls, you can build your own ActiveX controls with Visual Basic. The ability to build and deploy your own custom controls is a powerful method of encapsulating and distributing functionality. In the next chapter we will explore creating our own custom control.*

Controls are also objects. They are encapsulated functionality nicely packed in a component you can add to your project. When we talk about working with controls, we are talking about working with objects.

Working with Objects

As mentioned earlier, Visual Basic is object based. Controls you add to your form are objects, forms are objects, classes are objects, and data connections are objects. Visual Basic comes with a tool called Object Browser found on the View menu. This tool allows you to view all of the properties, methods, and events of any objects referenced in your project.

To get started with object exploration, let's create a new project. To do that, follow these steps:

1. Click Start on the task bar.

2. Select Programs and then Microsoft Visual Basic 6.0.

3. Click the Visual Basic icon.

4. Start a new Standard EXE project, as shown in Figure 2-8.

Tip *You can also create a shortcut to Visual Basic and double-click the shortcut from your desktop. Simply click on the Visual Basic icon in step 3 above and drag it to your desktop. A shortcut is then created on your desktop.*

The next step is to add a couple of component (read "object") references. On the Project menu select Components. Figure 2-9 shows the Components dialog box. The first tab, Controls, allows you to add controls installed on your system into your project. Here you will find options to add data controls, common Windows controls, multimedia controls, and much more. As mentioned, it is these controls that will be the building blocks of the user interface for your application.

You can also add designer objects. ActiveX designers can provide visual interfaces for tasks that otherwise might require a great deal of code. For example, the UserConnection designer (Enterprise Edition) provides visual tools for defining complex database queries. At run time, these queries can be invoked with very little code. Other designers include the data designer, web class designer, and DHTML designer.

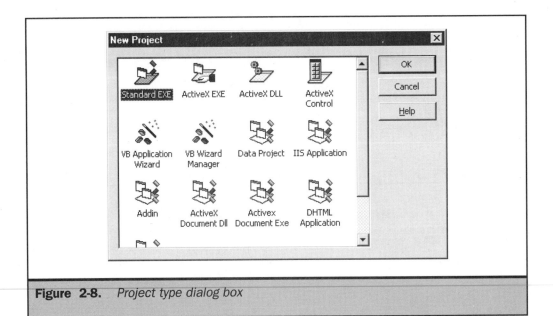

Figure 2-8. Project type dialog box

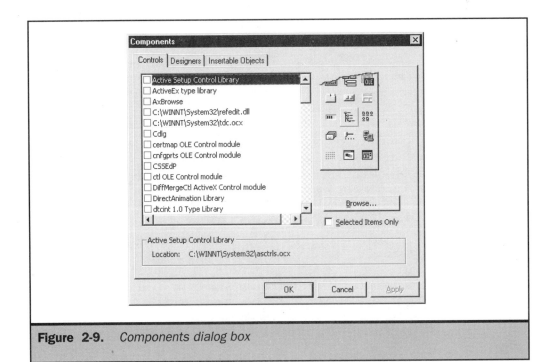

Figure 2-9. Components dialog box

Last on the Components menu, you can add "insertable objects." Examples include Microsoft Excel worksheet objects, Microsoft Word documents, and Microsoft Project Calendar objects. Since these can be added to the toolbox, they can be considered controls. Some of these objects also support Automation (formerly called OLE Automation), which allows you to program another application's objects within a Visual Basic application. But the basic idea is that these are all objects you can include and utilize in your project.

The Object Browser becomes useful in exploring the object model (see Chapter 3 for more information). Let's go ahead and add a couple of components to the new project so we can then explore them in the Object Browser. Go to the Components tab and add Microsoft Windows Common Controls – 2 6.0. And on the Insertable Objects tab, let's add an Excel spreadsheet.

Now we are ready to do a little object exploration. Go ahead and load the Object Browser, as shown in Figure 2-10. Currently showing are all object libraries. But we can specifically explore the Windows common controls and the Excel spreadsheet.

Click the upper-left drop-down box and select ComCtl2 for the common controls. You will see in the left pane of the browser a listing of classes. For example, the MonthView control is one of the common controls. Select MonthView, and the right pane will show all of the properties, events, and methods (subroutines) that are accessible in the control. And it will list the parameters for the event or method plus a description.

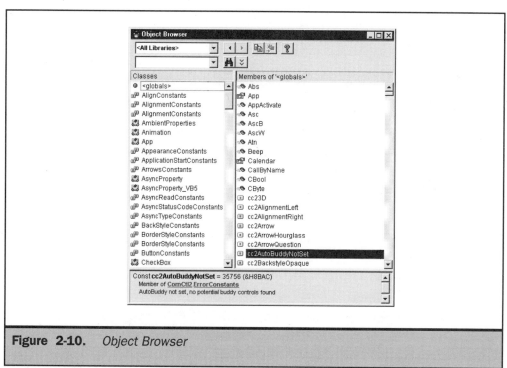

Figure 2-10. *Object Browser*

Now select ExcelCtl from the drop-down box. Then click on Sheet to see the properties, events, and methods for the spreadsheet. This capability can be especially powerful if you are building your own object libraries in Visual Basic using the class module. You have the ability to add business objects created in VB by another user and then view the object model in the browser. As you will see in this book, the concept of building applications based on objects is key to successful Visual Basic development.

One more topic related to components is references. References allow you to select another application's objects that you want available in your code by setting a reference to that application's object library. Figure 2-11 shows the References dialog box. A reference has a file with an .olb extension that provides documentation information about available objects to something called *Automation controllers*. You can retrieve property descriptions and descriptions on how to call methods, arguments, and so on. Visual Basic is an example of an Automation controller. Once a reference is added, you can use the Object Browser to examine the contents of an object library and get information about the objects provided.

Scroll through the list of references available to your applications. You want to ensure you only have references you need, since they add overhead to your project. There are several standard references made in each project, such as links to the Visual Basic for Applications objects, the Visual Basic run time, and so on. One of the key references you need to make for most database work is to the Microsoft ActiveX Data Objects 2.0 Library for using Microsoft's new ADO technology. In fact, when you add a data environment to your project, the reference is made automatically. (See "Data Environment Designer" later in the chapter.)

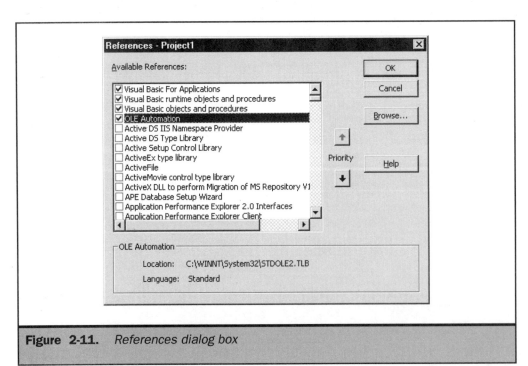

Figure 2-11. *References dialog box*

Visual Basic Modules

Another key development tool is the use of code-encapsulating tools called *modules*. You can add standard modules and class modules. If you start a new project and right-click on the project frame, you can add one of each. Note that forms are really a special type of module–form modules.

Standard modules (.bas file name extension) are containers for procedures and declarations commonly accessed by other modules within the application. They can contain global (available to the whole application) or module-level declarations of variables, constants, types, external procedures, and global procedures. The code you write in a standard module isn't necessarily tied to a particular application; if you're careful not to reference forms or controls by name, a standard module can be reused in many different applications.

Class modules (.cls file name extension) are the foundation of object-oriented programming in Visual Basic. You can write code in class modules to create new objects. These new objects can include your own customized properties and methods. Actually, forms are just class modules that can have controls placed on them and can display form windows. In the next chapter we will take a close look at creating object-oriented applications in Visual Basic.

A primary goal for Microsoft has been to build in the ability to encapsulate code for later reuse in other applications and deployment in remote servers. And with the advent of the Internet, this concept becomes even more essential. Corporations more and more will need to be able to deploy business logic both internally in the client/server context and externally on public Internet sites and private intranet/extranet sites. Visual Basic 6.0 provides the capability to deploy the same code in both environments.

Building Event-Driven Code

Now that we have reviewed the basics of the development environment, let's get started with an example. Start Visual Basic and select Standard EXE when the program asks what kind of project you would like to create (as outlined in the steps under "Working with Objects").

Note *You can read in Appendix C about the different application types and what each is.*

Once we have our new application created, let's go ahead and set some of the project property settings. Follow these steps:

1. Select the Project menu.

2. Select Project1 Properties. The first tab (General) is shown in Figure 2-12.

Project1 - Project Properties

General | Make | Compile | Component | Debugging

Project Type: Startup Object:
Standard EXE   Form1

Project Name:
Project1

Help File Name: Project Help
                                       Context ID:
                              [...]   0

Project Description:

□ Unattended Execution   ┌─ Threading Model ─────────────
☑ Upgrade ActiveX Controls │
□ Require License Key   │ ○ Thread per Object
□ Retained In Memory   │ ● Thread Pool   1   threads

              OK   Cancel   Help

Figure 2-12. *Project Properties tabbed dialog box*

3. Set Project Name to be "Sample1Proj." Note the drop-down box of application types. Ours defaults to Standard EXE.

4. Switch to the Make tab, shown in Figure 2-13.

5. Set the application title to be "Sample1."

Note *On the Make tab you can track version numbers for your program. This is helpful if you know you are going to be implementing several releases of the program in the future. You can also set command line startup arguments if your program needs certain startup indicators. And you can set your default icon for the program.*

Now we are ready to do a little programming in our application. First let's set the caption of our form to be something different from Form1. Follow these steps:

1. Click on the form.

2. In the Properties window on the right, find the Caption property.

3. Set it to "Chapter 2 - Sample 1."

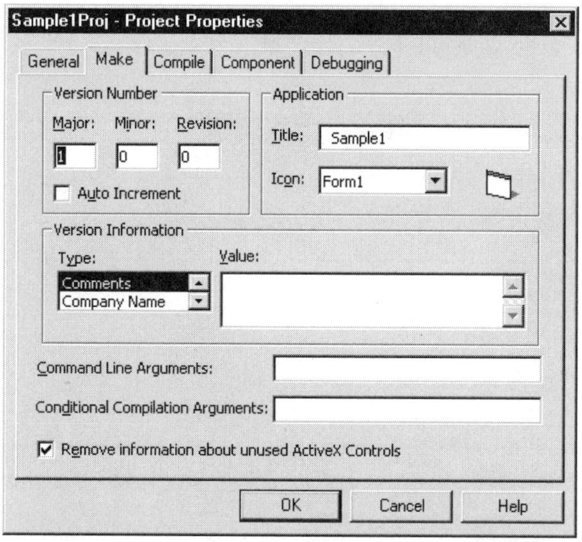

Figure 2-13.   *The Make tab on Project Properties*

4. Save the current project to your system by clicking on the floppy disk icon on the toolbar.

Now we need to add a couple of controls to our form. Let's first add a text box by clicking on the text box control on the left toolbar and then drawing the toolbox on our form. Figure 2-14 shows the form.

Since we don't want the user to see "Text1" when the form starts up, let's change that property. Follow these steps:

1. Click on the text box control.

2. Go to the Properties window and find the Text property.

3. Change the text to read "Hello World!" (of course—what else!).

Note   *Go ahead and explore the programming options for the text box. Double-click on it, and the code view will pop up. You should see the Text1_Change() event. If you want to see just how much control you have over the user's actions with the text box, click on the drop-down box in the upper right that reads "Change." You will see all the events the user can initiate on the text box that you have control over—all the way down to mouse movements. That gives you a lot of power to react to events initiated by the user on the text box.*

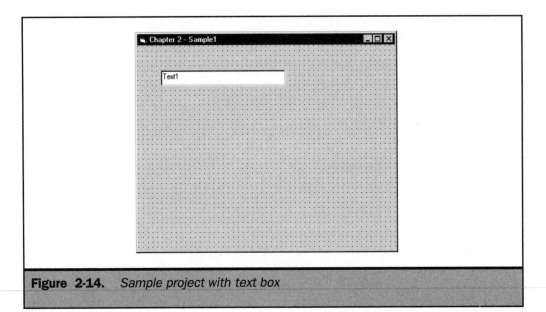

Figure 2-14. *Sample project with text box*

4. To finish our sample program, go ahead and add one more text box and a command button to the form.

5. Follow the same steps for adding the text box control above.

6. For the new text box, clear the Text property completely for the second text box.

7. Set the Caption property to "Click Me" for the command button. Figure 2-15 shows the new form.

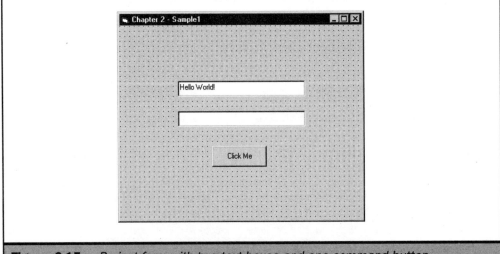

Figure 2-15. *Project form with two text boxes and one command button*

Now we are ready to put a little code behind our application. Below is the code:

```
'  Global variable to indicate whether or not
'  the command button was clicked
Dim intClick As Integer

'  Click event of the command button
Private Sub Command1_Click()

'  Set our global variable to true to indicate
'  the command button was clicked.
intClick = True

End Sub

'  Click event of the text box
Private Sub Text1_Click()

'  Change the text in the text box by accessing
'  its text property.
Text1.Text = "Hello World - You Clicked Me!"

End Sub

'  Change event of the second text box
Private Sub Text2_Change()

'  Check to see if the global click
'  variable is set to True or not
If intClick <> True Then
    '  If not then clear the text box
    Text2.Text = ""
End If

End Sub
```

Tip

Code documentation and commenting is critical for long-term support of an application. Visual Basic uses the single quote (') for providing code comments. When a single quote is encountered in the code, everything after it is ignored by the compiler. Make good use of code comments. It will save you time and a little hair pulling later when you or someone else needs to revisit your code.

The first thing to note in our code is the setting of a global integer variable, intClick. This variable is defined outside of any function and is thus globally accessible to any subroutine or procedure on the form. This variable is used in the click event of the button.

When the user clicks on the command button, the code in the Command1_Click event is fired off. In this case we simply set the intClick variable to have the system value of True. Then in the Text2_Change event for the text2 text box, we check the value of the variable. If the value is not set to True, then the text entered into the text box is cleared by setting the text property of text2 (text2.text) to an empty string (""). If, on the other hand, the variable is true, the text box is cleared, and you are allowed to type in the text box. This is a good example of event-driven programming and sequence of events to affect flow control. The user can type in the text box anytime, but only after the user has fired off the click event of the button will the text be allowed.

Finally, for the first text box, when the user clicks on it, the text is changed. In fact, you can type anything in the text box, but if you click on it again, it is reset. That is because each time the text box is clicked on, the click event code runs, regardless of what was typed in previously. Perhaps this click event setting should only be done once; that could become annoying if your changes keep getting overwritten! Figure 2-16 shows the form at run time, and Figure 2-17 shows the effects of using the program.

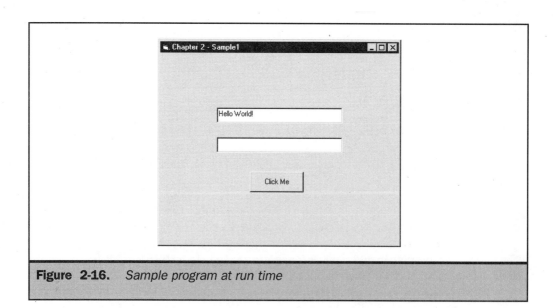

Figure 2-16.   *Sample program at run time*

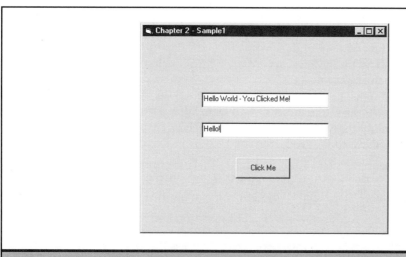

Figure 2-17.   *Sample program with the first text box clicked, the button clicked, and data entered in the second text box*

Building a Database Project

Powerful database development is a key feature of Visual Basic and is right up there with event-driven programming, use of controls and objects, and the rapid application development IDE. Before we jump into the Visual Basic side of things, we need to have a quick overview of Open Database Connectivity (ODBC).

Open Database Connectivity (ODBC)

The first thing we are going to need is an ODBC connection to the database. ODBC provides a universal interface for accessing data in a database. Database developers will write ODBC-compliant drivers to interface with their database management system (DBMS). Then tools developers can write one interface for working with ODBC. This makes for an elegant universal interface for accessing data.

For the example we will work on below, we want to connect with the biblio.mdb Access database provided with Visual Basic. To create the data connection, follow these steps:

1. Go to Start, click on Settings and then Control Panel, and open the ODBC Setup item.

2. In the dialog box select the option marked ODBC and click on the User DSN tab so we can add a data source.

Note   *An ODBC data source is any collection of data that can be indexed and referenced for data retrieval. Keep in mind that the ODBC client requires the proper drivers for each data type (Access, SQL, tab delimited text, FoxPro, etc.). For more information on ODBC, you can visit Microsoft's Data Access Web site at http://www.microsoft.com/odbc.*

3. Click on the Add button, and the Add Data Source dialog box will appear with a list of available drivers. Select Microsoft Access Driver from the list. A dialog box will appear (see Figure 2-18).

4. Enter **Biblio** in the Data Source Name field. Click on Select and locate the copy of biblio.mdb that was installed with Visual Basic 6.0 (try c:\Program Files\Microsoft Visual Basic\dir\dir\filename.mdb).

5. Click OK to save your new driver configuration and close ODBC.

This DSN (data source name) will point to the access file and provide the link between our Visual Basic program and the database. ODBC is a system-level interface (driver) to a database application. An application achieves independence from a database by working through an ODBC driver written specifically for a type of database rather than working directly with the database. The driver translates the database calls into commands its database can use. In this case, our data source will allow Visual Basic to talk with Access, and we won't have to worry about how Access works in its database implementation.

Note   *In Chapter 4 we will also take a look at Microsoft's new universal data connectivity tool, OLE DB.*

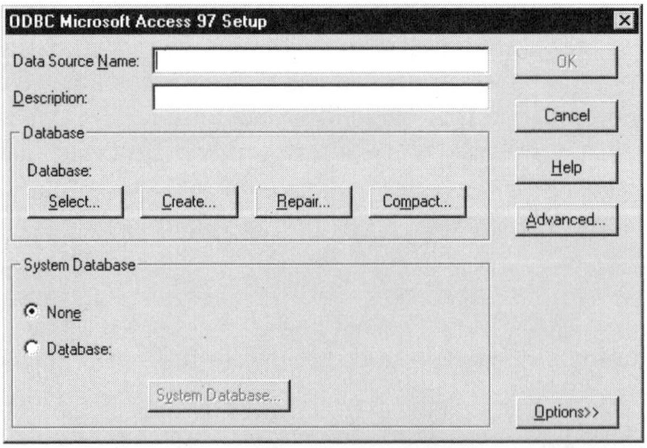

Figure 2-18.   *Microsoft Access ODBC DSN Add screen*

Data Environment Designer

One more powerful tool, as mentioned in Chapter 1, has been added to the Visual Basic development environment—the data environment designer. The data environment enables you to build encapsulated access to your database for easy access in your Visual Basic program. We will be using the data designer throughout the book and will look further into its capabilities and programming interface. In the example here, we will build a simple program for accessing data in the biblio.mdb file included with Visual Basic.

The data environment designer provides an interactive environment for creating data access interfaces for your application. At design time, you set property values for Connection and Command objects, write code to respond to ActiveX Data Object events (data events that are similar to user events), execute commands, and so on. You can also drag data environment objects onto forms or reports to create data bound controls.

Now we are ready to begin our database programming. Our goal will be to perform some queries for various author data from the Biblio database.

Author! Author!

Go ahead and start a new Visual Basic Standard EXE application (as outlined in the steps earlier). The first thing we want to do is add the data environment designer to the application. To get started, click the Project menu and select Add a 'Data Environment' to your project.

When the designer opens, you will see two options, Connections and Commands. The first step will be to create a connection to the Biblio database using the ODBC DSN we created. Follow these steps:

1. Right-click on the Connection1 listing. A dialog box will pop up that gives several options. The first tab shows providers for connecting to the database.

2. Select Microsoft OLE DB Provider for ODBC Drivers. This will allow us to use the ODBC Biblio DSN we created.

3. Click on the Connection tab.

4. The first drop-down box shows our data sources on the system. Select Biblio to connect to our Biblio Microsoft Access database. Figure 2-19 shows the dialog box.

5. Click the Test Connection button to ensure success. If you do not get a successful connection, go back to your ODBC DSN and double-check its settings.

That is it for connecting to an Access database. Just in case, click on the Test Connection to ensure success.

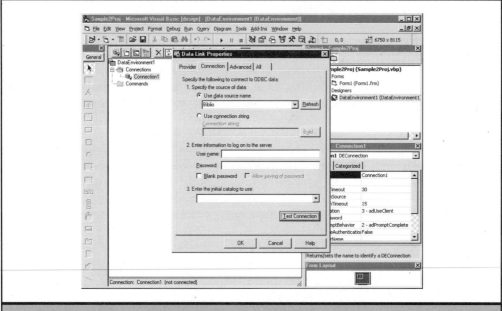

Figure 2-19.   *The Data Environment Connection interface*

Building the Data Environment Commands

Now we are ready to add our first command to the data environment. A command is a query to the database. Examples include selecting data from the tables, updating information, or inserting new records.

Before we add our first command, let's do a quick review of the data structure of the database. Table 2-3 defines each of the tables, and Figure 2-20 shows their relationships.

Table	Description
Authors	List of authors, each identified uniquely with Au_ID.
Publishers	List of publishers, each identified uniquely by PubID.
Title Author	Lookup table of book title ISBNs and author IDs.
Titles	List of book titles with a link to the publisher (PubID).

Table 2-3.   *Biblio Table Structure*

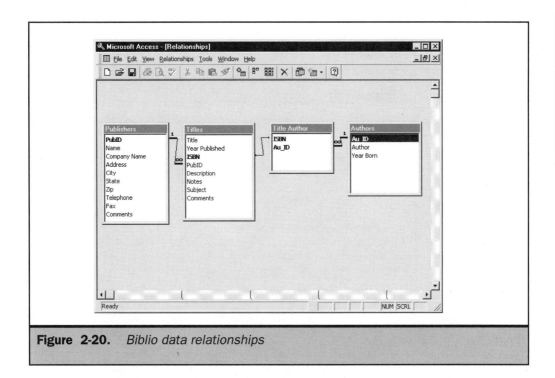

Figure 2-20.   *Biblio data relationships*

Let's create two commands in our data environment. The first will simply return a list of authors, and the second will return a list of books written by yours truly (Noel Jerke). The first one is rather easy—follow these steps:

1. Right-click on Command.

2. Select Add Command from the menu.

3. When the command is added, rename it to "Authors" by right-clicking and selecting Rename.

Following the steps above, go ahead and add our second command and name it "FavAuthor." Figure 2-21 shows the data designer after adding the commands.

Right-click on the Authors command and select Properties. The Properties tab allows us to define the data that will be returned from the database for this command. To make the first one, simply follow these steps:

1. On the Connection list, select our connection, Connection1.

2. For the database object, select Table.

3. For the object name (table), select Authors.

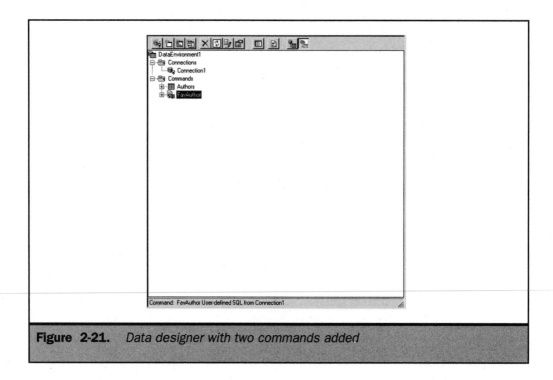

Figure 2-21.   *Data designer with two commands added*

The list of authors will be returned from the table when the Authors command of the data environment is accessed (a demonstration is coming soon). Click OK, and let's go to the second query. This one will be a bit more complicated.

Once you have selected the Properties dialog box of the FavAuthor command, ensure that Connection1 is selected for the connection (see the preceding steps). This time we want to use a SQL statement for our command.

Note   *SQL is short for Standard Query Language. Any serious database development in Visual Basic requires some fundamental knowledge of SQL database programming. If you are new to SQL, you might want to check out Osborne's SQL Programmer's Reference, by Kishore Bhamidpati, or LAN Times Guide to SQL, by Jim Groff and Paul Weinberg.*

Click the SQL Statement radio button, and then click on the SQL Builder button. The SQL Builder is a great GUI tool for creating SQL queries. Those of you who have been doing Access programming for a while will find some similarity to the query builder. The Data View screen is brought up, as shown in Figure 2-22.

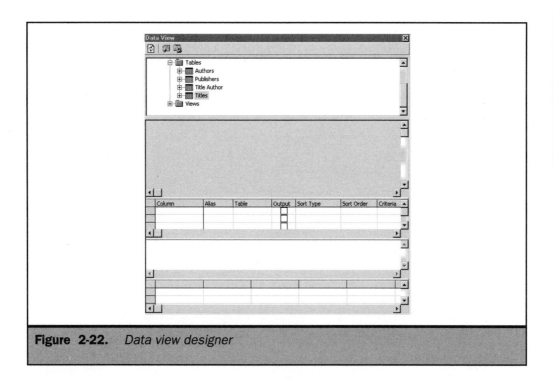

Figure 2-22.   *Data view designer*

To build our query, we need to add three tables to get a list of books for a specific author. According to our data diagram for Biblio, we will need to add Authors, Title Author, and Titles. This is because the Title Author table links the Titles and Author tables together. Thus, we can find the list of titles for an author by looking up their cross-reference. Add the tables to the query by dragging each of these tables onto the design background. Once this is done, your screen should look like Figure 2-23.

Note   *The query window begins to build the SQL code for returning all of the titles and authors. You can see the SQL code being built in the designer.*

We need to decide what fields are going to be displayed. For this query, let's return Author, ISBN, Title, and Year Published. To add these, click on the check box next to each field in the table boxes. When you do that, each will show up on the field grid.

The last thing we need to do is set our criteria to return books authored by Jerke, Noel. In the Criteria cell for the Author field, type **'Jerke, Noel'** (with the single

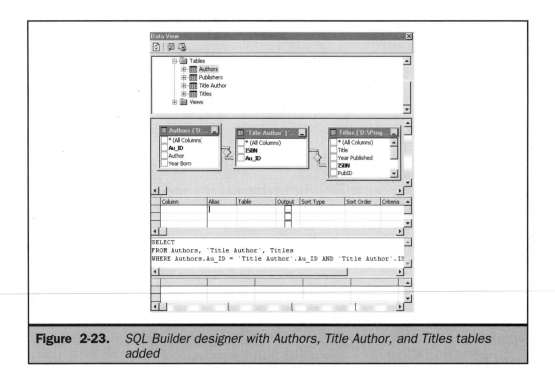

Figure 2-23.   SQL Builder designer with Authors, Title Author, and Titles tables added

quotes). Note that again the SQL code is updated to reflect the new query parameter. Your SQL code should look something like the following:

```
SELECT Authors.Author,
       'Title Author'.ISBN,
       Titles.Title,
       Titles.'Year Published'
FROM   Authors, 'Title Author', Titles
WHERE
       Authors.Au_ID = 'Title Author'.Au_ID AND
       'Title Author'.ISBN = Titles.ISBN AND
       (Authors.Author = 'jerke, noel')
```

Now we are ready to test the query. Right-click on the field grid and select Run. In the bottom frame the results will be returned. And, unless Microsoft decided to update their Books database, you should see one book show up. Figure 2-24 shows the final output of the command designer.

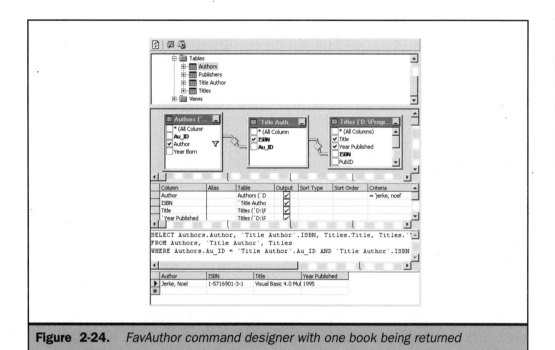

Figure 2-24. *FavAuthor command designer with one book being returned*

Finally, close out the command designer, and you will be back at the primary data environment screen. Be sure to save the changes you have made. There is much more to a data environment than just the design tools. In fact, there is an entire programming interface behind each data command and connection. Double-click on any one of them and review the events available. You can have a great deal of control over how transactions are processed.

Let's move on to the form for our program and utilize our data environment. The first thing to do is add some data bound controls to our project that can easily connect to our data environment. Data bound controls can be intrinsically bound to a database field. In this case, we could attach a text box to the Name field in the Author table. For each record reviewed, the text box would show the author's name—all without a lot of programming!

Select Components from the Project menu and add Microsoft DataList Controls 6.0 (OLEDB). The DataList and DataCombo boxes are added. Select the DataCombo control and draw one on the form. We will hook this control to the Authors command of the data environment. Set the following properties of the DataCombo box:

DataMember	Authors
DataSource	DataEnvironment1
ListField	Author
RowMember	Authors
RowSource	DataEnvironment1

These data settings hook up the primary data source and row source to the Authors command of the data environment. The data source indicates where the combo box should get its data. The list field will be the Author field. This is the data that will show up in the combo box. We could have just as easily selected any other field in the Author table to display.

At this point, go ahead and run the project. You will see that the combo box shows all of the authors' names. Figure 2-25 shows the project at run time. The next thing we can do in our project is call our FavAuthor query. Add a command button to the form. Change the caption property to Click Me!, and double-click on the button to go to its click event. Note the object and event list boxes automatically show the command button and click event. In that event, add the following code:

```
Private Sub Command1_Click()

'   Execute the query
DataEnvironment1.FavAuthor

'   Show the results by accessing the
'   resultset
MsgBox DataEnvironment1.rsFavAuthor("Author")
MsgBox DataEnvironment1.rsFavAuthor("Title")

'   Close the resultset
DataEnvironment1.rsFavAuthor.Close

End Sub
```

Figure 2-25.   *Combo box with authors listed*

The first thing we do in the click event is execute our FavAuthor command. That is done by referencing our data environment, DataEnvironment1, and then subreferencing with a '.' the FavAuthor command. When the command is executed, it will open a result set with our query results. A *result set* is the data from the database that was returned to our query. We can then access the rsFavAuthor result set. Note the "rs" moniker added to the FavAuthor name to indicate the result set.

In the result set, we can then access the value of each returned field by name (remember the Author, ISBN, Title, and Year Published fields from the query). Finally, when we have displayed the results in a message box, the result set closes. If we don't close the result set, the next time the command button is clicked, an error will occur because the result set is still open. You can't run a query and return a result set if the result set you want to return the data to is already open and has other data assigned to it. Figure 2-26 shows the application in action.

As you can see, the data environment provides an excellent way to encapsulate data access to your databases, whether they are Microsoft Access, SQL Server, Oracle Server, or others. If you think about it, your Visual Basic form really knows nothing about what kind of data is being accessed, where it is located, or how it is structured (beyond field names). If at some point you want to move your Biblio database to Oracle or Microsoft SQL Server, there is little reason your form code would have to change.

In fact, you can easily encapsulate access to different databases in the same data environment interface. If you really want to get serious about data development, take a look at the new project type, Data Project, that even includes a report designer. Visual Basic has always been a powerful tool for database development projects, and Microsoft just keeps adding more features. In Chapter 4 we will take a closer look at Visual Basic's data access capabilities.

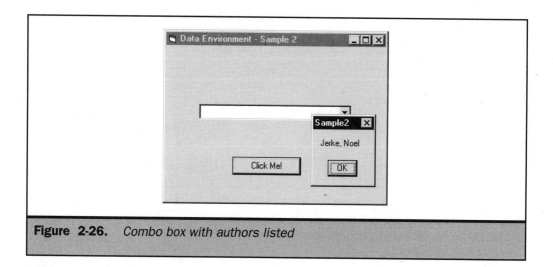

Figure 2-26.   *Combo box with authors listed*

Summary

The Visual Basic integrated development environment has many features and tools that can aid you in development. The data designer, Object Browser, standard module, and class module are just the beginning. If you are a hard-core Visual Basic programmer, version 6.0 has plenty of new features for you—from the new Internet capabilities, to the ability to create your own add-ins, custom controls, and data projects.

If you are new to event-driven programming, you will get into the swing of things in terms of knowing when and where to write code. Getting started with a few simple applications will set you on your way. The rest of Part I will introduce additional key concepts such as object-oriented programming, database development, and Internet development.

What's Next?

In the next chapter we will take a close look at building object-based applications. An exploration of object models, the class designer, class modules, and building custom controls will be undertaken.

Chapter 3

Building Objects in Visual Basic

This chapter will review the foundation of building object-based applications in Visual Basic. When you program in Visual Basic, you will inherently be using objects such as components, designers, forms, modules, and so on. But it is not just about using objects; Visual Basic has powerful tools for creating objects, including business objects and custom controls. In this chapter we will explore the use of the VB class module for creating objects. Specifically, we will model a favorite collector's item, sports cards. Our class modules will model their properties and methods. We will also explore the concept of building an object model and how objects can interact with each other. If you are new to objects and classes, it may seem a bit daunting. But work through the example of building a single class, then a series of classes that work together (an object model), and you will get the basics of building your own objects.

Object Basics

Building object-based applications in Visual Basic is one of its primary strengths. In fact, VB is all about using objects to construct applications, whether it takes the form of referencing visual objects such as controls (components), building data environments for easy reuse, or building visual interface forms.

Objects are something that help to hide the complexity of an underlying process or thing. Think of a radio, for example. You know how to set its properties: AM or FM, on or off. And you know how to manipulate its methods: change frequency, change volume, change bass, change treble, and so on. But you certainly don't need to understand what happens "under the covers." For example, when you set the on/off property to on, you don't worry about underlying events that take place to get power and receive frequency. Or when you increase the volume, you don't worry about making any changes to the speakers directly. In other words, the radio object has presented an interface to you as the user, but it has abstracted away the complexity of actually running the radio.

As mentioned in Chapter 2, the class module is one of the key tools for building object-based applications in Visual Basic. It allows VB code to be encapsulated (abstracted) into an easy interface for reference and reuse in other applications. Class modules allow you to define an object's properties, methods, and events. But the calling application does not need to understand the complexity behind the object.

Building Our First Object—The Sports Card

To get started with building an example of an object-based application that utilizes class modules, we are going to use the Visual Basic Class Builder add-in utility to design the methods and properties of our class module. Once the class is created, we can then fill in the properties and methods with appropriate code to build the functionality of the application. Finally, we will see how to integrate the use of the class module into our forms interface.

Select Add-In Manager on the Add-Ins menu. Figure 3-1 shows the Add-In Manager dialog box. Select VB 6 Class Builder Utility. Once you have added the Class Builder utility, go ahead and start it by selecting it on the Add-Ins menu. Figure 3-2 shows the utility at startup.

With the Class Builder utility, we can define classes that will be added to our project. Certainly, you could go ahead and write the code directly in a class module, but you will most likely find it much easier to have the code framework generated for you from the utility. Right-click on Project 1, select New, and then select Class. Figure 3-3 shows the dialog box for creating a new class.

Go ahead and add a new class called "SportsCard." The class we are going to build will encapsulate common properties and methods of a sports card. For example, the player's name, the team, and the purchase price are all properties. Methods will include calculating a quality rating for the card, calculating the card value, and calculating a retail markup.

To get started creating these properties and methods, select the SportsCard class, and then select the Properties tab. Right-click in the property frame and select New Property. A dialog box pops up (see Figure 3-4) and asks for the property's name and data type. The Declaration options indicate how you would like the property to be accessed. If it is a public property, it will be exposed to other applications. The Let, Get, Set settings indicate that the property value can be set and retrieved externally. If it can only be retrieved and not set, then it is read-only. The Set option also indicates whether the property will contain an object when setting the property.

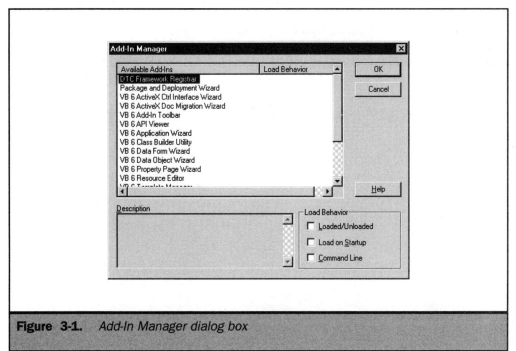

Figure 3-1.   *Add-In Manager dialog box*

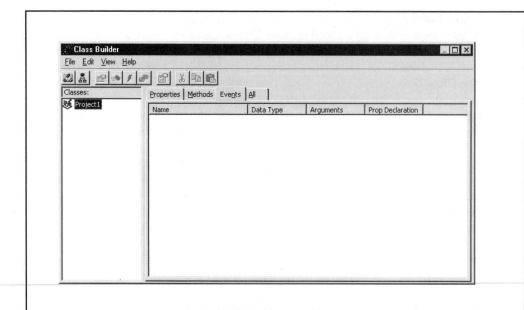

Figure 3-2. *The Class Builder utility*

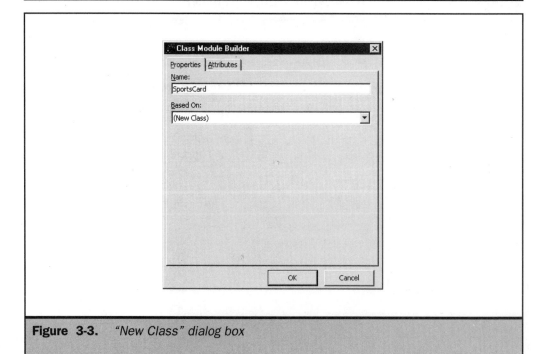

Figure 3-3. *"New Class" dialog box*

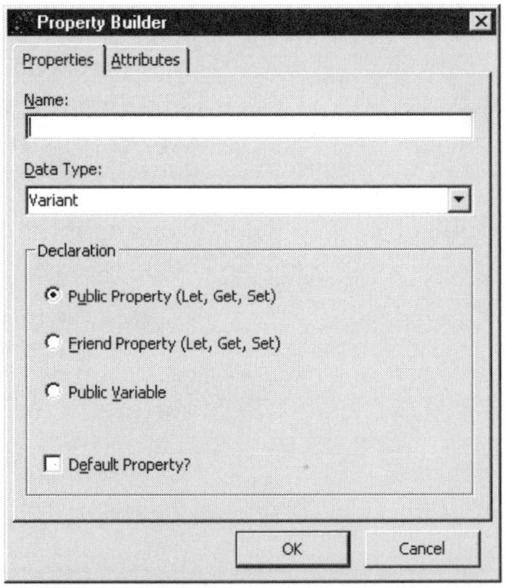

Figure 3-4. *"New Property" dialog box*

Go ahead and add the properties to the SportsCard class as outlined in Table 3-1. Note that all of the properties are public properties.

Name	Data Type	Description
First Name	String	First name of the player on the card.
Last Name	String	Last name of the player on the card.
Imperfections	Integer	Number of card imperfections.
League	String	The league the player is in.
Manufacturer	String	Manufacturer of the card.
MiscDescription	String	Comments/description.

Table 3-1. *Properties of the SportsCard Class*

Name	Data Type	Description
PlayerBasePrice	Currency	The base card price for the player. This is an arbitrary field for the starting price of all cards for that player.
PlayerDemandRating	Integer	A rating of the current demand for the player's cards.
PurchasePrice	Currency	Original purchase price of the card.
Rookie	Integer	Indication of whether this is a rookie card for the player.
Team	String	The team the player is on.
Year	Date	Year the card was issued.

Table 3-1.   *Properties of the SportsCard Class* (continued)

The next thing we need to do is add the methods outlined earlier for our class. Click on the Methods tab of the Class Builder dialog box once the properties have been added. Right-click on the methods pane and select New Method. A dialog box for adding a new method will pop up, as shown in Figure 3-5. Also shown in Figure 3-5 is the Add Argument dialog box for adding arguments (passed-in values) to our method. For each method, add the name and arguments as outlined in Table 3-2.

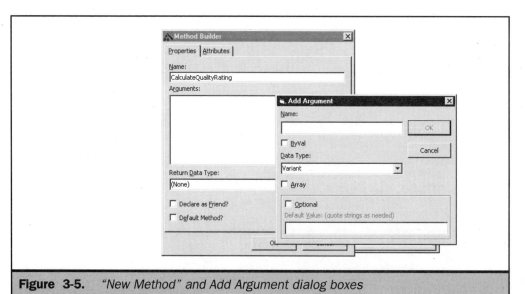

Figure 3-5.   *"New Method" and Add Argument dialog boxes*

Name	Argument	Description
CalculateMarkup	MarketTension as Integer	Calculates the retail markup on the card based on the card's value.
CalculateQualityRating	MarketTension as Integer	Calculates the quality of the card based on the number of imperfections.
CalculateValue	MarketTension as Integer	Calculates the value of the card based on several criteria, including quality and ratings for the player.

Table 3-2.   *Methods for the SportsCard Class*

The MarketTension argument is used to indicate the overall current demand for sports cards. If it is a soft market, the value will be higher; in a tight market, it will be lower. If demand is extremely high, the value will be 0.

That is it for creating the class. Now we are ready to have the class created in our project. On the File menu of the Class Builder, select Update Project. When you do that, the class is created in the project. To see the results, double-click on the SportsCard class that is created, and review the properties and methods. In fact, we can use the Object Browser to review the class. Click on the View menu and select Object Browser. In the drop-down box, select the name of the project. In the classes, select the SportsCard class. In the right pane you will see a list of your properties and methods just added to the class, as shown in Figure 3-6.

Now that we have our class created, let's dissect it and put some code behind it. In the global declarations section we see a list of variables that relate to our properties. Note the "mvar" moniker on the beginning of each one. This indicates that it is a *member variable* of the class. This is how the class properties are stored and referenced internally in the class.

```
'local variable(s) to hold property value(s)
Private mvarManufacturer As String 'local copy
```

```
Private mvarYear As Date 'local copy
Private mvarLeague As String 'local copy
Private mvarImperfections As Integer 'local copy
Private mvarFirstName As String 'local copy
Private mvarLastName As String 'local copy
Private mvarTeam As String 'local copy
Private mvarMiscDescription As String 'local copy
Private mvarPurchasePrice As Currency 'local copy
Private mvarPlayerDemandRating As Integer 'local copy
Private mvarRookie As Integer 'local copy
Private mvarPlayerBasePrice As Currency 'local copy
```

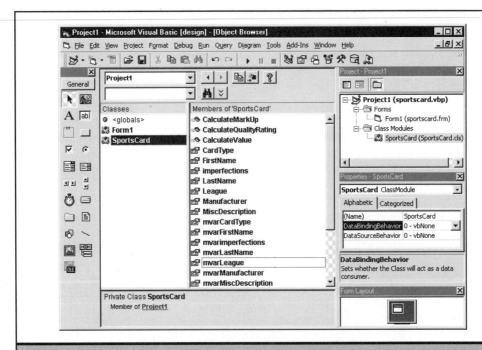

Figure 3-6. *Object Browser view of the SportsCard class*

Each property has a Let and Get definition that defines how the property is set and how it is read. Within each property, you can perform any type of logic necessary on the passed-in variable (vData). In this case we simply set the passed-in value (for Let) to the corresponding member variable of the class.

```
Public Property Let PlayerBasePrice(ByVal vData As Currency)
'used when assigning a value to the property, on the left side of
'an assignment.
'Syntax: X.PlayerBasePrice = 5
    mvarPlayerBasePrice = vData
End Property
```

For the Get property, we retrieve the data in the member variable and return it. Note that PlayerBasePrice defines the base card price for the player. (I know this is a bit arbitrary, but it serves the purpose of demonstration.)

```
Public Property Get PlayerBasePrice() As Currency
'used when retrieving value of a property, on the right side of an
'assignment.
'Syntax: Debug.Print X.PlayerBasePrice
    Set PlayerBasePrice = mvarPlayerBasePrice
End Property
```

The next section of our class defines the rest of the properties. Note the same format for each property as generated by the Class Builder utility. For the Rookie property, you might want to consider adding some validation on the code to ensure the property is only set to a 0 or 1. In fact, for all the properties, such as PlayerDemandRating, Purchase Price, and Year, you could perform data validation in the Let procedure to ensure only valid data is set for the class.

```
Public Property Let Rookie(ByVal vData As Integer)
'used when assigning a value to the property, on the left side of
'an assignment.
'Syntax: X.Rookie = 5
    mvarRookie = vData
End Property

Public Property Get Rookie() As Integer
'used when retrieving value of a property, on the right side of an
'assignment.
'Syntax: Debug.Print X.Rookie
```

```
      Set Rookie = mvarRookie
End Property

Public Property Let PlayerDemandRating(ByVal vData As Integer)
'used when assigning a value to the property, on the left side of
'an assignment.
'Syntax: X.PlayerDemandRating = 5
    mvarPlayerDemandRating = vData
End Property

Public Property Get PlayerDemandRating() As Integer
'used when retrieving value of a property, on the right side of an
'assignment.
'Syntax: Debug.Print X.PlayerDemandRating
    Set PlayerDemandRating = mvarPlayerDemandRating
End Property

Public Property Let imperfections(ByVal vData As Integer)
'used when assigning a value to the property, on the left side of
'an assignment.
'Syntax: X.imperfections = 5
    mvarImperfections = vData
End Property

Public Property Get imperfections() As Integer
'used when retrieving value of a property, on the right side of an
'assignment.
'Syntax: Debug.Print X.imperfections
    imperfections = mvarImperfections
End Property

Public Property Let League(ByVal vData As String)
'used when assigning a value to the property, on the left side of
'an assignment.
'Syntax: X.League = 5
    mvarLeague = vData
End Property

Public Property Get League() As String
'used when retrieving value of a property, on the right side of an
'assignment.
'Syntax: Debug.Print X.League
```

```
        Set League = mvarLeague
End Property


Public Property Let Year(ByVal vData As Date)
'used when assigning a value to the property, on the left side of
'an assignment.
'Syntax: X.Year = 5
    mvarYear = vData
End Property}


Public Property Get Year() As Date
'used when retrieving value of a property, on the right side of an
'assignment.
'Syntax: Debug.Print X.Year
    Year = mvarYear
End Property


Public Property Let Manufacturer(ByVal vData As String)
'used when assigning a value to the property, on the left side of
'an assignment.
'Syntax: X.Manufacturer = 5
    mvarManufacturer = vData
End Property


Public Property Get Manufacturer() As String
'used when retrieving value of a property, on the right side of an
'assignment.
'Syntax: Debug.Print X.Manufacturer
    Manufacturer = mvarManufacturer
End Property


Public Property Let PurchasePrice(ByVal vData As Currency)
'used when assigning a value to the property, on the left side of
'an assignment.
'Syntax: X.PurchasePrice = 5
    mvarPurchasePrice = vData
End Property


Public Property Get PurchasePrice() As Currency
'used when retrieving value of a property, on the right side of an
'assignment.
'Syntax: Debug.Print X.PurchasePrice
```

```
      PurchasePrice = mvarPurchasePrice
End Property

Public Property Let MiscDescription(ByVal vData As String)
'used when assigning a value to the property, on the left side of
'an assignment.
'Syntax: X.MiscDescription = 5
      mvarMiscDescription = vData
End Property

Public Property Get MiscDescription() As String
'used when retrieving value of a property, on the right side of an
'assignment.
'Syntax: Debug.Print X.MiscDescription
      Set MiscDescription = mvarMiscDescription
End Property

Public Property Let Team(ByVal vData As String)
'used when assigning a value to the property, on the left side of
'an assignment.
'Syntax: X.Team = 5
      mvarTeam = vData
End Property

Public Property Get Team() As String
'used when retrieving value of a property, on the right side of an
'assignment.
'Syntax: Debug.Print X.Team
      Set Team = mvarTeam
End Property

Public Property Let LastName(ByVal vData As String)
'used when assigning a value to the property, on the left side of
'an assignment.
'Syntax: X.LastName = 5
      mvarLastName = vData
End Property

Public Property Get LastName() As String}
'used when retrieving value of a property, on the right side of an
'assignment.
'Syntax: Debug.Print X.LastName
```

```
        Set LastName = mvarLastName
End Property

Public Property Let FirstName(ByVal vData As String)
'used when assigning a value to the property, on the left side of
'an assignment.
'Syntax: X.FirstName = 5
        mvarFirstName = vData
End Property

Public Property Get FirstName() As String
'used when retrieving value of a property, on the right side of an
'assignment.
'Syntax: Debug.Print X.FirstName
        Set FirstName = mvarFirstName
End Property
```

That finishes the properties for the class. We have extensively defined the "what" of the sports card; now we are ready to work on the "how."

The Class Functions

First, we will add a little code to our methods. While our class is now well defined in terms of properties, it is ready to be able to perform some functionality. We are going to add three methods to our class that will allow the SportsCard class to calculate its quality rating, value, and retail value. These calculations will be partly done based on property settings of the class.

The CalculateQualityRating Function

Let's start with CalculateQualityRating. The purpose of this method is to determine the quality rating of the card. Note that the MarketTension variable is sent into the function. This will indicate how tight the marketplace is for sports cards. With a high demand, quality ratings may go up. The first thing we do is check to ensure that the number of imperfections on the card has been set. This would include bad printing, wear and tear, marks, and so on. The quality rating of the card is then based on a set rating with regard to the number of imperfections. And a value is subtracted based on the market tension times the number of imperfections. If the market tension is 0 (very tight), then basically nothing is subtracted. Note that 0 imperfections always gives a quality rating of 5. And anything over 5 imperfections returns a rating of 0. The value returned is the quality rating.

```vb
' The market tension parameter describes the current volatility
' of the marketplace. In other words, how hot is demand for the
' moment.
Public Function CalculateQualityRating(MarketTension As Integer) _
As Integer
' If no imperfections value has been set then exit with a -1
' result
If mvarImperfections = -1 Then
    CalculateQualityRating = -1
    Exit Function
End If

' Ultimately the quality rating is set by the number of
' imperfections
' and the current market tension. In a hot market the quality
' rating
' may be higher (less stringent) than in a loose market.
Select Case mvarImperfections

    ' If there are no imperfections it gets a top rating of 5
    Case 0
        CalculateQualityRating = 5

    ' For one imperfection the rating would be 4.5 in a very
    ' tight market (0 value for MarketTension).
    Case 1
        CalculateQualityRating = 4.5 - (MarketTension * _
        mvarImperfections)

    ' For two imperfections the rating would be 3.5 in a very
    ' tight market (0 value for MarketTension).
    Case 2
        CalculateQualityRating = 3.5 - (MarketTension * _
        mvarImperfections)

    ' For three imperfections the rating would be 2.5 in a very
    ' tight market (0 value for MarketTension).
    Case 3
        CalculateQualityRating = 2.5 - (MarketTension * _
        mvarImperfections)

    ' For four imperfections the rating would be 1.2 in a very
    ' tight market (0 value for MarketTension).
```

```
   Case 4
       CalculateQualityRating = 1.2 - (MarketTension * _
       mvarImperfections)

    '  For five imperfections the rating would be 1 in a very
    '  tight market (0 value for MarketTension).
   Case 5
       CalculateQualityRating = 1 - (MarketTension * _
       mvarImperfections)

    '  Anything more than 5 imperfections automatically has
    '  a quality rating of 0.
   Case Else
       CalculateQualityRating = 0

End Select

End Function
```

The CalculateMarkup Function

Our next method calculates the markup value of the card for retail. It returns the dollar value of the card. And the market tension variable is passed in since that will have a bearing on what we can actually get for the card. Basically, the markup value is calculated based on the day of the week (a bit odd, but makes for a good demo!). For the less active retail days of the week (Monday through Thursday), the multiplier is lower than Friday, Saturday, and Sunday. The current day of the week is retrieved using the new Weekday function against today's date. The CalculateValue method of the class is used to determine the wholesale value of the card.

```
'  Calculate the markup of the value of the card depending on the
'  shopping day
Public Function CalculateMarkUp(MarketTension As Integer) As _
Currency
'  Get the day of the week and multiply the value
'  times a markup percentage. Note that Friday, Saturday and Sunday
'  are the biggest markup days
Select Case Weekday(Date)
    Case 1
```

```
        CalculateMarkUp = CalculateValue(MarketTension) * 1.8
    Case 2
        CalculateMarkUp = CalculateValue(MarketTension) * 1.5

    Case 3
        CalculateMarkUp = CalculateValue(MarketTension) * 1.6

    Case 4
        CalculateMarkUp = CalculateValue(MarketTension) * 1.7

    Case 5
        CalculateMarkUp = CalculateValue(MarketTension) * 1.75

    Case 6
        CalculateMarkUp = CalculateValue(MarketTension) * 1.9

    Case 7
        CalculateMarkUp = CalculateValue(MarketTension) * 1.9

End Select

End Function
```

The CalculateValue Function

Our last method is the CalculateValue function. This will calculate the base (or wholesale) value of the card. The formula for calculating the value is based on the quality of the card, whether or not it is a rookie card, the base card price for the player, and the demand for the player's cards (player demand rating). The first calculation is to determine whether the player base price needs to be multiplied by the rookie markup (since rookie cards are always more valuable for a player). Then the demand rating for the player is multiplied by the current calculated value and added to the value. Finally, based on the quality rating of the card, a percentage of the card's value is subtracted. And voila, you have a card value just like magic (really). What this method in particular points out is that the calling application does not have to understand the underlying logic behind the calculation of the card value (thank goodness!).

```vb
Public Function CalculateValue(MarketTension As Integer) As _
Currency

'  Declare our variables
Dim RookieMult As Double
Dim Quality As Double

'  Get the quality rating for the card
Quality = CalculateQualityRating(MarketTension)

'  Ensure the quality didn't return a -1, if
'  so, we can't calculate the value
If Quality = -1 Then
    CalculateValue = -1
    Exit Function
End If

'  If this is a rookie card for the player,
'  the value will be multiplied by 3 since
'  rookie cards are generally more valuable
If mvarRookie = 1 Then
    RookieMult = 3
Else
    RookieMult = 1
End If

'  Take the base player card price and
'  multiply by the rookie multiplier. Note
'  that the base player price takes into account
'  age of the cards for the player, etc.
CalculateValue = mvarPlayerBasePrice * RookieMult

'  Take that value and then multiply by the
'  current card demand rating for the player
CalculateValue = CalculateValue + (mvarPlayerDemandRating * _
CalculateValue)

'  Check the quality of the card. For anything other
'  than a quality rating of 5 a percentage of the
'  current calculated value is subtracted.
If Quality >= 4.5 And Quality < 5 Then
    CalculateValue = CalculateValue + (0.1 * CalculateValue)
End If
```

```
If Quality >= 4 And Quality < 4.5 Then
    CalculateValue = CalculateValue + (0.2 * CalculateValue)
End If

If Quality >= 2 And Quality < 4 Then
    CalculateValue = CalculateValue + (0.35 * CalculateValue)
End If

If Quality >= 0 And Quality < 2 Then
    CalculateValue = CalculateValue + (0.5 * CalculateValue)
End If

End Function
```

The initialize event of the class is fired off when the class is created in the application. In this case, we want to ensure that the Imperfections property is initially set to –1. That way, if someone tries to calculate quality or values, it will fail until an imperfection value has been set.

```
Private Sub Class_Initialize()
mvarImperfections = -1
End Sub
```

Adding Controls

Now we are ready to begin using our class in an application. On the form currently in your project, we are ready to add some controls that will allow us to interface with the class. Table 3-3 outlines each control and its key properties. Figure 3-7 shows how the form should be laid out.

Component/Property	Setting
Form	Form1
Caption	"Sports Cards"
Text Box	TxtMarketTension
Text	""

Table 3-3. *Components and Properties for the Sports Cards Form*

Component/Property	Setting
Text Box	TxtBasePrice
Text	""
Text Box	TxtRookieCard
Text	""
Text Box	TxtPlayRate
Text	""
Text Box	TxtPurchasePrice
Text	""
Text Box	TxtDescription
Text	""
MultiLine	-1 'True
Text Box	TxtTeam
Text	""
Text Box	TxtLastName
Text	""
Text Box	TxtFirstName
Text	""
Text Box	TxtNumImp
Text	""
Text Box	TxtLeague
Text	""
TextBox	TxtYear
Text	""
Text Box	TxtManufacturer
Text	""

Table 3-3. *Components and Properties for the Sports Cards Form* (continued)

Component/Property	Setting
Command Button	CmdCalculateMarkup
Caption	"Calculate Markup"
Command Button	CmdCalculateValue
Caption	"Calculate Value"
Command Button	CmdQuality
Caption	"Calculate Quality"
Label	label1 – label13
Caption(s)	"Market Tension:", "Rookie Card:", "Player Demand Rating:", "Purchase Price:", "Player Base Price:", "Description:", "Team:", "Last Name:", "First Name:", "Number of Imperfections:", "League:", "Year:", "Manufacturer:"
AutoSize	-1 'True
Label	LblMarkup
Caption	"$0.00"
AutoSize	-1 'True
Label	LblValue
Caption	"$0.00"
AutoSize	-1 'True
Label	LblQuality
Caption	"0"
AutoSize	-1 'True

Table 3-3. *Components and Properties for the Sports Cards Form* (continued)

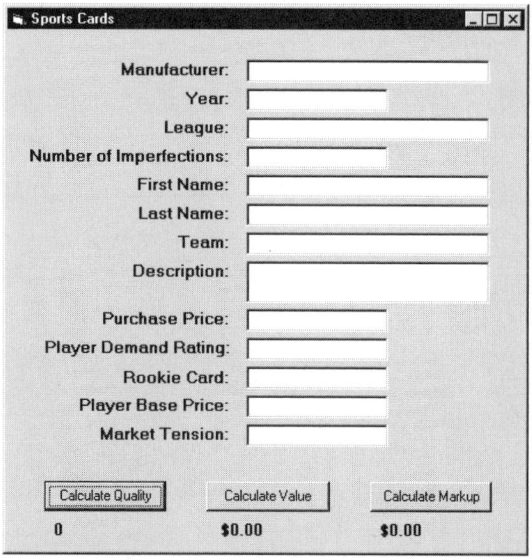

Figure 3-7.   *Sports Cards project form with controls added*

Adding Interface Functionality

The next step is to add some code behind our user interface to connect to our class. The first item in the global declarations is the creation of an instance of our SportsCard class. A variable named SC is used to point to an instance of an object created from our class. Following that is a subroutine, SetClassProperties, that takes the data out of the text boxes and sets the properties of the class with the data. Note, little data validation is done, so it is important that each field is filled out properly.

```
'   Globally declare an instance of our
'   class that will be referenced as SC
Dim SC As New SportsCard

'   This subroutine sets the properties
'   of the class
Private Sub SetClassProperties()
```

```
'   Set each by referencing the property name
'   and getting the value from the text box
SC.Manufacturer = txtManufacturer.Text
SC.Year = txtYear.Text
SC.League = txtLeague.Text
SC.imperfections = txtNumImp.Text
SC.FirstName = txtFirstName.Text
SC.LastName = txtLastName.Text
SC.Team = txtTeam.Text
SC.MiscDescription = txtDescription.Text
SC.PurchasePrice = txtPurchasePrice.Text
SC.PlayerDemandRating = txtPlayRate.Text
SC.Rookie = txtRookieCard.Text
SC.PlayerBasePrice = txtBasePrice.Text

End Sub
```

The Calculate Markup command button first calls the SetClassProperties subroutine to set our class properties. Once that is done, the CalculateMarkup method of the class is called with the market tension variable entered by the user passed in. Note the $ added to the beginning of the value returned.

```
'   Click event
Private Sub cmdCalculateMarkup_Click()
'   Set the class properties before calculation
SetClassProperties

'   Set the label caption value to the result of
'   the CalculateMarkup function. Note that we
'   pass in the market tension variable
lblMarkup.Caption = "$" & SC.CalculateMarkUp(txtMarketTension.Text)

End Sub
```

The click event of the Calculate Value button sets the class properties and then calls the CalculateValue method of the class. This returns and displays the value of the card. Note, the market tension value the user entered is passed into the method call.

```
' Click event
Private Sub cmdCalculateValue_Click()

' Set the class properties before calculation
SetClassProperties

' Set the label caption value to the result of
' the CalculateValue function. Note that we
' pass in the market tension variable
lblValue.Caption = "$" & SC.CalculateValue(txtMarketTension.Text)

End Sub
```

Finally, the click event of the Calculate Quality button once again sets the class properties and then calls the CalculateQualityRating method of the class with the market tension passed in. This will return the quality of the card.

```
Private Sub cmdQuality_Click()

' Set the class properties before calculation
SetClassProperties

' Set the label caption value to the result of
' the CalculateQualityRating function. Note that we
' pass in the market tension variable
lblQuality.Caption = _
SC.CalculateQualityRating(txtMarketTension.Text)

End Sub
```

And with that, you have successfully created your first object-based project. The SportsCard class is created via the Class Builder utility with properties and methods added. Then the basic structure that was created for the class is modified with our code to add appropriate functionality. You will find that this process of building the outlines of your object and then filling in the "meat" of the code will be effective in designing your applications.

Once the class is created, we can then create it in our application and begin setting its properties and calling its methods to add the specific functionality to our application. But we have really only begun to see the power objects can provide.

Welcome to VBCard Pro!

Go ahead and run the application. Figure 3-8 shows sample data entered with calculations on the quality, value, and markup for the card. Try setting different values for the number of imperfections, player demand rating, rookie card, player base price, and market tension to see how they affect the value of the card. Figure 3-9 shows a different set of values and results for the card.

And with that, you have built and deployed your first class object! But you don't get off that easy. The real power of objects is their ability to relate to each other and "model" functionality. We will explore this type of functionality in the next section.

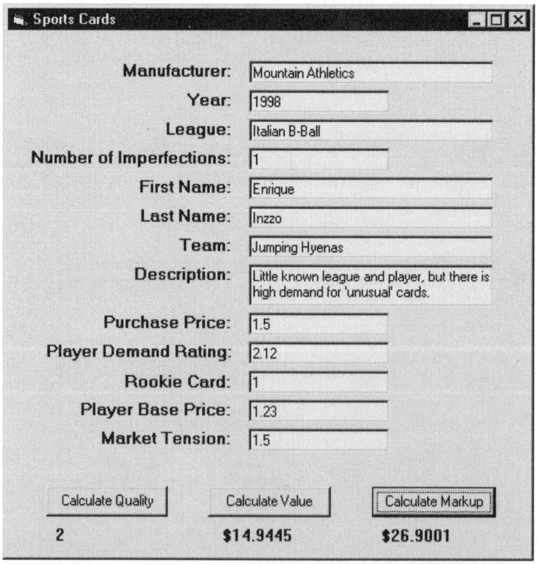

Figure 3-8. Sports Cards application with values set and calculations completed

Figure 3-9. *Sports Cards application with different values set and updated calculations*

Building Object Models

Building one object is fairly straightforward, but what about a series of related objects? Creating the relationships between the objects and interrelating them in your application can provide for powerful capabilities.

Object Model Design

In this section we are going to extend our object model using the class designer and then deploy it to our interface. The following diagram shows an extension to our SportsCard object.

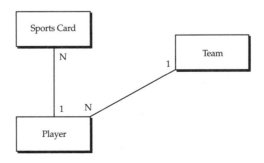

Here we have three objects, Sports Card, Player, and Team. You can see the relationships between each object with the connecting lines. The Player object relates to one or more (N) Sports Card objects. In other words, a player can have multiple sports cards. Conversely, the Sports Card object relates to one player. The third object, Team, defines a sports team. A sports team has multiple players on it. But a player can only be on one sports team (except for Bo Jackson and Dion Sanders).

Building Our Object Framework

Now that we have our object model conceptually created, we are ready to build the structure of our classes. To create our new objects, let's open the Class Builder add-in again. We will first need to define the Player class. Select the project and right-click on it. Then select New and Class. Name the class "Player," and add the properties in Table 3-4 to the class. Note that many of these properties used to be in the SportsCard class but shifted with our new model.

There are no methods for the Player class, just properties. Now that we have defined it, we need to relate the Player class to the SportsCard class. To do that, drag the Player class on top of the SportsCard class. The Player class is then added as a property of the SportsCard class and can be subreferenced.

Name	Data Type	Description
College	String	College where the player plays or played.
Comments	String	Comments on the player.
First Name	String	First name of the player.
Height	String	Height of the player.
Last Name	String	Last name of the player.
PlayerBasePrice	Currency	Base card price.
PlayerDemandRating	Integer	Card demand rating for the player.
Position	String	Position on the team.
Team	String	Team name.
Weight	Integer	Weight of the player.

Table 3-4.   *Player Class Properties*

Last of all, we need to create our Team class. This class is a little different from the others. It actually needs to contain a collection of players. The Class Builder can help us with that. Instead of adding a new class to the project, we want to add a new collection. Right-click on the project and select New and then Collection. In the Collection dialog box, name the collection "Team." Select Player from the drop-down box as the collection of existing class. That will indicate that the Team class will be a collection of Player classes.

When that happens, you will see a number of properties and methods added automatically to the Team class. Properties include count, item, and newenum. The count property indicates the number of items (players) in the collection. The item property allows you to reference an object in the collection by index or key. And newenum allows you to enumerate the collection easily.

The methods added are fairly straightforward. The first is the Add method for adding a new player to the team. The second is Remove for removing items from the list of players. These methods, combined with the properties, make it easy to manage a collection of players in our team. We still need some other properties for our team. Add the properties in Table 3-5.

Finally, we still need a few properties and methods for the SportsCard class. Add the Imperfections, League, Manufacturer, MiscDescription, PurchasePrice, Rookie, and Year properties. We will also still need the CalculateMarkup, CalculateQualityRating, and CalculateValue methods as outlined in the previous project. Once you have completed all of these updates, the Class Builder should be set up as shown in Figure 3-10.

Name	Data Type	Description
City	String	City where the team plays.
Coach	String	Coach for the team.
League	String	League in which the team plays.
Mascot	String	Mascot for the team.
TeamName	String	Team name.

Table 3-5. *Properties for the Team Class*

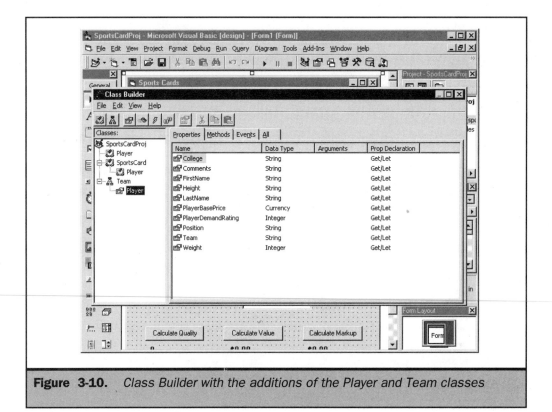

Figure 3-10.   *Class Builder with the additions of the Player and Team classes*

Building the Object Model Functionality

Now that we have our framework in place, we are ready to build the functionality in our classes. Let's go ahead and take a look at the Team class. The first item declared in the class is the mCol variable as a collection. This will hold the collection of players on the team. Followed by that declaration are the member variable properties of the class.

```
'local variable to hold collection
Private mCol As Collection

'local variable(s) to hold property value(s)
Private mvarTeamName As String 'local copy
Private mvarMascot As String 'local copy
Private mvarCoach As String 'local copy
Private mvarCity As String 'local copy
Private mvarLeague As String 'local copy
```

We then have a listing of the properties for the team. These are defined with the standard Let and Get procedures. Three properties—count, item, and newenum—only have Get procedures. This means they are read-only. An outside program cannot directly set any of these properties.

```
Public Property Let League(ByVal vData As String)
'used when assigning a value to the property, on the left side of
'an assignment.
'Syntax: X.League = 5
    mvarLeague = vData
End Property

Public Property Get League() As String
'used when retrieving value of a property, on the right side of an
'assignment.
'Syntax: Debug.Print X.League
    League = mvarLeague
End Property

Public Property Let City(ByVal vData As String)
'used when assigning a value to the property, on the left side of
'an assignment.
'Syntax: X.City = 5
    mvarCity = vData
End Property

Public Property Get City() As String
'used when retrieving value of a property, on the right side of an
'assignment.
'Syntax: Debug.Print X.City
    Set City = mvarCity
End Property

Public Property Let Coach(ByVal vData As String)
'used when assigning a value to the property, on the left side of
'an assignment.
'Syntax: X.Coach = 5
    mvarCoach = vData
End Property

Public Property Get Coach() As String
'used when retrieving value of a property, on the right side of an
'assignment.
```

```
'Syntax: Debug.Print X.Coach
    Set Coach = mvarCoach
End Property

Public Property Let Mascot(ByVal vData As String)
'used when assigning a value to the property, on the left side of
'an assignment.
'Syntax: X.Mascot = 5
    mvarMascot = vData
End Property

Public Property Get Mascot() As String
'used when retrieving value of a property, on the right side of an
'assignment.
'Syntax: Debug.Print X.Mascot
    Set Mascot = mvarMascot
End Property

Public Property Let TeamName(ByVal vData As String)
'used when assigning a value to the property, on the left side of
'an assignment.
'Syntax: X.TeamName = 5
    mvarTeamName = vData
End Property

Public Property Get TeamName() As String
'used when retrieving value of a property, on the right side of an
'assignment.
'Syntax: Debug.Print X.TeamName
    TeamName = mvarTeamName
End Property

Public Property Get Item(vntIndexKey As Variant) As Player
    'used when referencing an element in the collection
    'vntIndexKey contains either the Index or Key to the
    'collection,
    'this is why it is declared as a Variant
    'Syntax: Set foo = x.Item(xyz) or Set foo = x.Item(5)
    Set Item = mCol(vntIndexKey)
End Property
```

```
Public Property Get Count() As Long
    'used when retrieving the number of elements in the
    'collection. Syntax: Debug.Print x.Count
    Count = mCol.Count
End Property

Public Property Get NewEnum() As Iunknown
    'this property allows you to enumerate
    'this collection with the For...Each syntax
    Set NewEnum = mCol.[_NewEnum]
End Property
```

The Add method of our class allows us to define a new player on the team. Note that the arguments for the class are each of the property settings for the Player class. Note that the last argument defines a *key* for the item in the collection so it can be referenced by name and not just by index. However, that argument is optional. The method basically defines a new instance of the Player class and sets each of the properties. Then the Player class is added to the global member collection for Team, and the temporary object is returned and then destroyed. One minor addition is setting the team name for the player. That references the teamname member variable of the class.

```
Public Function Add(FirstName As String, LastName As String, _
Position As String, _
College As String, Height As String, Weight As Integer, Comments _
As String, _
PlayerBasePrice As Currency, PlayerDemandRating As Double, _
Optional sKey As _
String) As Player

    'create a new object
    Dim objNewMember As Player
    Set objNewMember = New Player

    'set the properties passed into the method
    objNewMember.FirstName = FirstName
    objNewMember.LastName = LastName
    objNewMember.Position = Position
    objNewMember.College = College
    objNewMember.Height = Height
```

```
    objNewMember.Weight = Weight
    objNewMember.Team = mvarTeamName
    objNewMember.Comments = Comments
    objNewMember.PlayerBasePrice = PlayerBasePrice
    objNewMember.PlayerDemandRating = PlayerDemandRating

    If Len(sKey) = 0 Then
        mCol.Add objNewMember
    Else
        mCol.Add objNewMember, sKey
    End If

    'return the object created
    Set Add = objNewMember
    Set objNewMember = Nothing

End Function
```

The remove method will delete one of the objects in the collection as indicated by either its key or index.

```
Public Sub Remove(vntIndexKey As Variant)
    'used when removing an element from the collection
    'vntIndexKey contains either the Index or Key, which is why
    'it is declared as a Variant
    'Syntax: x.Remove(xyz)
    mCol.Remove vntIndexKey
End Sub
```

When the class is initialized, the collection is created. When the class is terminated, the class is destroyed.

```
Private Sub Class_Initialize()
    'creates the collection when this class is created
    Set mCol = New Collection
End Sub

Private Sub Class_Terminate()
    'destroys collection when this class is terminated
    Set mCol = Nothing
End Sub
```

The following is the Player class created by the Class Builder utility. You will see the standard member variables at the top of the class with a listing of the Let and Get procedures for each property. Note that the comments added by the Class Builder have been deleted.

```
'local variable(s) to hold property value(s)
Private mvarFirstName As String 'local copy
Private mvarLastName As String 'local copy
Private mvarPosition As String 'local copy
Private mvarCollege As String 'local copy
Private mvarHeight As String 'local copy
Private mvarWeight As Integer 'local copy
Private mvarComments As String 'local copy
Private mvarPlayerDemandRating As Integer 'local copy
Private mvarPlayerBasePrice As Currency 'local copy
Private mvarTeam As String 'local copy

Public Property Get Team() As String
    Team = mvarTeam
End Property


Public Property Let Team(ByVal vData As String)
    mvarTeam = vData
End Property

Public Property Let PlayerDemandRating(ByVal vData As Integer)
    mvarPlayerDemandRating = vData
End Property

Public Property Get PlayerDemandRating() As Integer
    PlayerDemandRating = mvarPlayerDemandRating
End Property

Public Property Let PlayerBasePrice(ByVal vData As Currency)
    mvarPlayerBasePrice = vData
End Property

Public Property Get PlayerBasePrice() As Currency
    PlayerBasePrice = mvarPlayerBasePrice
End Property
```

```
Public Property Let Comments(ByVal vData As String)
    mvarComments = vData
End Property

Public Property Get Comments() As String
    Comments = mvarComments
End Property

Public Property Let Weight(ByVal vData As Integer)
    mvarWeight = vData
End Property

Public Property Get Weight() As Integer
    Set Weight = mvarWeight
End Property

Public Property Let Height(ByVal vData As String)
    mvarHeight = vData
End Property

Public Property Get Height() As String
    Set Height = mvarHeight
End Property

Public Property Let College(ByVal vData As String)
    mvarCollege = vData
End Property

Public Property Get College() As String
    Set College = mvarCollege
End Property

Public Property Let Position(ByVal vData As String)
    mvarPosition = vData
End Property

Public Property Get Position() As String
    Set Position = mvarPosition
End Property
```

```
Public Property Let LastName(ByVal vData As String)
    mvarLastName = vData
End Property

Public Property Get LastName() As String
    LastName = mvarLastName
End Property

Public Property Let FirstName(ByVal vData As String)
    mvarFirstName = vData
End Property

Public Property Get FirstName() As String
    FirstName = mvarFirstName
End Property
```

Last but not least, we have our updated SportsCard class. The first part of the class has the usual member variable declarations for properties. But you will see one critical addition, mvarPlayer. This is actually a reference to the Player class we just created. This will be one of the properties of our SportsCard class. Note that the Manufacturer property, Imperfections property, League property, Year property, Rookie property, MiscDescription property, Purchase Price property, CalculateMarkup method, and CalculateQualityRating method are not included in this code since they are the same as the code in the last project.

```
'local variable(s) to hold property value(s)
Private mvarManufacturer As String 'local copy
Private mvarYear As Date 'local copy
Private mvarLeague As String 'local copy
Private mvarImperfections As Integer 'local copy
Private mvarMiscDescription As String 'local copy
Private mvarPurchasePrice As Currency 'local copy
Private mvarRookie As Integer 'local copy
Private mvarPlayer As Player
```

The Get procedure for the Player class returns a reference to the Player object created and stored in mvarPlayer. Note that the Set syntax is used when setting the return value since we are dealing with an object. If the object instance has not yet been created for Player, then it is created now. This is a good example of using the property settings for additional processing.

```
Public Property Get Player() As Player
    If mvarPlayer Is Nothing Then
        Set mvarPlayer = New Player
    End If

    Set Player = mvarPlayer
End Property
```

We can also set the value of the Player class to an externally created instance of the class. Instead of using Let, we use Set to indicate that an object is being passed in as the property.

```
Public Property Set Player(vData As Player)
    Set mvarPlayer = vData
End Property
```

As before, when the class is initialized, the imperfections value is set to –1. When the class is terminated, the Player object created in the class is destroyed.

```
Private Sub Class_Initialize()
    mvarImperfections = -1
End Sub

Private Sub Class_Terminate()
    Set mvarPlayer = Nothing
End Sub
```

The CalculateValue method has to be updated. Previously, we accessed member variables of this class for the PlayerBasePrice and PlayerDemandRating properties. Now we need to subreference these properties in the Player class property of the SportsCard class. The code below has been updated appropriately.

```
Public Function CalculateValue(MarketTension As Integer) As
Currency

'  Declare our variables
Dim RookieMult As Double
Dim Quality As Double

'  Get the quality rating for the card
Quality = CalculateQualityRating(MarketTension)
```

```
'  Ensure the quality didn't return a -1, if
'  so, we can't calculate the value
If Quality = -1 Then
    CalculateValue = -1
    Exit Function
End If


'  If this is a rookie card for the player,
'  the value will be multiplied by 3 since
'  rookie cards are generally more valuable
If mvarRookie = 1 Then
    RookieMult = 3
Else
    RookieMult = 1
End If


'  Take the base player card price and
'  multiply by the rookie multiplier. Note
'  that the base player price takes into account
'  age of the cards for the player, etc.
CalculateValue = mvarPlayer.PlayerBasePrice * RookieMult

'  Take that value and then multiply by the
'  current card demand rating for the player
CalculateValue = CalculateValue + (mvarPlayer.PlayerDemandRating * _
CalculateValue)


'  Check the quality of the card. For anything other
'  than a quality rating of 5 a percentage of the
'  current calculated value is subtracted.
If Quality >= 4.5 And Quality < 5 Then
    CalculateValue = CalculateValue + (0.1 * CalculateValue)
End If

If Quality >= 4 And Quality < 4.5 Then
    CalculateValue = CalculateValue + (0.2 * CalculateValue)
End If

If Quality >= 2 And Quality < 4 Then
    CalculateValue = CalculateValue + (0.35 * CalculateValue)
End If
```

```
If Quality >= 0 And Quality < 2 Then
    CalculateValue = CalculateValue + (0.5 * CalculateValue)
End If

End Function
```

Updating the Interface and Building the Implementation

Our object model is set with our classes, and we are ready to update the code in our user interface to take advantage of the changes. We need to add a couple of components to our user interface. A combo box will be placed on the form for listing a set of players. From this, users can select players and define cards for them. Included with the combo box will be a label control. Table 3-6 outlines the names and properties for each.

Next we need to update our form code from the previous project. In the global declarations section, we are going to declare an additional variable for our Team class. And we are going to have a global variable, PlayerIndex, that will indicate which player in the collection of team players we are currently working with.

```
'   Globally declare an instance of the
'   sports card and teams class that will
'   be referenced as SC & TM. PlayerIndex
'   is a global variable that indicates the
'   current player being referenced in the
'   team collection.
Dim SC As New SportsCard
Dim TM As New Team
Dim PlayerIndex As Integer
```

Component/Property	Setting
Combo Box	CboPlayers
Style	2 'Dropdown List
Label	Lbl14
Caption	"Player"
AutoSize	-1 'True

Table 3-6. *Additional Components and Properties for the Sports Cards Project*

Now that the user can select from a list of players, we need to be able to reference the team player's properties and display them in our form text boxes. A generic function, DisplayPlayer, has been created for retrieving these property values and updating the appropriate text boxes. Note that we use the Item property of the Team class to retrieve the specified player on the team. The global PlayerIndex variable is used to indicate which item in the players collection should be referenced. Also, we can easily pass all of the current player properties to the SportsCard class by simply setting the Player property of the SportsCard class to the current Player class for the form.

```
'   Display player gets the data from the current
'   player selected in the combo box
Private Sub DisplayPlayer()

'   Display the league
txtLeague.Text = TM.League

'   Display the first and last name by indexing
'   into the teams collection
txtFirstName.Text = TM.Item(PlayerIndex).FirstName
txtLastName.Text = TM.Item(PlayerIndex).LastName

'   Display the team name
txtTeam.Text = TM.TeamName

'   Display the player demand rating and player
'   base price by indexing into the teams collection
txtPlayRate.Text = TM.Item(PlayerIndex).PlayerDemandRating
txtBasePrice.Text = TM.Item(PlayerIndex).PlayerBasePrice

'   Copy into the sports card class player object (class)
'   the player class currently being indexed on the team
Set SC.Player = TM.Item(PlayerIndex)

End Sub
```

We have had to update the SetClassProperties subroutine from the previous example. Now we don't need to pass in all of the properties including the player data since that is already stored in the Player object. So, as before, the basic properties of the SportsCard class are read in from the text box variables.

```
'   This subroutine sets the properties
'   of the class
Private Sub SetClassProperties()
```

```
'   Set each by referencing the property name
'   and getting the value from the text box
SC.Manufacturer = txtManufacturer.Text
SC.Year = txtYear.Text
SC.League = txtLeague.Text
SC.imperfections = txtNumImp.Text
SC.MiscDescription = txtDescription.Text
SC.PurchasePrice = txtPurchasePrice.Text
SC.Rookie = txtRookieCard.Text

End Sub
```

When the user clicks on the combo box and selects a player, we need to retrieve the current index in the combo box to know which player in the Team collection to reference. Note that the combo box starts its index counting at 0, and our collection starts at 1. Thus, the global PlayerIndex variable is equal to the index of the combo box plus 1.

```
'   Click event of the list box
Private Sub cboPlayers_Click()

'   Set the global player index value
'   to be the index currently selected in the
'   list box. Note we add 1 to the value since
'   the collection does not start at 0.
PlayerIndex = cboPlayers.ListIndex + 1

'   Display the player data
DisplayPlayer

End Sub
```

When the form is loaded, we need to set up our Team class. First, we set the standard properties of the Team class to appropriate data. Following that, the players on the team are set up. The Add method of the Team class is utilized with each of the parameters appropriately filled out. Following each addition, the player's first and last names are added to the combo box.

```
Private Sub Form_Load()

'  Set up the team values for the class
TM.City = "San Antonio"
TM.Coach = "Noel Jerke"
TM.League = "USA B-Ball"
TM.Mascot = "Flyer"
TM.TeamName = "Flyer Athletics"

'  Add in our first player by accessing the Add
'  method of the class
TM.Add "Maria", "Jerke", "Center", "Trinity", _
        "5 Foot", 100, "A great center!", 3.5, 4

'  Add the player name to the list box
cboPlayers.AddItem "Maria Jerke"

'  Add in the second player
TM.Add "Sherrie", "Jerke", "Forward", "Bucknell", _
        "5 Foot 5", 101, "What a forward!", 3.25, 2

'  Add the player to the list box
cboPlayers.AddItem "Sherrie Jerke"

'  Add in the third player
TM.Add "Edna", "Jerke", "Forward", "Greeley Tech", _
        "5 foot 7", 120, "An excellent forward!", 1, 2

'  Add the player to the list box
cboPlayers.AddItem "Edna Jerke"

'  Add in the fourth player
TM.Add "Aubrey", "Jerke", "Point", "Grapevine", _
        "3 foot 8", 90, "An outstanding point!", 5, 8

'  Add the player to the list box
cboPlayers.AddItem "Aubrey Jerke"
```

```
'  Add in the fifth player
TM.Add "Ashley", "Jerke", "Guard", "Mustangs", _
        "5 foot 1", 100, "An amazing guard!", 2, 1

'  Add the player to the list box
cboPlayers.AddItem "Ashley Jerke"

End Sub
```

Going to Home Plate

Let's run the application now that we have all of our code in place. Figure 3-11 shows the application at run time. Note the label and combo box at the top of the form for selecting a player. Go ahead and select Maria Jerke. The updated form is shown in Figure 3-12. The data that is displayed came directly from our Player class with the properly indexed player.

Now fill in the appropriate data to finish the Sports Cards information and click the quality, value, and markup buttons to make your calculations. Figure 3-13 shows the program with appropriate calculations.

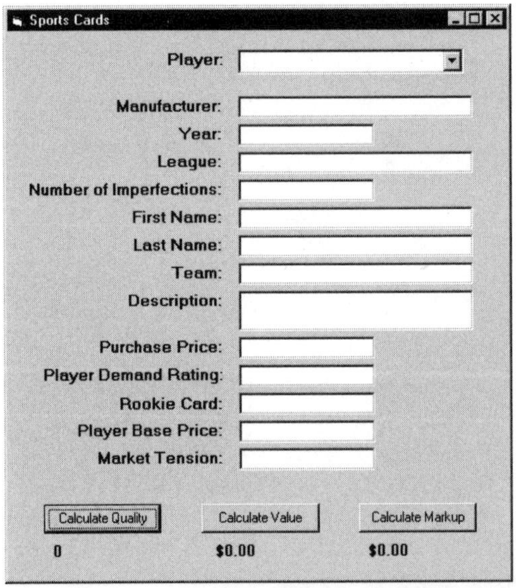

Figure 3-11. *Sports Cards program at run time*

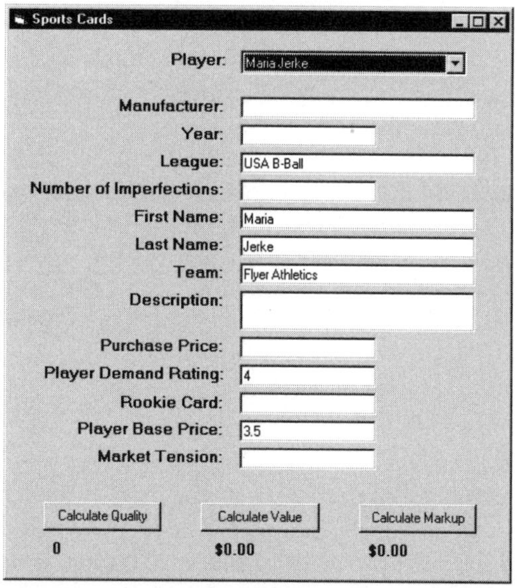

Figure 3-12.   *Sports Cards program with a player selected*

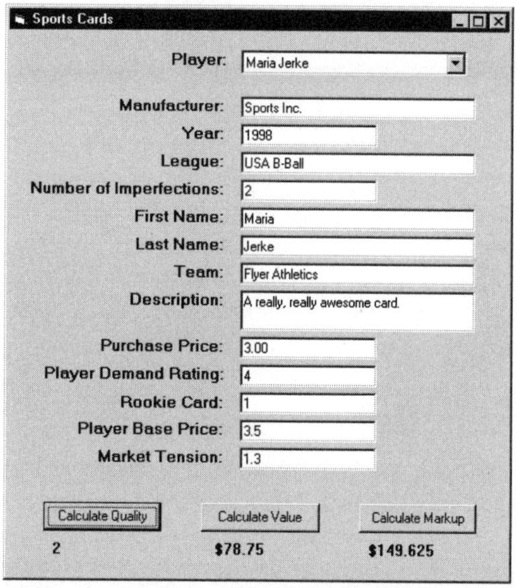

Figure 3-13.   *Sports Cards program with complete data and calculations*

Note that the three buttons to calculate quantity, value, and markup did not change (in fact are not referenced above in the form code list). The key here is that they did not require any change in the way they called the underlying methods in the class. In fact, the CalculateValue function did change to reference the Player subclass. If there is any change in logic or calculation methods for the SportsCard class, the calling application does not need to change its reference. That is part of the power of object-based applications and logic encapsulation. If the underlying business rules change, the calling application should only have to change minimally if at all.

Our object model successfully implements a team made up of subclasses of players. And our SportsCard class uses a single Player subclass to define the athlete on the card. Of course, our player could have multiple SportsCards (as indicated in the object model diagram). If we wanted to rework our implementation around a bit, we could have the Player class have a collection of SportsCards.

Can It Be Better?

You may be wondering about all of that hard-coded data in the application, such as markup multipliers, the data in the Form_Load event for the players, and so on. You are right in thinking that data should be in a database. In fact, all of the team, player, and sports card data should be implemented from an underlying data store. As we get into the next chapter and further into the book, using databases for just these purposes will be essential.

Encapsulating ActiveX Controls

Finally, let's take a look at another type of encapsulation of code we can create in our Visual Basic applications. The ActiveX control or custom control can be a powerful method of allowing our programming to be easily portable and encapsulated. Of course, in this case we are primarily talking about a set of code that has some type of user interface.

We're going to build a simple program that demonstrates the construction of ActiveX controls. Go ahead and start a new ActiveX control project. When the project starts, you will see a familiar development environment. You will note that the "form" has no header bar at the top. The "design" space is what the user will see as the interface to your control.

The ActiveX Progress Bar

Our simple demonstration program will implement a progress bar that will increase in value with each tick of the timer control. The speed of the progress bar will be based on the interval set in a text box. The timer and progress bar will be enabled and disabled with a check box and reset with a command button. Figure 3-14 shows the interface with the controls placed on it. Table 3-7 shows the names and properties for the controls.

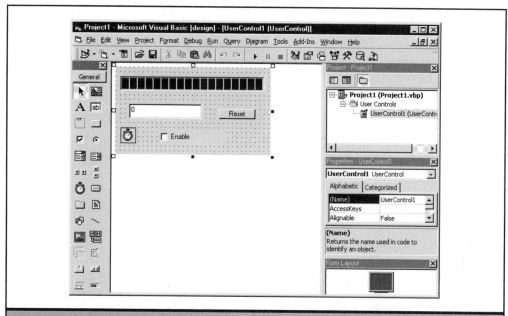

Figure 3-14. *ActiveX control interface with components placed on it*

Component/Property	Setting
Check Box	ChkEnable
Caption	"Enable"
Command Button	CmdReset
Caption	"Reset"
Text Box	TxtInterval
Text	"0"
Progress Bar	PrgBar
Appearance	1
Timer	Timer1
Enabled	0 'False

Table 3-7. *Components for the User Control Interface*

Note that the controls/components placed on the design interface will be "wrapped" into the control we are building. At this point, go ahead and run the control to see how we test our handiwork. When you go to run the project, the Project Properties dialog box pops up asking how you want to test the control. By default, the control will be run in a browser (Internet Explorer). Go ahead and accept these defaults and run the program. You will see your control with the components on it in the browser.

Now we are ready to go ahead and place some code behind the control interface. The first we can do is set up the check box to handle enabling and disabling the timer control. When the check box is on with a value of 1, the timer is enabled. When it is off (0), the timer is disabled.

```
'  Click event of the check box
Private Sub chkEnable_Click()

'  Check to see if the check box is on
If chkEnable.Value = 1 Then
    '  Enable the timer
    Timer1.Enabled = True
Else
    '  Disable the timer
    Timer1.Enabled = False
End If

End Sub
```

The Reset button simply sets the value of the progress bar back to 0 and disables the timer control by setting the Enable check box to unchecked. That in turn disables the timer control.

```
'  Click event of the reset button
Private Sub cmdReset_Click()

'  Set the progress bar to 0
prgBar.Value = 0

'  Uncheck the check box
chkEnable.Value = 0

End Sub
```

The timer event is fired after the specified interval property (in milliseconds) has been counted off. The progress bar value is increased by 5 with each tick. We check to ensure that the progress bar does not exceed 100. When it reaches 100, the timer is disabled.

```
'  Timer event
Private Sub Timer1_Timer()

'  Increase the value by 5
prgBar.Value = prgBar.Value + 5

'  If we are at 100 then disable the timer
If prgBar.Value = 100 Then

    '  Disable timer
    Timer1.Enabled = False

End If

End Sub
```

Finally, when the text in the text box is changed, the value of the timer interval is updated, thus changing the speed of the progress bar.

```
Private Sub txtInterval_Change()

'  When the text box changes, change the
'  timer interval to the new time entered
Timer1.Interval = txtInterval.Text

End Sub
```

Making Progress

Now go ahead and run the control in the browser and test its features. Figure 3-15 shows the control in use. Take a second to view the source of the page. In the page, you will see a pair of object tags with a classid identifying the ActiveX control. Of course, you can use your ActiveX control on Visual Basic forms as well. Using the Package and Deployment wizard, you can build an installation package for both the Internet and Visual Basic development and distribution. The possibilities are wide open for encapsulating business logic and deploying to your end user.

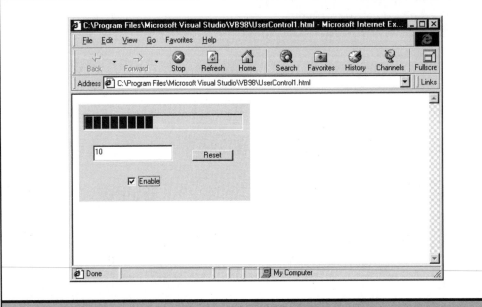

Figure 3-15.   *ActiveX control in use in Internet Explorer*

Summary

Using and building objects in Visual Basic is the key to understanding and utilizing the language. If you want to access databases, you will need to use the ActiveX Data Object (ADO). Breaking down complexity of extensive development projects will require use of class modules for abstraction and encapsulation. Even using components and controls requires the use of properties, methods, and events. When we build business objects in Part III and Internet applications that are based on special web classes in Part IV, we will be creating and using objects. Throughout the rest of the book, we will build and use objects to build powerful, flexible, and reusable applications.

What's Next

The next chapter will serve to introduce database applications in more detail. Visual Basic has always been a strong database application development tool and is only getting stronger. The data environment example we touched on in this chapter is just the beginning of what is possible.

Chapter 4

Connecting to Databases

One could easily argue that a Visual Basic application without a database behind it is no Visual Basic application at all. Of course, that is not true, but databases are the lifeblood of many corporate-level applications. In this chapter we will explore the different options in Visual Basic to get connected to your database.

Getting Connected

Visual Basic in its many different incarnations has provided many different features for accessing data. Its roots begin with Data Access Objects (DAO), and Microsoft continues to develop and enhance DAO. A couple of versions ago, Microsoft then introduced Remote Data Objects (RDO). RDO was built to deal with remote data access and not having a local query processor (such as the JET engine). Finally, Microsoft has introduced ActiveX Data Objects (ADO) as its new data access method of choice.

Data Access Objects

DAO enables you to use a programming language to access and manipulate data in local or remote databases and to manage databases, their objects, and their structure. DAO supports two different database environments, or *workspaces*. The first is Microsoft JET workspaces, which include databases created in Microsoft Access. You can also connect to JET databases via ODBC drivers. And finally, you can support ISAM databases such as Paradox or Microsoft Excel. Use the Microsoft JET workspace when you open a Microsoft JET database (.mdb file) or other desktop ISAM database. The second is ODBCDirect workspaces. With this option you can bypass the Microsoft JET database engine and go directly to the back-end server to execute queries against the database. The ODBCDirect workspace provides an alternative when you only need to execute queries or stored procedures against a back-end server, such as Microsoft SQL Server or Oracle.

> **Note**   *You may be more familiar with the term "SQL Passthrough." This is the same as DAO's ODBCDirect concept.*

One of the most powerful features of Visual Basic since data access was introduced to the language is the *data control*. This control encapsulates basic functionality for creating applications that display, edit, and update information. As you will see in our first example for the chapter, a lot of database manipulation functionality is packed into this little control. One of its key functions is providing an interface for data bound controls (list box, text box, etc.). This functionality in certain situations can save hours of database interface programming. Microsoft has added many new features to DAO, including the ODBCDirect capabilities. For further reference on the new features and documentation on DAO's many properties, methods, and events, see the MSDN DAO 3.5 SDK.

Remote Data Objects

After DAO there was RDO, and all was good in the universe of data access. In fact, RDO was a significant leap forward in enterprise-level data access and management for Visual Basic. RDO provides an information model for accessing remote data sources through ODBC. RDO offers a set of objects that make it easy to connect to a database, execute queries and stored procedures, manipulate results, and commit changes to the server.

The RDO programming model is similar to the DAO programming model in many respects. However, far more emphasis is focused on handling stored procedures and their result sets, and less emphasis is placed on data access retrieval methods used solely by ISAM programming models.

Note	*Stored procedures are SQL queries that are stored on the database server instead of in the Visual Basic application code.*

RDO was developed as part of Microsoft's initiative to develop n-tier applications, with the primary tiers being the user interface, the business object (business programming), and the data access layer. The separation of data from the user interface and direct access in the Visual Basic GUI front end required a robust model for accessing remote data (on another server).

ActiveX Data Objects

As part of its Web initiative, Microsoft launched a new type of data access, ADO. ADO is the successor to DAO and RDO. Functionally, ADO 2.0 is most similar to RDO. Anyone familiar with RDO programming will note the similarities between the two models. ADO "flattens" the object model used by DAO and RDO, meaning that it contains fewer objects and more properties, methods (and arguments), and events. For example, ADO has no equivalents to the rdoEngine and rdoEnvironment objects that exposed the ODBC driver.

Much of the functionality contained in the DAO and RDO models was consolidated into single objects in the model, making for a much simpler object model. If you are used to DAO or RDO programming, working with ADO may take some getting used to.

Note	*ADO currently doesn't support all of DAO's functionality. ADO mostly includes RDO-style functionality to interact with OLE DB data sources. So if you are trying to convert existing DAO code to ADO, you will have problems with conversion of data definition language (DDL) features.*

As outlined in Chapter 1, ADO consists of three primary objects. The Data Connection object defines the connection to the database. The Data Command object defines access to database objects such as tables, stored procedures, or SQL queries. The Recordset object contains the set of records returned from the database server.

Later in the chapter, we will dig into a couple different examples of programming with ADO, including an example using the data environment and our SportsCard class.

OLE DB

A key addition in ADO is OLE DB support. OLE DB is a set of COM interfaces that provide applications with uniform access to data stored in a wide variety of information sources, both relational and nonrelational. These interfaces support the amount of DBMS functionality appropriate to the data source, enabling it to share its data through a standard database interface format. Thus, you can use ADO to potentially access data in fairly unstructured formats. ADO is the way that programmers access OLE DB. All the new data bound controls, the data environment, and the data report designer are OLE DB aware.

COM stands for component object model. This is Microsoft's platform-independent technology for linking objects with a consistent interface. For more information on COM, visit Microsoft's COM Web site at http://www.microsoft.com/com/.

The idea behind OLE DB is universal data access. There are no restrictions to JET, relational database sources, and so on. With this type of data access, you can access unstructured data such as text files and Excel spreadsheets. The key to this flexibility is using ADO—the programmatic interface to OLE DB. OLE DB supports ODBC connections (see Chapter 2) and JET connections, and it provides a wide-open specification for database management system developers to provide connectivity to their software.

To learn a lot more about the gory inner workings of OLE DB, see the Microsoft OLE DB Overview on the MSDN.

If you are new to Visual Basic, the good news is that data access is getting easier with ADO and OLE DB. If you are an advanced developer, the good news is that your life is getting easier and your programming more flexible with ADO and OLE DB.

Confused or unfamiliar with these different database options? Don't worry, stick to ODBC connections (the second option) as outlined in Chapter 3, and you will be able to easily access your databases as needed. And for that matter, if you are working on a new database project, stick to ADO. There are only a few cases when working with JET- and ISAM-based databases in which you will need to work with DAO.

Data Bound Controls

Controls that you can directly bind to a database for viewing, editing, adding, and deleting data are known as data bound controls. These controls can provide extensive functionality right out of the box.

- **DataGrid:** This control is a spreadsheet-like control that displays a series of rows and columns representing records and fields from a Recordset object. You can use the DataGrid control to create an application that allows the end user to read and write to most databases.

- **Bound controls:** These can be quickly configured at design time with little or no code. When you set the control's DataSource property at design time, the control is automatically filled in and automatically set from the data source's recordset. In the case of the DataGrid control, you can then edit the grid's columns: delete, rearrange, add column headers, or adjust any column's width.

Combining these controls with the data control (DAO), remote data control (RDO), or the ActiveX data control (ADO), you can build quick interfaces for working with a database. In our first example below, we will see the power of combining data bound controls and data controls to build database applications.

Using DAO to Build a Simple Database Interface

To get started, let's build a simple DAO application using the DataGrid control and data bound controls. First, of course, we will need a database to access. For this chapter, we will use Microsoft Access 97 MDB files.

Building the Database

Our database will be simple name, address, and phone contact storage. Table 4-1 outlines the fields. Go ahead and create your database and save it as address.mdb. We will use the database as a simple address management system.

Building Our Project with the DAO Data Control

Now that we have the database, we are ready to begin our sample project. The first step is building the user interface with the appropriate controls. In this case we are going to use bound controls with the data control. We will have to place a bit of code behind our application to support adding new records to the database.

Field Name	Data Type	Description
IdAddress	AutoNumber	Primary key that increments automatically (AutoNumber).
TxtFirstName	Text	First name of the contact.
TxtLastName	Text	Last name of the contact.
txtAddress	Text	Address of the contact.
txtCity	Text	City where the contact lives.
txtState	Text	State where the contact lives.
txtZipCode	Text	Zip code for the contact.
txtPhone	Text	Phone number for the contact.
txtFax	Text	Fax number for the contact.

Table 4-1. *Address Database Structure*

Building the Interface

Start a Standard EXE project and save it to your system. We are going to need several command buttons for adding new addresses and updating the database. Also, we will need one data control and several text boxes to display the data. Table 4-2 outlines the controls to be placed on the form. Figure 4-1 shows the form at design time.

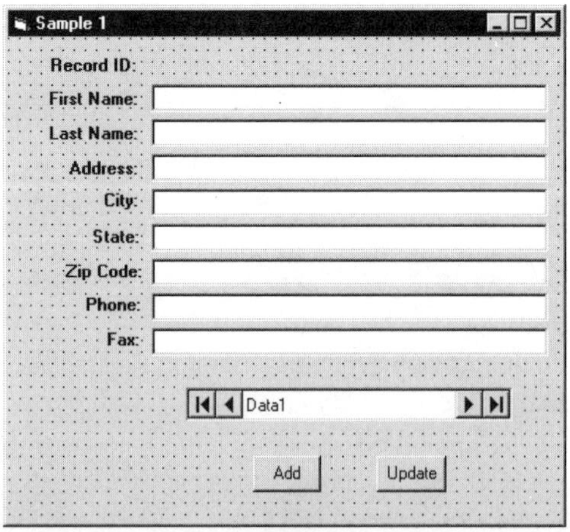

Figure 4-1. *Sample data access project at design time*

Component/Property	Setting
Form	Sample1
Caption	"Sample 1"
CommandButton	CmdUpdate
Caption	"Update"
Visible	0 'False
CommandButton	CmdAdd
Caption	"Add"
Data	Data1
Caption	"Data1"
Connect	"Access"
DatabaseName	(Point to Access Database on Your System/CD)
DefaultCursorType	0 'DefaultCursor
DefaultType	2 'UseODBC
Exclusive	0 'False
ReadOnly	0 'False
RecordsetType	1 'Dynaset
RecordSource	"Address"
TextBox	TxtFax
DataField	"txtFax"
DataSource	"Data1"
Text	""
TextBox	TxtPhone
DataField	"txtPhone"
DataSource	"Data1"
Text	""
TextBox	TxtZipCode

Table 4-2.   *Interface Form and Control Properties*

Component/Property	Setting
DataField	"txtZipCode"
DataSource	"Data1"
Text	""
TextBox	TxtState
DataField	"txtState"
DataSource	"Data1"
Text	""
TextBox	TxtCity
DataField	"txtCity"
DataSource	"Data1"
Text	""
TextBox	TxtAddress
DataField	"txtAddress"
DataSource	"Data1"
Text	""
TextBox	TxtLastName
DataField	"txtLastName"
DataSource	"Data1"
Text	""
TextBox	TxtFirstName
DataField	"txtFirstName"
DataSource	"Data1"
Text	""
Label	LblIdAddress
AutoSize	-1 'True
DataField	"idAddress"

Table 4-2. *Interface Form and Control Properties* (continued)

Component/Property	Setting
DataSource	"Data1"
Label	Label1 – Label 9
Alignment	1 'Right Justify
AutoSize	-1 'True
Caption	"Record ID:", "Fax:", "Phone:", "Zip Code:", "State:", "City:", "Address:", "Last Name:", "First Name:"

Table 4-2. *Interface Form and Control Properties* (continued)

Note that the LblIDAddress label will be used to display the unique ID (autonumber primary key). The data is displayed in a label since it is neither entered nor updated by the user. It is also important to place the data control and set its properties before placing the data bound text and label controls on the form. Each of these requires binding to the data control by settings its data source property. Finally, the Update button is not visible upon startup of the form. It can only be used after the Add button has been clicked and the user is entering a new record.

To lay out your user interface in a consistent way, with all the controls aligned properly, use the options on the Format menu for lining up your controls.

That's it for building a simple data-aware interface! Of course, we have not yet implemented the functionality of the Add and Update buttons. But, if you want to go ahead and run the project, you will be able to move back and forth through the existing records and update the data.

Building the Code Behind the Interface

Now let's put some code behind our application. First, for the click event of the Add button, we will want to tell the data control to add a new record. That is done by accessing the Recordset property and calling the AddNew method. Once that is done, the bound controls are automatically cleared and ready for data entry. To ensure the user doesn't try and add a new record in the middle of adding a new record, we hide the Add button. Then to provide a method for updating the database with the new data, the Update button is displayed.

```
'  Click event of the add command
'  button
Private Sub cmdAdd_Click()

'  Add a new record to the record set
Data1.Recordset.AddNew

'  Hide the add button
cmdAdd.Visible = False

'  Display the Update button
cmdUpdate.Visible = True

End Sub
```

When the user clicks the Update button, the Update method of the Recordset object for the data control is invoked. That will cause the data control to insert the new data into the database. After that is done, the Add button is displayed again, and the Update button is hidden. That is it—you have just created a database application that is about as simple and easy to implement as is possible.

```
'  Click event of the Update command
'  button
Private Sub cmdUpdate_Click()

'  Update the data control
Data1.Recordset.Update

'  Make the add command button
'  visible
cmdAdd.Visible = True

'  Hide the update button
cmdUpdate.Visible = False

End Sub
```

Thus we have code for initiating an insert into the database and then finishing the insert with an update of the data to the database. Note that we did not have to write any code for browsing the data in the database or any code for updating records. Visual Basic's data bound controls and data controls provide a significant amount of functionality right out of the box.

Testing and Running Our Application

Go ahead and run the application. Figure 4-2 shows the form loaded, with the address data displayed. Click on the arrow buttons of the data control to scroll through the records. Type changes into one of the records, move to a new record, and then go back. You will note your changes are automatically saved. Figure 4-3 shows the form with data changes.

Finally, click on the Add button to insert a new record. When you do that, the Update button is displayed, and the contents of the bound controls are cleared. Figure 4-4 shows the form after the Add button has been clicked. Once you are done entering data, click on the Update button, and your record will be added to the database. The Add button will reappear, and you can scroll through your records and find the new one you entered.

You could just as easily have used the remote data control or the ActiveX data control to make the connection to the database, show the contents of the address table, and allow updates and inserts. Data controls are nice for making simple connections to a database. But if you want to go deeper and be able to break out the data access from the user interface, you will have to use ADO directly or, at a minimum, work with the data environment. In large corporate systems or Internet systems, you don't have the luxury of assuming you can do all the database programming at the client's desktop, and in that case data controls cannot be used.

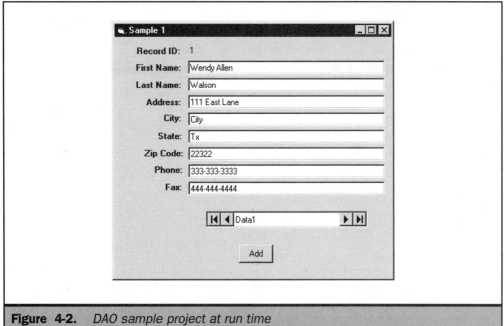

Figure 4-2.   *DAO sample project at run time*

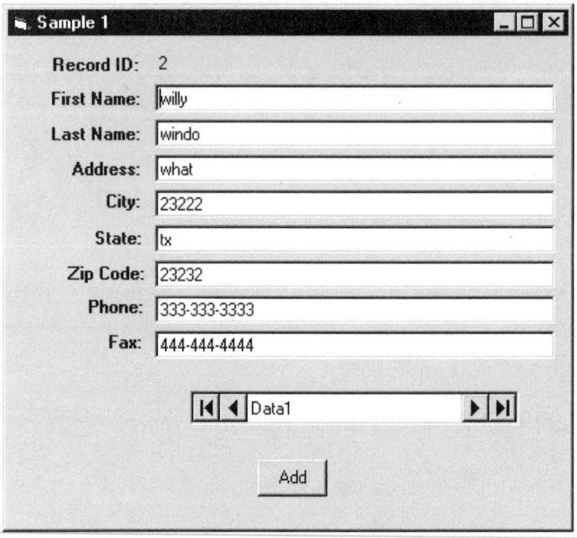

Figure 4-3. DAO sample project with an updated record

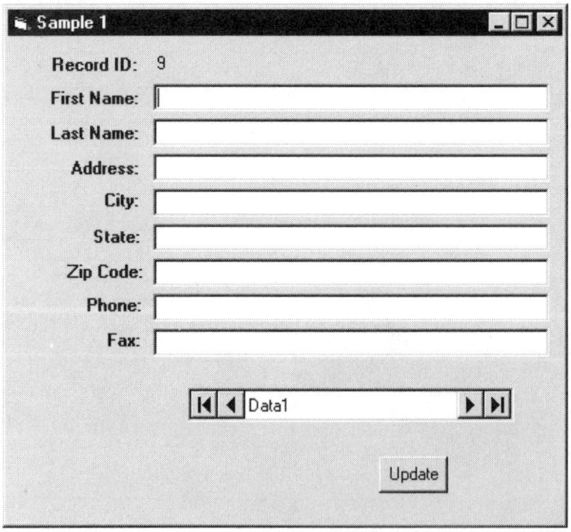

Figure 4-4. DAO sample project after the Add button has been clicked

Programming with ADO—In Depth

To get a feel for a bit of raw ADO programming, let's create our second example for the chapter. Using the same address database, we are going to create the same functionality as the first example, but we are going to do it using ADO directly—no data controls or data bound controls.

Updating the Interface

We will use the same user interface as the first example, but we will add a couple of new options. Table 4-3 outlines the updated and additional controls for the project. Note that the data control has been removed from the interface. Figure 4-5 shows the project at design time.

In the first example, we did not implement a way to delete records or a way to cancel the addition of a new record. In our user interface, we have added two buttons for these features. And, since we are not using a data control, we are going to need some easy way to select addresses. That is what the combo box is for.

Building the ADO Code Behind the Interface

Of course, this project, unlike the first project, will have no functionality when you run it. We are going to have to put code behind each of the functions. To get started, we need a couple of global variables. The first, intCurrAddress, will store the ID of the

Component/Property	Setting
Form	Sample2
Caption	"Sample 2"
CommandButton	CmdCancel
Caption	"Cancel"
Enabled	0 'False
CommandButton	CmdDelete
Caption	"Delete"
ComboBox	CboAddresses
Style	2 'Dropdown List

Table 4-3. *New User Interface Property Settings for the Second Sample Project*

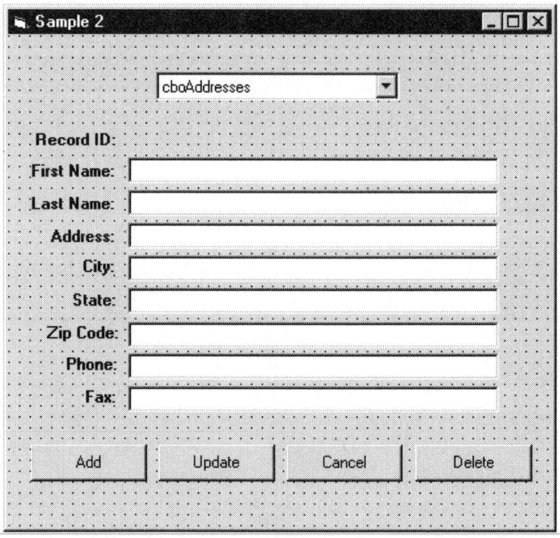

Figure 4-5. *ADO sample project at design time*

current address selected in the drop-down box. The intSaveUpdate variable indicates when changes to the current record should be updated. As we will see, there are some cases when we don't need to save any changes typed into the text boxes.

```
'   Stores the id of the current address
Dim intCurrAddress As Integer

'   Indicates whether a change in the
'   list box should invoke a save of the
'   data in the text boxes
Dim intSaveUpdate As Integer
```

The combo box will need to be loaded with the addresses in the database. If you have not already done so, be sure to select Microsoft ActiveX Data Objects 2.0 Library in your references. The LoadAddresses subroutine will be called when we need to load the current set of addresses out of the database. The first two variables declared are ActiveX Data Objects. The first is an ADO connection object, and the second is an ADO recordset object. The connection object will create a connection to our database. The easiest way to define this for Access is through an ODBC connection. Go ahead and create a data source name called "address" that points to the Access database (see the steps for this in Chapter 3).

Once the DSN is created, the connection string for the Open method is quite simple. The connection string simply designates the data source name to be the name of our ODBC DSN (address).

When the connection is established, we are ready to load the addresses. The Clear method of the combo box is called to clear any current contents in the list. After that we are ready to execute a SQL statement that will return all of the addresses sorted by last name. That is done by using the Execute method of the connection object. The results from this query execution are returned in a recordset object. Those results are then set to the rsAddress recordset object declared in the beginning of our subroutine.

Since the first address displayed in the list box is the current address ID, the intCurrAddress global variable is set. We are then ready to loop through the recordset and load the addresses in the combo box. Each address is loaded with the AddItem method. The first and last names are displayed. We then load the address ID in the ItemData field property. The ItemData property stores information about the current item in the list box. Note that the reference to the last item added is done by using the NewIndex property, which is the index of the last item added. Once that is done, we close the connection to the database.

Finally, we need to select an address for display once the list is filled out. When an index is set for the list box, the click event is fired off. In this case, we don't want to go through the data save routine in the click event of the combo box, so we need to indicate that step should be bypassed. That is where the intSaveUpdate global variable comes into play. It is set to 0 to indicate the save should *not* be done. Then the index is set. After that, intSaveUpdate is set back to 1.

```
'   This subroutine should be called to load or
'   refresh the combo box of addresses
Private Sub LoadAddresses()

'   Declare our variables
Dim dbAddress As New ADODB.Connection
Dim rsAddress As New ADODB.Recordset

'   Make the connection
dbAddress.Open "dsn=address"

'   Clear the combo box
cboAddresses.Clear

'   Request the addresses with a SQL statement
'   executed by the connection to the database
```

```vb
Set rsAddress = dbAddress.Execute("select * from" & _
    "address order by txtLastName")

' Set the global variable to the first address
' since that is the one that will be displayed
intCurrAddress = rsAddress("idAddress")

' Loop through the addresses
Do Until rsAddress.EOF

    ' Add the address to the list by showing the
    ' person's first name and last name
    cboAddresses.AddItem _
        rsAddress("txtFirstName") & " " & _
        rsAddress("txtLastName")

    ' Add the id of the address to the item data
    ' property for the address
    cboAddresses.ItemData(cboAddresses.NewIndex) = _
        rsAddress("idAddress")

    ' Move to the next record
    rsAddress.MoveNext

Loop

' Close the DB
dbAddress.Close

' Set our save variable to indicate no saves should
' be done when the index is set
intSaveUpdate = 0

' Set to the first address
cboAddresses.ListIndex = 0

' Set back to allow updates
intSaveUpdate = 1

End Sub
```

The next step in the process is to respond to clicks on the combo box. When the click event is fired off, we need to do a couple of things. First, we need to save any changes. A check is done of the intSaveUpdate variable to ensure it is not set to 0 to indicate the save should be skipped. In the beginning of the event, our database connection and recordset variables are declared, and the connection is opened.

When the data for the current address is saved, an update SQL query is created to update the current address. The ID of the current address is stored in intCurrAddress. The values for the fields in the database are read from the corresponding text boxes. Once the SQL query is built, the Execute method of the ADO connection is run for the SQL statement. Note in this case we are not expecting any results back from an update, so a result set object is not needed to hold the return of the Execute method.

Once the data is saved, we can display the address selected by the user. The current address is retrieved from the ItemData field of the combo box. Then a SQL statement is created to retrieve the address in the database based on the ID. The results are stored in our rsAddress result set variable. Then each of the text boxes and the ID label are updated with the new values, and voila, we have saved any changes to the last address and have displayed the new one.

```vb
'   Click event of the combo box. Note that this
'   is fired as well when the listindex property
'   is set.
Private Sub cboAddresses_Click()


'   Declare our variables
Dim dbAddress As New ADODB.Connection
Dim rsAddress As New ADODB.Recordset


'   Open our connection
dbAddress.Open "dsn=address"


'   Check the global variable to see if we are supposed
'   to save any changes entered by the user
If intSaveUpdate = 1 Then


    '   Build the SQL update query
    sql = "update address set " & _
        "txtFirstName = '" & txtFirstName.Text & "', " & _
        "txtLastName = '" & txtLastName.Text & "', " & _
        "txtAddress = '" & txtAddress.Text & "', " & _
        "txtCity = '" & txtCity.Text & "', " & _
        "txtState = '" & txtState.Text & "', " & _
```

```
            "txtZipCode = '" & txtZipCode.Text & "', " & _
            "txtPhone = '" & txtPhone.Text & "', " & _
            "txtFax = '" & txtFax.Text & "' where idaddress = " & _
            intCurrAddress

    '   Execute the query
        dbAddress.Execute sql

End If

'   Set the id of the current address
intCurrAddress = cboAddresses.ItemData(cboAddresses.ListIndex)

'   Build the query to retrieve the address
'   data
Set rsAddress = dbAddress.Execute("select * " & _
    "from address where idAddress = " & intCurrAddress)

'   Display the data
lblIDAddress.Caption = rsAddress("idAddress")
txtFirstName.Text = rsAddress("txtFirstName")
txtLastName.Text = rsAddress("txtLastName")
txtAddress.Text = rsAddress("txtAddress")
txtCity.Text = rsAddress("txtCity")
txtState.Text = rsAddress("txtState")
txtZipCode.Text = rsAddress("txtZipCode")
txtPhone.Text = rsAddress("txtPhone")
txtFax.Text = rsAddress("txtFax")

'   Close the database
dbAddress.Close

End Sub
```

The Add button click event will initiate the process of adding a new address to the database. The first thing done is to enable the Cancel and Update buttons. The Cancel button will allow the user to cancel a new addition, and the Update button will save the new addition. Also, the Add button will need to be disabled as well as the combo box. We don't want someone trying to select an address in the middle of an add. Once that is done, all the input text boxes are cleared for new data entry.

> **Note** *You could put abort logic in the click event of the combo box to abort any current attempts to add a new address. That way, if the user had clicked the Add button but then clicked the combo box, we could cancel the add process and allow the user to select one of the addresses.*

```
'  Click event of the add button
Private Sub cmdAdd_Click()

'  Enable the cancel and update buttons
cmdCancel.Enabled = True
cmdUpdate.Enabled = True

'  Disable the add button
cmdAdd.Enabled = False

'  Disable the combo list
cboAddresses.Enabled = False

'  Clear the input text boxes
lblIDAddress.Caption = ""
txtFirstName.Text = ""
txtLastName.Text = ""
txtAddress.Text = ""
txtCity.Text = ""
txtState.Text = ""
txtZipCode.Text = ""
txtPhone.Text = ""
txtFax.Text = ""

'  Ensure no saves are done (not really possible
'  since the combo box is disabled)
intSaveUpdate = 0

End Sub
```

The Cancel button allows the user to cancel the addition of a new address. The first thing done is to load the new address into the combo box, which will correspondingly display the address data. After that, the appropriate controls are enabled and disabled to return to the original address browsing and updating state. You also may want to consider using the Cancel button to cancel any changes typed in for a current address.

> **Note**
> *If you have a large number of rows in your database, you may want to consider saving the ID of the address currently being viewed when the Add button was clicked and then show that address if the Cancel button is clicked. That way, you don't have to reload the data.*

```
' Click event of the cancel button
Private Sub cmdCancel_Click()

' Load the address into the combo box
LoadAddresses

' Enable the combo box
cboAddresses.Enabled = True

' Enable the add button
cmdAdd.Enabled = True

' Disable the update button
cmdUpdate.Enabled = False

' Disable the cancel button
cmdCancel.Enabled = False

End Sub
```

When the Delete button is clicked, we will delete the current address from the database. Like any good interface, we will give the user one last chance to cancel the delete operation. To do that, we will use a message box with a yes or no response option. If the response is yes (6), then open our database connection, build a SQL query to delete the current address, and execute the query. After that, we reload the combo box with the updated list of addresses.

```
' Click event of the delete button
Private Sub cmdDelete_Click()

' Declare our variables
Dim dbAddress As New ADODB.Connection
Dim intResponse As Integer

' Query to ensure the user wants to
' delete the record
strResponse = MsgBox("Are you sure?", vbYesNo, "Delete Query")
```

```
'  Check to see if the response was a yes
If strResponse = 6 Then

    '  Open the connection
    dbAddress.Open "dsn=address"

    '  Delete the address
    sql = "delete from address where idaddress = " & intCurrAddress

    '  Execute the SQL statement
    dbAddress.Execute sql

    '  Load the addresses
    LoadAddresses

    '  Close the DB
    dbAddress.Close

End If

End Sub
```

Once the user has finished the data entry for a new address, the user will click on the Update button. When that is done, the appropriate command buttons are enabled and disabled. Then our database connection is opened. A SQL query is built to insert the new record into the database. Note that, in this example, no data validation is done to ensure the proper or required fields have been filled out. This could be done to any specification you may require. Once the record has been inserted, we need to reload the combo box with the latest set of addresses.

```
'  Click event of the Update button
Private Sub cmdUpdate_Click()

'  Declare the variables
Dim dbAddress As New ADODB.Connection
Dim rsAddress As New ADODB.Recordset

'  Disable the update button
cmdUpdate.Enabled = False
```

```
'  Enable the add button
cmdAdd.Enabled = True

'  Enable the combo boxes
cboAddresses.Enabled = True

'  Open the database connection
dbAddress.Open "dsn=address"

'  Build the insert SQL statement
sql = "insert into address(txtFirstName, txtLastName," & _
      "txtAddress, " & _
      "txtCity, txtState, txtZipCode, txtPhone, txtFax)" & _
      " values('" & _
      txtFirstName.Text & "', '" & _
      txtLastName.Text & "', '" & _
      txtAddress.Text & "', '" & _
      txtCity.Text & "', '" & _
      txtState.Text & "', '" & _
      txtZipCode.Text & "', '" & _
      txtPhone.Text & "', '" & _
      txtFax.Text & "')"

'  Execute the SQL statement
dbAddress.Execute sql

'  Close the DB connection
dbAddress.Close

'  Load the addresses
LoadAddresses

End Sub
```

When the form is loaded, we need to load the combo box with addresses.

```
Private Sub Form_Load()

'  Load the addresses
LoadAddresses

End Sub
```

All of what was done for us in the first example with data bound controls and the data control has been replaced here with Visual Basic code and the ADO interface. While this is not as simple or elegant as the first set of code, you do have complete control over the process of managing the address data.

Running and Testing Our Application

Now that you have your code and controls in place, you are ready to run the application. You will find that it doesn't behave all that differently from the first example. But this time you have created the code behind the functionality instead of relying on the built-in functionality of a data control. Figure 4-6 shows the application at run time.

Click on the combo box to select a new address, and all the right processes should take place to save any changes to the previous record and then display the new record. Figure 4-7 shows the application after an update and selection of a new record. If speed is a crucial factor of your application for browsing through records, you may want to eliminate the automatic save of a record when the combo box is clicked. You could set a global flag in the change event for each text box that would indicate a data change for that record. If the global flag had not been set, you could bypass the record update logic in the combo box click event. That would make the application a bit snappier.

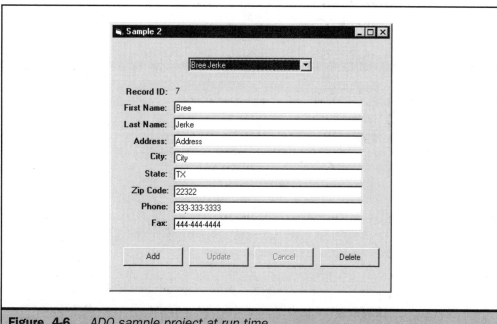

Figure 4-6. *ADO sample project at run time*

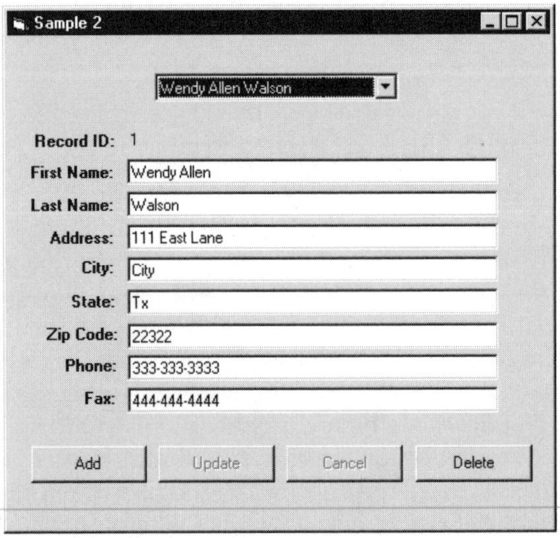

Figure 4-7.   *ADO sample project after a record update and selection of a new record*

Figure 4-8 shows the application when a new record is being updated. Finally, Figure 4-9 shows the message box after the Delete button has been clicked.

You have built your first ADO application from the ground up. But many facets of ADO have not been touched on, such as parameterized queries, calling stored procedures, and much more. In Parts III and IV of the book, we will explore the use of ADO in building n-tier distributed applications. You may be wondering, why go through all the work in the second example when it was so easy in the first one? In fact, there are cases when the ADO control is perfect for simple database manipulation. However, if you are building enterprise-level distributed applications, you are going to want to be able to divorce the data interface from your user interface. A perfect example is building Internet applications. While you can in some cases reach across the Net from the browser and access the database, in most instances you will want to (or have to) have the data access abstracted away on the server.

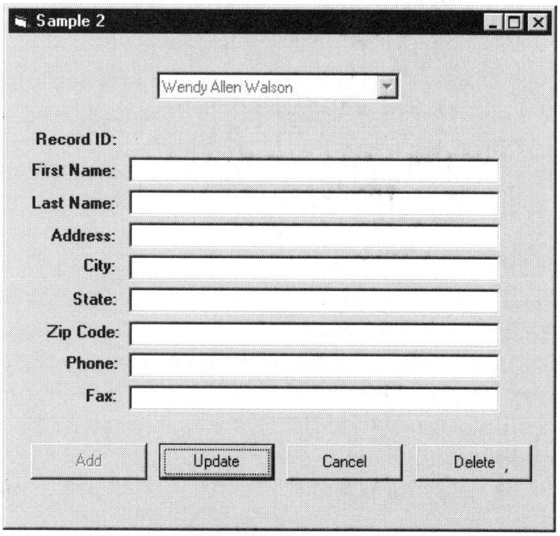

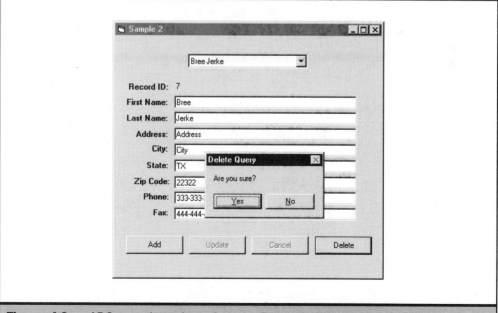

Figure 4-8.   *ADO sample project after the Add button has been clicked*

Figure 4-9.   *ADO sample project when the Delete button has been clicked*

Adding a Data Interface to Your Object Models

Let's take the use of ADO one step further and resurrect our Sports Cards example from Chapter 3. In the last example in the chapter, the team and player data was hard coded into the application. Of course, and as noted, it would be much more useful if the data came from a database. So let's go ahead and build a database interface for the Sports Cards project.

Designing the Database

We will need two tables in our database. The first will hold team data, and the second will hold player data. Table 4-4 outlines the fields for the team database.

You will recognize that the fields in the team table relate to the properties of the Team class. In fact, they are the same. Essentially, we are building in "persistent" storage for the object properties. When the class is instantiated, the properties will be read in from our persistent storage—the database.

Table 4-5 outlines the fields for the player table. Note that the player table stores the ID of the team the player is on. This is related to the team table.

Go ahead and create the tables in Access (or your favorite database). Once you have the database created, we are going to update our original Sports Cards program.

Updating the Sports Cards User Interface

First off, we will add a couple of extra controls on our interface to those we had in Chapter 3. The original program did not support multiple team selection. We only created one Team class that had multiple players. With the database, we will need to support selection of multiple teams. Table 4-6 adds a combo box for selecting teams. Figure 4-10 shows the updated interface.

Field Name	Data Type	Description
idTeam	AutoNumber	Unique identifier for the team.
TxtTeamName	Text	Team name.
txtMascot	Text	Mascot name for the team.
txtCoach	Text	Coach for the team.
txtCity	Text	City where the team plays.
txtLeague	Text	League in which the team plays.

Table 4-4.   *Team Database Structure*

Field Name	Data Type	Description
IdPlayer	AutoNumber	Unique ID for the player.
txtFirstName	Text	First name of the player.
txtLastName	Text	Last name of the player.
txtPosition	Text	Position of the player.
txtCollege	Text	College of the player.
nbrHeight	Number – Integer	Height of the player.
nbrWeight	Number – Integer	Weight of the player.
memComments	Memo	Comments on the player.
nbrDemandRating	Number – Double	Demand rating for the player.
nbrPlayerBasePrice	Number – Double	Base card price for the player.
idTeam	Number	ID of the player's team. This relates to the ID of the team table.

Table 4-5. *Player Database Structure*

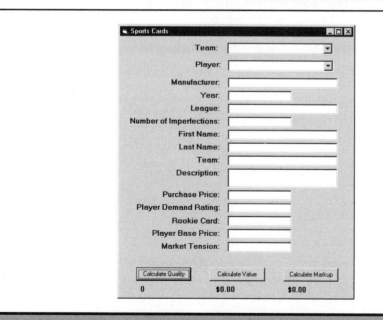

Figure 4-10. *Updated Sports Cards example interface*

Component/Property	Setting
Form	Form1
Caption	"Sports Cards"
ComboBox	CboTeams
Style	2 'Dropdown List

Table 4-6. *Update to the Sports Cards Project Interface*

Now that we have our database in place (the back end), and we have our user interface in place (the front end), we are ready to work on the middle-tier business code to interface with the database.

Updating the Object Model Implementation Code

In order to support multiple teams, we need an easy way to store multiple instances of the Team class (one for each team entry in the database). To do that, we will use the collection object to store each class. In the general declarations of the form for our Sports Cards project, add a colTeam variable as a collection.

```
'  Globally declare an instance of the
'  sports card class
Dim SC As New SportsCard

'  Collection of team classes representing
'  our teams in the database
Dim colTeam As New Collection

'  Index of the current player selected
Dim PlayerIndex As Integer
```

The first subroutine we will add to our project is LoadTeams. You will find this similar to the LoadAddresses subroutine in the previous example. But we have a lot of work to do in this function. Not only does the combo box have to be loaded, but our classes for the teams need to be created and the players for each team set up.

The team data will be retrieved from our database using ADO. Be sure and have an ODBC DSN defined for connecting to your database. The connection is opened to the database. Our SQL statement retrieves the list of teams from the database. The SQL statement is executed, and the results are stored in the rsTeams recordset.

As we loop through the recordset, we create a new team object for our class during each iteration of the loop. Then we set the team properties from the database. Each team name is then added to the combo box. And, just like the previous example, the ID of the team is stored in the ItemData property for that item in the combo box.

Next we need to get the list of players from the current team. A SQL query is created that retrieves all of the players from the database where the ID of the team matches the current team we are working with. That query is then executed with the same connection object, and the results this time are stored in the rsPlayers recordset. Now we are ready to loop through the players and add them to our Team class. The same method, Add, is utilized for adding the players to the team. So, in effect, neither our team nor our Player class had to be updated to support our persistent data store. And ideally, none of the functions that the user interface implements need to be updated because of any underlying functionality changes in the classes.

Once all the players have been set up for the team, we then add the Team class to our colTeam collection and loop to the next team in the database. Finally, the database connection is closed once all the teams have been processed.

```
' Loads the teams into the display combo box
' and stores the team classes in a collection
Private Sub LoadTeams()

' Declare our variables
Dim dbTeams As New ADODB.Connection
Dim rsTeams As New ADODB.Recordset
Dim rsPlayers As New ADODB.Recordset
Dim SQL As String
Dim TM As Team

' Open our connection
dbTeams.Open "dsn=SportsCard"

' Set our SQL statement
SQL = "Select * from team"

' Get our record set of teams
Set rsTeams = dbTeams.Execute(SQL)

' Loop through the teams
Do Until rsTeams.EOF

    ' Create a new team object
    Set TM = New Team
```

```
'  Set the properties of the class to the data
'  in the database
TM.City = rsTeams("txtCity")
TM.Coach = rsTeams("txtCoach")
TM.League = rsTeams("txtLeague")
TM.Mascot = rsTeams("txtMascot")
TM.IDTeam = rsTeams("idTeam")
TM.TeamName = rsTeams("txtTeamName")

'  Add the team to the combo box
cboTeams.AddItem TM.TeamName

'  Set the item data to be the id of the team
cboTeams.ItemData(cboTeams.NewIndex) = TM.IDTeam

'  Build the SQL statement to retrieve players
'  for the current team
SQL = "Select * from player where idTeam = " & _
      TM.IDTeam & _
      " order by txtLastName"

'  Retrieve the record set
Set rsPlayers = dbTeams.Execute(SQL)

'  Loop through the players
Do Until rsPlayers.EOF

    '  Add the player to the collection
    TM.Add _
        rsPlayers("txtFirstName"), _
        rsPlayers("txtLastName"), _
        rsPlayers("txtPosition"), _
        rsPlayers("txtCollege"), _
        rsPlayers("nbrHeight"), _
        rsPlayers("nbrWeight"), _
        rsPlayers("memComments"), _
        rsPlayers("nbrPlayerBasePrice"), _
        rsPlayers("nbrDemandRating")

    '  Loop through the players
    rsPlayers.MoveNext
```

```
    Loop

    '  Add the team to our collection
    colTeam.Add TM

    '  Loop to the next team
    rsTeams.MoveNext

Loop

rsTeams.Close

End Sub
```

Our DisplayPlayer function from the previous example has to be updated a bit. In order to display the player's data, we need to reference the proper team in the teams collection and then reference the appropriate associated player data. Remember that the ItemData field of the cboTeams combo box stores the ID of the current team. That ID corresponds to the index of the team object in the colTeam collection.

To make referencing the team syntactically simple, we create a local copy of a team object, curTeam, and will retrieve the stored copy of the referenced team in the collection object. That makes subreferencing the team much easier to read in our code. The same will be done for the current player to be referenced. The curPlayer object will store the current player referenced by the cboPlayers combo box. In order to retrieve that player, we have to subreference the Player class in the Team class of the currently selected team (it gets a bit tricky since we are referencing data in a combo box, then referencing data in a class, and finally, subreferencing data in a class in that class.... Whew!). But, once we have our curTeam and curPlayer local classes set properly, we can easily set the display text boxes to the appropriate data and move on. Note as before, we copy the Player class into the global SportsCard class, SC.

```
'  Display player gets the data from the current
'  player selected in the combo box
Private Sub DisplayPlayer()

Dim curTeam As Team
Dim curPlayer As New Player
```

```
' Retrieve the current team from the collection
Set curTeam = colTeam(cboPlayers.ItemData(cboPlayers.ListIndex))

' Retrieve the current player from the team
Set curPlayer = _
colTeam(cboPlayers.ItemData(cboPlayers.ListIndex)) _
.Item(PlayerIndex)

' Display the league
txtLeague.Text = curTeam.League

' Display the first and last name by indexing
' into the teams collection
txtFirstName.Text = curPlayer.FirstName
txtLastName.Text = curPlayer.LastName

' Display the team name
txtTeam.Text = curTeam.TeamName

' Display the player demand rating and player
' base price by indexing into the teams collection
txtPlayRate.Text = curPlayer.PlayerDemandRating
txtBasePrice.Text = curPlayer.PlayerBasePrice

' Copy into the sports card class player object (class)
' the player class currently being indexed on the team
Set SC.Player = curPlayer

End Sub
```

When the user clicks on the cboTeams combo box, we have to update the players combo box with the list of players for that team. So, hold onto your hat—we have another set of referencing and subreferencing. As in DisplayPlayer, we have to break out the new team selected by the user by referencing the appropriate team in our team collection, which is based on the data in the ItemData field. Note that the players combo box is cleared of any current players.

Once we have that, we need to loop through the players in the team and display them in the cboPlayers combo box. The count property of the teams class tells us how many players are associated with the team. We can loop through that set and load the players combo box. With each iteration of the loop, the local curPlayer variable is set to the player, and the first and last names are added to the combo box. The item data for each player is set to the ID of the team so that the appropriate team data can be referenced later when the player data is loaded. Finally, once the players are loaded, we need to clear any current player data displayed in our data entry text boxes.

```
'  Click event of the teams combo box
Private Sub cboTeams_Click()

'  Declare variables
Dim curTeam As New Team
Dim curPlayer As Player

'  Clear the players list box
cboPlayers.Clear

'  Set to the current team
Set curTeam = colTeam(cboTeams.ItemData(cboTeams.ListIndex))

'  Loop through the players for the team
For n = 1 To curTeam.Count

    '  Get the current player
    Set curPlayer = curTeam.Item(n)

    '  Add the first and last name to the combo box
    cboPlayers.AddItem curPlayer.FirstName & " " & _
    curPlayer.LastName

    '  Set the id of the team in the item data of the player
    cboPlayers.ItemData(cboPlayers.NewIndex) = curTeam.IDTeam

Next

'  Clear out the text boxes
txtManufacturer.Text = ""
txtFirstName.Text = ""
txtLastName.Text = ""
txtTeam.Text = ""
txtLeague.Text = ""
txtYear.Text = ""
txtBasePrice.Text = ""
txtMarketTension.Text = ""
```

```
txtRookieCard.Text = ""
txtPlayRate.Text = ""
txtPurchasePrice.Text = ""
txtDescription.Text = ""
txtNumImp.Text = ""

End Sub
```

The Form_Load event has changed substantially from the example in the last chapter. Before, we hard coded both our team and player data for our classes. Now we call the LoadTeams function to retrieve the data from the database.

```
Private Sub Form_Load()

    '  Load the teams in the combo box
    LoadTeams

End Sub
```

In effect, we have added into the form code the ability to interface with the database and feed our classes the appropriate data. If you wanted, you could consider accessing the data directly from the classes or have some type of "League" class that would load the Team classes from the database.

Running the New Data-Driven VB Sports Cards Program

Let's go ahead and run the program. Figure 4-11 shows the program at run time with a team and player selected. You can run the same calculation functions as in Chapter 3 and indeed should get the same results. Figure 4-12 shows the calculations run with data filled in for the user input fields.

This time, you have a complete persistent database behind the team and player data being loaded into the application. Of course, the next step would be to build a maintenance interface for adding, updating, and deleting team and player data. If you review the code carefully, you will note that the only database interface has been added in the LoadTeams subroutine. In reality, you could decide where this database functionality would be placed. There is certainly nothing that requires it to be in the form object. You may want to have it in a separate class for abstraction of the data layer. In fact, the data functions could be called within the Team and Player classes to completely hide from the user interface where or how the data is stored.

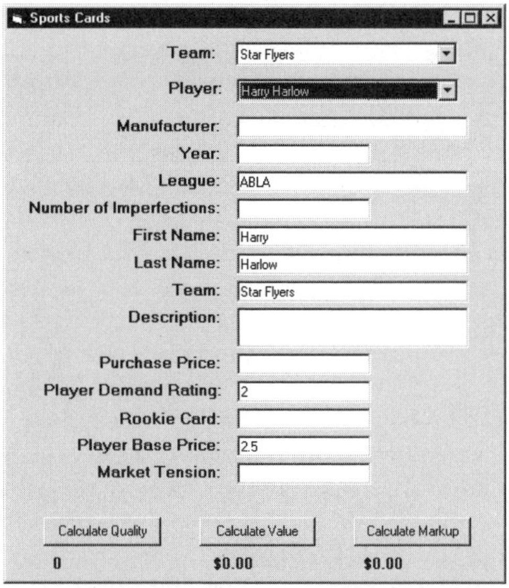

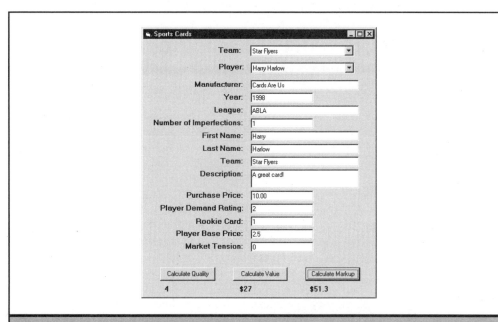

Figure 4-11.   *Sports Cards example with a team and player selected*

Figure 4-12.   *Sports Cards program after running the Calculate Quality, Calculate Value, and Calculate Markup functions*

Deploying Business Objects

If you put the data into its own class, that "business object" could be deployed on a data server. The benefits of separating the data access from the Team and Player classes as well as the user interface is that you have control over changing the underlying database implementation without breaking the class business logic or user interface. For example, the database created here was done in Microsoft Access. But suppose you needed to scale it up to SQL server at a later date. You could change the data class, and if done properly, neither the user interface code nor the business logic code (team and player) would have to change; whereas in our current implementation, the user interface code might have to be updated and redeployed. In the client/server section of the book, we will explore application partitioning in more detail along with different design methods.

Also, it is important to understand that the database model is far from complete. Most likely, you would want some kind of database lookup on leagues, colleges, cities, and so on. In fact, you may want to change the object model around a bit to support selecting leagues, then teams, and finally, players. This would entail a League class being a collection of properties and Team classes, with the Team classes being a collection of properties and Player classes. Then you could store sports card data and have the Player class contain a collection of cards for the player. But, for now, you can begin to see the elegance of an object model that is supported by a robust database interface.

Working with the Visual Basic Report Designer

The last topic for the chapter will be reporting—something that has always been a little weak in Visual Basic itself. In fact, this author has heard many a programmer groan that they wished the Microsoft Access reporting engine was available in Visual Basic. Well, to some extent, that wish has come true. One of the new designers available in Visual Basic 6.0 is the data report designer. And in fact, it is very similar to the Access report engine interface. There are differences, but you can finally add simple and easy reporting to your application.

To get started with an example, let's start a new data project. A data project is one of the new types of projects for Visual Basic. In reality, this is like a Standard EXE project, but it is set up for database development. The project includes a form, a data environment designer, and a data report designer.

Tip *You can add both data environment designers and data report designers to any of your standard projects.*

Setting Up a Data Environment for Our Database

In order to build reports, we need access to data. So, to get started with building our reports, let's work with the data environment in our project. We will go ahead and build two commands to our Sports Cards database. The first command will simply return all the teams in the Team database. The second will return a join of the Team and Player tables.

These commands correlate directly to the commands we worked with (executed) in our ADO programming. The data designer puts a nice interface on building queries with the query builder, working with stored procedures and the ADO object model in general.

Set up the connection properties of the data environment to access your sports card database. If you set up the ODBC connection outlined earlier, then reference the DSN in the connection. Once you have that done, create two commands from the connection. Name one of them "Teams" and the other "Players."

For the Teams command, set the properties to retrieve a "Database Object," and set the object to be the "Team" table. That will automatically retrieve all the rows in the team table.

For the second command, we need to build a SQL query. Follow these steps:

1. Right-click on the command object and select Properties.

2. Select the SQL Statement option.

3. Go to the SQL Builder to build the query.

4. Add both the Team and Player tables to the query builder by double-clicking on each.

5. Ensure that there is a link between the idTeam field in Team and the idTeam field in Player. If not, drag one field onto the other to create the link. When you do this, the SQL Builder will create a query joining the two tables.

6. Add * in all fields, for both tables, by double-clicking on the * symbol in the field listing for the tables. Close the query.

Below is the SQL code if you would like to paste it into the properties directly:

```
SELECT Player.*, Team.*
FROM Player, Team
WHERE Player.idTeam = Team.idTeam
```

With that, you have the necessary database connectivity via ADO to create your reports on the Team and Player tables.

Building Reports in the Designer

Now you are ready to begin building your reports. Double-click on the data report in your project. The first thing to do is rename it "rptTeams." As with forms and almost any other object in Visual Basic, you will find a set of properties for the report. And, just like forms, you will find a set of controls you can drag onto the report. But, unlike forms, reports have several components. There are headers that only display at the top of the report or the top of the page. And there are footers that display only at the bottom of each page. There are also report headers and footers that only display at the top and bottom of the report. The Detail section is where you will build the fields to be reported for each row in your recordset.

Figure 4-13 shows the report at design time. You have some basic controls for placement on the form. Table 4-7 outlines each.

Go ahead and add labels and text boxes for each field in the players and teams database, as shown in Figure 4-13. You will need to ensure that the data source for the report is set to the data environment in your project. Then set the data member for the report to be "Teams." Once that is done, you can set each of the text boxes to point to the appropriate "teams" data member. Then you can tie each appropriate text box to the proper field (for example, Team name to txtTeamName). You will note that the report header and footer are not showing on the report design page since in this case we didn't set them up. If you like, add an appropriate set of identifying text.

The second report, rptPlayers, will be tied to the Players command we created. As with the Teams report, you will need to set the data source property to the data environment. And the data member is set to players. Set up the report as shown in Figure 4-14.

Control	Description
RptLabel	Label control for the report interface.
RptTextBox	Text box control, which can be data bound.
RptImage	Image control for placing images on your report. Note that you cannot bind this field to database field.
RptLine	Ability to draw lines on the report.
RptShape	Shape control for drawing shapes on the report.
RptFunction	Can only be placed in the report footer. This function can calculate sums, mins, maxs, averages, standard deviation, standard error, value count, and row count. This can be very useful for automatically summing up a field, calculating averages, etc.

Table 4-7. *Report Controls*

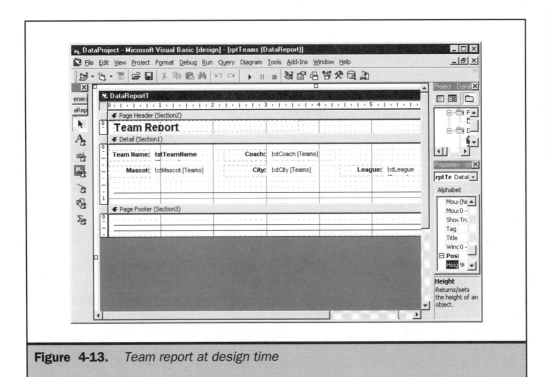

Figure 4-13.   Team report at design time

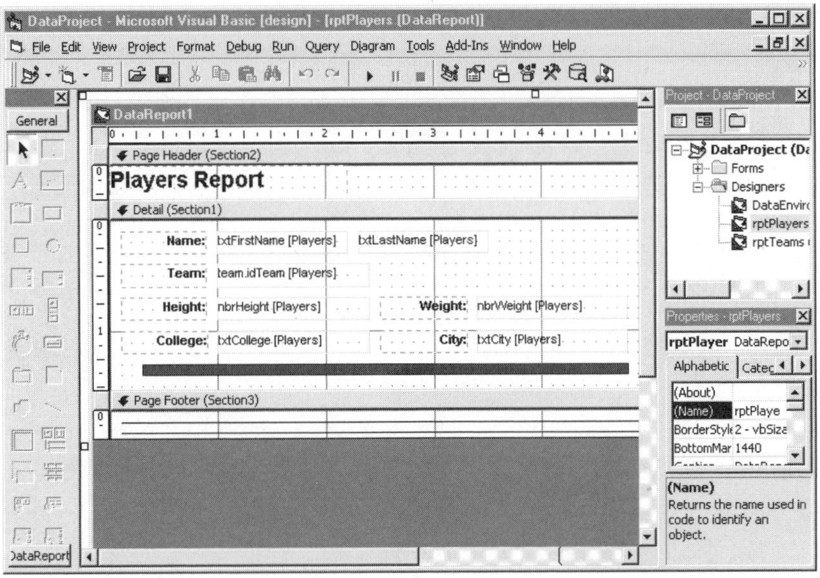

Figure 4-14.   Players report at design time

Go ahead and add some formatting on the report with shapes and other graphics. The red box or two livens up the report a little. Although not on the example, you might want to place a min and max function control to calculate the tallest and shortest heights on the team.

Building an Interface to the Reports

The next step is to create an interface for calling our reports. On the form in the project, add the command buttons shown in Table 4-8. The first button will call the teams report. The second will call the players report.

The following is the code for the application. The report is simply shown by calling the Show method. In each click event, the appropriate report is called. When that happens, the reports are displayed in a separate window.

```
Private Sub cmdPlayers_Click()

'   Show the players report
rptPlayers.Show

End Sub


Private Sub cmdTeams_Click()

'   Show the teams report
rptTeams.Show

End Sub
```

Testing and Running Our Reports

Now we are ready to run the application. Figure 4-15 shows the form at run time. Go ahead and click on each of the buttons. Figures 4-16 and 4-17 show the reports at run time. The player report has a shape control dividing each player. Note the navigation controls at the bottom of the page. Also note that the player report combines both team and player data from our query.

Component/Property	Setting
Form	FrmDataEnv
Caption	"Data Reporting"
Command Button	CmdTeams
Caption	"Show Teams"
Command Button	CmdPlayers
Caption	"Show Player"

Table 4-8.   *Report Interface Properties*

The team report has a line dividing each record. The bottom of each page is marked with double lines and placed at design time.

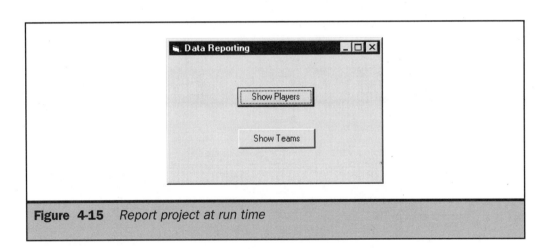

Figure 4-15   *Report project at run time*

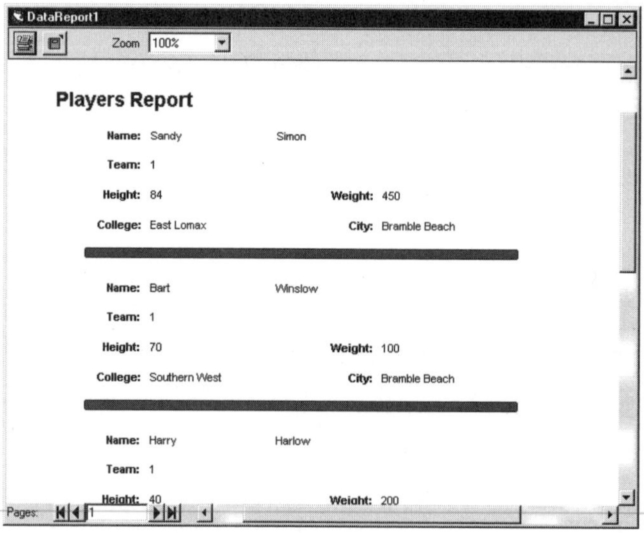

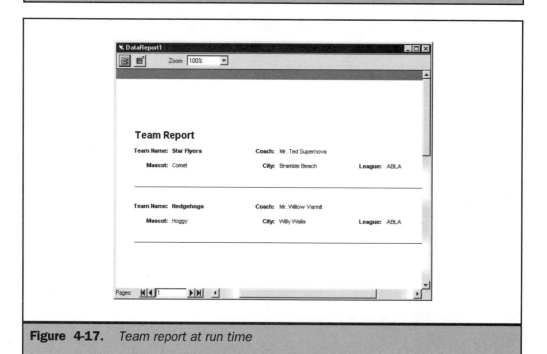

Figure 4-16. Players report at run time

Figure 4-17. Team report at run time

Summary

Visual Basic provides rich and powerful data access methods. And it now provides flexible reporting capabilities. Microsoft continues to develop and evolve data access methods and tools for developing data projects. There is no doubt that the ADO model is much more robust and simplified than the DAO and RDO implementations. And, with version 6.0, Microsoft has finally married its Web data access strategy to its enterprise-level data programming strategy and ADO.

What's Next

Heard (or read) a lot about Microsoft's new Internet programming capabilities? Been wondering when good old VB would get around to building great Internet applications? Wait no longer. In the next chapter we will explore Visual Basic's new IIS application and DHTML application capabilities.

VISUAL BASIC 6.0
OVERVIEW

Visual
Basic 6

Chapter 5

Introduction to Building Internet Applications

T he Internet in the last four to five years has really taken off as a medium for application development. The rise of the corporate intranet and extranet has been fast and furious. With the release of VB 6, Microsoft has added significant functionality for building Internet applications. In this chapter we will introduce these new capabilities in preparation for the last part of the book.

Internet Basics

Volumes and volumes of books have been written on the fundamentals of the Internet. We certainly cannot cover all that is to be said about Internet technology in the beginning of this chapter. The good thing is that once you get the basics down, you will find that building Internet applications with VB is not all that different from building standard forms-based applications. It is just a different interface.

Traditional networks are client/server based. The client is a desktop of some type that is connected via a network to a server. The network has "private" wires run between the computers to connect them. Sometimes those private wires may include phone lines between different facilities. The "language" spoken by the computers on these private wires can be any one of a number of network protocols. The Internet is no different, except that the wires are publicly owned and accessible (including phone and cable lines). You can send traffic between your Web browser (the client) to a server somewhere on the Net. A standard communication protocol, TCP/IP, ensures all traffic can be properly handled.

An *intranet* is simply a secure internal business network that has implemented the TCP/IP protocol. The key to the intranet is that it runs on the private lines within the organization and is not accessible via the public lines. And, if you have heard the term *extranet*, that is simply a protected intranet that runs on public wire. Security measures are in place to ensure the general public can't access the extranet.

Internet technology allows for transfer of data in various agreed upon (for the most part, anyway) formats. One common format is the HyperText Transfer Protocol, or HTTP. On that protocol, you can send HyperText Markup Language, or HTML, pages back and forth between the client and the server. You can also use the File Transfer Protocol, or FTP, to send files back and forth between the client and the server. The amazing thing about the Internet is that everyone on the public wire agrees to these transfer protocols, so a common language can be spoken by all the different machines that are hooked up. On those machines, there are specific pieces of software that handle the translation of the data being sent to and fro. On the server, there is typically a "Web server." In the case of Microsoft, the Web server is Internet Information Server (IIS). You may have heard of other Web servers, such as Apache or Netscape's Suite Spot. On the client side, you have the browser or FTP client that supports retrieving and sending information. For Web browsers, of course, you have the big two, Internet Explorer and Netscape Navigator. A wide range of FTP clients are available in the marketplace.

If you need more of a backgrounder or primer on Internet technology to get you started, take a look at Osborne/McGraw-Hill's The Internet Complete Reference, Second Edition, *by Harley Hahn.*

When the Internet was started way back in the 1970s, it was mostly built to support sending and receiving static content. There was nothing dynamic, interactive, or programmatic about the Web. This was useful for sharing raw data, but it did not provide a dynamic environment for application creation. The first real interactive addition to the Web was the Common Gateway Interface (CGI). Through this interface you could build script programs in languages such as PERL that could dynamically update Web content. Microsoft came up with its own gateway interface called Internet Server Application Programming Interface (ISAPI).

With the advent of ISAPI, Microsoft supported Active Server Pages programming and developed VBScript as the script language for the programming. This code would execute on the server in the framework of their IIS Web server. At the same time, Web browsers were beginning to support client-side scripting that was embedded directly in the Web page. So, instead of going to the server to run a script, the script could be run in the browser. There are limitations to client-side scripting. For example, you cannot universally access databases back on the server. Or, from client-side scripts, you are not allowed to interact directly with the client's system (you can with ActiveX controls). If you want to do data processing, you need to run scripts on the server. Common client-side script languages include VBScript and JavaScript. And the latest development is the creation of Dynamic HTML (DHTML) applications, which combine the browser object model, scripting language, and a special extension to HTML, Stylesheets, to create dynamic client-side Web pages.

The Internet Comes to Visual Basic

The next evolution in Internet development is direct Internet capabilities in Visual Basic. Now you can also build full-blown Visual Basic applications that return HTML, instead of the traditional forms interface, to the browser. Visual Basic integrates directly into Internet Information Server and ISAPI.

On the client side, you can create DHTML applications (script-based applications) in Visual Basic 6.0. Of course, when they are built in VB 6, they are no longer script based. In other words, you get the full power of VB behind your programming. One note of caution here: VB 6 only supports DHTML development for Internet Explorer 4 running on a Windows platform. You will not get cross-platform and cross-browser compatibility. However, if you are running on a Windows-based intranet, this will not be an issue.

The Internet is an exciting development platform. And Visual Basic is only going to make it that much more fun. Once you get the basics of HTML and Internet technology under your belt, you will be deploying VB Internet apps before you know it. If you are already an Internet guru, VB will be a welcome addition to your development toolkit.

HTML Basics

We won't spend much time going over HTML tagging basics—just enough to get into the swing of "tagging." HTML is built on a foundation of tags that mark up the page and tell the browser how to render the content. They describe page elements such as tables, images, input text boxes, buttons, and fonts. The combination of these tags defines how the page will be structured.

In addition to describing the structural relationships among page elements, some HTML tags also contain attributes. *Attributes* provide details about a particular tag. For example, if you want your text to be red, you set a color attribute on your font tag.

For a good guide to HTML development, check out HTML: The Complete Reference, *by Thomas A. Powell, published by Osborne/McGraw-Hill. If you want to learn more about the official language specification and review additions to the specification, check out the Web site for the World Wide Web Consortium at http://www.w3.org.*

HTML has a standard document structure that defines the beginning and ending of the page. The following code defines this structure:

```
<HTML>
<HEAD>
<TITLE>Title Tags</TITLE>
</HEAD>
<body>
</body>
</HTML>
```

The document starts and closes with the <HTML> and </HTML> tags. Almost all tags have a beginning and ending pair. The beginning tag is the name of the tag, such as <HTML>, and the ending is marked by a / character in the tag.

HTML tags are not case sensitive.

An HTML document traditionally contains a head section that can contain page titles and headings. Again, note the head section is marked by a beginning <HEAD> tag and then closed by a </HEAD> tag. In the example above, our document head contains a title. The title will show up on the top of the browser (for most browsers) and not directly on the page.

Creating HTML code comments is simple. The comment is one tag with the comments included in the tag. The tag begins with <!- - and ends with - ->. In fact, in the last sentence, the text "and ends with" would be the comment text for the tag.

Following the header in the sample code is the body of the document, designated by the <BODY> </BODY> tags. This is where the core of the document will be created. In fact, attributes of the body tag can control the overall appearance of your document. Table 5-1 reviews several of these attributes.

A sample of the body tag set with attributes would be as follows:

```
<BODY bgcolor="red" text="blue" link="yellow">
```

Attribute	Description
background	Designates an image resource. The image generally tiles the background (for visual browsers). The location can be relative on the same Web site or an absolute URL.
bgcolor	Sets the background color for the document body.
text	Sets the foreground color for text.
link	Sets the color of text marking unvisited hypertext links.
vlink	Sets the color of text marking visited hypertext links.
alink	Sets the color of text marking hypertext links when selected by the user.

Table 5-1.   *Body Tag Attributes*

In this case the background color will be red. The text on the page will be blue, and all unvisited links will be yellow. The ending body tag would still be </BODY>.

Tip   *Use the <BR> tag to designate line breaks in your document. Pressing RETURN between text does not make a line break. Note that there is no closing </BR> tag.*

There are many more constructs to review in HTML, but let's take a quick look at building document tables. You will find tables to be one of the more powerful page formatting tools in standard HTML. The following document defines a table with two rows and three columns:

```
<HTML>

<head>
<title>Table Sample</title>
</head>

<body bgcolor="white">

<table border="1">
  <tr>
    <td>Row 1 Column 1</td>
    <td>Row 1 Column 2</td>
    <td>Row 1 Column 3</td>
  </tr>
  <tr>
```

```
    <td>Row 2 Column 1</td>
    <td>Row 2 Column 2</td>
    <td>Row 2 Column 3</td>
  </tr>
  <tr>
    <td>Row 3 Column 1</td>
    <td>Row 3 Column 2</td>
    <td>Row 3 Column 3</td>
  </tr>
</table>

</body>
</html>
```

Go ahead and open good old Notepad and create the above listing (or open the file on the CD in Notepad). Once you have done that, save it to your system as table.html. Now double-click on the file, and your browser will display it. Figure 5-1 shows the page. In this case you can see the document title in the top left of the browser. On the page itself, the background color of the document is white, based on the body tag.

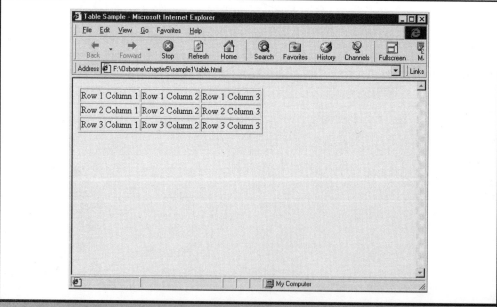

Figure 5-1. *Table HTML file displayed in Internet Explorer*

A table begins with a <table> tag and, of course, ends with a corresponding </table> tag. In this case we have set one attribute for our table, the border style (1). In Figure 5-1 you can see the border around the table rows and columns. Nested inside the table tags are the tags that define the rows and columns. Rows are designated by beginning and ending <TR> </TR> tags. Columns are designated by table data cell tags, <TD> </TD>. You place the contents you would like displayed in the cell between the table data cell tags.

Be sure all of your table rows have the same number of columns, even if you have to put in a blank column. Note that you can have a column span multiple columns by using the COLSPAN attribute.

Basic HTML tagging is fairly easy to master. There are more complex document-building code structures, such as cascading style sheets (CSS), that can add richness to the interface of your Web pages. Cascading style sheets give you the ability to define a set of styles that overrides the browser's standard methods for rendering HTML. This lets you give your pages a unique and consistent design. For example, you can set the font style for specific elements on all of your pages. Or you can define border properties for all your tables, including color and width. In the last part of the book, we will touch more on the use of CSS when designing DHTML applications.

The World Wide Web Consortium has set a standard for CSS, which both Netscape 4.x and Internet Explorer 4.x follow.

Our final topic in HTML basics is the use of Dynamic HTML. DHTML is a set of language additions to HTML that allow page developers to dynamically change the attributes of HTML page elements. With DHTML, you can also add, update, and delete elements on a Web page after it has been loaded. The key thing to note is that the two leading browsers on the market, Netscape 4.x and Internet Explorer 4.x, do not use the same DHTML specification.

As we will see in this chapter and in the last part of the book, we can create DHTML applications for Internet Explorer 4.x in VB 6. We will be able to manipulate the Internet Explorer 4 document object model (DOM) to interact with the Web page directly in the client's browser. It is important to note that DHTML applications do not run on the server; they run on the client's computer. In this case the computer needs to be running Windows 95/98 or Windows NT.

HTML, CSS, and DHTML are rich and powerful Web document building tools. As we will see in the rest of this chapter, combining them with VB 6 provides an exciting new application building paradigm.

IIS and Active Server Pages

Before we jump directly into building IIS applications, it is important to review the foundation upon which our IIS applications will run. First and foremost, we have to fulfill the IIS part of the equation.

For Windows NT 4.0, you will need Internet Information Server 3.0 or later with the Active Server Pages component installed. In fact, you don't need Internet Information Server unless you have Windows NT 4.0. If you are running Windows NT 4.0 Workstation, you will need to be running Peer Web Server 3.0 or later with the Active Server Pages module installed. And for Windows 95/98, you will need the Personal Web Server 3.0 or later with the Active Server Pages component installed.

That takes care of the server side, but what about the client side? For IIS applications, you can control what browser will be able to support your application by determining the level of HTML support required by the browser. If, for example, you are going to be using CSS, then you will need Netscape 4.x and Internet 3.x or higher to support the application. If you are only sending out basic HTML, then most browsers will be able to support your application.

You may be wondering what the difference is between Active Server Pages (ASP) and IIS applications. ASP runs on the server side as well. You can program ASP with VBScript. The unique thing about ASP is that you can intermingle your HTML code with your VBScript code on the same page. When the page is requested from the server, the Active Server Pages component in IIS will run the code and send the results to the browser.

IIS applications are really Visual Basic applications that have a Web interface. Instead of designing a form as the interface, you will design Web pages and create Web pages on the fly from your VB code to define your application interface. IIS applications allow you to build your application using all the robustness of VB, the IDE, wizards, classes, and so on, that are not available in a scripting environment.

You will notice, however, that your IIS application is actually run within an ASP Web page at run time. The ASP interface is the host for your IIS application. It acts as the programmatic proxy to calling your application.

For more information on IIS, check out Microsoft Internet Information Server 4: The Complete Reference, *by Tom Sheldon and John Mueller, published by Osborne/ McGraw-Hill.*

Building IIS Applications

Now we are ready to get started with building our first IIS application. There are several steps in this process. First we will take a look at the web class designer. This is similar to the familiar form designer, but as you would suspect, we will be defining the Web-based interface.

Second, we will build our required interface pages for our application. This will be done externally and then imported into our application. Once we have our interface defined, we will begin building our functionality. Finally, we will be ready to run and test our application.

Our example application will be a simple quiz that asks a series of questions, evaluates the answers, and provides a response. With that, let's get started!

Web Class Designer

Web classes are the fundamental building blocks of IIS applications. The web class runs on the server and responds to input from the user in the Web browser. To define your web classes, Microsoft has provided the web class designer.

Web classes are made up of two fundamental components, HTML pages and custom web items. The HTML page(s) is used as a template for defining the user interface for your web class. As we will see in the last part of the book, you can also use special custom tags in the HTML template page to allow your VB code to insert custom code that is then sent to the browser.

Custom web items are very similar to events on a traditional form. You can define what types of response or processing you need to do in your custom web item and then attach it to any number of HTML template pages. For example, perhaps there is a link on all of your pages that takes you back to the home page for your Web application. You could define a custom web item that would handle the click event when the user selects that link. That custom web item would then indicate to your application that the response should be the HTML template page for the home page of the application. The following illustration demonstrates this concept:

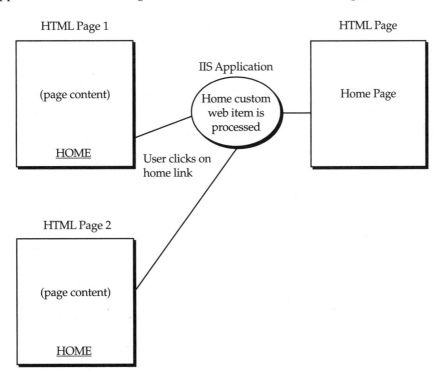

In the illustration we have two pages, HTML Page 1 and HTML Page 2, that have a link to the application's home page. When that link is clicked on, the Home custom web item in the IIS application is called, which then returns the application's home page.

Note *Each web class will have a corresponding ASP page that is generated by Visual Basic. By calling this page, the user will invoke your IIS application.*

Now that we have touched on events for our application and custom web items, there are three types of events in an IIS Application. They are defined in Table 5-2.

Using web classes may be a foreign concept depending on your level of familiarity with Internet technology. But just remember the first time you sat down to develop form-based VB applications. Now that seems old hat. Once you get through the example provided in this chapter and dive into the last part of the book, using web classes and building Internet interfaces will seem as easy as building form-based applications.

Note *If you are not familiar with building Web-based applications, you will hear a lot about keeping "state." No, that doesn't mean knowing what state your user is located in. It means remembering data from Web page to Web page about the "state" of the application. For example, if the user clicks to edit a record in a database, you will need to know the ID of the record when you go to the editing page. This is a natural function in a Visual Basic application but takes a bit more work in an IIS application. This will be explored further in the last part of the book.*

Event	Description
Standard	These are automatically included for each template and web item. Included are the Respond event, ProcessTag event, and User event. These will be explored further later in the chapter.
Template	These events are directly tied to tags on the HTML template page. For example, you can define an event for a form tag or link tag. You connect these template events to the tags. Note that a template event can be connected to a custom web item, as shown in our home page example above. In that case, the custom web item is the event handler for the template event (such as clicking on a link).
Custom	Custom events are just that—custom. You can add a custom event to an HTML template or custom web item. These events are in addition to the standard events defined by the system. An example might be a custom event that does a database call and returns the data in a Web page.

Table 5-2. *Web Class Event Types*

IIS Object Model

As mentioned earlier, IIS applications are hosted by an .asp file. In order to read and write data to the HTML interface, we will need to make use of several of the objects in the Active Server Pages object model. Table 5-3 outlines the objects we will be using in our web classes.

As we will see in our application, these objects become the interface through which you interact with the browser. Remember that IIS applications marry traditional Internet technology with your back-end Visual Basic code. The web class provides the interface to your application, and the ASP objects provide the interface to the browser.

Building the Interface

As already mentioned, our sample application will be an on-line quiz. The interface will consist of a Web page with a series of questions. The page will need to contain an

Object	Description
Request	Retrieves requests from end users submitted in their browser. Data retrieved in the request can include HTTP header request, form elements, URL query strings, and cookie data.
Response	Sends information to the browser in order to display it to the user. With the Response object, you can write HTML to the user's browser, set cookie values, and redirect the user to a specific Web page.
Session	Maintains information about the current user session and stores and retrieves state information. As mentioned in the note above, you have to explicitly store state values between pages for a particular user. Sessions are created per user when an ASP page is requested.
Application	Works the same as the Session object but stores data at a global level for all users, not just for a specific user.
Server	Creates other objects and determines server-specific properties that might influence the web class's processing. You can use the Server object to create business objects on the server for use in your IIS application.
BrowserType	Allows you to determine the specific capabilities of a browser. This can be critical if you are building applications that use capabilities (such as DHTML) that are browser specific.

Table 5-3.   *Web Class Objects*

HTML form and elements for users to input responses and then submit them to our IIS application.

To build the interface, we will need to use an external editor. Once the .html page is created, we will then import it into a web class in our application. Since we will have a fairly simple page to work with, you can use Notepad to type in your HTML code.

Tip   *There are a wide variety of HTML page building tools on the market. Two of the more advanced products are Microsoft's FrontPage and Visual InterDev. FrontPage employs a WYSIWYG interface for page building. Visual InterDev is traditionally used for ASP development but can also be used for basic HTML coding.*

The following HTML listing shows the code for the quiz interface:

```
<HTML>

<HEAD>
<TITLE>Quiz IIS Application</TITLE>
</HEAD>

<BODY BGCOLOR="WHITE">

<!-- Form that will post the data to the server. Note that
     we have defined no 'action' for the form since the
     action will be defined in the IIS Application
-->
<FORM method="post">

<!-- First question -->
1. What is the Web Class Designer?<BR><BR>

<!-- Radio buttons to ask the web class question. Correct
     answer is number 3.
-->
<input type="radio" name="webclass" value="1">A Species of
Moose<BR>
<input type="radio" name="webclass" value="2">A terrible plague<BR>
<input type="radio" name="webclass" value="3">A new web interface
building tool for VB

<BR><BR>
```

```
<!--   Second question -->
2. What is state?<BR><BR>

<!--   Radio buttons to ask the state question. Correct
       answer is number 3.
-->
<input type="radio" name="state" value="1">A unit of government<BR>
<input type="radio" name="state" value="2">A new slang term for
cool<BR>
<input type="radio" name="state" value="3">The status of an
application at any moment in time

<BR><BR>
<!--   Third question -->
3. What is Mitochondria?<BR><BR>

<!--   Radio buttons to ask the mitochondria question. Correct
       answer is number 3
-->

<input type="radio" name="mito" value="1">Something you definitely
don't want to get<BR>
<input type="radio" name="mito" value="2">An awesome rock band<BR>
<input type="radio" name="mito" value="3">Structures in the human
cell
<BR><BR>

<!--   Submit button for the form -->
<input type="submit" value="submit" name="submit">
</form>

</body>
</html>
```

Our page has the familiar document header and body. In this case the body of our document contains our quiz form. The quiz form defines the interactive part of our page. Within the form we have a series of radio buttons that define the quiz questions. Figure 5-2 shows the page in Internet Explorer.

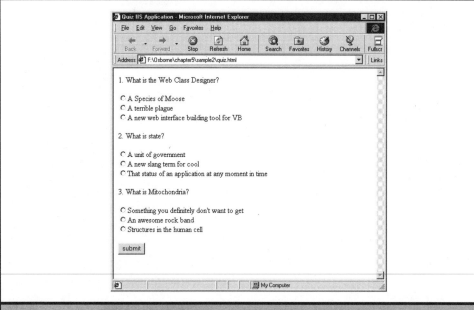

Figure 5-2. Quiz Web page in Internet Explorer

The first set of radio buttons are named "webclass" to identify the question. When the user selects one of the responses, we will use the request object in our code to read the selected value. The next two questions also have their set of radio buttons defined. The form ends with a submit button that will send the responses to the server, where we can respond to them in our application. Finally, the page is completed with the ending tags.

Building the Functionality

We are finally ready to get started with the Visual Basic portion of this exercise. The first step is to start a new IIS application in Visual Basic. When you do, you will see the web class designer. The application at design time is shown in Figure 5-3.

The first step is to import the HTML page we created into a template in our project. Before you do that, save the application. Once saved, follow these steps to import the page:

1. Right-click on HTML Template WebItems.

2. Select Add HTML Template. When you do, a File dialog box is shown to locate the HTML page.

3. Locate your saved HTML page and select it in the dialog box.

4. Once imported, change the name from Template1 to "Quiz."

After you have finished these steps, your web class should look like Figure 5-4.

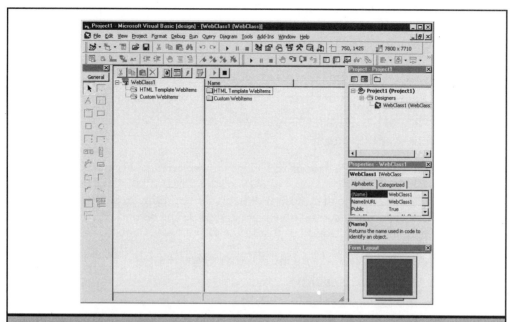

Figure 5-3. *IIS application at design time*

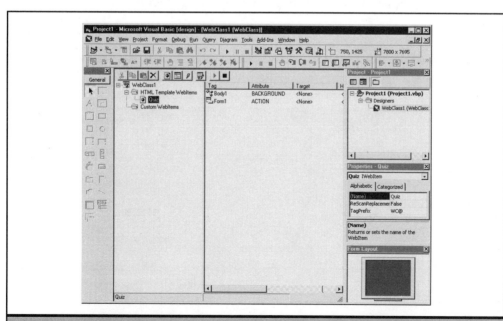

Figure 5-4. *IIS application with the quiz HTML page imported into the web class designer*

The first thing we will need to do is add a custom event to handle the submission of the page to the server with the user's responses. To add the custom event, follow these steps:

1. Right-click on the Form1 tag in the web class designer.

2. Select Connect to Custom Event. A form1 event will be added to the web class.

3. Right-click on the form1 custom event and select Rename.

4. Name the event "Evaluate."

Once you have that finished, your web class should look like Figure 5-5.

When users submit their responses to the questions, we will need to respond. In this case, let's define a couple of custom web items for handling those responses. The first will be "Congrats" for a successful set of responses. The second will be "Sorry" for incorrect responses. Follow these steps to add the custom web items:

1. Right-click on Custom WebItems in the web class designer.

2. Select Add Custom WebItem.

3. Rename the custom web item to "Congrats."

4. Follow the same steps to add the second custom web item and rename it "Sorry."

Once you are finished, your web class should look like Figure 5-6.

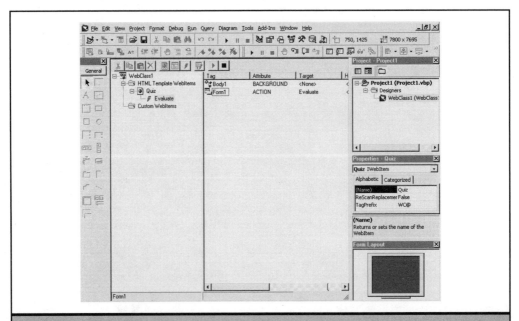

Figure 5-5.   *Web class with the Evaluate event connected to the form1 tag*

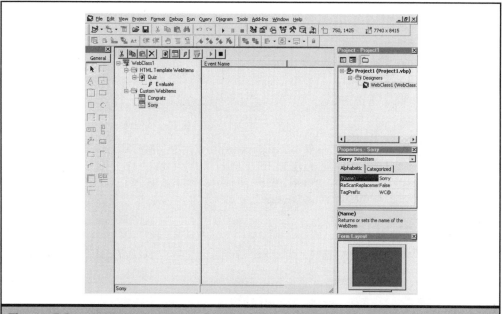

Figure 5-6.   *Web class with the Congrats and Sorry custom web items added*

With that we have completed the setup for our application. We are now ready to dive into the code to make it all work. The first item we want to deal with is the web class start event. This is the first set of code processed when the application starts up. The start event is analogous to the form load event of a form.

```
Private Sub WebClass_Start()

'  When the webclass starts up, we want the
'  first item to be processed to be the quiz
'  page
Set NextItem = Quiz

End Sub
```

In the event, we use the NextItem property of the web class to define the next item to be processed. In this case we want to show the quiz template page, so NextItem is set to Quiz.

When that happens, the respond event of the Quiz template web item is fired off. In that event, we want to display the page. To do that, the WriteTemplate method of the web item is called.

```
Private Sub Quiz_Respond()

'  Write out the HTML page
Quiz.WriteTemplate

End Sub
```

Once the template is displayed, we are basically waiting for the user to fill out her or his responses and submit the page to the server. When that happens, the Evaluate custom web event, which we defined as the response to form1, will be fired off. That is our chance to evaluate the user's answers.

```
Private Sub Quiz_Evaluate()
'  Variable to track correct responses
Dim Flag As Integer

'  Start at 0 - all responses are correct
Flag = 0

'  Use the request variable to retrieve the value
'  of the radio button selections. Note we reference
'  the name of the Radio HTML elements
If Request("webclass") <> 3 Then Flag = 1
If Request("state") <> 3 Then Flag = 1
If Request("mito") <> 3 Then Flag = 1

'  Check for a correct set of responses
If Flag = 0 Then

    '  Go to the Congrats custom webitem
    Set NextItem = Congrats

Else

    '  Go to the Sorry custom webitem
    Set NextItem = Sorry

End If

End Sub
```

Here is our first look at using the ASP objects to interface with the user. Remember that the HTML template had three sets of radio buttons defined for each question. Each set had a unique name (WebClass, State, and Mito). We can reference this name using the Request object to see the value of the response. Each of the radio buttons had a number for its value attribute indicating the response. If that radio button was selected, that number was returned to the server. In the Evaluate event, we simply process the responses to check to see if all questions have been answered correctly. If so, the Congrats custom web item is set as the next item. If not, the Sorry custom web item is set as the next item to process.

```
Private Sub Congrats_Respond()

'  Build the HTML tag
Response.Write "<HTML>"

'  Build the document head
Response.Write "<HEAD>"
Response.Write "<TITLE>Congratulations!</TITLE>"
Response.Write "</HEAD>"

'  Build the body
Response.Write "<BODY BGCOLOR=""WHITE"">"

'  Build the body contents
Response.Write "<FONT SIZE=""5"" COLOR=""RED"">"
Response.Write "<B>CONGRATULATIONS!!! YOU SCORED A 100!!!</B>"
Response.Write "</font>"

'  End the document
Response.Write "</body>"
Response.Write "</html>"

End Sub
```

When the Congrats custom web item is set as the next web item to process, the respond event is called. In that event, we can write out our response to the user. In this case we will use the Response ASP object to write HTML code to the browser. The page we will write will be created on the fly; it will not be based on an HTML template. So we need to construct the entire document, including the HTML header and body. Note we use the <font> tag to set the font attribute for the text to be large and red. Also, the bold <B> tag is used to make the font bold.

```
Private Sub Sorry_Respond()

'  Write the beginning HTML tag
Response.Write "<HTML>"

'  Build the header
Response.Write "<HEAD>"
Response.Write "<TITLE>Congratulations!</TITLE>"
Response.Write "</HEAD>"

'  Start the body
Response.Write "<BODY BGCOLOR=""WHITE"">"
'  Build the document body
Response.Write "<FONT SIZE=""5"" COLOR=""RED"">"
Response.Write "<B>Sorry ... Click "

'  The URLFor method used to create a custom URL
'  that will point to the Quiz template webitem.
'  We want the user to return to the quiz to take
'  it again
Response.Write "<a href=""" & URLFor(Quiz) & """>here</a>"

Response.Write "to try again.</B>"
Response.Write "</font>"

'  Close the document
Response.Write "</body>"
Response.Write "</html>"

End Sub
```

The Sorry custom web item functions in much the same way as the Congrats custom web item. But, in this case, we want the user to be able to return to the Quiz page and take the quiz again. The best way to return is a link on the page the user can click on. But how do we build a link to a template page?

The URLFor method of the web class is just what the doctor ordered. The URLFor method will build a URL to a custom web item or HTML template in your application. The first parameter it takes is the object to link to. In this case it was the Quiz HTML template. The second parameter indicates the event for the object to call. The default is the Respond event. In our code, we want the Respond event of the Quiz template to be called, so the second parameter is not specified.

Tip   *As we will see later in the book, the URLFor method is used to create custom events at run time. When would you want to do this? Imagine you are querying a database of addresses and listing them on a Web page. You then want users to be able to click on the person's name in the address and go to a page where they can edit the address. That link URL created for the person's name would be custom based on the ID of the address. And it would need a custom response in your application. URLFor would allow us to create that custom URL and respond to it in our application.*

With the last bit of code, we have our application ready for prime time. Users can take the quiz and find out whether they answered the questions correctly. Let's go ahead and test our application.

Testing Our IIS Application

Now we are ready to run our application. Of course, we are going to need a Web browser for our application's user interface. Go ahead and click the Run button to start your application. When you do, the dialog box in Figure 5-7 will show up.

When your application starts, you want your web class to be the first component called. Second, you want to use a browser to demonstrate your application. The check box Use Existing Browser indicates that VB should first look for an existing browser to run the application; if it can't find one, it will start a new instance. Click OK to continue.

The next dialog box, Figure 5-8, has to do with where your project is located. By default, Visual Basic is going to set up your project to run under the default Web site in your Web server. But it wants to create a different path (*virtual root*) to call it from rather than /. It takes the default name that you see in the box from the project properties. In this case, change the default to "Quiz." Click OK to continue.

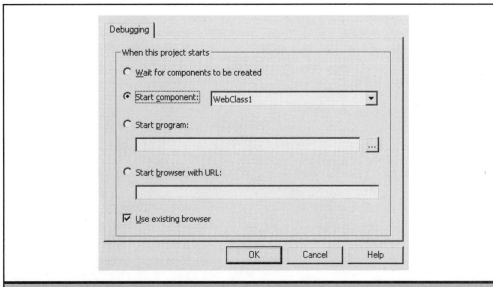

Figure 5-7.   *Debugging dialog box*

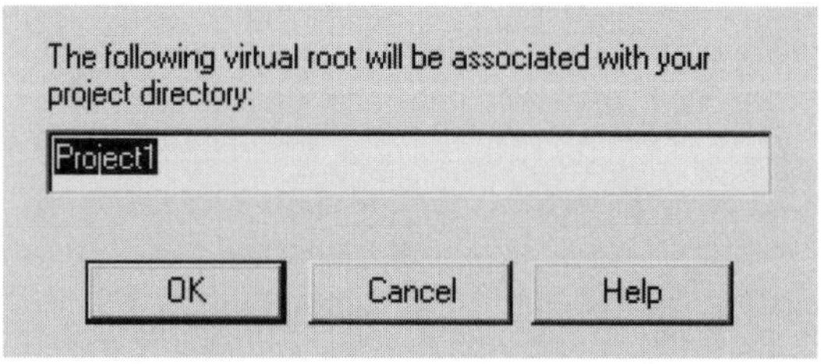

The following virtual root will be associated with your project directory:

Project1

| OK | Cancel | Help |

Figure 5-8.   *VB Virtual Root Creation dialog box*

Finally, you have your first IIS application running! You should see the quiz in the browser. Note in the URL the "quiz" virtual root designation. If you encounter problems getting your application to run, you will need to review your Web server setup. Try hitting the default Web site on your Web server and ensure you can properly access it.

Go ahead and take the quiz. Of course, your answers will be moose, slang term for cool, and an awesome rock band. When you submit those responses, you will see the Sorry page, as shown in Figure 5-9.

Note the "here" link indicates the same ASP page but sets querystring parameters to indicate the Quiz template should be called. Go ahead and click on the link back to the quiz and take the quiz again. This time, respond with the correct answers (Web interface tool, status of an application, structures in human cell). You will see the Congratulations page, as shown in Figure 5-10.

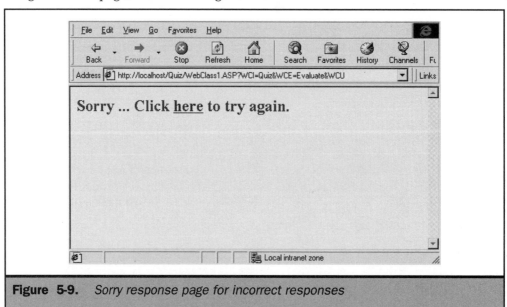

Figure 5-9.   *Sorry response page for incorrect responses*

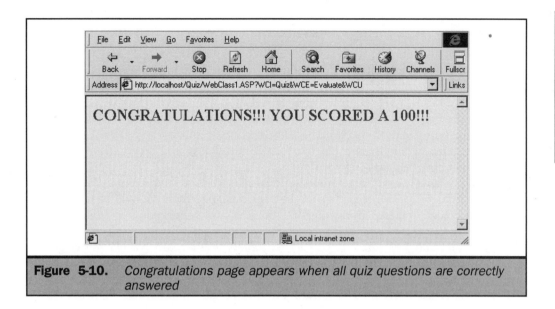

Figure 5-10.   *Congratulations page appears when all quiz questions are correctly answered*

Indeed, congratulations are in order. You have just built your first Internet application using VB 6. Now we are ready to move away from building server-based IIS applications to building client-based DHTML applications.

Building DHTML Applications

A DHTML application is a Visual Basic application that uses a combination of DHTML and compiled Visual Basic code in a browser-based application. A DHTML application resides on the browser machine, where it interprets and responds to actions the end user performs in the browser.

A DHTML application uses Visual Basic code and the Dynamic HTML object model to instantly respond to actions that occur on the page. This could involve responding to user-initiated actions such as mouse movements and clicks, or responding to browser-based events such as page loads.

You can get very creative and make the Web page dynamic. For example, you can create HTML elements on the fly in response to user actions, update the appearance of the page, change default behavior for elements, and much more. The benefit of DHTML applications is that you can do more processing on the client side of the equation and make fewer time-consuming trips back to the server to process the user's actions. An example could be validating a data entry form on the client side instead of having to validate the data on the server and then send a response back to the user.

In our example, we are going to take our quiz application built in the previous example and move it over to the client side into a DHTML application.

Using the DHTML Page Designer

The page designer corresponds to a single HTML page in your project and acts as the base on which you create its user interface. If you want to include more than one HTML page in your application, you can insert additional designers into your project. Figure 5-11 shows a DHTML application started. You will note the toolbar on the left has several elements available to us. These correspond to the standard HTML elements, including text boxes, radio buttons, text areas, images, and links. You can use these in a similar fashion to controls on a form. Simply drag and drop each onto the page designer and start creating your page.

You really have two options for designing your interface. If you have simple projects that can be quickly designed in the page designer, then you will be in good shape. If you need to create highly customized graphical pages, you may wish to use an external designer and import the pages into your project.

When you build pages in your project, externally or internally, you have two save options for how the page should be stored. The first is to save the page as part of the project. The second is to save it in an external file. To set these options, click on the DHTML Page Designer Properties button on the page designer toolbar. Figure 5-12

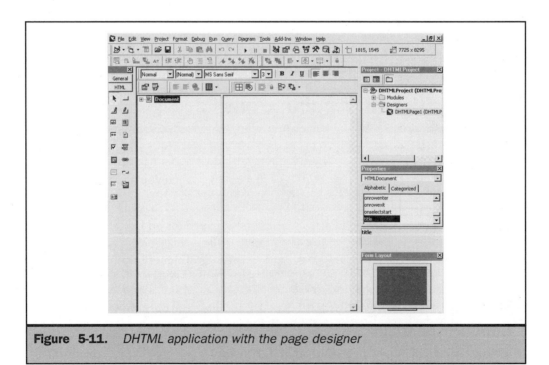

Figure 5-11.   *DHTML application with the page designer*

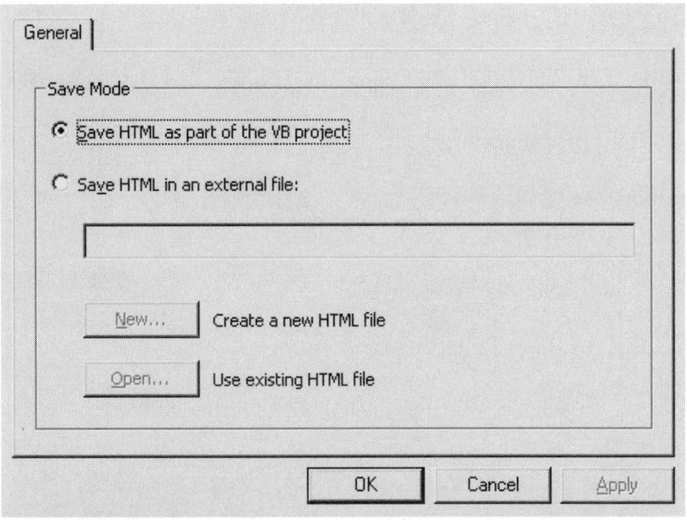

General

Save Mode

⊙ Save HTML as part of the VB project

○ Save HTML in an external file:

[   ]

New...   Create a new HTML file

Open...   Use existing HTML file

[OK]   [Cancel]   [Apply]

Figure 5-12.   *Page designer's Save Mode settings*

shows these options. If you choose to save the file externally, you have the option of indicating the file name, creating a new file, or importing an existing file. In most cases you are going to want to save to an external file.

Building the Interface

To make our lives a bit simpler for this project, let's go ahead and import the quiz.html page we created in the earlier example. Select the second option on the Save Mode frame, and then use the Open dialog box to find the file. When you are finished, the page designer should look like Figure 5-13.

In order to make our page work, we have to make some adjustments to the HTML code. Specifically, we need to identify the option buttons for our DHTML application. That is done by setting an ID attribute for each. To edit the page once it has been imported, click on the Launch Editor button on the page designer toolbar. The default editor launched is Notepad. Below is the listing for the updated page code.

If you don't want to use Notepad as your default editor, you can change the editor in the Options dialog box on the Tools menu. Select the Advanced tab, and you can change the external HTML editor to be your favorite page-editing program.

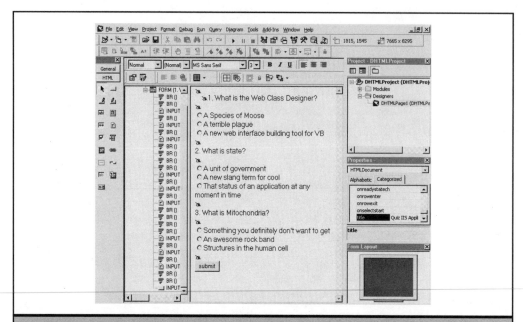

Figure 5-13. *Page designer with the Quiz file imported*

```
<HTML>
<HEAD>
<TITLE>Quiz IIS Application</TITLE>
</HEAD>

<BODY BGCOLOR="white">

<!--  First question -->
<p id=pwebclass>
   1. What is the Web Class Designer?
</p>
<BR>
<!--  Radio buttons to ask the web class question. Correct
      answer is number 3. Note the ID is included for the DHTML
      Application.
-->
<input id=WebClass1 type="radio" name="webclass" value="1">A
Species of Moose<BR>
```

```
<input id=WebClass2 type="radio" name="webclass" value="2">A
terrible plague<BR>
<input id=WebClass3 type="radio" name="webclass" value="3">A new
web interface building tool for VB
<BR><BR>

<!--   Second question -->
<p id=pstate>
   2. What is state?
</p>
<BR>
<!--   Radio buttons to ask the state question. Correct
       answer is number 3. Note the ID is included for the DHTML
       Application.
-->
<input id=State1 type="radio" name="state" value="1">A unit of
government<BR>
<input id=State2 type="radio" name="state" value="2">A new slang
term for cool<BR>
<input id=State3 type="radio" name="state" value="3">The status of
an
application at any moment in time
<BR><BR>

<!--   Third question -->
<p id=pmito>
    3. What is Mitochondria?
</p>
<BR>

<!--   Radio buttons to ask the mitochondria question. Correct
       answer is number 3. Note the ID is included for the DHTML
       Application.
-->
<input id=Mito1 type="radio" name="mito" value="1">Something you
definitely don't want to get<BR>
<input id=Mito2 type="radio" name="mito" value="2">An awesome rock
band<BR>
<input id=Mito3 type="radio" name="mito" value="3">Structures in
the human cell
<BR><BR>
```

```
<!-- Submit button for the form -->
<INPUT id=Button1 name=Button1 type=button value="Check Quiz">

<!-- Paragraph tags displaying the quiz status. -->
<P id=Status>Quiz Status:  </P>

</BODY>
</html>
```

You will notice a few more changes than just identifying IDs in the radio option buttons. You will also notice that the form is gone from the page. That is because we will not actually need to submit the page to the server for processing. Thus, we need no form.

Since we need no form for the page, we do not need a submit button. Instead, we have changed the submit button to be an HTML button element and have given it an appropriate ID for reference in our application. Finally, you will also notice a set of paragraph tags. One set is around each question in the quiz. We have given the paragraph an ID beginning with "p" to separate it from the radio buttons. And the Quiz Status text also has a set of paragraph tags. We will use this text for dynamically displaying the quiz status to the user.

That finalizes the HTML interface for the application. Now we are ready to put some functionality behind the interface.

Building the Functionality

Certainly our goal on the application is to check whether the user has entered correct responses and to give some feedback. That doesn't mean we can't jazz up the interface a bit and make taking the quiz a little more exciting than just a "yes, you answered correctly" type response.

We are going to start using the document object model for Internet Explorer in the development of this sample. The DOM is a rich multilevel model that allows for highly customized development of the Web page interface. The Microsoft Web site and MSDN provide extensive reference to the many attributes, properties, and methods available in Internet Explorer and cascading style sheets.

First, let's work on a little user interface development. When users move their mouse over a question on the page, let's make the text change color and turn bolder so the question will stand out.To do this, we will reference the paragraph ID we put in our HTML document. For the mitochondria question, that would be "pmito." In the object listing drop-down box of the page designer code view interface, select the pmito object. Then in the procedure drop-down box, select the "onmouseover" event. Note while you are doing this the many events you have available to you for programming the paragraph tag interface alone!

Now that you have the onmouseover event available for programming, we are ready to change the properties of the pmito tag. In this case we are going to work with the style of the tag. So our first "." reference on the tag is Style. When you select Style, you can see all of the many properties and methods we can set and call for style. In particular, we are interested in the color and fontweight properties.

To change the text color, simply set the property to your desired color. Likewise, set the fontweight property to your desired weight—400 is typically a medium weight, while 700 is a bold weight.

You will want to follow the same procedures on the "onmouseout" event. Following is the listing for the pmito object for both the onmouseout and onmouseover events. In this case the text will be changed to blue and bold when the mouse is over the text and then back to black medium when the mouse moves out of the text.

```
Private Sub pmito_onmouseout()

'   Change the text color back to black
pmito.Style.Color = "BLACK"
'   Change the font weight to medium
pmito.Style.fontWeight = 400

End Sub


Private Sub pmito_onmouseover()

'   Change the color to blue
pmito.Style.Color = "BLUE"
'   Change the font weight to bold
pmito.Style.fontWeight = 700

End Sub
```

Follow the same procedures for the pstate object. In this case the mouse over text will turn to green bold and then back to black medium when the mouse leaves.

```
Private Sub pstate_onmouseout()

'   Change the font color to black
pstate.Style.Color = "BLACK"
'   Change the font weight back to medium
pstate.Style.fontWeight = 400

End Sub
```

```
Private Sub pstate_onmouseover()

'  Change the font color to green
pstate.Style.Color = "GREEN"
'  Change the font weight to bold
pstate.Style.fontWeight = 700

End Sub
```

Finally, set the pclass object to change the text to red and bold when the mouse is over text and back to black medium when the mouse leaves.

```
Private Sub pwebclass_onmouseout()

'  Change the font color back to black
pwebclass.Style.Color = "Black"
'  Change the font weight back to medium
pwebclass.Style.fontWeight = 400

End Sub

Private Sub pwebclass_onmouseover()

'  Change the font color to red
pwebclass.Style.Color = "RED"
'  Change the font weight to bold
pwebclass.Style.fontWeight = 700

End Sub
```

Now that we have some of the flashier items out of the way, let's build the functionality to test our quiz takers. As in the earlier example, we will utilize a flag to indicate whether or not the questions have been answered properly.

To test the responses, we can directly access the checked property of the radio buttons. In this case, nothing is submitted to the server, so there are no request values to be evaluated. In fact, our radio button elements could skip the value attribute completely since our test is to see whether the correct answer has been selected.

To access the radio buttons, we use the ID placed in the HTML coding. Since the proper response for each question is the third answer, we will be evaluating the checked property of the third ID for each (webclass3, state3, mito3). If any one of them is unchecked, we need to set the flag and notify the user.

To notify the user, we are going to change the question text to contain two **
characters plus the original question. That is done by using the innerText property of
the paragraph object. The innerText property allows us to retrieve and update the
"inner text" in the paragraph tags. Thus, we can update the question text quite easily
and provide instant feedback for the user.

```vb
Private Function Button1_onclick() As Boolean

' Declare our variables
Dim Flag As Integer

' Set the flag = 0 assuming all responses are correct
Flag = 0

' Check to see if the third radio button on the web
' class question is checked
If WebClass3.Checked <> True Then

    ' Set the flag to indicate a false response
    Flag = 1

    ' Change the text on the question to indicate
    ' an incorrect response with two **. InnerText
    ' changes the text inside of the <p></p> tags
    ' and will not process the text for any HTML
    ' tags
    pwebclass.innerText = "**" & pwebclass.innerText

End If

If State3.Checked <> True Then

    ' Set the flag to indicate a false response
    Flag = 1

    ' Change the text on the question to indicate
    ' an incorrect response with two **
    pstate.innerText = "**" & pstate.innerText

End If
```

```
If Mito3.Checked <> True Then
    ' Set the flag to indicate a false response
    Flag = 1

    ' Change the text on the question to indicate
    ' an incorrect response with two **
    pmito.innerText = "**" & pmito.innerText

End If
```

The last section of our button click code is to display the quiz evaluation response. If the user has answered the questions properly, we are going to display a colorful, bright, scrolling marquee in place of the "Quiz Result:" paragraph. Are you wondering how the paragraph tags and text can magically turn into a marquee? It is simple with the outerHTML property of the paragraph object. Much like the innerText property, we can update the outerHTML property to change all the text *and* the tags. When the outerHTML property is set, it forces the browser to replace and evaluate the new HTML code being placed on the page. Voila, you now have a marquee instead of a paragraph.

Finally, for an incorrect response, we will replace the inner text again, but in this case we want to include some HTML tags to be processed. Instead of using the innerText property, we will use the innerHTML property. The paragraph tags stay in place, but when the inner text is replaced, any HTML tags are processed and appropriate results are displayed.

```
' Check to see if all responses were correct
If Flag = 0 Then

    ' Build a MARQUEE tag set of HTML tags. The font size will be
    ' 4 and the font color will be green. It may look complex, but
    ' the HTML string is simple
    MHTML = "<font size=""4"" color=""GREEN"">"
    MHTML = MHTML & "<B><MARQUEE BGCOLOR=""YELLOW"""
    MHTML = MHTML & " DIRECTION=RIGHT BEHAVIOR=SCROLL"
    MHTML = MHTML & " SCROLLAMOUNT=10 SCROLLDELAY=200>"
    MHTML = MHTML & "Correct Response!  Congratulations!."
    MHTML = MHTML & "</MARQUEE></b></font>"
```

```
        '  Use the innerHTML function of the paragraph element
        '  to change the entire paragraph to a Marquee!  InnerHTML
        '  forces the HTML tagging to be recompiled.
        Status.outerHTML = MHTML

    Else

        '  Changes the text between the <p></p> tags
        '  but in this case it will process any HTML
        '  tags.
        Status.innerHTML = "<B>Quiz Result:  **You have an " & _
        " incorrect response.</b>"

    End If

End Function
```

You have now built your first client-side DHTML application with VB. You have probably realized from this exercise that learning the DHTML document object model is going to be essential for building great DHTML applications. The fortunate thing is that Microsoft's object coding tools are excellent, and combined with MSDN, you have all the resources you need to build powerful client-side DHTML applications.

Testing Our DHTML Application

Now that we have built all of this functionality, let's see it in action! Go ahead and run the application. As with IIS applications, you will get a Debugging dialog box prompting you for the object to display first (in this case only our one page designer is available) and whether to use an existing version of Internet Explorer. Go ahead and accept the defaults. Figure 5-14 shows the page at startup.

To test the capabilities, let's first answer all the questions incorrectly, then click the Check Quiz button. When you do that, you should see all the quiz questions get updated with the **, indicating incorrect answers. Figure 5-15 shows the page.

Finally, let's answer all the questions correctly (the third response on each). Then click the Check Quiz button again. That is when the scrolling marquee shows up on the page congratulating us on our successful responses. Figure 5-16 shows the page.

One thing we didn't do was to delete the ** in front of the question when the answer was corrected. You can go to the button click event and add an else option on the answer checking to clear the ** and return the questions to their original state.

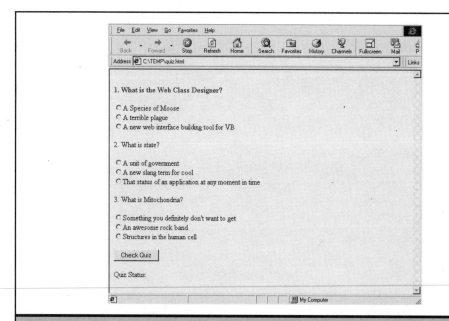

Figure 5-14. DHTML Quiz application at startup in Internet Explorer

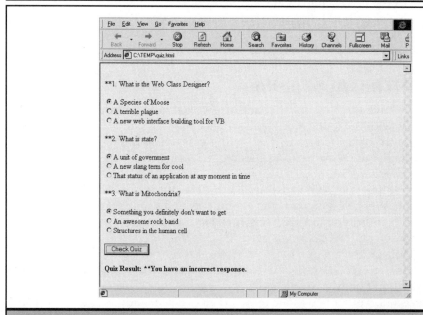

Figure 5-15. DHTML Quiz application with incorrect responses to all questions

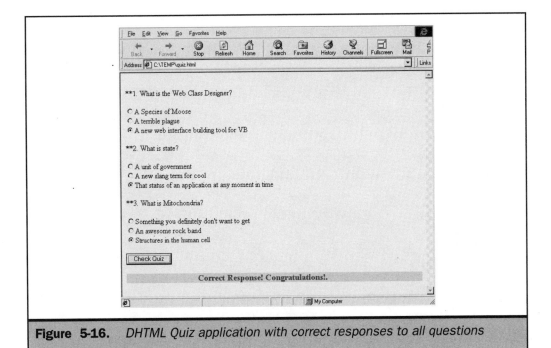

Figure 5-16.   *DHTML Quiz application with correct responses to all questions*

Summary

If you are at all interested in developing applications based on Internet technology, you will be excited about what Visual Basic 6.0 has to offer. If you have a wide range of browsers to target, IIS applications will open up a whole new world of Internet development. And, you can use already created server-based business objects and databases that are right in your IIS Applications. If you know your browser audience is Internet Explorer 4 on a PC and want to combine server-side Internet capabilities with powerful client-side programming tools, DHTML applications will deliver good-looking and user-friendly applications.

This chapter is just to whet your appetite. The last part of the book is devoted to building and deploying these new kinds of applications.

What's Next

The next part of the book will move on to building Visual Basic applications in the Windows environment. We will explore topics such as utilizing the Windows API, building user interfaces, deploying applications, and working with Internet technology within your application.

The
Complete
Reference

Visual
Basic 6

Part II

Working with Windows

In this part we will explore the ins and outs of using the Visual Basic integrated development environment. We will also explore how to build your Visual Basic applications to integrate into the Windows environment. We will explore user interfaces, Windows API programming, building setup installation programs, printers, debugging, error handling, and much more. The goal of this part is to provide you with a good reference to all of the capabilities of building great Windows-based Visual Basic programs.

The Complete Reference

Visual
Basic 6

Chapter 6

Designing User Interfaces

In Part I we had a good overview of many key capabilities and new features in Visual Basic 6.0. Now it is time to get down to doing some application building. In this chapter, we are going to take a close look at building user interfaces for our applications using VB. A good user interface correctly utilizes menus, toolbars, help, and much more. User interface design can be an art in itself. Many companies such as Microsoft, Apple, Netscape, and others have spent millions of dollars to study consumers' utilization of program user interfaces. Books have been written on interface design, and many a user has lamented at the poor design in some applications. This chapter will help you get the basics under your belt so you can be well-equipped to build an interface that is elegant and functional for your user base.

The first section of this chapter reviews the fundamental elements of a Windows-based user interface. Then we will deploy these into a sample application.

Visual Elements of a Visual Basic Application

Several key elements make up a successful user interface. Each has become familiar to the user and is typically expected in an interface. User interface elements have been designed to help the user either utilize functionality already learned or explore new functionality without too much difficulty. In some cases user interfaces have become extensive and highly customizable. Examples include the suite of Microsoft Office applications. Users ranging from novice to expert can get going easily with the interface. Power users can customize the toolbars to have exactly the features they use frequently and in the spot where they want them on the screen.

Keep in mind that the user interface is the *only* way a user can access the functionality of your application. While you may certainly outline a feature in your manual or in on-line help, if it can't be easily found or accessed in your application, then it will probably not be utilized by the user. Other items to consider as you build your interface are the number of clicks required to take an action in your application.

Also critical is how far the user has to move the mouse pointer to reach specific functionality. Many constructs, such as toolbars, tab strips, right mouse buttons, and floating toolbars, have all been designed to simplify and minimize the amount of mouse activity required to reach a set of functionality in an application.

Menus

Menus have traditionally been the primary interface to an application. The menu bar appears immediately below the title bar on the form and contains one or more titles. You will be familiar with standard menus such as File, Edit, Window, and Help. When you click a menu title, a window containing a list of menu options drops down. On that window you can have direct commands (such as cut, copy, and paste) or submenus that pull up additional window and divider bars to help organize the different items on the menu.

To make your application easy to use, you should group menu items according to their function. Typically, the File menu organizes the application and any files it is working on. For example, in VB the File menu gives you options for working with your project files. The Edit menu provides a large list of features for editing code, searching code, and so on.

From a programmatic standpoint, a menu control is an object; like other objects, it has properties that can be used to define its appearance and behavior within your application. You can set the Caption property, the Enabled and Visible properties, the Checked property, and others at design time or at run time. Menu controls contain only one event, the click event, which is invoked when the menu control is selected with the mouse or from the keyboard.

Fortunately, Microsoft provides a great tool for developing menus in your application, the menu editor. The menu editor, shown in Figure 6-1, can be found on the Tools menu in VB. The menu editor allows you to create a list of menu items organized by top-level menu titles and subitems. Each subitem can then have its own subitems.

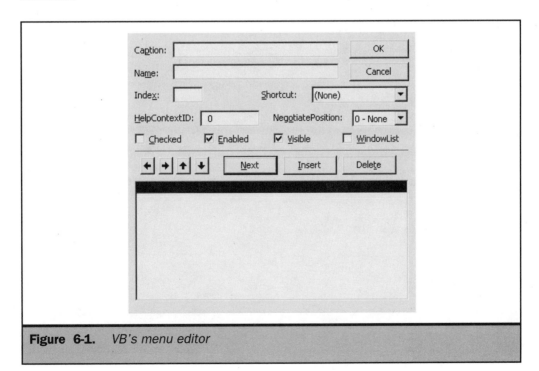

Figure 6-1. *VB's menu editor*

Follow these steps to create a File menu with one submenu:

1. In the caption field, enter **&File**. The & will indicate that "F" is the hot key for accessing the title menu through the ALT-F keyboard sequence.

2. Name the menu "mnuFile."

3. That is it for adding the File title menu. Now click on the Next button.

4. We want the next menu item to be a subitem of the File menu. To do this, we need to indent the next item. Do this by clicking on the right arrow icon.

5. Now type **&Open** in the caption.

6. Set the menu name to be "mnuOpen."

7. In the Shortcut drop-down list, select CTRL-O as the keyboard shortcut sequence. Once that is done, the menu editor should look like Figure 6-2.

8. Click on the Next button to go to the next item.

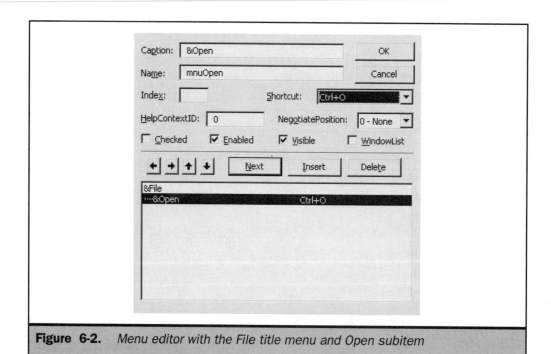

Figure 6-2.   *Menu editor with the File title menu and Open subitem*

9. Let's add a break bar in the menu by typing - (dash) in the caption and setting the menu name to "mnuDash." This will show up as a break line on the menu.

10. Select the Next button, type **&Save Options** for the caption, and name the menu item "mnuSaveOptions."

11. Now click Next again and click the right arrow one more time. This will create a submenu off Save Options.

12. Type **&Export** as the caption and set the menu name to "mnuExport." Set the shortcut to be CTRL-E.

13. Type **Save &As** for the next caption and set the menu name to "mnuSaveAs." Set the shortcut to be CTRL-A.

14. Type **&Save** for the next caption and set the menu name to "mnuSave." Set the shortcut to be CTRL-S.

Now your menu editor should look like Figure 6-3.

In the Visual Basic IDE, you can select the menu as though it were run time, but you can then get access to the click method of each menu item and put the appropriate programming behind the interface. Figure 6-4 shows the form at run time with the submenu displayed. Note that the - has turned into a dividing line on the menu.

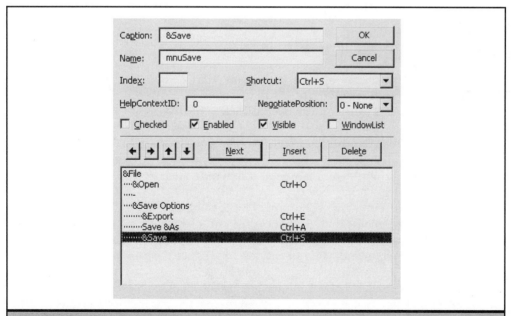

Figure 6-3.   *Menu editor with File title menu, two subitems with a submenu*

WORKING WITH WINDOWS

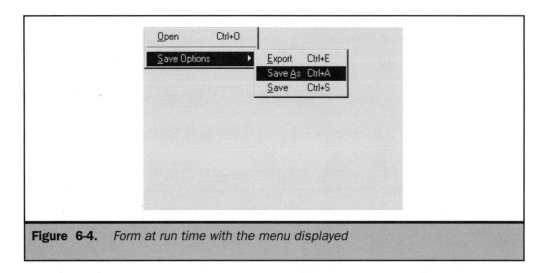

Figure 6-4. *Form at run time with the menu displayed*

That is all there is to building menus for your application. Pay careful attention to the use of shortcut control sequences. You will certainly want to try and follow standard Windows conventions for user interface design. For example, almost all users know they can type CTRL-S to save whatever they are currently working on. CTRL-C, CTRL-X, and CTRL-V are the standard copy, cut, and paste shortcuts for Edit menus, and so on.

Toolbars and Tab Strips

You can further enhance your application's menu interface with toolbars and tab strips. Tab strips provide multiple pages for viewing content in your application. Many of the dialog boxes we have reviewed in Visual Basic's IDE have used tab strips to organize and display many options in a small amount of screen space.

Toolbars contain toolbar buttons, which provide quick access to the most frequently used commands in an application. For example, the Visual Basic toolbar contains toolbar buttons to perform commonly used commands, such as running projects or saving the current project.

A Toolbar control contains a collection of Button objects used to create the toolbar. Typically, a toolbar contains buttons that correspond to items in an application's menu, providing a graphic interface for the user to access an application's most frequently used functions and commands. It is an easy way to reduce the number of clicks to reach functionality on a menu and to put it into an easy-to-use graphical context.

All that sounds good, but what about a coolbar? A CoolBar control contains a collection of Band objects used to create a configurable toolbar that is associated with a form. You can place many different controls on a coolbar. Specifically, you can place toolbar controls to create button menus for your application. Coolbars are great because they allow the user to easily slide and organize "bands" of functionality.

Build an Interface Using Tab Strips, Coolbars, and Toolbars

The best way to get familiar with these tools is to work with an example. In our example, we will create a tab strip as the main element on our application. On the first tab we will place a calendar control and on the second a text box for taking notes.

We will also create a coolbar that will contain three toolbars. The first will have open, save, and print options; the second will have cut, copy, and paste options; and the third will have bold and italic options. We would be remiss in building the user interface if we did not include a corresponding menu for our toolbar buttons, so a menu will be added.

Start your new application and save it to your system. You will need to include several of the standard components that come with VB. Specifically, add the Microsoft Windows Common Controls 6.0, Microsoft Windows Common Controls-2 6.0, and the Microsoft Windows Common Controls-3 6.0. This will add the tab strip, coolbar, toolbar, and other standard Windows controls to your toolbox.

BUILDING THE TAB STRIP   Let's get started by building the tab strip. Add the controls shown in Table 6-1 to your user interface.

Control	Setting
TabStrip	TbsDialogue
NumTabs	2
Tab1	
Caption	"Calendar"
Tab2	
Caption	"Notes"
Frame	FrmTabStrip
BorderStyle	0 'None
Caption	"Frame1"
Index	1
TextBox	TxtNotes (contained in the Frame1, index 1 control)
MultiLine	-1 'True

Table 6-1.   *Control Properties for the Tab Strip Interface*

Control	Setting
Frame	FrmTabStrip
BorderStyle	0 'None
Caption	"Frame1"
Index	0
MonthView	MnthCalendar (contained in Frame1, index 0 control)

Table 6-1.   *Control Properties for the Tab Strip Interface* (continued)

The tab strip control is set up with two tabs for the user. The first will hold a monthview calendar control for picking calendar dates, and the second will hold a notes text box. You can configure the tab strip by right-clicking on the tab strip and selecting Properties. Figure 6-5 shows the Tabs management tab on the properties interface (notice the use of a tab control in this setting).

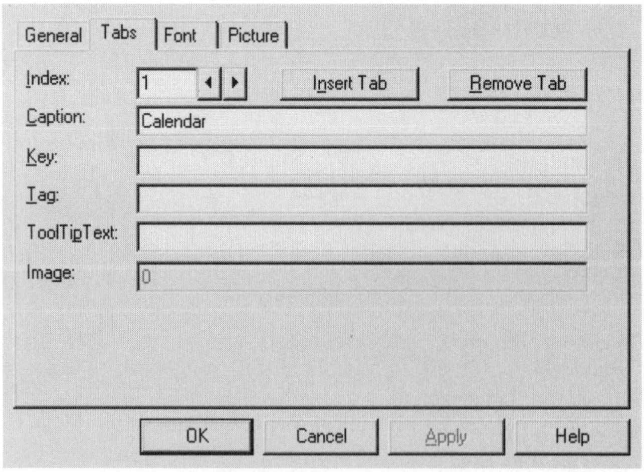

Figure 6-5.   *Tabs management tab for the tab strip control*

Now, you are probably wondering what all that business is about using frame controls with no borders. Typically, each tab on a tab strip will need to show multiple controls. We need an easy way to contain all of these controls in one easy-to-use interface. This can be done quite simply with a frame control. In this case we have drawn the monthview and textbox controls on the frame control array. What we can then do at run time is size the frame controls to the size of the client area on the tab strip and then simply change the z-order (layering) of the frame to make one or the other visible depending on the tab selected. And the index of the frame in the control array will correspond to the tab selected on the tab strip. This makes for simple tab strip control display management.

BUILDING THE COOLBAR INTERFACE   Next let's work on building the coolbar interface. Place the controls outlined in Table 6-2 on your application interface.

Control	Setting
ImageList	ImlButtons
NumListImages	8
ListImage1 – ListImage8	(local graphics on machine)
CoolBar	CblToolBar
CBHeight	375
Child1	TlbFile
NewRow1	0 'False
Toolbar	TlbFile (contained in the tlbFile band)
Style	1
ImageList	ImlButtons
NumButtons	3
Button1	
ImageIndex	1
Button2	
ImageIndex	2
Button3	
ImageIndex	3

Table 6-2.   *Coolbar, Toolbar, and Image List Properties*

Control	Setting
Child2	TlbEdit
NewRow2	0 'False
Toolbar	TlbEdit (contained in the tlbEdit band)
Style	1
ImageList	ImlButtons
NumButtons	3
Button1	
ImageIndex	4
Button2	
ImageIndex	5
Button3	
ImageIndex	6
Child3	TlbFormat
NewRow3	0 'False
Toolbar	TlbFormat (contained in the tlbFormat band)
Style	1
ImageList	ImlButtons
NumButtons	2
Button1	
ImageIndex	7
Button2	
ImageIndex	8

Table 6-2. *Coolbar, Toolbar, and Image List Properties* (continued)

To build the coolbar containing the toolbars, you want to follow these steps. It can get a little tricky if things are not done in the right order (as you may have already found out).

1. Place the ImageListcontrol on the form.

2. Right-click on the ImageList control and select Properties.

3. Go to the Images tab and insert a series of button graphics into the image list. Specifically, we need the graphics provided with VB in the OffCtlBr\Small\B&W folder. In that folder we need the new.bmp, save.bmp, print.bmp, cut.bmp, copy.bmp, and paste.bmp graphics, in that order.

4. The last two bold and italic graphics should be inserted and can be found in the tlbr_w95 folder. The files are bld.bmp and itl.bmp.

That sets up the list of bitmap buttons we will need for the three toolbars that will be on our coolbar. To set up the coolbar, follow these steps:

1. Place the coolbar on the form. Ideally, it will be placed at the top of the form and span the width of the form.

2. Draw three toolbar controls, as outlined above, on the coolbar.

3. The trick is to "bind" each of the toolbars to one of the bands.

4. Right-click on the coolbar and select Properties.

5. Select the Bands tab, as shown in Figure 6-6.

6. On the first band, select the tlbFile toolbar as the child.

7. On the second band, select the tlbEdit toolbar as the child.

8. On the third band, select the tlbFormat toolbar as the child.

Once you have toolbars set up on the coolbar, you can go into each and set up the buttons. Simply insert buttons as appropriate and set the indexes as outlined in Table 6-2.

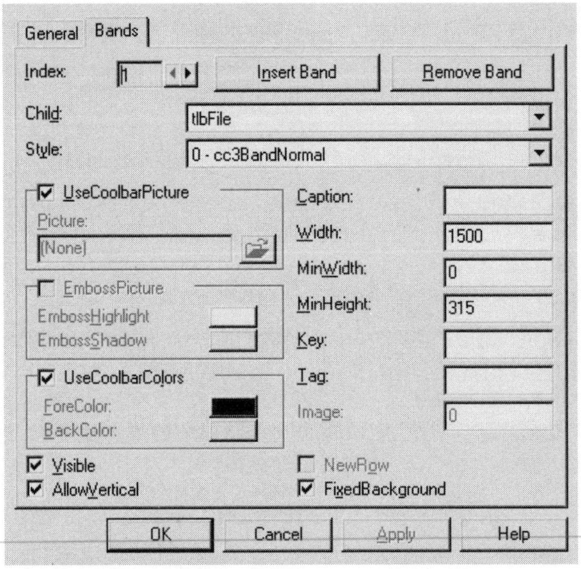

Figure 6-6.   *Bands tab of the coolbar*

BUILDING THE MENU INTERFACE   The last step is to create our menu. Table 6-3 outlines the menu setup for the form.

Control	Setting
Menu	mnuFile
Caption	"&File"
Menu	mnuOpen
Caption	"&Open"
Shortcut	CTRL-O
Menu	mnuPrint
Caption	"&Print"
Shortcut	CTRL-P

Table 6-3.   *Menu Setup for the Application*

Control	Setting
Menu	mnuSave
Caption	"&Save"
Shortcut	CTRL-S
Menu	MnuEdit
Caption	"&Edit"
Menu	mnuCut
Caption	"Cu&t"
Shortcut	CTRL-X
Menu	mnuCopy
Caption	"&Copy"
Shortcut	CTRL-C
Menu	mnuPaste
Caption	"&Paste"
Shortcut	CTRL-V
Menu	mnuDash
Caption	"-"
Menu	mnuBold
Caption	"&Bold"
Shortcut	CTRL-B
Menu	mnuItalic
Caption	"&Italic"
Shortcut	CTRL-I

Table 6-3. *Menu Setup for the Application* (continued)

And with that, we have built our user interface. To review, we placed our tab strip on the form and configured two "frame" container windows for our controls to display on each tab. Second, we set up a coolbar control with three bands and a toolbar on each band. The toolbar's button icons are set in the ImageList control. Finally, we built a corresponding menu interface to match the buttons on our coolbar.

CODING THE TAB STRIP   The last step is to place a little bit of code in the application to handle the tab strip interface.

```
Option Explicit

Private Sub Form_Load()

Dim intCnt As Integer

'  Loop through the tabs on the tabstrip
For intCnt = 0 To frmTabStrip.Count - 1

    '  Move the frame controls to cover the
    '  client area of the tabstrip
    frmTabStrip(intCnt).Move _
    tbsDialogue.ClientLeft, _
    tbsDialogue.ClientTop, _
    tbsDialogue.ClientWidth, _
    tbsDialogue.ClientHeight

Next intCnt

'  Ensure the frame associated with the current tab is set
'  to the top of the page and is visible.
frmTabStrip(tbsDialogue.SelectedItem.Index - 1).ZOrder 0

End Sub

Private Sub tbsDialogue_Click()

    '  When the user selects a new tab, we
    '  will make the corresponding frame at the
    '  top in the zorder.
    frmTabStrip(tbsDialogue.SelectedItem.Index - 1).ZOrder 0

End Sub
```

When the form is loaded, the frame control array is sized to fit on the tab strip client area. A loop is created to go through the frame control array. Finally, the frame corresponding to the currently selected tab is set to the top of the z-order (on top of everything else on the form).

When the user clicks on a new tab, in the click event of the tab strip control, we change the z-order of the corresponding frame to be on the top of the tab strip.

TESTING THE INTERFACE   Now that we have put all this hard work into building the interface, we are finally ready to test. Start the application. Figure 6-7 shows the form at run time. As you can see, we have built a pretty nice standard Windows interface. The coolbar is set up to act as our application toolbar. We have corresponding menu functionality, and the tab strip is set up with the monthview control placed properly on the tab strip. Now go ahead and click on the Notes tab of the tab strip. Figure 6-8 shows the tab change.

When the Notes tab was selected, the frame with the text box was placed on top of the frame with the monthview control. The old frame is still there, it is just hidden from view. Finally, play around with the coolbar. You can also change the coolbar from being one row to multiple rows. Figure 6-9 shows the coolbar with two rows and the bands moved around.

The toolbar, coolbar, and tab strip controls can be powerful and elegant user interface options for your application. Microsoft is certainly setting the coolbar/toolbar combination as the standard for application interfaces. Tab strip controls are great for organizing a lot of user interface items into compact screen space and providing some order to the interface.

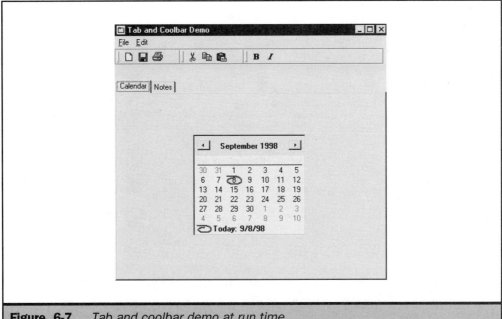

Figure 6-7.   *Tab and coolbar demo at run time*

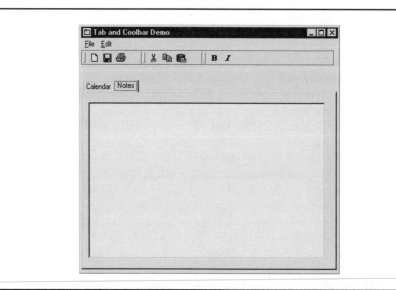

Figure 6-8. Application with the Notes tab selected

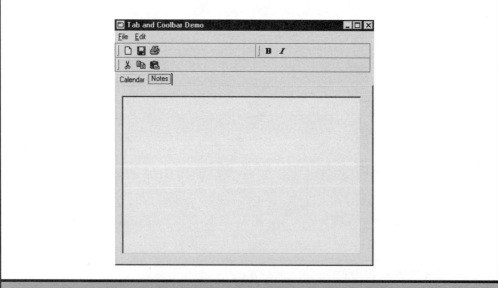

Figure 6-9. Coolbar with two rows and the bands manipulated

ActiveX and Other Controls

There have been volumes and volumes of articles and books written on the many controls in the market for VB developers. Controls can range from the generic list box to highly customized lines of business controls. As we saw in the previous example, there are standard sets of controls available to the developer that will provide the primary user interface elements.

When you start Visual Basic, you get a standard set of controls that includes labels, text boxes, command buttons, check boxes, option buttons, combo boxes, list boxes, and scroll bars. These should be fairly straightforward and familiar to the developer. You may have also heard of these as "intrinsic" controls. They are included in the Visual Basic .exe file; you do not have to add them into the project as you do ActiveX controls.

There are also a series of ActiveX controls provided with Visual Basic that you can put at your disposal. You have already seen a number of these, including the coolbar and monthview controls. Appendix C provides an overview of these controls as well as the data bound controls.

You should explore the many different controls provided with Visual Basic. They can provide a rich set of user interface options. Controls such as MultiMediam, MSChart, and RichTextBox provide extended sets of functionality right in a simple user interface.

Some controls such as the MAPI, Internet Transfer, and communications controls provide connectivity features that would otherwise take a considerable amount of programming to accomplish. You can add mail, Internet, and serial communications capabilities simply through using these controls.

As we continue to work through the chapters in this book, many of these out-of-the-box controls will be demonstrated in various uses. Have fun with them, and explore their capabilities and how they can provide elegant user interface solutions for your applications. If you don't find what you need in VB, check out the rich third-party development market.

Status Bars

Another key interface feature you will find in almost any Windows application is status bars. These bars typically reside at the bottom of the application interface and provide feedback on the status of the application. For example, in Microsoft Word, the bottom status bar shows the current page, section, number of total pages, line on the page, and column. That status bar is a provider of immediate and unobtrusive feedback to the user. Figure 6-10 shows the Word status bar.

In Visual Basic, you can build status bars using (of course) the status bar ActiveX control. The control provides you with the ability to build in multiple panels (a collection) on the bar and programmatically control each at run time. In the next example in the chapter—a complete interface design—we will build a status bar to give the user active feedback in the application.

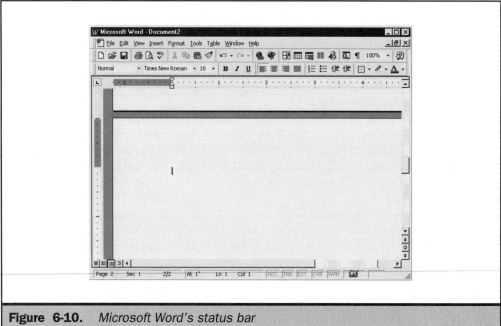

Figure 6-10.   *Microsoft Word's status bar*

Adding Help

Help is a critical part of any application and can take many forms. Traditionally, help is an external document that provides an interactive interface for searching for specific topics. Adding support for help to your Visual Basic application is fairly straightforward.

But help can also take the form of context-sensitive help by associating help topics with aspects of the application interface. All you need to do is set one property, HelpFile, to display help when the user presses the F1 key or requests help from a menu. An additional property, HelpContextID, can be set to provide a contextual help topic for any user interface element in your application.

There are two types of help formats available for your application. The first is traditional WinHelp, and the second is HTML help based on Web technology. If you are deploying new applications, consider using HTML help as your primary help support method.

The process of hooking up help is essentially the same for both WinHelp and HTML help. Follow these steps to hook up a help file for your application:

1. Select Project Properties from the Project menu.

2. In the Help File Name field of the General tab, enter the path and file name for your application's help file (.hlp or .chm).

The HelpContextID property is used to link a user interface element such as a control or form to a related topic in a help file. The HelpContextID property must be a Long data type that matches the Context ID of a topic in a WinHelp (.hlp) or HTML help (.chm) file. For example, you might enter 500 in the HelpContextID property of a list box. When the user selects the list box and presses F1, a search will be done for a help topic with a Context ID of 500 in the help file. When it is found, a Help window will open and display the topic.

Carefully consider building help into your system. Users will rely on it as a quick and easy way to find answers to their questions about your application. A good help interface can make or break a great piece of software. All the functionality in the world won't make a difference if the user doesn't understand how to use it.

> **Note** *Creating a help file in your application is fairly straightforward. There are excellent third-party tools in the marketplace, such as RoboHelp and others, that can assist you in building your help system. Visual Basic also comes with two supported formats, WinHelp and HTML help. Check out the MSDN CD to find out more about help compiler tools for creating help files.*

Design Tools and Guidelines

Now that we have reviewed the major user interface elements of an application, there are several tools and guidelines you should consider using to enhance and refine your interface. Small things such as setting control focus, aligning controls, and so on, can have a big impact on how intuitive and usable your application interface is to use.

Animation and Timed Events

There are a million uses for timed events and animation in your applications. You will rarely see simple animation and timing techniques used, but if done properly, they can enhance an application's usability and acceptance. A small demonstration is given in the last example of the chapter. A "You Win!" banner scrolls across a form in response to the user correctly solving a quiz. Traditionally, that might have been just a simple message box or some other method of displaying the notification. But the combination of timer control and a label control that moves from left to right adds a little pizzazz to the interface.

The timer control counts off time in specified milliseconds. For example, perhaps you are building a query-by-example interface to a database and you want to give the user feedback on time spent performing the query. Or perhaps you need a reminder to users every so often to save their application data. Tracking time intervals in an application can provide many different ways of giving users time-based feedback.

Along the same lines, animation feedback with the progress bar control can be very useful. If you are performing a series of activities such as connecting with a modem or transferring a file, the progress bar can give valuable feedback on the progress of the operation. Again, this gives the user excellent visual feedback on a process that may not be readily traceable.

Another nifty tool is the animation control. This control can play AVI videos and yet act as a button. If you have something in your application that you really want the user to click, set it up as an animated button, and the user is sure to notice. Figure 6-11 shows the Search.avi file provided with Visual Basic. When the user clicks on the button, the common dialog box is shown to find a file on the system.

You don't want to add too much flash to your interface, especially if a user will be using it day in and day out. That can get annoying. But if you need to get the user's attention or to track or initiate time-based events, these tools can be invaluable.

Aligning Controls, Setting Focus and Tab Order

Have you ever used an application whose interface has controls that are inconsistently sized or out of alignment? Or how about one in which you jump all over the place when you tab through the input elements? Building a consistent, well-laid-out interface helps to make your application visually appealing and easy on the eye. In VB 5.0, Microsoft had an Align Controls add-in that was immensely useful in lining up and sizing controls consistently. In VB 6, these features are standard menu options.

The Format menu gives you options for aligning controls left, center, right, top, middle, bottom, and to the form grid. You can make controls the same width, height, or both. And you can even control the horizontal and vertical spacing between controls to ensure it is uniform. All these functions make what can be a tedious layout task much simpler.

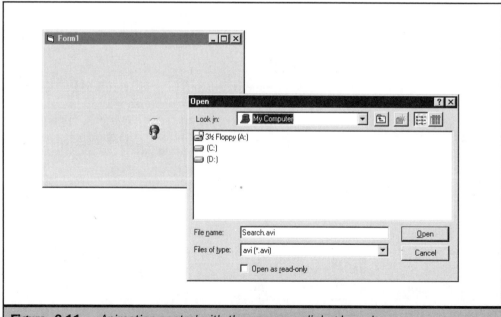

Figure 6-11.   *Animation control with the common dialog box shown*

You can also precisely move and size controls using the CTRL and SHIFT keys in combination with the arrow keys. SHIFT plus the arrow keys will size the control. CTRL plus the arrow keys will move the control. These can be immensely helpful in exact placement of controls.

Ever start an application only to find that you have to click on another section of the interface before starting? Setting the *focus* of a control can be crucial in saving keystrokes for the user as well as indicating where to get started. For example, on a name and address form, the control you probably want to get the focus first at run time is the First Name text box, not the submit button. Likewise, if the user submits the new address data to the database, and during validation you find that the address is missing, you will want to set the application focus on the Address text box.

Last but not least, always ensure the tab order properties of the page make sense. You want to be sure users can maneuver logically through the interface using the TAB key. It can greatly confuse and frustrate users when they tab to the next control on the screen only to find they have jumped halfway across the page.

Aligning controls and setting focus and tabs may be subtle and minor details when you are in the throes of developing that next great application, but when it comes to implementation and convenience for the user, they can be crucial.

Designing for Different Display Types

Unfortunately, we don't live in a world where everyone has 20-inch monitors with 1024×768 screen resolution and support for 16 million–plus colors. In fact, many people are still running 13-inch monitors that support 640×480 screen resolution and only 256 colors. So, that application that looks great on your 20-inch monitor with that large screen resolution and number of colors might not even be usable or visible on a lower-end system.

First and foremost, know your application audience and what type of hardware they have available. If they do have the high-end 20-inch monitors, then go for it in terms of design. If they don't, you will need to think about form layout size and screen real estate. Typically, it is safe to ensure your application is not larger in display size than 640×480. Second, if you are setting color properties in your application, you might want to use only 16 standard colors from the standard Windows palette—that way, the colors will be consistent on all platforms.

Microsoft has added the form layout tool to Visual Basic to assist developers with both placing their form at startup and understanding where it will be placed at different screen resolutions. If you are not careful, you can design your application such that it will not be visible on a 640×480 screen. If you design on a 1024×768 screen and place the form outside the 640×480 screen area, the user will not be able to reach your application on a 640×480 screen! Figure 6-12 shows the form layout tool. Notice the resolution guide. The form layout tool also provides four options for laying out your screen: Manual, Center Owner, Center Screen, and Windows Default. Thus, you can easily control the startup behavior of your application.

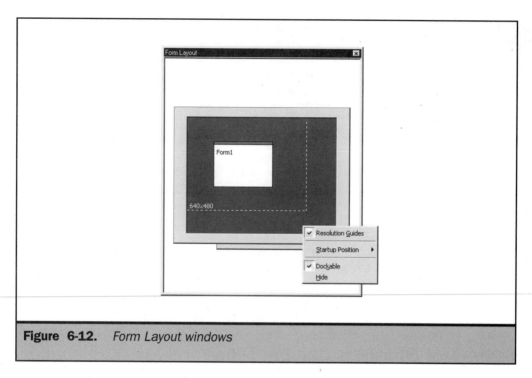

Figure 6-12.   *Form Layout windows*

The best method is to deploy and test your application on various systems to ensure it looks good and makes sense. Even though you may know your application will fit on a 640×480 screen resolution with 16 standard Windows colors, it simply may not look good. If it takes up the whole screen and everything looks exceedingly large, you may need to pare down the display size of the interface. But you will have to balance that against designing the interface in too compact a fashion for higher screen resolutions.

Right Mouse Button Support

Mouse support is a natural for any Windows application. It is very important to think about right mouse support as a type of context help and feature access for your application. Today in Windows you can right-click on just about anything and get a context-sensitive menu for your use.

You can add pop-up menu support in your application by accessing the mouse_down event of any control that supports it. Simply check the button that was clicked, and if it is the second mouse button, use the PopUpMenu method and the name of any menu in your application to provide a menu option.

You can control which menus on that pop-up are enabled by directly accessing the enabled property of any of the menu items. This provides an effective way, with minimal mouse movement and mouse clicks, to get context-sensitive menu functionality in your application.

Many controls have mouse menu support as part of their basic functionality. For example, the text box control provides standard cut, copy, and paste features in a context-sensitive menu that is activated with a right button click.

Building Our Sample Application

Now it is time to put our interface knowledge to work. Our review of VB's design features will guide us in building a well-rounded user interface application. Our sample application is going to be a simple matching game quiz. But what may be simple as a complete user interface will take some development. Core features of our interface will include

- Menus
- Toolbar buttons
- Cut, copy, and paste edit features
- Status bar feedback
- Clean interface layout
- Help
- Animation

We are going to build the matching feature using check boxes in the interface. On the face of it, this may sound great and easy to implement. The user will click on an item in one list and then click on the matching item (or at least their guess) in the second list. But watch out! In fact, we have a host of user interface issues to work with in order to make the interface clean and simple. What if the user clicks on another check box in the same pick list? How do we indicate a correct response? What about indicating an incorrect response? And, if this were a complex list of items, how would we facilitate the user tracking through notes on incorrect responses? All of these questions and more will be answered as we get started.

Application Outline and Features

We will build our application in three stages. First, we will build the primary interface of our quiz, which will define the core functionality of the application. This will include check boxes for taking the quiz and note boxes for assisting the user. It will also include the "You Win!" animation.

Following that, we will build the supporting framework that will include menus, a status bar, and toolbar. Finally, we will build the programming functionality behind the interface. That will take place in several stages to build the key features of the application. The end result will be a nifty little game that shows off key user interface design and elements as well as the sometimes tricky and extensive code behind making a user interface elegant and responsive to the user.

Building the User Interface

Start a new application in Visual Basic and save it to your system. The first order of building a good interface will be to ensure the project property settings are appropriately set. Follow these steps to set the project properties:

1. Select the Project menu and select Project1 Properties.

2. On the General tab, change the project name to "SportsMatch."

3. Select the Make tab.

4. Change the application's title to "Sports Match."

With these settings, when the application is run and installed, the project will be properly referenced by name rather than an innocuous "Project1" title. The next step is to set up our form with the proper identifying properties. Specifically, we need to ensure the caption is appropriately set, as well as the icon identifying the form. In fact, the default icon for the application will come from the default form unless otherwise specified. Table 6-4 shows the form properties for our application.

The icon is set to the bullseye.ico file provided with Visual Basic and installed in the \Graphics\Icon\Misc folder. Also note that the default startup position of the application is centered on the screen. That way, regardless of the resolution of the monitor, the application will be centered.

The next step is to define the core interface items. The primary match items will consist of a series of three basketball players and three teams. The goal will be to match the basketball player with the team he plays on (at least as of 1998!). The user will select a single player or a single team and try and make the match. The idea behind the Notes boxes by each is for users to keep track of their incorrect selections. It may be a bit of

Property	Setting
Form	Form1
Caption	"Sports Match"
Icon	(local file)
StartUpPosition	1 'CenterScreen

Table 6-4.   *Form Properties for the Sports Match Application*

overkill in this simple application, but it highlights support features and ideas to consider in your applications. Add the items in Table 6-5 to the user interface.

Property	Setting
Timer	tmrAnimate
Enabled	0 'False
Interval	100
CheckBox	chkPlayer
Captions	"Michael Jordan", "David Robinson", "Patrick Ewing"
Index	0, 1, 2
CheckBox	ChkTeam
Captions	"San Antonio Spurs", "Chicago Bulls", "New York Knicks"
Index	0, 1, 2
TextBox	TxtNotes
Index	0, 1, 2, 3, 4, 5
Label	lblNotes2
AutoSize	-1 'True
Caption	"Notes"
Label	LblNotes1
AutoSize	-1 'True
Caption	"Notes"
Label	lblWinner
AutoSize	-1 'True
Caption	"You Win!"

Table 6-5.   *Interface Objects and Properties for Sports Match*

Property	Setting
Font Name	"Arial Black"
Size	12
Weight	700 (Bold)
Color	Red
Visible	0 'False

Table 6-5.   *Interface Objects and Properties for Sports Match* (continued)

Our interface has two sets of check boxes, one for players and one for teams. Note that we have built each as a control array. As will be evident when our programming is put behind the interface, the control array provides us some programmatic flexibility in working with the check box controls and also makes our application much more scalable. If we want to add ten more players and teams to our interface, this will require less programming than if each check box needed to be programmatically handled individually.

The same concept is followed for the text boxes. Even though we will be doing little work with them programmatically, it will simplify management of their interface. In fact, we will be building some cut, copy, and paste functionality to match up with our Edit menu, and this is made easier by using a control array.

We have a couple of label controls for identifying our Notes text boxes. The third label control, lblWinner, is our animated text that will let users know they have successfully finished the matching game. Note that at startup, the visible property is false, since we do not want the user to see the label control until the match is completed. Ensure on your user interface that the label control is positioned near the left edge of the form so it can travel from left to right.

We also have in our interface a timer control. The timer will be used to tick off each movement of the lblWinner control and give the effect of animated text. The enabled property is set to false to ensure the animation doesn't start when the application starts. Figure 6-13 shows the form design interface at this stage.

Be sure and use the tools mentioned earlier in the chapter to align your text boxes and check boxes and make them the same size. This can save hours of tedious mouse layout and frustration!

The next step is to define the supporting structure for our interface, including the toolbar, menu, and status bar. Add the items in Table 6-6 to the user interface.

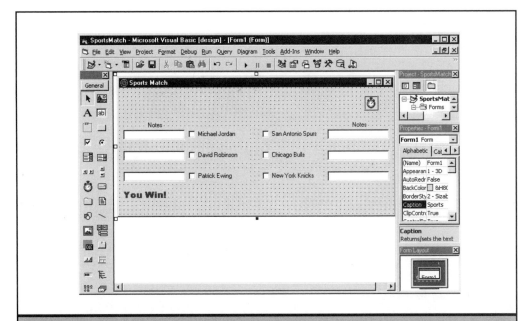

Figure 6-13.   *Form interface at design time with the match check boxes, Notes text boxes, label controls, and timer*

Control	Setting
ImageList	ImlButtons
NumListImages	2
Picture	(local file)
Picture	(local file)
Toolbar	tblFunctions
Align	1 'Align Top
Style	1
ImageList	ImlButtons

Table 6-6.   *Supporting Framework Objects and Properties of the User Interface*

Control	Setting
NumButtons	2
Toolbar – Button1	
ToolTipText	"Exit the Application"
ImageIndex	1
Toolbar – Button2	
ToolTipText	"Game Settings"
ImageIndex	2
Style	5 (menu)
Toolbar - Button2 – Button Menus	
NumButtonMenus	2
ButtonMenu1	
Text	"Clear"
ButtonMenu2	
Text	"Hints"
StatusBar	StbHelp
Align	2 'Align Bottom
NumPanels	2
Panel1	
AutoSize	1
ToolTipText	"Answer Feedback"
Panel2	
AutoSize	1
ToolTipText	"Hints"

Table 6-6. *Supporting Framework Objects and Properties of the User Interface*
(continued)

The first item in the list is the ImageList control. This holds the graphics that will be referenced in our toolbar. In this case we have two buttons on the interface. The first will be a dimmed lightbulb that will be used to end the application. The second will be a spade graphic that will indicate game options. You can find these graphics in the \Common\Graphics\Icons\Misc folder installed with Visual Basic.

The toolbar will then utilize the ImageList control as its index of buttons on the interface. As mentioned, the toolbar has two buttons on the interface. The second button is actually a menu style that allows the user to select two options from the button. In this case the options are Clear and Hints. The menu toolbar button can be especially effective for providing grouped options in one button. If your interface has a multitude of options and buttons, consider using this feature. Note that tool tip text is set for the buttons as well. When the user moves the mouse over the button, the tool tip information is shown to let the user know what the button is for.

The last item is the StatusBar control. The status bar allows you to define information panels at the bottom of your application. In this case we have two panels. One is for matching hints, and the second is for general feedback. We can also define tool tip text for our users. If they are wondering what the data they are seeing in the panel is for, the tool tip text will help. Figure 6-14 shows the form interface at this stage.

Finally, we are ready to finish off our user interface with appropriate menu buttons.

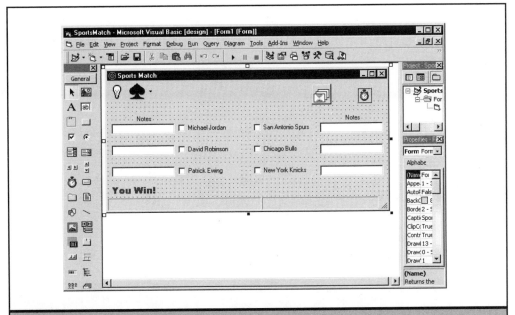

Figure 6-14. *Form interface with toolbar, image list, and status bar added*

Building Menu Structures

As demonstrated early in the chapter, you use the menu editor on the Tools menu in VB to build the toolbar. Set the menus up as shown in Table 6-7.

Control	Setting
Menu	MnuFile
Caption	"&File"
Menu	mnuExit
Caption	"E&xit"
Menu	mnuEdit
Caption	"&Edit"
Menu	mnuCut
Caption	"Cu&t"
Shortcut	CTRL-X
Menu	MnuCopy
Caption	"&Copy"
Shortcut	CTRL-C
Menu	MnuPaste
Caption	"&Paste"
Shortcut	CTRL-V
Menu	MnuGame
Caption	"&Game"
Menu	MnuClear
Caption	"&Clear"
Shortcut	CTRL-L

Table 6-7. *Menu Items*

Control	Setting
Menu	Hints
Caption	"&Hints"
Checked	-1 'True
Shortcut	CTRL-H
Menu	MnuHelp
Caption	"&Help"
Menu	MnuHow
Caption	"&How to Play"
Shortcut	CTRL-P

Table 6-7. *Menu Items* (continued)

And with the menus in place, our user interface is finally all set up and ready for programming. We are going to have to hook up code behind the menus, toolbar, status bar, and, of course, the match check boxes.

Programming the User Interface

To get started, let's first tackle the programming of the check boxes to get the heart of our application's functionality built. This is going to entail tracking user clicks and checking for matches. We have to do all of this in an event-driven environment where the user can do anything. Obviously, our ideal scenario would be for the user to play nice and select an item on the left and then an item on the right and continue to completion. But users can do just about anything. They can select an item on the left, change their mind, then check another item on the left, and so on.

The first thing we will need in our application is a set of global tracking variables. The following code defines these variables:

```
Option Explicit

'   Track the click status of our two series of
'   check boxes
```

```
Dim intPlayerClickStatus As Integer
Dim intTeamClickStatus As Integer

'  Track the index of the last check box clicked
Dim intPlayerClickIndex As Integer
Dim intTeamClickIndex As Integer

'  Indicates whether or not to ignore
'  the processing code in the check box
'  click events
Dim intIgnoreFlag As Integer

'  Indicates whether or not to show hints
Dim intHints As Integer

'  Stores the original background color of
'  the check boxes
Dim lngOrgColor As Long
```

Every time a user selects a check box, we want to track which control array was selected and the index of the control selected. Then when the user clicks on the next check box, we can match the two up and check for an incorrect or correct response.

The control array is tracked by intPlayerClickStatus and intTeamClickStatus, and the corresponding index variables track the index of the check box selected. The next variable, intIgnoreFlag, is a crucial one. As you will see below, every time a check box is selected, the click event is fired. Even if we change the value in code, the click event is fired off. There are going to be times when we simply want to change the check box value and not run the check matching code. The intIgnoreFlag global variable will tell us when to ignore the click code in the application.

The intHints global variable tracks whether the user wants to see hints in the status bar. And finally, the lngOrgColor will track the default background color value for the check boxes.

Tackling Check Boxes

Let's start with our two core events, the click events of our check box control arrays. This is where the primary logic of the application takes place. The basic idea of handling the check boxes is this: when the first in the two-click sequence is initiated, we want to store the selection in our global variables. Also, to prevent the user from selecting another control in the same control array, we disable the rest of the controls in the array.

Then the user can only select a check box from the second set of controls. But we have to be careful to ensure we don't process a request for an already checked (and correctly matched) check box. A check is done to see if a proper match has been made; if it has, the background colors of the check boxes are updated. If it has not, both check boxes are unchecked.

The following is the code for the player check box control array click event. Note that the index of the control array clicked on is passed into the event. The first section of our code checks to see if the intIngnoreFlag has been set. If so, the flag is reset and the subroutine is exited.

```
Private Sub chkPlayer_Click(index As Integer)

Dim intClearFlag As Integer

'  If the global Ignore Flag is set then we don't
'  want to process the rest of the code in the
'  subroutine
If intIgnoreFlag = 1 Then

    '  Exit the subroutine
    Exit Sub

End If
```

The next section of our code checks to see if this is the first click in the two-click matching sequence. If it is, the DisableCheckBoxes function is called with the index of the current check box passed in. That will disable the rest of the check boxes in the control array. Finally, we set the value of our global variables to indicate the player check box was first in the sequence and the index of the box selected.

```
'  We check to see if a player check box has
'  been clicked first. If not, we set the
'  appropriate global variables to indicate
'  a first click selection has been made
'  on one of the player check boxes
If intTeamClickStatus <> 1 Then

    '  Disable all but the current
    '  check box.  That way users
    '  cannot try and select another player;
    '  they are forced to select a team
    DisableCheckBoxes index, 1
```

```
'   Indicate that a player check box has been
'   selected
intPlayerClickStatus = 1

'   Store the index of the player selected
intPlayerClickIndex = index

Else
```

If the player check box array was the second in the two-click sequence, we need to check for a correct match. A select case is done on the index of the check box selected, and then the global variables for the team check box are compared for a correct match. If there was a correct match, the background colors of the two correct check boxes are changed. And the check boxes that were disabled are enabled by calling the enablecheckboxes subroutine. If it was an invalid selection, a flag is set to clear the check boxes later in the subroutine.

```
'   If we are in the else section then the person
'   has tried to make a match.  We must check to see if
'   the match is correct.

'   Process based index of the player selected
Select Case index

    Case 0 '  San Antonio Spurs
        '   Check to see if David Robinson was selected
        If intTeamClickIndex = 1 Then
            '   Change the back color
            chkPlayer(index).BackColor = RGB(255, 0, 0)

            '   Change the back color
            chkTeam(intTeamClickIndex).BackColor = _
            RGB(255, 0, 0)

            '   Enable the check boxes for further selection
            EnableCheckBoxes

        Else
```

```
        '  Wrong selection ... we will clear later
        intClearFlag = 1

    End If

    Case 1  '  Chicago
    '  Check to see if Michael Jordan was selected
    If intTeamClickIndex = 0 Then

        '  Change the back color
        chkPlayer(index).BackColor = RGB(0, 255, 0)
        '  Change the back color
        chkTeam(intTeamClickIndex).BackColor = _
        RGB(0, 255, 0)
        '  Enable the check boxes for further selection
        EnableCheckBoxes

    Else

        '  Wrong selection ... we will clear later
        intClearFlag = 1

    End If

    Case 2  '  New York
        '  Check to see if Patrick Ewing was selected
        If intTeamClickIndex = 2 Then

        '  Change the back color
        chkPlayer(index).BackColor = RGB(0, 0, 255)
        '  Change the back color
        chkTeam(intTeamClickIndex).BackColor = _
        RGB(0, 0, 255)
        '  Enable the check boxes for further selection
        EnableCheckBoxes

    Else
```

```
            '  Wrong selection ... we will clear later
            intClearFlag = 1

        End If

End Select
```

If the clear flag was set, we need to uncheck the two selections the user made. Since we are going to change the value of the check boxes, this event is going to be fired off again. That may seem a bit recursive, but actually it is fairly straightforward. What we don't want is to have this set of code run again. That is why the intIgnoreFlag is set to 1. When the values are set to false, this code will not run again. Finally, we still need to enable the check boxes, and a status message is shown to the user that this was an incorrect response.

```
'  Check to see if the clear flag is set
  If intClearFlag = 1 Then
      '  Set the ignore flag
      intIgnoreFlag = 1

      '  Change the player value to false ... this may be
      '  a bit confusing since we are in the click event that
      '  is going to set it to true.  It will be unchecked.
      chkPlayer(index).Value = False
      intIgnoreFlag = 0

      intIngnoreFlag = 1
      '  Set the original team box to false
      chkTeam(intTeamClickIndex).Value = False
      intIgnoreFlag = 0

      '  Enable all check boxes
      EnableCheckBoxes

      '  Indicate an incorrect response
      stbHelp.Panels(1).Text = "Incorrect Selection!"

  Else
```

If it was a correct selection, we need to check to see if the user has successfully completed all of the matches with the CheckForComplete subroutine. If so, the ShowWinnerMessage subroutine is called to initiate the animation. Also, we want to indicate in the status bar that a correct selection was made.

```
        '  Check for a completed quiz
        If CheckForComplete = 0 Then ShowWinnerMessage
        '  Show a correct response
        stbHelp.Panels(1).Text = "Correct Selection!"

    End If
```

Finally, we clear the global variables indicating the team check box was first clicked.

```
'  Clear the global variables
    intTeamClickStatus = 0
    intTeamClickIndex = 0

End If

End Sub
```

We have virtually the same function for the team check box array. The first section makes the same check to ensure we are not to ignore the code in the application and exit.

```
Private Sub chkTeam_Click(index As Integer)

Dim intClearFlag As Integer

'  If the global Ignore Flag is set then we don't
'  want to process the rest of the code in the
'  subroutine
If intIgnoreFlag = 1 Then

    '  Exit the subroutine
    Exit Sub

End If
```

We next check to see if the team check box is the first one to be clicked in the two-click sequence. If it is, the check boxes other than the one clicked are disabled with the DisableCheckBoxes procedure to ensure that they cannot be clicked. Finally, our global variables indicate a team check box and its index were clicked first.

```
'  We check to see if a team check box has
'  been clicked first. If not we set the
'  appropriate global variables to indicate
'  a first click selection has been made
'  on one of the team check boxes
If intPlayerClickStatus <> 1 Then

    '  Disable all but the current check box
    DisableCheckBoxes index, 2

    '  Indicate the team check box has been
    '  clicked to initiate an attempt at a match
    intTeamClickStatus = 1

    '  Store the index of the check box
    intTeamClickIndex = index

Else
```

Otherwise, we are in the second stage of the two-click process for making a match. As in the last set of code, a select case statement is used to check for a correct match based on the player selected. If it is a successful match, the background color is changed to indicate a correct match. Then the check boxes are enabled for the initially selected control array. If an unsuccessful match is made, we set the clear flag to indicate the selections should be cleared.

```
'  If we are in the else section then the person
    '  has tried to make a match.  We must check to see if
    '  the match is correct.

    '  Process based index of the team selected
    Select Case index

        Case 0 ' Michael Jordan
            '  Chicago Bulls
            If intPlayerClickIndex = 1 Then
                '  Change the back color
                chkPlayer(intPlayerClickIndex).BackColor = _
                RGB(0, 255, 0)
```

```
                    '  Change the back color
                    chkTeam(index).BackColor = RGB(0, 255, 0)
                    '  Enable all of the check boxes
                    EnableCheckBoxes

                Else

                    '  If an incorrect match then clear the selection
                    intClearFlag = 1

                End If

        Case 1   ' David Robinson
            '  Check for a match with San Antonio
            If intPlayerClickIndex = 0 Then

                    '  Change the back color
                    chkPlayer(intPlayerClickIndex).BackColor = _
                    RGB(255, 0, 0)
                    '  Change the back color
                    chkTeam(index).BackColor = RGB(255, 0, 0)
                    '  Enable the check boxes
                    EnableCheckBoxes

                Else

                    '  If an incorrect match then clear the selection
                    intClearFlag = 1

                End If

        Case 2   ' Patrick Ewing
            If intPlayerClickIndex = 2 Then
                    '  Change the back color
                    chkPlayer(intPlayerClickIndex).BackColor = _
                    RGB(0, 0, 255)
                    '  Change the back color
                    chkTeam(index).BackColor = RGB(0, 0, 255)
                    '  Enable the check boxes
                    EnableCheckBoxes

                Else
```

```
                    '  If an incorrect match then clear the selection
                    intClearFlag = 1

            End If

    End Select
```

If the clear flag is set, we need to cancel the selection because it is incorrect. That means clearing the clicks on the two check boxes. Of course, before the value is changed, we need to set the ignore flag to ensure the code in the click event is not run again. And of course, we need to display an error message on the status bar and enable the check boxes that were disabled.

```
'  Check to see if we need to clear the check boxes due to
'  an incorrect selection
If intClearFlag = 1 Then

        '  Ignore processing when we set the check box
        '  value back to false
        intIgnoreFlag = 1
        chkPlayer(intPlayerClickIndex).Value = False
        intIgnoreFlag = 0

        '  Ignore processing when we set the check box
        '  value back to false
        intIgnoreFlag = 1
        chkTeam(index).Value = False
        intIgnoreFlag = 0

        '  Indicate an incorrect selection
        stbHelp.Panels(1).Text = "Incorrect Selection!"
        '  Enable all of the check boxes
        EnableCheckBoxes

Else
```

If we have a successful match, we need to check to see if all matches have been correctly made and display the animated message. Also, we need to be sure and show a correct selection in the status bar.

```
' Check to see if the quiz is finished
        If CheckForComplete = 0 Then ShowWinnerMessage

        ' Indicate a correct response
        stbHelp.Panels(1).Text = "Correct Selection!"

    End If
```

We need to clear the global variables to reset for the user to make the next match.

```
' Reset the global variables
    intPlayerClickStatus = 0
    intPlayerClickIndex = 0

End If

End Sub
```

That handles the basic process for checking for valid matches. But there are a couple of other events we need to utilize to refine our interface. Once a successful match is made, we need to ensure that the user doesn't uncheck a successful match. We can ensure that happens in the mouse down event of the check box.

A check is done to see if the check box has been checked already. If so, we need to uncheck the box so that when the mouse down event moves into the click event, it will be checked once again.

```
Private Sub chkPlayer_MouseDown(index As Integer, Button As
Integer, Shift As Integer, X As Single, Y As Single)

' If the user tries to unclick a check box that is
' already clicked, we stop the user by resetting
' the value
If chkPlayer(index).Value = 1 Then
    ' Don't process the click code
    intIgnoreFlag = 1
    ' Set the value back
    chkPlayer(index).Value = 0
End If

End Sub
```

```
Private Sub chkPlayer_MouseUp(Index As Integer, Button As Integer, _
Shift As Integer, X As Single, Y As Single)

'   Set flag
intIgnoreFlag = 0

End Sub
```

The same code applies to the mouse move event of the team check boxes.

```
Private Sub chkTeam_MouseDown(index As Integer, Button As Integer, _
Shift As Integer, X As Single, Y As Single)

'   If the user tries to unclick a check box that is
'   already clicked, we stop the user by resetting
'   the value
If chkTeam(index).Value = 1 Then
    '   Don't process the click code
    intIgnoreFlag = 1
    '   Set the value back
    chkTeam(index).Value = 0
End If

End Sub

Private Sub chkTeam_MouseUp(Index As Integer, Button As Integer,  _
Shift As Integer, X As Single, Y As Single)

'   Set back
intIgnoreFlag = 0

End Sub
```

Our next code is for the mouse move event of the check boxes. If hints are turned on for the check boxes, then in the mouse move event we want to show hints for the user. The TeamHint and PlayerHint procedures are called to show the hints in the status bar.

```
Private Sub chkPlayer_MouseMove(index As Integer, Button As _
Integer, Shift As Integer, X As Single, Y As Single)

'  Show hints
stbHelp.Panels(2).Text = TeamHint(index)

End Sub
Private Sub chkTeam_MouseMove(index As Integer, Button As _
Integer, Shift As Integer, X As Single, Y As Single)

'  Show the hints
stbHelp.Panels(2).Text = PlayerHint(index)

End Sub
```

Now we have a series of support functions for the check boxes as called from our event code. The EnableCheckBoxes function loops through all of the check boxes in the control array and ensures they are enabled.

```
'  This subroutine enables all of the check boxes
Private Sub EnableCheckBoxes()

Dim intCnt As Integer

'  Loop through the check boxes in the control
'  array
For intCnt = 0 To chkPlayer.Count - 1

    '  Enable the check boxes
    chkPlayer(intCnt).Enabled = True
    chkTeam(intCnt).Enabled = True

Next intCnt

End Sub
```

The DisableCheckBoxes function loops through the specified control array and disables all of the check boxes except the one indicated by the index. This procedure is used for disabling the rest of the check boxes in a control array when one has been selected as the first check box in the two-click sequence. That way, when they are disabled, the user cannot select a second one in the same control array.

```
'  This subroutine disables all but the selected check box
'  indicated by the index argument.  The boxset argument
'  indicates which set of check boxes to work on (player or team)
Private Sub DisableCheckBoxes(index As Integer, boxset As Integer)

Dim intCnt As Integer

'  Process Player or Team Check Boxes
If boxset = 1 Then

    '  Loop through the check boxes
    For intCnt = 0 To chkPlayer.Count - 1

        '  Do not disable the current check box
        If intCnt <> index Then chkPlayer(intCnt).Enabled = False

    Next intCnt

Else

    '  Loop through the check boxes
    For intCnt = 0 To chkTeam.Count - 1

        '  Do not disable the current check box
        If intCnt <> index Then chkTeam(intCnt).Enabled = False

    Next intCnt

End If

End Sub
```

As you can see, effective use of the check box events turns them into effective tools for our matching game. Had we not limited use of the control to specific series of actions and actions based on state, our user interface would not have been effective. Also, the use of the control array makes our task much simpler by being able to manipulate the controls based on index and not specific name.

Next we will take a look at the implementation of the "You Win!" animation.

You Win!

In the click events of the functions, one task we performed was to check for a successful match of all choices and then show the winning message. The message is enabled by use of the timer control and a label control that is hidden at startup.

The following code performs the check on the two control arrays to see if correct matches have been made.

```
'  This function will check to see if the test
'  has been completed
Private Function CheckForComplete() As Integer

Dim intFlag As Integer
Dim intCnt As Integer

intFlag = 0

'  Loop through the players
For intCnt = 0 To chkPlayer.Count - 1

    '  Check the value of the check boxes.  If
    '  any are not checked, then we are not complete
    If chkPlayer(intCnt).Value = False Then intFlag = 1
    If chkTeam(intCnt).Value = False Then intFlag = 1

Next intCnt

'  Return the value
CheckForComplete = intFlag

End Function
```

The check is quite simple. A loop is done to go through the two control arrays and ensure each check box is selected. Then the success value is returned. If we have made a successful match, the ShowWinnerMessage subroutine is called.

In the message, we call the DisableCheckBoxes function. Note that the index passed in is a –1 value. That way all three check boxes will be disabled for both control arrays. Once that is done, the label control is made visible, and the Enabled property on the timer control is set to true. When that happens, the timer will start ticking off its intervals.

```
'  This subroutine takes care of enabling the timer
'  and setting in motion the winner animation
Private Sub ShowWinnerMessage()
```

```
Dim intCnt As Integer

'  Disable all of the check boxes by passing
'  in a -1 for the index
DisableCheckBoxes -1, 1
DisableCheckBoxes -1, 2

'  Make the label visible
lblWinner.Visible = True

'  Enable the timer
tmrAnimate.Enabled = True

End Sub
```

In the timer event, we move the winner label to the right 60 twips. Thus, with each tick of the clock, the label control animates across the form. A check is done to see if the label has moved off the form by checking the left value of the label against the width of the form. The animation will continue until the Clear menu/toolbar option is selected.

```
Private Sub tmrAnimate_Timer()

'  Move 60 twips to the right with each tick
lblWinner.Left = lblWinner.Left + 60

'  check to see if we have moved off of the form
If lblWinner.Left > Form1.Width Then lblWinner.Left = 0

End Sub
```

The animation interface is fairly straightforward, yet it provides an effective and catchy method of letting users know they have won!

Menus and Toolbars

Next we are ready to move on to the menu functionality. Each menu added to the interface has a click event associated with the menu item. The following is the click event for the Exit menu item.

```
Private Sub mnuExit_Click()

'  End the program
End

End Sub
```

In the Exit menu, we simply end the program. If we wanted, we could use a message box function to query users and ensure they really want to exit. The following code is for the Clear menu option. When the game is cleared, we need to ensure the winner label is not visible and is moved back to the left, the timer is disabled, our global variables are reset and all of our check boxes are enabled, and background colors are reset and unchecked.

```
Private Sub mnuClear_Click()

Dim intCnt As Integer

'  Hide the winner label and move it back to the
'  left of the form
lblWinner.Visible = False
lblWinner.Left = 0

'  Disable the timer
tmrAnimate.Enabled = False

'  Clear the global variables
intPlayerClickStatus = 0
intTeamClickStatus = 0
intPlayerClickIndex = 0
intTeamClickIndex = 0

'  Loop through the check boxes
For intCnt = 0 To chkPlayer.Count - 1

    '  Set the ignore flag
    intIgnoreFlag = 1

    '  Enable, uncheck and reset the back color
    '  on the player check boxes
    chkPlayer(intCnt).Enabled = True
    chkPlayer(intCnt).Value = False
```

```
      chkPlayer(intCnt).BackColor = lngOrgColor
      intIgnoreFlag = 0

      '   Set the ignore flag
      intIgnoreFlag = 1

      '   Enable, uncheck and reset the back color
      '   on the player check boxes
      chkTeam(intCnt).Enabled = True
      chkTeam(intCnt).Value = False
      chkTeam(intCnt).BackColor = lngOrgColor
      intIgnoreFlag = 0

Next intCnt

End Sub
```

The next set of menu options will build the Edit menu features. The copy, cut, and paste functionalities will utilize the clipboard object. The clipboard object allows us to store and retrieve text from the Windows clipboard. In this case the only field we need to be concerned about is the text box notes control array. We want the user to be able to use the Edit menu on text in the text boxes.

Let's start with the Copy menu option. The first thing we need to do when we copy text onto the clipboard is to clear the clipboard object with the clear method. Following that, the clipboard text is set to the current active control (Screen.ActiveControl) selected text. The SelText property of the current active control is then set on the clipboard using the SetText method.

```
Private Sub mnuCopy_Click()

'   Clear the clipboard
Clipboard.Clear

'   Get and store the text from the active control on our form
Clipboard.SetText Screen.ActiveControl.SelText

End Sub
```

The Cut menu follows the same process as the Copy menu. But the last step will be to clear the selected text of the current active control. The clearing of the text performs the cut.

```
Private Sub mnuCut_Click()

'  Clear the clipboard
Clipboard.Clear

'  Get and store the text from the active control on our form
Clipboard.SetText Screen.ActiveControl.SelText

'  Clear the selected text in the control
Screen.ActiveControl.SelText = ""

End Sub
```

The Paste menu uses the GetText method of the clipboard to retrieve the current text on the clipboard object. This time the SelText property of the current active control is set to the clipboard text.

```
Private Sub mnuPaste_Click()

'  Set the currently selected text in the active
'  control to the text on the clipboard
Screen.ActiveControl.SelText = Clipboard.GetText()

End Sub
```

With that, we have our Edit menu functions in place. It should be noted that you can also right-click on any of the text boxes and automatically get a context-sensitive Edit menu. That is built in as a standard part of the control itself.

The following menu click event is for the Hints menu. This allows the user to turn on and off the display of hints in the application. With each click, we toggle the checked property of the menu item and set the intHints global variable appropriately.

```
Private Sub mnuHints_Click()

'  Check the current status
If mnuHints.Checked = True Then

    '  Uncheck the menu
    mnuHints.Checked = False
```

```
    '   Reset the global variable to 0
        intHints = 0

Else

    '   Check the menu
        mnuHints.Checked = True

    '   Set the global variable to 1 to display
    '   the hints
        intHints = 1

End If

End Sub
```

The How menu item shows help for the application. In this case we are showing a simple message box with basic instructions on how the matching game works.

```
Private Sub mnuHow_Click()

'   Show a message box help dialogue
MsgBox "Simply try and match" & _
       " up what player plays" & _
       " on what team.  When you" & _
       " have a correct match," & _
       " the background color of" & _
       " the match set will change. " & _
       " Be sure and turn on the Hint" & _
       " feature on the Game menu" & _
       " if you need assistance."

End Sub
```

Next we move on to the toolbar functions. Remember that these mirror the menu functions for the application. The toolbar click event passes in the reference to the button object that was clicked on. In this case we are only concerned about a click on the first button. The second button will automatically show the drop-down menu for the button. Below, we end the application when the user selects the first button.

```
Private Sub tblFunctions_ButtonClick(ByVal Button As _
MSComctlLib.Button)

'  If the first button is clicked then end
'  the program
If Button.index = 1 Then End

End Sub
```

When one of the button menus is clicked on, the ButtonMenuClick event is called, and a reference to the button menu object of the menu items is passed in. A simple check is done to find out which menu item was selected. For the Clear button menu item, we simply call the click event of the mnuClear menu.

For the Hints menu, we call the mnuHints click event to handle toggling the event capability. This will ensure the primary Hints menu is properly checked/unchecked. Also, in order to indicate the current status to the user, the text of the ButtonMenu is set to either include or exclude an "(x)" to indicate whether hints are turned on or off.

```
Private Sub tblFunctions_ButtonMenuClick(ByVal ButtonMenu As _
MSComctlLib.ButtonMenu)

'  Check to see which menu item was clicked
If ButtonMenu.index = 1 Then

    '  Fire off the clear menu click event
    mnuClear_Click

Else

    '  Fire off the hints menu click event
    mnuHints_Click

    '  Change the button menu text based on the current
    '  hints checked status
    If mnuHints.Checked = True Then
        ButtonMenu.Text = "(x)Hints"
    Else
        ButtonMenu.Text = "Hints"
    End If

End If

End Sub
```

That is it for implementing the toolbar in our example. We have a few final supporting procedures that need to be reviewed. The TeamHint procedure will return a hint string based on the value of the hint requested. Note that the intHints global variable is checked to ensure that hints are turned on. If not, the function is exited with no return value. Note that the TeamHint function is called from the mouse move event of the team check box array.

```
'  This function returns team hints
Private Function TeamHint(intHint As Integer) As String

'  If the intHints flag is not set then exit
If intHints = 0 Then Exit Function

'  Show the appropriate hint based on the index of the
'  check box passed in
Select Case intHint

    Case 0
       TeamHint = "It gets awfully windy there."

    Case 1
       TeamHint = "The stars at night are big and bright...."

    Case 2
       TeamHint = "He plays in Madison Square Garden."

End Select

End Function
```

The PlayerHint function works the same as the TeamHint function. It is called from the mouse move event of the player check box control array.

```
'  This function returns player hints
Private Function PlayerHint(intHint As Integer) As String

'  If the intHints flag is not set then exit
If intHints = 0 Then Exit Function

'  Show the appropriate hint based on the index of the
'  check box passed in
Select Case intHint
```

```
   Case 0
     PlayerHint = "They call him the Admiral."

   Case 1
     PlayerHint = "The greatest player of all time."

   Case 2
     PlayerHint = "He played for John Thompson."

End Select

End Function
```

Finally, in the load event of the form, we ensure the Hints menu is not checked so hints are not shown at startup, and we store the original background color of the check boxes. That way when the game is cleared, we can reset the backcolor property of the check boxes.

```
Private Sub Form_Load()

'   Uncheck the hints menu item so hints are not on when
'   the program starts
mnuHints.Checked = False

'   Store the original back color of the check boxes
lngOrgColor = chkTeam(1).BackColor

End Sub
```

Surprised? What may seem like a small matching game actually turns out to be quite a few lines of code to implement a well-rounded user interface design that not only provides intuitive use and flexibility for the end user but also anticipates potential pitfalls the user may encounter.

Testing Our Application

Now that we have the user interface and all of the code in place, let's test our application. Figure 6-15 shows the form when the application is started. Start the game by selecting Michael Jordan and Chicago Bulls. When you do, you will have made a successful selection. Note the left panel on the status bar and the message telling the user "Correct Selection!" Figure 6-16 shows the successful selection.

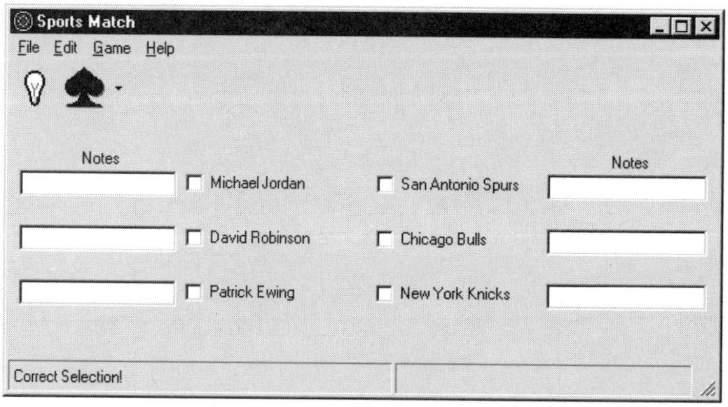

Figure 6-15. *Sports Match application at run time*

Let's turn on hints in our application. Click on the Game menu or select the drop-down menu on the toolbar. Then select the Hints option. When the menu item is checked or the menu bar has an (x) on it, the hints will be showing. When you hold your mouse over one of the check boxes, a hint will be shown in the second panel on the status bar. Figure 6-17 shows the Hints menu with a hint shown in the status bar.

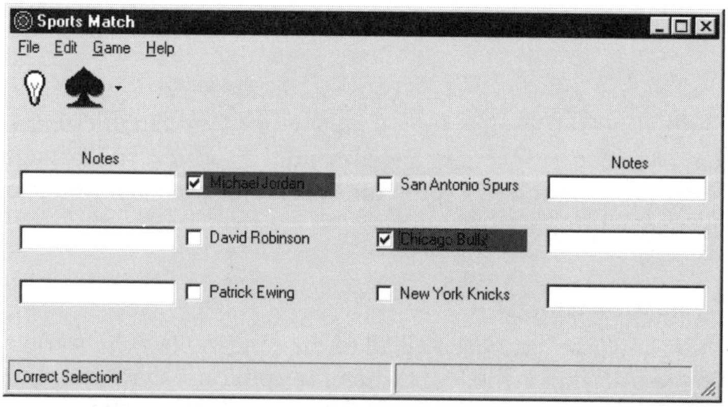

Figure 6-16. *Sports Match application after a successful selection*

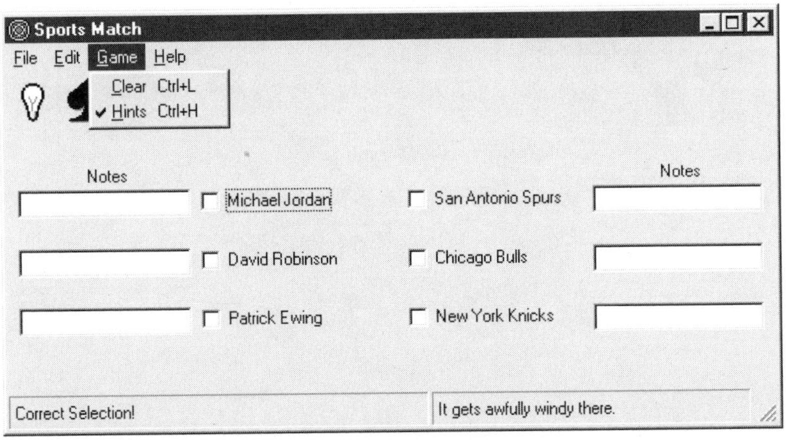

Figure 6-17. *Sports Match application with the Game menu shown and a hint in the status bar*

Let's follow the process to select an incorrect match. First select David Robinson. When you do, note that the Michael Jordan and Patrick Ewing check boxes are grayed out because they are disabled. That way users cannot select either one of these players; they are forced to select a team. Note that the Notes section next to David Robinson indicates that New York is not the correct selection for David Robinson. Figure 6-18 shows the application with just the player selected.

Now go ahead and select San Antonio Spurs. When you do, the background colors on the check boxes change. The status bar indicates a "Correct Selection!" While you are at it, try and select an already selected check box. You will note that the check box stays selected, and nothing happens. Figure 6-19 shows the application with the selection and the status bar message.

Well, it is time for a little winning. Go ahead and make all the correct selections to finish the matching game. When you do, all of the check boxes will be disabled, and the winning animation will be displayed. Figure 6-20 shows the animation.

The last step is to clear the game and start over. Click on the Clear option on the Game menu or the toolbar. That will clear the animation and reset all of the check boxes.

Believe it or not, that is it! The whole package comes together into an interface that has all the right tools to support the user. If you are still new to event-driven programming, you may be surprised at the amount of code that goes behind the check boxes to ensure the user follows the right steps.

There is probably even more we can add to the interface to make it simpler and more effective. One thing you will notice is that we give the user immediate feedback on correct selections. We may want to change the interface so it does not give feedback but simply allows users to check to see if they have made the correct selections. There

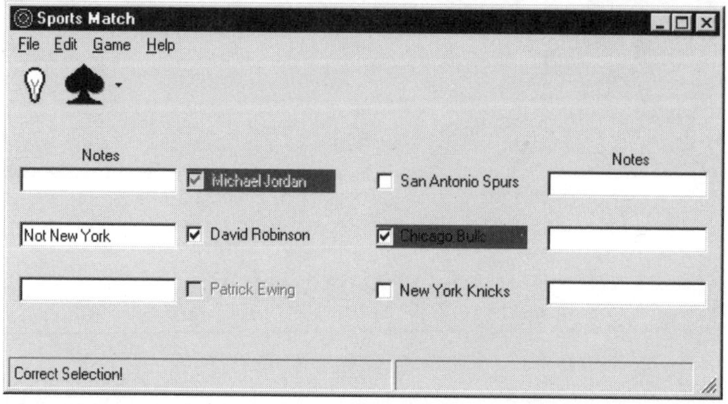

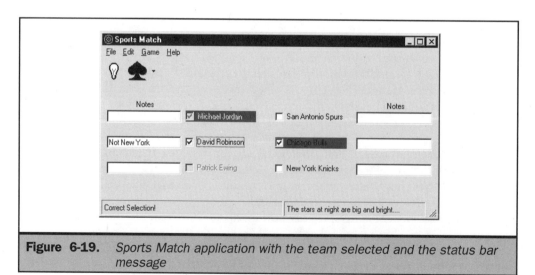

Figure 6-18. *Sports Match application with just one player selected*

could even be options on the Game menu to quickly flash the current correct selections as a hint.

If you want to expand the application, you can easily add more check box options. That is the value of the control array. It makes things much more scalable and doesn't require hard coding of check box names for individual selections. In fact, you could load the text and corresponding correct responses from a database and make the application scalable to any type of matching quiz.

Figure 6-19. *Sports Match application with the team selected and the status bar message*

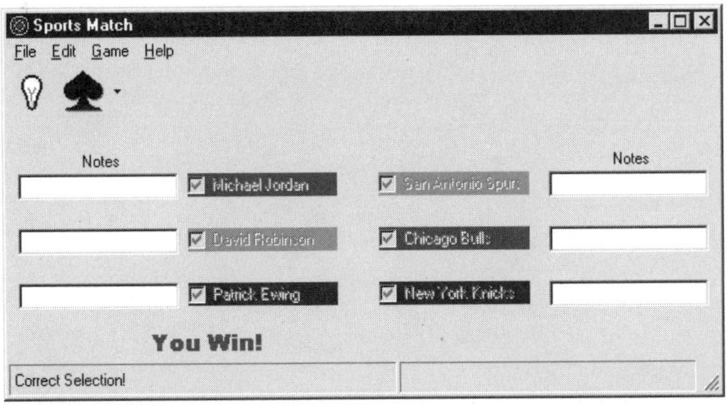

Figure 6-20. *Sports Match application with the correct matches and the winning animation*

Summary

User interface design is a key element of building great applications. Visual Basic became wildly popular when it was first introduced because of its ability to easily and quickly build Windows-based user interfaces. Since its release, there have been many improvements, and the latest enhancements of the coolbar and new controls only provide more options.

Explore the many options available for building highly interactive interfaces that can help your application come alive for the user. Explore the many controls provided with Visual Basic and the items on the third-party marketplace. Also consider the use of multiple forms for your interface. For example, you can build your own dialog boxes using the tab control. Simply pop up another form within your application as a dialog box with tab controls. Also explore the use of MDI applications that can have multiple forms on top of a background form (similar to Word or Excel).

What's Next

In the next chapter we will explore how you can integrate your application with the Windows environment. There are many tools that can provide for an integrated application. Capabilities such as printing, dragging and dropping, working with the file system and files, plus much more are covered.

Chapter 7

Building Programs in the Windows Environment

The applications you build in Visual Basic are not limited to the tools provided in the development environment. There are external tools that can enrich your application. Some of the more obvious ones include printers, keyboards, and the new file system object for working with drives and directories. But you can add many more features, such as drag-and-drop support, the clipboard, and multimedia. Each will help to complete the integration of your application with Windows and will allow you to add extended functionality to your application for the user.

Working with Windows

Visual Basic provides many standard objects for interfacing with Windows. For example, there is a printer object, which will allow us to work through installed printer drivers to build printed pages from our applications. Or you can build a standard common dialog box that allows the user to choose from a dialog box for printers, font selection, and much more. Let's get started with a review of the printer object.

Working with Printers

The printer object enables you to communicate with a system printer (initially, the default system printer). The printers collection enables you to gather information about all the available printers on the system.

The printers collection is fairly easy to use. You simply iterate through the collection to retrieve specific printer data. The following code loops through the printers collection and shows the device (printer) name for each printer:

```
For Each x In Printers

     msgbox x.DeviceName

Next
```

A For ... Each loop is used to iterate through the collection. Then the device name for the printer is displayed using the message box function. Table 7-1 outlines the various properties of the printer object.

Property	Description
DrawWidth	Returns or sets the line width for output from graphics methods. This sets the width of any lines drawn to the printer.
FontBold	Makes the font currently selected bold for text printing.

Table 7-1. *Printer Object Properties*

Property	Description
FontItalic	Makes the font currently selected italic for text printing.
FontStrikeThru	Adds a strike-through adornment to the text for printing.
FontUnderline	Underlines the font for text printing.
FontName	Returns or sets the font to be printed.
FontSize	Sets the point size of the font for text printing.
Height	Returns and sets the height dimensions of the paper in the printer.
Width	Returns and sets the width dimensions of the paper in the printer.
ColorMode	Returns or sets a value that determines whether a color printer prints output in color or monochrome.
Copies	Returns or sets the number of copies to be printed.
CurrentX	Returns the horizontal coordinates for the next printing.
CurrentY	Returns the vertical coordinates for the next printing.
DeviceName	Returns the name of the printer.
DrawMode	Returns or sets the appearance of the graphics output. Different pens are used for drawing. For example, vbInvert is the inverse of the print color.
DrawStyle	Determines the line style to draw with. For example, vbDash will draw a dashed line on the page.
DriverName	Returns the driver name for the printer.
Duplex	Returns or sets the value to determine whether the page is printed on both sides of the paper. Note, this is only available for printers that support duplex printing.
FillColor	Returns or sets the color used to fill in shapes.
FillStyle	Returns or sets the pattern used to fill a shape.
FontCount	Returns the number of fonts available on the printer.
Fonts	Returns all the font names for the printer.
HDC	Returns a handle to the printer device context.

Table 7-1.   *Printer Object Properties* (continued)

WORKING WITH WINDOWS

Property	Description
Orientation	Returns or sets the value indicating which orientation, landscape or portrait, will be used for printing the page.
Page	Returns the current page number being printed. This is useful for tracking the status of a print job.
PaperBin	Returns or sets the paper bin to be used when printing.
PaperSize	Returns or sets a value indicating the paper size for the current printer.
Port	Returns the name of the port to which the printer is connected.
PrintQuality	Returns or sets the printer resolution.

Table 7-1.   *Printer Object Properties* (continued)

If you have done any drawing in Visual Basic forms, many of the printer properties will seem familiar. In fact, Visual Basic treats the printer as just another device. The only difference is specific properties utilized by the printer, such as paper bins, paper size, and so on. A few key methods for use with the printer object are outlined in Table 7-2.

Note that the circle and line methods can be used on a form for drawing as well. Use of the printer object is fairly straightforward, although you will find complex drawing can require tedious tracking and minute placement, depending on what type of printing you need to do.

Method	Description
EndDoc	Ends the print operation and releases the document.
Circle	Draws a circle on the page.
Line	Draws a line on the page.
KillDoc	Deletes the current print job.
PaintPicture	Draws a graphics file on the printer.
NewPage	Ends the current page and starts a new page.

Table 7-2.   *Printer Object Methods*

Tip   *If you need to print reports based on a database, use the new report designer in Visual Basic 6. This is much more flexible and takes the difficulty out of tracking print placement.*

Let's work on an example of interfacing with the printer object. Our example application will enumerate the printers installed on the system and show them in a list box. Then we can select a printer from the system and print a circle or show selected properties. Table 7-3 shows the interface properties for the form.

Component/Property	Setting
Form	frmPrinters
Caption	"Printers"
TextBox	txtFontCount
Text	""
TextBox	txtPaperSize
Text	""
Textbox	txtPrintQuality
Text	""
CommandButton	cmdGetInfo
Caption	"Get Info"
CommandButton	cmdPrintCircle
Caption	"Print Circle"
ListBox	lstPrinters
Label	lblFontCount
AutoSize	-1 'True
Caption	"Font Count:"
Label	LblPaperSize
AutoSize	-1 'True
Caption	"Paper Size"
Label	lblDeviceName
AutoSize	-1 'True
Caption	"Print Quality:"

Table 7-3.   *Control Interface Properties for the Printer Object Project*

The print quality, paper size, and font count properties will be shown in the appropriate text boxes. Following is the code behind the interface for the project:

```
Private Sub cmdGetInfo_Click()

'  Show the print quality property
txtPrintQuality.Text = Printers(lstPrinters.ListIndex).DeviceName
'  Show the font count property
txtFontCount.Text = Printers(lstPrinters.ListIndex).FontCount
'  Show the paper size property
txtPaperSize.Text = Printers(lstPrinters.ListIndex).PaperSize

End Sub

Private Sub cmdPrintCircle_Click()

'  Print a circle on the page
Printers(lstPrinters.ListIndex).Circle (1, 2), 122

'  End the Page
Printers(lstPrinters.ListIndex).EndDoc

End Sub

Private Sub Form_Load()

'  Loop through the printers collection
For Each x In Printers

    '  Add the printers to the list box
    lstPrinters.AddItem x.DeviceName

Next

End Sub
```

When the form loads, we loop through the printers collection and add the device name to the list box. We can then select a printer from the list and perform operations on it. The printer will be selected based on the list count property of the list box. That will serve as the index into the printers collection. Figure 7-1 shows the form at run time with the list box populated.

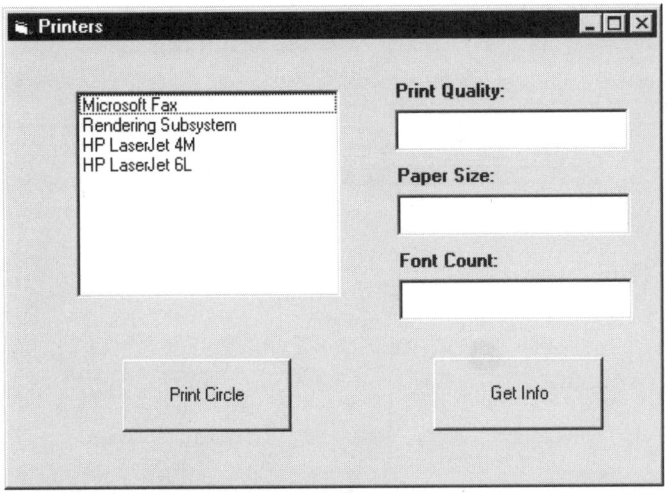

Figure 7-1.   *Printers populated in a list box*

The first command button will print a circle on the device. It uses the circle method of the printer object. The center point is indicated as the first parameter. The second parameter identifies the radius for the circle. Once the circle is drawn, we will need to end the document so the page is printed.

The second command button will display the print quality, paper size, and font count properties of the printer object. We index into the printers collection to retrieve the properties for the selected printing device. Figure 7-2 shows the properties for the HP 6L printer.

That is all there is to working with the printer object. If you need simple and straightforward printing capabilities, the printer object is your direct access to the printer installed on the user's system (or network). Next, we will move on to building common dialog boxes using the common dialog control.

Let's Have a Common Dialog

Anyone who has used Windows for any length of time will be familiar with common dialog boxes such as the Open/Save As dialog, printer dialog, and font settings dialog. Certainly, we can build these directly in Visual Basic in a forms-based environment. But Microsoft has provided a custom control, *common dialog*, that will allow us to add this functionality into our applications with little custom programming.

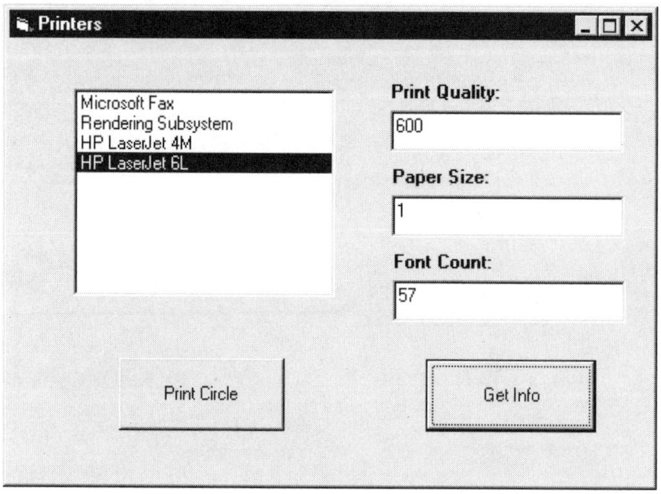

Figure 7-2. *Printer properties shown in the text boxes*

The common dialog control has several properties, which can be referenced in MSDN. Most important are the methods for showing different types of dialog boxes. Table 7-4 shows the different methods for the common dialog box.

Method	Description
ShowColor	Shows a color selection dialog box.
ShowFont	Shows a font selection dialog box.
ShowHelp	Starts the Windows help system.
ShowOpen	Shows a file open dialog box.
ShowPrinter	Shows the printer selection and properties dialog box.
ShowSave	Shows the file save as dialog box.

Table 7-4. *Common Dialog Box Methods*

Of course, properties need to be set for some of the methods to work. And some properties are set based on the results of one of the methods. The best way to see the common dialog work is in live code.

Let's build a sample application that will test each type of dialog box. A series of buttons will be created that will invoke each method. In the click events of each button, appropriate properties will be set. And return values will be displayed in a text box. Start your application and create the objects in Table 7-5 with the specified properties on the form.

The interface has six buttons, one for each method. The text box will display any results from the method. Now let's put some code behind the interface. Figure 7-3 shows the form at run time.

Component/Property	Setting
Form	cdlForm
Caption	"Common Dialog"
TextBox	txtReturn
MultiLine	-1 'True
CommandButton	cmdShowHelp
Caption	"Show Help"
CommandButton	cmdShowPrinter
Caption	"Show Printer"
CommandButton	cmdShowFont
Caption	"Show Font"
CommandButton	cmdShowColor
Caption	"Show Color"
CommandButton	cmdShowSave
Caption	"Show Save"
CommandButton	cmdShowOpen
Caption	"Show Open"
CommonDialog	CommonDialog1

Table 7-5.   *Control Properties for the Common Dialog Project*

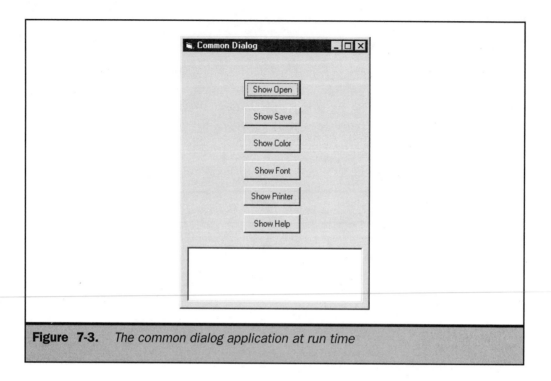

Figure 7-3. *The common dialog application at run time*

The first event is the ShowOpen click event. In the event, we call the ShowOpen method of the dialog box. The user will see the dialog box in Figure 7-4. Select a file from the system and click OK.

```
Private Sub cmdShowOpen_Click()

'   Show the open dialog box
CommonDialog1.ShowOpen

'   Show the filename selected
txtReturn.Text = "FileName = " & CommonDialog1.FileName

End Sub
```

The file name of the file to be opened is returned. We could then use that to open the file. The next event is the ShowSave click event. The ShowSave method of the common dialog box is called. Figure 7-5 shows the dialog box.

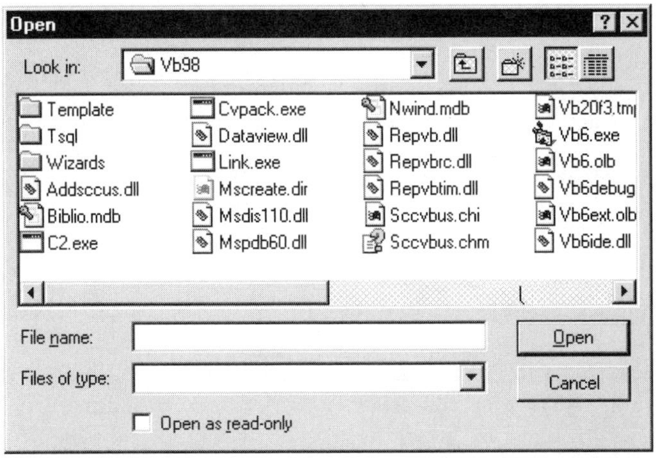

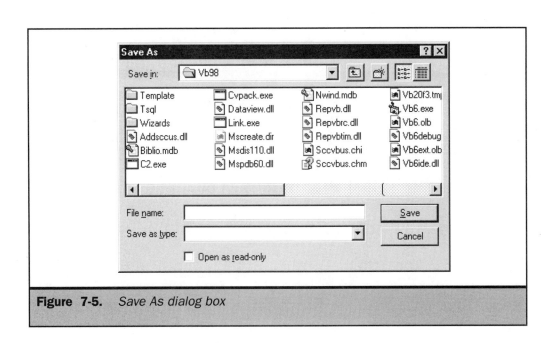

Figure 7-4. *Open dialog box*

Figure 7-5. *Save As dialog box*

```
Private Sub cmdShowSave_Click()

'  Show the save as dialog
CommonDialog1.ShowSave

'  Show the save as filename
txtReturn.Text = "Filename = " & CommonDialog1.FileName

End Sub
```

When the user types in the name of the file to save to, the file name property is set and returned. We could then save a file in our program to the specified file name.

The next dialog box is the color selection. In the color selection, we can pick a standard color or a custom color based on the color spectrum currently supported by the screen color settings. Figure 7-6 shows the color selection dialog box.

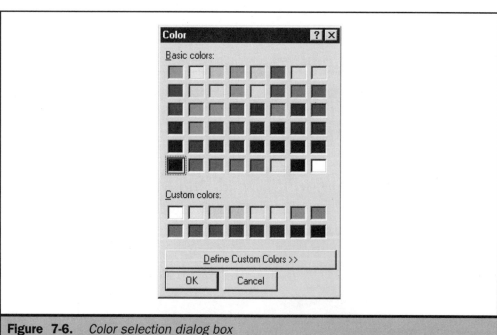

Figure 7-6.   *Color selection dialog box*

```
Private Sub cmdShowColor_Click()

'  Show the color dialog
CommonDialog1.ShowColor

'  Show the color value selected
txtReturn.Text = "Color = " & CommonDialog1.Color

End Sub
```

When the user makes a selection, the value returned is of the color selected. That can then be used for an appropriate color setting elsewhere.

The next event is the ShowFont click event. In the click event, we have to indicate which fonts we want to make available to the user. In this case we indicate both screen and printer fonts with the cdlCFBoth constant. The dialog box is then shown (see Figure 7-7).

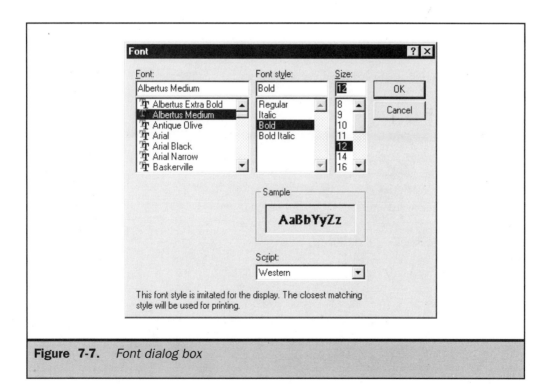

Figure 7-7.   *Font dialog box*

```
Private Sub cmdShowFont_Click()

'   Show screen and printer fonts
CommonDialog1.Flags = cdlCFBoth

'   Show the font dialog
CommonDialog1.ShowFont

'   Get the font bold value
txtReturn.Text = "FontBold = " & CommonDialog1.FontBold

'   Get the font italic value
txtReturn.Text = txtReturn.Text & Chr(13) & Chr(10) & _
                "FontItalic = " & _
                CommonDialog1.FontItalic

'   Get the font size value
txtReturn.Text = txtReturn.Text & Chr(13) & Chr(10) & _
                "FontSize = " & _
                CommonDialog1.FontSize

'   Show the font name
txtReturn.Text = txtReturn.Text & Chr(13) & Chr(10) & _
                "FontName = " & _
                CommonDialog1.FontName

End Sub
```

When the user makes font selections, the font-related properties of the common
dialog control are set. In this case we are showing the bold, italic, size, and name
properties of the font selected. Each is displayed in the text box.

Note   *We are placing carriage return and line feed characters in our text that will display the
font properties. This is done by using the ASC function and the ASCII value for the
carriage return (13) and line feed (10).*

The next function shows the printer dialog box. This allows the user to select which
printer to use, printer settings, number of copies, and so on. Figure 7-8 shows the
dialog box.

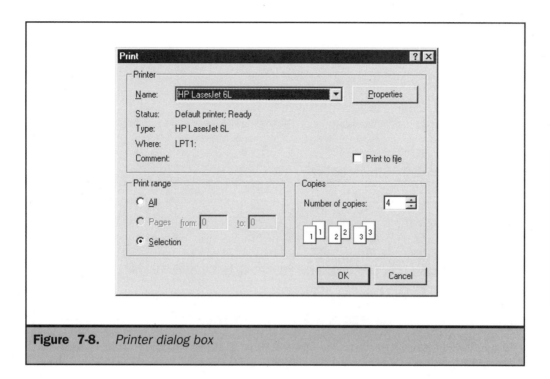

Figure 7-8.   *Printer dialog box*

```
Private Sub cmdShowPrinter_Click()

'   Show the printer dialog
CommonDialog1.ShowPrinter

'   Return the orientation
txtReturn.Text = "Orientation = " & CommonDialog1.Orientation

'   Return the copies
txtReturn.Text = txtReturn.Text & Chr(13) & Chr(10) & _
                "Copies = " & _
                CommonDialog1.Copies

End Sub
```

We subsequently display the paper orientation and number of copies to be printed. The final dialog box is for help. This shows the standard help interface. We have to indicate what help file should be displayed with the HelpFile property. And we need to specify the command, which in this case shows the help contents and the standard Windows help file.

```
Private Sub cmdShowHelp_Click()

    ' Set the help file to be displayed
    CommonDialog1.HelpFile = "windows.hlp"

    ' Show the contents
    CommonDialog1.HelpCommand = cdlHelpContents

    ' Show the help dialog
    CommonDialog1.ShowHelp

End Sub
```

With that, you have added six new sets of functionality to your application, all wrapped up in one little control. Typically, you will want to use the standard common dialog box formats in your applications. These will be familiar to your users and are simple to implement.

Working with Drives, Folders, and Files

You now have the ability to build a common dialog box to find files on the system. What about reading and writing data files? Visual Basic 6 has a new file system object (FSO) for working with the local file system.

The FSO object model is contained in a type library called Scripting, which is located in the file Scrrun.Dll. To utilize the DLL, you will need to create a reference to it. To do this, check Microsoft Scripting Runtime in the References dialog available from the Properties menu. You can then use the Object Browser to view its objects, collections, properties, methods, and events, as well as its constants. The scripting object has been a part of Active Server Pages programming and the VBScript language.

The FSO contains several objects that provide the interface to the file system. Table 7-6 outlines the different objects.

Object	Description
Drive	Provides information about drives attached to the system. You can get basic data such as share names, space available, etc.
Folder	Provides the ability to create, delete, and move folders.

Table 7-6. *File System Objects*

Object	Description
File	Provides the ability to create, delete, and move files.
FileSystemObject	Parent object of the group with extended methods.
TextStream	Enables reading and writing of files.

Table 7-6. *File System Objects* (continued)

There are legacy file support tools including sequential file access, random file access, and binary file access. If you wish to use these traditional methods, MSDN provides extended documentation. In most cases the file system object will meet your needs. Table 7-7 outlines the methods of the file system object.

The file system object has one property, Drives. This will return a list of drives on the system.

Method	Description
BuildPath	Appends a name to an existing path.
CopyFile	Copies one or more files from one location to another.
CopyFolder	Recursively copies a folder from one location to another.
CreateFolder	Creates a folder.
CreateTextFile	Creates a text file.
DeleteFile	Deletes a file.
DeleteFolder	Deletes a folder.
DriveExists	Checks to see if the specified drive exists.
FileExists	Checks to see if the specified file exists.
FolderExists	Checks to see if the specified folder exists.
GetAbsolutePathName	Provides a complete path from the root of a drive.
GetBaseName	Returns the base name of a component without file extension or path.
GetDrive	Returns a drive object.

Table 7-7. *File System Methods*

Method	Description
GetDriveName	Returns the name of the drive.
GetExtensionName	Returns the extension name of the last component.
GetFile	Returns a file object.
GetFileName	Returns the name of the file.
GetFolder	Returns a folder object.
GetParentFolderName	Returns the name of the parent folder of the last component in a specified path.
GetSpecialFolder	Returns either a Windows, system, or temporary folder for the system.
GetTempName	Returns a randomly generated temporary file or folder name.
MoveFile	Moves a set of files from one location to another.
MoveFolder	Moves a set of folders from one location to another.
OpenTextFile	Opens a text file and returns a text stream object that can be used to read, write, and append to the file.

Table 7-7. *File System Methods* (continued)

With FSO you can easily work with drives, folders, and files. To demonstrate, let's build a simple application that will get basic drive information, create folders, and do a little file creating, reading, and deleting. To get started, add the objects in Table 7-8 to a new project. Don't forget to add a reference to Microsoft Scripting Runtime in your project.

Component/Property	Description
Form	Form1
Caption	"File System Object"
Command Button	CmdReadFile
Caption	"Read File"

Table 7-8. *FSO Project Object Properties*

Component/Property	Description
Command Button	CmdFileFuncs
Caption	"File Functions"
Command Button	CmdCreateFile
Caption	"Create File"
Command Button	CmdDeleteFile
Caption	"Delete File"
Command Button	CmdDeleteFolder
Caption	"Delete Folder"
Command Button	CmdCreateFolder
Caption	"Create Folder"
Command Button	CmdDriveFuncs
Caption	"Drive Functions"
Label	LblFileFuncs
AutoSize	-1 'True
Caption	"File Functions"
Label	LblDateCreated
AutoSize	-1 'True
Caption	"Date Created"
Label	LblDateModified
AutoSize	-1 'True
Caption	"Date Modified"
Label	LblFileSize
AutoSize	-1 'True
Caption	"File Size"
Label	LblFreeSpace
AutoSize	-1 'True
Caption	"Free Space"

Table 7-8.   *FSO Project Object Properties* (continued)

Component/Property	Description
Label	LblSize
AutoSize	-1 'True
Caption	"Size"
Label	LblVolume
AutoSize	-1 'True
Caption	"Volume"
Label	LblDriverFuncs
AutoSize	-1 'True
Caption	"Drive Functions:"

Table 7-8. *FSO Project Object Properties* (continued)

Our interface is shown in Figure 7-9. On the left is the drive and folder set of functions; on the right is the set of file functions.

The first function in our interface is the command button to get basic drive data. The first thing we do is declare a file system object variable. We also declare a drive variable that will be our interface to the specified file system object—in this case a drive.

The drive object is retrieved using the GetDrive method in combination with the GetDriveName method to designate the drive. Once we have that drive object, we can get the rest of the data. The next three calls get the volume name, drive space, and free space, and the values are set in the label controls.

```
Private Sub cmdDriveFuncs_Click()

Dim FSO As New FileSystemObject
Dim DRV As Drive

'  Get the drive
Set DRV = FSO.GetDrive(FSO.GetDriveName("c:"))

'  Show the volume name
lblVolume.Caption = DRV.VolumeName
```

```
'  Show the total drive space
lblSize.Caption = "Total Space: " & _
                FormatNumber(DRV.TotalSize / 1024, 0) & _
                " Kb"

'  Show the free space
lblFreeSpace.Caption = "Free Space: " & _
                    FormatNumber(DRV.FreeSpace / 1024, 0) & _
                    " Kb"

End Sub
```

The next function in our list creates a new folder. Again, we create a file system object. Then we use the CreateFolder method to create a new folder. Note that an error

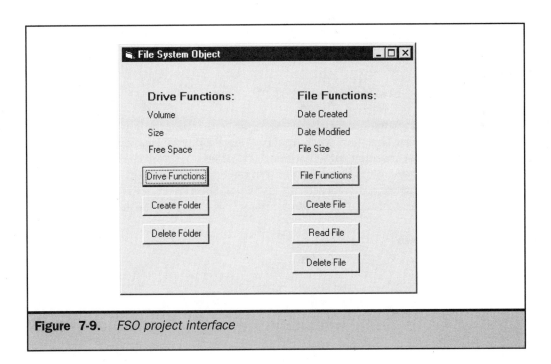

Figure 7-9. *FSO project interface*

will occur in the program if the folder already exists. You could use the FolderExists method to see if the folder already exists.

```
Private Sub cmdCreateFolder_Click()

Dim FSO As New FileSystemObject

'  Create a new folder
FSO.CreateFolder "c:\vb6fsotest"

End Sub
```

The last button in our drive and folder tools is to delete the folder we just created. We are going to use the DeleteFolder method. Be sure and click these folders in order. In this case, if the folder does not exist, an error will occur.

```
Private Sub cmdDeleteFolder_Click()

Dim FSO As New FileSystemObject

'  Delete the folder
FSO.DeleteFolder "c:\vb6fsotest"

End Sub
```

Next we move on to the file functions. We create our standard file system object, but we also create a file object for working with files. Be sure you have an autoexec.bat file on your system or change the file specified for retrieving information. We use the GetFile method to retrieve the file and store it in the FileInfo file object. Using the file object, we can get various properties about the file, including DateCreated, DateLastModified, and FileSize. The values are set in the captions of the label controls.

```
Private Sub cmdFileFuncs_Click()

Dim FSO As New FileSystemObject, FileInfo As File

'  Get the autoexec file
Set FileInfo = FSO.GetFile("c:\autoexec.bat")

'  Show the date created
lblDateCreated.Caption = FileInfo.DateCreated
```

```
'  Show the date last modified
lblDateModified.Caption = FileInfo.DateLastModified

'  Show the file size
lblFileSize.Caption = FileInfo.Size

End Sub
```

Our next button for the functions is to create a file on the system. As in the last subroutine, we also create a file object and a file system object. The first step is to create a text file using the CreateTextFile method of the FSO. We will introduce a new object into our project—the text stream. We open a text stream object, which is used for reading and writing from a file.

Once the text stream is created, three sets of text are written to the new file. The first uses the WriteLine method, which will create a line in the file and put a line break (return) at the end of the text written. Following that, we execute two write functions to the file that will be on the same line since there is no line break put in the file when the write is done. After that, we close the text stream, and voila, we have a new file on the system.

```
Private Sub cmdCreateFile_Click()

Dim FSO As New FileSystemObject
Dim txtFile As File
Dim txtStream As TextStream

'  Create the text file.
Set txtFile = FSO.CreateTextFile("c:\testfile.txt", True)

'  Open a text stream for writing
Set txtStream = txtFile.OpenAsTextStream(ForWriting)

' Write a line with a newline character.
txtStream.WriteLine ("Line with Line Break....")

'  Write a line with no newline character
txtStream.Write ("No Line Break 1.... ") ' Write a line.

'  Write a second line with no newline character
txtStream.Write ("No Line Break 2.... ") ' Write a line.
```

```
'  Close the text stream
txtStream.Close

End Sub
```

The next logical step is to read the file. The text stream object will allow us to read or write from the file easily. We use the GetFile object to retrieve the file. Then the OpenAsTextStream method of the file object is used to create a text stream to the file. Once the text stream is open, we can use the ReadLine method to read data from the file. In this case we will read the two lines written to the file when it was created and display the data in a message box. When we are done with the text stream, it is closed.

```
Private Sub cmdReadFile_Click()

Dim FSO As New FileSystemObject
Dim txtFile As File
Dim txtStream As TextStream

'  Get the file
Set txtFile = FSO.GetFile("c:\testfile.txt")

'  Open the file for reading
Set txtStream = txtFile.OpenAsTextStream(ForReading)

'  Display the first line
MsgBox txtStream.ReadLine

'  Display the second line
MsgBox txtStream.ReadLine

'  Close the text stream
txtStream.Close

End Sub
```

The last function to put in place is deleting the file we created. The DeleteFile method of the file system object is used to delete the file.

```
Private Sub cmdDeleteFile_Click()

Dim FSO As New FileSystemObject

'  Delete the new file
FSO.DeleteFile "c:\testfile.txt"

End Sub
```

OK, let's run the project and do a little file system work. Figure 7-10 shows the file drive data for the local C drive. Go ahead and click on the create and delete folder buttons. Before deleting, double-check your system to see that the folder is created.

Now let's move to the file functions. Figure 7-11 shows the file data for the local autoexec.bat file. Also go ahead and click on the Create File button. Once the file is created, you can click on the Read File button to display both lines written to the file. When that is done, click on the Delete File button to remove the file from the system.

Working with drives, files, and folders is easy. The file system object is straightforward to use and if you need to work with files in your system, FSO is an excellent tool for the job. Explore the many different methods and properties available in the file system objects in the Object Browser.

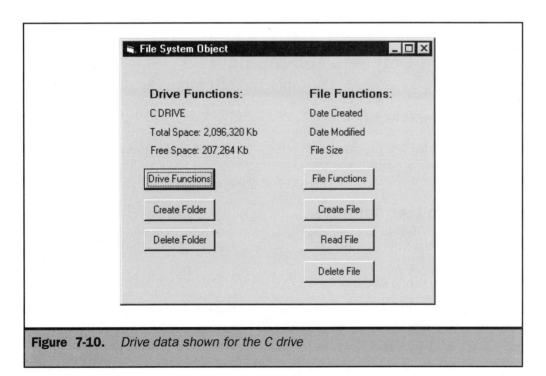

Figure 7-10. *Drive data shown for the C drive*

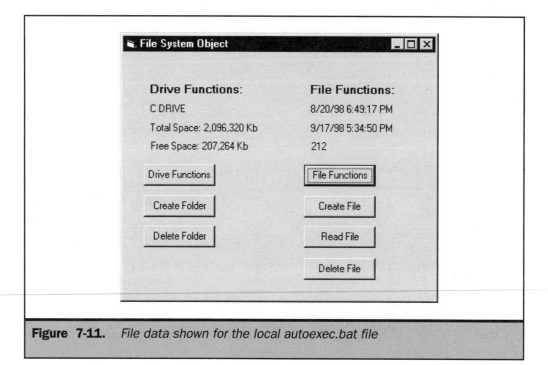

Figure 7-11.   *File data shown for the local autoexec.bat file*

Adding a Little Graphics and Multimedia

Multimedia and graphics are key parts of any good Windows program today. What application doesn't look dull without at least a spinning icon of some kind in the upper-right corner of the interface?

Two controls provided in VB 6, multimedia control and picture control, make working with video and graphics fairly straightforward. In the demonstration we will build for this section, we will also introduce two other key tools: the drive, directory, and file controls and the use of drag and drop in our applications.

Building the User Interface

Table 7-9 outlines the interface for our program. Place the objects listed in the table on the form and set their properties.

Component/Property	Description
Form	Form1
Caption	"AVI and Bitmap Viewer"
File List Box	FileControl
Pattern	"*.avi;*.bmp"
DirListBox	DirControl
DriveListBox	DrvControl
PictureBox	PctDisplay
AutoSize	-1 'True
BorderStyle	0' None
MMControl	mmControl
DeviceType	"AVIVideo"
FileName	""
Label	LblControl
Caption	"test"
Visible	0 'False

Table 7-9.   *Object Properties for the Multimedia and Bitmap Project*

You will note on the file list box control that we are defaulting the control to look only for files with a .bmp or .avi extension. The label control on the form will provide the interface for dragging and dropping images.

For the multimedia control, we need to specify a device type. There are many, including sound and video. In this case we want to play AVI video files. Thus, our device type is AVIVideo.

Placing Code Behind the User Interface

Our first event is the change event of the directory control. When the directory is changed, we need to update the file control to point to the new path.

```
Private Sub dirControl_Change()

'  Set the directory path for the file control
fileControl.Path = dirControl.Path

End Sub
```

When the drive changes, we need to update the directory control to look at the new drive. That will then fire off a change in the file list box control.

```
Private Sub drvControl_Change()

'  Set the directory to the root of the drive
dirControl.Path = drvControl.Drive & "\"

End Sub
```

When a user clicks on a file in the file control, we have to initiate several events. First we look to see if the extension is .avi. If it is, we close the multimedia control in case a previous file was opened. Then the file name of the multimedia control is set to the new file. The picture is cleared and set to a default size for showing the video. Finally, the multimedia control is opened and ready for playing.

```
Private Sub fileControl_Click()

'  Check to see if we are working with an AVI file
If LCase(Right(fileControl.FileName, 3)) = "avi" Then

    '  Close the previous AVI playing
    mmControl.Command = "close"

    '  Set the filename to be displayed
    mmControl.FileName = fileControl.Path & "\" & _
                        fileControl.FileName

    '  Clear the current picture
    pctDisplay.Cls
```

```
       '   Set the width and height
       pctDisplay.Width = 4000
       pctDisplay.Height = 4400

       '   Open the control
       mmControl.Command = "open"

End If

End Sub
```

When the mouse button is pressed while over the file control, we are ready to initiate a drag-and-drop sequence. The label control on our form will be moved to where the mouse pointer is. That is done by calculating the text height of a capital "M." Then we use the move method of the label control to move the label to the coordinates of the mouse that are passed into the mousedown event. Finally, the drag event of the label control is initiated.

```
Private Sub fileControl_MouseDown(Button As Integer, Shift As _
Integer, X As Single, Y As Single)

    Dim TH

    '   Get the maximum text height
    TH = TextHeight("M")

    '   Move the control to the current mouse location
    '   on the file control
    lblControl.Move fileControl.Left, _
                fileControl.Top + Y - TH / 2, _
                fileControl.Width, TH

    '   Start the drag process
    lblControl.Drag

End Sub
```

When the form is loaded, the multimedia control is opened and the picture control is set as the display device for the multimedia control. We will discuss in the next chapter the use of handles. If we did not set the picture control to be the multimedia display device, the video would play in its own window.

```
Private Sub Form_Load()

'  Open the control for play
mmControl.Command = "open"

'  Set the picture control as the display device
mmControl.hWndDisplay = pctDisplay.hWnd

End Sub
```

The drag-and-drop event of the picture control is fired off when something is dropped onto it. In this case it will be a bitmap file from the list box control. We have to put in an "on error resume next" statement in case the user decided to try and drop something other than a supported image type for the picture control.

Next we load the picture based on the file name and path from the directory and file list box controls. If there is an error, we notify the user that an invalid file was dropped on the picture control.

```
Private Sub pctDisplay_DragDrop(Source As Control, X As Single, Y _
As Single)

    '  Close the previous AVI playing
    mmControl.Command = "close"

    '  Allow us to continue if we try and drag an invalid
    '  bitmap file to the picture control
On Error Resume Next

    '  Load the picture dragged to the picture
    pctDisplay.Picture = LoadPicture(fileControl.Path + "\" + _
                    fileControl.FileName)

    '  Display a message that the image can't be
    '  loaded.
    If Err Then MsgBox "The image can't be loaded, may be an " & _
    "invalid file."

End Sub
```

That is it for our application. We have a lot of functionality in the form of multimedia, displayed bitmaps, drag and drop, and file system browsing. But we have very little code because the basic controls provided in Visual Basic give us a lot of inherent functionality. The only tricky or unusual piece of code is dragging and dropping using the label control as a visual proxy. But even then, it is only a matter of moving the control to the mouse and initiating the drag method of the control.

Demonstration Time

Now we are ready to go ahead and run the project. Figure 7-12 shows the project at run time. The current active drive and directory will be displayed. Go ahead and change to a directory you know has valid bitmap graphics. The \windows directory always has quite a few.

Once you have found a bitmap, go ahead and click on it. Immediately you will see the outline of the label control. Drag it toward the picture box. Figure 7-13 shows the drag in midprocess. Now drop the bitmap on the picture control. When you do so, the image will be shown. Figure 7-14 shows the Windows forest.bmp file.

Our last step is to test the playing of AVI video files. Go ahead and browse your system for an AVI file. Typically the \windows\help directory will have several AVI video files. When you find one, go ahead and click on it. When you do, the multimedia control will be activated and ready for play. The VCR-style buttons will be enabled. In this case the record and eject buttons will not be enabled at all since we are not actually dealing with a recordable device. Figure 7-15 shows the Windows explorer.avi file being played in the picture control.

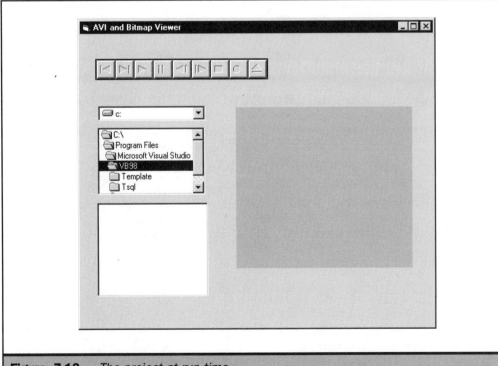

Figure 7-12.   *The project at run time*

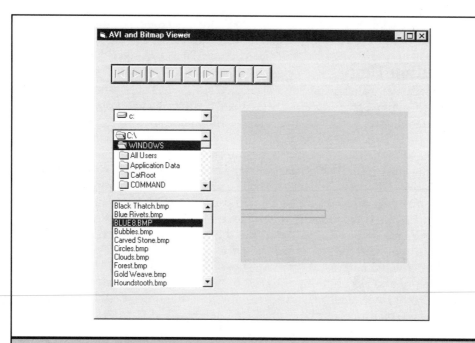

Figure 7-13. Dragging a bitmap to the picture box

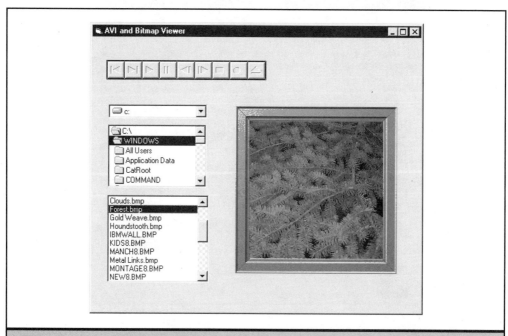

Figure 7-14. Bitmap dropped on the picture control

You might want to try and play video files that do not show up in the picture box. The only downside to this is sizing the picture control properly. In the Form_Load event, take out the line of code that sets the display window to be the picture control.

This application demonstrates some key functionality and techniques for Windows that can come in handy in building your applications.

Summary

The printer, the ability to drag and drop, the file system, multimedia, images, and much more, all add significant functionality to your application. Each can play a key role, depending on the type of application you are building. Combine these capabilities with the features outlined in the previous chapter, and before you know it, you will have professional application interfaces and capabilities that will rival world-class applications on the market today.

What's Next

In this chapter we explored how to add functionality that integrates our applications with the Windows environment. In the next chapter we will explore how to use the Windows application programming interface (API) to add the complete power of hard-core Windows programming into our applications.

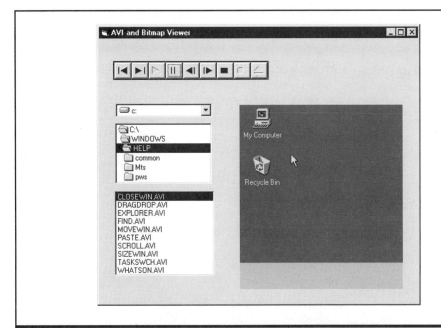

Figure 7-15. *AVI video running in the picture control*

The Complete Reference

Visual
Basic 6

Chapter 8

Working with the Windows API

Depending on your level of programming experience with Visual Basic and Windows, programming the Windows API may strike fear into your heart. But in reality, the basics of using the Windows API aren't so bad and can really open up a rich set of programming tools. In this chapter we will review the basics of utilizing the Windows API.

Application Programming Interface—What Is It?

The Windows 32-bit application programming interface (API) is an extensive set of functions, messages, and structures that allow programmers to build applications that run on the Windows platform. The API has a similar foundation for Windows 95, Windows 98, Windows NT Workstation, and Windows NT Server. There are some differences between the platforms that will be specific to the capabilities of the system. For example, Windows NT Server has a host of API calls that have been developed for running a server.

The Windows API functions, messages, data structures, and constants can be categorized as shown in Table 8-1.

Category	Description
Window management	The window management features give your applications the means to create and manage a user interface. Using the window management functions, you create and use windows to display output, prompt for user input, and carry out the other tasks necessary to support interaction with the user. Nearly all applications create at least one main window. Support is also included for using the clipboard, a mouse, and keyboard.
Graphics device interface (GDI)	The graphics device interface (GDI) provides functions and related structures that your applications can use to generate graphical output for displays, printers, and other devices. Using GDI functions, you can draw lines, curves, closed figures, paths, text, and bitmapped images. The color and style of the items you draw depend on the drawing objects. These include pens, brushes, and fonts of all different styles and formats.

Table 8-1.   *Categories of the API Tool Set*

Category	Description
System services	System services are a set of functions that give applications access to the resources of the computer and the features of the underlying operating system such as memory and the file system. These functions are essential to the basic operation of the system. For example, memory management takes care of memory allocation. There are processes to manage programs that are running and much more.
Multimedia	The multimedia functions give your applications access to audio and video. Multimedia functions let you enhance and expand the capabilities of your application, giving users the ability to combine these forms of communication with more traditional forms of computer output. With these functions, you can add video, music, synthesized music, and animation to your applications.
Remote procedure calls (RPC)	Remote procedure calls (RPC) give applications the means to carry out distributed computing, letting the applications tap the resources and computational power of computers on a network. RPC is a crucial aspect of building client/server applications. It allows clients to manipulate server-based data and processes that have an impact on the client.

Table 8-1. *Categories of the API Tool Set* (continued)

Note *Windows 3.1 is a 16-bit operating system that uses the 16-bit version of the Windows API. If you need to develop for Windows 3.1 as well, strongly consider looking into the third-party tool market for well-tested solutions.*

Working with DLLs

The Windows API is accessible through a series of system DLL files installed with Windows. These API functions, constants, and structures are all encapsulated in the DLLs and have to be declared in your application.

A key to understanding the use of these DLL files is that the functions were written in C code, not Visual Basic. That means we are going to have to do some translations to ensure we call the functions correctly as well as define type structures appropriately. That is where things get a little tricky. Also, we have to ensure that we use the DLL functions in the appropriate order and that we clean up after ourselves.

Just remember that Visual Basic made Windows programming easy. There was a reason VB became so popular—primarily because developers didn't have to know all the ins and outs of API programming. Now you are going to step up a level of complexity to work with the API directly.

Note   *If you have done C++ programming, the Microsoft Foundation Classes (MFC) also help to encapsulate the complexity of Windows programming.*

Declaring a DLL

Using functions in a DLL is not limited to the Windows API. Visual Basic comes with an API Viewer utility that will build the declare statements for you (see below), but it is important to understand how the declarations have been built. That way, if you work with third-party DLL tool sets, you will be able to create your own declarations.

To declare a DLL procedure, you add a declare statement to the declarations section of your code. If the procedure returns a value, write the declare as a function; if not, declare it as a subroutine. Most Windows API calls return some type of value. The following is an example of the CreateDC function that creates a device context.

```
Public Declare Function CreateDC Lib "gdi32" Alias "CreateDCA"
(ByVal lpDriverName As String, ByVal lpDeviceName As String,
ByVal lpOutput As String, lpInitData As DEVMODE) As Long
```

In this case we are publicly declaring the function (it returns a value) with a return type of Long.

DLL procedures declared in standard modules are public by default and can be called from anywhere in your application. DLL procedures declared in any other type of module are private to that module, and you must identify them as such by preceding the declaration with the Private keyword. In general, you may want to put your API procedures in a BAS module for wide use. In our strings example below, the functions are only to be used in the form they are being called in, so they are declared in the form.

Tip   *Procedure names are case sensitive in 32-bit versions of Visual Basic. In previous, 16-bit versions, procedure names were not case sensitive. So if you are ever stumped as to why an API function isn't working, and you have ruled out the obvious, be sure and check to see if you are declaring and calling the function with the correct case (the even more obvious!).*

The Lib clause in the declare statement tells Visual Basic where to find the DLL file that contains the procedure. In our example above, it will look for GDI32.dll. When you're referencing one of the core Windows libraries, such as User32, Kernel32, or GDI32, you don't need to include the file name extension. But for any other functions, you will want to indicate where the DLL file is located and its extension.

If you do not specify a path for the DLL library, Visual Basic will search for the file by first looking in the programs directory, then in the current directory (if different), the windows system directory, and finally, the windows directory.

Table 8-2 lists the common Windows API library files. As you will see throughout your use of the API, different calls will come from different DLLs depending on the particular task at hand.

Using Strings with the Windows API

When working with Windows API procedures that use strings, you'll need to add an alias clause to your declare statements to specify the correct character set. Windows API functions that contain strings actually exist in two formats: ANSI and Unicode. In the Windows header files, therefore, you'll get both ANSI and Unicode versions of each function that contains a string.

Dynamic Link Library	Description
Advapi32.dll	Advanced API services library supporting numerous APIs, including many security and registry calls.
Comdlg32.dll	Common dialog API library.
Gdi32.dll	Graphics device interface API library.
Kernel32.dll	Core Windows 32-bit base API support.
Lz32.dll	32-bit compression routines.
Mpr.dll	Multiple provider router library.
Netapi32.dll	32-bit network API library.
Shell32.dll	32-bit shell API library.
User32.dll	Library for user interface routines.
Version.dll	Version library.
Winmm.dll	Windows multimedia library.
Winspool.drv	Print spooler interface that contains the print spooler API calls.

Table 8-2.   *Windows API Files*

For example, following are the two C-language descriptions for the sndPlaySound function. You'll note that the first description defines the function as sndPlaySoundA, where the trailing "A" identifies it as an ANSI function.

```
Private Declare Function sndPlaySound Lib "winmm.dll" _
Alias "sndPlaySoundA" (ByVal lpszSoundName As String, _
ByVal uFlags As Long) As Long
```

The second declaration defines it as SetWindowTextW, where the trailing "W" identifies it as a wide, or Unicode, function.

```
Private Declare Function sndPlaySound Lib "winmm.dll" _
Alias "sndPlaySoundW" (ByVal lpszSoundName As String, _
ByVal uFlags As Long) As Long
```

As you can see, neither library function is actually named sndPlaySound. That is why we have an alias in our declaration to indicate the original name.

For API functions you use in Visual Basic, you should specify the ANSI version of a function. Windows NT only supports the Unicode versions. Use the Unicode versions only if you can be certain that your applications will be run only on Windows NT-based systems.

DLL Parameters

Calling a DLL is about knowing how to call its parameters and send in the right types of data formats. You can't pass in a string when a long is required, and you can't pass in an integer when a long pointer to a string is needed. And sometimes you don't want to pass a value at all, just a reference. Let's take a look at how a variable can be passed to a function.

By Value, by Reference, by George

By default, Visual Basic passes all arguments by reference. This means that instead of passing the actual value of the argument, Visual Basic passes a 32-bit address where the value is stored in memory. Note that you do not need to include the ByRef keyword in your declare statement.

Many DLL procedures expect an argument to be passed as a value. That means the function expects the actual value, instead of its memory location. If you pass an argument by reference to a procedure that expects an argument passed by value, the function will not work.

To pass an argument by value, place the ByVal keyword in front of the argument declaration in the declare statement. For example, the rectangle function accepts its arguments by value:

```
Private Declare Function Rectangle Lib "gdi32" _
(ByVal hdc As Long, ByVal X1 As Long, _
ByVal Y1 As Long, ByVal X2 As Long, ByVal Y2 As Long) As Long
```

But the CreateFontIndirect function accepts its argument by reference:

```
Private Declare Function CreateFontIndirect Lib "gdi32" Alias _
"CreateFontIndirectA" (lpLogFont As LOGFONT) As Long
```

You will note that the CreateFontIndirect function has a parameter of type LogFont. That is actually a type structure, so the function wants a reference to the structure in memory.

Table 8-3 outlines the standard conversion between C argument types found in the Windows API functions and the appropriate Visual Basic declaration. This chart can be very handy if you are trying to build a function call on your own.

C Data Type	Visual Basic Declaration	Call With
ATOM	ByVal variable As Integer	An expression that evaluates to an Integer.
BOOL	ByVal variable As Long	An expression that evaluates to a Long.
BYTE	ByVal variable As Byte	An expression that evaluates to a Byte.
CHAR	ByVal variable As Byte	An expression that evaluates to a Byte.
COLORREF	ByVal variable As Long	An expression that evaluates to a Long.
DWORD	ByVal variable As Long	An expression that evaluates to a Long.
HWND, HDC, HMENU, etc. (Windows handles)	ByVal variable As Long	An expression that evaluates to a Long.

Table 8-3.   *C Data Types and Visual Basic Declarations*

C Data Type	Visual Basic Declaration	Call With
INT, UINT	ByVal variable As Long	An expression that evaluates to a Long.
LONG	ByVal variable As Long	An expression that evaluates to a Long.
LPARAM	ByVal variable As Long	An expression that evaluates to a Long.
LPDWORD	variable As Long	An expression that evaluates to a Long.
LPINT, LPUINT	variable As Long	An expression that evaluates to a Long.
LPRECT	variable As type	Any variable of that user-defined type.
LPSTR, LPCSTR	ByVal variable As String	An expression that evaluates to a String.
LPVOID	variable As Any	Any variable (use ByVal when passing a string).
LPWORD	variable As Integer	An expression that evaluates to an Integer.
LRESULT	ByVal variable As Long	An expression that evaluates to a Long.
NULL	As Any or ByVal variable As Long	ByVal Nothing or ByVal 0& or vbNullString.
SHORT	ByVal variable As Integer	An expression that evaluates to an Integer.
VOID	Subprocedure	Not applicable.
WORD	ByVal variable As Integer	An expression that evaluates to an Integer.
WPARAM	ByVal variable As Long	An expression that evaluates to a Long.

Table 8-3.   *C Data Types and Visual Basic Declarations* (continued)

Fortunately, the builders of Visual Basic have left a way for your VB applications to interface fairly easily with the API. Even if the C data types are unfamiliar to you, you can quickly get the hang of calling API functions and retrieving return values.

PASSING STRINGS   As mentioned above, there is one set of data that needs special handling, strings. Passing a string by value means you are passing the address of the first data byte in the string; passing a string by reference means you are passing the memory address where another address is stored; the second address actually refers to the first data byte of the string.

As you've seen, strings should be passed to APIs using ByVal. Visual Basic uses a String data type known as a BSTR. A BSTR is made up of a header, which includes information about the length of the string, and the string itself, which may include embedded nulls. A BSTR is passed as a pointer, so the DLL procedure can modify the string because it knows where it is located in memory.

Note   *A pointer is a variable that contains the memory location of another variable, rather than the actual data. C programmers are very familiar with the use and dangers of pointers. If you get a bad pointer, you may overwrite critical sections of memory and crash your system.*

BSTRs are Unicode formatted, which means that each character takes two bytes. BSTRs typically end with a two-byte null character. All procedures in the Windows API recognize LPSTR types, which are pointers to standard null-terminated C strings. LPSTRs have no prefix. If a procedure expects an LPSTR (a pointer to a null-terminated string) as an argument, pass the BSTR by value. Because a pointer to a BSTR is a pointer to the first data byte of a null-terminated string, it looks like an LPSTR to the DLL procedure.

Tip   *It may sound complicated, but in reality, you are just passing in the string to the function—nothing special. Just make sure the declaration passes the string by value.*

For example, the sndPlaySound function accepts a string that names a digitized sound (.wav) file and plays that file.

```
Private Declare Function sndPlaySound Lib "winmm.dll" _
Alias "sndPlaySoundA" (ByVal lpszSoundName As String, _
ByVal uFlags As Long) As Long
```

Because the string argument for this procedure is declared with ByVal, in your code you will want to pass the string value to point to the first data byte for the string.

In general, use the ByVal keyword when passing string arguments to DLL procedures that expect LPSTR strings. If a DLL expects a pointer to an LPSTR string, pass the Visual Basic string by reference.

When passing binary data (such as an image) to a DLL procedure, pass a variable as an array of the Byte data type, instead of a String variable. Strings are assumed to contain characters, and binary data may not be properly read in external procedures if passed as a String variable. Binary data does not require two bytes to define each "character"—only one.

Procedures That Modify String Arguments

A DLL procedure can modify data in a string variable that it receives as an argument. However, if the changed data is longer than the original string, the procedure writes beyond the end of the string, probably corrupting other data. Typically, that is something neither you nor your users will appreciate! You can avoid this problem by making the string argument long enough so that the DLL procedure can never write past the end of it. When you declare a variable to be used as a modifiable string argument, be sure and specify the length of the string. You can do this in the following two ways:

Path = String(255, vbNullChar)
Dim Path As String * 255

Both of these processes have the same result: they create a fixed-length string that can contain the longest possible string the procedure might return. The first one will fill the string with NULLs.

Note *Windows API DLL procedures generally do not expect string buffers longer than 255 characters. You are safe to set the modifiable string sizes to 255.*

PASSING ARRAYS   As with strings, array data needs to be handled a little differently than you would expect in VB. Certainly you can pass individual elements of an array the same way you pass a variable of the same type. When you pass an individual element, it will be passed as the base type of the array. But sometimes you may want to pass an entire array to a DLL procedure. You can still pass an entire array if it is a numeric array. You pass an array by passing the first element of the array by reference. This works because numeric array data is always laid out sequentially in memory. If you pass the first element of an array to a DLL procedure, that DLL then has access to all of the array's elements.

Note *If the DLL procedure was written especially for Automation, you may be able to pass an array to the procedure the same way you pass an array to a Visual Basic procedure. Because Visual Basic uses Automation data types, including SAFEARRAYs, the DLL must be written to accommodate Automation for it to accept Visual Basic array arguments. For further information, consult the MSDN documentation.*

PASSING USER-DEFINED TYPES   Some DLL procedures take user-defined types, or structures, as arguments. As with arrays, you can pass the individual elements of a user-defined type the same way you would pass ordinary numeric or string variables.

You can pass an entire user-defined type as a single argument if you pass it by reference. User-defined types cannot be passed by value. Visual Basic passes the address of the first element, and the rest of the elements of a user-defined type are stored in memory following the first element. For example, the CreateFontIndirect function accepts a user-defined type for a logical font, which has the following structure:

```
Private Type LOGFONT
        lfHeight As Long
        lfWidth As Long
        lfEscapement As Long
        lfOrientation As Long
        lfWeight As Long
        lfItalic As Byte
        lfUnderline As Byte
        lfStrikeOut As Byte
        lfCharSet As Byte
        lfOutPrecision As Byte
        lfClipPrecision As Byte
        lfQuality As Byte
        lfPitchAndFamily As Byte
        'lfFaceName(1 To 256) As Byte
        lfFaceName As String * 50
End Type
```

One procedure that accepts a LogFont structure is CreateFontIndirect, which creates a font object. The CreateFontIndirect function is defined as follows:

```
Private Declare Function CreateFontIndirect Lib "gdi32" Alias _
"CreateFontIndirectA" (lpLogFont As LOGFONT) As Long
```

Once you have your logical font structure set up, you simply pass the name of your variable for the structure into the function as follows:

```
lngResult = CreateFontIndirect(LF)
```

The structure is then read from memory based on the pointer passed to the CreateFontIndirect function.

User-defined types can contain objects, arrays, and BSTR strings, although most DLL procedures that accept user-defined types do not expect them to contain string data. If the string elements are fixed-length strings (as in the LogFont structure), they look like null-terminated strings to the DLL and are stored in memory like any other value. Variable-length strings are incorporated in a user-defined type as pointers to string data. Four bytes are required for each variable-length string element.

Note	*When passing a user-defined type that contains binary data, such as image data, to a DLL procedure, store the binary data in a variable of an array of the Byte data type, instead of a String variable. Strings are assumed to contain characters, and binary data may not be properly read in external procedures if passed as a String variable.*

HANDLES   What is your handle, good buddy? You will find that a lot of API functions need a handle to some kind of object. A *handle* refers to a memory handle, which is essentially an index into an array of pointers. The pointers point to blocks of memory.

There are all kinds of objects that have handles to them. They include device contexts, windows, palettes, fonts, pens, and brushes. It is these objects that will be created and utilized to work with various aspects of the API.

In many cases, objects in Visual Basic have handles available for reference in API functions. For example, the form object has a handle to its device context as well as a handle to the form window.

Use of handles, or references, to objects in your Visual Basic application or that you create for use in your application will be the key to building your applications. The terminology may be a bit new, but once you get the hang of using pointers and handles in your applications, you will be ready for Windows API programming.

API Demonstration Time

OK, now that you have been overloaded with all of the ins and outs of the API, let's roll up our sleeves and build an example to put some of these concepts to work. We will have a little bit of fun working with different aspects of the API. Our example program will allow us to play a sound, build a rectangle, invert bitmap colors, manipulate fonts, set properties on a text box, and copy the screen image to a picture box. Sound like fun?

Windows API Viewer Add-in

A key tool that will aid development of our application is the Windows API Viewer add-in. On the Add-In menu, select Add-In Manager. From the list, select the API Viewer. Once you have the Viewer in place, go ahead and start it. Figure 8-1 shows the Viewer.

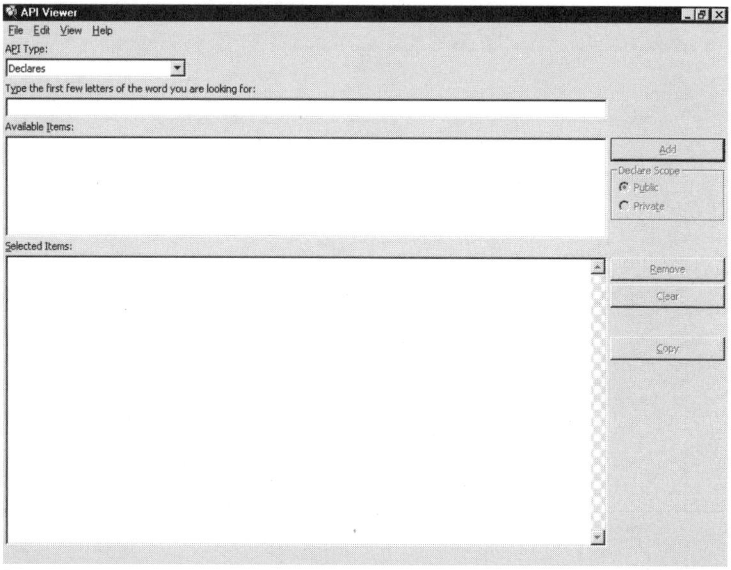

Figure 8-1.   *API Viewer*

You will want to load the Win32API.txt file. When you do so for the first time, it will ask if you want to create an Access file out of the text file. You will definitely want to do so because the searching speed will be much faster.

In the Viewer, you can search on three different classes of API elements: declares, constants, and types. Follow these steps to copy a declare into your VB code:

1. Select what you are looking for—a constant, type, or declare.

2. In the first text box, simply start typing the name of the item you are looking for, and matches will show up in the first listing.

3. When you find the item you are looking for, double-click on it.

4. The declaration is automatically added in the last text box.

5. Click on the Copy button to copy the declaration to the clipboard.

6. Go to your VB application and paste the declaration in the general declarations section of your form or module.

Figure 8-2 shows a function selected with the appropriate declare statement. The Viewer provides invaluable help in building applications that need a bit of API magic.

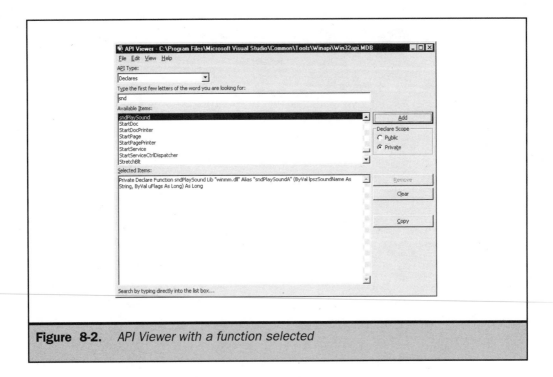

Figure 8-2. *API Viewer with a function selected*

Instead of trying to figure out how to declare all of the arguments, and so on, properly for Visual Basic, the declarations from the API Viewer have for the most part already been set up correctly. You may have a problem or two with some of the functions, especially when it comes to strings and their use.

Building the Interface

Our form will have a series of command buttons on it for testing each feature as well as a text box and picture box. Figure 8-3 shows the application at run time. Table 8-4 outlines the controls placed on the interface and their properties.

You will note on the form and the picture box control the use of the ScaleMode property. This property identifies the scale used for calculating the scalewidth and scaleheight properties. The default is twip, which is Visual Basic's internal coordinate system. But the Windows API doesn't know a twip from a bump in the road. It does know what a pixel is though. Thus, we want to change the scale mode of the objects on which we will be performing graphical functions to be pixels. That will make any calculations based on the size of the objects calculate properly using the API functions.

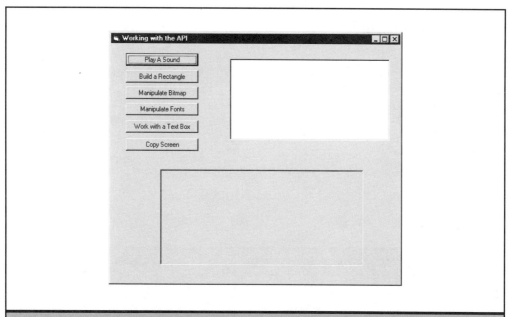

Figure 8-3.   *Windows API testing program at run time*

Component/Property	Setting
Form	Form1
Caption	"Working with the API"
ScaleMode	3 'Pixel
Command Button	CmdCopyScreen
Caption	"Copy Screen"
Text Box	TxtSample
MultiLine	-1 'True
Command Button	CmdText
Caption	"Work with a Text Box"
Command Button	CmdBitmap
Caption	"Manipulate Bitmap"

Table 8-4.   *Objects and Properties for the Windows API Program Interface*

Component/Property	Setting
Picture Box	pctSample
ScaleMode	3 'Pixel
Command Button	cmdFonts
Caption	"Manipulate Fonts"
Command Button	cmdRect
Caption	"Build a Rectangle"
Command Button	cmdPlaySound
Caption	"Play A Sound"

Table 8-4. *Objects and Properties for the Windows API Program Interface (continued)*

Making Our Declarations

Now that we have the interface built, we need to determine what declarations we are going to need for our code. Let's review each one along with the necessary API tools.

Playing Sounds

Let's start with the ability to play a sound. In this case we are going to use the sndPlaySound API function. In the API Viewer, select Declares and this function. When you do, you will get the following declaration:

```
Private Declare Function sndPlaySound Lib "winmm.dll" Alias _
"sndPlaySoundA" (ByVal lpszSoundName As String, _
ByVal uFlags As Long) As Long
```

Our function takes in two arguments: the first is the file name and the second is a set of flags for how to play the sound. The first argument can be a standard string. The second will be standard long integer values, in both cases sent by value. The flags will be represented by constant values and can also be retrieved from the API Viewer. Table 8-5 outlines each flag.

Flag	Description
SND_ASYNC	The sound is played asynchronously, and the function returns immediately after beginning the sound.
SND_LOOP	The sound plays repeatedly until sndPlaySound is called again, with the lpszSoundName parameter set to NULL. You must also specify the SND_ASYNC flag to loop sounds.
SND_MEMORY	The parameter specified by lpszSoundName points to an image of a waveform sound in memory.
SND_NODEFAULT	If the sound cannot be found, the function returns silently without playing the default sound.
SND_NOSTOP	If a sound is currently playing, the function immediately returns False, without playing the requested sound.
SND_SYNC	The sound is played synchronously, and the function does not return until the sound ends.

Table 8-5.   *uFlags Constants for the sndPlaySound API Function*

WORKING WITH WINDOWS

Again, the API Viewer will come in handy for retrieving the declarations for these constant values for your VB code.

You can use the multimedia command interface (MCI) functions and commands for playing multimedia files of all types. The sndPlaySound function is a quick and easy tool for playing .wav files. For more in-depth multimedia, consider using the MCI.

Building Rectangles

Building rectangles is pretty straightforward. We just need to use one function and no constants or structures. In the API Viewer, select the Rectangle function. The declaration is as follows:

```
Private Declare Function Rectangle Lib "gdi32" Alias _
"Rectangle" (ByVal hdc As Long, ByVal X1 As Long, _
ByVal Y1 As Long, ByVal X2 As Long, ByVal Y2 As Long) As Long
```

The first parameter is one of our good old handle friends. In this case it needs to be a handle to a device context on which to draw the rectangle. In our sample program, a picture box will be the device context. The rest of the parameters define the coordinates for the upper-left point and lower-right point of the rectangle.

Manipulating Bitmaps

We are going to do a little pattern manipulation on a bitmap in our picture box. To do this, we will use the PatBlt function. The PatBlt function paints a given rectangle using the brush that is currently selected into the specified device context. The brush color and the surface color(s) are combined by using the given raster operation.

Raster operations simply define how combinations of graphical bits will be performed. There are two basic raster operations that give you either black or white when bits are combined—not very useful, but none the less possible in binary math.

Don't worry too much about the brush. You can read more about API brushes in MSDN and the Windows SDK documentation. We will use the default brush already being utilized in the picture box. Our raster operation will simply be to invert the colors in the destination bitmap. Raster operations perform bit-level manipulation on images to affect the desired pattern outcome. The following is the declaration for PatBlt:

```
Private Declare Function PatBlt Lib "gdi32" Alias _
"PatBlt" (ByVal hdc As Long, ByVal x As Long, _
ByVal y As Long, ByVal nWidth As Long, ByVal nHeight As Long, _
ByVal dwRop As Long) As Long
```

The first parameter is (surprise, surprise) the handle of the device context we want to operate on. The next two parameters specify the upper-left point of the image area where we want to perform our pattern changes. It does not have to be 0,0. But it does need to be in the image boundaries. The following two parameters indicate the width and height of the rectangular area to operate on (from our x,y starting point). The final parameter is the raster operation to be performed. Table 8-6 outlines the different raster operation parameters. Even though we are using DSTInvert in our example, try the other ones to see their effects.

Parameter	Description
PATCOPY	Copies the specified pattern into the destination bitmap.
PATINVERT	Combines the colors of the specified pattern with the colors of the destination rectangle by using the Boolean OR operator.

Table 8-6.   *Raster Operation Parameters*

Parameter	Description
DSTINVERT	Inverts the destination rectangle.
BLACKNESS	Fills the destination rectangle using the color associated with index 0 in the physical palette. (This color is black for the default physical palette.)
WHITENESS	Fills the destination rectangle using the color associated with index 1 in the physical palette. (This color is white for the default physical palette.)

Table 8-6.   *Raster Operation Parameters* (continued)

Manipulating Fonts

There is more than one way to have fun with fonts. Using the Windows API is yet another. In fact, we can build font objects on our own and use them in our application. The following is the declaration for CreateFontIndirect:

```
Public Declare Function CreateFontIndirect Lib "gdi32" Alias
"CreateFontIndirectA" (lpLogFont As LOGFONT) As Long
```

The LogFont structure will define the various attributes of the font object to be created. And the CreateFontIndirect function will create the font object and return a handle of the font to us. Table 8-7 outlines the fields of the LogFont structure.

Once we have the font, we can select it into our picture box for display and then write some text to the picture box. Finally, when we are done with the font, we can delete it. Outlined next are the TextOut, SelectObject, and DeleteObject functions.

Property	Description
LfHeight	Specifies the height of the character cell.
LfWidth	Specifies the average width of characters in the font.
LfEscapement	Specifies the angles in tenths of degrees for the rotation of the font.
LfOrientation	Specifies the angle of the rotation of each character.

Table 8-7.   *LogFont Field Properties*

Property	Description
LfWeight	Specifies the weight of the font; 400 is normal and 700 is bold.
LfItalic	Specifies whether the font is italicized.
LfUnderline	Specifies whether the font is underlined.
LfStrikeOut	Specifies whether the font has a strikeout.
LfCharSet	Specifies the character set. This is critical for international font settings.
LfOutPrecision	Specifies how closely the output device must match the font settings.
LfClipPrecision	Specifies how to clip characters that are outside of the clipping region.
LfQuality	Specifies how closely the GDI must match the font attributes to the actual font.
LfPitchAndFamily	Specifies the pitch and family of the font.
LfFaceName	Specifies the face name of the font.

Table 8-7. *LogFont Field Properties* (continued)

```
Private Declare Function TextOut Lib "gdi32" Alias "TextOutA" _
(ByVal hdc As Long, ByVal x As Long, ByVal y As Long, _
ByVal lpString As String, ByVal nCount As Long) As Long

Private Declare Function SelectObject Lib "gdi32" _
(ByVal hdc As Long, ByVal hObject As Long) As Long

Private Declare Function DeleteObject Lib "gdi32" _
(ByVal hObject As Long) As Long
```

The TextOut function will draw text on the specified device context at the given coordinates. The lpString argument will contain the text to be written, and the last parameter indicates the number of characters in the text. The select object function selects an object into a specified device context. In this case it will be our font object into the picture box. Finally, when we are done with our font object that we created, we can delete it using DeleteObject.

Work with a Text Box

Have you ever wanted to force someone to type in all uppercase or lowercase? Well, with the API you can make a couple of quick calls, and you will have it done. The GetWindowLong function retrieves information about the specified window. The function also retrieves the long value at the specified offset into the extra window memory of a window. We need to specify the particular data about the window we want to retrieve. In our case it will be the style data represented by the GWL_STYLE constant. The following is the declaration for the function:

```
Private Declare Function GetWindowLong Lib "user32" Alias _
"GetWindowLongA" (ByVal hwnd As Long, ByVal nIndex As Long) As Long
```

The first parameter is the handle to the window we want to get information about. The second is the data about the window we want to retrieve. The SetWindowLong function changes an attribute of the specified window. The function sets a long value at the specified offset into the extra window memory of a window.

```
Private Declare Function SetWindowLong Lib "user32" _
Alias "SetWindowLongA" (ByVal hwnd As Long, _
ByVal nIndex As Long, ByVal dwNewLong As Long) As Long
```

The first parameter is the handle of the window, the second is the offset value to be set (GWL_STYLE), and the third is the new value for the setting. It is through these different settings that we can change the behavior and style of a window.

Copying Images

Our last Windows API sample will be to make a copy of the screen images and place it on a picture box. We will literally do a screen capture. We will also ensure the image is stretched to fit into the picture box and not be cut off. The function we will use is StretchBlt. The following is the declaration:

```
Private Declare Function StretchBlt Lib "gdi32" _
(ByVal hdc As Long, ByVal x As Long, ByVal y As Long, _
ByVal nWidth As Long, ByVal nHeight As Long, _
ByVal hSrcDC As Long, ByVal xSrc As Long, _
ByVal ySrc As Long, ByVal nSrcWidth As Long, _
ByVal nSrcHeight As Long, ByVal dwRop As Long) As Long
```

The StretchBlt function copies a bitmap from a source rectangle into a destination rectangle, stretching or compressing the bitmap to fit the dimensions of the destination rectangle, if necessary. The system stretches or compresses the bitmap according to the stretching mode currently set in the destination device context.

All of those parameters may look daunting. But they can be broken down into three sets. The first five apply to the rectangle of the destination context. The second five apply to the source image. And the last is the type of raster copy to make. In our case we will simply copy the bitmap with any effects (other than the stretching). Table 8-8 outlines the different raster operations.

Raster Operation	Description
SRCCOPY	Copies the source bits to the destination rectangle.
SRCPAINT	Combines the source and destination bits using the bitwise OR operator.
SRCAND	Combines the source and destination bits using the bitwise AND operator.
SRCINVERT	Combines the source and destination bits using the bitwise exclusive OR operator.
SRCERASE	Combines the source and inverse of destination bits using the bitwise AND operator.
NOTSRCCOPY	Copies the inverse of the destination bits to the destination rectangle.
NOTSRCERASE	Combines the inverse of the source and destination bits using the bitwise AND operator.
MERGECOPY	Combines the source and brush bits using the bitwise AND operator.
MERGEPAINT	Combines the destination and inverse of the source bits using the bitwise OR operator.
PATCOPY	Copies the brush bits to the destination rectangle.
PATPAINT	Combines the destination, pattern, and the inverse of source bits using the bitwise OR operator.
PATINVERT	Combines the pattern and destination bits using the bitwise exclusive OR operator.
DSTINVERT	Copies the inverse of the destination bits.
BLACKNESS	Sets all bits to black.
WHITENESS	Sets all bits to white.

Table 8-8.   *Raster Operations*

Building the Code

Now that we have a good overview of the different API tools, we are going to put them to work. The first section of our program code overviews the declarations. The first declarations are the sound-playing functions and constants. Note the supporting constants for playing the sound differently.

```
Option Explicit

'******************* Sound Functions and Constants

'  Declare our function.  Note the alias to indicate
'  the ASCII version of the function.  The first parameter
'  is the sound name.  The second parameter is to set any
'  flags for playing the sound (see below).
Private Declare Function sndPlaySound Lib "winmm.dll" _
Alias "sndPlaySoundA" (ByVal lpszSoundName As String, _
ByVal uFlags As Long) As Long

'  Constants for the sndPlaySound function
Const SND_ASYNC = &H1
Const SND_LOOP = &H8
Const SND_MEMORY = &H4
Const SND_NODEFAULT = &H2
Const SND_NOSTOP = &H10
Const SND_SYNC = &H0
```

The next section is the rectangle function call. We do not need any particular structures or constants for the rectangle call.

```
'*********************** Rectangle Functions
'  Rectangle Function - Creates a rectangle on a
'  device context
Private Declare Function Rectangle Lib "gdi32" _
(ByVal hdc As Long, ByVal X1 As Long, _
ByVal Y1 As Long, ByVal X2 As Long, ByVal Y2 As Long) As Long
```

The text box functions GetWindowLong and SetWindowLong are declared along with the constants needed for changing the window settings.

```
'****************** TextBox Functions and Constants
'   Used to set a window's properties
Private Declare Function SetWindowLong Lib "user32" _
Alias "SetWindowLongA" (ByVal hwnd As Long, _
ByVal nIndex As Long, ByVal dwNewLong As Long) As Long

'   Get the window properties
Private Declare Function GetWindowLong Lib "user32" Alias _
"GetWindowLongA" (ByVal hwnd As Long, ByVal nIndex As Long) As Long

'   Constants indicating uppercase and lowercase
'   for a window
Const ES_UPPERCASE = &H8&
Const ES_LOWERCASE = &H10&
Const GWL_STYLE = (-16)
```

The next section is the pattern-copying functionality. The PatBlt function is declared along with our constant for inverting the pattern.

```
'*********************** Bitmap Pattern Copy
'   Copies a pattern on a bitmap
Private Declare Function PatBlt Lib "gdi32" _
(ByVal hdc As Long, ByVal x As Long, ByVal y As Long, _
ByVal nWidth As Long, ByVal nHeight As Long, ByVal dwRop As Long) _
As Long

'   Constant indicating that the destination should be inverted
Const DSTINVERT = &H550009
```

The next section is our font functionality. The CreateFontIndirect function is declared along with the LogFont type structure. Note that the lfFaceName field is set to be a fixed-length string. The TextOut function will be used to display text in an object, and the SelectObject function will select the font into a device context.

```
'*********************** Font Functions

'   Creates a font object from a logfont structure
Private Declare Function CreateFontIndirect Lib "gdi32" Alias _
"CreateFontIndirectA" (lpLogFont As LOGFONT) As Long

'   Logfont structure that defines
'   a font object to be created
```

```
Private Type LOGFONT
        lfHeight As Long
        lfWidth As Long
        lfEscapement As Long
        lfOrientation As Long
        lfWeight As Long
        lfItalic As Byte
        lfUnderline As Byte
        lfStrikeOut As Byte
        lfCharSet As Byte
        lfOutPrecision As Byte
        lfClipPrecision As Byte
        lfQuality As Byte
        lfPitchAndFamily As Byte
        lfFaceName As String * 50
End Type


'  Outputs text on a device context
Private Declare Function TextOut Lib "gdi32" Alias "TextOutA" _
(ByVal hdc As Long, ByVal x As Long, ByVal y As Long, _
ByVal lpString As String, ByVal nCount As Long) As Long


'  Selects a windows object into a device context
Private Declare Function SelectObject Lib "gdi32" _
(ByVal hdc As Long, ByVal hObject As Long) As Long
```

The last general declarations section is the screen capture. The StretchBlt function is declared along with the GetDC function. GetDC will be used to retrieve the device context for the screen. And the DeleteObject function is declared for cleaning up any objects created from our API calls.

```
'******************** Screen Capture Functions
'  Copies an image and stretches it onto another
'  device context
Private Declare Function StretchBlt Lib "gdi32" _
(ByVal hdc As Long, ByVal x As Long, ByVal y As Long, _
ByVal nWidth As Long, ByVal nHeight As Long, _
ByVal hSrcDC As Long, ByVal xSrc As Long, _
ByVal ySrc As Long, ByVal nSrcWidth As Long, _
ByVal nSrcHeight As Long, ByVal dwRop As Long) As Long
```

```
'   Retrieves a device context
Private Declare Function GetDC Lib "user32" _
(ByVal hwnd As Long) As Long

'   DeleteObject will delete any windows object
Private Declare Function DeleteObject Lib "gdi32" _
(ByVal hObject As Long) As Long

'   Constant indicating how to copy an image
Const SRCCOPY = &HCC0020
Const SRCPAINT = &HEE0086
Const SRCAND = &H8800C6
Const SRCINVERT = &H660046
Const SRCERASE = &H440328
Const NOTSRCCOPY = &H330008
Const NOTSRCERASE = &H1100A6
Const MERGECOPY = &HC000CA
Const MERGEPAINT = &HBB0226
Const PATCOPY = &HF00021
Const PATPAINT = &HFB0A09
Const PATINVERT = &H5A0049
'Const DSTINVERT = &H550009 already declared above
Const BLACKNESS = &H42
Const WHITENESS = &HFF0062
```

Our first command button is for the bitmap manipulation that will invert the pattern bitmap. To make things a bit interesting, we will randomly generate the two points that will define our rectangle for the pattern.

The first thing that is done is to seed the random number generator. We don't want to exceed the bounds of the picture box, so we will ensure the numbers are within the pixel bounds. We generate the upper-left point and lower-right point on the rectangle. So we use the ScaleWidth and ScaleHeight properties of the picture box. Remember that we set the scale mode property to be pixels so that the measurements will be in pixels, which the PatBlt function will require.

The next step is to load a picture into our picture box. That is done with the VB LoadPicture function. In this case we are loading the clouds.bmp file that comes with Windows. Change appropriately to an image on your system. Once the picture is loaded, the PatBlt function is called with all of the randomly generated components.

```
Private Sub cmdBitmap_Click()
'  Declare Variables
Dim Result As Long
Dim X1 As Integer
Dim Y1 As Integer
Dim X2 As Integer
Dim Y2 As Integer

'  Seed the random number generator
Rnd

'  Generate an X, Y point that will define the upper
'  left corner of the pattern
X1 = Int((pctSample.ScaleWidth - 0 + 1) * Rnd + 0)
Y1 = Int((pctSample.ScaleHeight - 0 + 1) * Rnd + 0)

'  Generate an X, Y point that will define the lower
'  right corner of the pattern

X2 = Int((pctSample.ScaleWidth - X1 + 1) * Rnd + X1)
Y2 = Int((pctSample.ScaleHeight - Y1 + 1) * Rnd + Y1)

'  Load our picture
pctSample.Picture = LoadPicture("c:\windows\clouds.bmp")

'  Display the pattern.  Note that in this case we are
'  inverting the current image
Result = PatBlt(pctSample.hdc, X1, Y1, X2, Y2, DSTINVERT)

End Sub
```

Our next command button is for building fonts. The first step is to declare a variable for our LogFont structure. Then we set the values. Play around with the height, width, escapement, and other values. The font name is set to a string, and we terminate the string with a null character. That will indicate to the CreateFontIndirect function where the font name ends.

Once the structure is set up, a font object is created from the CreateFontIndirect function. A pointer to the object is returned from the function. The next step is to select the font object into our picture box device context. That will replace the current font object that Visual Basic created in the picture box.

When the font object is selected, the return value is a pointer to the original font object in the picture box. We will store that so we can reselect it into the picture box once we are done with the font object we created.

Now that our font is in place, we can show text on the picture box. This is done using the TextOut function. We indicate the device context for the text to be displayed and the coordinates to start the text drawing. The last two parameters indicate the text to be shown and the number of characters. Finally, we do a little cleanup by selecting the original font into the picture box and then deleting our font so it doesn't continue to take up memory in the system.

```vb
Private Sub cmdFonts_Click()

'   Declare our variables
Dim LF As LOGFONT
Dim Result As Long
Dim lngNewFont As Long
Dim lngOrgFont As Long

'   Build the font structure
LF.lfHeight = 140
LF.lfWidth = 23
LF.lfEscapement = 20
LF.lfOrientation = 0
LF.lfWeight = 700
LF.lfItalic = 0
LF.lfUnderline = 1
LF.lfStrikeOut = 1
LF.lfFaceName = "Coronet" & Chr(0)

'   Create our font object
lngNewFont = CreateFontIndirect(LF)

'   Select that font into the device context.

'   The handle to the original font is returned
lngOrgFont = SelectObject(pctSample.hdc, lngNewFont)

'   Display text on the picture box starting at coordinates
'   0, 0.  The last parameter indicates the number of characters
'   to be displayed.
Result = TextOut(pctSample.hdc, 0, 0, "HELLO", 5)

'   Put back original font
Result = SelectObject(pctSample.hdc, lngOrgFont)

'   Delete the new font once we are done with it.
Result = DeleteObject(lngNewFont)

End Sub
```

The next command button is to play sounds. This is a fairly straightforward set of steps. We first indicate the .wav file we want to play by putting it into a string. Be sure and change the directory and file to an appropriate one for your system.

The next call is to the sndPlaySound function. The first parameter is our string that points to the file. The second indicates how the file should be played. In this case we use the SND_ASYNC constant. You might want to try the other settings to see the effect on playing the file.

```
Private Sub cmdPlaySound_Click()

'  Declare our Variables
Dim Result As Long
Dim SoundFile As String

'  Set the file name
SoundFile = "c:\Windows\media\" & "ding.wav"

'  Play the sound asynchronously
Result = sndPlaySound(SoundFile, SND_ASYNC)

End Sub
```

The rectangle command button will generate randomly sized rectangles on our picture box. As with the bitmap pattern function, we are going to randomly generate the x,y coordinates to define the rectangle.

Next, to make things interesting, we are also going to randomly generate RGB values for the forecolor property of the picture box. The forecolor will be used when the rectangle is drawn to determine the pen color that will be used to draw the rectangle.

Finally, we make our call to the rectangle function to draw the rectangle on our picture box. The first parameter is the device context to the window where we want to draw our rectangle, in this case the picture box. The last four parameters are the coordinates of our rectangle.

```
Private Sub cmdRect_Click()

'  Declare our Variables
Dim Result As Long

Dim X1 As Integer
Dim Y1 As Integer
Dim X2 As Integer
Dim Y2 As Integer
```

```
Dim R As Integer
Dim G As Integer
Dim B As Integer

'  Seed the random number generator
Rnd

'  Randomly generate an x and y starting point
X1 = Int((pctSample.ScaleWidth - 0 + 1) * Rnd + 0)
Y1 = Int((pctSample.ScaleHeight - 0 + 1) * Rnd + 0)

'  Randomly generate the lower x and y coordinates
X2 = Int((pctSample.ScaleWidth - X1 + 1) * Rnd + X1)
Y2 = Int((pctSample.ScaleHeight - Y1 + 1) * Rnd + Y1)

'  Randomly generate RGB values for the forecolor of the
'  picture box
R = Int((255 - 0 + 1) * Rnd + 0)
G = Int((255 - 0 + 1) * Rnd + 0)
B = Int((255 - 0 + 1) * Rnd + 0)

'  Set the forecolor
pctSample.ForeColor = RGB(R, G, B)

'  Draw the rectangle.  The first coordinates are the
'  handle of the device context.  The rest of the
'  parameters are the coordinates of the rectangle
Result = Rectangle(pctSample.hdc, X1, Y1, X2, Y2)

End Sub
```

The text command button uses the GetWindowLong and SetWindowLong functions to ensure the text in the text box is all uppercase. The first thing we have to do is get the current style settings for the text box window.

The GetWindowLong function passes in the handle of the text box and the GWL_STYLE constant. The style settings for the text box are returned. The settings will be updated to include the uppercase flag.

Next we call the SetWindowLong function. The first parameter is the handle of the text box. The second is the constant indicating the settings to be updated. The last parameter is the updated settings. We have to pass in all of the original settings and update them at the same time. To do this, the Style variable, which holds the settings, is updated by combining the ES_UPPERCASE constant with an OR function. That will update the appropriate bit in the settings variable.

```
Private Sub cmdText_Click()

'  Declare our Variables
Dim Result As Long
Dim Style As Long

'  Get the current windows style
Style = GetWindowLong(txtSample.hwnd, GWL_STYLE)

'  Set the uppercase style.  Note we have to keep
'  the original style and set the uppercase bit
Result = SetWindowLong(txtSample.hwnd, GWL_STYLE, _
         Style Or ES_UPPERCASE)

End Sub
```

The final command button handles copying the screen image into the picture box control. Visual Basic has an object available called Screen, which gives basic information about the screen settings. It includes the width and height values in twips of the screen. It also includes properties for converting the twips value to pixels, which, again, is what the API functions will use. The twip width and height values are converted to pixels by dividing the number of twips by the number of twips per pixel.

The next step is to get a handle to the screen's device context. The screen object in Visual Basic does not have an .hDC property. So we will have to resort to the GetDC API function. By default, a 0 parameter will return the hDC value for the screen. And, voila, we have the handle to the screen device context.

Finally, we are ready for the StretchBlt function. We first pass in the device context handle for the picture box and the parameters for the upper-left corner and the width and height. Next we pass in the handle to the screen device that we retrieved. And we pass in the upper-left coordinate of the screen device and the width and height. Once that is done, the screen image is copied and stretched to fit into the picture box.

```
Private Sub cmdCopyScreen_Click()

'  Declare our variables
Dim lngResult As Long
Dim lngWidth As Long
Dim lngHeight As Long
Dim lngScreenHandle As Long
```

```
'  Get the width and height of the screen in
'  pixels.  We have to use the conversion properties
'  that tell us the number of twips per pixel.  The
'  width and height which are in twips are divided by
'  the corresponding conversion value to get the
'  width and height in pixels.  All Windows API functions
'  work in pixels.
lngWidth = Screen.Width / Screen.TwipsPerPixelX
lngHeight = Screen.Height / Screen.TwipsPerPixelY

'  Get the screen handle.  By default the GetDC function
'  returns the handle to the screen object if the value
'  passed in is 0.
lngScreenHandle = GetDC(0)

'  The StretchBlt function copies from one image to another.  In
'  this case the target is our picture box.  It will stretch the
'  image onto the target.
lngResult = StretchBlt(pctSample.hdc, 0, 0, _
pctSample.ScaleWidth, pctSample.ScaleHeight, lngScreenHandle, _
0, 0, lngWidth, lngHeight, SRCCOPY)

End Sub
```

And with that, we have built our API demonstration application. As you look through the different API calls in the application, you will see the different uses of the API discussed in the first section of the chapter.

The API in Action

Now that we have done all the hard work, let's see the fireworks in action. The first test will be to play a sound. Go ahead and click on the Play a Sound button. You should hear the sound play. Next, click on the Build a Rectangle button. When you do, a randomly generated rectangle will be drawn on the picture box. Figure 8-4 shows the application. Now click on the Build a Rectangle button several times. The picture box will fill up with rectangles of all sizes and colors. Figure 8-5 shows the picture box.

Next let's have some fun with the bitmap patterns. Click on the Manipulate Bitmap button. When you do, the bitmap will show up on the picture, and a randomly generated rectangle will be inverted using the PatBlt function. Figure 8-6 shows the bitmap with the inverted rectangle.

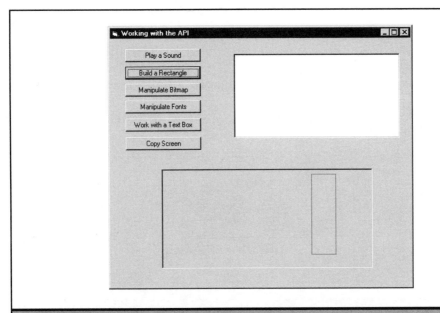

Figure 8-4. *API program with a randomly generated rectangle*

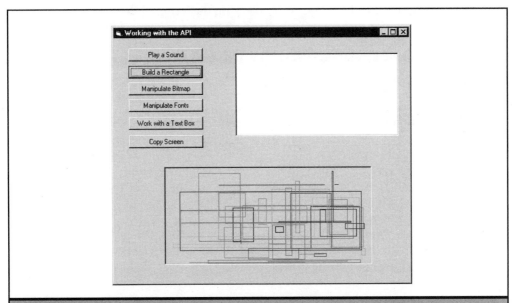

Figure 8-5. *API program with multiple randomly generated rectangles*

WORKING WITH WINDOWS

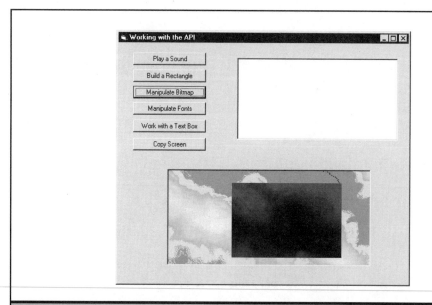

Figure 8-6.   *The bitmap image with a rectangle pattern inverted*

Now we are ready to build some fonts. Click on the Manipulate Fonts button. If you still have the bitmap and inverted pattern showing, the text will be shown over the image. Figure 8-7 shows the font.

Now we are ready to jump to the text box. First you will want to type some text in lowercase into the text box. Then click on the Work with a Text Box button, and type in the text box again. The text will be in uppercase. Figure 8-8 shows the text box with both lowercase and uppercase text.

The last function is to copy the screen to a picture box. Click on the Copy Screen button. That will copy the entire screen image into the picture box. Figure 8-9 shows the results.

Let's change the raster operation in the StretchBlt function to be a MERGECOPY. When you do so, the screen and the current image in the picture box will be merged. Figure 8-10 shows the effect.

And with that, you have successfully utilized the Windows API. Try playing around with variations on the functions. The text box can have many different settings, fonts can appear in all shapes and sizes, and much more can be done. You have just started to tap into the power of the Windows API.

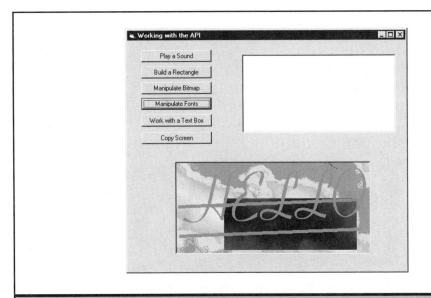

Figure 8-7.   *The bitmap image, inverted pattern with the font shown over it*

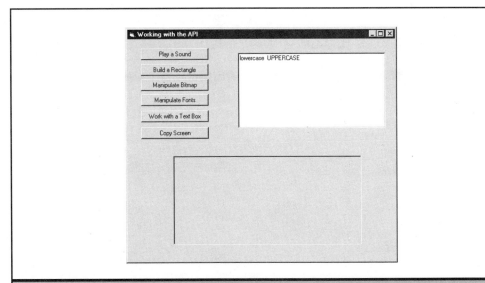

Figure 8-8.   *The text box with both lowercase and uppercase text*

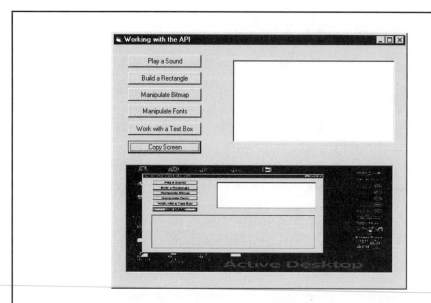

Figure 8-9. The picture box with the screen image captured

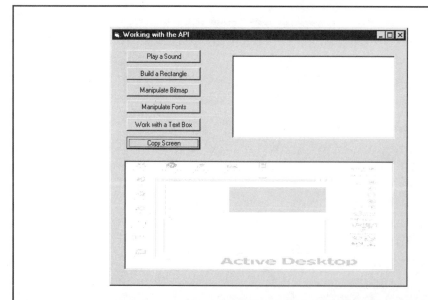

Figure 8-10. Screen image copied with a MERGECOPY raster operation

Summary

The Windows API is literally your window to working with the operating system. All programs in Windows, including Visual Basic, are written based on the API. If there is something you can't do in Visual Basic or through a third-party tool, you may need to roll up your sleeves and dig into the Windows API. There are a number of excellent references on the market to find out more about the hundreds of different API functions and structures.

What's Next

Now that we have built all of these great applications, how can we deploy them? In the next chapter we will review topics related to deploying Visual Basic applications. The Package and Deployment wizard will be reviewed, as well as options and issues for deploying different types of applications.

WORKING WITH WINDOWS

Chapter 9

Error Handling, Debugging, and Deploying Applications

317

Now that you have built that great application, are you wondering what you should do next? How do you debug and test for errors? How do you deploy the application to your audience? Fortunately, Visual Basic has a powerful set of tools for error handling, testing, and debugging your application. And the Package and Deployment wizard provides an elegant interface for preparing your application for installation on target machines.

Error Handling

The first thing you will need to think about as you begin to button up your application is handling errors. Whether you like it or not, your users may perform a set of actions that you have not anticipated, or non-user-related system problems, such as the network being down or the database not being available, could cause your application to bomb.

Err Object, Functions, and Statements

One key object and several functions and statements make up the core of Visual Basic's error handling capabilities. Let's first review the Err object. Table 9-1 outlines the different properties and methods of the object.

The error object is relatively easy to use; the implementing and handling of errors are the keys to its use. There are also several error functions and statements that go along with the error object. These are outlined in Table 9-2.

Property/Method	Description
HelpContext	Returns or sets a string expression containing the context ID for a topic in a help file.
HelpFile	The fully qualified path to the appropriate help file.
LastDLLError	System error code produced when a call to a DLL file is made and fails.
Number	Numeric value specifying the error.
Source	Name of the object or application that generated the error.
Clear	Clears all properties for the object.
Raise	Generates a run-time error.

Table 9-1. *Properties and Methods of the Err Object*

Function/Statement	Description
Error function	Returns the error message corresponding to an error code.
Error statement	Forces an error with the specified error code.
On Error statement	Enables an error handling routine and specifies the location of the routine.
Resume statement	Resumes execution after an error handling routine if finished.

Table 9-2.   *Error-Related Functions*

Ideally, Visual Basic procedures wouldn't need error handling code at all. Reality dictates that hardware problems or unanticipated actions by the user can cause run-time errors that halt your code, and there's usually nothing the user can do to resume running the application. Other errors might not interrupt code, but they can cause it to act unpredictably.

Building a Sample Project

The best way to get started with the error object is to dive directly into some code and see it in action. Let's resurrect our file system object example from Chapter 7. There were definite steps to using the program, and if you did one out of sequence, the program bombed and you had to start it again. We will beef it up with error handling.

Updating the Interface

Make a copy of the program and update the interface to have the objects and properties as shown in Table 9-3. You can see we have added a couple of command buttons for testing the error object as well as a list box that will be utilized for showing a list of error messages.

Component/Property	Setting
Form	Form1
Caption	"File System Object"
List Box	LstErrors

Table 9-3.   *Object Properties of the Error Program*

Component/Property	Setting
Command Button	CmdShowErrors
Caption	"Show Errors"
Command Button	CmdRaise
Caption	"Raise an Error"
Command Button	CmdReadFile
Caption	"Read File"
Command Button	CmdFileFuncs
Caption	"File Functions"
Command Button	CmdCreateFile
Caption	"Create File"
Command Button	CmdDeleteFile
Caption	"Delete File"
Command Button	CmdDeleteFolder
Caption	"Delete Folder"
Command Button	CmdCreateFolder
Caption	"Create Folder"
Command Button	CmdDriveFuncs
Caption	"Drive Functions"
Label	LblFileFuncs
AutoSize	-1 'True
Caption	"File Functions"
Label	LblDateCreated
AutoSize	-1 'True
Caption	"Date Created"
Label	LblDateModified
AutoSize	-1 'True

Table 9-3. *Object Properties of the Error Program* (continued)

Component/Property	Setting
Caption	"Date Modified"
Label	LblFileSize
AutoSize	-1 'True
Caption	"File Size"
Label	LblFreeSpace
AutoSize	-1 'True
Caption	"Free Space"
Label	LblSize
AutoSize	-1 'True
Caption	"Size"
Label	LblVolume
AutoSize	-1 'True
Caption	"Volume"
Label	LblDriveFuncs
AutoSize	-1 'True
Caption	"Drive Functions"

Table 9-3. *Object Properties of the Error Program* (continued)

Adding the Error Code

When a user creates a file, we need to ensure the file doesn't already exist. If it does, we need to ask the user if she or he wants to delete it. The On Error is set to go to the DeleteFile section of the subroutine. The CreateTextFile function will error if the file already exists, and the error code will be 58.

If the error pops up, we then show a prompt for the user to delete the file. If the user indicates yes, we call the delete command button click event and then use the Resume keyword for the subroutine to resume the file creation process.

Next we need to put in error handling if for some reason the write process fails. When that happens, we simply tell the program to continue (resume), and we check for any errors afterwards and simply indicate that the process failed.

> **Note** *You could set the second parameter on CreateTextFile to true, but that would overwrite the file without giving the user the option of whether to continue.*

```vb
Private Sub cmdCreateFile_Click()

Dim FSO As New FileSystemObject
Dim txtStream As TextStream
Dim Response As Integer

' Resume processing if an error continues
On Error GoTo DeleteFile

' Create the text file.
Set txtStream = FSO.CreateTextFile("c:\testfile.txt", False)

' Resume through the writing process
On Error Resume Next

' Write a line with a newline character.
txtStream.WriteLine ("Line with Line Break....")

' Write a line with no newline character
txtStream.Write ("No Line Break 1.... ") ' Write a line.

' Write a second line with no newline character
txtStream.Write ("No Line Break 2.... ") ' Write a line.

' Close the text stream
txtStream.Close

Exit Sub

DeleteFile:

    If Err.Number = 58 Then

    ' Find out if the user would like to create the file
    Response = MsgBox(Err.Description & " (" & Err.Number & ")" & _
    "Would you " & _
    "like to overwrite the existing file?", vbYesNo)
```

```
    '  If yes...
    If Response = vbYes Then
        '  Clear any error messages
        Err.Clear

        '  Execute the click event of the CreateFile
        '  command button
        cmdDeleteFile_Click

        '  Resume process of the create file
        Resume

    End If

    End If

Exit Sub

WriteError:

'  Indicate the file was not properly created
If Err.Number <> 0 Then

    '  Show an error
    MsgBox "File could not be written to properly."

    '  Delete the file in case the error was on the writes
    cmdDeleteFile_Click

End If

End Sub
```

In the create folder process, we have not added any error checking. So, if you try and create the folder twice, you will get an error indicating the folder already exists.

```
Private Sub cmdCreateFolder_Click()

Dim FSO As New FileSystemObject
```

```
'   Create a new folder
FSO.CreateFolder "c:\vb6fsotest"

End Sub
```

In the delete method, we will take a little different approach to error handling. If the user tries to delete a file that does not exist (error code 53), we will simply notify the user and continue. If it is another error code (besides 0), we indicate a fatal system problem. That ought to really scare the user!

```
Private Sub cmdDeleteFile_Click()

Dim FSO As New FileSystemObject

'   Resume on error
On Error Resume Next

'   Delete the new file
FSO.DeleteFile "c:\testfile.txt"

'   Indicate the file could not be found for deletion.
If Err.Number = 53 Then

    '   Show the error
    MsgBox "The file could not be found for deletion."

Else

    '   Check to ensure we did not have success
    If Err.Number <> 0 Then

        '   Indicate another fatal error popped up
        MsgBox "Serious system error, call administrator. (" & _
        Err.Number & ")"

    End If

End If

End Sub
```

As with the create folder function, we do no error checking on the delete folder option. It will raise an error if we try to delete a folder that does not exist, and, of course, the error is not handled.

```
Private Sub cmdDeleteFolder_Click()

Dim FSO As New FileSystemObject

'  Delete the folder
FSO.DeleteFolder "c:\vb6fsotest"

End Sub
```

This is standard drive information retrieval. We could add error handling if the drive did not exist.

```
Private Sub cmdDriveFuncs_Click()

Dim FSO As New FileSystemObject
Dim DRV As Drive

'  Get the drive
Set DRV = FSO.GetDrive(FSO.GetDriveName("c:"))

'  Show the volume name
lblVolume.Caption = DRV.VolumeName

'  Show the total drive space
lblSize.Caption = "Total Space: " & _
                  FormatNumber(DRV.TotalSize / 1024, 0) & _
                  " Kb"

'  Show the free space
lblFreeSpace.Caption = "Free Space: " & _
                       FormatNumber(DRV.FreeSpace / 1024, 0) & _
                       " Kb"

End Sub
```

In the standard file information retrieval, we add error handling in case the file does not exist. In this case we tell the user that the code needs to be changed. We also update the label controls to show "N/A."

```vb
Private Sub cmdFileFuncs_Click()

Dim FSO As New FileSystemObject
Dim FileInfo As File

'  Resume if there is an error
On Error Resume Next

'  Get the autoexec file
Set FileInfo = FSO.GetFile("c:\autoexec.bat")

'  Show the date created
lblDateCreated.Caption = FileInfo.DateCreated

'  Show the date last modified
lblDateModified.Caption = FileInfo.DateLastModified

'  Show the file size
lblFileSize.Caption = FileInfo.Size

If Err.Number <> 0 Then

    '  Indicate the file was not found
    MsgBox "You need to change the code to point to a valid file."

    '  Clear our variables and show N/As
    lblDateCreated.Caption = "N/A"
    lblDateModified.Caption = "N/A"
    lblFileSize.Caption = "N/A"

End If

End Sub
```

This command button demonstrates the Raise method of the error object.

```vb
Private Sub cmdRaise_Click()

'  Raise error 53
Err.Raise 53

End Sub
```

When we read the file, of course, we have to have a file to read. If we find there is no file to read, the program will show an error. In this case, we want to give the user the option of then creating the file and continuing with the read process. If the user indicates yes, the Resume statement is used to continue after the file is created.

```
Private Sub cmdReadFile_Click()

Dim FSO As New FileSystemObject
Dim txtFile As File
Dim txtStream As TextStream
Dim Response As Integer

'  If there is an error then go to the read error section
On Error GoTo ReadError

'  Get the file
Set txtFile = FSO.GetFile("c:\testfile.txt")

'  Open the file for reading
Set txtStream = txtFile.OpenAsTextStream(ForReading)

'  Display the first line
MsgBox txtStream.ReadLine

'  Display the second line
MsgBox txtStream.ReadLine

'  Close the text stream
txtStream.Close

'  Exit the sub so the read error code is not run
Exit Sub

ReadError:

    '  Find out if the user would like to create the file
    Response = MsgBox(Err.Description & " (" & Err.Number & ")" & _
    "Would you " & _
    "like to create the file?", vbYesNo)

    '  If yes...
    If Response = vbYes Then
```

```
     ' Clear any error messages
     Err.Clear

     ' Execute the click event of the CreateFile
     ' command button
     cmdCreateFile_Click

     ' Resume process of the read file
     Resume

   End If

End Sub
```

The ShowErrors command button simply loops through and uses the Error function to return the error description in a list box for values 0 through 500.

```
Private Sub cmdShowErrors_Click()

Dim N As Integer
' Loop through 500 error codes
For N = 0 To 500

    ' Add each to the list box
    lstErrors.AddItem N & " - " & Error(N)

Next N

End Sub
```

You will find this version of the program much easier to use than the last version in Chapter 7, at least for the file functionality. The drive functionality was intentionally left alone for comparative purposes.

Testing the Error of Our Ways

Let's see how our error functionality works. Figure 9-1 shows the program at run time. To remind ourselves of the errors of our past, click twice on the Create Folder button. You will get an error indicating the "file" (folder) already exists. Figure 9-2 shows the error.

In this case we have no error handling, and the program crashes. And we can, of course, simulate the same effect with the Raise method of the error object. Click on the Raise an Error command button. The results are shown in Figure 9-3.

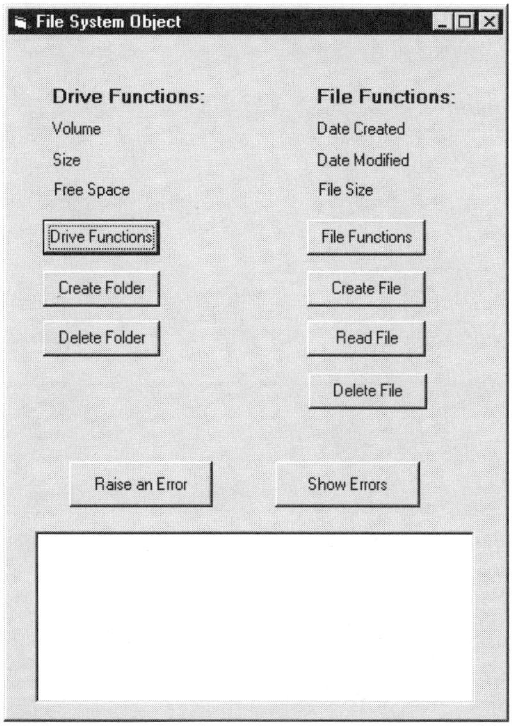

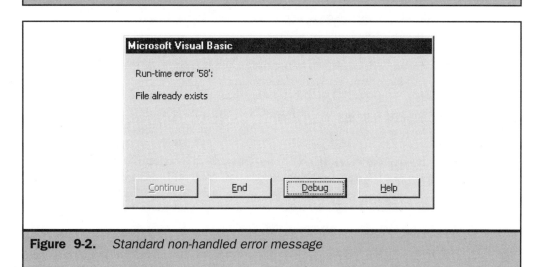

Figure 9-1. *Program at run time*

Figure 9-2. *Standard non-handled error message*

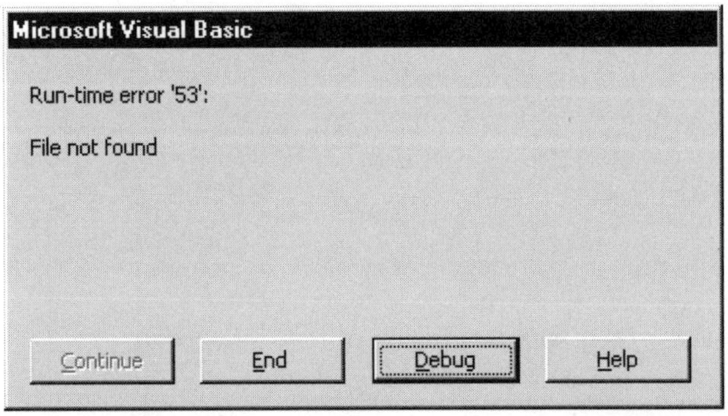

Figure 9-3. *Raise an error*

Raising errors can be useful if you want to use a standard error handling routine and know that an error message pertains to your needs. When we break the code on the error, you will see it is highlighted, as shown in Figure 9-4. Visual Basic is fairly helpful in providing information on what line of code caused the error. You can also immediately go to MSDN help for any additional information by pressing F1.

Now let's get into our new nifty error handling. Click twice on the Create File command button. When you do so, the error message shown in Figure 9-5 is displayed. Because of our error handling code in the program, the program doesn't bomb. In fact, it asks if we want to go ahead and overwrite the file. Click Yes to continue, and indeed the file is overwritten.

Go ahead and delete the file so we can test our read error handling. Click on the Read File command button. When you do so, there is no file to read since we have deleted it. Our error handler will then prompt for whether to go ahead and create the file, as shown in Figure 9-6. Click Yes to continue. When you do, you will go back into the file read code and continue with the processing.

Next, double-click on the Delete File command button. On the second click you will get an error message, as shown in Figure 9-7, indicating that no file could be found to delete. That is a far cry from our program bombing if we try to delete a nonexistent folder.

Finally, click on the Show Errors command button. That will build a list of error messages for numbers 0 through 500 (see Figure 9-8). You will find that many of the error values are undefined, but you also may find a few you haven't seen before.

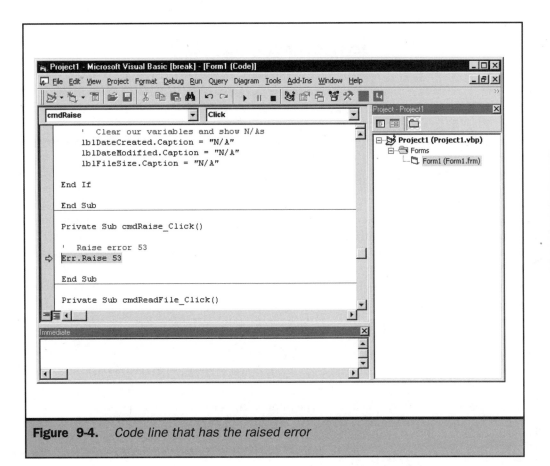

Figure 9-4.   *Code line that has the raised error*

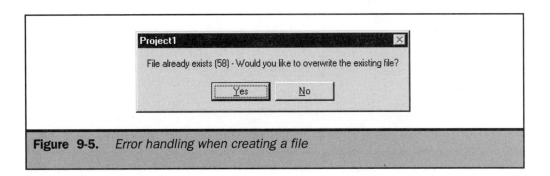

Figure 9-5.   *Error handling when creating a file*

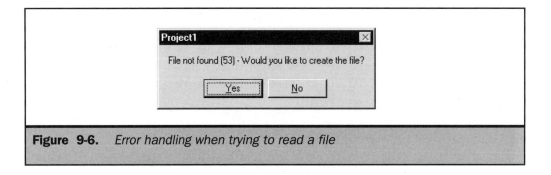

Figure 9-6. *Error handling when trying to read a file*

Error handling can make all the difference in the world on how your application handles failures. There is nothing worse for a user than to be working in a program, only to have an error pop up and then unexpectedly shut down. You never know when the network may crash, or the Internet link may close, or the database may time out. Gracefully handling these types of external errors will help to minimize user frustration.

Debugging Your Applications

Ever have the bug in your code you just can't figure out? Do you have 23 different variables that all have to be set just right to ensure your code works properly, and you know one is off, but not which one? The debugging tools in VB give you a robust set of options for tackling these problems head on.

Types of Application Errors

There are all kinds of errors you can debug for. One kind is syntax errors. These include forming an If...Then...Else incorrectly or misspelling a keyword such as Iteger

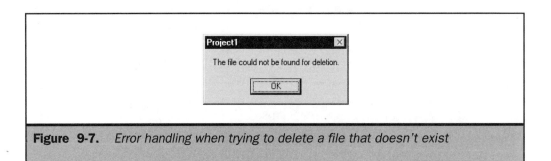

Figure 9-7. *Error handling when trying to delete a file that doesn't exist*

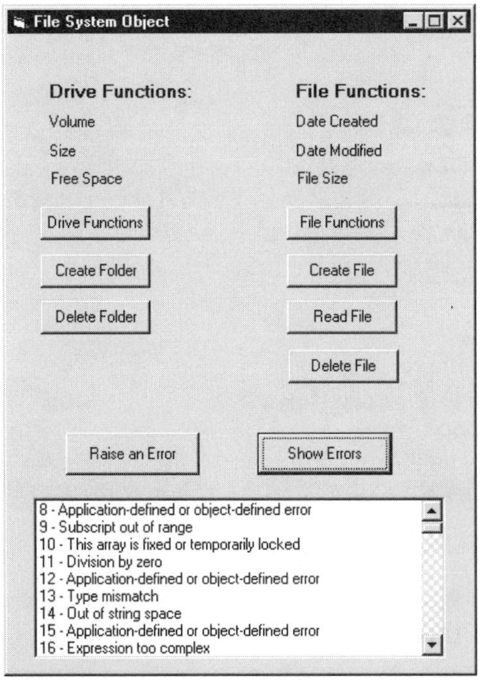

Figure 9-8. *List of error messages*

(instead of Integer). These will be caught automatically by turning on the Auto Syntax option in the IDE. This can be done with the following steps:

1. Select the Tools menu.
2. Select Options.
3. Select the Editor tab.
4. Select Auto Syntax Check.

By default this feature is turned on. This will help to ensure your code has the correct syntax when typed in. Of course, it doesn't ensure the code will work correctly! You can still have run-time errors, such as the ones we reviewed in the error handling section above. You can also have functionality errors because your program doesn't operate as intended. That is where the debugging tools come into play.

Debugging Tools

A review of the available debugging tools can be found in Table 9-4.

Fixing a Sick Calculator

Let's put these tools to work debugging some bad code in a sample calculator application. Our calculator looks and feels like a real calculator, but in reality the numbers don't add up (or multiply, divide, and subtract).

Tool	Description
Toggle Breakpoint	Defines a line in your code where Visual Basic suspends execution of the application. You can have multiple breakpoints defined.
Step Into	Executes the next executable line of code in the application and steps into any procedures encountered.
Step Over	Executes the next executable line of code in the application without stepping into a procedure. This can be helpful if you know the bug is in the current procedure; you don't have to laboriously step into other procedures. This can be especially helpful in loops.
Step Out	Executes the remainder of the current procedure and breaks at the next line in the calling procedure.
Locals window	Displays the current value of local variables.
Immediate window	Allows you to execute code or query values while the application is in break mode.
Watches window	Displays the values of selected expressions.
Quick Watch	Lists the current value of an expression while the application is in break mode.
Call Stack	While in break mode, presents a dialog box that shows all procedures that have been called but not yet run to completion. That way you can find out how far into a particular set of logic your code has gone.

Table 9-4.   *Debugging Tools*

Building the User Interface

Add the controls listed in Table 9-5 to your project. Our interface includes standard number buttons as a control array, the operator buttons, and a clear and clear error set of buttons. A text box is used as the display for the results of any operations. Figure 9-9 shows the interface.

Component/Property	Setting
Form	Form1
Caption	"Calculator"
Command Button	CmdClear
Caption	"Clear
Command Button	CmdDivide
Caption	"/"
Command Button	cmdMultiply
Caption	"*"
Command Button	cmdMenus
Caption	"-"
Command Button	cmdPlus
Caption	"+"
Command Button	cmdEqual
Caption	"="
Command Button	cmdDecimal
Caption	"."
Command Button	cmdNumber
Caption	"1", "2", "3", "4", "5", "6", "7", "8", "9", "0"
Index	0, 1, 2, 3, 4, 5, 6, 7, 8, 9, 10
Text Box	txtResults
Text	""

Table 9-5. *Objects and Properties for the Calculator Project*

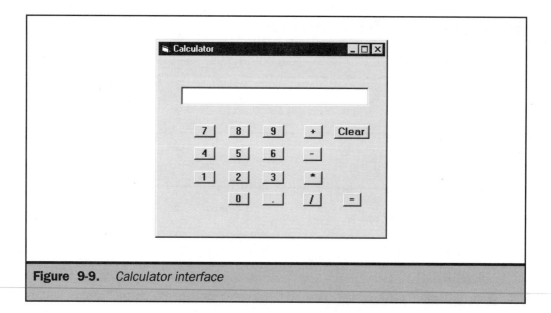

Figure 9-9. Calculator interface

Adding the Suspect (and Undocumented) Code

OK, now that we have the user interface built, let's go ahead and add the following code:

```
Dim intLeft As Integer
Dim intRight As Integer
Dim intInProg As Integer
Dim intOperator As Integer
Dim intPrevOperator As Integer
Dim intClear as Integer

Private Sub Calculate()

If intInProg = 0 Then

    intLeft = Int(txtResults.Text)
    intInProg = 1
    txtResults.Text = ""
    intPrevOperator = intOperator

    Exit Sub

Else
```

```
        intRight = Int(txtResults.Text)
        txtResults.Text = ""

End If

Select Case intPrevOperator

    Case 1 ' add
        intLeft = intLeft + intRight
        intRight = -1
        txtResults.Text = intLeft

    Case 2 ' subtract
        intLeft = intLeft - intRight
        intRight = -1
        txtResults.Text = intLeft

    Case 3 ' multiply
        intLeft = intLeft * intRight
        intRight = -1
        txtResults.Text = intLeft

    Case 4 ' divide
        intLeft = intLeft / intRight
        intRight = -1
        txtResults.Text = intLeft

End Select

intPrevOperator = intOperator

intClear = 1

End Sub

Private Sub cmdClear_Click()
txtResults.Text = ""
intLeft = 0
intRight = 0
intOperator = 0
intPrevOperator = 0
```

```
intInProg = 0

End Sub

Private Sub cmdDecimal_Click()

txtResults.Text = txtResults.Text & "."

End Sub

Private Sub cmdDivide_Click()

intOperator = 4

Calculate

End Sub

Private Sub cmdEqual_Click()

intOperator = 5

Calculate

End Sub

Private Sub cmdMinus_Click()

intOperator = 2

Calculate

End Sub

Private Sub cmdMultiply_Click()

intOperator = 3

Calculate

End Sub
```

```
Private Sub cmdNumber_Click(Index As Integer)

If intClear = 1 Then

    txtResults.Text = ""
    intClear = 1
End If

If Index <> 10 Then

    txtResults.Text = txtResults.Text & (Index + 1)

Else

    txtResults.Text = txtResults.Text & "0"

End If

End Sub

Private Sub cmdPlus_Click()

intOperator = 1

Calculate

End Sub

Private Sub Form_Load()

intInProg = False

End Sub
```

You have probably seen many of the errors already. But let's use the tools to ferret out some of them.

Sleuthing for Errors

The first thing we want to check for is whether we are properly handling division by 0. We need to be sure and notify the user and not crash due to an error. Use the interface to divide 9 by 0. The results are shown in Figure 9-10.

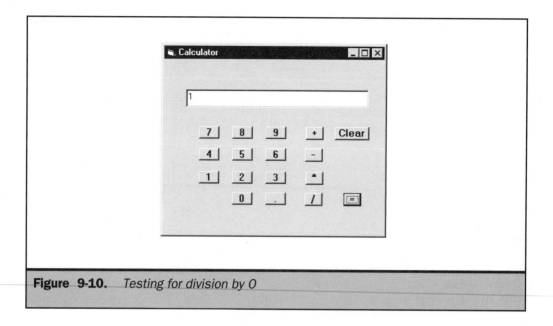

Figure 9-10. *Testing for division by 0*

As you can see, the result is not as suspected. In fact, the result is 1 and not an error. We definitely have a problem that we need to debug. Let's go ahead and put a breakpoint in the Calculate subroutine on the case for the divide. Figure 9-11 shows the setting.

Now run the application and perform the same operation. When you do so, the code will stop on the case for the divide. That will provide us with the opportunity to see what our variables are set to and do a little test code.

When the code breaks, we want to have the Immediate, Locals, and Watches debug windows visible in our application. First off, in the Locals window, navigate the tree until you see the intLeft and intRight variables. In fact, you will see all of the global variables.

You can also drag the variables to the Watches window. Simply double-click and highlight the entire variable name in code. Then drag the variable to the Watches window. Drag both the left and right variables. As you can see, the values are 9 and 10. But wait, they should be 9 and 0! So, we have something wrong in the way those two are being set. Figure 9-12 shows the current interface settings.

While we are in this section of code, we might as well check to see if there is a division by 0 error. In the Watches window, you can update the value of intRight to be 0, then continue with the code. In fact, you will then get the notorious division by 0 error. So, we know we need to add some error code to handle that situation. Use the error techniques outlined in the first part of the chapter.

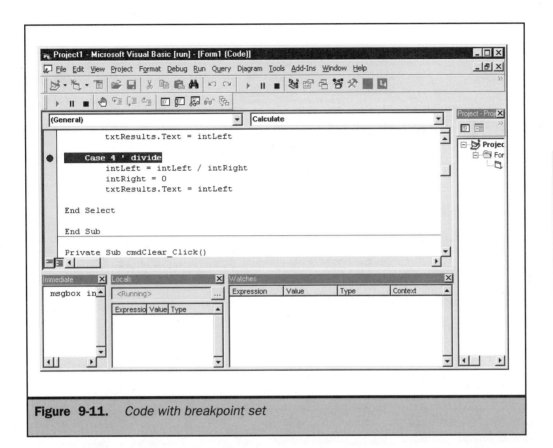

Figure 9-11. *Code with breakpoint set*

Now we need to check back in the click event for the numbers command button to see how the left and right variables are being set. In fact, we can put a breakpoint in the click event and see what is happening. Use the "step" tools to follow the variable settings through the code. If you do so and track your watch variables, you will see that the index for number 0 is actually 9, not 10. So we have a bug in our code when checking to see if the number 0 is being clicked. We need to update the If statements as follows:

```
If intInProg = 1 Then txtResults.Text = ""

If Index <> 9 Then

    txtResults.Text = txtResults.Text & (Index + 1)
Else
    txtResults.Text = txtResults.Text & "0"
End If
```

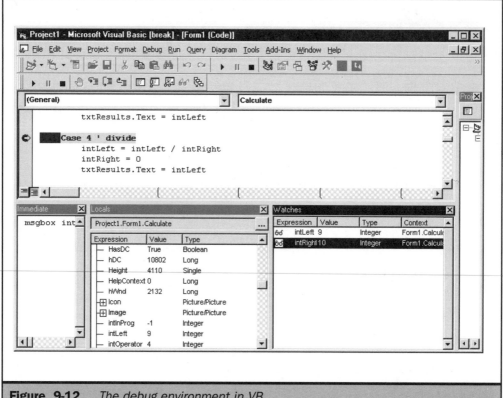

Figure 9-12. *The debug environment in VB*

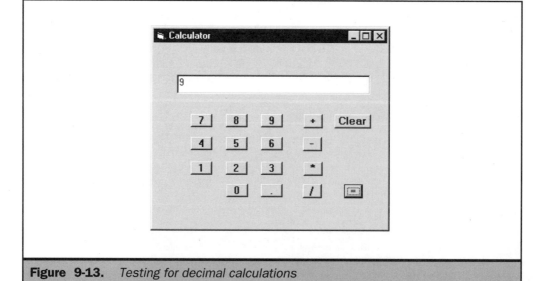

Figure 9-13. *Testing for decimal calculations*

The next item we should test is whether calculating decimal values is supported correctly. For example, 3.3 * 3.3 should be 10.89. When we process this calculation, Figure 9-13 shows the result. The result is, in fact, 9. Something is definitely wrong. Let's once again put a breakpoint in the multiply case in our code. This time we can use the Immediate window to do some testing. You will note first, though, that the left and right variables are 3, not 3.33! So, something is up.

In the Immediate window, let's check the math and type in the following:

```
Msgbox 3.33 * 3.33
```

When you do that, a message box will pop up showing that, indeed, the answer is 11.0889. Figure 9-14 shows the Watches window code set and the resulting message box.

In fact, you can test any snippet of code in the Watches window to test the current system state and code results. Of course, the problem is that we are doing our math with Integer data types and not Double data types. So we need to update our intLeft and intRight to be Double data types. When you do that, the calculations will start coming out correct. Figure 9-15 shows the Watches window with the proper 3.33 values.

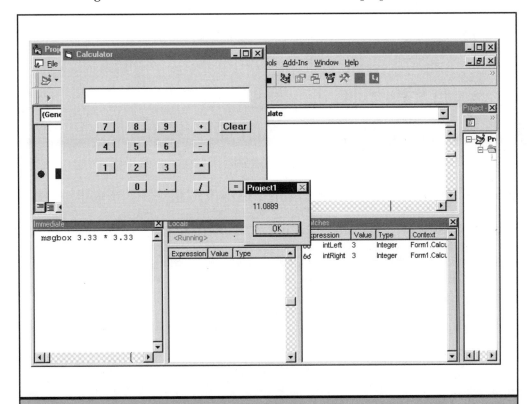

Figure 9-14.   *Watches window set with results*

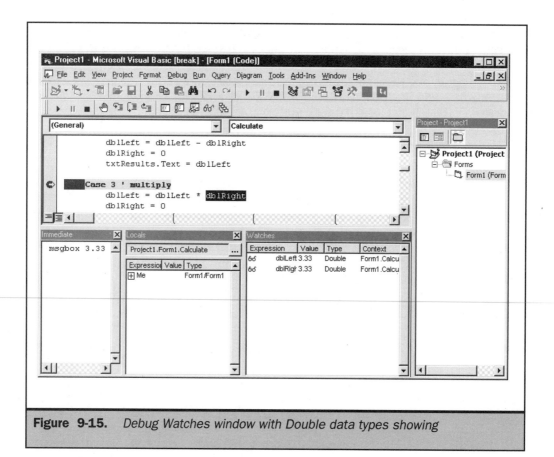

Figure 9-15. Debug Watches window with Double data types showing

Good Medicine for a Sick Calculator

The following is a listing of the updated code with appropriate comments and a review of the functionality and changes.

The first thing we have is our global variables. And, as outlined above, we have to ensure that the variables that will store our data values for the calculations can store floating point numbers. Following that are our tracking variables.

```
'   Hold the left and right values
'   of the calculation
Dim dblLeft As Double
Dim dblRight As Double
```

```
' Tracks where in the calculation progress we are
Dim intInProg As Integer

' Stores the current operator selected
Dim intOperator As Integer

' Store the previous operator selected
Dim intPrevOperator As Integer

' Indicates when the text field should be cleared
Dim intClearText As Integer
```

The calculate subroutine tracks the operation order and will perform the appropriate operation once we have both the left and right values for the operator. It is important to remember that the result of one operation serves as the left value for the next operation except when the calculator is in a cleared state (intInProg = 0).

The primary change in this subroutine is the use of the Error functionality to track a division by 0. We might also want to add some error checking to see if we overflow any of the variables.

```
Private Sub Calculate()

' Check to see if we are just getting started with
' the first numbers entered for this calculation
If intInProg = 0 Then

    ' Get the number entered
    dblLeft = txtResults.Text

    ' Set the next stage
    intInProg = 1

    ' Clear the text box
    txtResults.Text = ""

    ' Store the current operator as the previous
    ' one clicked
    intPrevOperator = intOperator

    Exit Sub
```

```
Else

    ' Get the right-hand side of the operation
    dblRight = txtResults.Text

    ' Clear the text box
    txtResults.Text = ""

End If

' Perform the last operation

Select Case intPrevOperator

    Case 1 ' add
        dblLeft = dblLeft + dblRight
        dblRight = 0
        txtResults.Text = dblLeft

    Case 2 ' subtract
        dblLeft = dblLeft - dblRight
        dblRight = 0
        txtResults.Text = dblLeft

    Case 3 ' multiply
        dblLeft = dblLeft * dblRight
        dblRight = 0
        txtResults.Text = dblLeft

    Case 4 ' divide
        ' Check for a divide by 0 error
        On Error GoTo DivideZero
        dblLeft = dblLeft / dblRight
        dblRight = 0
        txtResults.Text = dblLeft

End Select
' Take the current operator as the previous operator
' Next time we calc we will need to perform the operation
' that fired off this calculation. Note we still need the
' value on the right of the operator
intPrevOperator = intOperator
```

```
'  Indicate  the text field should be cleared
intClearText = 1

'  Exit the subroutine
Exit Sub

'  Divide by Zero Support
DivideZero:

    '  Notify the user
    MsgBox "You cannot divide a number by 0."

    '  Clear the calculator
    cmdClear_Click

End Sub


Private Sub cmdClear_Click()

'  Clear all values
txtResults.Text = ""
dblLeft = 0
dblRight = 0
intOperator = 0
intPrevOperator = 0
intInProg = 0
intClear = 0

End Sub
```

Now add a decimal to the number.

```
Private Sub cmdDecimal_Click()

'  Add a decimal to the value
txtResults.Text = txtResults.Text & "."

End Sub
```

Next comes a series of operator clicks. You might want to think about using a constant defined globally instead of numbers to indicate the operator that was clicked.

```
Private Sub cmdDivide_Click()

'   Indicate the operator
intOperator = 4

'   Make the calculation
Calculate

End Sub

Private Sub cmdEqual_Click()

'   Indicate the operator
intOperator = 5

'   Make the calculation
Calculate

End Sub

Private Sub cmdMinus_Click()

'   Indicate the operator
intOperator = 2

'   Make the calculation
Calculate

End Sub

Private Sub cmdMultiply_Click()

'   Indicate the operator
intOperator = 3

'   Make the calculation
Calculate

End Sub
```

```
Private Sub cmdPlus_Click()

'   Indicate the operator
intOperator = 1

'   Make the calculation
Calculate

End Sub
```

The number click event will need to support adding the appropriately clicked value to our number in the text box. We first check to see if the text box should be cleared because we are going to enter a new number, not append to an existing one. If so, the text box is cleared. Next, we convert the index into the appropriate value for display.

```
Private Sub cmdNumber_Click(Index As Integer)

'   If set, clear the text
If intClearText = 1 Then

    '   Clear the text
    txtResults.Text = ""

    '   Reset the value
    intClearText = 0

End If

'   Check to see if our index is not 0
If Index <> 9 Then

    '   Set the number value
    txtResults.Text = txtResults.Text & (Index + 1)

Else

    '   Add 0
    txtResults.Text = txtResults.Text & "0"

End If

End Sub
```

When the form loads, we ensure the calculation progress is at stage 0.

```
Private Sub Form_Load()

'  Start out at 0
intInProg = 0

End Sub
```

The calculator will be a great tool for playing around with the debugging tools. Track different operations, calculated values, global values, and try different sets of code in the Intermediate window. Plus, all of the step tools will come in handy for following the exact code process.

You could start the control array index at 0 with the number 0. It was done in reverse in this case for demonstration purposes. The calculator would be a bit more straightforward if the indexes followed the numbers.

Deploying Your Applications

Now that we have built our world-class calculator—one that will rival calc.exe that is delivered with Windows—let's prepare to deploy it to the world. That calls for the new Package and Deployment wizard provided with Visual Basic.

The Package and Deployment Wizard

The Package and Deployment wizard provides options for distributing your application. Examples include the creation of standard packages that are installed as executables, Internet packages that can be downloaded from a Web site, etc. You can also create dependency files that can be distributed with components. Dependency files list the run-time components that must be distributed with your application's project files. For example, if your project uses ActiveX controls, they will need to be distributed with your application. When you purchase a third-party ActiveX control, you should have a dependency file provided. Likewise, when you create a control, you will need to provide a dependency file. Dependency files tell where on a machine files should be loaded and other pertinent installation data.

Creating an Installation Package

Creating installation packages is fairly straightforward. To demonstrate, let's walk through the process for our calculator program.

1. Start the Package and Deployment wizard, which is provided with the Visual Studio 6.0 tools. Figure 9-16 shows the wizard at startup.

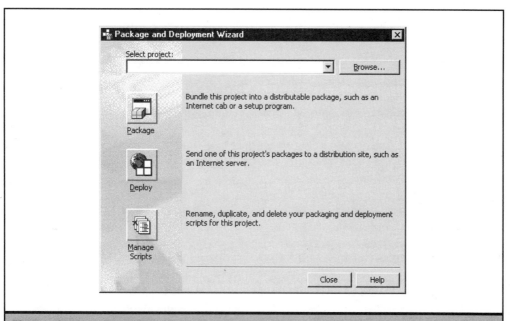

Figure 9-16.   *Package and Deployment wizard*

2. Select the Browse button, and find the project for the updated and correct calculator code.

3. Once you have found the project, click on the Package button. Figure 9-17 shows the next screen.

4. Since we did not create an executable for our program, the wizard asks you either to find the executable or create it. Go ahead and click on Compile.

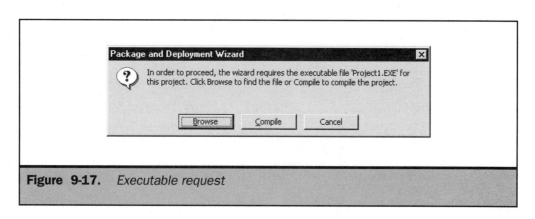

Figure 9-17.   *Executable request*

5. Once it is done compiling, you are asked to select a packaging script. You only have one option, Standard Setup Package 1.

Note *You do have the option of creating your own installation programs. Visual Basic provides a setup1.vbp project, which is used by the Package and Deployment wizard to create the installation program for your application. This is a standard Visual Basic project that you can modify to suit your installation needs.*

6. The next screen, shown in Figure 9-18, shows the options for a package type. The two displayed are Standard Setup Package and Dependency File. In this case, select Standard Setup Package.

Note *You can only create Internet packages for ActiveX projects such as ActiveX EXE, ActiveX DLL, and ActiveX Controls.*

The next screen prompts you for the location in which to create the package. By default it is in a subdirectory under your code directory. Next, the wizard gives you a list of files to be included in your package. This will be based on its review of all references, controls, and so on, found in your application. You can add files such as documentation, images, and databases. Figure 9-19 shows the dialog.

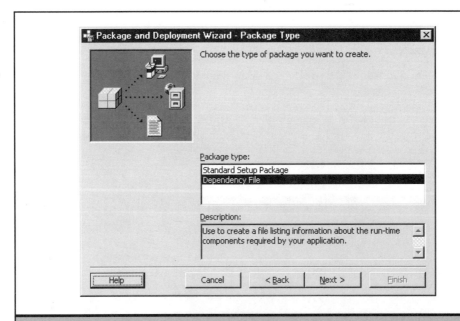

Figure 9-18. *Package options*

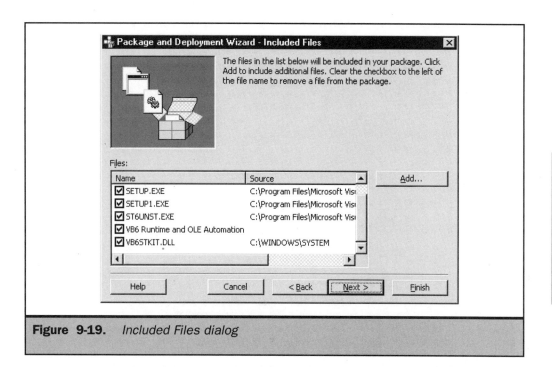

Figure 9-19.   *Included Files dialog*

7. Click Next to continue. You then have the option of building one CAB file or multiple CAB files that will fit on floppies. Select the Single Cab option.

8. Next you will be asked to input the installation title. Make sure it is "Calculator."

9. Now, as shown in Figure 9-20, you have the option of defining where on the Windows Start menu the program links should be installed. In our case, the default will work fine.

10. The next dialog gives you the option of determining where the program should be installed. Typically, you will want to install it in the default application path selected by the user.

11. The Shared Files dialog gives you the option of determining which files may be shared and used in more than one program. In this case, our calculator will not be used by any other programs, so simply continue.

12. That is it for the necessary information. You can enter some setting names for the session and click on Finish.

The wizard will then create appropriate CAB and setup files for deploying your calculator. Figure 9-21 shows the final screen once finished. The wizard also creates a batch file, which can be used to re-create the CAB file should you update your project files. But keep in mind that any new files or additional items will not be included.

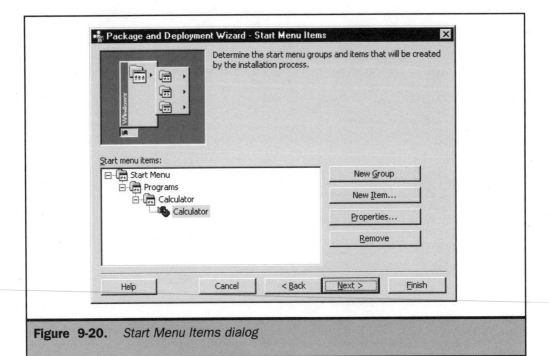

Figure 9-20. Start Menu Items dialog

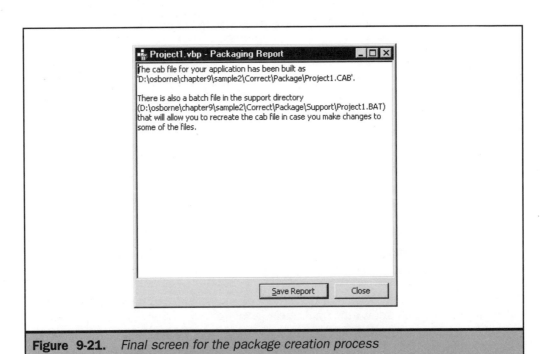

Figure 9-21. Final screen for the package creation process

Testing the Installation

You can go ahead and run the setup file created by the wizard. You will find that it is a standard Windows installation program and should look quite familiar. Figure 9-22 shows the installation screen.

When the program is installed, the application removal utility, st6unst.exe, is installed in the system. An application removal log is created with the installation in the application directory for removal of the program.

The next step would be to deploy our package for installation over a network or via the Web. To do that, you would select the Deploy option and follow the steps for placing it on a network or Web site. That will allow you to easily distribute your application other than via floppy.

The wizard is intuitive and easy to use, and for all but the most complex projects where you truly need a customized installation process, it will meet your needs right out of the box.

Deployment Considerations

There are many items to consider when deploying your application. For example, Visual Basic applications do not work on anything but Windows systems. And even then, you have to watch out for Alpha-based systems, which need the code compiled for the Alpha chip.

If you are distributing your application on the public Internet, you will want to be sure that your targeted users know the installation requirements. Also a consideration for Internet deployment is the size of download. How long will that user at 28.8 bps be willing to wait for your download?

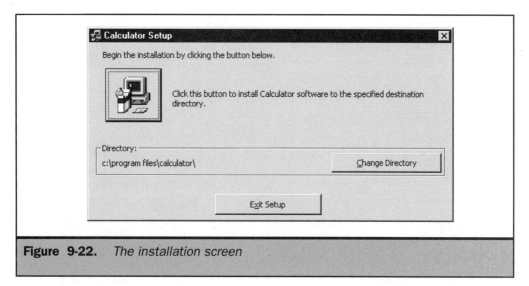

Figure 9-22. *The installation screen*

WORKING WITH WINDOWS

Tools that install as business objects on servers will also need to be well tested in terms of remote access and ensuring your client applications can talk successfully with these objects. Updating and maintaining business logic in components requires careful tracking of release revisions and versions, updates needed elsewhere in the system, and so on. In fact, versioning is an issue you need to pay careful attention to so that you do not have mass confusion in your software deployment. On the Make tab of the project properties you can set Major, Minor, and Revision values.

Summary

Error handling, debugging, and delivering your application are the last three steps in ensuring your application is primed and ready for delivery. While they may not be the most exciting part of the application development process, they are crucial to ensuring that your application will be successful and easy to use and install.

Take time to explore and play with the error, debugging, and deployment tools. With a little familiarity and practice, you will be able to improve your applications and ensure the best experience for users, from installation to use.

What's Next

In the next part of the book, we will take a look at building client/server applications—one of the primary strengths of Visual Basic. We will review all aspects of client/server development, including building multitier applications covering the user interface to the back-end database and everything in between. Many of the new tools in the VB development environment will enhance and speed up client/server development.

The Complete Reference

Visual
Basic 6

Part III

Client/Server Development

One of the great strengths of Visual Basic is the ability to build applications into multiple "partitions." Client/Server and multitier application development is a powerful paradigm for building enterprise-level applications. Visual Basic supports this model with the ability to build both server side and client side applications that integrate across a network. And, Visual Basic's powerful data access capabilities integrate in the "third tier," data access. In this part we will explore multitier development by building an enterprise-level project tracking application.

Chapter 10

Building Multitier
Applications

One of Visual Basic's primary strengths is the way it lets you build applications that can span your network, from the server to the client and everything in between. In this part of the book, we are going to explore how to utilize all the tools in Visual Basic to build great applications.

There are three core pieces to our n-tier development model. The first is the piece we have all seen—the user interface. This is what users will see as their interface to the application, which may be distributed to multiple servers on a disparate network. The second piece is made up of the classes that define the business logic of the application. For example, in our sports card project in Part I, that would be the classes that encapsulated the player, team, and sports card. Those classes could be deployed on servers and accessed from the client instead of being deployed in the same project. That way, if you need to update the business logic, you don't necessarily have to redeploy the user interface.

The last piece is the database itself. Typically, this will be deployed on a database server that is dedicated to this purpose. In the business logic layer, you will need to encapsulate the data interface to hide the data access from the business logic.

The "n" in n-tier means that you can partition your project across multiple servers and multiple applications. The user interface resides on one tier, the business objects can reside on many tiers, and the database is on a data tier. If your application is being deployed in a small business with a few people, or in a small group, all three tiers might be on one server. If you are in a megacorporation that is going to have widespread access to the application, the application may need to be deployed across many servers. This can be the same for Internet applications, but in that case the client is across the Internet or intranet, not on the same network.

Building and Deploying a Project Tracking System

In this part of the book, we are going to build a sample project tracking system. In doing so, we will explore building and deploying an object model, building business objects, defining and interfacing with a database, and much, much more.

Design Steps for Building the System

The n-tier design process can follow eight common steps for design. But keep in mind that each step will be a work in progress and may need to be revisited while the system is being developed. Following are the steps:

1. Design the top-level object model for the system.

2. Design the database structure that will hold the persistent data from the object model.

3. Design appropriate stored procedures in the database to perform the basic functions required to add, update, and delete data from the data structure.

4. Implement the database in a data environment in Visual Basic.

5. Design a prototype user interface for the system.

6. Implement the functionality of the system. Note that this may include appropriate reports.

7. Test and update the system.

8. Deploy the system.

The idea is to define the structure of your application, including the object model and data structure, in the first four steps. Certainly, you will not get it 100 percent correct up front, and it may require modifications and tweaks. But you should begin the foundation of your project up front. Following that, you begin to implement the first tier of the application—the user interface. That will serve to "cement" the functionality into a visible form. From that interface design, you may have some changes to both the object and database models.

Once you have the foundation and interface laid out, you are ready to begin implementing functionality in the system. The key thing to keep in mind here is that the object model and database may be deployed on different servers. You will want to be sure and partition any data access away from your user interface.

Once you have the functionality in place, you will certainly need to go through a series of debug testing, user testing, and so on. Once that is done, you are ready for deployment. In Chapter 16, we will review how you deploy the different pieces of your application to the different logical tiers.

As we will see in this chapter and the next three chapters, the Visual Basic development environment is rich in providing support for the development process outlined above. Certainly, the Class Builder tool can be helpful in defining the object model. The data environment provides a powerful and encapsulated interface into the database. Of course, we will utilize the familiar form design tools and language to implement the functionality. And finally, we can break our application into logical units using the different application types and then deploy with the Package and Deployment wizard.

Defining the Object Model

In Part I we defined an object model for sports cards. Now we are going to need an object model for tracking projects. Once we have that, we will work on the user interface tier in the next chapter. That will be followed by database and business object building in Chapter 12. Finally, we will deploy our tiers in standard EXEs and ActiveX EXEs, and we will implement an installation process.

Our project tracking system will focus on a programming development project. The system will have developers, tasks, roles, and so on. The key elements include projects, tasks, developers, and roles (for the developers). The projects will have multiple tasks for each project. And each task can have multiple developers assigned to the tasks. The developers on each task will fill a role. On some tasks they may be a database administrator, on other tasks they may be a project manager, and on another, a developer. The following illustration outlines the object diagram for the project tracking system.

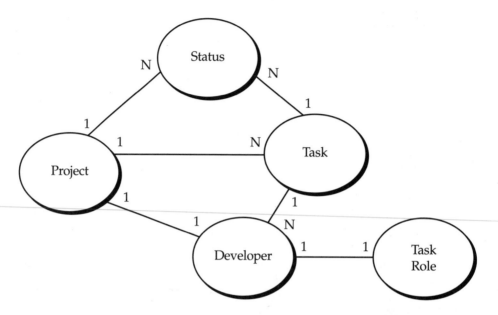

As mentioned, we have our project object, task object, developer object, and task role object. From the diagram, we can see that there are multiple tasks for each project, multiple developers for each task, and one task role for each developer, per task. One additional object is status. Status will be set for a given task or project and will be time based. So a task, in its life cycle from start to finish, may have any number of status settings. By keeping them in a separate object, we can see the status history of a project or task.

These basic objects will define our business logic structure and the database behind it. Next we will define the methods and properties needed for each object. Once we have that, we will define our classes.

Let's first take a look at the project class. We are going to need the properties shown in Table 10-1. The properties are fairly self-explanatory and combine the basic information you would want to know about a project. Appropriate methods will be defined for managing the projects as we develop the functionality of the project in later chapters.

Note   *As we go through the development cycle on this project, we may find that we need more properties and methods than defined in this chapter. The goal is to build the primary class interfaces so we can begin designing the user interface, database, and business logic.*

Property	Description
Project Name	Name of the project.
Project Description	Description of the project.
Project Start Date	Overall starting date for the project.
Project End Date	Targeted end date of the project.
Project Manager	Developer assigned as the project manager. Note this may in fact be an ID pointing to the developer class, which identifies the developer who is the project manager.
Percent Complete	Percentage of the project that is complete.
Count Task	Number of tasks assigned to the project.
Project ID	ID of the project.
Task Collection	Collection of tasks for the project.
Status	Status of the project.

Table 10-1.   *Properties of the Project Class*

Next let's take a look at the task object. Table 10-2 outlines the basic properties for defining our project tasks. Again, the task properties are fairly typical for describing a task of a project. Note that both the task ID and project ID will actually be defined by database fields. Of course, the rest of the data will ultimately be stored in a database.

The next class is for the developer. We need to be able to define basic data about a developer. Developers will be assigned to various aspects of the project, including project manager. Table 10-3 defines the properties for the developer object.

Property	Description
Developer Count	Number of developers assigned to the task.
End Date	End date of the task.
Hours Completed	Number of hours completed on the task.
Task ID	ID of the task.
Projected End Date	Projected end date of the task.
Projected Hours	Number of projected hours for the task.
Start Date	Start date of the task.
Status	Status of the task.
Task Name	Name of the task.
Task Notes	Notes on the task.

Table 10-2.   *Properties of the Task Object*

Property	Description
First Name	Developer's first name.
Last Name	Developer's last name.
Developer ID	ID of the developer.
Role	The role the developer plays in the task.
Task Hours	Number of hours spent on the task.

Table 10-3. *Properties of the Developer Object*

Certainly, we could add quite a few more properties to define a developer. For example, we may want to define the hourly rate paid for determining labor cost on a project. We could add other information such as strengths or a description. Of course, some of this data would need to be protected from certain application users.

The next object is the task role. We need to define the different roles a developer can have in the project. Table 10-4 defines the properties for the object. As with the other objects, the role ID will be database driven. We also define a description of the role and a role name.

That defines our four primary objects for the system. We will in fact add one more, called "projects." The projects object will simply be a convenient way of encapsulating a collection of objects in a Visual Basic class. We may wish to store summary project data such as total cost, general notes, and so on.

Building Our Class Templates

The next step is to define a series of classes for our Visual Basic project. Before we do that, start a new project. Set the project name to be "ProjectTrack" and the application title to "Project Track." We could use the Class Builder utility, but unfortunately, it will not allow us to easily define hierarchies of class collections. If you think about it, the project class has a collection of tasks, which in turn has a collection of developers. Instead, we will need to utilize collection management code to build our collection relationships. Let's start at the bottom of the hierarchy with the developer class.

Property	Description
Description	Description of the task role.
Role Name	Name of the role.
Role ID	ID of the role.

Table 10-4. *Properties of the Task Role Object*

The first section contains the general declarations for the class. The key will be the identifying key for the collection of developers assigned to a class. Our local variables define the properties.

```
'  Key for the task class that has a developer collection
Public Key As String


'  Local variables
Private mvarFirstName As String 'local copy
Private mvarLastName As String 'local copy
Private mvarRole As String 'local copy
Private mvarTaskHours As Double 'local copy
Private mvarIDDeveloper As Integer 'local copy
```

The next section contains the property declarations for each of our class properties. Each has the appropriate Let and Get statements. These will be used as we begin to develop the program for validating data and the additional logic based on property settings.

```
'  Sets the id of the developer
Public Property Let idDeveloper(ByVal vData As Integer)
   '  Set the local variable
   mvarIDDeveloper = vData
End Property


'  Retrieve the developer id
Public Property Get idDeveloper() As Integer
   idDeveloper = mvarIDDeveloper
End Property


'  Set and retrieve the role
Public Property Let Role(ByVal vData As String)
   mvarRole = vData
End Property

Public Property Get Role() As String
   Role = mvarRole
End Property


'  Set and retrieve the task hours
Public Property Let TaskHours(ByVal vData As Double)
   mvarTaskHours = vData
End Property
```

```
Public Property Get TaskHours() As Double
    TaskHours = mvarTaskHours
End Property

'  Set and retrieve the last name
Public Property Let LastName(ByVal vData As String)
    mvarLastName = vData
End Property

Public Property Get LastName() As String
    LastName = mvarLastName
End Property

'  Set and retrieve the first name
Public Property Let FirstName(ByVal vData As String)
    mvarFirstName = vData
End Property

Public Property Get FirstName() As String
    FirstName = mvarFirstName
End Property
```

Our next class is the task class. This class defines the properties as outlined in Table 10-2. It also defines the properties and methods necessary for managing an assigned collection of developers for the class.

As with the developer class, we define a key for managing a collection of tasks assigned to a project. We also define a collection, mColDeveloper. This collection will have a series of developer classes defined for it. These will be the developers assigned to the task. Following that are our local variables for storing the class property values.

```
'local variable to hold collection
Private mColDeveloper As Collection

'  Public key for the collection of tasks in the project class
Public Key As String

'  Local property variables
Private mvarStatus As String 'local copy
Private mvarTaskName As String 'local copy
```

```
Private mvarStartDate As Date 'local copy
Private mvarProjectedEndDate As Date 'local copy
Private mvarEndDate As Date 'local copy
Private mvarProjectedHours As Integer 'local copy
Private mvarHoursCompleted As Integer 'local copy
Private mvarTaskNotes As String 'local copy
Private mvarIDTask As Integer 'local copy
```

Next we define the property statements for the class. Each has the appropriate Let and Get statements that set and retrieve the local property variables. These will be used for validating property values and taking appropriate additional actions when a property is set.

```
'  Set and retrieve the task id
Public Property Let idTask(ByVal vData As Integer)
    mvarIDTask = vData
End Property

Public Property Get idTask() As Integer
    idTask = mvarIDTask
End Property

'  Set and retrieve the status
Public Property Let status(ByVal vData As String)
    mvarStatus = vData
End Property

Public Property Get status() As String
    status = mvarStatus
End Property

'  Set and retrieve the hours complete
Public Property Let HoursCompleted(ByVal vData As Integer)
    mvarHoursCompleted = vData
End Property

Public Property Get HoursCompleted() As Integer
    HoursCompleted = mvarHoursCompleted
End Property
```

```
'  Set and retrieve the projected hours
Public Property Let ProjectedHours(ByVal vData As Integer)
    mvarProjectedHours = vData
End Property

Public Property Get ProjectedHours() As Integer
    ProjectedHours = mvarProjectedHours
End Property

'  Set and retrieve the end date
Public Property Let EndDate(ByVal vData As Date)
    mvarEndDate = vData
End Property

Public Property Get EndDate() As Date
    EndDate = mvarEndDate
End Property

'  Set and retrieve the projected end date
Public Property Let ProjectedEndDate(ByVal vData As Date)
    mvarProjectedEndDate = vData
End Property

Public Property Get ProjectedEndDate() As Date
    ProjectedEndDate = mvarProjectedEndDate
End Property

'  Set and retrieve the start date
Public Property Let StartDate(ByVal vData As Date)
    mvarStartDate = vData
End Property

Public Property Get StartDate() As Date
    StartDate = mvarStartDate
End Property

'  Set and retrieve the task notes
Public Property Let TaskNotes(ByVal vData As String)
    mvarTaskNotes = vData
End Property
```

```
Public Property Get TaskNotes() As String
    TaskNotes = mvarTaskNotes
End Property

'  Set and retrieve the task name
Public Property Let TaskName(ByVal vData As String)
    mvarTaskName = vData
End Property

Public Property Get TaskName() As String
    TaskName = mvarTaskName
End Property
```

The AddDeveloper function is the first method for our class. It will add another developer class to our collection of developers. The key or ID for the new developer is passed in. Once we have that, a new developer class is created. The key property for the developer class is set, and the class is added to the collection.

```
'  Add a developer to the task
Public Function AddDeveloper(Key As String, Optional sKey As
String) As Developer

'  create a new object
Dim objNewMember As Developer
Set objNewMember = New Developer

'  set the properties passed into the method
objNewMember.Key = Key

'  Set the key
If Len(sKey) = 0 Then
    mColDeveloper.Add objNewMember
Else
    mColDeveloper.Add objNewMember, sKey
End If

'  Return the object created
Set AddDeveloper = objNewMember
Set objNewMember = Nothing

End Function
```

The ItemDeveloper property will return a developer class based on the index into the developers collection for the task. This is the method you will want to use to reference developers assigned to a task.

```
Public Property Get ItemDeveloper(vntIndexKey As Variant) As _
Developer
    'used when referencing an element in the collection
    'vntIndexKey contains either the Index or Key to the
    'collection,
    'this is why it is declared as a Variant
    'Syntax: Set foo = x.Item(xyz) or Set foo = x.Item(5)
    Set ItemDeveloper = mColDeveloper(vntIndexKey)
End Property
```

The CountDeveloper property defines the number of developers assigned to the task.

```
Public Property Get CountDeveloper() As Long
    'used when retrieving the number of elements in the
    'collection. Syntax: Debug.Print x.Count
    CountDeveloper = mColDeveloper.Count
End Property
```

The RemoveDeveloper method of the class will remove a developer from the collection of developers assigned to the task.

```
Public Sub RemoveDeveloper(vntIndexKey As Variant)
    'used when removing an element from the collection
    'vntIndexKey contains either the Index or Key, which is why
    'it is declared as a Variant
    'Syntax: x.Remove(xyz)
    mColDeveloper.Remove vntIndexKey
End Sub
```

The NewEnumDeveloper property allows you to easily enumerate the developer collection.

```
Public Property Get NewEnumDeveloper() As Iunknown
    'this property allows you to enumerate
    'this collection with the For...Each syntax
    Set NewEnumDeveloper = mColDeveloper.[_NewEnum]
End Property
```

When the class is initialized and terminated, the developer collection is created and destroyed.

```
Private Sub Class_Initialize()
    'creates the collection when this class is created
    Set mColDeveloper = New Collection
End Sub

Private Sub Class_Terminate()
    'destroys collection when this class is terminated
    Set mColDeveloper = Nothing
End Sub
```

The task class will provide and track task-related data for projects. There will be multiple tasks assigned to a project, with various developers assigned to each task. Note that the same developer can be assigned to different tasks in the same project and have the same or different roles.

Next we will move to the project class. The project class will contain a collection of tasks assigned to the project. And our project class is in turn going to be part of a collection class called projects, which will hold all the projects in the system.

The key property is the key for the projects class collection. Following that is the collection for the tasks assigned to the project. And we then have the standard member property variables for holding property data for the class. One property is a developer class that will hold the manager data for the project.

```
'   Public key for the projects class which has
'   a collection of projects
Public Key As String

'   Local variable to hold task collection
Private mColTask As Collection

'local variable(s) to hold property value(s)
Private mvarProjectName As String 'local copy
Private mvarStartDate As Date 'local copy
Private mvarDescription As String 'local copy
Private mvarEndDate As String 'local copy
Private mvarPercentComplete As Double 'local copy
Public Manager As New Developer   'local copy
Private mvarIDProject As Integer 'local copy
Private mvarIDManager As Integer 'local copy
Private mvarStatus As String 'local copy
```

CLIENT/SERVER
DEVELOPMENT

Next we define the property declarations for the class. Each has the appropriate Let and Get statements that define the property. As the properties are set, we can do validation and additional processing.

```
'  Sets and retrieves the id of the project
Public Property Let idproject(ByVal vData As Integer)
    mvarIDProject = vData
End Property

Public Property Get idproject() As Integer
    idproject = mvarIDProject
End Property

'  Sets  and retrieves the project manager
Public Property Let idManager(ByVal vData As Integer)
    mvarIDManager = vData
End Property

Public Property Get idManager() As Integer
    idManager = mvarIDManager
End Property

'  Sets and retrieves the percent complete
Public Property Let PercentComplete(ByVal vData As Double)
    mvarPercentComplete = vData
End Property

Public Property Get PercentComplete() As Double
    PercentComplete = mvarPercentComplete
End Property

'  Sets and retrieves the end date
Public Property Let EndDate(ByVal vData As String)
    mvarEndDate = vData
End Property

Public Property Get EndDate() As String
    EndDate = mvarEndDate
End Property
```

```
'  Sets and retrieves the status
Public Property Let status(ByVal vData As String)
    mvarStatus = vData
End Property

Public Property Get status() As String
    status = mvarStatus
End Property

'  Sets and retrieves the description
Public Property Let Description(ByVal vData As String)
    mvarDescription = vData
End Property

Public Property Get Description() As String
    Description = mvarDescription
End Property

'  Sets and retrieves the start date
Public Property Let StartDate(ByVal vData As Date)
    mvarStartDate = vData
End Property

Public Property Get StartDate() As Date
    StartDate = mvarStartDate
End Property

'  Sets and retrieves the project name
Public Property Let ProjectName(ByVal vData As String)
    mvarProjectName = vData
End Property

Public Property Get ProjectName() As String
    ProjectName = mvarProjectName
End Property
```

The AddTask method of the class is similar to the AddDeveloper method for the task class. This method will add another task to the collection of tasks assigned to the project. The class is created, the key for the item in the collection is set, and the task is added to the collection.

```
' Add a task to the collection of tasks for the project
Public Function AddTask(Key As String, Optional sKey As String) As _
Task
    'create a new task object
    Dim objNewMember As Task
    Set objNewMember = New Task

    'set the properties passed into the method
    objNewMember.Key = Key

    ' Set the key
    If Len(sKey) = 0 Then
        mColTask.Add objNewMember
    Else
        mColTask.Add objNewMember, sKey
    End If

    'return the object created
    Set AddTask = objNewMember
    Set objNewMember = Nothing

End Function
```

The ItemTask property returns a task object relating to the key passed into the property.

```
Public Property Get ItemTask(vntIndexKey As Variant) As Task
    'used when referencing an element in the collection
    'vntIndexKey contains either the Index or Key to the
    'collection,
    'this is why it is declared as a Variant
    'Syntax: Set foo = x.Item(xyz) or Set foo = x.Item(5)
  Set ItemTask = mColTask(vntIndexKey)
End Property
```

The CountTask property returns the number of tasks assigned to the project.

```
Public Property Get CountTask() As Long
    'used when retrieving the number of elements in the
    'collection. Syntax: Debug.Print x.Count
    CountTask = mColTask.Count
End Property
```

The RemoveTask subroutine will remove the specified task from the collection of tasks.

```
Public Sub RemoveTask(vntIndexKey As Variant)
    'used when removing an element from the collection
    'vntIndexKey contains either the Index or Key, which is why
    'it is declared as a Variant
    'Syntax: x.Remove(xyz)
    mColTask.Remove vntIndexKey
End Sub
```

The NewEnumTask property allows you to easily enumerate the task collection.

```
Public Property Get NewEnumTask() As Iunknown
    'this property allows you to enumerate
    'this collection with the For...Each syntax
    Set NewEnumTask = mColTask.[_NewEnum]
End Property
```

Finally, the initialize and terminate methods of the class take care of creating and destroying the task collection.

```
Private Sub Class_Initialize()
    'creates the collection when this class is created
    Set mColTask = New Collection
End Sub

Private Sub Class_Terminate()
    'destroys collection when this class is terminated
    Set mColTask = Nothing
End Sub
```

That is it for the project class. Next we have our projects class, which will hold a collection of projects. The only private property variable is mCol, which will hold our collection of project classes. You will find that the rest of the methods and properties directly relate to the same class collection management properties and methods we have seen in the previous classes. We will be able to add and remove projects, get the project count, enumerate the collection, and so on.

> **Note**
>
> *We will not be adding much more functionality to this class in this section. This class is primarily being utilized as a logical method for organizing all the projects in the system. But you may wish to consider some aggregate functionality for the class. For example, you may want to do some overall project loading calculations such as tracking open time slots, number of hours allocated, and so on.*

```vb
'  Local variable to hold collection
Private mCol As Collection
'  Add a new project
Public Function Add(Key As String, Optional sKey As String) As _
Project

'  Create a new object
Dim objNewMember As Project
Set objNewMember = New Project

'set the properties passed into the method
objNewMember.Key = Key

'  Set the key
If Len(sKey) = 0 Then
    mCol.Add objNewMember
Else
    mCol.Add objNewMember, sKey
End If

'  return the object created
Set Add = objNewMember
Set objNewMember = Nothing

End Function

Public Property Get Item(vntIndexKey As Variant) As Project
    'used when referencing an element in the collection
    'vntIndexKey contains either the Index or Key to the
    'collection,
    'this is why it is declared as a Variant
    'Syntax: Set foo = x.Item(xyz) or Set foo = x.Item(5)
    Set Item = mCol(vntIndexKey)
End Property
```

```
Public Property Get Count() As Long
    'used when retrieving the number of elements in the
    'collection. Syntax: Debug.Print x.Count
    Count = mCol.Count
End Property

Public Sub Remove(vntIndexKey As Variant)
    'used when removing an element from the collection
    'vntIndexKey contains either the Index or Key, which is why
    'it is declared as a Variant
    'Syntax: x.Remove(xyz)
    mCol.Remove vntIndexKey
End Sub

Public Property Get NewEnum() As Iunknown
    'this property allows you to enumerate
    'this collection with the For...Each syntax
    Set NewEnum = mCol.[_NewEnum]
End Property

Private Sub Class_Initialize()

'  creates the collection when this class is created
Set mCol = New Collection

End Sub

Private Sub Class_Terminate()
    'destroys collection when this class is terminated
    Set mCol = Nothing
End Sub
```

The TaskRole class is fairly simple. We don't have any particular functionality other than to store the role name, description, and role ID properties. The appropriate Let and Get declarations are made, with private member variables declared.

```
'  Local property variables
Private mvarRoleName As String 'local copy
Private mvarDescription As Variant 'local copy
Private mvarIDTaskRole As Integer 'local copy
```

```
'  Set and retrieve the ID of the task role
Public Property Let idTaskRole(ByVal vData As Integer)
    mvarIDTaskRole = vData
End Property

Public Property Get idTaskRole() As Integer
    idTaskRole = mvarIDTaskRole
End Property

'  Set and retrieve the description
Public Property Let Description(ByVal vData As Variant)
    mvarDescription = vData
End Property

Public Property Get Description() As Variant
    Description = mvarDescription
End Property

'  Set and retrieve the role name
Public Property Let RoleName(ByVal vData As String)
    mvarRoleName = vData
End Property

Public Property Get RoleName() As String
    RoleName = mvarRoleName
End Property
```

That defines the base structure for our classes. Keep in mind this is by no means all of the functionality that our classes will encapsulate. In the next several chapters, we will build additional methods and some properties for supporting the overall functionality of the application. Next we need to define the core database structure for the application.

Designing the Database

All of the properties in our classes will need to be embodied in an appropriate database structure. We will need a relational structure that will in turn encapsulate the different relational structures for the project tracking system.

Building the Table Structure

First we need to define the tables that will store the persistent data from our object model. The following illustration shows the database structure for the project tracking system.

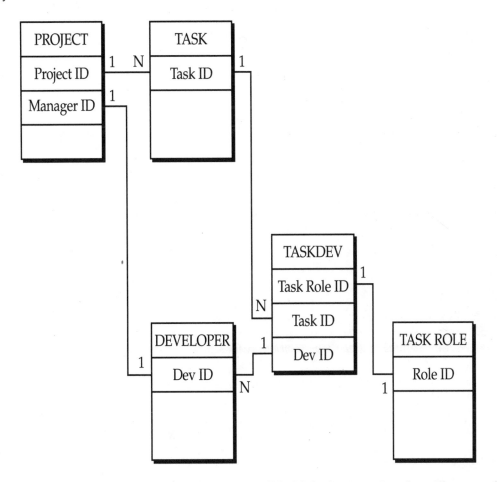

Our first table is the Project table, which will hold the basic project data. The second table is the Task table. We can have multiple tasks assigned to each project. The relational identifier is the project ID, which will be stored in the Task table.

Next we have a table called TaskDev. TaskDev will track the developers assigned to the task. We could store the developer data in each task, but that would be inefficient and would not produce a database that could be easily maintained if a developer's name or pertinent data has changed. With the TaskDev table, we can assign a developer to multiple tasks as well.

Each TaskDev row will contain identifiers indicating the developer and his or her role in the task. The TaskDev table stores the ID of the task. The last two tables are the TaskRole and Developer tables. These are lookup tables of developers and task roles.

You will note that the Project table stores a Manager ID field. We can assign one of the developers to be the project manager. The ID of the developer is stored in the Project table as a lookup.

The SQL code for the tables and appropriate properties needs to be created. The first table, Project, is as follows:

```
/****** Object:  Table dbo.Project ******/
CREATE TABLE dbo.Project (
    idProject int IDENTITY (1, 1) NOT NULL ,
    txtDescription text NULL ,
    dtEndDate datetime NULL ,
    idManager int NULL ,
    dtStartDate datetime NULL ,
    chrProjectName varchar (255) NULL ,
    fltPercentComplete float NULL ,
    intArchived tinyint NULL ,
    txtStatus text NULL
)
GO
```

Tip   *To create the tables in your SQL database, simply run the scripts in a query window. Be sure you have a database device and database created for the project tracking system. The scripts will then create the appropriate tables.*

The idProject property is the primary key for the table. It is also an identity column, which means it will auto-increment with every insert into the table. After that, we have the properties as defined above for our project class object.

The next table, Task, defines the data to be stored for the tasks assigned to a project.

```
/****** Object:  Table dbo.Task ******/
CREATE TABLE dbo.Task (
    idTask int IDENTITY (1, 1) NOT NULL ,
    dtEndDate datetime NULL ,
    fltHoursComplete float NULL ,
    dtProjectedEndDate datetime NULL ,
    fltProjectedHours float NULL ,
    dtStartDate datetime NULL ,
    chrTaskName varchar (255) NULL ,
```

```
    txtTaskNotes text NULL ,
    idProject int NULL ,
    txtStatus text NULL
)
GO
```

The task ID is also an identity column and a primary key for the table. Note that the ID of the project is stored in the table to make the relational link to the Project table. Next is the SQL code for the TaskDev table.

```
/****** Object:   Table dbo.TaskDev ******/
CREATE TABLE dbo.TaskDev (
    idDeveloper int NULL ,
    idTask int NULL ,
    idRole int NULL ,
    fltHours float NULL
)
GO
```

The only nonrelational property we are storing in the TaskDev table is the number of hours the assigned developer has on the task. The idRole, idTask, and idDeveloper fields all relate to the appropriate table. The primary key is the combination of the idTask and idDeveloper fields.

The Developer table defines the first and last names of the developer. Included is a unique identifier, idDeveloper, that is an identity column and a primary key.

```
/****** Object:   Table dbo.Developer ******/
CREATE TABLE dbo.Developer (
    idDeveloper int IDENTITY (1, 1) NOT NULL ,
    chrFirstName varchar (255) NULL ,
    chrLastName varchar (255) NULL
)
GO
```

Finally, we have the TaskRole table, which defines task roles for the developers. A description and name is provided. And, as with all the tables, an identity column is provided as a primary key for the table.

```
/****** Object:  Table dbo.TaskRole ******/
CREATE TABLE dbo.TaskRole (
    idTaskRole int IDENTITY (1, 1) NOT NULL ,
    txtDescription text NULL ,
    chrRoleName varchar (255) NULL
)
GO
```

Now that we have our tables defined, we are going to need stored procedures to interface with the database. Part of the strategy of building n-tier applications is to hide the underlying database structure from our class business objects.

 You will want to seed the Developer and TaskRole tables with appropriate test data.

Building Stored Procedures

Once the stored procedures are built, we can encapsulate the code into a data environment in our application. We are going to need a series of stored procedures for performing appropriate functions on our database. Table 10-5 outlines each of the procedures.

Stored Procedure	Description
sp_AddNewProject	Adds a new project and returns the new project ID.
sp_AddNewTask	Adds a new task and returns the new task ID.
sp_DeleteProject	Deletes a project.
sp_DeleteTask	Deletes a task.
sp_DeleteTaskDeveloper	Deletes a developer assigned to a task.
sp_RetrieveActiveProjects	Retrieves active projects.
sp_RetrieveDeveloper	Retrieves a developer by ID.
sp_RetrieveDevelopers	Retrieves all developers.
sp_RetrieveInactiveProjects	Retrieves inactive projects.
sp_RetrieveProject	Retrieves projects.
sp_RetrieveTask	Retrieves a task by task ID.
sp_RetrieveTaskByProject	Retrieves a task by project.
sp_RetrieveTaskDevelopers	Retrieves a task's developers.

Table 10-5. *Stored Procedures for the Project Tracking Database*

Stored Procedure	Description
sp_UpdateProject	Updates a project.
sp_UpdateTask	Updates a task.
sp_RetrieveTaskRoles	Retrieves all task roles.
sp_RetrieveTaskRole	Retrieves a task role by ID.
sp_DeleteTaskDevelopers	Deletes a task's developers.
sp_UpdateTaskDev	Updates a task developer.
sp_AssignTaskDeveloper	Assigns a developer to a task.

Table 10-5. *Stored Procedures for the Project Tracking Database* (continued)

CLIENT/SERVER
DEVELOPMENT

Let's review the stored procedures code. Our first procedure adds a new project. In this case the project name is passed in, and we use the SQL Server @@identity global variable to return the new idProject value for the inserted row.

Note   *If you are not using Microsoft SQL Server 6.5, you may need to update some of the stored procedures to work with your DBMS.*

```
/****** Object:  Stored Procedure dbo.sp_AddNewProject ******/
CREATE PROCEDURE sp_AddNewProject

@chrProjectName varchar(255)

AS

insert into project(chrProjectName)
values(@chrProjectName)

select idProject = @@identity

GO
```

The AddNewTask stored procedure is very similar to AddNewProject. In this case though, we need to pass in the task name as well as the ID of the project to which the task is assigned. The stored procedure returns the ID of the new task using the @@identity global variable.

```
/****** Object:  Stored Procedure dbo.sp_AddNewTask ******/
CREATE PROCEDURE sp_AddNewTask
@chrTaskName varchar(255),
@idProject integer

AS

insert into task(chrTaskName, idProject)
values(@chrTaskName, @idProject)

select idTask = @@identity
GO
```

The AssignTaskDeveloper stored procedure will link a task with a developer and the developer's role. The ID of the task is passed in along with the ID of the developer and the ID of the role. Also, the number of initial hours the developer has worked on the task is passed in. The ID of the new TaskDev row is returned using the @@identity global variable.

```
/****** Object:  Stored Procedure dbo.sp_AssignTaskDeveloper
******/
CREATE PROCEDURE sp_AssignTaskDeveloper

@idTask integer,
@idDeveloper integer,
@idRole integer,
@fltHours float

AS

insert into TaskDev(idTask, idDeveloper, idRole, fltHours)
values(@idTask, @idDeveloper, @idRole, @fltHours)
GO
```

The DeleteProject stored procedure simply deletes the project from the Project table. The ID of the project is passed in.

Note *If we delete a project, we logically want to delete any tasks assigned to the project as well as any developers assigned to the project in the TaskDev table. In this case we could implement a cascading delete in the stored procedure to remove assigned tasks and developers. Instead, as will be demonstrated in Chapter 15, we have implemented the cascading delete in the class structure of the project. It could logically be implemented either way. For performance considerations, you may wish to place it in the stored procedure, but keep in mind the objects in the project will also need to be properly updated.*

```
/****** Object:  Stored Procedure dbo.sp_DeleteProject ******/
CREATE PROCEDURE sp_DeleteProject

@idProject integer

AS

delete from Project where idProject = @idProject
GO
```

The DeleteTask stored procedure deletes the appropriate rows from the Task table based on the ID of the task.

```
/****** Object:  Stored Procedure dbo.sp_DeleteTask ******/
CREATE PROCEDURE sp_DeleteTask

@idTask integer

AS

delete from task where idTask = @idTask
GO
```

The DeleteTaskDeveloper stored procedure will delete an assigned developer from a task. In order to do that, we will pass in the id of the task and the id of the developer.

```
/****** Object:  Stored Procedure dbo.sp_DeleteTaskDeveloper
******/
CREATE PROCEDURE sp_DeleteTaskDeveloper

@idTask integer,
@idDeveloper integer
```

CLIENT/SERVER
DEVELOPMENT

```
AS

delete from TaskDev where idTask = @idTask and idDeveloper =
@idDeveloper
GO
```

In the DeleteTaskDevelopers stored procedure, the developers assigned to a given task (defined by the ID) are deleted from the TaskDev table.

```
/****** Object:   Stored Procedure dbo.sp_DeleteTaskDevelopers
******/
CREATE PROCEDURE sp_DeleteTaskDevelopers

@idTask integer

AS

delete from taskdev where idTask = @idTask
GO
```

RetrieveActiveProjects returns all projects where the intArchived flag is 0.

Note

In the prototype system we are developing, the ability to archive projects will not be implemented. But you could easily do this by setting the intArchived flag in the database to 1. This will be useful for implementing a project system to allow for management of live and inactive projects.

```
/****** Object:   Stored Procedure dbo.sp_RetrieveActiveProjects
******/
CREATE PROCEDURE sp_RetrieveActiveProjects

 AS

select * from project where intarchived = 0
GO
```

In the RetrieveDeveloper stored procedure, all the developer data is returned for a given developer, designated by the ID of the developer.

```
/****** Object:  Stored Procedure dbo.sp_RetrieveDeveloper ******/
CREATE PROCEDURE sp_RetrieveDeveloper

@idDeveloper  integer

AS

select * from developer where idDeveloper = @idDeveloper
GO
```

The RetrieveDevelopers stored procedure returns all the developers in the database and orders them by first name.

```
/****** Object:  Stored Procedure dbo.sp_RetrieveDevelopers ******/
CREATE PROCEDURE sp_RetrieveDevelopers AS

select * from developer order by chrfirstname
GO
```

In RetrieveProject the project data is returned for a given project, which is designated by the ID passed into the stored procedure.

```
/****** Object:  Stored Procedure dbo.sp_RetrieveProject ******/
CREATE PROCEDURE sp_RetrieveProject

@idProject integer

 AS

select * from project where idProject = @idProject
GO
```

In RetrieveTask the task data is returned for a given task, which is designated by the ID passed into the stored procedure.

```
/****** Object:  Stored Procedure dbo.sp_RetrieveTask ******/
CREATE PROCEDURE sp_RetrieveTask

@idTask integer

AS

select * from task where idTask = @idTask
GO
```

CLIENT/SERVER DEVELOPMENT

RetrieveTaskByProject retrieves all tasks assigned to a given project. The ID of the project is passed in.

```
/****** Object:  Stored Procedure dbo.sp_RetrieveTaskByProject
******/
CREATE PROCEDURE sp_RetrieveTaskByProject

@idProject integer

AS

select * from task where idProject = @idProject
GO
```

The RetrieveTaskDevelopers table returns all developers assigned to a specific task. We have to join the TaskDev and TaskRole tables to return the role name and description along with the assigned developer. The ID of the task is passed in.

```
/****** Object:  Stored Procedure dbo.sp_RetrieveTaskDevelopers
******/
CREATE PROCEDURE sp_RetrieveTaskDevelopers

@idTask integer

as

select * from TaskDev, taskrole where taskdev.idTask =
    @idTask and taskdev.idrole = taskrole.idtaskrole
GO
```

In the RetrieveTaskRoles stored procedure, we return all the roles in the TaskRole table.

```
/****** Object:  Stored Procedure dbo.sp_RetrieveTaskRoles ******/
CREATE PROCEDURE sp_RetrieveTaskRoles AS

select * from taskrole
GO
```

The UpdateProject stored procedure will update all fields of the project designated by the ID of the project, which is passed in.

Tip *You could write SQL code to update only the appropriate fields based on what data is passed into the stored procedure. That would not require the Visual Basic code to pass in a value (other than NULL) for each parameter. This applies to both the UpdateProject and UpdateTask stored procedures.*

```
/****** Object:  Stored Procedure dbo.sp_UpdateProject ******/
CREATE PROCEDURE sp_UpdateProject

@idProject integer,
@txtDescription text,
@dtEndDate datetime,
@idManager integer,
@dtStartDate datetime,
@chrProjectName varchar(255),
@fltPercentComplete float,
@txtStatus text

AS

update project set

  txtDescription = @txtDescription,
  dtEnddate = @dtEndDate,
  idManager = @idManager,
  dtStartDate = @dtStartDate,
  chrProjectName = @chrProjectName,
  fltPercentComplete = @fltPercentComplete,
  txtStatus = @txtStatus

where

  idProject = @idProject
GO
```

The UpdateTask stored procedure will update all fields of the task designated by the ID of the task, which is passed in.

```
/****** Object:  Stored Procedure dbo.sp_UpdateTask ******/
CREATE PROCEDURE sp_UpdateTask

@idTask integer,
@dtEndDate datetime,
```

```
@fltHoursComplete float,
@dtProjectedEndDate datetime,
@fltProjectedHours float,
@dtStartDate datetime,
@chrTaskName varchar(255),
@txtTaskNotes text,
@txtStatus text

AS
update task set
  dtEndDate = @dtEndDate,
  fltHoursComplete = @fltHoursComplete,
  dtProjectedEndDate = @dtProjectedEndDate,
  fltProjectedHours = @fltProjectedHours,
  dtStartDate = @dtStartDate,
  chrTaskname = @chrTaskname,
  txtTaskNotes = @txtTaskNotes,
  txtStatus = @txtStatus

where

  idTask = @idTask
GO
```

In the UpdateTaskDev stored procedure, we update the TaskDev table with the new number of hours on the task for the specific developer. The IDs of the developer and task are passed in as well as the number of hours.

```
/****** Object:  Stored Procedure dbo.sp_UpdateTaskDev ******/
CREATE PROCEDURE sp_UpdateTaskDev

@idTask integer,
@idDeveloper integer,
@fltHours float

AS

update taskdev set
    fltHours = @fltHours
where
    idTask = @idTask and idDeveloper = @idDeveloper
GO
```

The RetrieveTaskRole stored procedure will return a specific role's data based on the ID of the role.

```
/****** Object:  Stored Procedure dbo.sp_RetrieveTaskRole ******/
CREATE PROCEDURE sp_retrievetaskrole

@idtaskrole integer

AS

select * from taskrole where idtaskrole = @idtaskrole
GO
```

Note *Why all the stored procedures? Why not implement the database functionality in a data environment or directly in our classes? As much as possible, we want to be able to hide the underlying database functionality from the business logic and the rest of the application. By implementing the basic database tools in stored procedures, we can later change the underlying database functionality with minimal disruption to Visual Basic code. In terms of maintenance and scalability of our application, this can provide extensive flexibility in our system.*

Now that we have our stored procedures and database structure in place, we are going to build a data environment in Visual Basic to encapsulate the database connectivity and functionality.

Building the Data Environment

To our project with the class shells defined, let's add a new data environment. Follow these steps:

1. Select the Project menu.

2. Select Add Data Environment on the Project menu.

3. Rename the data environment to "dbProjectTrack."

Next we need to set up our connection to the project tracking database created above. You will need to create an ODBC DSN called "ProjTrack" that points to your database server. Once that is done, we need to set up our connection as follows:

1. Select Connection1 in the data environment.

2. Rename the connection to "ProjectTrack."

3. Right-click on ProjectTrack and select Properties.

4. Select Microsoft OLE DB Provider for ODBC on the Provider tab.

5. Select the Connection tab.

6. In the "Use data source name" option, select your ProjTrack ODBC data source.

7. Enter the appropriate username and password.

8. Test the data connection.

Figure 10-1 shows the connection set up properly.

Our next step is to import the stored procedures we have created into our data environment. Fortunately, the data environment makes this easy by allowing us to import stored procedures. Follow these steps:

1. Right-click on the Commands option. This will open the connection to the database and display the Insert Stored Procedures dialog box, as shown in Figure 10-2.

2. Select the >> option to move all the stored procedures from the Available pane to the Add pane.

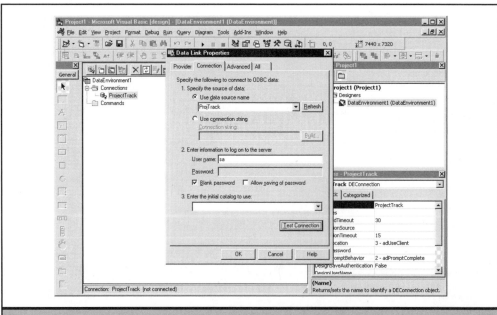

Figure 10-1. *ProjectTrack connection set up*

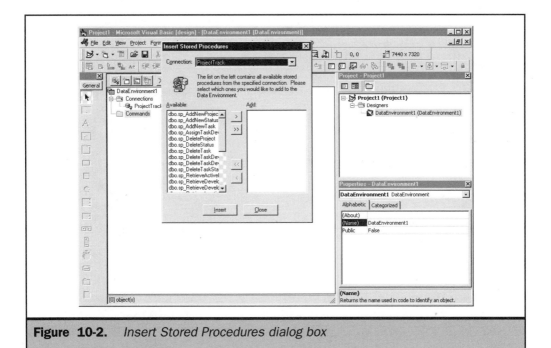

Figure 10-2.   *Insert Stored Procedures dialog box*

3. Click on the Insert button to insert the stored procedures into the data
   environment. Several dialog boxes will pop up and request that the stored
   procedure be executed. The data environment needs to do this before it can
   retrieve the fields that must be sent into the stored procedure and returned.

When you are done with these steps, the stored procedures will be inserted into the
data environment and ready for use. You will note that each stored procedure begins
with "dbo_sp_." For ease of readability in code, this has been removed from the names of
the stored procedures. Figure 10-3 shows the project with the data environment set up.

The last step is to automatically open and close our connection when the data
environment is created. Double-click on the ProjectTrack connection. When you do so,
the Code window for the data environment is brought up. The following is the
connection code for the initialize event:

```
Private Sub DataEnvironment_Initialize()

    ProjectTrack.Open "DSN=ProjTrack;UID=sa;PWD=;"

End Sub
```

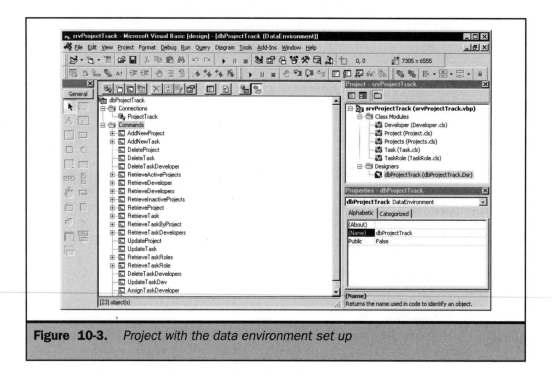

Figure 10-3. *Project with the data environment set up*

We will automatically open the connection when the data environment is created. The connection string indicates the DSN, user ID, and password. When the data environment is destroyed, the connection will be closed as follows:

```
Private Sub DataEnvironment_Terminate()

    ProjectTrack.Close

End Sub
```

With that, we have finished the design of the object structure and database for our project. This is the foundation upon which the entire application will be built. The classes will encompass the business logic in the application. The database will provide the persistent storage of the application. And the data environment will provide the connection between the two. If we decide to scale or change our database, we can change the data environment, keep the same stored procedure names and parameters, and the rest of the application does not have to change. At worst, the business logic will need minor updates and reinstallation.

Summary

In this chapter we have built the foundation of our project tracking system. That fulfills the first four steps of our eight steps to design the system. Certainly, the classes are going to need to be filled out with business logic. And we can add functionality to our database if need be and simply import it into the data designer.

What's Next

Now that we have the class structure and database structure defined for our application, we are ready to move to the next step, which is to design the user interface for the application. The user interface will be crucial to ensuring that our application is easy to use.

The Complete Reference

Visual
Basic 6

Chapter 11

Building the User Interface

The next step is to build the user interface for our project tracking system. This will define how the user interacts with the application and how our user interface must interface with the business logic. We could take many different approaches to implementing the interface. One method would be to define an MDI form and have two subforms, one for projects and one for tasks. The potential problem with this approach is that you will typically need to see both project and task information at the same time. Thus, the ability to tile and overlap the project and task window may not be very useful and perhaps annoying.

For our implementation, we are going to use one form for the interface. But the form will be divided into subframes using the frame control. The first frame will be for project data, and the second will be for task data. One thing to note is that task and project data must always be in sync. In other words, we don't want to have project A displayed while project B's tasks are showing.

Defining the Interface

We will build the interface in four steps. In the first step we will build the form and toolbar. The second step will be to design a project frame that will provide the interface for the project data. The third step is to build the task frame that will provide the interface for the task data. The final step will be to do some coding behind the interface to implement basic interface functionality.

Designing the Form

Let's start with the basic form. We will need a toolbar to provide necessary interface functionality. Our interface will have one coolbar with two bands. The first band will contain project- and program-related buttons. The second band will contain task-related buttons.

Table 11-1 outlines the form and coolbar properties. Also included is the image list control for defining the button images. The coolbar will contain two toolbars for each band.

Component/Property	Setting
Form	FrmProjects
Frame	FrmTasks
Caption	"Project Tasks"

Table 11-1.   *Objects and Properties for the Form and Toolbar*

Component/Property	Setting
Frame	FrmProjects
Caption	"Projects"
ImageList	ImgProject
Images	ListImage1 – ListImage5
CoolBar	CblProjectTrack
Align	1 'Align Top
BandCount	2
Child1	TblTask
NewRow1	0 'False
Toolbar	tblTask
Appearance	1
Style	1
ImageList	imgProject
NumButtons	3
Button1	
Caption	"Delete Task"
ToolTipText	"Delete Task"
ImageIndex	1
Button2	
Caption	"Save Task"
ToolTipText	"Save Task"
ImageIndex	2
Button3	
Caption	"New Task"
ToolTipText	"New Task"
ImageIndex	3
Child2	tblProject

CLIENT/SERVER DEVELOPMENT

Table 11-1. *Objects and Properties for the Form and Toolbar* (continued)

Component/Property	Setting
NewRow2	0 'False
Toolbar	tblTask
Appearance	1
Style	1
ImageList	imgProject
NumButtons	3
Button1	
Caption	"Exit"
ToolTipText	"Exit the Program"
ImageIndex	5
Button2	
Caption	"Delete"
ToolTipText	"Delete Project"
ImageIndex	1
Button3	
Caption	"Save"
ToolTipText	"Save Project"
ImageIndex	2
Button4	
Caption	"New"
ToolTipText	"New Project"
ImageIndex	3
Button5	
Caption	"Report"
ToolTipText	"Projects Report"
ImageIndex	4

Table 11-1. *Objects and Properties for the Form and Toolbar* (continued)

The image list buttons can be found in the \common\graphics\bitmaps\tlbr_w95 folder. For the project, we are defining the ability to exit the program, delete a task or project, save a task or project, start a new project or task, and show reports. We could add a menu bar if necessary, but our form is already going to be fairly large. And in fact, it should be sized to about 800×600 pixels to make everything fit. The toolbar functionality is fairly straightforward for the project. One option would be to implement a menu bar only and not the toolbar. That would save some screen real estate. If you do have to design for 640×480, the MDI form with subforms may be the best option.

When you save a project, you will also want to save any tasks that have been changed. This will be implemented when we code the project.

Figure 11-1 shows the form with the coolbar implemented with the image list.

Designing the Project Frame

The next step is to define the project frame. We need to build a facility to select any one of the projects in the system. A combo box listing the projects can be used for project

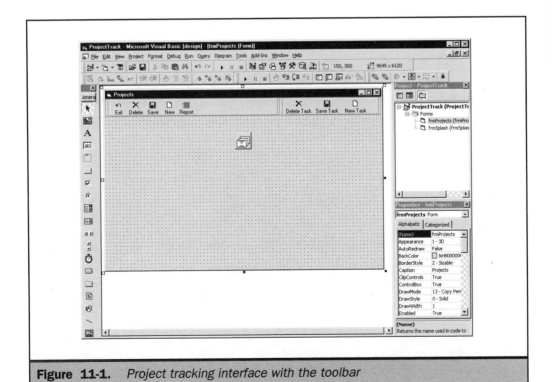

Figure 11-1.   *Project tracking interface with the toolbar*

selection. Then we will have a series of text boxes that will display the project properties. Table 11-2 defines the frame's objects and properties.

Component/Property	Setting
Frame	FrmProjects
Combo Box	CboProjects
Style	2 'Dropdown List
Text Box	txtStartDate
Text	''
Text Box	txtEndDate
Text	''
Text Box	txtProjectManager
Locked	-1 'True
Text Box	txtDescription
Text	''
Multi Line	-1 'True
Scroll Bars	2 'Vertical
Text Box	txtStatus
Text	''
Multi Line	-1 'True
Text Box	txtPercentComplete
Text	''
Combo Box	cboDevelopers
Style	2 'Dropdown List
Text Box	txtProjectName
Text	''
Label	lblNewManager

Table 11-2. *Objects and Properties for the Project Frame*

Component/Property	Setting
AutoSize	-1 'True
Caption	"Select New Manager"
Label	lblProjects
AutoSize	-1 'True
Caption	"Select Project"
Label	lblStartDate
AutoSize	-1 'True
Caption	"Start Date:"
Label	lblEndDate
AutoSize	-1 'True
Caption	"End Date:"
Label	lblProjectManager
AutoSize	-1 'True
Caption	"Project Manager:"
Label	lblDescription
AutoSize	-1 'True
Caption	"Description:"
Label	lblStatus
Caption	"Status:"
Label	lblPercentComplete
AutoSize	-1 'True
Caption	"% Complete:"
Label	lblProjectName
AutoSize	-1 'True
Caption	"Project Name:"

Table 11-2.   *Objects and Properties for the Project Frame* (continued)

One feature we will need to provide for users is the ability to select a new manager for the project. This is facilitated through the use of a drop-down combo box of developers. The currently assigned manager will be shown in a text box, and a new manager can be selected.

If the New project option is selected, all the fields on the project frame will be cleared. The delete option will do the same, but the project will be removed from the database. Figure 11-2 shows the project at design time with the project frame.

Designing the Task Frame

The task frame will pack in a lot of functionality. Not only do we need to be able to implement the basic task properties, but we also need to support assigning developers to the task. Table 11-3 outlines the objects and properties on the task frame.

As with the project frame, we have a select list combo box, which will allow us to quickly review the tasks assigned on the project. With each selection of a task, the text boxes for the task properties are cleared, including the developer data, and the new task data is loaded.

The developer section of the task frame will allow us to manage the developers, roles, and hours worked on the task. We can add, update, and delete developers. Note that the list of developers will show the developer's name, hours, and role for the task.

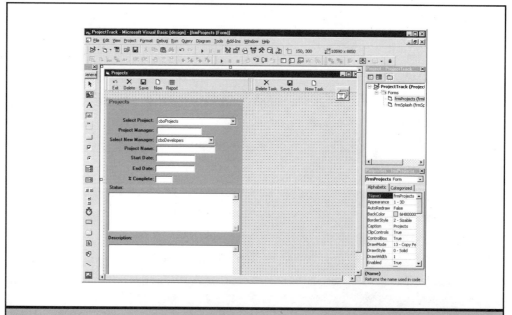

Figure 11-2.   *The project with the project frame*

Component/Property	Setting
Frame	frmTasks
Combo Box	cboRoles
Style	2 'Dropdown List
Combo Box	cboTasks
Style	2 'Dropdown List
Text Box	txtTaskStartDate
Text	''
Text Box	txtTaskEndDate
Text	''
Text Box	txtTaskNotes
MultiLine	-1 'True
ScrollBars	2 'Vertical
Text	''
Text Box	txtTaskProjectedEndDate
Text	''
Text Box	txtProjectedHoursComplete
Text	''
Text Box	txtHoursComplete
Text	''
Text Box	txtTaskStatus
MultiLine	-1 'True
ScrollBars	2 'Vertical
List Box	lstDevelopers
Command Button	cmdDeleteDeveloper
Caption	"Delete"
Combo Box	cboTaskDevelopers
Style	2 'Dropdown List

Table 11-3.   *Objects and Properties for the Task Frame*

Component/Property	Setting
Command Button	cmdUpdateDeveloper
Caption	"Update Developer"
Command Button	cmdAddDeveloper
Caption	"Add Developer"
Text Box	txtHours
Text	""
Label	lblDeveloper
AutoSize	-1 'True
Caption	"Developer – Hours – Role"
Line	lnDivide
Border Width	2
X1	75
X2	5805
Y1	5265
Y2	5265
Label	lblTasks
AutoSize	-1 'True
Caption	"SelectTask:"
Label	lblTaskStartDate
AutoSize	-1 'True
Caption	"Start Date:"
Label	lblTaskEndDate
AutoSize	-1 'True
Caption	"End Date"
Label	lblTaskNotes
AutoSize	-1 'True

Table 11-3. *Objects and Properties for the Task Frame* (continued)

Component/Property	Setting
Caption	"Task Notes"
Label	-1 'True
AutoSize	-1 'True
Caption	"Task Name:"
Label	lblProjectedEndDate
AutoSize	-1 'True
Caption	"Projected End Date:"
Label	lblProjHoursComplete
AutoSize	-1 'True
Caption	"Projected Hours to Complete"
Label	lblHoursComplete
AutoSize	-1 'True
Caption	"Hours Completed:"
Label	lblTaskStatus
AutoSize	-1 'True
Caption	"Status:"
Label	lblHours
AutoSize	-1 'True
Caption	"Hours on Task:"

Table 11-3.   *Objects and Properties for the Task Frame* (continued)

When a task is deleted, all the task properties will be cleared and deleted from the database, including the developers. Also, the data displayed will be cleared. If a new task is created, all the task data will be cleared on the screen. Figure 11-3 shows the project at design time with the task frame laid out.

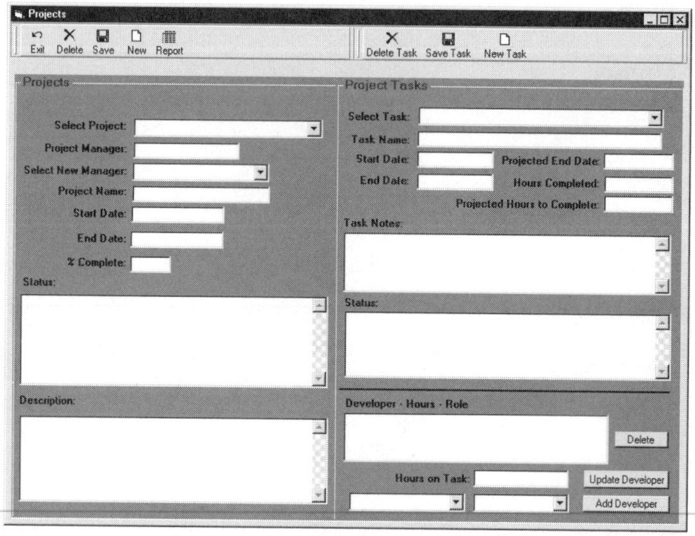

Figure 11-3. The project tracking system with the task frame

Let's review the basic processes for creating projects, tasks, and assigning developers. The general process for adding a new project will be defined as follows:

1. The New button will be selected on the project toolbar.

2. The name of the task will be requested from the user.

3. A new project will be inserted into the database, and the fields will be cleared on the form. The new project name will be selected in the Projects list box.

4. Any tasks loaded in the task combo box will be cleared, since there will be no tasks for the new project.

5. The user will select a manager and fill out the appropriate project data and save the project.

To add a new task, these steps will be followed:

1. The New button will be selected on the task toolbar.

2. The name of the task will be requested from the user.

3. A new task will be inserted into the database, and the fields will be cleared on the form. The new task name will be selected in the task combo box.

4. Any developers listed in the developer list box will be cleared, since no developers will have yet been assigned to the task.

5. The user will fill out the task properties and assign developers to the task. Then the task will be saved.

The user interface provides for a quick all-in-one view of projects and tasks. And it provides a simple interface to quickly review projects and assigned tasks. Finally, the ability to manage projects and tasks is easily facilitated through the use of the task bar. Figure 11-4 shows the project with the toolbar, projects, and project tasks.

When the project is loaded, there is going to be quite a bit of loading of project data into the application. In fact, the larger the use of the application and numbers of projects, and depending on the load, the user may believe the application is not functioning at startup. We'll provide some ideas to work around slowdowns in the next section.

Designing the Splash Screen

To add a little pizzazz to the interface, we can create a splash screen at startup that will notify the user the project is loading. Then, once the project has been fully loaded, the project tracking form will be displayed. Table 11-4 defines the form's properties and objects.

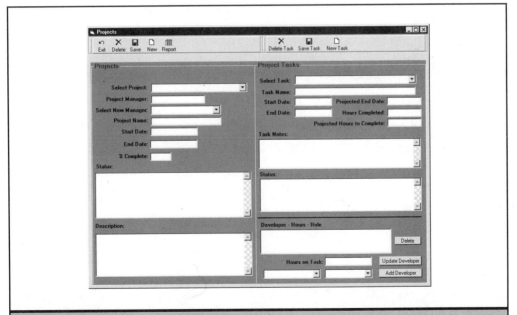

Figure 11-4. *The project at run time*

Component/Property	Setting
Form	frmSplash
Border Style	0 'None
Caption	"Form1"
Start Up Position	2 'CenterScreen
Label	LblMessage
AutoSize	-1 'True
Caption	"Loading…."

Table 11-4. *Objects and Properties for the Splash Screen*

Our splash form has no frame and will simply appear on the screen with the message "Loading…." when the application starts up. Figure 11-5 shows the splash screen. The screen will only be displayed while the classes and data are retrieved from the database. The appropriate list boxes, and so on, on the project tracking form will be loaded while the splash screen is displayed.

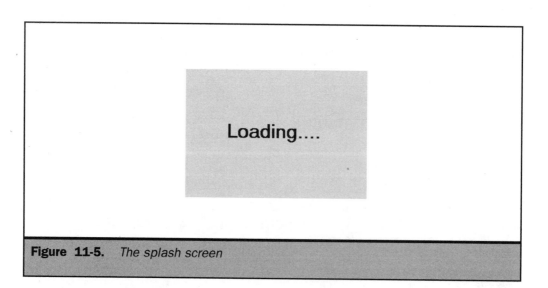

Figure 11-5. *The splash screen*

Building the Interface Code

In the next chapter, we will build the core of the application. But let's take a look at some of the fundamental interface programming. First, let's review the splash code, as follows:

```
Option Explicit

'  Global variable for loading projects.
Dim intPaintFlag As Integer

Private Sub Form_Load()

'  Only show once
intPaintFlag = 0

End Sub

Private Sub Form_Paint()

'  Check to see if the flag is set
If intPaintFlag = 0 Then

    '  Reset flag
    intPaintFlag = 1

    '  Refresh to ensure the label is showing
    frmSplash.Refresh

    '  LOAD PROJECT HERE

    '  Show the projects form once
    '  loaded
    frmProjects.Show

    '  Hide this form
    frmSplash.Hide

End If

End Sub
```

If we start processing the project loading in the Form_Load event, the form will not be displayed until the loading is done. That would defeat the purpose. So instead, we want to load the project once the form has been painted on the screen. Thus, we can use the Form_Paint event. But, at the same time, if the form should refresh for some reason, we don't want to reload the project. Thus, we have set up a global flag, intPaintFlag, that will indicate when the form has been painted one time. The first time, we will execute the load code (written in the next chapter). Note that we also execute a refresh to ensure that the label control indeed had time to display before we start loading the projects.

After the projects are loaded, we then hide the splash screen and show the projects form. And, voila, we have our splash screen for the project at startup.

In the projects form, we know we are going to need a couple of supporting functions for clearing the task and project frame text field and list boxes. To support that functionality, let's write two subroutines, ClearTaskFields and ClearProjectFields. Following is the code for the ClearTaskFields subroutine:

```
'  Subroutine to clear the task frame fields
Public Sub ClearTaskFields()

'  Clear the text fields
txtTaskNotes.Text = ""
txtTaskEndDate.Text = ""
txtTaskProjectedEndDate.Text = ""
txtTaskName.Text = ""
txtTaskStartDate.Text = ""
txtTaskStatus.Text = ""
txtHoursComplete.Text = ""
txtProjectedHoursComplete.Text = ""
txtHours.Text = ""

'  Clear the developer list
lstDevelopers.Clear

End Sub
```

Each of the text boxes on the task frame interface is cleared of any settings. And the list box of assigned developers is cleared as well. Note that the combo box of task names is not cleared. This is because we may be adding a new task, in which case we will not want the task list cleared.

Following is the code for the ClearProjectFields subroutine:

```
'  Subroutine to clear project frame fields
Public Sub ClearProjectFields()

'  Clear the text box fields
txtDescription.Text = ""
txtEndDate.Text = ""
txtPercentComplete.Text = ""
txtProjectManager.Text = ""
txtProjectName.Text = ""
txtStartDate.Text = ""
txtStatus.Text = ""

'  Clear the tasks list
cboTasks.Clear

'  If we clear a project, we need to
'  clear the task fields
ClearTaskFields

End Sub
```

As with the tasks, we clear out all the text fields for the project data. And, as with the tasks, we will not clear the combo box of projects since we may be adding a new project.

Next we clear the combo box of tasks. If we are starting a new project or deleting a project, we will need to clear any tasks as well. Followed by clearing the tasks combo box, we will call the ClearTaskFields subroutine to clear out the rest of the tasks frame.

We will also need to do some checking when our project is ended. We don't want users to be able to exit the program if they are in the middle of updating a project. To do this, we will use Form_UnLoad.

When the form is unloaded, we will need to check to see if a project is selected in the project combo box. If a project is selected, we will need to query the user about whether they want to save the project data. Following is the code:

```
'  Unload event of the form
Private Sub Form_Unload(Cancel As Integer)

'  Declare our variables
Dim intResult As Integer
```

```
' Check to see if a project is selected
If cboProjects.ListIndex <> -1 Then

    ' Query the users if they want to save the project
    intResult = MsgBox("Save any changes to the project and task?" _
            , vbYesNoCancel)

    ' Check the result
    Select Case intResult

        ' If cancel was selected we set the
        ' cancel argument of the function
        ' to True so the project end is
        ' canceled
        Case vbCancel
            Cancel = True

        ' If yes then save the project and tasks
        Case vbYes
            ' SAVE THE PROJECT
            End

        Case Else
            End

    End Select

Else

    End

End If
```

To query the user, we utilize the message box function to ask whether they wish to save the project. The vbYesNoCancel parameter with the MsgBox function will give the user a yes, no, or cancel option.

We then build a select case statement based on the response. If the user responds with a yes, for the moment we will end the project. But that is also where our "save" code will go. If the user responds with a cancel, we set the cancel parameter of the Form_Unload procedure to stop the program from unloading. If the user answers no, the program is simply ended. Figure 11-6 shows the message box.

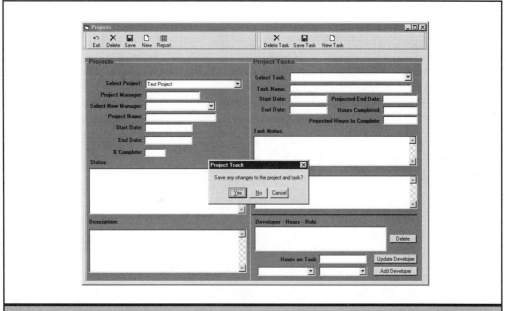

Figure 11-6. *Project save message box*

Note   *A test project is loaded in the Projects combo box for testing.*

We can also go ahead and define some of the user interface functionality for the toolbar. When we add a new project, we will need to query the user for a project name. And when we delete a project, we will need to query the user to confirm the action. This will all take place in the ButtonClick event of the project toolbar. The code is as follows:

```
'  Button click of the project toolbar
Private Sub tblProject_ButtonClick(ByVal Button As _
MSComctlLib.Button)

'  Declare our variables
Dim strResults As String
Dim intResults as Integer

'  Select case on the button index
Select Case Button.Index
```

```
    ' The first button ends the project
    Case 1
        End

    ' The second button deletes the project
    Case 2

        ' Only delete if a project is selected
        If cboProjects.ListIndex <> -1 Then

            ' Ensure the user wants to delete the
            ' project
            intResult = MsgBox("Are you sure?", vbYesNo)

            ' If yes
            If intResult = vbYes Then

                ' DELETE PROJECT

            End If
        End If

    ' Add a new project
    Case 4

        ' Query the user for the project name
        strResults = InputBox("Enter the project name:", _
                    "Project Name", "New Project")

        ' Ensure a project name was entered
        If strResults <> "" Then

            ' ADD NEW PROJECT
        Else
            ' Indicate the project name cannot be empty
            MsgBox "You cannot have an empty project name."
        End If

End Select

End Sub
```

In the select case statement, we can process several of the options. First, we can end the program if the first button is selected. When the delete button is selected, we first need to check to see if a project is selected in the Projects list box. If not, we cannot delete a project. Users are queried about whether they are sure they want to delete the project. Figure 11-7 shows the query.

We also need to query users for the new project name if they click on the new project button. In that case we utilize the InputBox function to retrieve the project name. A check is then done to ensure that a project name has been entered. Figure 11-8 shows the input box query.

If users do not enter a project name, they are notified that they must enter one. Figure 11-9 shows the message box.

We will follow a very similar set of steps for the task toolbar. As with the project toolbar, we will want to query the user about whether they are going to delete a task. And with a new task, we will need to retrieve the task name from the user.

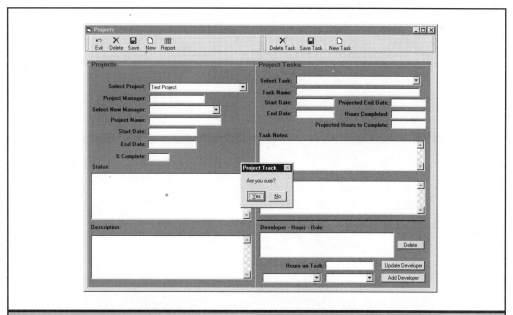

Figure 11-7.   *Message box with the delete project query*

CLIENT/SERVER DEVELOPMENT

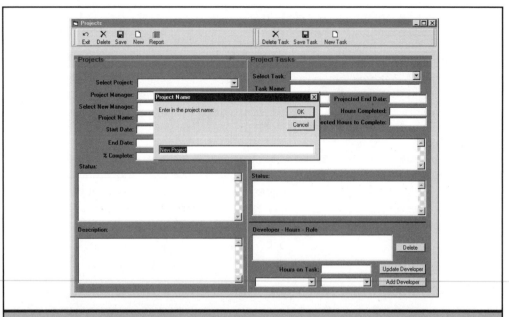

Figure 11-8. *The new project input box*

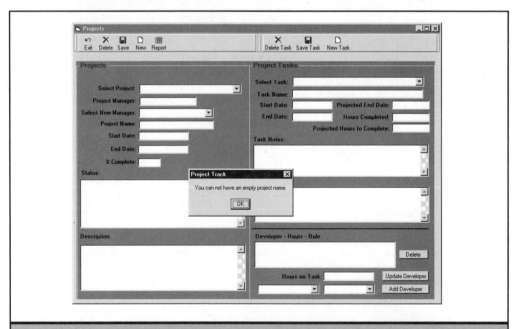

Figure 11-9. *Message box if users do not enter a project name*

```
'  Button click of the task toolbar
Private Sub tblTask_ButtonClick(ByVal button As MSComctlLib.button)

'  Declare a variable
Dim strResults As String
Dim intResult As Integer

'  Process by the button selected
Select Case button.Index

    '  Delete task button
    Case 1

        '  Ensure a project is selected
        If cboProjects.ListIndex <> -1 Then

            '  Ensure a task is selected
            If cboTasks.ListIndex <> -1 Then

                '  Ensure the user wants to delete the
                '  project
                intResult = MsgBox("Are you sure?", vbYesNo)

                '  If yes
                If intResult = vbYes Then

                    '  DELETE PROJECT

                End If

            End If

        End If

    '  Save the task
    Case 2

    '  Add a new task
    Case 3

    '  Ensure a project is selected
    If cboProjects.ListIndex <> -1 Then
```

```
      ' Ask for the task name
      strResults = InputBox("Enter the task name:", _
                  "Task Name", "New Task")

      ' Ensure we do not have an empty task name
      If strResults <> "" Then

          ' ADD NEW TASK

      Else

          ' Indicate the task cannot be empty
          MsgBox "You cannot have an empty task name."

      End If

    End If

  End Select

  End Sub
```

If a task is to be deleted, we have to ensure that a project and a task are selected. We can't delete a task if none is selected. If the user responds with a yes, we can delete the project. Figure 11-10 shows the message box.

For a new task, we will need to query the user for the task name. But it is important to ensure that we have a project selected to assign the task to. If a project is selected, the input box is utilized again to retrieve the task name from the user. And we have to verify that the user has entered a name. Figure 11-11 shows the input box.

With that, we have all the elements of our user interface defined. The user will be able to navigate easily through projects and tasks. And we have implemented appropriate interface design to query the user to save projects and tasks and to delete projects and tasks.

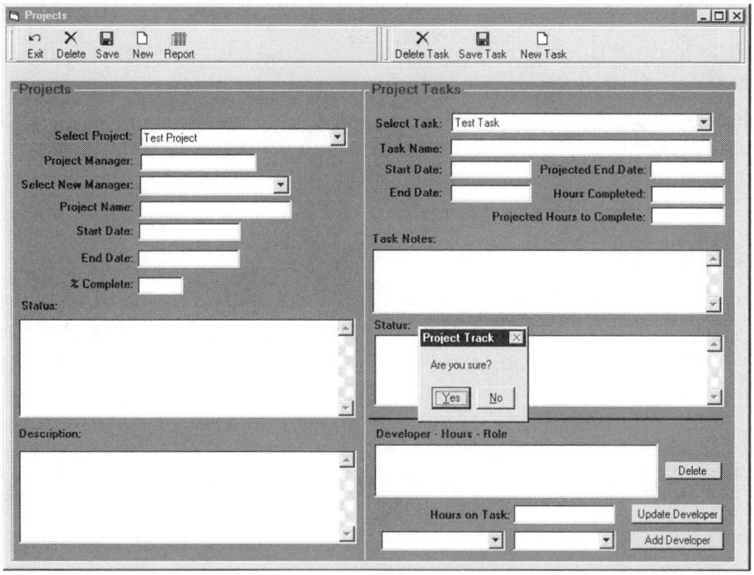

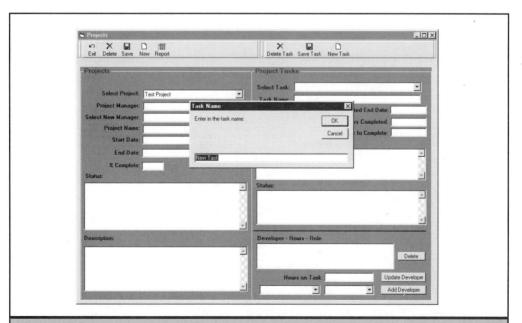

Figure 11-10. *The delete task message box*

Figure 11-11. *The new task name input box*

Summary

In Chapter 10 we built the class structure and database for our project. In this chapter we have designed the key elements of the user interface. Now that we have a good feel for the basic structure and interface of our project, we are ready to begin building the primary business logic to make the project tracking system function.

What's Next

In the next chapter we will begin filling in the structure of our application with code that will make it function and hook up with the database. Following that, in Chapter 13, we will implement the code in multiple tiers and prepare it for deployment.

Chapter 12

Building the Business Logic

W e have our class foundation, database, and user interface built. It is time to build the core functionality on the foundation and behind the interface. We need to connect the classes to the database to provide reading and writing of persistent data. And we need to connect our user interface to the class structure.

We will start with the projects class and ensure we can load all of the projects loaded in the database along with appropriate tasks and developers. Once we have all the classes created and the data loaded, we will work on representing the data in the user interface.

Implementing the Class Structure

The primary task we will need to perform in our classes is to build database functionality that will allow us to add, update, and delete appropriate data for each class. We will add more methods to our classes to complete functionality beyond basic class and structure management.

Projects Class

The projects class holds a collection of project classes. We will need to loop through the database and retrieve all active projects in the system. With each project we find in the database, we will need to create a new project class.

 Many properties of the projects class developed in Chapter 10 are not repeated in the code listed here.

In the general declarations section of the projects class, we will add the dbPT variable, which will contain our project track data environment. This will be used throughout the class to connect to the database.

```
Option Explicit

'   Local variable to hold collection and the
'   database
Private mCol As Collection
Private dbPT As dbProjectTrack
```

The AddNew method of the class will add a new project to the system. This is one of the new classes for the projects class. We need to be able to add a new project. This function is different from the Add function in that this one not only adds another project class but also creates a new project in the database. The project name is passed into the function. This will be received from the user interface.

The key for the new class will be set to the current count of projects plus one. Then the AddNewProject method of the project class is classed. This will insert the new data into the database. Once that is done, we add our project to the projects collection for the class, and we have successfully added a new project to the system.

```
Public Function AddNew(strProjectName As String) As Project

'  Create a new object
Dim sKey
Dim objNewMember As Project

Set objNewMember = New Project

'  Set the properties passed into the method
objNewMember.Key = Me.Count + 1

'  Add a new project into the database and pass in
'  the project name
objNewMember.AddNewProject strProjectName

'  Set the key
If Len(sKey) = 0 Then
    mCol.Add objNewMember
Else
    mCol.Add objNewMember, sKey
End If

'  Return the object created
Set AddNew = objNewMember
Set objNewMember = Nothing

End Function
```

The Add method is similar to the one outlined in Chapter 10. But we now need to load all the properties of the project from the database. In the class initialize event of the class, we open the connection to the database. Thus when the Add event is called, the database connection is open, and we can read the recordset returned from the RetrieveActiveProjects stored procedure. Otherwise, we still create a new project class and add it to our projects collection.

```
'   Add a new project
Public Function Add(Key As String, Optional sKey As String) As
Project

'   Create a new object
Dim objNewMember As Project

Set objNewMember = New Project
'set the properties passed into the method

objNewMember.Key = Key

'   Set the id of the project
objNewMember.idproject = _
   dbPT.rsRetrieveActiveProjects("idProject")

'   Set the description
objNewMember.Description = _
   dbPT.rsRetrieveActiveProjects("txtDescription") & ""

'   Set the end date
objNewMember.EndDate = _
   dbPT.rsRetrieveActiveProjects("dtEndDate") & ""

'   Set the ID of the manager
objNewMember.idManager = _
   dbPT.rsRetrieveActiveProjects("idManager")

'   Set the percent complete
objNewMember.PercentComplete = _
   dbPT.rsRetrieveActiveProjects("fltPercentComplete")

'   Set the project name
objNewMember.ProjectName = _
   dbPT.rsRetrieveActiveProjects("chrProjectName")

'   Set the status
objNewMember.status = _
   dbPT.rsRetrieveActiveProjects("txtStatus") & ""

'   Set the start date
objNewMember.StartDate = _
   dbPT.rsRetrieveActiveProjects("dtStartDate") & ""
```

```
'  Set the key
If Len(sKey) = 0 Then
    mCol.Add objNewMember
Else
    mCol.Add objNewMember, sKey
End If

'  return the object created
Set Add = objNewMember
Set objNewMember = Nothing

End Function
```

The Remove function needs one addition to its functionality. We need to delete the project data from the database before we remove it from the projects collection. To delete the project from the database, the DeleteProject method of the project class is called (developed later in the chapter).

```
Public Sub Remove(vntIndexKey As Variant)

    '  Remove the project
    mCol.Item(vntIndexKey).DeleteProject

    'used when removing an element from the collection
    'vntIndexKey contains either the Index or Key, which is why
    'it is declared as a Variant
    'Syntax: x.Remove(xyz)
    mCol.Remove vntIndexKey

End Sub
```

The Initialize event of the class will retrieve all the active projects from the database. The returned recordset is looped through, and the Add method of the projects class is called to add the new project to the collection. That will in turn set up the properties of the new project class from the database (as outlined above).

```
Private Sub Class_Initialize()

'  Declare our variables
Dim intCnt As Integer
```

CLIENT/SERVER DEVELOPMENT

```
' creates the collection when this class is created
Set mCol = New Collection

Set dbPT = New dbProjectTrack

' Retrieve the active projects
dbPT.RetrieveActiveProjects

' Loop through the active projects
Do Until dbPT.rsRetrieveActiveProjects.EOF

    ' Increment the counter
    intCnt = intCnt + 1

    ' Add the class
    Add CStr(intCnt)

    ' Move to the next row
    dbPT.rsRetrieveActiveProjects.MoveNext

Loop

Set dbPT = Nothing

End Sub
```

The sum result of the projects class is that the project data is retrieved from the database, and a collection of projects is created. Within each step of creating the project classes, cascading events will be called to create task and developer classes as appropriate for each project.

Project Class

The project class will load the appropriate task classes for the project. The properties for the project class are set by the projects superclass. We also declare in this class, in the general declarations section project class, a dbPT variable for our project track data environment. This will be used for retrieving, storing, and deleting appropriate data from the database.

Note   *Many of the property declarations created in Chapter 10 are not repeated here.*

```
Option Explicit

'  Public key for the projects class which has
'  a collection of projects
Public Key As String

'  Local variable to hold task collection
Private mColTask As Collection

'  Local database connection
Private dbPT As dbProjectTrack

'local variable(s) to hold property value(s)
Private mvarProjectName As String 'local copy
Private mvarStartDate As Date 'local copy
Private mvarDescription As String 'local copy
Private mvarEndDate As String 'local copy
Private mvarPercentComplete As Double 'local copy
Public Manager As New Developer   'local copy
Private mvarIDProject As Integer 'local copy
Private mvarIDManager As Integer 'local copy
Private mvarStatus As String 'local copy
```

When the ID property of the project class is set, we can then load the tasks for the projects. We call the private LoadProjectTasks method of the class to load all the task classes for the project.

```
'  Sets and retrieves the id of the project
Public Property Let idproject(ByVal vData As Integer)
    mvarIDProject = vData

    '  Loads the project's tasks
    LoadProjectTasks

End Property

Public Property Get idproject() As Integer
    idproject = mvarIDProject
End Property
```

When the ID of the manager for the class is set, we will set up the manager class, which will retrieve the first and last names of the developer. Thus, if we have to retrieve the manager data for the project, we can reference a developer subclass.

```
'  Sets  and retrieves the project manager
Public Property Let idManager(ByVal vData As Integer)
    mvarIDManager = vData
    Manager.idDeveloper = mvarIDManager
End Property

Public Property Get idManager() As Integer
    idManager = mvarIDManager
End Property
```

The public AddNewTask method will create a new task for the project. The name of the task is passed into the method. This will be retrieved from the user interface. We create a new task object in the method. The key for the task will be the number of tasks (count) plus one. Once the task object is created, the AddNewTask method of the task object is called, with the ID of the project and the name of the task passed in as arguments. Finally, the task class is added to the collection of tasks for the project.

```
'  Add a new task to the project
Public Function AddNewTask(strTaskName As String) As Task

    '  Create a new task object
    Dim sKey
    Dim objNewMember As Task

    Set objNewMember = New Task

    '  Set the count passed into the method
    objNewMember.Key = Me.CountTask + 1

    '  Add the new task with the task name and id of the project
    '  Note this is the Task class method, not the project
    '  method we are currently in
    objNewMember.AddNewTask strTaskName, mvarIDProject

    '  Set the key
    If Len(sKey) = 0 Then
        mColTask.Add objNewMember
    Else
        mColTask.Add objNewMember, sKey
    End If
```

```
'return the object created
Set AddNewTask = objNewMember
Set objNewMember = Nothing

End Function
```

The AddTask method is similar to the original, but we need to update the functionality to include reading the task data from the database. The database connection is opened and the recordset retrieved in the LoadProjectTasks private method of the class.

The recordset data is read from the RetrieveTaskByProject stored procedure setup in the data environment. The properties for the task are set to the data returned, and the task is added to the collection.

```
'  Add a task to the collection of tasks for the project
Public Function AddTask(Key As String, Optional sKey As String) As _
Task

    'create a new task object
    Dim objNewMember As Task

    Set objNewMember = New Task

    'set the properties passed into the method
    objNewMember.Key = Key

    '  Set the hours complete from the database
    objNewMember.HoursCompleted = _
        dbPT.rsRetrieveTaskByProject("fltHoursComplete")

    '  Set the id of the task
    objNewMember.idTask = _
        dbPT.rsRetrieveTaskByProject("idTask")

    '  Set the end date
    objNewMember.EndDate = _
        dbPT.rsRetrieveTaskByProject("dtEndDate")
```

```
    '  Set the projected end date
    objNewMember.ProjectedEndDate = _
        dbPT.rsRetrieveTaskByProject("dtProjectedEndDate")

    '  Set the projected hours
    objNewMember.ProjectedHours = _
        dbPT.rsRetrieveTaskByProject("fltProjectedHours")

    '  Set the start date
    objNewMember.StartDate = _
        dbPT.rsRetrieveTaskByProject("dtStartDate")

    '  Set the task name
    objNewMember.TaskName = _
        dbPT.rsRetrieveTaskByProject("chrTaskName")

    '  set the task notes
    objNewMember.TaskNotes = _
        dbPT.rsRetrieveTaskByProject("txtTaskNotes")

    '  Set the status
    objNewMember.status = _
        dbPT.rsRetrieveTaskByProject("txtStatus") & ""

    '  Load the task developers
    objNewMember.LoadTaskDevelopers

    '  Set the key
    If Len(sKey) = 0 Then
        mColTask.Add objNewMember
    Else
        mColTask.Add objNewMember, sKey
    End If

    'return the object created
    Set AddTask = objNewMember
    Set objNewMember = Nothing

End Function
```

The RemoveTask method of the class will remove a task from the project. Before the task is removed from the task collection, the DeleteTask method of the task class is called. This will delete the task data from the database.

```
Public Sub RemoveTask(vntIndexKey As Variant)
    '  Call the delete task function of the task object
    '  to remove the task
    mColTask.Item(vntIndexKey).DeleteTask

    'used when removing an element from the collection
    'vntIndexKey contains either the Index or Key, which is why
    'it is declared as a Variant
    'Syntax: x.Remove(xyz)
    mColTask.Remove vntIndexKey
End Sub
```

In the projects class, we called the AddNewProject method of the project class to add a new project to the database. This method takes in as its only argument the name of the project that will be retrieved from the user interface. The data environment is created, which will automatically create the connection. The AddNewProject stored procedure is called with the project name passed in. Returned in the recordset from the insert is the ID of the new project. That value is set for the private project ID member variable. The project name is also stored in the properties. The rest of the properties are all defaulted. Specifically, the dates for the project are defaulted to the current date.

```
'  Add a new project into the database
Public Sub AddNewProject(strProjectName As String)

'  Create the database object
Set dbPT = New dbProjectTrack

'  Call the stored procedure
dbPT.AddNewProject strProjectName

'  Set the project name
mvarProjectName = strProjectName

'  Set the id of the project
mvarIDProject = dbPT.rsAddNewProject(0)
```

```
'  Default the rest of the values
mvarDescription = ""
mvarIDManager = 0
mvarStatus = ""
mvarEndDate = Date
mvarStartDate = Date

End Sub
```

The StoreProject public method will take the temporary data stored in the project class properties and save it to the database. The UpdateProject stored procedure of the project track data environment is called, with the private property member variables passed into the stored procedure.

```
'  Saves the project properties in the database
Public Sub StoreProject()

Set dbPT = New dbProjectTrack

'  Update the project
dbPT.UpdateProject _
    mvarIDProject, _
    mvarDescription, _
    mvarEndDate, _
    mvarIDManager, _
    mvarStartDate, _
    mvarProjectName, _
    mvarPercentComplete, _
    mvarStatus

Set dbPT = Nothing

End Sub
```

The DeleteProject method will delete the current project from the database. A check is done to ensure that the ID of the project is set. If it is, then we call the DeleteProject stored procedure and pass in the ID of the project.

```
'  Delete the project from the database
Public Sub DeleteProject()

'  Ensure the id for the project is set to a valid value
If mvarIDProject <> -1 Then

    Set dbPT = New dbProjectTrack

    '  Delete the project
    dbPT.DeleteProject mvarIDProject

    Set dbPT = Nothing

End If

End Sub
```

LoadProjectTasks will retrieve the tasks assigned to the project and create a collection of tasks. The RetrieveTaskByProject stored procedure is called, with the ID of the project passed in. A recordset of the task data is returned from the database.

With each record returned, the AddTask method of the project class is called to add a new task object to the task collection. In the AddTask method, the properties of the task class are set from the recordset returned in LoadProjectTasks.

```
'  Load the project's tasks
Private Sub LoadProjectTasks()

'  Declare our variables
Dim intCnt As Integer

Set dbPT = New dbProjectTrack

'  Retrieve the tasks
dbPT.RetrieveTaskByProject mvarIDProject

'  Loop through the listing
Do Until dbPT.rsRetrieveTaskByProject.EOF

    '  Increment the count
    intCnt = intCnt + 1
```

```
'  Add the task
AddTask CStr(intCnt)

'  Move to the next row
dbPT.rsRetrieveTaskByProject.MoveNext

Loop

Set dbPT = Nothing

End Sub
```

When the class is initialized, the ID property is set to −1 to indicate no class is loaded.

```
Private Sub Class_Initialize()
    'creates the collection when this class is created
    Set mColTask = New Collection

    '  Default the id of the project
    mvarIDProject = -1

End Sub
```

The project class will define the primary properties of each project. And in turn it loads the appropriate tasks assigned to the project. We have added several methods over our basic structure, which primarily defined the properties and task collection management. Now we can add, update, and delete tasks and have the propagation continue to the database level.

We have also added functions to the project class that will operate on the project directly. These include adding a new project, deleting the project, and storing the project properties. Next we will take a look at the task class.

Task Class

The task class will encapsulate the tasks assigned to a project. And in turn the task class has a collection of developers assigned to each task. As with the projects and project classes, we define a global instance of the project track data environment for accessing data about the task.

> **Note**   *Many of the property declarations defined in Chapter 10 have been removed since they are redundant.*

```
Option Explicit

'local variable to hold collection
Private mColDeveloper As Collection

'   Public key for the collection of tasks in the project class
Public Key As String

'   Database Object
Private dbPT As dbProjectTrack

'   Local property variables
Private mvarStatus As String 'local copy
Private mvarTaskName As String 'local copy
Private mvarStartDate As Date 'local copy
Private mvarProjectedEndDate As Date 'local copy
Private mvarEndDate As Date 'local copy
Private mvarProjectedHours As Integer 'local copy
Private mvarHoursCompleted As Integer 'local copy
Private mvarTaskNotes As String 'local copy
Private mvarIDTask As Integer 'local copy
```

The AddDeveloper method will add a new developer class to the developer collection for the task. The properties of the developer class will be set from the recordset returned by the RetrieveTaskDevelopers stored procedure. Once the developer class is set up, it is added to the collection.

```
'   Add a developer to the task
Public Function AddDeveloper(Key As String, Optional sKey As _
String) As Developer

'   create a new object
Dim objNewMember As Developer

Set objNewMember = New Developer

'   set the properties passed into the method
objNewMember.Key = Key
```

```
'  Set the id of the developer
objNewMember.idDeveloper = _
    dbPT.rsRetrieveTaskDevelopers("idDeveloper")

'  Set the task hours
objNewMember.TaskHours = _
    dbPT.rsRetrieveTaskDevelopers("fltHours")

'  Set the developers role
objNewMember.Role = _
    dbPT.rsRetrieveTaskDevelopers("chrRoleName")

'  Set the key
If Len(sKey) = 0 Then
    mColDeveloper.Add objNewMember
Else
    mColDeveloper.Add objNewMember, sKey
End If

'  Return the object created
Set AddDeveloper = objNewMember
Set objNewMember = Nothing

End Function
```

The RemoveDeveloper method of the class has been updated to remove the developer data from the database as well. The DeleteDeveloper method of the developer class is called, with the ID of the task passed in. Once the data is deleted, the developer is removed from the collection.

Note *This will not delete the developer from the developer table, but will remove the developer's assignment to the task in the TaskDev table.*

```
Public Sub RemoveDeveloper(vntIndexKey As Variant)
    '  Delete the assigned developer from the database
    mColDeveloper.Item(vntIndexKey).DeleteDeveloper mvarIDTask
```

```
        'used when removing an element from the collection
        'vntIndexKey contains either the Index or Key, which is why
        'it is declared as a Variant
        'Syntax: x.Remove(xyz)
        mColDeveloper.Remove vntIndexKey

End Sub
```

The AddNewTask method will insert a new task into the database. The parameters
for the method identify the task name and ID of the project. The AddNewTask stored
procedure is called to insert the new task into the database. The ID of the new task is
returned and is set to the local property. The rest of the class's properties are defaulted.
The data properties are defaulted to the current date.

```
'  Add a new task to the project
Public Sub AddNewTask(strTaskName As String, idproject As Integer)

set dbPT = new dbProjectTrack

'  Add the new task
dbPT.AddNewTask strTaskName, idproject

'  Set the task name
mvarTaskName = strTaskName

'  Set the ID of the task
mvarIDTask = dbPT.rsAddNewTask(0)

'  Default the rest of the values
mvarTaskNotes = ""
mvarEndDate = Date
mvarStartDate = Date
mvarProjectedEndDate = Date
mvarHoursCompleted = 0
mvarProjectedHours = 0

End Sub
```

The AddNewDeveloper method adds a new developer to the task. The ID of the developer and the ID of the role the developer is to play are passed into the function. These will be determined by the user interface.

The developer class is created, and the AddNewDeveloper method of the developer class is called. In addition to the developer ID and the role ID, the ID of the task is passed in as well. The key for the new developer class will be the current number of tasks plus one. The class is then added to the developer's collection.

```vb
' Add a new developer to the task
Public Function AddNewDeveloper(idDeveloper As Integer, idRole As _
Integer) As Developer

' Create a new object
Dim sKey
Dim objNewMember As Developer

Set objNewMember = New Developer

' Set the properties passed into the method
objNewMember.Key = Me.CountDeveloper + 1

' Add the new developer with the assigned role for the
' specified task
objNewMember.AddNewDeveloper idDeveloper, idRole, idTask

' Set the key
If Len(sKey) = 0 Then
    mColDeveloper.Add objNewMember
Else
    mColDeveloper.Add objNewMember, sKey
End If

' Return the object created
Set AddNewDeveloper = objNewMember
Set objNewMember = Nothing

End Function
```

The StoreTask method of the class will save the task data to the database. The private member variable properties of the class are passed into the UpdateTask stored procedure of the data environment.

```
'   Store the task
Public Sub StoreTask()

Set dbPT = New dbProjectTrack

'   Update the task
dbPT.UpdateTask mvarIDTask, _
    mvarEndDate, _
    mvarHoursCompleted, _
    mvarProjectedEndDate, _
    mvarProjectedHours, _
    mvarStartDate, _
    mvarTaskName, _
    mvarTaskNotes, _
    mvarStatus

Set dbPT = Nothing

End Sub
```

The LoadTaskDevelopers method will retrieve the recordset of developers from the database using the RetrieveTaskDevelopers stored procedure. The ID of the task is passed into the stored procedure. The recordset is looped through, and the AddDeveloper method of the class is called to set up the developer class properties and add the class to the collection.

```
'   Load the task's developers
Public Sub LoadTaskDevelopers()

'   Declare our variables
Dim intCnt As Integer

Set dbPT = New dbProjectTrack

'   Retrieve the task developers
dbPT.RetrieveTaskDevelopers mvarIDTask

'   Loop through the task developers
Do Until dbPT.rsRetrieveTaskDevelopers.EOF

    '   Increment our counter
    intCnt = intCnt + 1
```

```
     '  Add the developer
     AddDeveloper CStr(intCnt)

     '  Move to the next row
     dbPT.rsRetrieveTaskDevelopers.MoveNext

Loop

Set dbPT = Nothing

End Sub
```

The delete task method of the class will remove the task data from the database. This function is called before the task class is removed from the project. The DeleteTask stored procedure is called, with the ID of the task passed into it.

```
'  Delete the task
Public Sub DeleteTask()

Set dbPT = New dbProjectTrack

'  Delete the task
dbPT.DeleteTask mvarIDTask

'  Delete the task developers
dbPT.DeleteTaskDevelopers mvarIDTask

Set dbPT = Nothing

End Sub
```

The task class is designed to define the tasks assigned to a project and retrieve the developers assigned to a task. As with the project class, we have added several methods over our original creation of the class. Several methods have been added for managing the task developers and for interfacing the task class with the database. Next we will take a look at the developer class.

Developer Class

The developer class serves several purposes in our program. First, it will define the basic developer data by task the developer is assigned to. Second, it will also define the manager for the project. And finally, it will detail the role and the number of hours the developer has for the task.

The general declarations section of the class, as with the past set of classes, defines a global instance of the project track data environment. This will be utilized for interfacing with the developer data in the database.

Note *Many of the properties defined in Chapter 10 are not shown here because they have not changed.*

```
Option Explicit

'   Key for the task class that has a developer collection
Public Key As String

'   Local database connection
Private dbPT As dbProjectTrack

'   Local variables
Private mvarFirstName As String 'local copy
Private mvarLastName As String 'local copy
Private mvarRole As String 'local copy
Private mvarTaskHours As Double 'local copy
Private mvarIDDeveloper As Integer 'local copy
```

When the ID of the developer is set for the class, the first and last names of the developer are retrieved from the database. The RetrieveDeveloper stored procedure is utilized to retrieve the data with the ID passed in. The data for the property in particular is retrieved because the developer class will be used to set the manager data for the project as well. Thus, regardless of when or why the developer class is used, when the ID is set, the name will be retrieved.

```
'   Sets the id of the developer
Public Property Let idDeveloper(ByVal vData As Integer)

Set dbPT = New dbProjectTrack

'   Set the local variable
mvarIDDeveloper = vData
```

```
'  Check to ensure the ID is not 0
If mvarIDDeveloper <> 0 Then

    '  Retrieves the developer
    dbPT.RetrieveDeveloper mvarIDDeveloper

    '  Retrieves the first name
    mvarFirstName = dbPT.rsRetrieveDeveloper("chrFirstName") & ""

    '  Retrieves the last name
    mvarLastName = dbPT.rsRetrieveDeveloper("chrLastName")

End If

Set dbPT = Nothing

End Property

'  Retrieve the developer id
Public Property Get idDeveloper() As Integer
    idDeveloper = mvarIDDeveloper
End Property
```

The DeleteDeveloper method will delete a developer from the specified task. The ID of the task is passed into the function. The DeleteTaskDeveloper stored procedure is called to delete the assigned developer, and the ID of the task and ID of the developer are passed in.

```
'  Delete the developer
Public Sub DeleteDeveloper(idTask As Integer)

Set dbPT = New dbProjectTrack

'  Delete the task developer
dbPT.DeleteTaskDeveloper idTask, mvarIDDeveloper

Set dbPT = Nothing

End Sub
```

The AddNewDeveloper method will assign a developer to the specified task. The ID of the developer, the ID of the role for the developer, and the ID of the task are passed into the subroutine. The iddeveloper property of the class is set to read in the developer's name. Then the AssignTaskDeveloper stored procedure is called to assign the developer to the task with the specified role.

Following that, the RetrieveTaskRole stored procedure is called to return the role data for the specified role, and the role name property is set. The number of task hours for the developer is defaulted to 0.

```
'  Add a new developer to the database
Public Sub AddNewDeveloper(idDeveloper As Integer, idRole As _
Integer, idTask As Integer)

'  Set the id of the developer
Me.idDeveloper = idDeveloper

Set dbPT = New dbProjectTrack

'  Assign the developer to the task and set the role
dbPT.AssignTaskDeveloper idTask, idDeveloper, idRole, 0

'  Retrieve the task role
dbPT.retrievetaskrole idRole

'  Set the role name
mvarRole = dbPT.rsRetrieveTaskRole("chrRoleName")

'  Default the hours
mvarTaskHours = 0

Set dbPT = Nothing

End Sub
```

StoreDeveloper calls the UpdateTaskDev stored procedure to update the number of task hours for the developer on the task.

```
'  Store the developer
Public Sub StoreDeveloper(idTask As Integer)

Set dbPT = New dbProjectTrack
```

```
'  Update the TaskDev table
dbPT.UpdateTaskDev idTask, mvarIDDeveloper, mvarTaskHours

Set dbPT = Nothing

End Sub
```

In our program, we want to be able to retrieve all the developers in the system. We will need to provide a list for the user to select a manager and assign developers to a task. In this case we will define a metafunction in the developer class that will return the list of developers in the database.

It is called a *metafunction* because it doesn't operate on a single developer, but across several developers. In this case the list is read into a series of developer classes and returned as a collection to the calling application.

```
'  Retrieve the developers in the database
'  This is a metafunction that is performed on all
'  developers. A collection is returned.
Public Function RetrieveDevelopers() As Collection

'  Declare our variables
Dim RD As New Collection
Dim Dev As Developer

Set dbPT = New dbProjectTrack

'  Retrieve the developers
dbPT.RetrieveDevelopers

'  Loop through the developers
Do Until dbPT.rsRetrieveDevelopers.EOF

    '  Create a new developer class
    Set Dev = New Developer

    '  Retrieve the ID of the developer
    Dev.idDeveloper = _
        dbPT.rsRetrieveDevelopers("idDeveloper")
```

```
     '  Add the developer to the collection
     RD.Add Dev

     '  Move to the next row
     dbPT.rsRetrieveDevelopers.MoveNext

Loop

Set dbPT = Nothing

'  Return the collection
Set RetrieveDevelopers = RD

End Function
```

The developer class makes a few twists from the model defined in the project and task classes. In this case there is not a one-to-one relationship between the developer class and the developer table. In fact, the developer class will encapsulate data from the developer, taskdev, and taskrole tables. The developer class represents developers assigned to tasks and appropriate data from each of these tables.

Task Role Class

Finally, we have the task role class. This class is fairly straightforward because it primarily serves as a lookup of roles in the database. The project track data environment is declared globally.

```
Option Explicit

'  Declare our database object
Private dbPT As dbProjectTrack

'  Local property variables
Private mvarRoleName As String 'local copy
Private mvarDescription As Variant 'local copy
Private mvarIDTaskRole As Integer 'local copy
```

The RetrieveTaskRoles method is a metafunction similar to the metafunction of the developer class that retrieves all the developers in the system. In this case we create a series of task role class objects and populate their properties from the database. The task role objects are returned in a collection to the calling application.

```vb
' Retrieve the task roles. This is a metafunction
' for all roles
Public Function RetrieveTaskRoles() As Collection

' Create the collection of task roles to be returned
Dim RTR As New Collection
Dim TR As TaskRole

Set dbPT = New dbProjectTrack

' Retrieve the task roles
dbPT.RetrieveTaskRoles

' Loop through the task roles
Do Until dbPT.rsRetrieveTaskRoles.EOF

    ' Create a new task role class
    Set TR = New TaskRole

    ' Set the description
    TR.Description = _
        dbPT.rsRetrieveTaskRoles("txtdescription")

    ' Set the ID
    TR.idTaskRole = _
        dbPT.rsRetrieveTaskRoles("idTaskRole")

    ' Set the role name
    TR.RoleName = _
        dbPT.rsRetrieveTaskRoles("chrRoleName")

    ' Add the class to the collection
    RTR.Add TR

    ' Move to the next row
    dbPT.rsRetrieveTaskRoles.MoveNext
```

```
Loop

Set dbPT = Nothing

'  Return the collection
Set RetrieveTaskRoles = RTR

End Function
```

That finishes the class functionality. We have in effect encapsulated the functionality of managing our projects, tasks, and developers in our classes. The data interface is hidden away in the database and interfaced with the data environment. Next we will build the user interface for the application to be built upon the class structure we have created.

General Functions

Our interface will use a series of "standard" functions that will be placed in a new module in our application, modPT.bas. The rest of the "event" functionality will be defined in the projects form.

First in our modPT module we define a global projects class. This will be our primary interface into the entire class structure. In fact, we will never independently access task, developer, project, or task role classes. We will always utilize all of the project tracking system business logic via the top-level projects class.

```
Option Explicit

'  The clsProjects class will hold all of
'  the project classes and in turn will reference
'  all of the task and developer classes.
Public clsProjects As New Projects
```

The DeleteDeveloper subroutine will interface with the class structure to delete a developer from a task. The "with" syntax is utilized to simplify the access to the objects on the projects form. Also, we cannot delete a developer if a project, task, and developer are not selected.

Users are queried as to whether they are sure they want to delete the developer before the developer is deleted. We have to traverse the class structure to make the appropriate call to remove the developer. First we must indicate which project we are working with by getting the list index of the cboProjects combo box. We need to add one to this index since the list starts at 0 and not 1.

Next we reference the ItemTask property of the project class to reference the current task that we wish to delete the developer from. In this case we reference the list index of the cboTasks combo box and add one. The RemoveDeveloper method of the task is referenced.

But we do have to reference the ID of the developer we wish to remove from the task. The list index of the developers list is passed into the RemoveDeveloper method. Once all of that is done, the developer has been removed within our class structure as well as within the database. Finally, the LoadDevelopers subroutine is called to reload the developers list box and clear out the one we have deleted.

```
'  Subroutine to delete a developer
Public Sub DeleteDeveloper()

Dim intResult As Integer

'  Use the With statement to shorten calls'
'  to objects on the form
With frmProjects

'  Ensure a project is selected
If .cboProjects.ListIndex <> -1 Then
 If .cboTasks.ListIndex <> -1 Then
  If .lstDevelopers.ListIndex <> -1 Then

    '  Ask users if they are sure they want to
    '  delete the developer
    intResult = MsgBox("Are you sure?", vbYesNo)

    '  Check for a yes answer
    If intResult = vbYes Then

        '  Call the RemoveDeveloper method of the
        '  task object for the currently selected
        '  project
        clsProjects(.cboProjects.ListIndex + 1). _
        ItemTask(.cboTasks.ListIndex + 1).RemoveDeveloper _
            .lstDevelopers.ListIndex + 1
```

```
        '  Load the developers list
        LoadDevelopers

    End If
  End If
 End If
End If

End With

End Sub
```

The LoadDevelopers subroutine will load the developers associated with the currently displayed task. Since we have several references to make to the cboProjects and cboTasks combo boxes, we will get the current list index from each.

The current list is cleared. Then the number of developers assigned to the current task is retrieved. We will loop through the list and retrieve the first name, last name, number of hours, and role for each developer. The data is then loaded into the list box.

```
'  Load the developers
Public Sub LoadDevelopers()

'  Declare our variables
Dim intCnt As Integer
Dim strFirstName As String
Dim strLastName As String
Dim strRole As String
Dim intTaskHours As Integer
Dim intIndexProject As Integer
Dim intIndexTask As Integer

'  Use the With statement to shorten calls'
'  to objects on the form
With frmProjects

'  Retrieve the project and task indexes
intIndexProject = .cboProjects.ListIndex + 1
intIndexTask = .cboTasks.ListIndex + 1
```

```
' Clear the list of developers
.lstDevelopers.Clear

' Loop through the number of developers for the task
For intCnt = 1 To clsProjects(intIndexProject). _
                ItemTask(intIndexTask).CountDeveloper

    ' Retrieve the first name from the first developer
    strFirstName = clsProjects(intIndexProject). _
            ItemTask(intIndexTask). _
            ItemDeveloper(intCnt).FirstName

    ' Retrieve the last name from the first developer
    strLastName = clsProjects(intIndexProject). _
            ItemTask(intIndexTask). _
            ItemDeveloper(intCnt).LastName

    ' Retrieve the task hours for the developer
    intTaskHours = clsProjects(intIndexProject). _
            ItemTask(intIndexTask). _
            ItemDeveloper(intCnt).TaskHours

    strRole = clsProjects(intIndexProject). _
        ItemTask(intIndexTask).ItemDeveloper(intCnt).Role

    .lstDevelopers.AddItem strFirstName & " " & strLastName & _
    Chr(9) & intTaskHours & Chr(9) & strRole

    .lstDevelopers.ItemData(.lstDevelopers.NewIndex) = _
    clsProjects(intIndexProject). _
    ItemTask(intIndexTask).ItemDeveloper(intCnt).idDeveloper

Next

End With

End Sub
```

The LoadTasks subroutine will retrieve all of the tasks for the current project and load the tasks combo box. A check is first done to ensure that a project is selected. Then any current tasks in the combo box are cleared.

The number of tasks for the current project is retrieved, and we loop through the tasks. Each task name is loaded into the cboTasks combo box. And the item data field for the combo box is set to store the database ID of the task.

```
'  Load the tasks for the current project
Public Sub LoadTasks()

'  Declare our variables
Dim intCnt As Integer
Dim intIndexProject As Integer
Dim intIndexTask As Integer

'  Use the With statement to shorten calls'
'  to objects on the form
With frmProjects

'  Retrieve our project index
intIndexProject = .cboProjects.ListIndex + 1

'  Clear the tasks list box
.cboTasks.Clear

'  Loop through the tasks for the current project
For intCnt = 1 To clsProjects(intIndexProject).CountTask

    '  Retrieve the task name
    .cboTasks.AddItem clsProjects.Item(intIndexProject). _
        ItemTask(intCnt).TaskName

    '  Add the id of the task to the item data field
    .cboTasks.ItemData(.cboTasks.NewIndex) = _
      clsProjects.Item(intIndexProject).ItemTask(intCnt).idTask

Next

End With

End Sub
```

The LoadProjects subroutine is utilized to load the system when the program is started. It will be called from the splash screen with the splash screen displayed. When the clsProjects class was created, the project system was loaded. Now we are ready to load the user interface with the appropriate data.

First we loop through the series of projects in the system and load the cboProjects combo box with the project names. Next we use the RetrieveDevelopers metafunction of the developers class to retrieve a collection of developers from the database. This collection is then looped through and added to our two developer listings on the form. The ID of the developers is stored in the item data field of the controls.

Finally, we also use the RetrieveTaskRoles metamethod of the TaskRole class to return a collection of roles that we can load into the cboRoles combo box. The ID of the role is stored in the item data field of each listing in the combo box.

```
'  Load the projects
Public Sub LoadProjects()

'  Declare the developer and taskrole classes
Dim clsDev As New Developer
Dim clsTaskRole As New TaskRole
Dim colTaskRole As Collection

'  Two collections for our developers and task roles
Dim colDev As New Collection
Dim ColTaskRol As New Collection

'  Two variables for looping through the collections
Dim CD
Dim CTR

Dim intCnt As Integer

'  Use the With statement to shorten calls'
'  to objects on the form
With frmProjects

'  Clear all of the list boxes
.cboProjects.Clear
.cboDevelopers.Clear
.cboTaskDevelopers.Clear
```

```
'  Loop through the projects in the projects class
For intCnt = 1 To clsProjects.Count

    '  add the project name to the projects list box
    .cboProjects.AddItem clsProjects.Item(intCnt).ProjectName

Next intCnt

'  Retrieve the class of developers using the
'  retrieve developers metamethod of the developers
'  class
Set colDev = clsDev.RetrieveDevelopers

'  Loop through the developers
For Each CD In colDev

    '  Add the first name and last name to the developers
    '  list box
    .cboDevelopers.AddItem CD.FirstName & " " & CD.LastName

    '  Add the id of the developer to the item data property
    .cboDevelopers.ItemData(.cboDevelopers.NewIndex) = _
    CD.idDeveloper

    '  Add the first name and last name to the task developers
    '  list box
    .cboTaskDevelopers.AddItem CD.FirstName & " " & CD.LastName

    '  Add the id of the developer to the item data property
    .cboTaskDevelopers.ItemData(.cboDevelopers.NewIndex) = _
    CD.idDeveloper

Next

'  Retrieve the collection of task roles
Set colTaskRole = clsTaskRole.RetrieveTaskRoles
```

```
'  Loop through the task roles
For Each CTR In colTaskRole

    '  Add the task role to the roles list box
    .cboRoles.AddItem CTR.RoleName

    '  Set the id of the role to the item data property
    .cboRoles.ItemData(.cboRoles.NewIndex) = CTR.idTaskRole

Next

End With

End Sub
```

The DeleteTask subroutine will remove the current task displayed in the cboTasks combo box. Before the task is deleted, we ask users if they are sure they want to delete the task.

If the user wishes to retrieve the task, we first have to delete all developers assigned to the task. The developers assigned are looped through, and the RemoveDeveloper method of the task is called with the key of the developer passed in.

Once the developers for the task are removed, we can remove the task as well. The RemoveTask function of the project class is called, and the task is removed. Once the task and developers have been removed, we clear the task fields by calling our ClearTaskFields subroutine created in Chapter 11. Following that, the LoadTasks subroutine is called to reload the remaining tasks.

```
'  Delete the current task
Public Sub DeleteTask()

'  Declare our variables
Dim intResult As Integer
Dim intCnt As Integer

'  Use the With statement to shorten calls'
'  to objects on the form
With frmProjects
```

```
'  Query the user
intResult = MsgBox("Are you sure?", vbYesNo)

'  Check the result
If intResult = vbYes Then

    '  Loop through the developers and delete each one
    For intCnt = 1 To clsProjects(.cboProjects.ListIndex + 1). _
            ItemTask(.cboTasks.ListIndex + 1).CountDeveloper

        '  Remove the developer
        clsProjects(.cboProjects.ListIndex + 1). _
            ItemTask(intCnt).RemoveDeveloper intCnt

    Next intCnt

    '  Remove the task
    clsProjects(.cboProjects.ListIndex + 1).RemoveTask _
    .cboTasks.ListIndex + 1

End If

'  Clear the task fields
.ClearTaskFields

'  Reload the tasks
LoadTasks

End With

End Sub
```

The DeleteProject subroutine will delete a project, its assigned tasks, and the developers assigned to the tasks. Users are asked if they are sure they want to delete the project. If they are, we start by looping through the tasks assigned to the project.

For each task we loop through the developers assigned to the task and remove the developers from the system. Then each task is deleted and finally the project. Next, both of the frames are cleared of any data, and the projects combo box is reloaded.

```vb
'  Delete the project
Public Sub DeleteProject()

'  Declare our variables
Dim intResult As Integer
Dim intCnt As Integer
Dim intCnt2 As Integer

'  Use the With statement to shorten calls'
'  to objects on the form
With frmProjects

    '  Ensure the user wants to delete the
    '  project
    intResult = MsgBox("Are you sure?", vbYesNo)

    '  If yes
    If intResult = vbYes Then

        '  Loop through the tasks
        For intCnt = 1 To clsProjects(.cboProjects.ListIndex + _
        1).CountTask

            '  Loop through the developers
            For intCnt2 = 1 To clsProjects(.cboProjects.ListIndex + 1). _
                        ItemTask(intCnt).CountDeveloper

                '  Delete the developers
                clsProjects(.cboProjects.ListIndex + 1). _
                ItemTask(intCnt).RemoveDeveloper intCnt2

            Next intCnt2

            '  Delete the task
            clsProjects(.cboProjects.ListIndex + 1).RemoveTask intCnt

        Next intCnt

        '  Remove the project
        clsProjects.Remove .cboProjects.ListIndex + 1

    End If
```

```
'  Clear the project and task fields
.ClearProjectFields
.ClearTaskFields

'  Load the projects list box
LoadProjects

End With

End Sub
```

The SaveProject subroutine will retrieve the appropriate data from the project frame set and set the properties of the selected project class. Note, for the manager, we ensure a manager is selected before setting the ID of the manager. Finally, the StoreProject method of the project class is called, and the database is updated.

```
'  Save the project
Public Sub SaveProject()

'  Declare our variables
Dim intIndexProject As Integer

'  Use the With statement to shorten calls
'  to objects on the form
With frmProjects

'  Get the project index
intIndexProject = .cboProjects.ListIndex + 1

'  Set the project description, end date and start date
clsProjects(intIndexProject).Description = .txtDescription.Text
clsProjects(intIndexProject).EndDate = .txtEndDate.Text
clsProjects(intIndexProject).StartDate = .txtStartDate.Text

'  Check to see if a manager has been selected
If .cboDevelopers.ListIndex <> -1 Then
```

```
        '  Set the id of the manager to the id of the developer
        '  selected.
        clsProjects(intIndexProject).idManager = _
          .cboDevelopers.ItemData(.cboDevelopers.ListIndex)

  End If

  '  Set the status of the project
  clsProjects(intIndexProject).status = .txtStatus.Text

  '  Set the percent complete
  clsProjects(intIndexProject).PercentComplete = _
    .txtPercentComplete.Text

  '  Set the project name
  clsProjects(intIndexProject).ProjectName = _
    .txtProjectName.Text

  '  Save the project
  clsProjects(intIndexProject).StoreProject

  End With

  End Sub
```

The SaveTask subroutine works much the same as the SaveProject procedure. Each of the fields on the task frame and the appropriate properties in the task class are set. Finally, the StoreTask method of the task class is called to update the task table in the database.

```
'  Save the task
Public Sub SaveTask()

'  Declare our variables
Dim intIndexProject As Integer
Dim intIndexTask As Integer

'  Use the With statement to shorten calls
'  to objects on the form
With frmProjects
```

```
If .cboTasks.ListIndex <> -1 Then

'   Get the project and task indexes
intIndexProject = .cboProjects.ListIndex + 1
intIndexTask = .cboTasks.ListIndex + 1

'   Set the task notes
clsProjects(intIndexProject). _
  ItemTask(intIndexTask).TaskNotes = _
  .txtTaskNotes.Text

'   Set the end date
clsProjects(intIndexProject). _
  ItemTask(intIndexTask).EndDate = _
  FormatDateTime(.txtTaskEndDate.Text, vbShortDate)

'   Set the end date
clsProjects(intIndexProject). _
  ItemTask(intIndexTask).ProjectedEndDate = _
  FormatDateTime(.txtTaskProjectedEndDate.Text, vbShortDate)

'   Set the task name
clsProjects(intIndexProject). _
  ItemTask(intIndexTask).TaskName = _
  .txtTaskName.Text

'   Set the start date
clsProjects(intIndexProject). _
  ItemTask(intIndexTask).StartDate = _
  FormatDateTime(.txtTaskStartDate.Text, vbShortDate)

'   Set the task status
clsProjects(intIndexProject). _
  ItemTask(intIndexTask).status = .txtTaskStatus.Text

'   Set the task hours completed
clsProjects(intIndexProject). _
  ItemTask(intIndexTask).HoursCompleted = .txtHoursComplete.Text

'   set the projected hours to complete
clsProjects(intIndexProject). _
```

```
    ItemTask(intIndexTask).ProjectedHours = _
    .txtProjectedHoursComplete.Text

'  Store the task
clsProjects(intIndexProject). _
    ItemTask(intIndexTask).StoreTask

End If

End With

End Sub
```

> **Note**
> *The SaveTask and SaveProject subroutines could be made much simpler if the class structure handled its own cascading saves. In other words, if a save was initiated on the project class, it would automatically invoke a save on its task classes, and so on. It is a matter of definition and where to partition the logic. If you are trying to build a very simple client, putting the save logic in the class structure in the business tier may make sense.*
>
> *These subroutines will be called from our form code to implement the functionality of the classes in the user interface. As you can see, most of the purpose of these procedures is to verify the correct events have taken place on the form, query the user, and then invoke the appropriate properties and methods of the classes to interface with our object model.*

Form Code

Last but not least, we have our form code. In Chapter 11 we built some of the functionality to finish off the user interface prototype. Now we can finalize functionality by interfacing with our module procedures and the project class structure.

The click event of the projects combo box will need to display a new project as well as retrieve the tasks for the project. Since we will be referencing the list index of the combo box frequently, the value (plus one) will be stored in a variable. We then retrieve the property values for the specified project and display them in the project frame.

Once the project data is set up, the ClearTaskFields function is called to clear out the task frame. Then the LoadTasks procedure is called to load the tasks for the specified project.

```
Option Explicit

'  Click event of the projects combo box
Private Sub cboProjects_Click()

'  Declare our variables
Dim intCnt As Integer
Dim intIndexProject As Integer
Dim intIndexTask As Integer

'  To reference the task data, we have to reference the project
'  selected in the cboProjects list box
intIndexProject = cboProjects.ListIndex + 1

'Set the project name
txtProjectName.Text = clsProjects(intIndexProject).ProjectName

'  Set the project manager
txtProjectManager.Text = clsProjects(intIndexProject). _
                         Manager.FirstName & " " & _
                         clsProjects(intIndexProject). _
                         Manager.LastName

'  Set the percent complete
txtPercentComplete.Text = clsProjects(intIndexProject). _
                          PercentComplete

'  Set the project start date
txtStartDate.Text = FormatDateTime( _
                    clsProjects(intIndexProject).StartDate _
                    , vbShortDate)

'  Set the project end date
txtEndDate.Text = FormatDateTime( _
                  clsProjects(intIndexProject).EndDate _
                  , vbShortDate)

'  Set the project status
txtStatus.Text = clsProjects(intIndexProject).status
```

```
'  Set the project description
txtDescription.Text = clsProjects(intIndexProject).Description

'  Clear the task fields
ClearTaskFields

'  Load the tasks
LoadTasks

End Sub
```

When the tasks combo box is selected, we will retrieve the task data from the selected task. As with the projects combo box, the list index property will be referenced several times but, in this case, for both the project and task combo boxes. The values (plus one) are retrieved for each in a variable.

The task frame is updated with the new data from the class. Once that is done, the LoadDevelopers procedure is called to retrieve the developers for the specified task and show them in the developers list box.

```
'  Click event to select a project
Private Sub cboTasks_Click()

'  Declare our variables
Dim intIndexProject As Integer
Dim intIndexTask As Integer

'  To reference the task data, we have to reference the project
'  selected in the cboProjects list box
intIndexProject = cboProjects.ListIndex + 1

'  Then we reference the task selected
intIndexTask = cboTasks.ListIndex + 1

'  Set the task notes
txtTaskNotes.Text = _
    clsProjects(intIndexProject). _
    ItemTask(intIndexTask).TaskNotes
```

```
'  Set the task end date
txtTaskEndDate.Text = FormatDateTime( _
    clsProjects(intIndexProject). _
    ItemTask(intIndexTask).EndDate _
    , vbShortDate)

'  Set the task projected end date
txtTaskProjectedEndDate.Text = FormatDateTime( _
    clsProjects(intIndexProject). _
    ItemTask(intIndexTask).ProjectedEndDate _
    , vbShortDate)

'  Set the task name
txtTaskName.Text = _
    clsProjects(intIndexProject). _
    ItemTask(intIndexTask).TaskName

'  Set the task start date
txtTaskStartDate.Text = FormatDateTime( _
    clsProjects(intIndexProject). _
    ItemTask(intIndexTask).StartDate _
    , vbShortDate)

'  Set the task status
txtTaskStatus.Text = _
    clsProjects(intIndexProject). _
    ItemTask(cboTasks.ListIndex + 1).status

'  Set the number of hours complete
txtHoursComplete.Text = _
    clsProjects(intIndexProject). _
    ItemTask(intIndexTask).HoursCompleted

'  Set the projected hours complete
txtProjectedHoursComplete.Text = _
    clsProjects(intIndexProject). _
    ItemTask(intIndexTask).ProjectedHours

'  Load the developers
LoadDevelopers

End Sub
```

The Add Developer command button will assign a new developer to the current task. As before, the list indexes of both the project and task combo boxes are retrieved to reference the proper project and task classes. But we also need to retrieve the index into the developers and roles combo boxes to determine who will be assigned to the task and in what role.

The AddDeveloper method of the current task is called to assign a new developer to the task. The ID of the developer and the ID of the role are passed in to the call. Once the developer is added, the LoadDevelopers procedure is called to refresh the developers list box.

```
'  Add developer command button
Private Sub cmdAddDeveloper_Click()

'  Declare our variables
Dim intIndexProject As Integer
Dim intIndexTask As Integer
Dim intIndexTaskDeveloper As Integer
Dim intIndexTaskRole As Integer

'  To reference the task data, we have to reference the project
'  selected in the cboProjects list box
intIndexProject = cboProjects.ListIndex + 1

'  Then we reference the task selected
intIndexTask = cboTasks.ListIndex + 1

'  The new developer is referenced from the task developer list box
intIndexTaskDeveloper = cboTaskDevelopers.ListIndex

'  The new role is referenced from the role list box
intIndexTaskRole = cboRoles.ListIndex

'  Ensure a project is selected before we add a developer
'  to a task
If cboTaskDevelopers.ListIndex <> -1 Then

    '  Ensure a task is selected before we add a developer
    If cboRoles.ListIndex <> -1 Then
```

```
'  For the current task in the given project we
'  will call the AddDeveloper method to add the
'  new developer selected. When we add the developer
'  we pass in the id of the developer and the id of
'  the role
clsProjects(intIndexProject). _
ItemTask(intIndexTask).AddNewDeveloper _
cboTaskDevelopers.ItemData(intIndexTaskDeveloper), _
cboRoles.ItemData(intIndexTaskRole)

'  Load the developers list box with the
'  new developer
LoadDevelopers

    End If

End If

End Sub
```

When the Delete Developer button is clicked, the DeleteDeveloper procedure is called.

```
'  Command button for deleting a developer
Private Sub cmdDeleteDeveloper_Click()

'  Call the DeleteDeveloper function
DeleteDeveloper

End Sub
```

The Update Developer command button will read the new number of hours entered in the task for the selected developer. First a check is done to ensure that a developer has been selected. If so, then the appropriate indexes into the project and task class are retrieved from the combo boxes.

Finally, the Task Hours property of the developer is updated to have the new number of hours. Then the StoreDeveloper method of the developer class is called to store the data in the database.

```
'  Command button to update the developer's hours
Private Sub cmdUpdateDeveloper_Click()

'  Declare our variables
Dim intIndexProject As Integer
Dim intIndexTask As Integer
Dim intIndexDeveloper As Integer

if lstDevelopers.ListIndex <> - 1 then

    '  To reference the task data, we have to reference the project
    '  selected in the cboProjects list box
    intIndexProject = cboProjects.ListIndex + 1

    '  Then we reference the task selected
    intIndexTask = cboTasks.ListIndex + 1

    '  The developer is referenced from the developer list box
    intIndexDeveloper = lstDevelopers.ListIndex + 1

    '  Set the task hours for the developer class
    clsProjects(intIndexProject). _
      ItemTask(intIndexTask).ItemDeveloper(intIndexDeveloper). _
      TaskHours = txtHours.Text

    '  Store the developer data. To do that, we need to know the
    '  id of the task to update the TaskDev table.
    clsProjects(intIndexProject).ItemTask(intIndexTask). _
      ItemDeveloper(intIndexDeveloper). _
      StoreDeveloper _
      clsProjects(intIndexProject). _
      ItemTask(intIndexTask).idTask

    LoadDevelopers

End If

End Sub
```

Not much has been added to the Form_Unload event other than the specific calls to
the SaveProject and SaveTask methods if the user opts to save the project before exiting
the application.

```
'  Unload event of the form
Private Sub Form_Unload(Cancel As Integer)

'  Declare our variables
Dim intResult As Integer

'  Check to see if a project is selected
If cboProjects.ListIndex <> -1 Then

    '  Query users if they want to save the project
    intResult = MsgBox("Save any changes to the project and task?" _
            , vbYesNoCancel)

    '  Check the result
    Select Case intResult

        '  If cancel was selected we set the
        '  cancel argument of the function
        '  to True so the project end is
        '  canceled
        Case vbCancel
            Cancel = True

        '  If yes then save the project and tasks
        Case vbYes
            SaveProject
            SaveTask
            End

        Case Else
            End

    End Select

Else

    End

End If

End Sub
```

The same is true for the button click on the project toolbar. The appropriate DeleteProject, SaveProject, and code for a new project are added to the case statements.

```
'   Button click of the project toolbar
Private Sub tblProject_ButtonClick(ByVal Button As _
MSComctlLib.Button)

'   Declare our variables
Dim strResults As String

'   Select case on the button index
Select Case Button.Index

    '   The first button ends the project
    Case 1
        End

    '   The second button deletes the project
    Case 2
        '   Only delete if a project is selected
        If cboProjects.ListIndex <> -1 Then

            '   Call the delete project subroutine
            DeleteProject

        End If

    '   Save the project
    Case 3

        '   Only save the project if a project is selected
        If cboProjects.ListIndex <> -1 Then

            '   Save the project
            SaveProject

        End If

    '   Add a new project
    Case 4
```

```
'  Clear the project fields
ClearProjectFields

'  Query the user for the project name
strResults = InputBox("Enter the project name:", _
            "Project Name", "New Project")

'  Ensure a project name was entered
If strResults <> "" Then

    '  Add a new project name to the projects
    '  class by calling the AddNew method of the
    '  class
    clsProjects.AddNew strResults

    '  Load the projects
    LoadProjects

Else

    '  Indicate the project name cannot be empty
    MsgBox "You cannot have an empty project name."

End If

'  Show the projects report
Case 5

    rptProjects.Show

End Select

End Sub
```

As with the project toolbar, the task toolbar has been updated with the appropriate calls to delete a task, save a task, and add a new task.

```vb
' Button click of the task toolbar
Private Sub tblTask_ButtonClick(ByVal Button As MSComctlLib.Button)

' Declare a variable
Dim strResults As String

' Process by the button selected
Select Case Button.Index

    ' Delete task button
    Case 1

        ' Ensure a project is selected
        If cboProjects.ListIndex <> -1 Then

            ' Ensure a task is selected
            If cboTasks.ListIndex <> -1 Then

                ' Delete the task
                DeleteTask

            End If

        End If

    ' Save the task
    Case 2

        ' Ensure a project is selected
        If cboProjects.ListIndex <> -1 Then

            ' Ensure a task is selected
            If cboTasks.ListIndex <> -1 Then

                ' Save the task
                SaveTask

            End If

        End If
```

```
    '  Add a new task
    Case 3

    ' Ensure a project is selected
    If cboProjects.ListIndex <> -1 Then

        '  Clear the task fields
        ClearTaskFields

        '  Ask for the task name
        strResults = InputBox("Enter the task name:", _
                    "Task Name", "New Task")

        '  Ensure we do not have an empty task name
        If strResults <> "" Then

            '  Add a new task by calling the AddNewTask
            '  method of the projects class.
            clsProjects(cboProjects.ListIndex + 1).AddNewTask _
            strResults

            '  Load the tasks list box
            LoadTasks

        Else

            '  Indicate the task cannot be empty
            MsgBox "You cannot have an empty task name."

        End If

    End If

End Select

End Sub
```

There is a lot of code behind the project tracking system. In the classes, we implement the functionality to manage the project relationships and data. In the user interface, we implement the class structure and connect it to the interface. Now it is time to finally see our application in action.

Running the Project Tracking System

For the moment, we have all of the application contained in one project, so we can go ahead and run the program. Figure 12-1 shows the program at run time. Ensure you have developer and role data loaded into your database. You will first see the splash screen before the project is actually loaded. First you will be able to see that the Select New Manager, developer, and role combo boxes are all filled with data from the database. Figure 12-2 shows the drop-down box for the developer.

Let's create a new project in our system. Click on the New button on the project toolbar. When you do so, you will get the project name input box we built in the previous chapter. Go ahead and enter **Project One** as the project name. When you do so, a new project class will be created and the project added to the project combo box. Select the Project One project in the project combo box (see Figure 12-3).

Now fill out the fields of the project form. Be sure and select a developer from the list of developers. Once you are finished, click the Save button. Figure 12-4 shows the completed project information.

Next let's add a couple of new tasks to the project. Click on the New Task button on the task toolbar. When you do so, the task name input box will require you to enter the task name. Enter **Project One Task One** as the task name, then click OK. Figure 12-5 shows the task selected in the task list box.

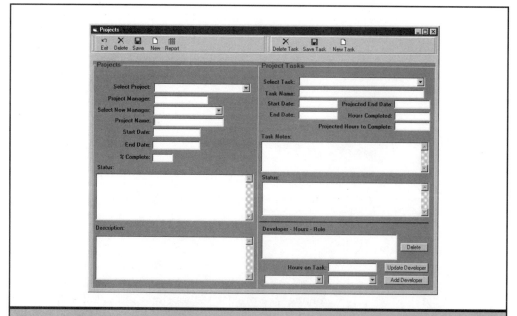

Figure 12-1. *Project tracking system at run time*

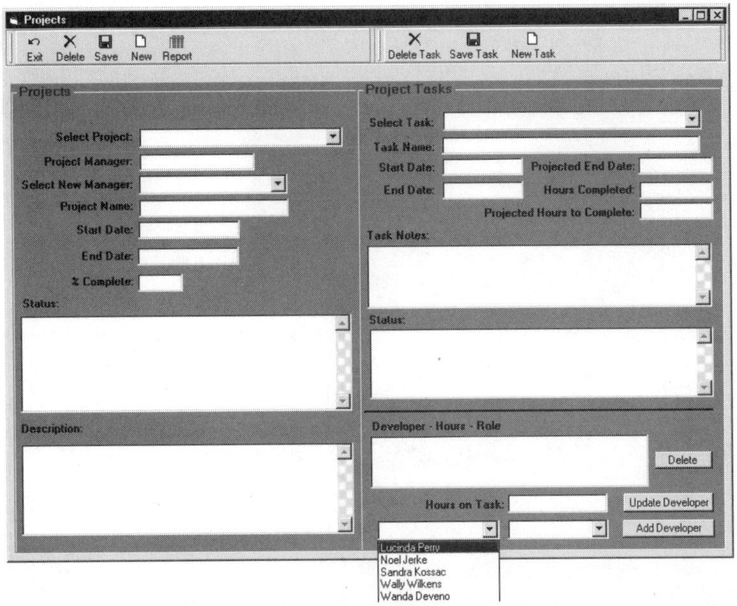

Figure 12-2.   Developer list box

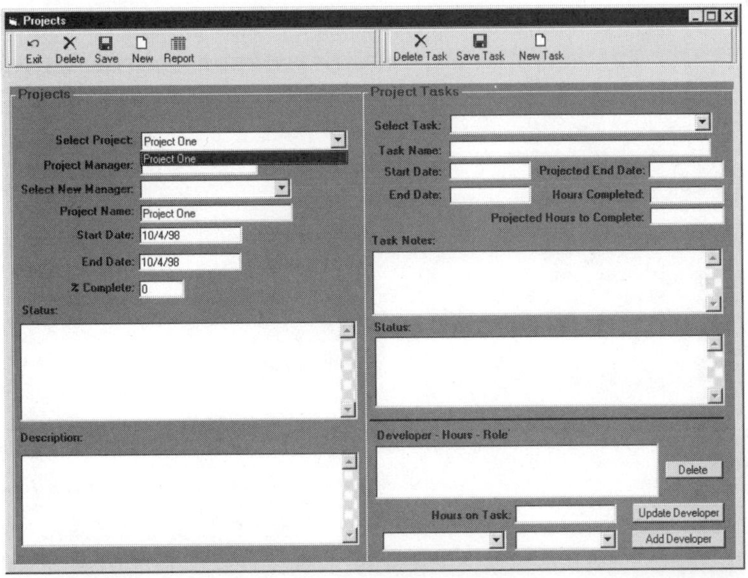

Figure 12-3.   Project selected in the project list

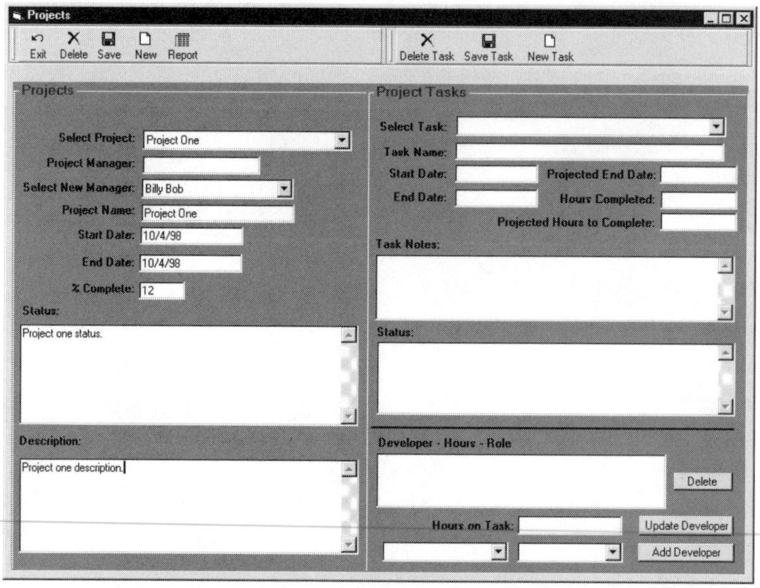

Figure 12-4. Project One information filled out and saved

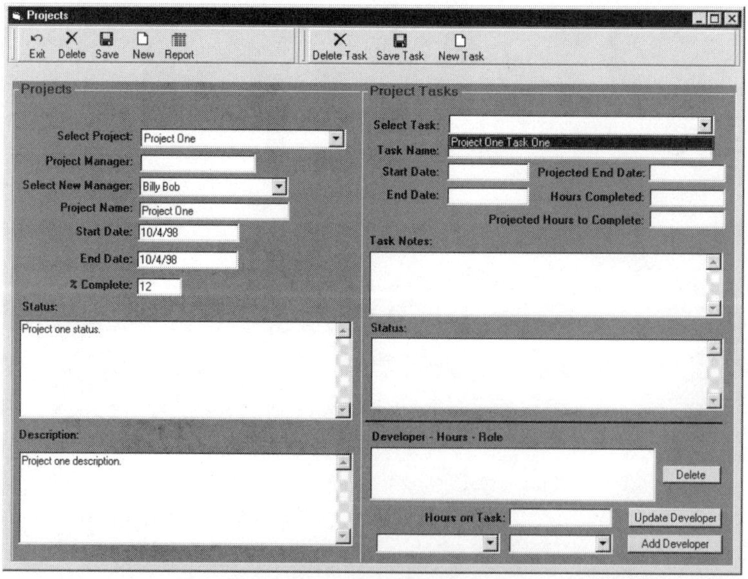

Figure 12-5. Task selected in the task list box

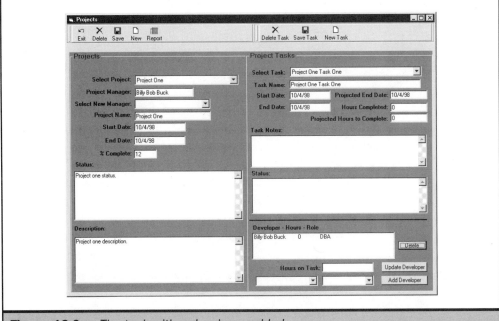

Figure 12-6.   *The task with a developer added*

Now go ahead and fill out the basic task data and save it. Next let's add some developers to the task. Select a developer from the developer list and select a role. If you only select one or the other, you will not be allowed to add a developer to the list. Figure 12-6 shows the task with one added developer.

Now let's update the developer's hours from 0 to 10. Type **10** into the Hours on Task text box. Then click the Update Developer command button. When you do, the hours for the developer will be updated in the list box. Figure 12-7 shows the update.

You can continue adding more tasks and developers to each task. The real test will come when you close the application and restart it. When you do so, you should have your project tasks and developers all loaded up. Note that the data is actually loaded when the project starts.

Once the application is reloaded, browse through the project and task data. You should be all set with each of the data elements falling into place. Now let's delete the work we just created. Figure 12-8 shows a second task in our project and two developers. Select the first developer and click on the Delete Developer command button.

The developer will then be deleted from the list of developers for the second task. Now let's delete the second task from the project. Ensure the second task is selected, and select the Delete Task button. Figure 12-9 shows the task list box with only one task left.

Finally, let's delete the complete project. When we do so, all subtasks and assigned developers will be deleted. Ensure the project is selected, and click on the Delete button on the project toolbar. When you do so, the system will essentially be cleared out (if only one project has been loaded). Figure 12-10 shows the project tracking system with all projects deleted.

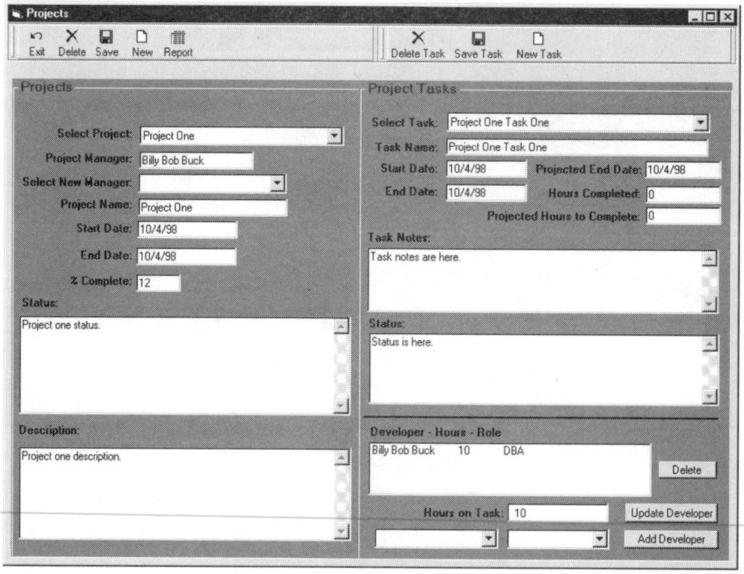

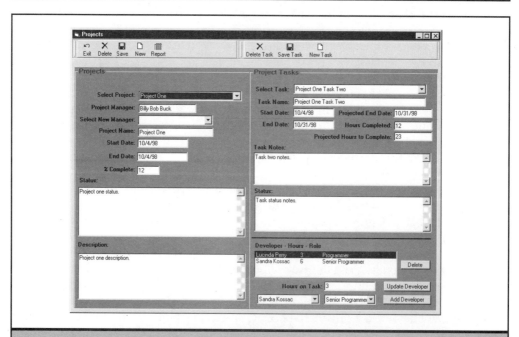

Figure 12-7. Task developer's hours updated

Figure 12-8. Project with a task showing and two developers

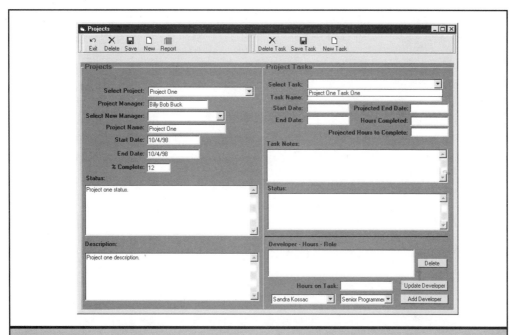

Figure 12-9.   *Task list minus one task*

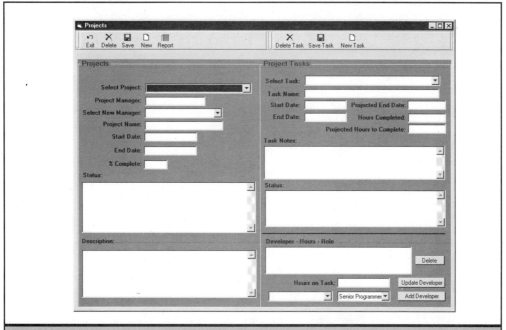

Figure 12-10.   *Project tracking system with all projects deleted*

And with that, we have built the core functionality of our tracking system, designed from the database and class structure up. Play around with the interface and use of the system. In the next chapter we will use VB to add more functionality to the application and deploy it.

Summary

In the previous two chapters we built the object model, database, and interface foundation for our project tracking system. In this chapter we filled out the business logic code in our class structure and added implementation code in our interface. By building our application this way, we have segmented it into multiple tiers. The first is the user interface, the second is the projects object model, and the third is the database interface.

We can now think about deploying our application in different segments. For example, the user interface will need to go to the client. The projects class structure could go to a business objects server. The data environment could go to a database objects server. And, of course, the database will be placed on a database server.

What's Next

In the next chapter we will finalize our application, first, by adding a basic report using Visual Basic's report designer. Then we will partition our application into logic segments. And finally, we will review how to deploy those segments using the Package and Deployment wizard.

Chapter 13

Deploying the Tracking System

In this chapter we will work on making our project tracking system "enterprise ready." The first step will be to partition the code into two logical units. After that, we will provide some basic reporting capabilities on projects in the system. We will see how to effectively use the data environment with the new reporting tools.

Once we have our application partitioned, we are ready for deployment. The Package and Deployment wizard will be utilized to create installation sets for our application. Finally, we will review some options for extending the application.

Splitting Up the Application

Breaking up can be hard to do, but with Microsoft Visual Basic and the different component types, we can easily take our class logic and database connectivity and create a component that can be called from our user interface.

Components are characterized by their location relative to clients. An *out-of-process* component is an EXE file that runs in its own process, with its own thread of execution. Communication between a client and an out-of-process component uses out-of-process communication.

An *in-process* component, such as a DLL or OCX file, runs in the same process as the client. It provides the fastest way of accessing objects, because property and method calls don't have to be marshaled across process boundaries. However, an in-process component must use the client's thread of execution.

Building the Server-Side ActiveX EXE Application

In our case, we can build the class logic and data environment into an out-of-process component that will be used in our interface application. Our intent is to deploy the DLL file to a machine other than the one on which the client is running. That means the component will be running on a remote server.

To partition our application, let's first build the remote business component with our classes and data environment. To work through this process, follow these steps:

1. Create a new Visual Basic project as an ActiveX EXE project.

2. Save the project as "srvProjectTrack."

3. Make copies of the developer.cls, project.cls, projects.cls, task.cls, and taskrole.cls files in the new project directory.

4. Copy the dbProjectTrack.DCA, dbProjectTrack.Dsr, and dbProjectTrack.dsx files to the directory as well. That will move the data environment into the new project directory.

5. Import the class files and dbProjectTrack.dsr file into the project.

That gets us where we need to be in terms of getting the proper files into the project. Table 13-1 shows the appropriate property settings for each of the imported files.

We want our classes to be publicly created in multiple instances. Our options are private, which means the calling application could not see the classes at all. PublicNotCreatable means that the classes are publicly visible but cannot be created. GlobalMultiUse is similar to MultiUse, but the objects are automatically created and can be used without creating an instance of the class. In our case, we simply want to be able to create multiple instances of our objects and utilize them.

> **Note** *You could set only the Projects task to be MultiUse and the rest of the classes to be PublicNotCreatable. In our interface we could avoid directly using and creating task, developer, project, and task role classes and let the projects class handle all of it.*

Next we need to set up the project properties for our ActiveX DLL. Follow these steps:

1. Select the Project menu.
2. Select the project properties options.
3. On the General tab, ensure the project name is srvProjectTrack. Note that the Project Type is ActiveX DLL.
4. Select the Make tab and ensure the application title is srvProjectTrack.
5. Select the Component tab. We want to ensure the Remote Server Files option is selected, as shown in Figure 13-1.

File	Setting
Developer	
Instancing	5 – Multiuse
Project	
Instancing	5 – Multiuse
Projects	
Instancing	5 – Multiuse
Task	
Instancing	5 – Multiuse
TaskRole	
Instancing	5 – Multiuse
DbProjectTrack	
Public	False

Table 13-1. *File Settings for the Server-Side Project Tracking Application*

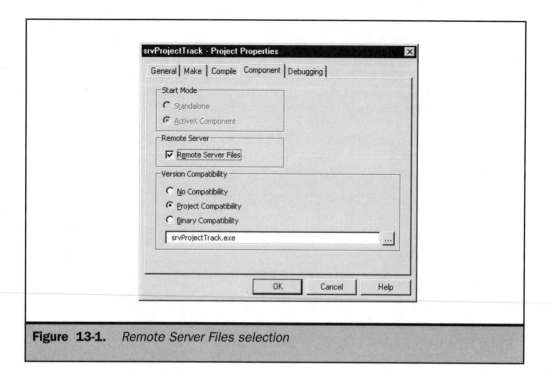

Figure 13-1.   *Remote Server Files selection*

With the remote server files installed, we can then deploy the srvProjectTrack application on a remote server and include the appropriate files with our client installation. That way we can have our business logic run on a remote server without being distributed or processed on the client's machine.

As we will see in the next part of the book, we can easily develop a new Internet interface for our application and still access the business logic on the remote server while utilizing much of the code developed in the basic module in our current interface.

Building the Client Interface Application

Now that we have our server application created, we will need to pare down our client-side application to exclude the data environment and business logic. We will want to reference the code on the remote server, but not actually include the code. Follow these steps to create the client application:

1. Open the project tracking application.

2. Remove the class files from the application.

3. Remove the data environment controls from the application. That will leave the two forms and the basic module in our application.

4. Select the Project menu.

5. Select the References option.

6. Select the srvProjectTrack reference, as shown in Figure 13-2. That will implement the functionality in our application for use.

Let's explore this new reference we just added to the application. Select the Object Browser option on the View menu. In the viewer, select the srvProjectTrack object from the list of objects in our application. Figure 13-3 shows the Object Browser.

You can see our classes in the browser. You can click on each and get a listing of properties and methods of the classes. By now those should all be quite familiar! Click on the developer class. You can see the properties and methods indicated. You can click on each of these to find out more about the type of property and the arguments and return values from the methods. Figure 13-4 shows the developer class listing.

One thing you will not see is the data environment. It is still visible privately to the rest of the classes in srvProjectTrack. So, for all intents and purposes, our client application has no idea where the database is located, how it is structured, on what technology it is placed, and so on.

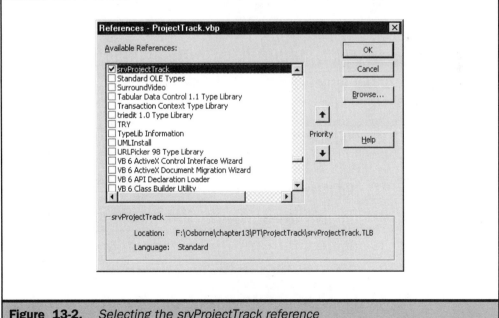

Figure 13-2.   *Selecting the srvProjectTrack reference*

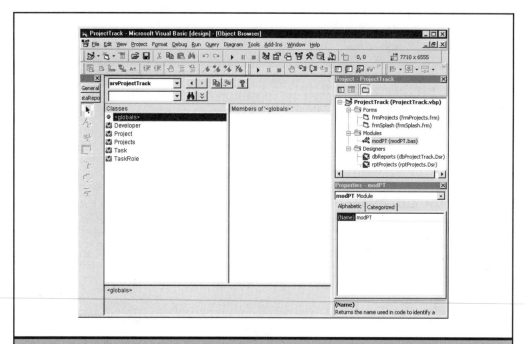

Figure 13-3. *Object Browser showing the srvProjectTrack object*

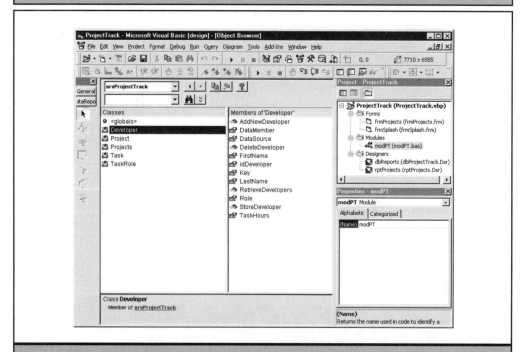

Figure 13-4. *Object Browser with the developer class selected*

With that, we have our application broken into three tiers. You may be wondering where n-tier development comes into play. Suppose we decided that our developer class needed to run on a different server and off a different database. We might decide to deploy that class and a data environment separately on a different server and in a different application. We then move beyond three tiers for our application. Here is a breakdown of our application:

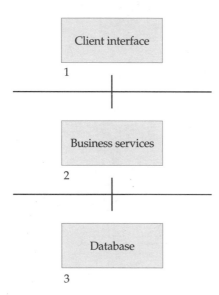

We have built the client interface that does not have our business logic classes and data interface. We have moved the classes and data interface into the second tier and kept it in one cohesive unit. Finally, our database is on a SQL server on the network and is accessed by the business services unit. And logic for accessing the underlying tables in the database is encapsulated in stored procedures that are stored and compiled on the database server.

Testing the Partition

Now that we have divided our application into partitions, we can go ahead and test, even though the components may still be on the same server. Go ahead and start the client application. The application should perform as usual. Just to be sure, let's add a new project and two tasks with a couple of developers to the system. Figure 13-5 shows the application with the additional data.

Go ahead and do a few deletes, and so on, for testing, but the application should run just as if the classes and data environment were still all in the same project. That lets us know that the application can correctly reference the server component locally, but can we connect to it remotely using remote automation? (Remote automation is discussed in more depth later in the chapter.)

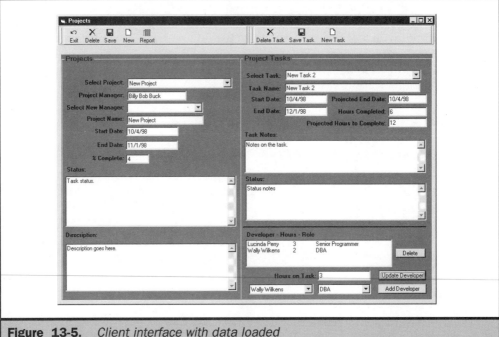

Figure 13-5. *Client interface with data loaded*

You will typically want to develop your multitier applications all in one project to simplify testing and debugging. It can be difficult to debug applications across multiple projects, although in some cases it certainly may be necessary.

You can test remote operation if you are running on Windows NT. You will want to have both projects open. Ensure the srvProjectTrack project is running. Provided with Visual Basic is a tool called the Remote Automation Connection Manager. This tool allows you to specify on the server how the connection to the object will be made. By default, it is not done by remote automation. Also, you can monitor the connections using the Automation Manager, also provided with Visual Basic.

Start both the Automation Manager and the Remote Automation Connection Manager. If you look down the list of COM classes in the Remote Automation Connection Manager, you will find the srvProjectTrack.Developer and other classes we created. For the moment, run the client application without making any changes. Figure 13-6 shows the results.

As you can see, the Automation Manager shows 0 connections to 0 objects. In other words, we are connecting directly to the object without using any proxies, such as remote automation or DCOM.

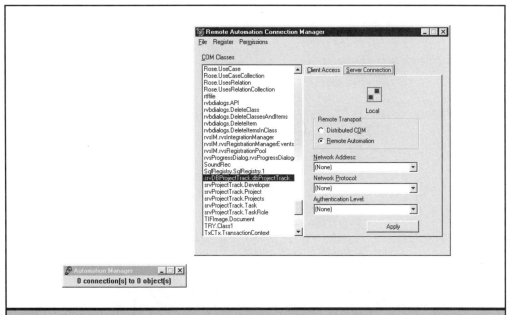

Figure 13-6.   *Client running without using remote automation for access to the server objects*

Note   *You will notice that you can handle your remote connectivity via remote automation or DCOM. DCOM is an application-level protocol for object-oriented remote procedure calls that is useful for distributed component-based systems of all types. More information can be found at hyperlink http://www.microsoft.com/com/dcom.asp*

Now let's make a couple of configuration changes to the Remote Automation Connection Manager for each of our classes, as follows:

1. Select the class.
2. Specify the network address to be the machine name you are currently working on (assuming that is where the server code is located as well).
3. Specify the network protocol your network typically runs on.
4. Set the authentication level to default.
5. Right click on the Local icon and change to Remote.
6. On the client tab for each class, ensure the Allow Remote Creates by Key option is selected and the Allow Remote Activation check box is checked.
7. Do this for all the classes. Figure 13-7 shows an example.

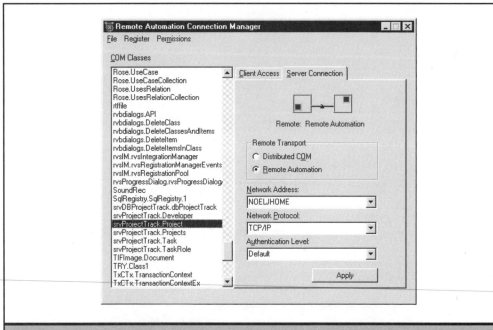

Figure 13-7. *Setting up the Remote Automation Connection Manager to test connecting via remote automation*

Now let's run the client application again. This time we will see very different results. The connections on the Automation Manager will come alive. Indeed, we are talking between the applications using remote automation. Figure 13-8 shows the results.

That is it. Our application is now partitioned and successfully running in separate pieces. Next let's add some reporting capabilities before we look at deploying the application.

Adding Report Capabilities

Before we work on deployment of our application, one more feature needs to be implemented in our application—the reports. The button has been sitting on the toolbar long enough; we ought to do something with it. Typically, in the development cycle, the reporting is done last because it is dependent upon the final database design.

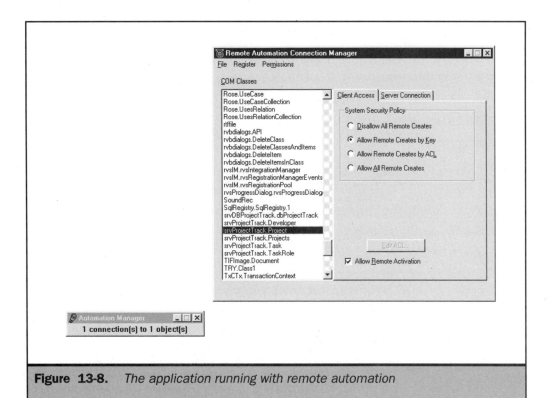

Figure 13-8.   *The application running with remote automation*

Building the Data Interface for the Report

We in some sense are going to break the "rules" of our three tiers to directly build the report in our Visual Basic application. While it is certainly desirable to partition all data access away from the client interface, it may not be prudent. In this case the data reporting capabilities of Visual Basic provide extensive functionality that will be useful to the end user. We will still have our primary business and data logic partitioned into other applications.

To do this, we are going to create a new data environment in our client interface called dbReports. Set up the connection as follows:

1. Set the name of the data environment to "dbReports."

2. Set the name of the connection to "Reports."

3. Ensure the connection uses the ProjTrack ODBC data source.

4. Set the username and password appropriately.

The report we want to build will be a report of projects, tasks assigned to projects, and developers assigned to tasks. In effect, we will have three levels of detail in our report—projects, tasks, and developers. Fortunately, the data environment makes it easy to build multitier queries that can be incorporated into the report. Here are the steps of this process:

1. Add a new command to the data environment.

2. Rename the command to "Projects."

   We need to return all of the projects in the system, but we have to join the project and developer tables to get the project manager for the project.

3. Right-click on the Projects command and select its properties.

4. Set the connection to Reports.

5. Select the SQL Builder option.

6. Add the project and developer tables to the query. Ensure there is a connection between the ID of the manager and the ID of the developer.

7. We want to return the project name, first name, last name, end date, start date, percent complete, and ID of the project. Select these fields into the results. Figure 13-9 shows the SQL Builder.

8. Close the SQL Builder and save the query. Following is the SQL code generated for the query.

```
SELECT Project.chrProjectName, Developer.chrFirstName,
Developer.chrLastName, Project.dtEndDate, Project.dtStartDate,
Project.fltPercentComplete, Project.idProject FROM Project INNER
JOIN Developer ON Project.idManager = Developer.idDeveloper
```

The query will return the project data for the query. But we do not yet have the appropriate task data associated with each project. What we can do next is create a subquery of the project query to return the tasks associated with each project. Follow these steps to create the subquery:

1. Right-click on the Projects query.

2. Select Add Child Command.

3. Rename the command to "Tasks."

4. Right-click on the Tasks command.

5. Select the properties option.

6. In this case we simply want to return data from the tasks table. On the General tab, set the Database Object to be Table.

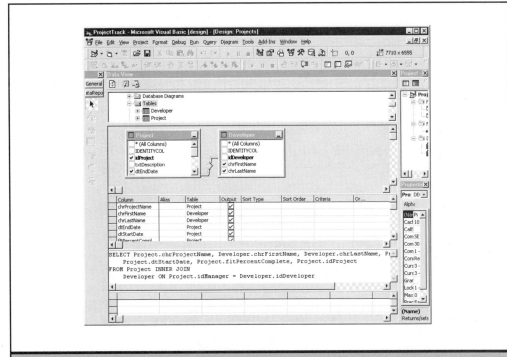

Figure 13-9. *SQL Builder designing the Projects query to return the project data joined with the manager data*

7. Set the Object Name to be dbo.Task for the task table. Figure 13-10 shows the settings.

8. We do need to relate the task table to the parent Projects query. Click on the Relation tab of the properties dialog.

9. In the Parent Fields list box, select idProject as the related field.

10. In the Child Fields/Parameters list box, select idProject as the related field.

11. Click on Add to add the relation. Figure 13-11 shows the relation set up.

By setting up the relationship between the Projects command and the Tasks command, we will only return tasks as they are related to projects returned in the project query. That way we have a related set of data for our report.

Next we need to return developer data for each task. This will require us to join the TaskDev, TaskRole, and Developer tables and relate them to our Tasks command. Follow these steps to set up the command:

1. Right-click on the Tasks query.

2. Select Add Child Command.

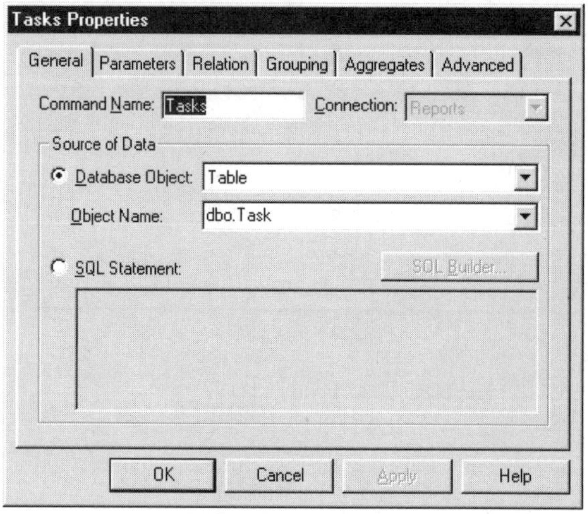

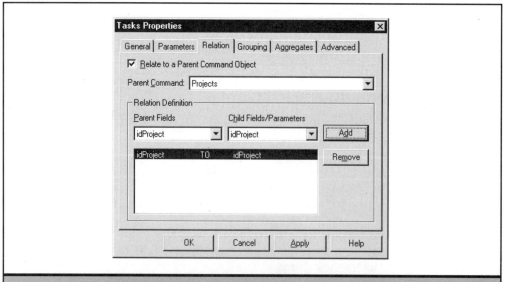

Figure 13-10. General settings for the Tasks command

Figure 13-11. Task to Project relationship set up for the Tasks command

3. Rename the new command to "Developers."

4. Right-click on the Developers command.

5. Select the properties option.

6. Set the connection to Reports.

7. Select the SQL Builder option.

8. Add the TaskDev, TaskRole, and Developer tables to the query. Ensure there is a connection between the ID of the developer in TaskDev and the ID of the developer in the Developer table. Also ensure there is a relationship between the idRole of the TaskDev table and the idTaskRole field of the TaskRole table.

9. In this case we simply want to return all the fields from the tables. Ensure the column setting is set to * return fields. Figure 13-12 shows the SQL Builder setup.

10. Close the SQL Builder and save the query. Following is the SQL query returned from the SQL Builder.

```
SELECT * FROM taskdev, developer, taskrole WHERE
taskdev.iddeveloper = developer.iddeveloper AND taskdev.idrole =
taskrole.idtaskrole
```

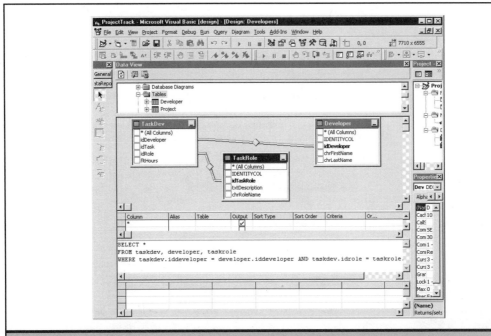

Figure 13-12.   *The SQL Builder setup for the Developers command*

11. We also have to relate our Developers command to the Tasks command in the same way we related the Tasks command to the Projects command. On the properties for the Developers command, select the Relation tab.

12. In the Parent Fields list box, select idTask as the related field.

13. In the Child Fields/Parameters list box, select idTask as the related field.

14. Click on Add to add the relation. Figure 13-13 shows the relation set up.

Last but not least, let's automatically open a database connection when the data environment is accessed. Add the following code to the connect object:

```
Private Sub DataEnvironment_Initialize()

Reports.Open "DSN=ProjTrack;UID=sa;PWD=;"

End Sub

Private Sub DataEnvironment_Terminate()

Reports.Close

End Sub
```

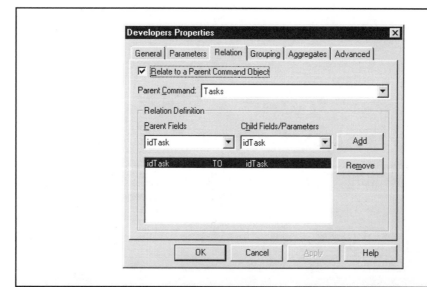

Figure 13-13. *Task to Developer relationship set up for the Tasks command*

This will automatically open our database connection when the data environment is created, and when it is terminated, the database connection is automatically closed.

And with that, we have set up a command in our data environment that will return projects with tasks grouped by project and developers grouped by task. We are now ready to begin building our projects report.

Building the Projects Report

Now we can build the projects report that is based on our Projects command in our data environment. From the Project menu, select Add Data Report to add a data report to your Visual Basic application.

Open the report designer. The first thing we will need to do is set several properties of our report. In the properties dialog of the report, set the DataSource to be our dbReports data environment. Then set the data member to be the Projects command in the data environment. Set the name of the report to be "rptProjects."

Next we are going to have the data report "retrieve" the structure of the data to be reported. Before we do that, take a look at Figure 13-14 to see the default report structure.

Now we are ready to import the structure of our data to be retrieved. Right-click on the report and select Retrieve Structure. When you do so, you will see a dialog box indicating that the current report will be cleared and the structure imported. Click Yes to continue.

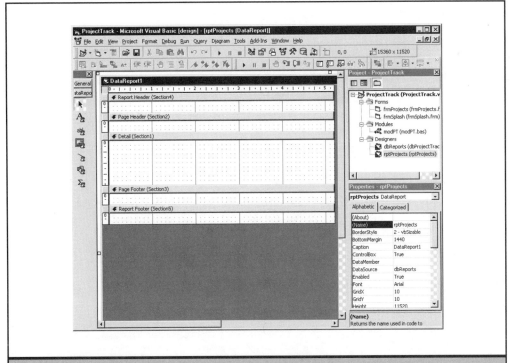

Figure 13-14.   *Report designer before the command structure is retrieved*

You will see that the report has been segmented into two group headers, Projects and Tasks. And there is one detail section for our Developers. Each of these correlates to a command we created in our Projects command. Figure 13-15 shows the new structure.

Now we are ready to place the appropriate report controls on the interface to lay out the project data we want to report. Top-level project data such as project name, manager, end date, percent complete, and so on, will be shown on the Projects_Header group header.

Task-level data such as task name, start date, end date, and so on, will be shown on the Tasks_Header group header. And finally, developers assigned to tasks will be shown on the Developers_Detail detail section of the report. We can add report and page header and footer data as needed. Figure 13-16 shows the design layout of the report.

Now all we have to do is hook up the report in our interface code. In the button click event of the projects toolbar, we need to implement Case 5, which is the report button. Following is the code:

```
'   Show the projects report
    Case 5
        rptProjects.Show
```

All we do to show the report is call the Show method of the report. When we do that, the report will pop up in a separate window. Figure 13-17 shows the report.

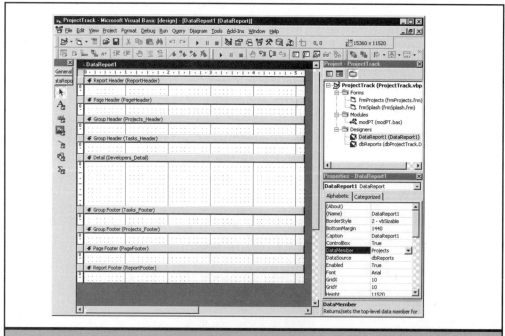

Figure 13-15.   *Report designer with the Projects command structure retrieved*

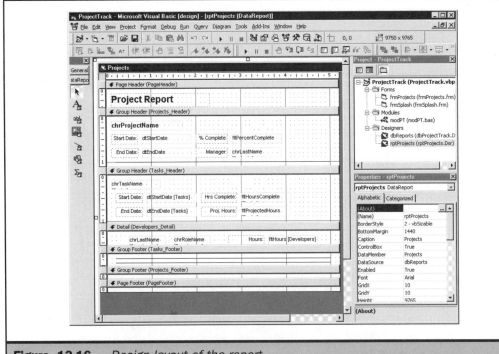

Figure 13-16. *Design layout of the report*

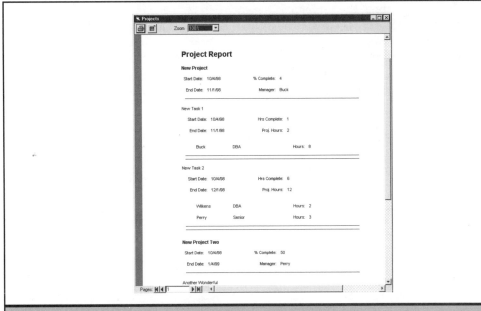

Figure 13-17. *The projects report*

You can, in fact, do extensive data reporting in your application. You might consider adding reports for developers assigned to tasks and project workload, charts on project loading, and so on.

Deploying the Application

Let's start with the data tier of our application. You will need to deploy the database to a production server from your development server. If you are working with Microsoft SQL Server, this is fairly simple. Simply create your new database devices on the production server. Then you can transfer all tables and any data (if desired) to the production server across the network using SQL Enterprise Manager. With regard to our ODBC DSNs, don't forget to deploy an ODBC DSN on both the client and the server that will point to the production server.

Out next step is to figure out how to deploy all this stuff to both the server and the client. We have to be able to tell the server that the component being installed will be accessed via remote automation. Remote automation is a technology through which COM components can communicate across network boundaries. Remote automation uses a combination of registry settings, proxies local to the client component (that translate the requests across the network), and an Automation Manager local to the server component.

Working with Remote Automation

When we checked Remote Server Files on our server-side project, that included the appropriate files for both the server and the client. In fact, one of those files is a VBR file, which is a text file of registry entries. These are almost identical to those that were created and entered in your registry on the development machine. The only difference is that file names have their full path names. Also created is a TLB file. This is a type library, which can be browsed using the Object Browser that comes with Visual Basic. The following illustration shows how remote automation will work across the network.

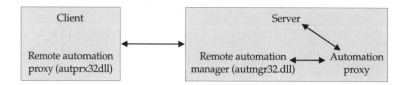

Our system will run on the client machine and access the remote server using a remote automation proxy. It will then talk to the server via the Remote Automation Connection Manager. The Remote Automation Connection Manager then works through the automation proxy on the server to interface with the server application.

Building the Server Installation

Let's get started setting all of this up. Open the server project and compile it to a new EXE file called "srvProjectTrack.exe." Once you have that finished, we are ready to start the Package and Deployment wizard provided with Visual Basic. Select your project. Figure 13-18 shows the wizard.

1. Click on the Package button.

2. Select None for packaging script (we have not yet created one for this project).

3. Select Standard Setup Package.

4. Indicate the directory where you would like to create the package.

5. You will next be given a prompt asking if this project will be used as a remote automation (RA) server. Figure 13-19 shows the message box.

6. Answer yes, since this will be used as a remote automation server.

7. Click Next to continue past the file list. We do not need to add any files.

8. Select Single Cab.

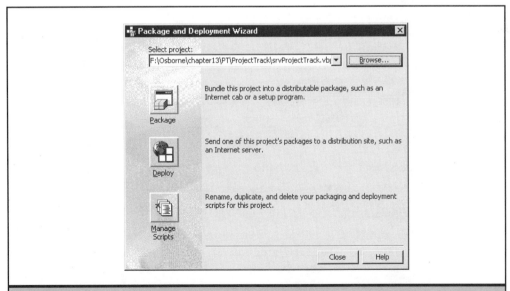

Figure 13-18. *Package and Deployment wizard with the srvProjectTrack project selected*

CLIENT/SERVER DEVELOPMENT

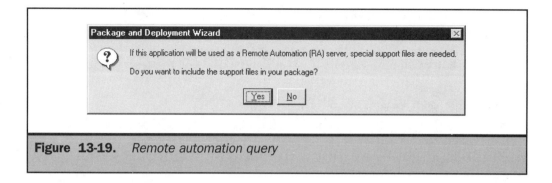

Figure 13-19. *Remote automation query*

9. Default the installation title to srvProjectTrack and click Next.

10. Default the Start menu location and click Next.

11. Keep the default installation location for each of the files and click Next.

12. Keep the defaults on shared files and click Next.

13. Set the script name to be "srvProjectTrack Setup" and click Finish.

14. If desired, use the Package and Deployment wizard to create a deployment installation package.

Now you will need to install the software on your server. On the server, you will want to be sure and configure the Remote Automation Connection Manager to allow access to the components. Once installed on the server, start the manager and then select the srvProjectTrack components in the manager. Set each component on the Client Access tab to Allow Remote Creates by Key, and ensure the Allow Remote Activation check box is selected. Figure 13-20 shows an example of setting this up.

Building the Client Installation

Now, on the client side, we will need to use the Package and Deployment wizard to create our installation package. Follow these steps:

1. Select your project in the wizard and click on Package.

2. Select None for the package script, then click Next.

3. Select Standard Setup Package and click Next to continue.

4. Indicate the location of the package. Figure 13-21 shows the dialog.

5. Select OK when prompted regarding missing dependency information for the srvProjectTrack.tlb file and any others.

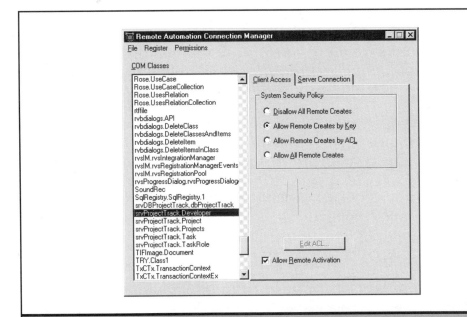

Figure 13-20.   *Setting up remote activation for our components*

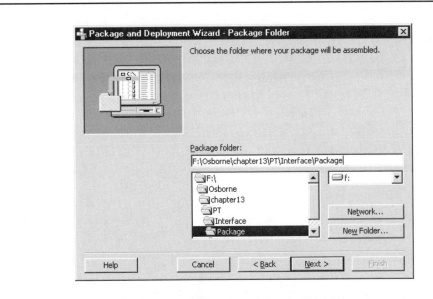

Figure 13-21.   *Package installation dialog*

6. The next dialog is where we need to add our VBR file from the srvProjectTrack project. This file will tell our client how to access the remote server. Figure 13-22 shows the dialog.

7. Click on Add. You will see the Add File dialog.

8. Find the VBR file that is created with the server project. Figure 13-23 shows the dialog.

9. Click Next to continue.

10. You will next be prompted with a Remote Servers dialog, as shown in Figure 13-24. This dialog will ask you to set the Net address, connection, protocol, and authentication. Set each as appropriate. Figure 13-25 shows a sample filled out. Click Next to continue.

11. Select Single Cab.

12. Default the installation title to Project Track and click Next.

13. Keep the default Start menu installation and click Next.

14. Keep the default installation locations and click Next.

15. Keep the defaults on Shared Files and click Next.

16. Save the setup script as Project Track Client and click Finish.

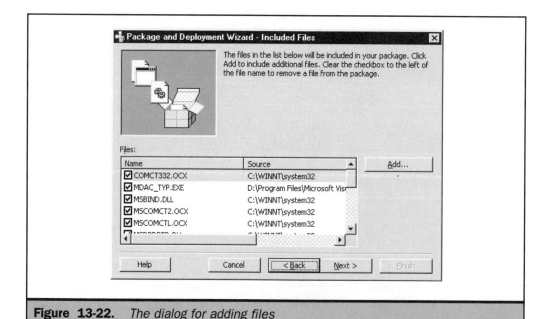

Figure 13-22. *The dialog for adding files*

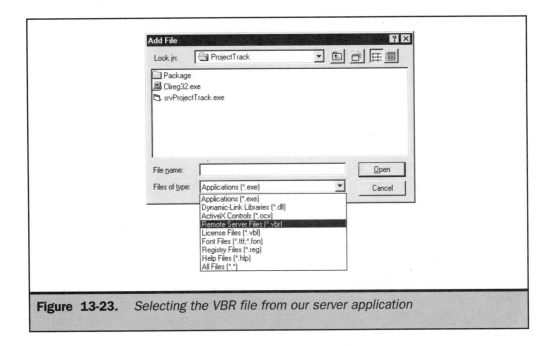

Figure 13-23. *Selecting the VBR file from our server application*

17. If desired, use the Package and Deployment wizard to create a deployment installation package.

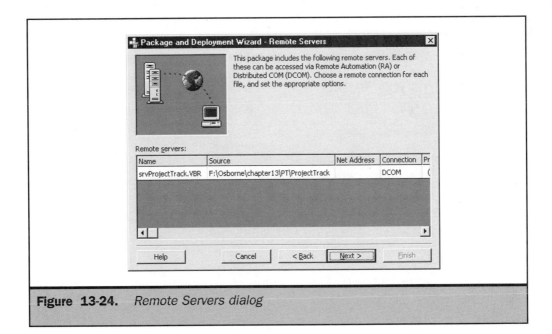

Figure 13-24. *Remote Servers dialog*

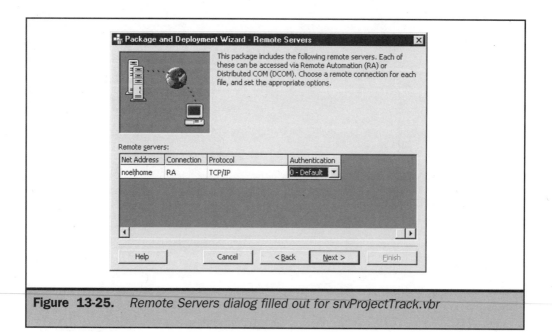

Figure 13-25. *Remote Servers dialog filled out for srvProjectTrack.vbr*

The next step is to install the client application. Simply double-click on the setup.exe file, and away things go. Figure 13-26 shows the setup at startup.

Click on OK to start the setup. Then click on the Installation button to begin the program installation. Note that behind the scenes the appropriate steps are taking place to set up the remote connectivity to the server via the VBR file and settings you put in the wizard.

Testing the Application

Finally, we are ready to begin testing. You can go to the Start menu and start the project track application. What will be of particular interest is the connections being made to the server. You can test this readily if you have the server component and the client component on the same machine. Figure 13-27 shows the client during application launch with the Automation Manager running.

You will note the two connections. Actually the number of connections jumps up and down as we create objects on the server. But that indicates we are truly talking to the server application using remote automation.

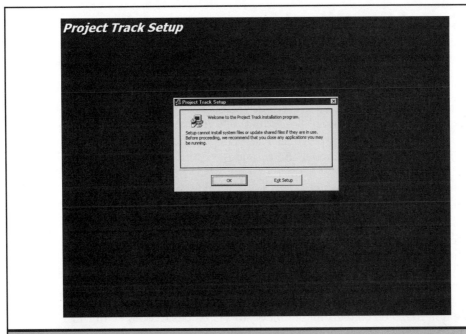

Figure 13-26.   *The client setup at startup*

Figure 13-27.   *The client with the Automation Manager running*

Additional Functionality

As you may have already realized, the project tracking sample application we have developed has really only scratched the surface of what is functionally possible. And there are a few pieces missing.

To add functionality, you may first want to consider using two additional tools in the design process. The first is the Microsoft Transaction Server (MTS). Microsoft Transaction Server is a component-based transaction processing system for developing, deploying, and managing high-performance, scalable, and robust server applications. MTS defines a programming model and provides a run-time environment and graphical administration tool for managing enterprise applications. If you are considering building mission-critical applications that require fault tolerant capabilities, you can combine Visual Basic 6.0 and MTS. For further information on this topic, review MSDN as well as http://www.microsoft.com/NTServer/Basics/AppServices/default.asp.

One other tool for building object-oriented systems is the Visual Modeler that comes with Visual Studio Enterprise Edition. Visual Modeler is a tool for designing three-tier distributed applications using class and component diagrams. With Visual Modeler, you can visually design models of the classes and components your application needs, then convert these models to Visual Basic code. Figure 13-28 shows our business services classes modeled in the Visual Modeler tool.

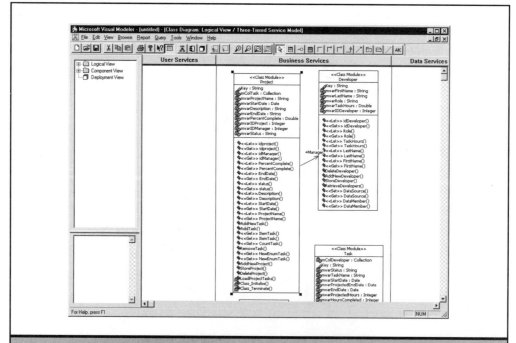

Figure 13-28. *Business services model of the project tracking application*

There are several application considerations to make as well. First off, the sample does not include a help system. You may wish to incorporate this as a toolbar button or perhaps stick with context-sensitive help for the different sections of the application.

Another consideration is data loading. To make the application simplistic, all of the classes are loaded up front in the application, with the data read from the database. In reality, this may be very slow. Consider selectively loading data based on access. For example, perhaps only the top-level project data needs to be loaded, and task and developer data is only loaded when a task is requested. That could save considerable loading time for the application. It would also reduce the memory requirements on the server.

In terms of project tracking capabilities, the sky is the limit. The implementation in this interface only does the basics of project data and tasks. There is only one report and very little analysis in the way of broad status tracking/review. A management piece of the application could be built to focus specifically on project planning that could in part be based on historical trends, and so on. Now that the foundation is built, the possibilities are wide open.

Summary

In this part of the book, we have covered everything from designing databases and object models to deploying via remote automation. As you can see, Visual Basic provides a powerful development environment for enterprise-level applications. Certainly Visual Basic will always be great for building and deploying stand-alone applications that have little system requirements. But Microsoft has focused heavily on the enterprise-level features of Visual Basic.

Many of the topics in this chapter regarding application partitioning and deployment will need careful consideration given the target environment you are developing for. You will also need to consider frequency of application updates and the deployment model. If you are only deploying to two or three computers, you probably do not need to worry as much about breaking up your application into different logical pieces. On the other hand, if you are deploying to thousands of desktops across a WAN, performance and cost to update and maintain the application are important considerations. But that is where the flexibility of Visual Basic can provide powerful options.

What's Next

We have covered a lot in terms of building n-tier client/server applications. But what about the Internet? What if we want to add an Internet interface to our project tracking system? In the next part of the book, we will further explore building IIS and DHTML applications. In fact, we will even build that Internet interface to our project tracking application.

The Complete Reference

Visual
Basic 6

Part IV

Internet Application Development

Microsoft has added significant functionality in Visual Basic 6.0 to develop Internet applications. In Chapter 5 we did a brief exploration of the new IIS application and DHTML application technology. In this section we are going to explore these technologies in more depth. If you are doing Internet or intranet development, Visual Basic has powerful new functionality to offer you.

Chapter 14

Building IIS Applications

In Chapter 10 we had a preview of building Internet applications with Visual Basic. Now we are ready to delve deeper into building Internet Information Server (IIS) applications. In this chapter we will build the "Daily Update," an application that will run in any Web browser and tracks who is in, who is out, and the hot list of action items for the day. In Chapter 16 we will take the project tracking system we built in earlier chapters and add a Web interface to the application.

Designing the Application

To build IIS applications, we need to design a series of HTML template pages that will define the basic interface structure of our application. The application will provide the following functionality:

- Ability to set the default user by cookie
- Ability to set the date, time, and contact information when an employee is out
- Ability to delete a date and time out for an employee
- Ability to add an item to the hot list
- Ability to edit an item on the hot list
- Ability to delete an item on the hot list

These capabilities will combine to build the Daily Update application. Certainly there are a number of different possibilities for the application. Once you get the hang of the programming, you can modify it to suit your needs.

Default Template Page

The first page we are going to need is a general navigation and reporting page. We will have three sections on the page. The first will be a quick set for the employee based on a cookie setting on the system. There will be a link to select a default employee and set the cookie.

The second section will be the "Daily Hot List." This will provide a link to add to the hot list as well as the list itself. The list will provide a link for editing and deleting items on the hot list.

The final section is the "Who's Out" list. This will show the in/out status of each employee who has been set up on the system. This will list each employee by name and show his or her in/out times and contact information. The user can click on the name of any employee to edit the status of the employee.

Following is the template HTML code for the default.html page. The page begins with a standard header.

```
<HTML>

<TITLE>The Daily Update</TITLE>

<BODY BGCOLOR=WHITE>

<H2><center><font color="red">The Daily Update</font></CENTER></H2>
```

The three sections will be placed in a table on the page. The first section is the "My Status" section, which will show the employee settings based on the cookie settings. You will note the <wc@mystatus> tag. The "wc" stands for web class. We will be able to process this tag in our IIS application web class and replace it with the appropriate information for the user.

```
<table border=1 cellpadding=3 cellspacing=3>

<tr>
  <th colspan=2><a href=" ">My Status</a></th>
</tr>

<WC@MYINOUT>/WC@MYINOUT>
```

The next section is for the daily hot list. We build a header row and then use, once again, a set of custom web class tags. These tags will be replaced with HTML code to show the hot list for the day.

```
<tr>
  <th colspan=2>Daily Hot List</th>
</tr>

<wc@HOTLIST></wc@HOTLIST>
```

Our last section is for the in/out status of each employee. As with the previous two sections, we have a header row followed by custom web tags for processing our Visual Basic application. Following that, the page is closed out.

```
<tr>
  <th colspan=2>Who's Out</th>
</tr>
```

```
<WC@OUT></WC@OUT>

</table>

</BODY>
</HTML>
```

The default page will give us the quick status of each section and allow us to easily access our personal settings. The next page will allow us to edit the employee setting.

Select Employee Template Page

Our next template will allow users to select their default employee setting for the default template page. The page will provide a list of users from which to select. Our page starts out with standard HTML header content.

```
<HTML>

<TITLE>The Daily Update</TITLE>

<BODY BGCOLOR=white>

<H2><center><font color="red">Select Your
Default Setting</font></center></H2>
```

Our page will have a form. Note that we do not set the action of the form. That will be defined in our application. The actual list of employees will be generated in the Visual Basic application. The custom tag wc@employees will be replaced with a select list.

```
<form method="post" action="">

Employee Listing:  <wc@EMPLOYEES></WC@EMPLOYEES>
```

Finally, the page is closed out with a Submit button, closing form tag, and the ending tags for the page.

```
<br><br>

<input type="submit" value="Submit">

</form>

</BODY>
</HTML>
```

That is it for the select employee page. As you can see, this page is really just a template for generating the employee data. Next we set up the add hot item page, which will add a hot item to the list.

Add Hot Item Template Page

The add hot item page will provide input fields for the user to add a new hot item to the page. Note that in our application, only items with the current date will be shown. The date, therefore, should be defaulted to the current date. The page begins with a standard set of page HTML tags.

```
<HTML>

<TITLE>The Daily Update</TITLE>

<BODY BGCOLOR=white>

<H2><center><font color="red">The Daily
Update</font></center></H2>
```

Our page has a form that will be submitted to the server. We will define the form action in our Visual Basic application. The first field will be the item description. The second will be the date of the hot item list. This will be filled in with a custom tag, wc@date. That way, we can default the date.

```
<form method="post" action="">

<table border=1>
  <tr>
    <td align=right>  Item:</td>
    <td><input name="chrDescription" ></td>
```

```
    </tr>
    <tr>
      <td align=right>  Date:</td>
      <td><wc@DATE></WC@DATE></td>
    </tr>
```

The page is finished with a closing submit tag and closing form, table, and page tags.

```
    <tr>
      <td align=middle colspan=2>
      <input type="submit" value="Submit" name="Submit"></td>
    </tr>
  </table>
  </form>
  </BODY>
  </HTML>
```

The add hot item page shows a good example of mixing HTML and Visual Basic together. Most of the form is built in HTML, but one of the input elements will be built from our application.

Edit Item Template Page

In contrast to the hot item page, the edit item page will allow the user to edit the contents of a hot list item. The primary difference between the two pages is that the description will be generated from the database and replaced when the application is run. Note again that the form has no action and will be handled in the Visual Basic application.

```
<HTML>

<TITLE>The Daily Update</TITLE>

<BODY BGCOLOR=white>

<H2><center><font color="red">The Daily
Update</font></center></H2>
<form method="post" action="">

<table border=1>
  <tr>
```

```
   <td align=right>  Item:</td>
    <td><wc@DESCRIPTION></WC@DESCRIPTION></td>
  </tr>
  <tr>
    <td align=right>  Date:</td>
    <td><wc@DATE></WC@DATE></td>
  </tr>
  <tr>
    <td align=middle colspan=2>
    <input type="submit" value="Submit" name="Submit"></td>
  </tr>

</table>

</form>
</BODY>
</HTML>
```

Note *The addhotitem.html and edititem.html pages could be combined into one template page. For demonstration purposes, they are not combined here, but it could be done with the Visual Basic code.*

Building the Database

Now that we have our template pages defined, we need to define the database that will sit behind the application. We will need a table of employees, hot items, and in/out statuses.

Defining the Tables

The first table, Employee, defines the first and last names of each employee for the system. A unique ID is defined for each.

```
CREATE TABLE dbo.Employee (
    idEmployee int IDENTITY (1, 1) NOT NULL ,
    chrFirstName varchar (255) NULL ,
    chrLastName varchar (255) NULL
)
GO
```

Our next table is HotList, which will contain the list of hot items by day. There is an ID for each item, the date it was entered, and a description.

```
CREATE TABLE dbo.HotList (
    idHotList int IDENTITY (1, 1) NOT NULL ,
    dtItemHot datetime NULL ,
    chrDescription varchar (255) NULL
)
GO
```

Our final table is the Out table, which will define the "out" status for each employee. Note that the idea is to have only one record for each employee that will define the employee's current status as appropriate.

The chrDayOut, chrDayIn, chrTimeOut, and chrTimeIn fields are defined as varchar data types. This will allow the user to input time ranges, instead of strictly tying a time in and out to a specific minute and hour.

```
CREATE TABLE dbo.Out (
    idOut int IDENTITY (1, 1) NOT NULL ,
    idEmployee int NOT NULL ,
    chrContactInfo varchar (255) NULL ,
    chrDayOut varchar (25) NULL ,
    chrDayIn varchar (25) NULL ,
    chrTimeOut varchar (25) NULL ,
    chrTimeIn varchar (25) NULL
)
GO
```

These tables will define the basis of our application. Next we will define the stored procedure interfaces to our tables that will be utilized in a data environment in our application.

Building the Stored Procedures

Our first stored procedure, DeleteHotItem, will delete a hot item from the hot list database. The ID of the item is passed into the stored procedure.

```
CREATE PROCEDURE sp_DeleteHotItem

@idHotList integer

AS

delete from hotlist where idHotList = @idHotList
GO
```

The next stored procedure, InsertHotItem, will add a new hot item to the database. The date of the hot item and the description are passed in as parameters. An insert statement is called to add the item.

```
CREATE PROCEDURE sp_InsertHotItem

@dtItemHot datetime,
@chrDescription varchar(255)

AS

insert into HotList(dtItemHot, chrDescription) values(@dtItemHot,
@chrDescription)
GO


CREATE PROCEDURE sp_RetrieveEmployeeStatus AS
select * from out, employee where out.idEmployee =
employee.idemployee
GO
```

An employee's data can be retrieved by ID with the RetrieveEmployeeByID stored procedure. The ID of the employee is passed into the stored procedure. In this example, the query joins the Out and Employee tables to retrieve the employee status.

```
CREATE PROCEDURE sp_RetrieveEmployeeByID

@idEmployee integer

AS

SELECT * FROM
    Out, Employee
WHERE
    employee.idemployee = @idemployee AND
    out.idemployee = employee.idemployee
GO
```

Our next stored procedure, RetrieveEmployees, will return a list of employees ordered by last name.

```
CREATE PROCEDURE sp_RetrieveEmployees AS

select * from employee order by chrLastName
GO
```

The RetrieveHotItem stored procedure will return the list of current hot items. To do that, the stored procedure will use the DatePart function to get all hot list entries that fall on the current date. The GetDate function returns down to the second, but we only want to check against the current day in the current year.

```
CREATE PROCEDURE sp_RetrieveHotItem AS

select * from hotlist where
datepart(yy, dtitemhot) = datepart(yy, getdate()) and
datepart(dy, dtItemHot) = datepart(dy, getdate())
GO
```

The RetrieveHotItemByID stored procedure returns a single hot item based on ID.

```
CREATE PROCEDURE sp_RetrieveHotItemByID

@idHotList integer

as

select * from hotlist where idHotList = @idHotList
GO
```

The SetEmployeeOut stored procedure will insert a new employee status into the database. This stored procedure should only be run if the employee does not have a current status. The value for the ID of the employee, contact information, day out, day in, time out, and time in are passed in. The record is then inserted into the database.

```
CREATE PROCEDURE sp_SetEmployeeOut

@idEmployee integer,
@chrContactInfo varchar(255),
@chrDayOut varchar(25),
@chrDayIn varchar(25),
@chrTimeOut varchar(25),
@chrTimeIn varchar(25)

AS

insert into out(idEmployee,
                chrContactInfo,
                chrDayOut,
```

```
            chrDayIn,
             chrTimeOut,
             chrTimeIn)
values(

             @idEmployee,
             @chrContactInfo,
             @chrDayOut,
             @chrDayIn,
             @chrTimeOut,
             @chrTimeIn)
GO
```

If the record is already inserted in the database for the employee status, we will
need to update the employee's record. As with the Set Employee Out stored procedure,
we pass in the ID of the employee, the contact information, day out, day in, time out,
and time in.

```
CREATE PROCEDURE sp_UpdateEmployeeOut

@idEmployee integer,
@chrContactInfo varchar(255),
@chrDayOut varchar(25),
@chrDayIn  varchar(25),
@chrTimeOut varchar(25),
@chrTimeIn  varchar(25)

AS

update out set
    chrContactinfo = @chrContactInfo,
    chrdayOut = @chrDayOut,
    chrdayIn = @chrDayIn,
    chrTimeOut = @chrTimeOut,
    chrTimeIn = @chrTimeIn

where
    idEmployee = @idEmployee
GO
```

The UpdateHotItem stored procedure will update a hot item in the database. The ID of the hot list item will be passed in, along with the day the item is hot and the description. Then the update SQL statement is built to update the record.

```
CREATE PROCEDURE sp_UpdateHotItem

@idHotList integer,
@dtItemHot datetime,
@chrDescription varchar(255)

AS

update hotlist set
   dtItemHot = @dtItemHot,
   chrDescription = @chrDescription
where
   idHotList = @idHotList
GO
```

That is the end of building the foundation of our application. We have the template pages and the database built. Now we are ready to begin building the IIS application Visual Basic infrastructure.

Building the IIS Application

The first step will be to import the templates into our application. Start a new IIS application. Set the project name to be "DailyUpdate" and the application title to "Daily Update." Once the application is started, save it as appropriate.

Importing Our Templates and Building the Data Environment

Now we are ready to add our templates. Right-click on the web class and click on the Add HTML Template option. Then select the default page. Follow the same procedures to add each template. Be sure and rename each template as it is imported. Figure 14-1 shows the application with the template pages imported.

Next we can build the data environment for our application. Click on the Project menu and select Add Data Environment. Rename the data environment to "dbDailyUpdate." Then rename the connection to "DailyUpdate."

Set the properties to set up the data source. Add an ODBC driver to your database called "DailyUpdate." That will create the connection for the data environment to the database.

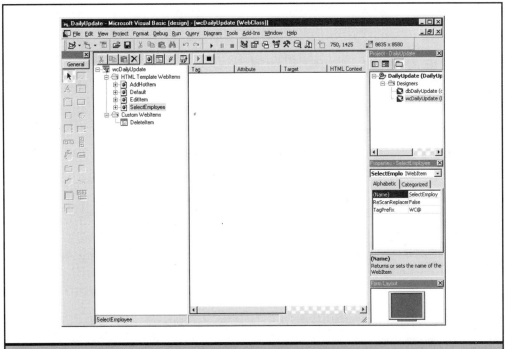

Figure 14-1. *Application with HTML pages imported*

Now we can import the stored procedures into our data environment. Right-click on the stored procedure, and select Insert Stored Procedures to add the stored procedures we created earlier in the chapter. That will insert each into the database.

Double-click on the connection object. We will want to create and delete the connection to the database when the data environment is created. In the Initialize event, the "open" method of the connection is called to create the connection. The Terminate event of the data environment will then close the connection.

```
Private Sub DataEnvironment_Initialize()
  DailyUpdate.Open "dsn=dailyupdate;uid=sa;pwd="
End Sub


Private Sub DataEnvironment_Terminate()
  DailyUpdate.Close
End Sub
```

That is it for our data environment and importing our templates. Through these two foundations, we will build our Visual Basic code.

Building the Visual Basic Code

The beginning of our application sets the coding parameters. We do have one global variable, idHotItem. That will define the ID of a hot item that the user has selected either to delete or edit.

```
Option Explicit
Option Compare Text

'  Global variable for the hot item
Dim idHotItem As Integer
```

The web class start event will be called when the application runs. The NextItem property of the class is set to the default page.

```
'  Start event of the web class
Private Sub WebClass_Start()

'  Set the next item to the default page
Set NextItem = Default

End Sub
```

The respond event of the default page is fired off when it is set as the next item. When the respond event is called, the WriteTemplate method of the default template is called to display the page.

```
'  Respond event of the default page
Private Sub Default_Respond()

'  Write out the template
Default.WriteTemplate

End Sub
```

In the Template interface, double-click on the hyperlink in the template. This will create a Hyperlink1 event for the default page. This event will allow the user to go to the SelectEmployee page, which in turn will allow the user to select the default employee for the application. When the Hyperlink1 event is fired off, the NextItem is set to the SelectEmployee template.

```
'  Hyperlink1 event of the default page
Private Sub Default_Hyperlink1()

'  Set the next item to be the SelectEmployee page
Set NextItem = SelectEmployee

End Sub
```

The ProcessTag event of the default page will process the custom tags on the default page. The wc@myinout tag will run the RetrieveCookieEmployee function that will return the tagging and database data for the default employee.

The wc@out custom tag will call the RetrieveOut function that will return the status list of all the employees in the database. Finally, the wc@hotlist custom tag will call the ListHotItems function to return the list of hot items in the database for the current date.

```
'  ProcessTag event of the default page
Private Sub Default_ProcessTag(ByVal TagName As String, TagContents _
As String, SendTags As Boolean)

'  Select by tag name
Select Case LCase(TagName)

    '  InOut listing for the defaulted page
    Case "wc@myinout"
        '  Retrieve the employee cookie data
        TagContents = RetrieveCookieEmployee

    '  Employee out list
    Case "wc@out"
        '  Retrieve the list of employees who are out
        TagContents = RetrieveOut

    '  Hot list
    Case "wc@hotlist"
        '  Retrieve the list of hot item
        TagContents = ListHotItems

End Select

End Sub
```

The UserEvent subroutine of the default page will process the different custom events. The first event is to update the status for the cookie default user. The second is to call the update and clear the status for the user. The last is to edit an employee. The EditEmployee subroutine is called to build the edit page on the fly.

```
'  User event for the default page
Private Sub Default_UserEvent(ByVal EventName As String)

'  Select by event name
Select Case EventName

    '  Update my status event. 0 indicates
    '  the record is not to be cleared. Indicate no employee
    '  ID is passed in, it should be read from the cookie.
    Case "UpdateMyStatus"
        UpdateEmployeeStatus 0, -1

    '  Clears the employee status by cookie value
    '  1 indicates the data is not to be cleared
    Case "ClearCookieStatus"
        UpdateEmployeeStatus 1, -1

    '  Anything else that comes in is a selection to
    '  edit a specific employee. Pass in the employee
    '  Id.
    Case Else
        EditEmployee CInt(EventName)

End Select

End Sub
```

The DeleteHotItem subroutine will utilize the data environment to remove a hot item from the list. The ID of the hot item is passed into the subroutine.

```
'  Deletes a hot item from the database
Private Sub DeleteHotItem(idHotList As Integer)

'  Declare a database environment
Dim dbDU As New dbDailyUpdate
```

```
'  Deletes an item from the list
dbDU.DeleteHotItem idHotList

'  Delete the data environment
Set dbDU = Nothing

End Sub
```

The ListHotItems function is called to build a list of HTML hot items in the database. It returns the HTML string to the calling function. A standard URL is put in place to add a new hot item to the list. The URLFor function is used to call the AddHotItem template page.

The Edit and Delete functions are built using the URLFor function. The first argument indicates the web item to be called, and the second specifies the value to be passed in as the user event. In each case, the ID of the hot item is passed in so appropriate action can take place on it.

```
'  List the hot items for today
Private Function ListHotItems() As String

'  Declare a database environment and variables
Dim dbDU As New dbDailyUpdate
Dim Tag As String

'  Retrieve the hot item
dbDU.RetrieveHotItem

'  Note we are building a table within a table
Tag = "<tr><td colspan=2>"
Tag = Tag & "<table width=""100%"" cellpadding=""3""" & _
"cellspacing=""3"">"
Tag = Tag & "<tr><td align=""center"" colspan=""3"">"

'  Build a link to the AddHotItem page
Tag = Tag & "<a href=""" & _
    URLFor(AddHotItem, "Display") & _
    """>Add Hot Item</a>"

Tag = Tag & "</tr></td>"
```

```
'  Loop through the list of hot items in the database
Do Until dbDU.rsRetrieveHotItem.EOF

    '  Show the description
    Tag = Tag & "<tr><td>"
    Tag = Tag & dbDU.rsRetrieveHotItem("chrDescription")
    Tag = Tag & "</td>"

    '  Build a link to edit the item
    Tag = Tag & "<td>" & "<a href=""" & _
        URLFor(EditItem, _
        Str(dbDU.rsRetrieveHotItem("idHotList"))) & _
        """>Edit</a>"

    Tag = Tag & "</td>"

    '  Build a link to delete the item. Note this link
    '  is to the DeleteItem custom web item
    Tag = Tag & "<td>" & "<a href=""" & _
        URLFor(DeleteItem, _
        Str(dbDU.rsRetrieveHotItem("idHotList"))) & _
        """>Delete</a>"

    Tag = Tag & "</td>"
    Tag = Tag & "</tr>"

    '  Move to the next item
    dbDU.rsRetrieveHotItem.MoveNext

Loop

'  Close the table
Tag = Tag & "</table>"
Tag = Tag & "</td></tr>"

'  Return the tagging
ListHotItems = Tag

'  Delete the data environment
Set dbDU = Nothing

End Function
```

Before we start working on the EditEmployee subroutine, we need to add three custom web items to the project. Two of them will be used in EditEmployee. Right-click on the CustomWebItems listing in the web class designer. Select Add Custom WebItem. Add three custom web items. The first should be named "ClearEmployee," the second is "DeleteItem," and the third is "UpdateEmployee." Figure 14-2 shows the project with the custom web items added.

EditEmployee handles editing an employee's in/out settings. The ID of the employee is passed in. This subroutine actually builds a complete page on the fly. The employee data is retrieved from the database. A table is built with a form for submitting the employee data. The form action goes back to the UpdateEmployee custom web item, and the ID of the employee will be the user event name.

A Submit button is built to submit the data to the server. Also, a clear link is built with the ID of the developer on the URL to clear the employee's in/out data. That will post to the ClearEmployee custom web item with the ID of the employee being the user event.

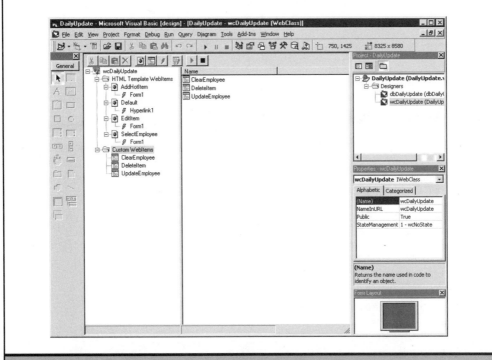

Figure 14-2. *Project with three custom web items added*

| Note | You could build a template page for the employee status editing. In this case we demonstrate the ability to build entire pages on the fly. |

```
' Edit Employee subroutine will show the data to edit an
' employee as the default. The id of the employee is
' passed in.
Private Sub EditEmployee(idEmployee As Integer)

' Declare our variables
Dim Tag As String
Dim dbDU As New dbDailyUpdate
Dim chrDayIn As String
Dim chrDayOut As String
Dim chrTimeIn As String
Dim chrTimeOut As String
Dim chrContactInfo As String

' Retrieve the employee's data
dbDU.RetrieveEmployeeByID idEmployee

' Check to ensure data was returned
If Not dbDU.rsRetrieveEmployeeByID.EOF Then

    ' Retrieve the day in, day out, time in
    ' time out and contact information
    chrDayIn = dbDU.rsRetrieveEmployeeByID("chrDayIn")
    chrDayOut = dbDU.rsRetrieveEmployeeByID("chrDayOut")
    chrTimeIn = dbDU.rsRetrieveEmployeeByID("chrTimeIn")
    chrTimeOut = dbDU.rsRetrieveEmployeeByID("chrTimeOut")
    chrContactInfo = dbDU.rsRetrieveEmployeeByID("chrContactInfo")

End If

' Build the beginning of the page
Tag = "<HTML><BODY BGCOLOR=""WHITE"">"

' Start the table
Tag = Tag & "<table border=""1"" cellpadding=""3""" & _
"cellspacing=""3"">"

' Build a form that will post back
' to the UpdateEmployee custom web item
' and call an UpdateMyStatus user event
```

```
Tag = Tag & "<form method=""post"" action=""" & _
     URLFor(UpdateEmployee, _
     CStr(dbDU.rsRetrieveEmployeeByID("idEmployee"))) & """>"

Tag = Tag & "<tr>"

Tag = Tag & "<td align=""center"" colspan=""2""><b>"

'  Show the last name and first name
Tag = Tag & dbDU.rsRetrieveEmployeeByID("chrLastName") & ", " & _
     dbDU.rsRetrieveEmployeeByID("chrFirstName")

Tag = Tag & "</b></td>"
Tag = Tag & "<tr>"
Tag = Tag & "<td align=""center"">Day Out: "

'  Show the day out time
Tag = Tag & "<input type=""Text"" value=""" & chrDayOut & """ & _
"name=""chrDayOut"">"
Tag = Tag & "</td>"

Tag = Tag & "<td align=""center"">Day In: "

'  Show the day in time
Tag = Tag & "<input type=""text"" value=""" & chrDayIn & """ & _
"name=""chrDayIn"">"
Tag = Tag & "</td>"
Tag = Tag & "</tr>"

Tag = Tag & "<tr>"
Tag = Tag & "<td align=""center"">Time Out: "

'  Show the time out time
Tag = Tag & "<input type=""Text"" value=""" & _
     chrTimeOut & """ name=""chrTimeOut"">"

Tag = Tag & "</td>"
Tag = Tag & "<td align=""center"">Time In: "

'  Show the time in time
Tag = Tag & "<input type=""text"" value=""" & _
     chrTimeIn & """ name=""chrTimeIn"">"
```

```
Tag = Tag & "</td>"
Tag = Tag & "</tr>"
Tag = Tag & "<tr>"

Tag = Tag & "<td align=""center"" colspan=""2"">Contact Info: "

'   Show the contact info.
Tag = Tag & "<input type=""text"" value=""" & _
        chrContactInfo & """ name=""chrContactInfo"">"

Tag = Tag & "</td>"
Tag = Tag & "</tr>"

'   Build the submit form
Tag = Tag & "<tr valign=""center"">"
Tag = Tag & "<td align=""center"">"
Tag = Tag & "<input type=""submit"" value=""Submit"">"
Tag = Tag & "</td><td align=""center"">"

'   Call the ClearEmployee custom web item with the ID of the
'   employee
'   as the user event
Tag = Tag & "<a href=""" & _
        URLFor(ClearEmployee, _
        CStr(dbDU.rsRetrieve EmployeeByID("idEmployee"))) & _
        """>Clear</a>"

Tag = Tag & "</td>"
Tag = Tag & "</tr>"

'   Close the page
Tag = Tag & "</table></form></body></html>"

'   Write out the tags
Response.Write Tag

End Sub
```

The next subroutine is the UpdateEmployeeStatus. This subroutine handles updating any employee status. The clear flag will clear the status with "IN" values. The idEmployee argument identifies the ID of the employee. If it is a –1 value, we will retrieve the ID from the cookie stored on the system.

A check is done to see if the employee has had a record inserted into the database yet. If not, we call the SetEmployeeOut stored procedure to add a new record. If the employee has a record, we call the UpdateEmployeeOut stored procedure to update with the new values. Once the update is done, the user is directed back to the home page.

```
'  Update the employee status
Private Sub UpdateEmployeeStatus(intClearFlag As Integer, _
idEmployee As Integer)

'  Declare our variables
Dim dbDU As New dbDailyUpdate
Dim chrDayIn As String
Dim chrDayOut As String
Dim chrTimeIn As String
Dim chrTimeOut As String
Dim chrContactInfo As String

If idEmployee = -1 Then
    '  Retrieve the employee data
    dbDU.RetrieveEmployeeByID Request.Cookies("idEmployee")
    idEmployee = Request.Cookies("idEmployee")

Else

    dbDU.RetrieveEmployeeByID idEmployee

End If

'  Check to see if we are to clear the data
If intClearFlag = 1 Then

    '  If so then set the date values to 'IN'
    chrContactInfo = "IN"
    chrDayIn = "IN"
    chrDayOut = "IN"
    chrTimeIn = ""
    chrTimeOut = ""

Else

    '  Otherwise set the data according to
    '  the database
    chrContactInfo = Request("chrContactInfo")
    chrDayIn = Request("chrDayIn")
```

```
    chrDayOut = Request("chrDayOut")
    chrTimeIn = Request("chrTimeIn")
    chrTimeOut = Request("chrTimeOut")

End If

'  If no data was returned then we need to insert
'  a new row for the employee
If dbDU.rsRetrieveEmployeeByID.EOF Then
    '  Call the SetEmployeeOut stored procedure
    dbDU.SetEmployeeOut idEmployee, _
                        chrContactInfo, _
                        chrDayOut, _
                        chrDayIn, _
                        chrTimeOut, _
                        chrTimeIn

Else

    '  Update the employee's record
    dbDU.UpdateEmployeeOut idEmployee, _
                        chrContactInfo, _
                        chrDayOut, _
                        chrDayIn, _
                        chrTimeOut, _
                        chrTimeIn

End If

'  Go back to the default page
Set NextItem = Default

'  clear out data environment
Set dbDU = Nothing

End Sub
```

The RetrieveOut function will retrieve the out status of employees in the database. The RetrieveEmployeeStatus subroutine is called to retrieve the status of all the employees in the database. A table is built with a row for each employee. A listing is built for each employee with the out, in, and contact information status showing.

The employee name is built as a hyperlink to edit the employee settings. The URLFor function is called to create a URL to the default page and pass in the ID of the employee as the user event name. When the user clicks on the name, the employee is identified, and the EditEmployee subroutine will be called.

```
'  Retrieve the list of employees who are out
Private Function RetrieveOut() As String

'  Declare our variables
Dim Tag As String
Dim dbDU As New dbDailyUpdate
Dim Flag As Integer

'   Retrieve the employee status
dbDU.RetrieveEmployeeStatus

'  Check to ensure we don't have an empty record
'  set
If Not dbDU.rsRetrieveEmployeeStatus.EOF Then

    '   Start our table within the primary table
    Tag = "<tr><td colspan=""2"">"
    Tag = Tag & "<TABLE width=""100%"" CELLPADDING=""3""" & _
    "CELLSPACING=""3"">"
    Tag = Tag & _
"<TR><th>Name</th><th>Out</th><th>In</th><th>Contact " & _
        "Info</th></tr>"

    Flag = 1

End If

'  Loop through the employees
Do Until dbDU.rsRetrieveEmployeeStatus.EOF

    '  Write out a row for each
    Tag = Tag & "<tr><td>"

    '  Build a link to the default page and pass in the
    '  id of the employee as the user event
    Tag = Tag & "<a href=""" & _
        URLFor(Default, _
```

```
CStr(dbDU.rsRetrieveEmployeeStatus("idEmployee"))) & _
        """>"

    '  Show the last and first name
    Tag = Tag & dbDU.rsRetrieveEmployeeStatus("chrLastName") & ", "
    Tag = Tag & dbDU.rsRetrieveEmployeeStatus("chrFirstName") & " "

    '  Close the link
    Tag = Tag & "</a>"
    Tag = Tag & "</td><td>"

    '  Show the day and time out
    Tag = Tag & dbDU.rsRetrieveEmployeeStatus("chrDayOut") & " "
    Tag = Tag & dbDU.rsRetrieveEmployeeStatus("chrTimeOut") & " "
    Tag = Tag & "</td><td>"

    '  Show the day in and out
    Tag = Tag & dbDU.rsRetrieveEmployeeStatus("chrDayIn") & " "
    Tag = Tag & dbDU.rsRetrieveEmployeeStatus("chrTimeIn") & " "
    Tag = Tag & "</td><td>"

    '  Show the contact info
    Tag = Tag & dbDU.rsRetrieveEmployeeStatus("chrContactInfo") & _
    " "
    Tag = Tag & "</tr>"

    '  Move to the next row
    dbDU.rsRetrieveEmployeeStatus.MoveNext

Loop

'  If our flag is set (data was returned)
'  then we close the table and row within
'  the larger table
If Flag = 1 Then

    Tag = Tag & "</table>"
    Tag = Tag & "</td></tr>"

End If
```

```
'  Return the tag info.
RetrieveOut = Tag


'  Delete our data environment
Set dbDU = Nothing


End Function
```

The RetrieveCookieEmployee function will retrieve the employee data. If the cookie is specified, the ID from the cookie is used. If not, we indicate that the user needs to set the cookie by selecting a default employee.

The form for the data will post to the default page as specified in the URLFor method. The user event name will be "UpdateMyStatus," which will indicate that the cookie user's status should be used. The clear link will also go to the default page with a user event name of ClearCookieStatus.

```
'  Retrieve the Employee data for the cookie
'  data set
Private Function RetrieveCookieEmployee() As String


'  Declare our variables
Dim Tag As String
Dim dbDU As New dbDailyUpdate
Dim chrDayIn As String
Dim chrDayOut As String
Dim chrTimeIn As String
Dim chrTimeOut As String
Dim chrContactInfo As String


'  Check to see if the cookie data
'  is set or not
If Request.Cookies("idemployee") <> "" Then

    '  Retrieve the employee data based on the cookie
    dbDU.RetrieveEmployeeByID Request.Cookies("idemployee")

    '  Check to see if data was returned
    If Not dbDU.rsRetrieveEmployeeByID.EOF Then
```

```
    '  Retrieve the employee data
    chrDayIn = dbDU.rsRetrieveEmployeeByID("chrDayIn")
    chrDayOut = dbDU.rsRetrieveEmployeeByID("chrDayOut")
    chrTimeIn = dbDU.rsRetrieveEmployeeByID("chrTimeIn")
    chrTimeOut = dbDU.rsRetrieveEmployeeByID("chrTimeOut")
    chrContactInfo = _
    dbDU.rsRetrieveEmployeeByID("chrContactInfo")

Else

    '  Default the employee data
    chrDayOut = FormatDateTime(Date, vbShortDate)
    chrDayIn = FormatDateTime(Date, vbShortDate)
    chrTimeIn = Time
    chrTimeOut = Time

End If

'  Build a form to post to the default page
'  and call the UpdateMyStatus user event
Tag = "<form method=""post"" action=""" & _
    URLFor(Default, "UpdateMyStatus") & """>"

'  Show the day out
Tag = Tag & "<tr>"
Tag = Tag & "<td align=""center"">Day Out: "
Tag = Tag & "<input type=""Text"" value=""" & chrDayOut & _
    """ name=""chrDayOut"">"

Tag = Tag & "</td>"

'  Show the day in
Tag = Tag & "<td align=""center"">Day In: "
Tag = Tag & "<input type=""text"" value=""" & chrDayIn & _
    """ name=""chrDayIn"">"

Tag = Tag & "</td>"
Tag = Tag & "</tr>"

'  Show the time out
Tag = Tag & "<tr>"
```

```
    Tag = Tag & "<td align=""center"">Time Out: "
    Tag = Tag & "<input type=""Text"" value=""" & chrTimeOut & _
        """ name=""chrTimeOut"">"
    Tag = Tag & "</td>"

    '  Show the time in
    Tag = Tag & "<td align=""center"">Time In: "
    Tag = Tag & "<input type=""text"" value=""" & chrTimeIn & _
        """ name=""chrTimeIn"">"

    Tag = Tag & "</td>"
    Tag = Tag & "</tr>"

    '  Show the contact info
    Tag = Tag & "<tr>"
    Tag = Tag & "<td align=""center"" colspan=""2"">Contact Info: "
    Tag = Tag & "<input type=""text"" value=""" & _
        chrContactInfo & _
        """ name=""chrContactInfo"">"
    Tag = Tag & "</td>"
    Tag = Tag & "</tr>"

    '  Show the submit button
    Tag = Tag & "<tr valign=""center"">"
    Tag = Tag & "<td align=""center"">"
    Tag = Tag & "<input type=""submit"" value=""Submit"">"
    Tag = Tag & "</td><td align=""center"">"

    '  Build a link to the default page and call the
    '  ClearCookieStatus event
    Tag = Tag & "<a href=""" & _
        URLFor(Default, "ClearCookieStatus") & _
        """>Clear</a>"

    Tag = Tag & "</td>"
    Tag = Tag & "</tr></form>"

Else

    '  If no cookie is set then indicate
    '  to the user to select a cookie
```

```
            Tag = Tag & "<tr><td colspan=""2"">Select your name from " & _
                "the list by clicking on ""My Status""</td></tr>"

    End If

    '  Return the tags
    RetrieveCookieEmployee = Tag

    End Function
```

The form event on the AddHotItem page will insert the new hot item into the list. The ID of the hot item and the description are passed into the InsertHotItem stored procedure. When the insert is done, the next item is set to the default page.

```
    '  Form1 event of the AddHotItem page
    Private Sub AddHotItem_Form1()

    '  Declare a data environment
    Dim dbDU As New dbDailyUpdate

    '  Insert the new hot item into the list
    dbDU.InsertHotItem Request("dtItemHot"), Request("chrDescription")

    '  Set the default page
    Set NextItem = Default

    '  Clear out data environment
    Set dbDU = Nothing

    End Sub
```

The ProcessTag event of the AddHotItem template page will default the date of the hot item to the current date. The page looks for the wc@date custom tag.

```
    '  Process the tags for the AddHotItem page
    Private Sub AddHotItem_ProcessTag(ByVal TagName As String, _
    TagContents As String, SendTags As Boolean)

    '  Process by tag name
    Select Case TagName
```

```
'  Show the current date
Case "wc@date"
    '  Show the current data and time in an input box
    TagContents = "<input type=""text"" value=""" & _
                  FormatDateTime(Date, vbShortDate) & _
                  """ name=""dtItemHot"">"

End Select

End Sub
```

When the respond event of the AddHotItem page is called, the page is written to the browser.

```
'  Respond event of the AddHotItem page
Private Sub AddHotItem_Respond()

'  Write out the page
AddHotItem.WriteTemplate

End Sub
```

The UserEvent for the AddHotItem template handles displaying the page when it is called.

```
'  User Event of the AddHotItem page
Private Sub AddHotItem_UserEvent(ByVal EventName As String)

'  Select by event name
Select Case EventName

    '  Display event
    Case "Display"
        '  Set the next item to be the AddHotItem page
        Set NextItem = AddHotItem

End Select

End Sub
```

The DeleteItem custom web event handles deleting a hot item from the database. The EventName argument identifies the ID of the item to be deleted. The DeleteHotItem subroutine is called to delete the item, and the user is returned to the default page.

```
'   DeleteItem user events
Private Sub DeleteItem_UserEvent(ByVal EventName As String)

'   The EventName will be the id of the item to
'   delete. Call the DeleteHotItem subroutine
'   and pass in the id.
DeleteHotItem CInt(EventName)

'   Set the default page as the next item
Set NextItem = Default

End Sub
```

The form1 event EditItem template page will handle submitting the updates to the hot item to the database. The UpdateHotItem stored procedure is called to update the specified item. Then the user is sent back to the default template page.

```
'   Form1 event of the EditItem page
Private Sub EditItem_Form1()

'   Create a data environment
Dim dbDU As New dbDailyUpdate

'   Call the UpdateHotItem stored procedure
'   to update the data
dbDU.UpdateHotItem Request("idHotItem"), _
    CDate(Request("dtItemHot")), _
    Request("chrDescription")

'   Set the next item to be the default page
Set NextItem = Default

'   Destroy our data environment object
Set dbDU = Nothing

End Sub
```

When the EditItem page encounters custom web tags on the page, the ProcessTag event is called. We will then retrieve the hot item settings by referencing the value set in the global variable.

In this case we are going to show the description and date of the item. An input text box will need to be created for each. Also, a hidden input element will be created on the page to store the ID of the hot item we are editing. That way we can update the item when the form is submitted by reading the hidden variable.

```
' Process tags for the EditItem page
Private Sub EditItem_ProcessTag(ByVal TagName As String, _
TagContents As String, SendTags As Boolean)
' Create a data environment
Dim dbDU As New dbDailyUpdate

' Retrieve the hot item by ID
dbDU.RetrieveHotItemByID idHotItem

' Select by tag name
Select Case LCase(TagName)

    ' Description
    Case "wc@description"
        ' Build the hot item description
        TagContents = "<input type=""text"" value=""" & _
                dbDU.rsRetrieveHotItemByID("chrDescription") & _
                """ name=""chrDescription"">"

        ' Build a hidden input that will store the ID _
        ' of the hot item
        TagContents = TagContents & _
        "<input type=""hidden"" value=""" & _
        idHotItem & """ name=""idHotItem"">"

    ' Date field
    Case "wc@date"
        ' Build the input for the date
        TagContents = "<input type=""text"" value=""" & _
        FormatDateTime(dbDU.rsRetrieveHotItemByID("dtItemHot"), _
        vbShortDate) & """ name=""dtItemHot"">"
```

```
End Select

'  Destroy our data environment
Set dbDU = Nothing

End Sub
```

In the respond event of the EditItem template, the page is written to the browser using the WriteTemplate method.

```
'  Respond event of the EditItem page
Private Sub EditItem_Respond()

'  Write out the page
EditItem.WriteTemplate

End Sub
```

The UserEvent of the edit item page will have passed into it the ID of the item to edit. The global variable is set. Then the next item is set to the edit item template for display.

```
'  User event of the Edit Item page
Private Sub EditItem_UserEvent(ByVal EventName As String)

'  The event name is the item to edit. We will set the global
'  variable
idHotItem = CInt(EventName)

'  Set the next item to be the edit item page
Set NextItem = EditItem

End Sub
```

When the SelectEmployee template is submitted to the server, the form1 event of the template is fired off. When that happens, the ID of the employee selected is stored in a cookie called "idemployee." Then the user is returned to the default template.

```
'  Form1 event of the select employee page
Private Sub SelectEmployee_Form1()

'  Set the cookie for the user to the ID of the employee
'  they selected
Response.Cookies("idemployee") = Request("idemployee")

'  set the next page to the default page
Set NextItem = Default

End Sub
```

The ProcessTag event of the SelectEmployee template page will build a select element list of employee names. The list is retrieved from the database using the RetrieveEmployees stored procedure.

```
'  Process tag event of the SelectEmployee page
Private Sub SelectEmployee_ProcessTag(ByVal TagName As String, _
TagContents As String, SendTags As Boolean)

'  Create a new data environment
Dim dbDU As New dbDailyUpdate

'  Retrieve the list of employees
dbDU.RetrieveEmployees

'  Start building the select
TagContents = "<select name=""idEmployee"">"

'  Loop through the retrieved employees
Do Until dbDU.rsRetrieveEmployees.EOF

   '  Build the option value for the employee. Store
   '  the ID of the employee and display the last name
   '  and first name
   TagContents = TagContents & _
     "<option value=""" & _
     dbDU.rsRetrieveEmployees("idEmployee") & """>" & _
     dbDU.rsRetrieveEmployees("chrLastName") & ", " & _
     dbDU.rsRetrieveEmployees("chrFirstName") & _
     "</option>"
```

```
    '  Move to the next row
    dbDU.rsRetrieveEmployees.MoveNext

Loop

'  End the select
TagContents = TagContents & "</select>"

'  Destroy the data environment
Set dbDU = Nothing

End Sub

'  Respond event of the SelectEmployee page
Private Sub SelectEmployee_Respond()

'  Write out the template
SelectEmployee.WriteTemplate

End Sub
```

The UserEvent of the clear employee custom web item will retrieve the ID of the employee and will call the UpdateEmployeeStatus subroutine. The clear flag and ID of the employee are passed in.

```
Private Sub ClearEmployee_UserEvent(ByVal EventName As String)

UpdateEmployeeStatus 1, CInt(EventName)

End Sub
```

The UserEvent of the update employee custom web item will call the UpdateEmployeeStatus subroutine and pass in the clear flag and the ID of the employee.

```
Private Sub UpdateEmployee_UserEvent(ByVal EventName As String)

UpdateEmployeeStatus 0, CInt(EventName)

End Sub
```

Once you start going through examples of building IIS applications, you soon get into the rhythm of using templates, custom web items, web events, and the Active Server Pages object model.

To review, we built our template HTML pages for our IIS application to define the user interface structure. Then we designed the database behind the application and implemented appropriate stored procedures. From the stored procedures, we implemented a data environment interface to our database. Now we are ready to test and run our application.

Running the Daily Update

We are now ready to run our IIS application. As mentioned previously in the book, you will need to be running Internet Information Server 3.0 (or higher) or the Personal Web Server 3.0 (or higher) on Windows NT Server, Windows NT Workstation, or Windows 98. The Active Server Pages (ASP) option must be installed with the Web server because the IIS application interfaces through Active Server Pages.

Once you have the application set up, go ahead and run it. When you do, you will be prompted to add a virtual root to the default Web site on the Web server. The virtual root name will default to the application name. Figure 14-3 shows the query dialog box.

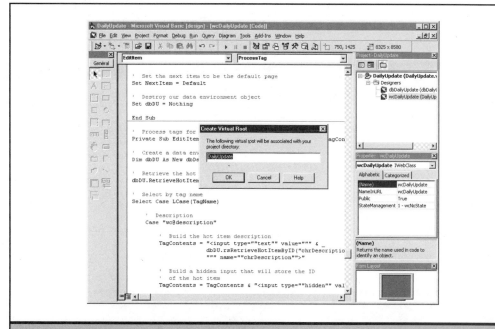

Figure 14-3. The virtual root query dialog box

When the application starts, you will have few options set except the ability to select a default employee setting and add a hot item to the list. Figure 14-4 shows the default template at startup. Let's start by selecting a default employee setting. Click on the My Status link at the top of the page. That will take you to the Select Employee template page. When that page is shown, the list of employees from the database will be displayed in a select box. Figure 14-5 shows the page.

Be sure your employee table is loaded with sample data.

Select an employee from the listing, and then click Submit. If you have your browser set to prompt to accept cookies, the browser will show you the cookie data. Figure 14-6 shows the cookie data in Internet Explorer.

Note the name of the cookie is "idEmployee," and the data in the example case is 3. That will be the ID from the database. Once the cookie is set, the default page will allow you to automatically set values on the default page for the default user. That way, you can easily set your own status without having to select from a list. Figure 14-7 shows the updated default page.

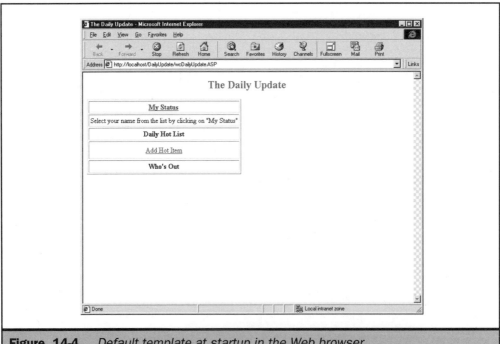

Figure 14-4. *Default template at startup in the Web browser*

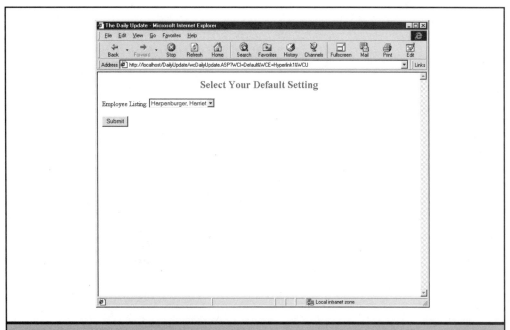

Figure 14-5.   *Select Employee page with a list of employees from the database*

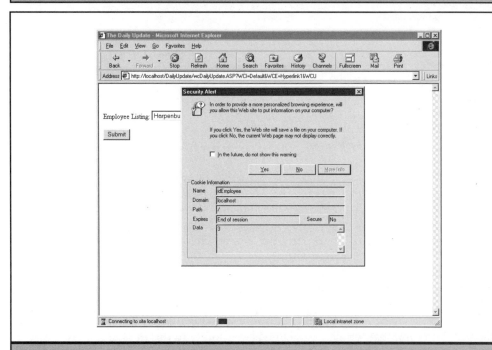

Figure 14-6.   *Cookie data sent to the browser when a default employee is selected*

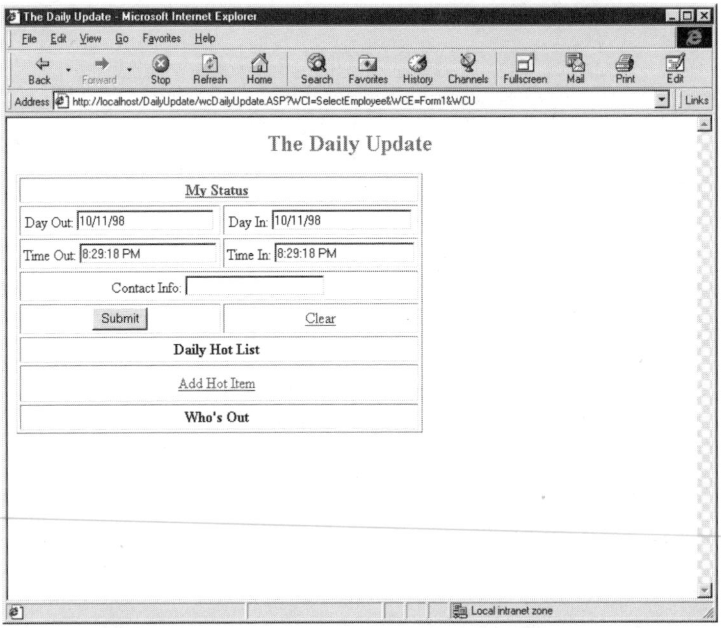

Figure 14-7. *Default page with a cookie set to define the default employee*

Let's go ahead and set some values for the default user to be out with appropriate contact information. Make the appropriate settings, and then submit the data. When you do so, the updated information will be added to the Who's Out list. Figure 14-8 shows the updated page.

Now let's move to the hot list section. Click on the Add Hot Item link on the default page. When you do so, you will go to the template page for adding a hot item to the list. Go ahead and fill out the form data as shown in Figure 14-9. The default page is updated to show the new hot list item. Figure 14-10 shows the updated hot list.

Now go ahead and add another hot list item and set the in/out status of a couple more employees. Then you can utilize the edit and delete links of the host list. And try clearing the in/out status of one of the employee settings. Figure 14-11 shows the default template page with several settings.

The IIS application provides an easy-to-use browser-based interface that can be supported by any browser. Try playing around with the application capabilities. You might try and build multiple day tracking for the hot list. The same could be done for the in/out list. You might also want to consider utilizing a select list for the in/out dates and times. But that would negate the user's ability to put in date ranges or any data that would differ from a standard date/time format.

Figure 14-8.   *Default page with an employee added to the Who's Out list*

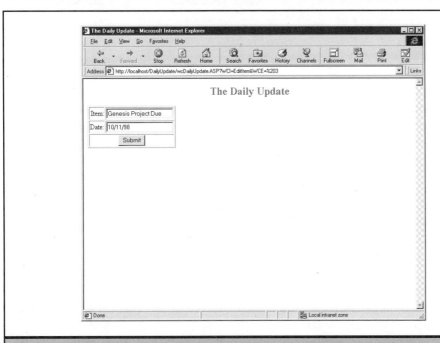

Figure 14-9.   *Add hot item page*

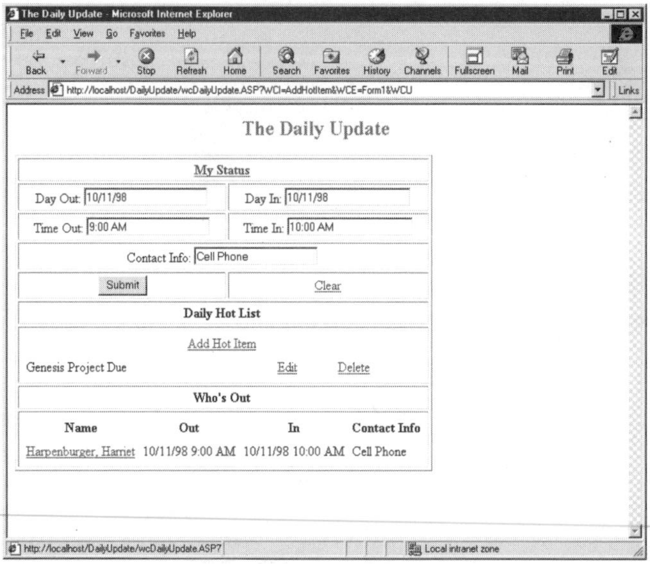

Figure 14-10. Default page with the new hot list item

Figure 14-11. Default page with multiple settings for the in/out status and hot list

Summary

IIS applications provide an elegant way of building Web browser interfaces to your applications. You can utilize familiar structures such as data environments, classes, modules, and so on. The primary difference is that we are not using a forms interface for the application.

Remember that you can interface with the application through the Active Server Pages interface. In fact, in our application, we build complete pages from our Visual Basic application. We can interface with cookies and replace custom tags in the HTML page, among other things, to build our Web pages. Interfacing with the database in our sample is done with a standard data environment and imported stored procedures.

What's Next

In the next chapter we will take a look at building DHTML applications in more depth. In fact, we can re-create the example in this chapter, only do it on the client side for the interface and interact with the database.

Chapter 15

Building Data Driven DHTML Applications

In Chapter 5 we reviewed how to build DHTML applications with Visual Basic. DHTML applications are great for intranets, when you want to combine the power of Visual Basic with the user interface of a browser. You can use all the data access tools we have learned about previously in the book, including the data environment, within your DHTML applications. The key requirement is that you will need to run this application on your local network, which will have direct data access via ODBC or some other method.

Remote Data Services (RDS) capabilities are also available to query a database over the Web instead of over a local network. You can learn more about using RDS in MSDN.

Designing the Application

In our example, we are going to build a simple data interface for an employee listing. We will want to be able to add, edit, update, and delete records as well as easily browse through the records. The database will reside on a remote server and can be accessed via ODBC.

Building the Database

Before we jump into the DHTML design, let's define the database and data environment that will sit behind our application—in other words, the data tier. Table 15-1 defines the database fields for our application.

Field	Description
idEmployee	Auto incrementing ID of the employee.
chrFirstName	First name of the employee.
chrLastName	Last name of the employee.
chrAddress	Address of the employee.
chrCity	City of the employee.
chrState	State of the employee.
chrZip	Zip code of the employee.
chrPhone	Phone number of the employee.

Table 15-1. *Employee Database Table*

The following is the SQL script for the employee table:

```
CREATE TABLE dbo.EmployeeData (
     idEmployee int IDENTITY (1, 1) NOT NULL ,
     chrFirstName varchar (255) NULL ,
     chrLastName varchar (255) NULL ,
     chrAddress varchar (255) NULL ,
     chrCity varchar (255) NULL ,
     chrState char (2) NULL ,
     chrZip varchar (20) NULL ,
     chrPhone varchar (25) NULL
)
GO
```

You will want to define an ODBC connection to the database called "EmployeeData." That will be used to connect to the database from our data environment.

Add a new data environment to the project. Name it "dbEmployeeData." Rename the connection "EmployeeData." Right-click on the connection and select Properties. For the OLE DB provider, select Microsoft OLE DB Provider for ODBC Drivers.

On the Connection tab, select EmployeeData from the list of data sources. Type in the appropriate username and password for your database. That will provide the connection to the database.

Now let's add one command to our database environment, called "Employees." We simply want this command to return the data in the EmployeeData table. We will then use the recordset returned by the data environment to work with the data.

Right-click on the Employees command and select Properties. In the connection property, select the EmployeeData connection we just created. For the Database Object, select the EmployeeData table.

We now have our data environment set up. We are ready to begin working on the user interface design for the Web browser.

Designing the Interface

Our interface just needs to be a simple data entry set of fields that match the fields in the database. We will also need a series of buttons to handle the navigation and manipulation of the database.

The simplest way to build the page with the various elements we need is to work directly in HTML. We will want to build a table that outlines a label and text input element for each field in the database (except for the employee ID). Following that, we will define HTML buttons for each of our functions: First, Previous, Next, Last, Delete, New, Update, Cancel. The page begins with the standard HTML tags to define the page.

```
<HTML>

<BODY>

<center>

<BR>
```

The first paragraph tags on the HTML page will define a status message for the page. Note the ID defined in the paragraph tag. The ID will allow us to identify it as an object on our page. Thus, we can manipulate it from our Visual Basic code.

```
<p id=pStatus></p>
```

Next the table is defined for the data entry. Our table has two columns. The first column contains the labels for the fields. These will be defined as paragraph tags with appropriate IDs. We will be able to manipulate each from our Visual Basic code.

The second column contains the text input elements for the user. Note that each defines a specific style for width and height. Each is given an ID for reference in our code.

```
<P>
<TABLE cellpadding=4 cellspacing=4 height=244 id=Table1
style="HEIGHT: 244px; WIDTH: 380px" width=380 name = Table1>

    <TR>
        <TD>
            <DIV align=right><p id=pFirstname>First Name:</p></DIV>
        </TD>
        <TD>
            <INPUT id=txtFirstname name=txtFirstName style="HEIGHT:
            22px; WIDTH: 251px">
        </TD>
    </TR>
    <TR>
        <TD>
            <DIV align=right><FONT style="BACKGROUND-COLOR:
            #ffffff">
            <p id=pLastName>Last Name:</p></FONT></DIV>
        </TD>
        <TD>
```

```
        <INPUT id=txtLastName name=txtLastName style="HEIGHT:
        22px;
        WIDTH: 251px">
    </TD>
</TR>
<TR>
    <TD>
        <DIV align=right><p id=paddress>Address:</p></DIV>
    </TD>
    <TD>
        <INPUT id=txtAddress name=txtAddress style="HEIGHT:
        22px;
        WIDTH: 251px">
    </TD>
</TR>
<TR>
    <TD>
        <DIV align=right><p id=pcity>City:</p></DIV>
    </TD>
    <TD>
        <INPUT id=txtCity name=txtCity style="HEIGHT: 22px;
        WIDTH: 251px">
    </TD>
</TR>
<TR>
    <TD>
        <DIV align=right><p id=pstate>State:</p></DIV>
    </TD>
    <TD>
        <INPUT id=txtState name=txtState style="HEIGHT: 22px;
        WIDTH:
        251px" size=2>
    </TD>
</TR>
<TR>
    <TD>
        <DIV align=right><p id=pZipCode>Zip Code:</p></DIV>
    </TD>
    <TD>
    <INPUT id=txtZipCode name=txtZipCode style="HEIGHT: 22px;
    WIDTH: 251px">
```

```
            </TD>
        </TR>
        <TR>
            <TD>
                <DIV align=right><p id=pPhone>Phone:</p></DIV>
            </TD>
            <TD>
                <INPUT id=txtPhone name=txtPhone style="HEIGHT: 22px;
                WIDTH: 251px">
            </TD>
        </TR>

    </TABLE>

    </P>
```

We next have an ID for the record count in the database. This will define the number of employee records. Again, we can manipulate this because we have defined an ID for the paragraph tags.

```
<p id=pRecordCount></p>
```

Now we are ready to define the buttons for the page. Each is an input element. In this case they are not Submit buttons, but regular buttons. And we have defined an ID for each so they can be referenced in our HTML code.

```
<P>
<INPUT id=btnFirst name=Button2 type=button value="    First    ">
<INPUT id=btnPrevious name=Button3 type=button value=Previous>
<INPUT id=btnNext name=button1 type=button value="   Next   ">
<INPUT id=btnLast name=Button2 type=button value="    Last    "><BR>
</P>

<INPUT id=btnDelete name=Button1 type=button value="  Delete  ">
<INPUT id=btnNew name=Button5 type=button value="    New    ">
<INPUT disabled id=btnUpdate name=Button1 type=button value=Update>
<INPUT disabled id=btnCancel name=Button1 type=button
value="Cancel">
```

Finally, we end the page with the appropriate closing tags.

```
</center>

</BODY>

</HTML>
```

Now we are ready to import the page into our page designer. Follow these steps:

1. Click on DHTML Page Designer Properties.
2. In the Save Mode dialog box, select "Save HTML in an external file."
3. Select the file in which you have placed the code.
4. Click OK. Figure 15-1 shows the dialog box.

Now we have the interface defined. You should see it in the page designer. Figure 15-2 shows the page imported into the application. We are ready to begin building code behind the interface and connect it to the database.

Building the Code

 We will have several global variables defined for our application. The first is the data environment. We will open a connection to our database for the entire session. That is why it is defined globally.

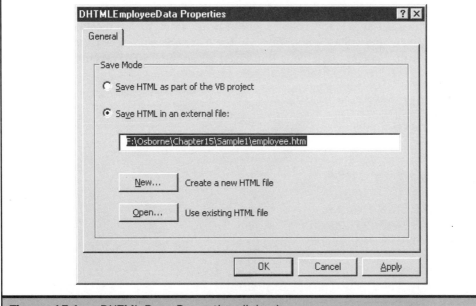

Figure 15-1. *DHTML Page Properties dialog box*

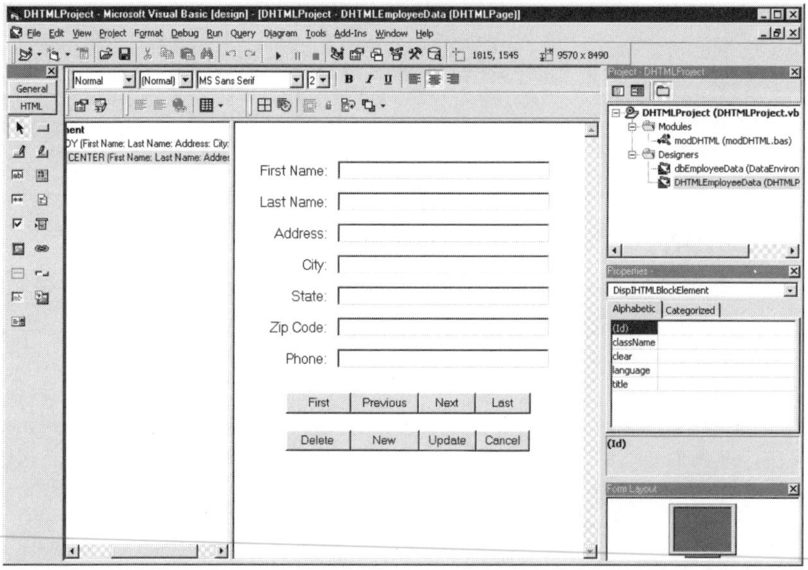

Figure 15-2. *The page imported into the application*

Next we have a series of three variables that will define the current state of the application. The intChangeFlag variables will indicate when the application is in a change state. The intInsertFlag will define when we are adding a new record to the database. The intDeleteFlag variable will indicate when the user wants to delete a record.

```
'  Global data source
Dim dbED As New dbEmployeeData

'  Flag to indicate when a change has been made
'  to any of the text boxes
Dim intChangeFlag As Integer

'  Insert flag indicates when a new
'  record is to be inserted
Dim intInsertFlag As Integer

'  Delete flag indicates when a delete
'  has been requested
Dim intDeleteFlag As Integer
```

We will have a series of supporting subroutines for our application. The first is the ConfirmDelete subroutine that will set up the navigation buttons when the user wants to delete a record. When the user clicks Delete, the record will not be immediately deleted. The user will have a chance to confirm the delete before it happens.

The Disabled property for each of the buttons is properly set. We only want the Delete and Cancel buttons to be enabled. The user will need to click the Delete button again to confirm the delete. The ResetButtonColors subroutine is called to set all the button colors back to grey.

```
'  This subroutine sets up the buttons to
'  confirm a delete
Private Sub ConfirmDelete()

    '  Set the disabled flags as appropriate
    btnNext.disabled = True
    btnPrevious.disabled = True
    btnFirst.disabled = True
    btnLast.disabled = True
    btnUpdate.disabled = True
    btnCancel.disabled = False
    btnDelete.disabled = False
    btnNew.disabled = True

    '  Ensure the buttons are reset back to grey
    '  If the button is disabled and the color was
    '  changed, then the color will not change back
    '  unless we explicitly set the color
    ResetButtonColors

End Sub
```

In the ShowRecordCount subroutine we will update the Record Count paragraph on the page. We reference the innerText method of the paragraph to change the text inside the paragraph tags. We show the appropriate label text and tack on the value returned by the RecordCount property of our employees recordset.

```
'  Shows the record count on the page
Private Sub ShowRecordCount()

    '  The pRecordCount object is updated. The
    '  innerText property is used which will just
```

```
'   change the text only in the tags
pRecordCount.innerText = "Record Count: " & _
dbED.rsEmployees.RecordCount

End Sub
```

SetFontColor will change the font color on an object to red or black. An object, such as a text box, is passed into the subroutine. A flag is passed in to indicate whether the color should be red or black.

Each time the function is called, the status paragraph is cleared by calling the innerHTML method. Then the Style settings and the color property of the object are referenced to set the font color.

```
'   Sets the FontColor of an object. An object such as
'   a paragraph is passed in to the subroutine and a flag is passed
'   in to indicate whether to turn the
'   text Red or Black
Private Sub SetFontColor(X As Object, intColorFlag)

    '   Clear the status message if we are changing font colors.
    '   That means we are not updating or inserting
    pStatus.innerHTML = ""

    '   Check the flag
    If intColorFlag = 1 Then

        '   Set the color property of the style
        '   object.
        X.Style.Color = "red"

    Else

        '   Set the color property of the style
        '   object
        X.Style.Color = "black"

    End If

End Sub
```

The SetButtonColor subroutine is similar to the SetFontColor subroutine. In this case we want to change the background color of the buttons. This is done by also referencing the Style property of the object passed into the subroutine. We then set the background property.

```
'   Sets the button colors. A button object is
'   passed in. The intOverFlag argument indicates
'   if the mouse is over the button
Private Sub SetButtonColor(X As Object, intOverFlag)

    '   Check to see if the mouse is over the button
    If intOverFlag = 1 Then

        '   If so then set the button color to white
        X.Style.backgroundColor = "white"

    Else

        '   Default to grey when mouse leaves
        '   the button
        X.Style.backgroundColor = ""

    End If

End Sub
```

ResetButtonColor sets all of the button colors back to grey by calling the SetButtonColor subroutine and passing in the different buttons.

```
'   The ResetButtonColor subroutine
'   will set all button colors back to grey
Private Sub ResetButtonColors()

    '   Utilize the SetButtonColor procedure
    SetButtonColor btnNext, 0
    SetButtonColor btnPrevious, 0
    SetButtonColor btnFirst, 0
    SetButtonColor btnLast, 0
    SetButtonColor btnUpdate, 0
    SetButtonColor btnCancel, 0
    SetButtonColor btnNew, 0

End Sub
```

DisableNavigation turns off the navigation buttons. This is done for the updating and inserting of a new record. We want only the Update and Cancel buttons to be visible. The button colors are reset to grey after the settings are finished.

```
'   Disable navigation turns off the
'   first, previous, next, last and
'   delete buttons
Private Sub DisableNavigation()

    '   Set the disabled flag as appropriate
    btnNext.disabled = True
    btnPrevious.disabled = True
    btnFirst.disabled = True
    btnLast.disabled = True
    btnUpdate.disabled = False
    btnCancel.disabled = False
    btnDelete.disabled = True
    btnNew.disabled = True

    '   Ensure the buttons are set back to grey
    '   If the button is disabled and the color was
    '   changed, then the color will not change back
    '   unless we explicitly set the color
    ResetButtonColors

End Sub
```

EnableNavigation will turn on the navigation buttons and turn off the Update and Cancel buttons. After the settings are done, the button colors are reset.

```
'   Enable navigation turns on the navigation buttons
'   and disables the update and cancel buttons
Private Sub EnableNavigation()

    '   Enable and disable the buttons
    '   as appropriate
    btnNext.disabled = False
    btnPrevious.disabled = False
    btnFirst.disabled = False
    btnLast.disabled = False
    btnUpdate.disabled = True
```

```
btnCancel.disabled = True
btnDelete.disabled = False
btnNew.disabled = False

'  Reset the button colors to grey to ensure
'  that all disabled button colors are grey.
ResetButtonColors

End Sub
```

The ClearTextBoxes subroutine clears the text boxes for entry of a new record in the database.

```
'  Clear Text Boxes deletes any text in the
'  HTML text input boxes
Private Sub ClearTextBoxes()

'  Clear the values
txtFirstname.Value = ""
txtLastName.Value = ""
txtAddress.Value = ""
txtCity.Value = ""
txtState.Value = ""
txtZipCode.Value = ""
txtPhone.Value = ""

End Sub
```

The InsertData subroutine handles adding a new record to the database. The AddNew method of the employees recordset is called. That will start the process for adding a new record. It sets the current record to the newly added record.

We then update each of the fields with the values in the text-input elements. Once that is done, the Update method of the recordset is called to add the data to the database. Finally, our global flags are cleared so the application is reset and taken out of insert mode.

Note *No data validation is done on the data entered by the user. This could be done before the new record is added.*

```
'   InsertData takes care of adding a new row
'   to the recordset of employees
Private Sub Insertdata()

'   Call the AddNew method of the recordset
'   to insert a new record
dbED.rsEmployees.AddNew

'   Retrieve the values and set the fields in the
'   database appropriately
dbED.rsEmployees("chrFirstName") = txtFirstname.Value
dbED.rsEmployees("chrLastname") = txtLastName.Value
dbED.rsEmployees("chrAddress") = txtAddress.Value
dbED.rsEmployees("chrCity") = txtCity.Value
dbED.rsEmployees("chrState") = txtState.Value
dbED.rsEmployees("chrZip") = txtZipCode.Value
dbED.rsEmployees("chrPhone") = txtPhone.Value

'   Update the database with the new record
dbED.rsEmployees.Update

'   Clear out insert and change flags
intInsertFlag = False
intChangeFlag = False

End Sub
```

SaveData handles updating records with updated data entered by the user for the current recordset. The values for each of the fields are set to the fields in the database for the current record. Then the Update method of the database is called to update the database. Finally, the global flags are cleared to indicate the save is done.

```
'   The SaveData subroutine will retrieve updated data in
'   the text input elements and update the current fields
'   referenced in the recordset.
Private Sub SaveData()

'   Update the fields in the recordset
dbED.rsEmployees("chrFirstName") = txtFirstname.Value
dbED.rsEmployees("chrLastname") = txtLastName.Value
dbED.rsEmployees("chrAddress") = txtAddress.Value
dbED.rsEmployees("chrCity") = txtCity.Value
```

```
dbED.rsEmployees("chrState") = txtState.Value
dbED.rsEmployees("chrZip") = txtZipCode.Value
dbED.rsEmployees("chrPhone") = txtPhone.Value

'  Update the row to the database
dbED.rsEmployees.Update

'  Clear our global flags
intInsertFlag = False
intChangeFlag = False

End Sub
```

The ShowRecord subroutine retrieves the current record data from the database and sets the text inputs as appropriate.

```
'  Show Record retrieves values from the
'  recordset and updates the text input
'  elements
Private Sub ShowRecord()

'  Retrieve and display the values
txtFirstname.Value = dbED.rsEmployees("chrFirstName")
txtLastName.Value = dbED.rsEmployees("chrLastname")
txtAddress.Value = dbED.rsEmployees("chrAddress")
txtCity.Value = dbED.rsEmployees("chrCity")
txtState.Value = dbED.rsEmployees("chrState")
txtZipCode.Value = dbED.rsEmployees("chrZip")
txtPhone.Value = dbED.rsEmployees("chrPhone")

End Sub
```

Next we move into the events for the buttons on the page. The first is the click event of the Cancel button. When users select the Cancel button, that means they no longer want to update or insert the record. If this is the case, the user is moved to the first record in the recordset. The record is shown, and global flags are reset. Finally, the navigation buttons are reset using the EnableNavigation subroutine.

```
'  Click event of the cancel button
Private Function btnCancel_onclick() As Boolean
```

```
'   Move to the first recordset
dbED.rsEmployees.MoveFirst

'   Show the record
ShowRecord

'   Clear the global flags
intInsertFlag = False
intChangeFlag = False

'   Enable the navigation buttons
EnableNavigation

'   Reset the text
btnDelete.Value = "Delete"

'  Set the text color back to black
btnDelete.Style.Color = "Black"

'   Reset the delete flag
intDeleteFlag = False

End Function
```

The mouse out event will set the button color back to grey.

```
'   Mouse out event of the cancel button
Private Sub btnCancel_onmouseout()

'   Reset the button color
SetButtonColor btnCancel, 0

End Sub
```

The mouse over event of the Cancel button will turn the button color to white.

```
'   Mouse over event of the cancel button
Private Sub btnCancel_onmouseover()
```

```
'   Set the button color to white
SetButtonColor btnCancel, 1

End Sub
```

The click event of the Delete button will start the delete process. A check is done to see if the process has been started. If not, the ConfirmDelete subroutine is called to set up the navigation for the user to confirm the record deletion. Next the text on the Delete button is changed to "Confirm?" to ask the user to confirm the delete. The button color is changed to red by calling the SetFontColor function. The delete flag is set to indicate a delete is in process.

If the delete is in process, the Delete method is called for the recordset, and the current record is deleted. The recordset is then moved to the first record, and the data is shown. Finally, the update status paragraph object is updated to indicate the delete was successful. The innerHTML function is called because we want to change text in the paragraph tags to include HTML tags. And we want the HTML tags to be processed appropriately.

```
'   Click event of the delete button
Private Function btnDelete_onclick() As Boolean

'   Check to see if we are in delete mode
If intDeleteFlag = False Then

    '   Set up the buttons to confirm a delete
    ConfirmDelete

    '   Change the delete button text
    btnDelete.Value = "Confirm?"

    '   Set the text color
    SetFontColor btnDelete, 1

    '   Set the delete flag
    intDeleteFlag = True

Else

    '   Call the Delete method of the recordset
    dbED.rsEmployees.Delete

    '   Move to the first record
    dbED.rsEmployees.MoveFirst
```

```
'   Show the data
ShowRecord

'   Change the status message. We will use the
'   InnerHTML property since we want the
'   HTML tags to be evaluated to show the
'   green font color
pStatus.innerHTML = _
    "<b><font color=""green"">Record Deleted " & _
    "Successfully</font></b>"

'   Update the record count display
ShowRecordCount

'   Reset the delete flag
intDeleteFlag = False

'   Enable the navigation
EnableNavigation

'   Change the text back
btnDelete.Value = "Delete"

'   Reset the text color
btnDelete.Style.Color = "Black"

End If

End Function
```

The mouse out event of the Delete button sets the background color back to grey.

```
'   Mouse out event of the delete button
Private Sub btnDelete_onmouseout()

'   Reset the button color
SetButtonColor btnDelete, 0

End Sub
```

The mouse over event of the Delete button sets the background color to white.

```
'  Mouse over event of the delete button
Private Sub btnDelete_onmouseover()

'  Set the button color to white
SetButtonColor btnDelete, 1

End Sub
```

The click event of the First button moves to the first record in the recordset by calling the MoveFirst method for the recordset. Then the data is shown by calling the ShowRecord subroutine.

```
'  Click event of the first button
Private Function btnFirst_onclick() As Boolean

'  Move to the first record
dbED.rsEmployees.MoveFirst

'  Show the record
ShowRecord

End Function
```

The mouse move event of the First button will set the background color to white.

```
'  Mouse move event of the First button
Private Sub btnFirst_onmousemove()

'  Set the button color to white
SetButtonColor btnFirst, 1

End Sub
```

The mouse out event of the First button will set the button color back to grey.

```
'  Mouse out event of the First button
Private Sub btnFirst_onmouseout()

'  Reset the button color to grey
SetButtonColor btnFirst, 0

End Sub
```

The click event of the last button moves to the last record in the recordset. The showrecord subroutine is called to display the data.

```
'   Click event of the last button
Private Function btnLast_onclick() As Boolean

'   Move to the last record
dbED.rsEmployees.MoveLast

'   Show the record
ShowRecord

End Function
```

The mouse move event of the Last button will set the button color to white.

```
'   Mouse move event of the last button
Private Sub btnLast_onmousemove()

'   Set the button color to white
SetButtonColor btnLast, 1

End Sub
```

The mouse out event of the Last button sets the button color back to grey.

```
'   Mouse out event of the last button
Private Sub btnLast_onmouseout()

'   Reset the color to grey
SetButtonColor btnLast, 0

End Sub
```

The click event of the New button will start the insert process for a new record. The DisableNavigation subroutine is called to set up the buttons to update the record or cancel the insert. The ClearTextBoxes subroutine is called to clear the text boxes for new data to be input. The insert global flag variable is set to indicate that an insert is in progress.

```
'  Click event of the New button
Private Function btnNew_onclick() As Boolean

'  Disable the navigation buttons
'  since we do not want record
'  navigation while the user is
'  entering a new record
DisableNavigation

'  clear the text input boxes for data
'  entry
ClearTextBoxes

'  Set our global insert flag to indicate when
'  the user clicks the 'Update' button that
'  the record should be inserted, not updated.
intInsertFlag = True

End Function
```

The mouse move event of the New button sets the background color to white.

```
'  Mouse move event of the New button
Private Sub btnNew_onmousemove()

'  Set the button color to white
SetButtonColor btnNew, 1

End Sub
```

The mouse out event of the New button sets the background color to grey.

```
'  Mouse out event of the New button
Private Sub btnNew_onmouseout()

'  Set the button color back to grey
SetButtonColor btnNew, 0

End Sub
```

The click event of the Next button will move to the next record in the recordset. Several checks have to be done to ensure we are not at the beginning of the file and end of the file. If we are at the end of the file, we cannot move forward. If we are at the beginning of the file, we need to move forward to go back to the first record (not past it). Finally, the record is shown.

```
'   Click event of the Next button
Private Function btnNext_onclick() As Boolean

'   Check to see if we are at the beginning of the
'   recordset. If so then we need to move back to
'   the first row
If dbED.rsEmployees.BOF Then dbED.rsEmployees.MoveNext

'   If we are not at the end of the recordset then
'   we cannot move forward a record
If Not dbED.rsEmployees.EOF Then dbED.rsEmployees.MoveNext

'   If we are not at the end
If Not dbED.rsEmployees.EOF Then

    '   Show the record
    ShowRecord

End If

End Function
```

The mouse move event of the Next button sets the background color to white.

```
'   Mouse move event of the Next button
Private Sub btnNext_onmousemove()

'   Set the button color to white
SetButtonColor btnNext, 1

End Sub
```

The mouse out event of the Next button sets the background color to grey.

```
'  Mouse out event of the Next button
Private Sub btnNext_onmouseout()

'  Set the button color back to grey
SetButtonColor btnNext, 0

End Sub
```

The click event of the Previous button will move to the previous record. A check is done to see if the user is at the end of the file or at the beginning of the file. If the user is at the end of the file, the recordset is moved back to the last record. If the recordset is at the beginning of the file, a move is made to the previous record. Finally, the record is shown by calling the ShowRecord subroutine.

```
'  Click event of the previous button
Private Function btnPrevious_onclick() As Boolean

'  Check to see if we are at the end of the file, if so then
'  we need to move to the last record
If dbED.rsEmployees.EOF Then dbED.rsEmployees.MovePrevious

'  If we are not at the beginning then move back a record
If Not dbED.rsEmployees.BOF Then dbED.rsEmployees.MovePrevious

'  Check to see if we are at the beginning
If Not dbED.rsEmployees.BOF Then

    '  Show the record
    ShowRecord

End If

End Function
```

The mouse move event of the Previous button will set the background color to white.

```
'  Mouse move event of the Previous button
Private Sub btnPrevious_onmousemove()

'  Set the button color to white
SetButtonColor btnPrevious, 1

End Sub
```

The mouse out event of the Previous button sets the button color to grey.

```
'  Mouse out event of the Previous button
Private Sub btnPrevious_onmouseout()

'  Set the button color back to grey.
SetButtonColor btnPrevious, 0

End Sub
```

The click event of the Update button will either insert a new record or update the current record. If we are updating a record, the SaveData subroutine is called to update the data in the database. Then the innerHTML property of the status paragraph object is set to show that the record was updated successfully. The font color is set with HTML tags in the text of the paragraph. The innerHTML property will tell the browser to interpret the HTML.

If the insert is in progress, the InsertData subroutine is called to insert the new record into the database. After the insert, the status paragraph is updated to indicate the insert was successful. Finally, the navigation buttons are enabled with the EnabledNavigation subroutine.

```
'  Click event of the Update button
Private Function btnUpdate_onclick() As Boolean

'  Check to see if the insert flag is set
If intInsertFlag = False Then

    '  Save the data to the recordset
    SaveData

    '  Update the status to indicate a successful update
    pStatus.innerHTML = "<b><font color=""green"">Updated " & _
    "Successfully</font></b>"

Else

    '  Insert the new data into the recordset
    Insertdata

    '  Update the display to show a successful insert
    pStatus.innerHTML = _
        "<b><font color=""green"">New Record Successfully " & _
        "Added</font></b>"
```

```
    '   Show the new record count
    ShowRecordCount

End If

'   Enable the navigation buttons
EnableNavigation

End Function
```

The mouse move event of the Update button sets the background color to white.

```
'   Mouse move event of the Update button
Private Sub btnUpdate_onmousemove()

'   Set the mouse color to white
SetButtonColor btnUpdate, 1

End Sub
```

The mouse out event of the Update button will set the button color back to grey.

```
'   Mouse out event of the Update button
Private Sub btnUpdate_onmouseout()

'   Set the button color back to grey
SetButtonColor btnUpdate, 0

End Sub
```

When the page is loaded, the employee recordset is retrieved by calling the Employees command of the global data environment. A check is done to ensure a record is available, and then the record is shown. If no record is available, the navigation is disabled, since there are no records to browse through and only an insert can be done. Finally, all the global flags are set to false, and the current record count is shown.

```
'   Load event for the page
Private Sub DHTMLPage_Load()

'   Retrieve the employees recordset
dbED.Employees

'   Check to ensure we are not at the end of the
'   recordset
If Not dbED.rsEmployees.EOF Then

    '   Show the record
    ShowRecord

Else

    '   Disable navigation
    DisableNavigation
    intInsertFlag = True

End If

'   Default the change and insert flags
intChangeFlag = False
intInsertFlag = False

'   Show the record count
ShowRecordCount

End Sub
```

Next we are going to move into the management of the text boxes. Each will follow the same pattern. The blur event of the text box is fired off when the text box loses the focus. When it loses focus, we want to set the paragraph label corresponding to the text box back to black.

```
'   Blur event of the address text box
Private Sub txtAddress_onblur()

'   Set the address text back to black
SetFontColor paddress, 0

End Sub
```

When the Address text box gets the focus, we will set the corresponding label paragraph to red. That will indicate the current text box is active for input.

```
'  Focus event of the text box
Private Sub txtAddress_onfocus()

'  Set the address text to red
SetFontColor paddress, 1

End Sub
```

The key press event of the Address text box is fired off when a character is typed into the box. That will indicate that the recordset is being updated. A check is done on the change flag, if it is not set, and then the DisableNavigation subroutine is called. The change flag is set to indicate the user is changing the current record. Finally, in order to ensure the character is displayed, the function value is set to true.

```
'  Key press event of the address box
Private Function txtAddress_onkeypress() As Boolean

'  Check to see if we are already in a
'  change event
If intChangeFlag = False Then

    '  Disable the navigation
    DisableNavigation

End If

'  Set the flag to indicate a record
'  is being updated by the user
intChangeFlag = True

'  Return true so the character will be displayed
txtAddress_onkeypress = True

End Function
```

The rest of the buttons will follow the same pattern. The effect is that anytime a user starts typing in a record, the application goes into "change mode." And each time a text box gets the focus, the corresponding label is turned to red to indicate that field is being accessed.

```
'   Blur event of the City text input
Private Sub txtCity_onblur()

'   Set the font color to black
SetFontColor pcity, 0

End Sub

'   Focus event of the City text input
Private Sub txtCity_onfocus()

'   Set the font color to red
SetFontColor pcity, 1

End Sub

'   Key press event of the City input
Private Function txtCity_onkeypress() As Boolean

'   Check to see if the update process has started
If intChangeFlag = False Then

    '   Disable navigation
    DisableNavigation

End If

'   Set the change flag to indicate an update
intChangeFlag = True

'   Set the return value to true so the character is displayed
txtCity_onkeypress = True

End Function

'   Blur event of the First Name input
Private Sub txtFirstname_onblur()

'   Set the font color back to black
SetFontColor pFirstname, 0

End Sub
```

```vbnet
' Key press event of the First Name input
Private Function txtFirstname_onkeypress() As Boolean

' Check to see if an update has been initiated
If intChangeFlag = False Then

    ' Disable the navigation
    DisableNavigation

End If

' Set the change flag to indicate an update is in progress
intChangeFlag = True

' Return true so the character is displayed
txtFirstname_onkeypress = True

End Function

' Focus event of the First Name input element
Private Sub txtFirstname_onfocus()

' Set the font color to grey
SetFontColor pFirstname, 1

End Sub

' Blur event of the last name input element
Private Sub txtLastName_onblur()

' Set the font color to black
SetFontColor pLastName, 0

End Sub

' Key press event of the last name element
Private Function txtLastName_onkeypress() As Boolean

' Check to see if an update has been initiated
If intChangeFlag = False Then
```

```vb
    '   Disable the navigation
    DisableNavigation

End If

'   Indicate an update is in progress
intChangeFlag = True

'   Return true so the character will be displayed
txtLastName_onkeypress = True

End Function

'   On focus event of the last name input element
Private Sub txtLastName_onfocus()

'   Set the font color to red
SetFontColor pLastName, 1

End Sub

'   Blur event of the Phone input element
Private Sub txtPhone_onblur()

'   Set the text to black
SetFontColor pPhone, 0

End Sub

'   Key press event of the Phone input element
Private Function txtPhone_onkeypress() As Boolean

'   Check the change flag to see if an update has
'   been initiated
If intChangeFlag = False Then

    '   Disable the navigation buttons
    DisableNavigation

End If
```

```
       Set the change flag to indicate an update is in
'    progress
intChangeFlag = True


'   Return true so the character will be displayed
txtPhone_onkeypress = True


End Function


'   Focus event of the Phone input element
Private Sub txtPhone_onfocus()


'   Set the font color to red
SetFontColor pPhone, 1


End Sub


'   Blur event of the state input element
Private Sub txtState_onblur()


'   Set the font color to black
SetFontColor pstate, 0


End Sub


'   Key press event of the state button
Private Function txtState_onkeypress() As Boolean


'   Check to see if an update has been initiated
If intChangeFlag = False Then


     '   Disable the navigation buttons
     DisableNavigation


End If


'   Set the change flag to indicate an update is in progress
intChangeFlag = True


'   Return true so the character is displayed
txtState_onkeypress = True


End Function
```

```vb
'   Focus event of the state button
Private Sub txtState_onfocus()

'   Set the font color to red
SetFontColor pstate, 1

End Sub

'   Blur event of the zip code button
Private Sub txtZipCode_onblur()

'   Set the font color back to black
SetFontColor pZipCode, 0

End Sub

'   Zip code input element key press event
Private Function txtZipCode_onkeypress() As Boolean

'   Check to see if an update has been initiated.
If intChangeFlag = False Then

    '   Disable the navigation buttons
    DisableNavigation

End If

'   Set the change flag to indicate an update
'   is in progress
intChangeFlag = True

'   Return true so the character is displayed
txtZipCode_onkeypress = True

End Function

'   Focus event of the zip code input element
Private Sub txtZipCode_onfocus()

'   Set the text to red
SetFontColor pZipCode, 1

End Sub
```

As you can see, in our application we have successfully combined the management of the user interface with our database. The user gets an interface in a Web browser that provides all the features, visual cues, and functionality you would expect in a standard Visual Basic application forms interface. And you have full data access capabilities with the data environment that easily integrates into the DHTML application.

Testing the Application

Now that we have the application built, we are ready to see it in action. You do not need to load the employee table with any data. The application will start in insert mode so you can add the first employee. Figure 15-3 shows the application at startup. Go ahead and start entering data. As soon as you click in the First Name text field, the First Name label will turn to red.

Now finish filling out the fields. Then click the Update button. That will insert the record into the database. Figure 15-4 shows the finished record after the update. Note the message that indicates the record was successfully added.

Next let's add a new record to the database. Click on the New button. When you do so, the navigation buttons are disabled. This time, click on the Cancel button. That will end the insert of the new record. Go ahead and add several more records.

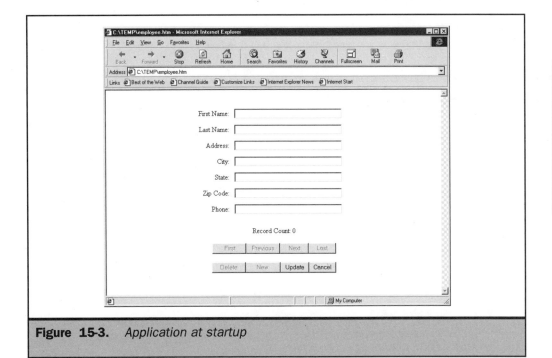

Figure 15-3.   *Application at startup*

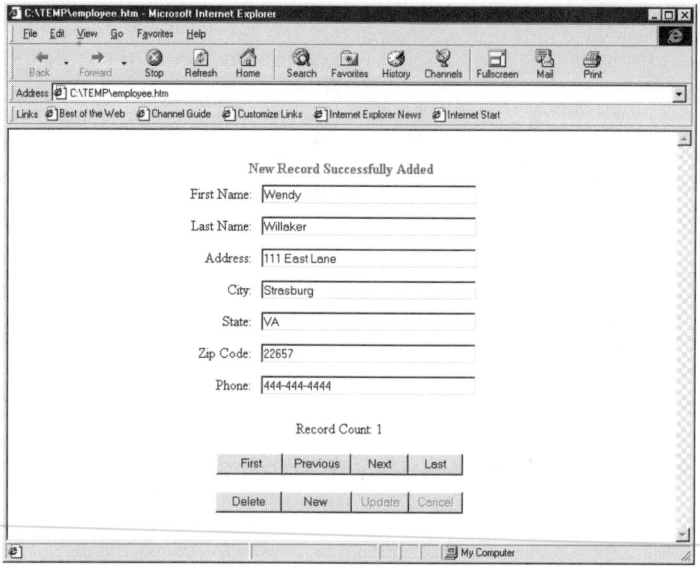

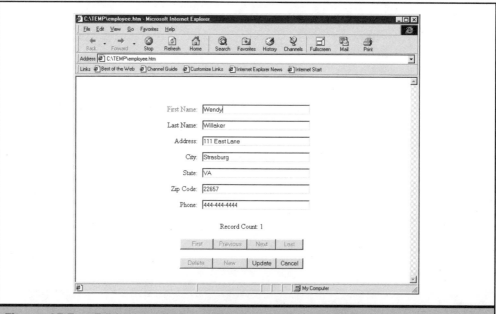

Figure 15-4. Newly inserted record

Figure 15-5. Editing an existing record

Now let's work on updating an employee's data. Page through the records until you find a record you want to update. Click on any of the text fields. Figure 15-5 shows the program in edit mode. Note that the navigation buttons are all disabled. Only the Update and Cancel buttons are active. Click on the Update button to update your changes in the database.

Finally, select a record to delete from the database. Click on the Delete button. When you do, the Delete button changes and turns to red. The Cancel button is still available if you do not want to delete the record. Figure 15-6 shows the delete in progress.

Go ahead and click on the Confirm? button to confirm the delete. When you do, the record is deleted. The page then shows a message indicating the record was successfully deleted (see Figure 15-7). Note that the record count is updated to show the deletion of the new record. Finally, when you begin to access a new record, the message is cleared from the display.

And with that, we have a DHTML application that runs on the client side in a browser and accesses a database on a back-end server.

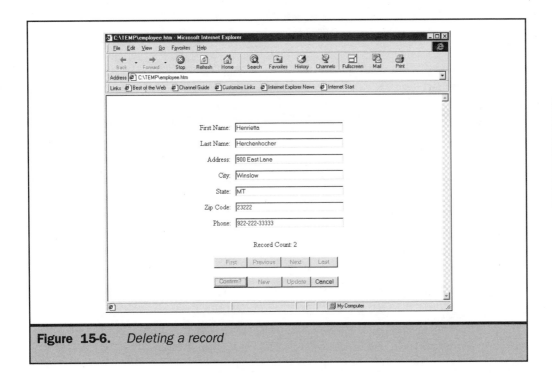

Figure 15-6. *Deleting a record*

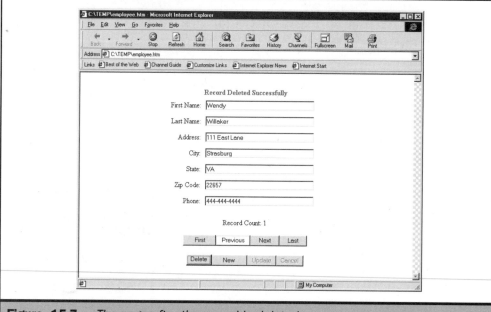

Figure 15-7. *The page after the record is deleted*

Summary

You will find many similarities between this application and a traditional forms-based client/server application. In reality we have replaced the form with a very active and programmable Web browser-based application.

We could add many other features to make this a more robust application. If you have a large number of employees, a search feature would be invaluable for finding employee records. You could add a button to the list that would allow the form to become a search interface for finding key words in each text field. That would require some fancy SQL query building and the ability to requery the entire database, but it would be a powerful feature to have in a browser.

What's Next

In the next chapter we will explore building ActiveX documents. ActiveX documents can be built in Visual Basic 6.0 and viewed in a browser. We will take the project tracking application and convert it into an ActiveX document that can be viewed in Internet Explorer. ActiveX documents provide a convenient way to deploy your forms-based applications on an intranet in a browser.

Chapter 16

Building ActiveX Documents

There is one more twist to delivering your applications in a browser. In Chapter 15 we explored building DHTML applications that are HTML based and manipulated through our Visual Basic code. ActiveX documents are forms that can appear within Internet browser windows. ActiveX documents are designed the same way you design Visual Basic forms. They can contain objects and controls. They can also show message boxes and secondary forms—all the things you would expect from a traditional application.

Overview of ActiveX Document Technology

Visual Basic ActiveX documents can appear in the Microsoft Office Binder and Internet Explorer. In the Office Binder, you can write code to save your document's data in Binder data files. With Internet Explorer 3.0 or later, you can also save properties of your ActiveX document by writing to and reading from the document's data file.

You may know that a Word document can be viewed in other containers. In that case, the Word application supplies the objects that enable another ActiveX container (such as Internet Explorer) to view and activate the document. And this same mechanism works for ActiveX documents created with Visual Basic. It will supply the objects necessary to display the interface.

When you create an ActiveX document-based project, you are creating a Visual Basic "document" that can be contained in an ActiveX container such as Internet Explorer. Compiling the ActiveX document creates both a Visual Basic document file (with the extension .vbd) and its corresponding server, which can be an ActiveX .dll or ActiveX .exe file. In other words, the .vbd file is to the .exe or .dll file what the .doc file is to the Winword.exe file.

ActiveX documents also support the Hyperlink object, which allows an ActiveX document to request that a hyperlink-aware container (such as Internet Explorer) navigate to another URL.

Running the ActiveX Document Migration Wizard

Fortunately, a wizard is provided with Visual Basic that will convert our standard forms-based application created in Part III of the book into an ActiveX document application. To make things simple, we are going to combine the splash page form with the projects form. That will make our application all self-contained in one document.

Make a copy of the project tracking code before it was segmented into client- and server-side code. In this case, we are going to combine it back into one project and have it delivered as an in-process DLL that will run on the client's machine.

INTERNET APPLICATION
DEVELOPMENT

Note *You will need an ODBC DSN on the client machine to support the data environment.*

Follow these steps to convert the project tracking system to an ActiveX document:

1. Select the Add-In Manager from the Add-Ins menu.

2. From the list of add-ins, select the VB 6 ActiveX Document Migration Wizard. Figure 16-1 shows the Add-In Manager, and Figure 16-2 shows the initial screen of the wizard.

3. Select the Next button to move to the next screen. The next screen requests the forms to be converted.

4. Select the frmProjects form. Figure 16-3 shows the wizard with the selection.

5. Click on the Next button to move to the next screen. The screen shows the options for conversion.

6. Select the "Comment out invalid code?" option. This will comment out any code that will no longer be valid in the application.

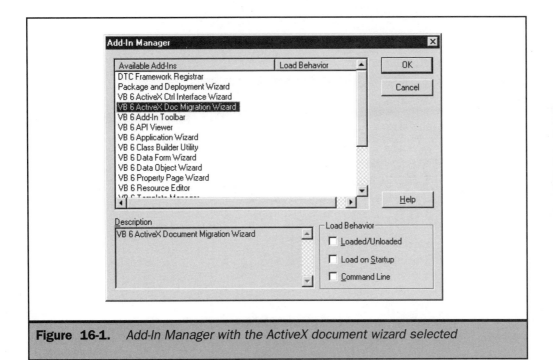

Figure 16-1. *Add-In Manager with the ActiveX document wizard selected*

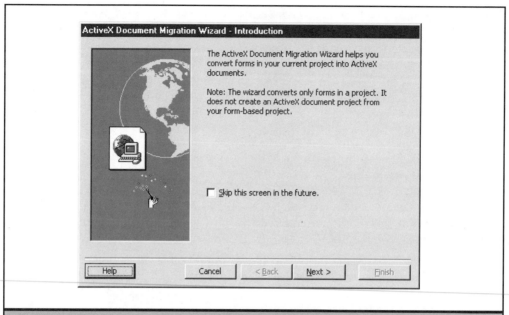

Figure 16-2. *Initial screen of the wizard*

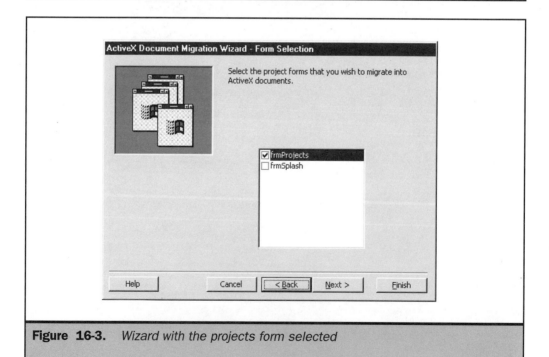

Figure 16-3. *Wizard with the projects form selected*

7. Select the "Remove original forms after conversion?" option. We will no longer need the original forms once the conversion is done.

8. The frame on the wizard indicates the current project type is invalid. Select the Convert to an ActiveX DLL? option. That will set the ActiveX document to run in-process. Figure 16-4 shows the selections.

9. Click Next to move to the next screen. You can then indicate whether you want to see the summary report. Select that option. Figure 16-5 shows the screen.

10. Click on the Finish button to start the conversion.

11. The wizard will indicate that some of the code is invalid and it will need to be flagged. The code will be flagged with [AXDW]. Figure 16-6 shows the message box.

12. When the conversion is finished, the screen in Figure 16-7 is shown. Click OK to continue.

Finally, the summary report is shown. The report includes good information regarding the use of the ActiveX document. Figure 16-8 shows the summary report.

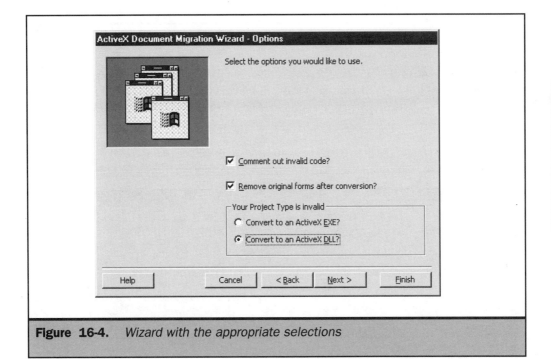

Figure 16-4. *Wizard with the appropriate selections*

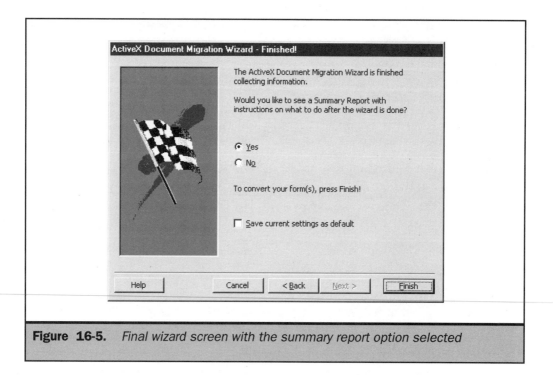

Figure 16-5. *Final wizard screen with the summary report option selected*

Once the conversion is finished, the frmProjects form is converted into a user document. We still have the frmSplash form in place. We will combine the code from the splash page with our new user document. Figure 16-9 shows the converted project.

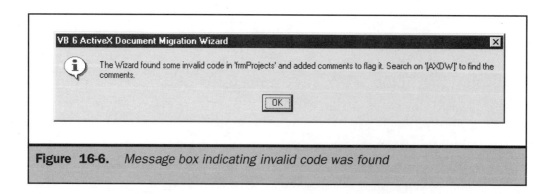

Figure 16-6. *Message box indicating invalid code was found*

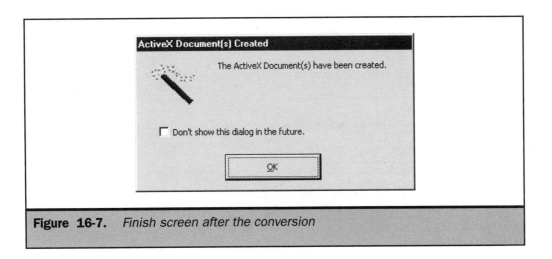

Figure 16-7. *Finish screen after the conversion*

As you can see, we still have our splash form, but we now have a new listing in the project window—user documents. And our projects form has been converted and moved to the user documents section.

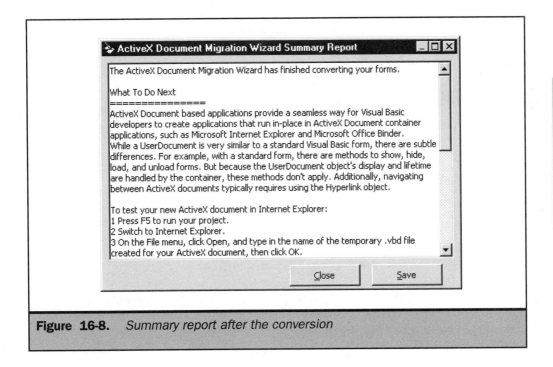

Figure 16-8. *Summary report after the conversion*

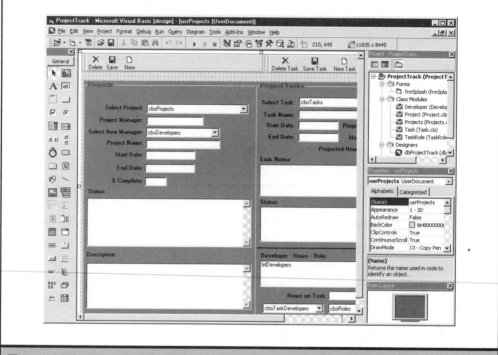

Figure 16-9. *Project with the newly converted ActiveX document*

Now that the form is converted, we are ready to begin the code conversion process to make our project functional as an ActiveX document.

Modifying the Code

Since we are now working with a DLL and not a standard EXE project, we will need to make some modifications to our project. Our interface is no longer a form, but a user document, so we should change the name from frmProjects to usrProjects. Select the properties for the user document and change the name appropriately. If you want, you can also save the document into a new file called "usrProjects.dob."

The first thing we need to do for the code is move it out of the basic module into our user document. We will want to directly reference the objects on the document instead of referencing the document and then the objects. Copy the code out of the module into the general declarations section of the new document. Then delete the module from the project.

We need to modify the code through our project so it does not use the With statement for the user document (formerly the form). Since we have moved the module code into the project, we can reference objects on the user interface directly without a dot (.) reference. For example, the LoadProjects code will need to be modified. The following shows the code before conversion:

```
'  Load the projects
Public Sub LoadProjects()

'  Declare the developer and taskrole classes
Dim clsDev As New Developer
Dim clsTaskRole As New TaskRole
Dim colTaskRole As Collection

'  Two collections for our developers and task roles
Dim colDev As New Collection
Dim ColTaskRol As New Collection

'  Two variables for looping through the collections
Dim CD
Dim CTR
Dim intCnt As Integer

'  Use the With statement to shorten calls
'  to objects on the form
With frmProjects

'  Clear all of the list boxes
.cboProjects.Clear
.cboDevelopers.Clear
.cboTaskDevelopers.Clear

'  Loop through the projects in the projects class
For intCnt = 1 To clsProjects.Count

    '  add the project name to the projects list box
    .cboProjects.AddItem clsProjects.Item(intCnt).ProjectName

Next intCnt
```

```vb
    ' Retrieve the class of developers using the
    ' retrieve developers meta method of the developers
    ' class
    Set colDev = clsDev.RetrieveDevelopers

    ' Loop through the developers
    For Each CD In colDev

        ' Add the first name and last name to the developers
        ' list box
        .cboDevelopers.AddItem CD.FirstName & " " & CD.LastName

        ' Add the id of the developer to the item data property
        .cboDevelopers.ItemData(.cboDevelopers.NewIndex) = _
        CD.idDeveloper

        ' Add the first name and last name to the task developers
        ' list box
        .cboTaskDevelopers.AddItem CD.FirstName & " " & CD.LastName

        ' Add the id of the developer to the item data property
        .cboTaskDevelopers.ItemData(.cboDevelopers.NewIndex) = _
        CD.idDeveloper

    Next

    ' Retrieve the collection of task roles
    Set colTaskRole = clsTaskRole.RetrieveTaskRoles

    ' Loop through the task roles
    For Each CTR In colTaskRole

        ' Add the task role to the roles list box
        .cboRoles.AddItem CTR.RoleName

        ' Set the id of the role to the item data property
        .cboRoles.ItemData(.cboRoles.NewIndex) = CTR.idTaskRole

    Next

End With

End Sub
```

Note the .cboRoles, .cboTaskDevelopers, and similar references and the beginning
With frmProjects code and ending With statements. We simply need to remove these
references. The following code is the converted LoadProjects subroutine:

```
'  Load the projects
Public Sub LoadProjects()

'  Declare the developer and taskrole classes
Dim clsDev As New Developer
Dim clsTaskRole As New TaskRole
Dim colTaskRole As Collection

'  Two collections for our developers and task roles
Dim colDev As New Collection
Dim ColTaskRol As New Collection

'  Two variables for looping through the collections
Dim CD
Dim CTR
Dim intCnt As Integer

'  Clear all of the list boxes
cboProjects.Clear
cboDevelopers.Clear
cboTaskDevelopers.Clear

'  Loop through the projects in the projects class
For intCnt = 1 To clsProjects.Count

    '  add the project name to the projects list box
    cboProjects.AddItem clsProjects.Item(intCnt).ProjectName

Next intCnt

'  Retrieve the class of developers using the
'  retrieve developers meta method of the developers
'  class
Set colDev = clsDev.RetrieveDevelopers

'  Loop through the developers
For Each CD In colDev

    '  Add the first name and last name to the developers
    '  list box
    cboDevelopers.AddItem CD.FirstName & " " & CD.LastName
```

```
        '  Add the id of the developer to the item data property
        cboDevelopers.ItemData(cboDevelopers.NewIndex) = CD.idDeveloper

        '  Add the first name and last name to the task developers
        '  list box
        cboTaskDevelopers.AddItem CD.FirstName & " " & CD.LastName

        '  Add the id of the developer to the item data property
        cboTaskDevelopers.ItemData(cboDevelopers.NewIndex) = _
        CD.idDeveloper

    Next

    '  Retrieve the collection of task roles
    Set colTaskRole = clsTaskRole.RetrieveTaskRoles

    '  Loop through the task roles
    For Each CTR In colTaskRole

        '  Add the task role to the roles list box
        cboRoles.AddItem CTR.RoleName

        '  Set the id of the role to the item data property
        cboRoles.ItemData(cboRoles.NewIndex) = CTR.idTaskRole

    Next

End Sub
```

Now we have updated the code to remove any dot (.) references for objects on the user interface. And we have removed the With statements. The downside of this, of course, is less modularity of code. But the user interface manipulation needs to take place within the user document. That is not to say that BAS modules cannot be used for other code use.

Many of the functions in the code will need to be changed. These include DeleteDeveloper, LoadDevelopers, LoadTasks, DeleteTask, DeleteProject, SaveProject, and SaveTask. Follow the same conversion process to migrate these functions.

There were several sections of code commented out because they are no longer valid in our new project type. Search on the string AXDW. When you do, you will find that all of the End statements are no longer valid. In fact, we will need to update our code to exit the project. We now have a new element in place—the browser is the container for the application. The user can close the browser, which will end our application.

In effect, we are going to simply eliminate the logic to end our application. That means eliminating the Exit button on the toolbar. Follow these steps to remove the button:

1. Right-click on the tblProject toolbar.

2. Select Properties.

3. Select the Buttons tab.

4. Click on the Remove Button button for the Exit button.

5. Click OK.

That removes the button from the interface. But we still need to update the ButtonClick event of the project toolbar. Following is the code for the function. Note that in the first case the End statement has been commented out with the appropriate note from the wizard. The rest of the code will still be valid.

```
'  Button click of the project toolbar
Private Sub tblProject_ButtonClick(ByVal Button As_
MSComctlLib.Button)

'  Declare our variables
Dim strResults As String

'  Select case on the button index
Select Case Button.Index

    '  The first button ends the project
    Case 1
'[AXDW] The following line was commented out by the ActiveX
'Document
'Migration Wizard.
'          End

    '  The second button deletes the project
    Case 2
```

```
              '  Only delete if a project is selected
             If cboProjects.ListIndex <> -1 Then
                  '  Call the delete project subroutine
                 DeleteProject

             End If

      '  Save the project
      Case 3

             '  Only save the project if a project is selected
             If cboProjects.ListIndex <> -1 Then

                  '  Save the project
                 SaveProject

             End If

      '  Add a new project
      Case 4

             '  Clear the project fields
             ClearProjectFields

             '  Query the user for the project name
             strResults = InputBox("Enter the project name:", _
                        "Project Name", "New Project")

             '  Ensure a project name was entered
             If strResults <> "" Then
                  '  Add a new project name to the projects
                  '  class by calling the AddNew method of the
                  '  class
                 clsProjects.AddNew strResults

                  '  Load the projects
                 LoadProjects

             Else
```

```
            '   Indicate the project name cannot be empty
            MsgBox "You cannot have an empty project name."

      End If

   '  Show the projects report
   Case 5

End Select

End Sub
```

Update the project as follows. We have deleted the first case from the code. And the rest of the cases have been shifted to start at 1 since we have removed the first button. Now the user will simply close the browser to exit the application.

```
'  Button click of the task toolbar
Private Sub tblTask_ButtonClick(ByVal Button As MSComctlLib.Button)

'  Declare a variable
Dim strResults As String

'  Process by the button selected
Select Case Button.Index

   '  Delete task button
   Case 1
      '  Ensure a project is selected
      If cboProjects.ListIndex <> -1 Then
         '  Ensure a task is selected
         If cboTasks.ListIndex <> -1 Then
            '  Delete the task
            DeleteTask
         End If
      End If

   '  Save the task
   Case 2
      '  Ensure a project is selected
      If cboProjects.ListIndex <> -1 Then
```

```
                    '   Ensure a task is selected
                If cboTasks.ListIndex <> -1 Then
                    '   Save the task
                    SaveTask
                End If
            End If

        '   Add a new task
        Case 3
        ' Ensure a project is selected
        If cboProjects.ListIndex <> -1 Then
            '   Clear the task fields
            ClearTaskFields

            '   Ask for the task name
            strResults = InputBox("Enter the task name:", _
                        "Task Name", "New Task")

            '   Ensure we do not have an empty task name
            If strResults <> "" Then
                '   Add a new task by calling the AddNewTask
                '   method of the projects class.
                clsProjects(cboProjects.ListIndex + 1).AddNewTask_
                strResults

                '   Load the tasks list box
                LoadTasks

            Else

                '   Indicate the task cannot be empty
                MsgBox "You cannot have an empty task name."

            End If

        End If

End Select

End Sub
```

We have one more set of End statements to take care of. In fact, you will find that the original Form_Unload event has been converted into UserDocument_Unload. And you will find that it is now in the general declarations section of the project. Updating this section of code is easy—simply delete it.

We really have no capability to end the program from the browser unless the user initiates it. Instead of querying the user (since we can't stop the exit) when the document is unloaded, we will automatically save the project data. The ExitFocus event will allow us to check to see if a project and task are selected and to set the appropriate save events.

```
'   The document is being exited
Private Sub UserDocument_ExitFocus()

'   Check to see if a project is selected
If cboProjects.ListIndex <> -1 Then

     '   Save the project
     SaveProject

End If

'   Check to see if a task is selected
If cboTasks.ListIndex <> -1 Then

     '   Save the task
     SaveTask

End If

End Sub
```

In the code, we check the cboProjects and cboTasks list boxes to ensure something is selected. If so, then the appropriate save procedure is called.

One last step should be done on our project. Most of the subroutines we have moved from the module to the user document should be changed from public to private. We do not necessarily want to expose this functionality publicly in our DLL. Change all of these to be private to ensure they are only accessible from the document.

Finally, we need to work on the loading of the project. Previously, we had a separate form for loading the project. The form showed the "Loading...." text while all of the classes where being initialized. Instead, we are going to put the "Loading...."

label on the user document we have created and hide the rest of the interface elements when data is finished loading. Follow these steps:

1. Start by placing a label called "lblMessage" in the center of the form.

2. Set the caption to read "Loading….".

3. Set the font color to blue.

Tip *You can copy the label off the original splash form onto the user document for the ActiveX document.*

Next we need to change the rest of the elements on the page to be invisible at load time. To do that, we just set the Visible property to false on the frmProjects frame, frmTasks frame, and the cblProjectTrack coolbar. Thus, at load time, only the label will be visible.

Now we need to move the load code out of the splash form into our user document. Previously, we had called the LoadProjects code in the paint event of the form. There is a similar event for our user document. Place the following code in the paint event of the user document.

```
Private Sub UserDocument_Paint()

If intPaintFlag <> 1 Then

    '  Refresh the label so it is visible
    lblMessage.Refresh

    '  Load the projects
    LoadProjects

    '  Set the paint flag so the code is not run
    '  again
    intPaintFlag = 1

End If

End Sub
```

You will also need to add a global integer variable, intPaintFlag, to the global declarations of the user document. When the paint event of the user document is fired off the first time, the label control is refreshed to ensure it is visible, and then the LoadProjects code is run.

We also have to modify the LoadProjects function to set up the interface once the data is loaded. We will add a new subroutine called LoadProjectInterface that will be called at the end of LoadProjects. Following is the code for the LoadProjectInterface subroutine:

```
'   Loads the project interface after the splash
'   screen has been shown
Private Sub LoadProjectInterface()

'   Hide the message label
lblMessage.Visible = False

'   Show the three elements of the interface
cblProjectTrack.Visible = True
frmProjects.Visible = True
frmTasks.Visible = True

End Sub
```

The subroutine will make the three primary elements on the user interface visible and will hide the label control. When the main elements are made visible, they will be loaded with all the project data from the system.

That should be it for the conversion of our forms-based application to an ActiveX document that will run in Internet Explorer.

Launching and Testing Our Document

Let's now test the application. The last step will be to remove the frmSplash form from the project. Then go to the Project menu and select Properties. On the Debugging tab, ensure the starting component is usrProjects. And ensure the Use Existing Browser check box is selected. That way, our user document will start in Internet Explorer. Now run the project. Figure 16-10 shows the project at load time.

Once the project is loaded, our user document will show up in Internet Explorer, complete with the toolbar and all the elements we would expect, just hosted in Internet Explorer. Figure 16-11 shows the interface.

Now you can go ahead and perform all the tasks you would normally do in the project tracking system. When you are finished, simply close the browser and exit. Note that when you do so, Visual Basic does not automatically end execution since we are working with a DLL project.

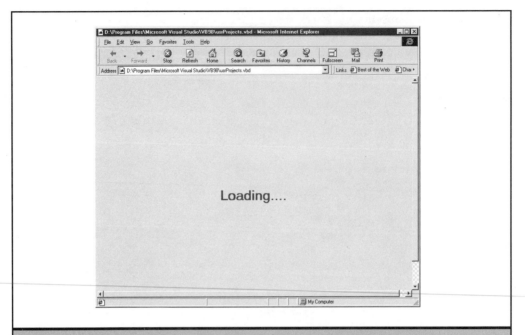

Figure 16-10. *Project screen while the project data is loading*

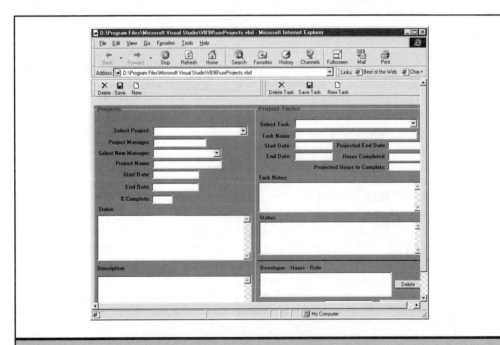

Figure 16-11. *Project interface within the browser*

Testing the DLL

Let's go ahead and make the DLL for the project. On the File menu, select the Make ProjectTrack.DLL option. That will create the in-process DLL file for the project tracking system. We can now easily test our application in the browser. A userProjects.vbd file is created with the project. You can drag and drop this .vbd file into a browser, and it will load the project tracking system. Figure 16-12 shows the drag-and-drop process.

The .vbd file is actually an OLE structured storage, which basically means that data in the file can be accessed and manipulated via standard OLE interfaces. Microsoft applications such as Word and Excel save data in this manner.

The DLL file is loaded in-process into the browser context. That is it. Of course, all the database pieces have to be in place on the back end, including the ODBC DSN. But you can deliver your applications in a browser interface.

Figure 16-12. *Project being dragged and dropped into the browser*

Summary

If you are building an intranet for your application and have times when standard HTML/DHTML interfaces are just not going to cut it or provide the robust user interface capabilities for your application, the ActiveX document provides an elegant way to build a traditional formlike interface for your application and host it in the browser. ActiveX documents give you one more way to provide your applications in an Internet environment.

What's Next

In the last section of the book, we will delve into one of the hottest topics on the Internet today, e-commerce. We will utilize Visual Basic's new Internet capabilities combined with traditional client/server programming to build a shopping basket application.

Chapter 17

Designing an E-Commerce System

One of the hottest topics today in development is the building of e-commerce systems. With Visual Basic's new Internet capabilities, we can create our own e-commerce system. In this chapter and the next we will pull together all the different techniques we have learned throughout the book to build a shopping basket e-commerce system.

Our system will allow us to review departments and products assigned to departments. Then we can add products to our shopping basket and, finally, check out and purchase the products. Our system will be built on a well-defined object model, database, and HTML interface.

Designing the Object Interface

Let's first take a look at the object model we will need as the foundation of our system. We will need a total of five objects to define all the "players" in our credit card shopping system. The following illustration shows the objects and their relationship to each other.

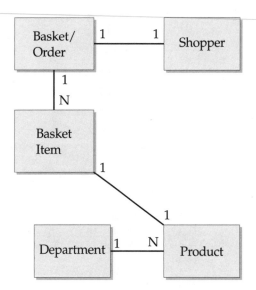

Overview of the Object Model

The first object is the shopping basket itself. You will note that it indicates the order data as well. We could define a separate object just for the order, but in our simple system, the basket and the order will contain roughly the same data.

Our shopping basket is made up of items placed in the basket. Keep in mind that a basket item is different from a product. The basket item will indicate quantity, price at the time of purchase, and so on. Our basket can contain multiple items.

The shopper in our system also needs to be represented. We have a shopper object that can at any one time relate to a basket. Note that a shopper in the database can have multiple baskets after repeat visits. But in our "live" object model, we will only allow one basket at a time for the shopper.

Finally, we have our product and department tables. A department groups multiple products together. And our product will directly relate to an item in the basket.

Defining Each Object

Let's take a look at each object in more detail starting with the department class. The department class will have a description and a unique ID (from the database) representing the department.

We will also have two methods for the class, ListDepartments and LoadProducts. The ListDepartments method is a meta method that operates on all departments. It will create a series of department objects for each department in the database. The LoadProducts method will load all the products related to the department. Note that the department class will contain a collection of product classes. Table 17-1 lists the properties and methods of our department class.

Next we have the product class. The product class will have several properties that define the data for the product, including name, price, and so on. In this case our product class does not have any methods. Table 17-2 lists the properties and methods of the product class.

Note *If we were to build an administration interface for our store, we could add methods to the product class for adding, updating, and deleting products from the database.*

Property/Method	Description
Description	Description/name of the department.
IdDepartment	ID of the department.
ListDepartments	Returns all departments in the database.
LoadProducts	Loads all products for the current department.

Table 17-1.   *Department Class*

Property/Method	Description
Active	Indicates whether the product is active.
Description	Description of the product.
IdDepartment	ID of the department to which the product is assigned.
IdProduct	ID of the product.
Price	Price of the product.
ProductImage	Image file for the product.
ProductName	Name of the product.
SaleEnd	Sale end date.
SalePrice	Sale price.
SaleStart	Sale start date.

Table 17-2.   *Product Class*

The next class is the basket. The shopping basket will contain quite a bit of data, including a collection of basket items assigned to the basket. Also, the basket will contain order data such as credit card owner's name, card type, number, and expiration date.

Our class will also need numerous methods for saving the basket, calculating tax and shipping, creating the order, and many more. The shopping basket is the heart of our system and tracks everything the shopper does. The properties and methods of the basket class are listed in Table 17-3.

Property/Method	Description
CardName	Name on the credit card.
CardType	Type of credit card (Visa, Mastercard, Discover, American Express)

Table 17-3.   *Basket Class*

Property/Method	Description
CreditCardNumber	Credit card number.
ExpDate	Credit card expiration date.
IdBasket	ID of the shopping basket.
IdOrder	ID of the order (when placed).
IdShopper	ID of the shopper assigned to the basket.
Shipping	Shipping amount.
ShipState	Shipping state (for calculating tax).
SubTotal	Shopping basket subtotal (without tax and shipping).
Tax	Tax amount.
Total	Basket total amount.
CalculateShipping	Calculates shipping charges.
CalculateSubTotal	Calculates the basket subtotal.
CalculateTax	Calculates tax on the order.
CalculateTotal	Calculates the order total.
ClearBasket	Clears the basket of all items.
SaveBasket	Saves the basket to the database. If the basket has not been previously saved, it is inserted into the database.
SaveCreditData	Saves credit card data and places the order.
UpdateQuantity	Updates quantity of each item in the basket.

Table 17-3. *Basket Class* (continued)

Next we have the basket item class. This will define the items added to the basket. Each basket item relates to a specific basket and a specific product. We have one method for our class that saves the basket item to the database. Table 17-4 lists the properties and methods of the basket item class.

Property/Method	Description
IdBasket	ID of the basket to which the basket item is assigned.
IdBasketItem	ID of the basket item.
IdProduct	ID of the product to which the basket item relates.
OnSale	Indicates whether the product is on sale and whether the price is a sale price.
Price	Indicates the price.
ProductName	Name of the basket item.
Quantity	Number the shopper wishes to purchase.
SaveBasketItem	Saves the basket item to the database. If the item has not been previously saved, a new record is inserted.

Table 17-4. *Basket Item Class*

Next we have our shopper class. This defines all the address data for both the shipping and billing address. The Password field will store the password for retrieving the shopper data later. That way repeat shoppers do not have to retype their shopper data.

The LoadShopper method will retrieve the shopper data based on the email billing address and the password. The SaveShopper method will save the shopper to the database. If the shopper has not been saved, a new record will be created. Table 17-5 lists the properties and methods of the shopper class.

Property/Method	Description
IdShopper	ID of the shopper.
ShipFirstName	Shipping first name.
ShipLastName	Shipping last name.
ShipAddress	Shipping address.
ShipCity	Shipping city.

Table 17-5. *Shopper Class*

Property/Method	Description
ShipState	Shipping state.
ShipZipCode	Shipping zip code.
ShipPhone	Shipping phone number.
ShipEmail	Shipping email address.
BillFirstName	Billing first name.
BillLastName	Billing last name.
BillAddress	Billing address.
BillCity	Billing city.
BillState	Billing state (tax will be calculated off this).
BillZipCode	Billing zip code.
BillPhone	Billing phone.
BillEmail	Email billing address.
Password	Password to retrieve the shopper data.
LoadShopper	Loads the shopper data from the database. The lookup will be done on the email billing address and the password.
SaveShopper	Saves the shopper to the database. If the shopper has not been saved yet, a new record is inserted.

Table 17-5. *Shopper Class* (continued)

The combination of these classes will provide us with a dynamic shopping environment for browsing through departments and products with the ability to add items to a shopping basket.

We will implement this class structure into an IIS application web class that will provide a shopping environment for the user. In the next chapter, we will use the Class Builder utility to define our classes and insert them into the project. Next, let's define the database that will store the shopping data.

Designing the Database

Our database structure is going to be very similar to the property structure of the classes. Here is a diagram of the database:

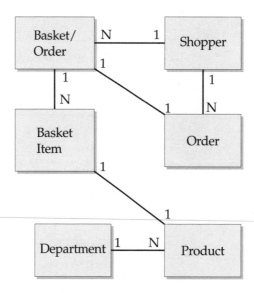

Our database will consist of six tables (versus five classes). Each will have the requisite properties to persist the class data into the database. There are also other subtle differences between the database structure and property structure. For example, the relationship between the shopper and basket tables is different. Because shoppers can look up their data by password, they can have multiple baskets and orders.

Also, we have a separate order table from the basket table. Even though there is still a one-to-one relationship between basket and order data, we probably want to store them separately. For example, you may wish to keep the two sets of data separate for security reasons. You may want to persist basket data longer than the details of the credit card data, and so on.

Let's take a look at each table in detail. First we have the department table. There are only two columns in the table. And we have two stored procedures for working with the data in the table. Table 17-6 lists the components of the department table.

Following is the SQL stored procedure to create the department table. The ID of the department is an identity column that will generate the next number in sequence with every insert and, of course, the description of the department.

Column/Stored Procedure	Description
IdDepartment	ID of the department, generated as an auto-incremented value.
ChrDescription	Description of the department.
Sp_GetDepartments	Stored procedure to retrieve departments.

Table 17-6.   *Department Table*

```
/****** Department ******/
CREATE TABLE dbo.Department (
    idDepartment int IDENTITY (1, 1) NOT NULL ,
     chrDescription varchar (255) NULL
)
GO
```

The sp_GetDepartments stored procedure retrieves all the departments from the database and orders them by the description.

```
/****** sp_GetDepartments ******/
CREATE PROCEDURE sp_GetDepartments AS

/*  Retrieve all of the departments and order
    by the description
*/
Select * from Department order by chrDescription
GO
```

Next we have the product table. The product table defines the basic data on the product. Of particular interest is the sale price. A product can be set on sale between the sale start and sale end date. Finally, the image file will be a string indicating the image file name and, if appropriate, the location on the Web server. Table 17-7 lists the components of the product table.

Field/Stored Procedure	Description
IdProduct	ID of the product.
BitActive	Flag to indicate whether the product is active.
ChrImage	Image file name.
FltPrice	Price of the product.
ChrProductName	Name of the product.
FltSalePrice	Sale price (based on the sale start and end date).
IdDepartment	ID of the department to which the product is assigned.
DtSaleStart	Sale start date.
DtSaleEnd	Sale end date.
TxtDescription	Description of the product.
Sp_GetDeptProducts	Stored procedure to receive products assigned to a particular department.

Table 17-7.   *Product Table*

The SQL code to create the table is fairly straightforward. Of course, the ID of the product is an auto-incrementing identity column in the database. The active flag is a bit field indicating yes or no if the product is active.

The description is a text field to allow unlimited length. In practical terms, there will need to be a limit within which the description data will show up on the product page in the store.

```
/****** Product ******/
CREATE TABLE dbo.Product (
    idProduct int IDENTITY (1, 1) NOT NULL ,
    bitActive bit NOT NULL ,
    chrImage varchar (255) NULL ,
```

```
    fltPrice float NULL ,
    chrProductName varchar (255) NULL ,
    fltSalePrice float NULL ,
    idDepartment int NULL ,
    dtSaleStart datetime NULL ,
    dtSaleEnd datetime NULL ,
    txtDescription text NULL
)
GO
```

Since each product will be assigned to a department, our query will retrieve all products that are assigned to a department based on an ID. The ID of the department is passed into the query, and the product listing is ordered by product name.

```
/****** sp_GetDeptProducts ******/
CREATE PROCEDURE sp_GetDeptProducts

@idDepartment integer

AS

/*  Retrieve the products assigned to the department ID
    passed in. Order by the product name.
*/
Select * from product where idDepartment = @idDepartment order by
chrProductName
GO
```

The basket table defines some of the data in the shopping basket class. Primarily, we are storing the basic basket data such as totals and fees and the shopper. The credit data that is accessed in our basket class will be stored in the order table (defined later). Table 17-8 lists components of the basket table.

The SQL code to create the table contains an Identity column for defining the basket ID. And the ID Shopper field will be directly related to the shopper table.

Field/Stored Procedure	Description
IdBasket	ID of the basket.
IdShopper	ID of the shopper assigned to the basket.
FltShipping	Shipping value.
FltSubTotal	Subtotal value.
FltTax	Tax total.
FltTotal	Total of the subtotal, tax, and shipping.
Sp_InsertBasket	Stored procedure to insert a basket into the database.
Sp_UpdateBasket	Stored procedure to update a basket in the database.

Table 17-8. *Basket Table*

Finally, we have several float values to charge the aggregate totals and fees in the basket.

```
/****** Basket ******/
CREATE TABLE dbo.Basket (
    idBasket int IDENTITY (1, 1) NOT NULL ,
    idShopper int NULL ,
    fltShipping float NULL ,
    fltSubTotal float NULL ,
    fltTax float NULL ,
    fltTotal float NULL
)
GO
```

The sp_InsertBasket stored procedure handles inserting a new basket into the database. When a new basket is created, we will presume the basket is essentially empty, and we just want an ID for the basket to begin tracking the shopper's actions.

Note   *The @@Identity SQL code will return the identity of the last inserted row into a table. In this case, the insert and the select all happen in the same transaction.*

```
/****** sp_InsertBasket ******/
CREATE PROCEDURE sp_InsertBasket

AS

/*  Insert a blank record /
insert into Basket(idShopper, fltShipping, fltSubTotal, fltTax,
fltTotal)
values(0, 0, 0, 0, 0)

/* Return the ID of the basket inserted */
select @@identity
GO
```

The sp_UpdateBasket stored procedure updates the values of the specified basket. Note that all values need to be passed in to do the update.

```
/****** sp_UpdateBasket ******/
CREATE PROCEDURE sp_UpdateBasket

@idShopper integer,
@fltShipping float,
@fltSubtotal float,
@fltTax float,
@fltTotal float,
@idBasket integer

AS

/*  Update the basket values where the ID of the basket
    equals the value passed into the stored procedure
*/
update basket set
    idShopper = @idShopper,
    fltShipping = @fltShipping,
    fltSubTotal = @fltSubTotal,
    fltTax = @fltTax,
    fltTotal = @fltTotal

where

    idBasket = @idBasket
GO
```

Next we move to the basket item table. This will store all the basket items related to a particular basket. The first field is the auto-incrementing ID of the basket item. We also assign the ID to the product that was added to the basket and the ID of the basket.

Note that we also store the price of the product in the basket item database. This is done in case the price of the product changes while the user is shopping. Essentially, if a product is on sale while the user is shopping and the clock ticks past the sale price end date, the user can still have the item in her or his basket at the time of the sale price. Keep in mind that a new basket will be created with every shopper visit. So there is no way the user can "store up" baskets with items on sale.

Also, the benefit of keeping the price in the basket is that over time, if the product price changes, you still have a record of the original purchase price of the product in case of any returns or credits. The components of the basket item table are listed in Table 17-9.

The basket item table defines the ID of the basket item as an identity column as well as the rest of the appropriate fields.

```
/****** BasketItem ******/
CREATE TABLE dbo.BasketItem (
    idBasketItem int IDENTITY (1, 1) NOT NULL ,
    idProduct int NOT NULL ,
    intQuantity int NULL ,
    idBasket int NULL ,
    fltPrice float NULL
)
GO
```

Field/Stored Procedure	Description
IdBasketItem	ID of the basket item.
IdProduct	ID of the product to which the basket item is related.
IntQuantity	Quantity to be purchased.
IdBasket	ID of the basket to which the basket item is assigned.
FltPrice	Price of the product at purchase time.
Sp_DeleteBasketItem	Stored procedure to delete a basket item.
Sp_InsertBasketItem	Stored procedure to insert a basket item.
Sp_UpdateBasketItem	Stored procedure to update a basket item.

Table 17-9. *Basket Item Table*

The sp_DeleteBasketItem stored procedure will delete the basket item based on the ID of the basket item passed into the stored procedure.

```
/****** sp_DeleteBasketItem ******/
CREATE PROCEDURE sp_DeleteBasketItem

@idBasketItem  integer

AS

/*  Delete from the basket item table where the ID equals
    the passed in value
*/
delete from basketitem where idBasketItem = @idBasketItem
GO
```

The sp_InsertBasketItem stored procedure handles inserting a new basket item into the database. We will assume the user has selected a product and clicked on the Add button on the product page. The ID of the product, quantity, ID of the basket, and the price are passed in. The item is inserted into the database, and the new ID of the basket item is returned.

```
/****** sp_InsertBasketItem ******/
CREATE PROCEDURE sp_InsertBasketItem

@idProduct integer,
@intQuantity integer,
@idBasket integer,
@fltPrice float

AS

/*  Insert a new basket item into the database /
insert into BasketItem(idProduct, intQuantity, idBasket, fltPrice)
values(@idProduct, @intQuantity, @idBasket, @fltPrice)

/*  Return the Id of the basket item inserted */
select @@identity
GO
```

INTERNET APPLICATION
DEVELOPMENT

The sp_UpdateBasketItem stored procedure will update a basket item. Primarily, this will only update the quantity. But we could have a need to update the price and other items depending on the action taken by the user.

```
/****** sp_UpdateBasketItem ******/
CREATE PROCEDURE sp_UpdateBasketItem

@idProduct integer,
@intQuantity integer,
@idBasket integer,
@fltPrice float,
@idBasketItem integer

AS

/*  Update the basket item based on the ID of the
    basket item passed into the stored procedure
*/
update BasketItem set
    idProduct = @idProduct,
    intQuantity = @intQuantity,
    idBasket = @idBasket,
    fltPrice = @fltPrice
where
    idBasketItem = @idBasketItem
GO
```

The shopper table defines all the basic data about the shopper, as listed in Table 17-10. We want to allow users to retrieve their shopper data after they have purchased once. The ChrPassword field will allow users to enter a password, which they can use to retrieve their data the next time.

Field/Stored Procedure	Description
IdShopper	Unique id of the shopper.
ChrShipFirstName	Shipping first name of the shopper.
ChrShipLastName	Shipping last name of the shopper.

Table 17-10. *Shopper Table*

Field/Stored Procedure	Description
ChrShipAddress	Shipping address.
ChrShipCity	Shipping city.
ChrShipState	Shipping state.
ChrShipZipCode	Shipping zip code.
ChrShipPhone	Shipping phone number.
ChrShipEmail	Shipping email address.
ChrBillFirstName	Billing first name.
ChrBillLastName	Billing last name.
ChrBillAddress	Billing address.
ChrBillCity	Billing city.
ChrBillState	Billing state.
ChrBillZipCode	Billing zip code.
ChrBillPhone	Billing phone number.
ChrBillEmail	Billing e-mail address.
ChrPassword	Billing password.
Sp_InsertShopper	Stored procedure to insert a shopper into the database.
Sp_RetrieveShopper	Stored procedure to retrieve a shopper from the database.
Sp_UpdateShopper	Stored procedure to update a shopper in the database.

Table 17-10.   *Shopper Table* (continued)

Note in the SQL code that the password field is only allowed to be ten characters long. You may also want to consider enforcing in code a minimum number of characters and requiring that the user enter characters other than alpha characters for extra security.

```
/****** Shopper ******/
CREATE TABLE dbo.Shopper (
    idShopper int IDENTITY (1, 1) NOT NULL ,
    chrShipFirstName varchar (100) NULL ,
    chrShipLastName varchar (100) NULL ,
    chrShipAddress varchar (150) NULL ,
    chrShipCity varchar (100) NULL ,
    chrShipState varchar (2) NULL ,
    chrShipZipCode varchar (15) NULL ,
    chrShipPhone varchar (25) NULL ,
    chrShipEmail varchar (255) NULL ,
    chrBillFirstName varchar (100) NULL ,
    chrBillLastName varchar (100) NULL ,
    chrBillAddress varchar (100) NULL ,
    chrBillCity varchar (100) NULL ,
    chrBillZipCode varchar (100) NULL ,
    chrBillState varchar (2) NULL ,
    chrBillPhone varchar (25) NULL ,
    chrBillEmail varchar (255) NULL ,
    dtShopping datetime NULL ,
    chrPassword varchar (10) NULL
)
GO
```

As with inserting a new basket into the database, when we insert a new shopper, we are going to essentially insert a blank shopper. We will store the date the shopper was created if we want to track shopper creation by date. The ID of the shopper is returned.

```
/****** sp_InsertShopper ******/
CREATE PROCEDURE sp_InsertShopper AS

/*  Insert a new shopper into the database.
    Indicate the date and time the shopper
    was entered
 */
insert into Shopper(dtShopping) values(getdate())

Select @@Identity
GO
```

The sp_RetrieveShopper stored procedure will retrieve the shopper data based on the email address and the password provided by the shopper. The stored procedure returns all the shopper data, including billing and shipping data as well as the password. You may wish to return only select subsets of this data. Specifically, you may wish to provide an alternative method for the user updating the password.

```
/****** sp_RetrieveShopper ******/
CREATE PROCEDURE sp_RetrieveShopper

@chrBillEmail varchar(255),
@chrPassword varchar(10)

AS

/*  Retrieve the shopper from the database based
    on the Billing email address and password
    passed into the stored procedure
*/
select * from Shopper where
    chrBillEmail = @chrBillEmail and
    chrPassword = @chrPassword
GO
```

The sp_UpdateShopper stored procedure updates the shopper table with the new data. Note that this update includes the password field. Again, you may wish to implement an alternative method of allowing users to update their password data.

```
/****** sp_UpdateShopper ******/
CREATE PROCEDURE sp_UpdateShopper

@idShopper integer,
@chrShipFirstName varchar(100),
@chrShipLastName varchar(100),
@chrShipAddress varchar(100),
@chrShipCity varchar(100),
@chrShipState varchar(2),
@chrShipZipCode varchar(15),
@chrShipPhone varchar(25),
@chrShipEmail varchar(255),
@chrPassword varchar(10),
@chrBillFirstName varchar(100),
@chrBillLastName varchar(100),
```

```
@chrBillAddress varchar(100),
@chrBillCity varchar(100),
@chrBillState varchar(2),
@chrBillZipCode varchar(15),
@chrBillPhone varchar(25),
@chrBillEmail varchar(255)

AS

/*  Update the shopper data where the ID of the Shopper
    equals the value of the shopper ID passed into the
    stored procedure.
*/
update shopper set
    chrShipFirstName = @chrShipFirstName,
    chrShipLastName = @chrShipLastName,
    chrShipAddress = @chrShipAddress,
    chrShipCity = @chrShipCity,
    chrShipState = @chrShipState,
    chrShipZipCode = @chrShipZipCode,
    chrShipPhone = @chrShipPhone,
    chrShipEmail = @chrShipEmail,
    chrPassword = @chrPassword,
    chrBillFirstName = @chrBillFirstName,
    chrBillLastName = @chrBillLastName,
    chrBillAddress = @chrBillAddress,
    chrBillCity = @chrBillCity,
    chrBillState = @chrBillState,
    chrBillZipCode = @chrBillZipCode,
    chrBillPhone = @chrBillPhone,
    chrBillEmail = @chrBillEmail

where
    idShopper = @idShopper
GO
```

The order table stores all the credit data for the order, as listed in Table 17-11. The standard credit card data is stored, including card number, name, type, and expiration date. Also, the appropriate links to the shopper and basket are provided. Note that through the basket items list for the basket, you can retrieve the list of products purchased.

Field/Stored Procedure	Description
IdOrder	ID of the order.
ChrCardName	Credit card name.
ChrCardNumber	Credit card number.
ChrExpDate	Expiration date of the credit card.
IdBasket	ID of the basket to which the order is assigned.
IdShopper	ID of the shopper to which the order is assigned.
ChrCardType	Type of credit card (Amex, Mastercard, Visa, and Discover)
SP_InsertOrder	Stored procedure to insert a new order.

Table 17-11.   *Order Table*

The SQL code for the order table is fairly straightforward. Note that the card number is stored in a variable character field, not an integer field. This way we can store the card number with spaces or dashes. Also, the expiration date is stored as a varchar since the format is MM/YY.

```
/****** Orders ******/
CREATE TABLE dbo.Orders (
    idOrder int IDENTITY (1, 1) NOT NULL ,
    chrCardName varchar (255) NULL ,
    chrCardNumber varchar (50) NULL ,
    chrExpDate varchar (255) NULL ,
    idBasket int NULL ,
    idShopper int NULL ,
    chrCardType varchar (255) NULL
)
GO
```

We have only one stored procedure for the order table. The sp_InsertOrder stored procedure inserts the order into the table. If we were to build reporting pages for the orders in the system, we would need additional stored procedures to retrieve data and link the basket, basket item, and shopper tables.

```
/****** sp_InsertOrder ******/
CREATE PROCEDURE sp_InsertOrder

@chrCardName varchar(255),
@chrCardNumber varchar(50),
@chrExpDate varchar(255),
@IDBasket integer,
@IDShopper integer,
@chrCardType varchar(255)

AS

/*  Insert a new order into the database /
insert into orders(chrCardName, chrCardNumber, chrExpDate,
                idBasket, idShopper, chrCardType)
values(@chrCardName, @chrCardNumber, @chrExpDate,
       @idBasket, @idShopper, @chrCardType)

/*  Return the order ID */
select @@identity
GO
```

That is it for the database structure of the shopping basket system. As you can see, it closely mirrors the class structure but varies in relationship and one-to-one correlation of specific classes.

We have also defined many of the stored procedures needed in a full shopping basket system and, certainly, the stored procedures needed for the shopping cart example we will be building in this part of the book. Additional ones would be needed for managing departments, products, and orders. Next, let's take a look at starting the project and building the HTML prototype interface.

Designing the Interface

For our shopping basket IIS project, we will need to define the basic template pages for the system. And we will need to import each template into our project and set up the appropriate custom events for each template.

Starting the Project

Before we start building the template, let's create our new project. You will want to start a new IIS application and save it to your system. Set the project name to be "prjShopping." And set the application title to be "Shopping Basket." Name the new web class that is created "Shopping." Also set the Name in URL property to be "Shopping."

Perhaps most important, we are going to set the StateManagement property of the web class to be "2- wcRetainInstance." This will essentially keep the instance of the web class alive between pages in the shopping basket. This will allow us to persist classes such as the basket, shopper, and so on, without having to re-create them with each new page.

The downside of keeping the web class instance alive is memory overhead. The server is going to have to store each web class instance in a session variable on the server. This could have an effect on scalability and server requirements. But you do lower the need to make trips to the SQL Server to query and requery for data.

Now, let's get started with our template interfaces.

Department Template

The first page in the shopping process is to select a department to browse. Each page will have a standard body and image logo header. And our department page will have appropriate welcoming text and instructions for the user.

```
<HTML>

<BODY bgcolor="#ffff99">

<center>
<img src="images/logo.bmp">
</center>

<!-- Show introduction text -->
<P><FONT size=5>Welcome to <EM>
  <STRONG style="COLOR: red">
   Shop Until You Drop
  </STRONG></EM>.
    Enjoy your shopping experience!!!
</FONT></P><BR>

<!-- Indicate that users should select their
      department -->
<P><STRONG><FONT size=4>
  Select your department:
</FONT></STRONG></P>
```

Our page will have a set of custom web class tags to indicate to our Visual Basic application that it needs to insert the list of departments.

```
<!-- Web class tags to indicate the
     department list should be shown
-->
<wc@DEPARTMENTLIST></WC@DEPARTMENTLIST>

<br>
```

Finally, our page closes out with a pair of custom web class tags to have the navigation bar for our shopping basket inserted into the page.

```
<!-- Web class tags to indicate the
     navigation bar should be shown
-->
<wc@NAVIGATION></WC@NAVIGATION>

</BODY>
</HTML>
```

The department page is fairly straightforward and does not require any special processing other than to provide a list of departments in the database and the standard navigation bar for our pages.

Go ahead and import the page into your application to create a new template. Be sure and name the template page "Department" once imported. Note that there are no custom web events for this page.

Product List Template

Once the user has selected a department from the list, he or she will get a listing of products assigned to that department. As with all pages, this one has the standard body and image logo bitmap.

```
<HTML>

<BODY bgcolor="#ffff99">

<!-- Header graphic -->
<center>
<img src="images/logo.bmp">
</center>
```

When the user reaches the page, we want to indicate which department was selected. Again, we use custom web class tags to tell the Visual Basic program to have the department name inserted into the page.

```
<!-- Web class tags that indicate the
     Department name for the current
     product list.
-->
<wc@DEPARTMENTNAME></WC@DEPARTMENTNAME>
<BR>

<!-- Indicate the user should select a
     product
-->
<P><STRONG><FONT face="" size=4>Select your
product:</FONT></STRONG></P>
```

And, as you would suspect, there is also a set of custom web class tags that will be replaced with the list of products in the department. Following that, the navigation bar is inserted into the page, and the page is closed out.

```
<!-- Web class tags that indicate the
     product list for the current
     department should be shown
-->
<wc@PRODUCTLIST></WC@PRODUCTLIST>

<br>

<!-- Web class tags that indicate the
     navigation bar should be shown
-->
<wc@NAVIGATION></wc@NAVIGATION>

</BODY>
</HTML>
```

Now import the page into the application. Be sure and name the template after it is imported to be "ProductList." Note that there are no custom web events for this template page.

Product Template

Next we have the product template page. This page will show the price, name, description, and image. The page begins with the standard page header items.

```
<HTML>

<BODY bgcolor="#ffff99">
<!-- Header Image -->
<center>
<img src="images/logo.bmp">
</center>
```

Our product page will need a form to add the item to the basket. Note that the form does not have any action. The action will be defined as a custom event in our IIS application.

```
<!-- Form to add the product to the
     basket
-->
<form method="post" action="" name="AddToBasket">
```

The product data will be displayed in a table. The only twist on the table is that the product description will be in a column that will span three rows. To the left of the description will be the name, price, an input for the quantity, and the Submit button to add to the basket.

```
<!-- Table that will lay out the product data -->
<table border=1 cellpadding=4 cellspacing=4>

 <!-- First row -->
 <tr>
   <!-- First column will show the product name
        through the web class tags
   -->
```

The product data will be inserted into the page with a series of custom web class tags. The product name, description, and price will be inserted.

```
<td><wc@PRODUCTNAME></WC@PRODUCTNAME></td>

  <!--  Second column will span three rows. The
        product description will be displayed
        through the web class tags
  -->
  <td rowspan="3"><wc@PRODUCTDESC></WC@PRODUCTDESC></td>
</tr>

<!-- Next row shows the product price through the
     web class tags. Note no second column is built
-->
<tr>
  <td><wc@PRODUCTPRICE></WC@PRODUCTPRICE></td>
</tr>
```

Users will be able to insert the quantity of items they would like to purchase in a text-input element. And a Submit button is built to send the page to the server.

```
<!--  Next row allows the user to set the
      quantity and builds a submit button
      to process the form
-->
<tr>
  <td>
    <!--  Quantity input element -->
    <input name="quantity" value="1" size=4 >

    <!--  Submit button for the form -->
    <input name="Submit" type="submit" value="Submit">

  </td>
</tr>
```

Finally, the product image is displayed, and the page is closed out with the navigation custom web class tags and the closing tags for the page.

```
<!--  The product image is shown through the
      processing of the web class tags
-->
<tr>
  <td colspan=2><wc@IMAGE></WC@IMAGE></td>
```

```
    </tr>

<!--  Close the table and form -->
</table>
</form>

<br>

<!--  Web class tags that indicate the
      navigation bar should be shown
-->
<wc@navigation></wc@navigation>

</BODY>
</HTML>
```

Import the product template page into the project and name the template "Product." We will also need one custom web event for our product page. Table 17-12 shows the event name and description.

Our IIS application code will need to process the quantity and product data requested when the product is submitted to the server.

Basket Template Page

Next we have the basket template page. When the user adds a product to the basket, the basket page will be displayed. The usual header tagging is present, including the logo image for the store.

```
<HTML>

<BODY bgcolor="#ffff99">

<!--  Header Image -->
<center>
<img src="images/logo.bmp">
</center>

<BR>

<!--  Indicate this is the shopping basket page -->
<font size="5" color="RED"><B>Shopping Basket</B></font>

<BR><BR>
```

Event Name	Description
AddtoBasket	The event will process the submission of the request to add the product to the basket.

Table 17-12.   *Product Page Custom Event*

A form is included on the page for submitting updated quantities of the products to purchase in the basket. Again, note that there is no action defined for the form. This will be defined as a custom web event in our application.

```
<!-- Form to submit the basket updates -->
<form method="post" action="" name="UpdateBasket">

<HR>
```

A table is built to organize the display of the items in the basket. The first row is a header row that identifies each column.

```
<!-- Table to display the products in
     the basket
-->
<table cellpadding=3 cellspacing=3>

<!-- Header row -->
<tr>
  <th>Product Code</th>
  <th>Product Name</th>
  <th>Price</th>
  <th>Quantity</th>
  <th>Delete</th>
</tr>
```

The basket items are inserted into the page via the BASKETITEMS custom web class tags. Included in the listing will be a link to delete the particular item from the basket.

```
<!-- Web class tags to process the basket items
     in the basket
-->
```

```
<wc@BASKETITEMS></WC@BASKETITEMS>

<!--  Close the table -->
</table>

<HR>
<BR>
```

Following the list of basket items are several options for the user. First will be a hyperlink to go to the checkout page. Second will be a hyperlink to clear the basket of all items. Note the hrefs have no target--these will be defined as a custom web event.

Finally, we have the Submit button for the form. This will submit the quantity updates on the items in the basket. Following that, the table and form are closed with the navigation bar showing.

```
<font size="4">

<!--  Hyperlink to the checkout page -->
<a href="">Check Out</a> |

<!--  Hyper link to clear the basket -->
<a href="">Clear Basket</a> |

</font>

<!--  Input to submit the basket updates -->
<input type="submit" value="Update">

</form>

<BR>
<HR>

<!--  Web class tags that indicate the
      navigation bar should be shown
-->
<wc@navigation></wc@navigation>

</BODY>
</html>
```

Import the page into the application and name it "Basket." Our basket page will have several custom events for the page, as shown in Table 17-13.

Event Name	Description
Update Basket	Updates the basket with the new quantities.
Hyperlink1	Moves the user to the checkout page.
Hyperlink2	Clears the basket of all items in the basket.

Table 17-13.   *Basket Page Custom Events*

The basket page is the center of the application. From this page, users can review the items they have added to the basket. And they can manage the items in the basket and choose to continue with the checkout process. Our three custom web events will be processed in the page with appropriate code.

Checkout Template

Next we have the checkout page. This page will allow users to enter their shipping and billing data into the page form. Also, users can enter their password so they can retrieve their shopper data later.

If users have looked up their shopper data, the form will automatically be filled out, including the password. But it will be displayed in password fields so the characters are not displayed.

```
<HTML>

<BODY bgcolor="#ffff99">

<center>
<img src="images/logo.bmp">
</center>
```

The page will indicate the shipping rates and the tax rates.

```
<!--  Indicate the shipping method -->
Shipping is calculated based on the total dollar amount
according to the following table:

<BR><BR>
```

```
<!--   Show the shipping table -->
   - $00.00 to $10.00 shipping is $5.00<BR>
   - $10.01 to $50.00 shipping is $7.50<BR>
   - $50.01 and up shipping is $15.00

<BR><BR>

<!--   Indicate the tax method -->
Tax is 4.5% in the state of Virginia

<BR><BR>
```

Our checkout page will have a form for submitting the shopper data to the database. Again, note that the form does not have an action defined. That will be defined in our custom web event. Following the form is a table to define the data entry structure for the form.

```
<!--   Form to submit the checkout data -->
<form method="post" action="" name="CheckOut">

<!--   Table to build the input of the
       name and address data
-->
<table border=0 cellpadding=3 cellspacing=3>
```

The first section of the page defines the shopper's shipping data. Each custom web tag will be replaced by an input element. Note that we do not provide text input elements in the HTML code directly, since if the shopper data is known, we will need to dynamically fill in the Value property of the text-input elements.

```
<!--   Shipping First Name -->
 <tr>
   <td><DIV align=right>Ship to First Name:</DIV></td>
   <td><wc@SHIPTOFIRSTNAME></WC@SHIPTOFIRSTNAME></td>
 </tr>

 <!--   Shipping Last Name -->
 <tr>
   <td><DIV align=right>Ship to Last Name:</DIV></td>
   <td><wc@SHIPTOLASTNAME></WC@SHIPTOLASTNAME></td>
 </tr>
```

```
<!-- Shipping Address -->
<tr>
  <td><DIV align=right>Ship to Address:</DIV></td>
  <td><wc@SHIPTOADDRESS></WC@SHIPTOADDRESS></td>
</tr>

<!-- Shipping City -->
<tr>
  <td><DIV align=right>Ship to City:</DIV></td>
  <td><wc@SHIPTOCITY></WC@SHIPTOCITY></td>
</tr>

<!-- Shipping State -->
<tr>
  <td><DIV align=right>Ship to State:</DIV></td>
  <td><wc@SHIPTOSTATE></WC@SHIPTOSTATE></td>
</tr>

<!-- Shipping Zip Code -->
 <tr>
  <td><DIV align=right>Ship to Zip Code:</DIV></td>
  <td><wc@SHIPTOZIPCODE></WC@SHIPTOZIPCODE></td>
</tr>

<!-- Shipping Phone -->
<tr>
  <td><DIV align=right>Ship to Phone:</DIV></td>
  <td><wc@SHIPTOPHONE></WC@SHIPTOPHONE></td>
</tr>

<!-- Shipping Email Address -->
<tr>
  <td><DIV align=right>Ship to Email:</DIV></td>
  <td><wc@SHIPTOEMAIL></WC@SHIPTOEMAIL></td>
</tr>

<!-- Spacer row -->
<tr>
   <td colspan=2> </td>
</tr>
```

We will provide a check box for the user to indicate that the billing data is the same as the shipping data.

```
<!-- Find out if the user wants to have the
      billing data be the same as the shipping
      data
  -->
<tr>
    <td colspan=2><input type="checkbox" value="1"
name="BillAddress">
                   Billing Same as Shipping?
    </td>
</tr>
```

The billing data and password are then provided in the same way, with each piece of data being inserted via a custom web class tag.

```
<!-- Billing First Name -->
 <tr>
   <td><DIV align=right>Bill to First Name:</DIV></td>
   <td><wc@BILLTOFIRSTNAME></WC@BILLTOFIRSTNAME></td>
 </tr>

<!-- Billing Last Name -->
 <tr>
   <td><DIV align=right>Bill to Last Name:</DIV></td>
   <td><wc@BILLTOLASTNAME></WC@BILLTOLASTNAME></td>
 </tr>

<!-- Billing Address -->
 <tr>
   <td><DIV align=right>Bill to Address:</DIV></td>
   <td><wc@BILLTOADDRESS></WC@BILLTOADDRESS></td>
 </tr>

<!-- Billing City -->
 <tr>
   <td><DIV align=right>Bill to City:</DIV></td>
   <td><wc@BILLTOCITY></WC@BILLTOCITY></td>
 </tr>
```

```
<!--  Billing State -->
<tr>
  <td><DIV align=right>Bill to State:</DIV></td>
  <td><wc@BILLTOSTATE></WC@BILLTOSTATE></td>
</tr>

<!--  Billing Zip Code -->
 <tr>
  <td><DIV align=right>Bill to Zip Code:</DIV></td>
  <td><wc@BILLTOZIPCODE></WC@BILLTOZIPCODE></td>
</tr>

<!--  Billing Phone -->
<tr>
  <td><DIV align=right>Bill to Phone:</DIV></td>
  <td><wc@BILLTOPHONE></WC@BILLTOPHONE></td>
</tr>

<!--  Billing Email Address -->
<tr>
  <td><DIV align=right>Bill to Email:</DIV></td>
  <td><wc@BILLTOEMAIL></WC@BILLTOEMAIL></td>
</tr>

<!--  Password to retrieve shopper data -->
<tr>
  <td><DIV align=right>Shopper Password:</DIV></td>
  <td><wc@PASSWORD></WC@PASSWORD></td>
</tr>
```

Finally, the page is ended with a Submit button and the closing of the table and form. And the navigation bar is shown and the page closed out.

```
<!--  Submit button for the form -->
 <tr>
   <td colspan=2><DIV align=center><br>
      <input type="submit" value="Submit" name="Submit"></DIV>
   </td>
 </tr>
```

```
<!--  Close the table and the form -->
</table>
</form>

<br>

<!--  Web class tags that indicate the
      navigation bar should be shown
-->
<wc@navigation></wc@navigation>

</BODY>
</HTML>
```

Insert the page into the project and name the template "CheckOut." We have one custom web event for submission of the form on the page, shown in Table 17-14.

Get Shopper Template

The get shopper template page will provide an input area for the user to retrieve a previous shopper record. This will save the shopper from having to retype all of the shipping and billing data into the checkout form.

```
<HTML>

<BODY bgcolor="#ffff99">

<!--  Header Image -->
<center>
<img src="images/logo.bmp">
</center>

<!-- Ask users to enter their email
     address and password
-->
<P>Enter your email address and password.</P>
```

Event Name	Description
Check Out	Custom web event to handle processing of the shopper data form submission.

Table 17-14. *Checkout Page Custom Event*

Our page has a form for submitting the shopper retrieval data to the server. The action will be defined by a custom web event. Our form has two input elements for the user to enter the email address and the password.

```
<!-- Form to submit the user's entries -->
<form method="post" action="" name="GetShopper">

<!-- Table to retrieve the user's entries -->
<table cellpadding=3 cellspacing=3>

<!-- Email Address -->
<tr>
  <td align="right">Billing Email Address:</td>

  <!-- Build an input element for the billing
       email address
  -->
  <td><INPUT name="chrBillEmail" value="" type="Text"></td>
</tr>

<!-- Password -->
<tr>
  <td align="right">Password:</td>

  <!-- Build an input element for the password  -->
  <td><input type="password" name="chrPassword" value="">
</tr>

<!-- Submit button -->
<tr>
```

```
<!-- Spans two columns -->
<td colspan=2 align="Center">
   <br>
   <!-- Submit input element -->
   <input type="Submit" value="Submit" name="Submit">
</td>
</tr>

<!-- Close the table and form -->
</table>
</form>

<BR>
```

The page ends with the navigation web class tags and the closing HTML tags for the page.

```
<!-- Web class tags that indicate the
     navigation bar should be shown
-->
<wc@NAVIGATION></wc@NAVIGATION>

</BODY>
</HTML>
```

Insert the template page into the project and name it "GoShopper." We have one event for the page to handle retrieving the shopper from the database, as shown in Table 17-15.

Event Name	Description
GetShopper	Handles the submission of the email billing address and password to retrieve the shopper data from the database.

Table 17-15. *Get Shopper Custom Event*

Credit Template

The credit template page is the final page in the process. This will allow users to enter their credit card data to process their order.

```
<HTML>

<BODY bgcolor="#ffff99">

<!-- Header image -->
<center>
<img src="images/logo.bmp">
</center>
```

On the page, we want to show the sum of the order, including the subtotal, tax, shipping, and order total. The SHOWTOTAL custom web tags will provide the placement for the IIS application in the page.

```
<!-- Web class tags to show the
     basket subtotal, shipping
     tax and total
-->
<wc@SHOWTOTAL></WC@SHOWTOTAL>

<BR>

<!-- Ask users to enter
     their credit card data
-->
<b>Enter your credit card data:</b>

<BR><BR>
```

Our page has a form on it for accepting input from the user. The form action will be defined as a custom web event. The form has a series of input elements for the card name and card number.

```
<!-- Form to process the credit card data -->
<form method="post" action="" Name="Credit">

<!-- Table to retrieve credit card data -->
<table border=0 cellpadding=3 cellspacing=3>
```

```
<!--   Name on the credit card -->
<tr>
  <td><DIV align=right>Card Name:</DIV></td>
  <td colspan=5>

    <!--  Input element to request the card name -->
    <input size="55" type="text" name="CardName" >

  </td>
</tr>

<!--   Number on the credit card -->
<tr>
  <td><DIV align=right>Card Number:</DIV></td>
  <td colspan=5>

    <!--  Input element to request the card number -->
    <input size="55" type="Text" name="CardNumber" >

  </td>
</tr>
```

The card type, expiration month, and expiration year are provided as select input elements. Note that the ID for each option is set to the appropriate value of the select input.

```
<!--  Card type, expiration month and year -->
<tr>
  <td><DIV align=right>Card Type:</DIV></td>
  <td>

    <!--  Select for the card type -->
    <select name="CardType">
          <option value="Amex" selected>American Express
          <option value="Visa">Visa
          <option value="MC">Master Card
          <option value="Discover">Discover
    </select>

  </td>
```

```
<td><DIV align=right>Month:</DIV></td>
<td>
 <!-- Select for the card month -->
 <select name="CardMonth">
         <option value="1">1
         <option value="2">2
         <option value="3">3
         <option value="4">4
         <option value="5">5
         <option value="6">6
         <option value="7">7
         <option value="8">8
         <option value="9">9
         <option value="10">10
         <option value="11">11
         <option value="12">12
 </select>

</td>
<td><DIV align=right>Year:</DIV></td>
<td>

 <!-- Select for the card year -->
 <select name="CardYear">
         <option value="1998">1998
         <option value="1999">1999
         <option value="2000">2000
         <option value="2001">2001
         <option value="2002">2002
 </select>

</td>

</tr>
```

The form is closed out with a Submit button to send the page to the server and the closing form and table tags. Finally, the navigation custom web tags are shown, and the page is closed out.

```
<!-- Input submit element -->
 <tr>
   <td colspan=6><br>
     <DIV align=center>
        <!-- Submit button for the form -->
        <input type="submit" value="Submit" name="submit">
     </DIV>
   </td>
 </tr>

<!-- Close the table and form -->
</table>
</form>

<br>

<!-- Web class tags that indicate the
     navigation bar should be shown
-->
<wc@navigation></wc@navigation>

</BODY>
</HTML>
```

Table 17-16 shows the Credit custom web event to process the form submission on the page. Insert the page into the project and define the event. Make sure the template name after it is imported is "Credit."

That is it for the template pages. Figure 17-1 shows the project with all the templates imported and the custom web events for each created. In the next chapter we will be ready to start placing the appropriate code into our project.

Event Name	Description
Credit	Custom web event to process the form submission of the credit data to the server.

Table 17-16. *Credit Page Custom Event*

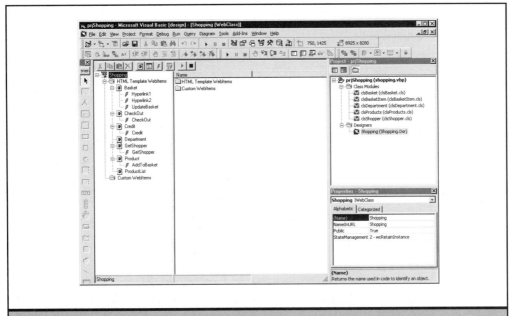

Figure 17-1.   *Shopping Basket Object Mode*

Summary

In this chapter we defined the class structure, database, and interface for the project. With that, we can now build the class code and web class functionality. In a solid Visual Basic application, this up-front design work is crucial to building great code that works efficiently, is expandable, scalable, and easily maintainable.

What's Next

In the next chapter, we will build the class code and web class structure on the foundation provided in this chapter. And we will test the interface and go shopping!

Chapter 18

Building an
E-Commerce System

In the previous chapter we built the foundation of our e-commerce system. In this chapter we are ready to dig into the heavy-duty coding of the class structure and web classes for the application. First we will flesh out the functionality of the classes based on the object model, properties, and methods laid out in Chapter 17. For each of the methods, we will build the appropriate code and, for the properties, the appropriate validation.

Note that in this application we will not be using a data environment object. Since we are keeping an instance of the web class alive in a session variable, which is stored in memory on the server, we will want to try and limit overhead as much as possible. Keeping additional database connections open with additional objects will only add more overhead.

You will also note a difference in this object model implementation over the project tracking system. In the project tracking system, all projects, tasks, developers, and so on, were loaded when the project was started. In this case, we cannot afford to store that overhead for potentially unlimited numbers of users on the server.

Once we have the class code built, we are ready to build the "glue" code in the web class to tie together the interface and our object model and database. So, let's get started with the class files.

Defining the Class Capabilities

In general, you can use the Class Builder utility to define the properties and methods of each class. Keep in mind that the basket class contains a collection of basket items. And the department class has a collection of products. The Class Builder will create the class files and will fill out the properties and subroutines/functions for the methods of the class.

Department Class

Our first class is the department class. This class defines department data for the shopping system. In the first section of the page, we have the mCol collection variable, which will hold a collection of product classes that are assigned to the department. Following that, we have the standard member variables for the class properties.

```
Option Explicit

'local variable to hold collection
Private mCol As Collection

'local variable(s) to hold property value(s)
Private mvarDescription As String 'local copy
Private mvaridDepartment As Integer 'local copy
```

Next we have the property definitions for the class. In this case, we have just two properties, idDepartment and Description. Both are defined with standard Let/Get property structures.

```
'  ID of the department
Public Property Let idDepartment(ByVal vData As Integer)
    mvaridDepartment = vData
End Property

Public Property Get idDepartment() As Integer
    idDepartment = mvaridDepartment
End Property

'  Description of the department
Public Property Let Description(ByVal vData As String)
    mvarDescription = vData
End Property

Public Property Get Description() As String
    Description = mvarDescription
End Property
```

Our first method is ListDepartments. This is a meta function of the class. In other words, it operates on all departments in the system, not just the current department defined for the class. The method will return a collection of department classes.

First in the method, the database connection is opened to our shopping basket database. Then we execute the sp_GetDepartments stored procedure to return the departments in the database. Once the recordset is returned, the recordset is looped through. With each iteration, a new department class is created and the ID and description set. The department is then added to the collection. Finally, the collection is returned.

```
'  Meta function to list all of the departments
'  in the database and return the list in a
'  collection
Public Function ListDepartments() As Collection

'  Collection of departments
Dim DeptList As New Collection
```

```vb
'  Declare our variables
Dim dbDepartment As New ADODB.Connection
Dim rsDepartment As New ADODB.Recordset
Dim SQL As String
Dim Dept As clsDepartment

'  Open our connection
dbDepartment.Open "dsn=prjShopping"

'  SQL statement that will retrieve the
'  departments in the database using the
'  sp_GetDepartments stored procedure
SQL = "execute sp_GetDepartments"

'  Execute the SQL statement
Set rsDepartment = dbDepartment.Execute(SQL)

'  Loop through the departments
Do Until rsDepartment.EOF

    '  Create a new department class
    Set Dept = New clsDepartment

    '  Retrieve the department ID
    Dept.idDepartment = rsDepartment("idDepartment")

    '  Retrieve the department's description
    Dept.Description = rsDepartment("chrDescription")

    '  Add to the collection
    DeptList.Add Dept

    '  Clear the class
    Set Dept = Nothing

    '  Move to the next row
    rsDepartment.MoveNext

'  Loop back
Loop
```

```
'  Return the collection of departments
Set ListDepartments = DeptList

End Function
```

Our next method is LoadProducts. This method retrieves all the product data assigned to the department and builds the collection of product classes.

First, a connection is opened to the shopping basket database. The sp_GetDeptProducts stored procedure is executed with the ID of the department passed in. The result set contains the products assigned to the department.

Each product is looped through with the properties of the product class set to the data in the database. Once the new product class is set up, the class is added to the mCol collection for the department class.

```
'  Loads the products for the department
Public Sub LoadProducts()

'  Declare our variables
Dim dbProducts As New ADODB.Connection
Dim rsProducts As New ADODB.Recordset
Dim SQL As String
Dim Prod As clsProducts

'  Open our connection
dbProducts.Open "dsn=prjShopping"

'  SQL statement that retrieves the products
'  for the current department using the
'  sp_GetDeptProducts stored procedure
SQL = "execute sp_GetDeptProducts " & mvaridDepartment

'  Execute the SQL statement
Set rsProducts = dbProducts.Execute(SQL)

'  Loop through the products
Do Until rsProducts.EOF

    '  Create a new product class
    Set Prod = New clsProducts
```

```
'  Set the department the product
'  belongs to
Prod.idDepartment = mvaridDepartment

'  Retrieve all of the values for the product
Prod.idProduct = rsProducts("idProduct")
Prod.Price = rsProducts("fltPrice")
Prod.ProductImage = rsProducts("chrImage")
Prod.ProductName = rsProducts("chrProductName")
Prod.SalePrice = rsProducts("fltSalePrice")
Prod.SaleEnd = rsProducts("dtSaleEnd")
Prod.SaleStart = rsProducts("dtSaleStart")
Prod.Description = rsProducts("txtDescription")

'  Add the product to the collection of products
'  for the current department class
mCol.Add Prod, CStr(Prod.idProduct)

'  Clear the product class
Set Prod = Nothing

'  Move to the next record
rsProducts.MoveNext

'  Loop back
Loop

End Sub
```

The Add method will add a new product to the collection. The appropriate product data is passed in to set up the new product.

```
'  Add a new product to the collection
Public Function Add(ProductName As String, Price As Double, _
                Description As String, ProductImage As String, _
                SalePrice As Double, Active As Boolean, _
                idProduct As Integer, idDepartment As Integer, _
                Optional sKey As String) As clsProducts
```

```
'create a new object
Dim objNewMember As clsProducts
Set objNewMember = New clsProducts

'set the properties passed into the method
objNewMember.ProductName = ProductName
objNewMember.Price = Price
objNewMember.Description = Description
objNewMember.ProductImage = ProductImage
objNewMember.SalePrice = SalePrice
objNewMember.Active = Active
objNewMember.idProduct = idProduct
objNewMember.idDepartment = mvaridDepartment

If Len(sKey) = 0 Then
    mCol.Add objNewMember
Else
    mCol.Add objNewMember, sKey
End If

'return the object created
Set Add = objNewMember
Set objNewMember = Nothing

End Function
```

The Item property allows us to index into the mCol collection to retrieve a specific product's data.

```
Public Property Get Item(vntIndexKey As Variant) As clsProducts
    'used when referencing an element in the collection
    'vntIndexKey contains either the Index or Key to the
    'collection,
    'this is why it is declared as a Variant
    'Syntax: Set foo = x.Item(xyz) or Set foo = x.Item(5)
    Set Item = mCol(vntIndexKey)
End Property
```

The Count property indicates the number of items in the products collection.

```
Public Property Get Count() As Long
    'used when retrieving the number of elements in the
    'collection. Syntax: Debug.Print x.Count
    Count = mCol.Count
End Property
```

The Remove method will delete a product from the collection assigned to the department. Note that this does not actually remove the class from the database.

```
Public Sub Remove(vntIndexKey As Variant)
    'used when removing an element from the collection
    'vntIndexKey contains either the Index or Key, which is why
    'it is declared as a Variant
    'Syntax: x.Remove(xyz)
    mCol.Remove vntIndexKey
End Sub
```

Use the NewEnum property to enumerate the products collection.

```
Public Property Get NewEnum() As Iunknown
    'this property allows you to enumerate
    'this collection with the For...Each syntax
    Set NewEnum = mCol.[_NewEnum]
End Property
```

When the class is initialized and terminated, the product collection is created and destroyed.

```
Private Sub Class_Initialize()
    'creates the collection when this class is created
    Set mCol = New Collection
End Sub

Private Sub Class_Terminate()
    'destroys collection when this class is terminated
    Set mCol = Nothing
End Sub
```

The department class will be our primary interface for browsing through the departments and products in the system. We can retrieve departments and products through this class. Next we will look at the product class.

Product Class

The product class holds the properties of the product. The beginning of the class
defines all the member variables for the class.

```
Option Explicit

'local variable(s) to hold property value(s)
Private mvarProductName As String 'local copy
Private mvarPrice As Double 'local copy
Private mvarDescription As String 'local copy
Private mvarProductImage As String 'local copy
Private mvarSalePrice As Double 'local copy
Private mvarActive As Boolean 'local copy
Private mvaridProduct As Integer 'local copy
Private mvaridDepartment As Integer 'local copy
Private mvardtSaleStart As Date 'local copy
Private mvardtSaleEnd As Date 'local copy
```

The SaleEnd property will hold the date the sale ends for the product (if one is set).

```
'  Sale Ends property
Public Property Let SaleEnd(ByVal vData As Date)
    mvardtSaleEnd = vData
End Property


Public Property Get SaleEnd() As Date
    SaleEnd = mvardtSaleEnd
End Property
```

The SaleStart property will hold the date the sale starts for the product
(if one is set).

```
'  Sale start property
Public Property Let SaleStart(ByVal vData As Date)
    mvardtSaleStart = vData
End Property


Public Property Get SaleStart() As Date
    SaleStart = mvardtSaleStart
End Property
```

The ID of the department will be stored in the product class. This is what defines its relationship to the parent department table.

```
'   ID of the department the product belongs to
Public Property Let idDepartment(ByVal vData As Integer)
    mvaridDepartment = vData
End Property

Public Property Get idDepartment() As Integer
    idDepartment = mvaridDepartment
End Property
```

The ID of the product is defined by the identity column in the product SQL database.

```
'   ID of the product
Public Property Let idProduct(ByVal vData As Integer)
    mvaridProduct = vData
End Property

Public Property Get idProduct() As Integer
    idProduct = mvaridProduct
End Property
```

The Active property defines whether or not the current product is active (or available).

```
'   Indicates whether the product is active or not
Public Property Let Active(ByVal vData As Boolean)
    mvarActive = vData
End Property

Public Property Get Active() As Boolean
    Active = mvarActive
End Property
```

The sale price is the price of the product between the sale end and start dates.

```
'   Sale price of the product
Public Property Let SalePrice(ByVal vData As Double)
    mvarSalePrice = vData
End Property
```

```
Public Property Get SalePrice() As Double
    SalePrice = mvarSalePrice
End Property
```

The product image will indicate where on the Web site the product images are located.

```
'   Product image
Public Property Let ProductImage(ByVal vData As String)
    mvarProductImage = vData
End Property

Public Property Get ProductImage() As String
    ProductImage = mvarProductImage
End Property
```

The Description property describes the product. Note that this is a text field in the database and can be of arbitrary length.

```
'   Product description
Public Property Let Description(ByVal vData As String)
    mvarDescription = vData
End Property

Public Property Get Description() As String
    Description = mvarDescription
End Property
```

The Price property is the standard price of the product. But it is not enforced during a sale period for the product.

```
'   Price of the product
Public Property Let Price(ByVal vData As Double)
    mvarPrice = vData
End Property

Public Property Get Price() As Double
    Price = mvarPrice
End Property
```

The product name is the standard name for the product. This is limited to 255 characters in the database.

```
'   Product name
Public Property Let ProductName(ByVal vData As String)
    mvarProductName = vData
End Property

Public Property Get ProductName() As String
    ProductName = mvarProductName
End Property
```

That is it for the product class. Its primary purpose in life is to represent the database data. But that is not to say, with further expansion of the system, certain methods for adding, updating, and deleting products from the database would not be appropriate.

Basket Class

Next we have the basket class. This class provides extensive functionality as the heart of the shopping basket interface. The first property defined in the class is a collection of basket items represented by the mCol variable. Following that are all the member variables for the properties of the class.

```
Option Explicit

'local variable to hold collection
Private mCol As Collection

'local variable(s) to hold property value(s)
Private mvarIDBasket As Integer 'local copy
Private mvarIDShopper As Integer 'local copy
Private mvarTotal As Double 'local copy
Private mvarTax As Double 'local copy
Private mvarSubTotal As Double 'local copy
Private mvarShipping As Double 'local copy
Private mvarShipState As String 'local copy
Private mvarCardName As String 'local copy
Private mvarCreditCardNumber As String 'local copy
Private mvarExpDate As String 'local copy
Private mvarCardType As Variant 'local copy
Private mvaridOrder As Integer 'local copy
```

The idOrder property is only set once the user has placed an order. Essentially, once the order is finalized, the basket is finished and now becomes the "order" data to report on and process the order.

```
'  ID of the order placed using the basket
Public Property Let idOrder(ByVal vData As Integer)
    mvaridOrder = vData
End Property

Public Property Get idOrder() As Integer
    idOrder = mvaridOrder
End Property
```

The Card Type defines the type of credit card the shopper is using.

```
'  Card Type used to place the order
Public Property Let CardType(ByVal vData As Variant)
    mvarCardType = vData
End Property

Public Property Get CardType() As Variant
    CardType = mvarCardType
End Property
```

The expiration date is in the format of MM/YY.

```
'  Card expiration date for the order
Public Property Let ExpDate(ByVal vData As String)
    mvarExpDate = vData
End Property

Public Property Get ExpDate() As String
    ExpDate = mvarExpDate
End Property
```

The CreditCardNumber property holds the card number entered by the user. Note that it is stored as a string and not as a number. That will allow the user to enter appropriate spaces and dashes without errors.

```
'  Credit card number for the order
Public Property Let CreditCardNumber(ByVal vData As String)
```

```
    mvarCreditCardNumber = vData
End Property

Public Property Get CreditCardNumber() As String
    CreditCardNumber = mvarCreditCardNumber
End Property
```

The card name is the name on the credit card the shopper is using.

```
'   Card name for the order
Public Property Let CardName(ByVal vData As String)
    mvarCardName = vData
End Property

Public Property Get CardName() As String
    CardName = mvarCardName
End Property
```

The shipping state indicates the state the order will be shipped to. This will be used to determine the tax for the order.

```
'   Shipping state
Public Property Let ShipState(ByVal vData As String)
    mvarShipState = vData
End Property

Public Property Get ShipState() As String
    ShipState = mvarShipState
End Property
```

Shipping holds the shipping charges for the basket/order.

```
'   Shipping charges
Public Property Let Shipping(ByVal vData As Double)
    Set mvarShipping = vData
End Property

Public Property Get Shipping() As Double
    Shipping = mvarShipping
End Property
```

SubTotal holds the basket subtotal for the basket/order.

```
'   Basket subtotal
Public Property Let SubTotal(ByVal vData As Double)
    Set mvarSubTotal = vData
End Property

Public Property Get SubTotal() As Double

    '   Calculate the current total
    CalculateTotal

    '   Return the subtotal value
    SubTotal = mvarSubTotal

End Property
```

Tax holds the tax charges for the basket/order.

```
'   Basket tax charges
Public Property Let Tax(ByVal vData As Double)
    Set mvarTax = vData
End Property

Public Property Get Tax() As Double
    Tax = mvarTax
End Property
```

Total holds the total charges for the basket/order.

```
'   Total basket cost
Public Property Let Total(ByVal vData As Double)
    Set mvarTotal = vData
End Property

Public Property Get Total() As Double
    Total = mvarTotal
End Property
```

The ID of the shopper that the basket/order belongs to is the next property.

```
'   ID of the shopper
Public Property Let idShopper(ByVal vData As Integer)
    mvarIDShopper = vData
End Property

Public Property Get idShopper() As Integer
    idShoppert = mvarIDShopper
End Property
```

The ID of the basket is determined by the Identity column in the SQL basket table.

```
'   ID of the basket
Public Property Let idBasket(ByVal vData As Integer)
    mvarIDBasket = vData
End Property

Public Property Get idBasket() As Integer
    idBasket = mvarIDBasket
End Property
```

The SaveCreditData method handles storing the credit card data the user enters to complete the order. When the data is inserted, the ID of the resulting order is returned, and the user is finished with this shopping basket.

The first section of the method opens the connection to the database. The sp_InsertOrder stored procedure will insert the data into the database. The ID of the order is returned.

```
'   Saves the credit card data set for the
'   class and returns an order
Public Sub SaveCreditData()

'   Declare our variables
Dim dbOrder As New ADODB.Connection
Dim rsOrder As New ADODB.Recordset
Dim SQL As String

'   Open our connection
dbOrder.Open "dsn=prjShopping"

'   Insert the order into the database
'   using the sp_InsertOrder stored
'   procedure
```

```
SQL = "execute sp_InsertOrder '" & _
        mvarCardName & "', '" & _
        mvarCreditCardNumber & "', '" & _
        mvarExpDate & "', " & _
        mvarIDBasket & ", " & _
        mvarIDShopper & ", '" & _
        mvarCardType & "'"

'  Execute the SQL statement
Set rsOrder = dbOrder.Execute(SQL)

'  Retrieve the returned order ID and
'  set the member variable for the
'  class
mvaridOrder = rsOrder(0)

End Sub
```

The SaveBasket method stores the basket in the database. When the basket is saved, we need to determine whether a new basket record has been inserted into the database. Otherwise, we cannot update the database if no record exists.

A check is done to see if the class has had an ID set for it. If so, we know the basket has been inserted since the ID only comes from the database. If there is no ID, we call the sp_InsertBasket stored procedure. Remember, in that stored procedure, we assumed the basket was being initialized with no data and only an ID was needed to be returned.

If the record has been inserted, we use the sp_UpdateBasket stored procedure to update the basket data. Before that is done, the subtotal, shipping, tax, and basket total are calculated by calling the CalculateTotal method.

```
'  Saves the shopping basket to the
'  database
Public Sub SaveBasket()

'  Declare our variables
Dim dbBasket As New ADODB.Connection
Dim rsBasket As New ADODB.Recordset
Dim SQL As String
```

```
'   Open our connection
dbBasket.Open "dsn=prjShopping"

'   Check to see if we have an assigned ID
'   for the basket yet. If we do not then
'   the basket data needs to be inserted
'   into the database
If mvarIDBasket = 0 Then

    '   SQL statement that will insert the basket data
    '   into the basket database using the sp_InsertBasket
    '   stored procedure
    SQL = "execute sp_InsertBasket"

    '   Execute the SQL statement
    Set rsBasket = dbBasket.Execute(SQL)

    '   Set IDBasket member variable to the
    '   ID returned from the insert
    mvarIDBasket = rsBasket(0)

Else

    '   Calculate the basket total (which
    '   also calculates subtotal, tax and shipping)
    CalculateTotal

    '   SQL statement that will update the basket
    '   data in the database using the sp_UpdateBasket
    '   stored procedure
    SQL = "execute sp_UpdateBasket " & _
              mvarIDShopper & ", " & _
              mvarShipping & ", " & _
              mvarSubTotal & ", " & _
              mvarTax & ", " & _
              mvarTotal & ", " & _
              mvarIDBasket

    '   Execute the SQL statement
    Set rsBasket = dbBasket.Execute(SQL)
```

```
End If

End Sub
```

Next we have the ClearBasket method. This will remove all basket items associated with the basket. The items are deleted from both the collection for the basket class and from the database. The Remove method of the basket class is called to remove the items.

```
'  Clear the basket of all basket items
Public Sub ClearBasket()

'  Declare our variables
Dim intCnt As Integer
Dim BskItem As clsBasketItem

'  Loop through each basket item class
'  in the collection
For Each BskItem In mCol

    '  Call the basket remove function and
    '  remove the basket item.
    Remove BskItem.idBasketItem

Next

End Sub
```

The UpdateQuantity subroutine handles updating the quantities for each of the basket items in the basket. The strQuantity argument will be formatted as follows:

```
1, 2, 1, 3, 1, 1
```

In this example, we would be updating six products with quantities of 1, 2, 1, 3, 1, and 1. The UpdateQuantity subroutine parses through the comma-delimited list and updates the products in succession.

Note   *The comma-delimited list comes from the basket page where the quantity updates are submitted to the server. Each quantity input is named "Quantity." The way the server handles the multiple input elements with the same name is to build them into a comma-delimited array.*

```
'   Updates the quantity of each item in the
'   basket. The strQuantity argument contains
'   the quantity for each item in the basket
'   in order and separated by a ','
Public Sub UpdateQuantity(strQuantity As String)

'   Declare our variables
Dim P As Integer
Dim P2 As Integer
Dim Cnt As Integer
Dim NewQuantity As Integer
Dim intCnt As Integer

'   Start our position counters at 1
P = 1
P2 = 1

'   Loop through each item in the basket
For intCnt = 1 To Count

    '   Find the next , in the string
    P = InStr(P2, strQuantity, ",")

    '   Check to see if one was found or not
    If P <> 0 Then

        '   Get the new quantity for the current item
        NewQuantity = Mid(strQuantity, P2, P - P2)

        '   Make sure the quantity is not 0. We cannot
        '   have a 0 quantity
        If NewQuantity <> 0 Then

            '   Call the update routine with the current basket item
            '    id and the new quantity
            Item(intCnt).Quantity = NewQuantity

            '   Save the basket
            Item(intCnt).SaveBasketItem

        End If
```

```
        '  Set our second string position pointer to be right after the
        '  , character just found.
        P2 = P + 1

    '  No more commas (last item in array)
    Else

        '  Get the new quantity
        NewQuantity = Mid(strQuantity, P2, Len(strQuantity))

        '  Make sure the quantity is not 0. We cannot
        '  have a 0 quantity
        If NewQuantity <> 0 Then

            '  Update the basket quantity
            Item(intCnt).Quantity = NewQuantity

            '  Save the basket
            Item(intCnt).SaveBasketItem

        End If

    End If

Next

End Sub
```

The CalculateTotal method handles calling the CalculateSubTotal, CalculateShipping, and CalculateTax methods. Then the total is calculated by summing up each one.

```
'  Calculate the basket total
Public Sub CalculateTotal()

'  First calculate the subtotal
CalculateSubTotal

'  Then calculate shipping
CalculateShipping
```

```
'   Then tax
CalculateTax

'   Finally the basket total is the sum of each
mvarTotal = mvarSubTotal + mvarShipping + mvarTax

End Sub
```

The CalculateTax method will check to see what the shipping state is for the shopping basket. In this case, we have only one state where tax is calculated, Virginia.

Tip   *If you have a more complicated tax model, you may wish to incorporate tax rates into a database, especially if they change frequently. Also, that would allow you to change the tax values without updating and recompiling the program. You also may wish to create a Server COM object, as outlined in Part III, that can be called from the IIS application. That way, you can just change the calculation COM object without updating the IIS application.*

```
'   Calculate the tax for the basket
Public Sub CalculateTax()

'   Tax is only charged in Virginia
If UCase(mvarShipState) = "VA" Then

    '   Multiply the subtotal times the
    '   tax rate
    mvarTax = mvarSubTotal * 0.045

End If

End Sub
```

The CalculateSubTotal method handles looping through the products in the basket item collection to total their prices. Note that the basket items' prices are set to the appropriate standard price or sale price.

```
'   Calculate the subtotal of the basket
Public Sub CalculateSubTotal()
```

```
'   Declare our variable
Dim intCnt As Integer

'   0 out the current subtotal
mvarSubTotal = 0

'   Loop through each item in the basket
For intCnt = 1 To Count

        '   Calculate the running subtotal. Note
        '   we need to multiply the item price times
        '   the quantity for each
        mvarSubTotal = mvarSubTotal + _
                        (Item(intCnt).Price * Item(intCnt).Quantity)

'  Loop back
Next intCnt

End Sub
```

The CalculateShipping method handles calculating the shipping total based on the subtotal basket value. There are different rates depending on that total.

As with the tax calculation, the shipping calculation could be database driven or done through a COM object. Also, there are many different ways of calculating shipping. Other examples could be based on the quantity of items (rather than the total basket value), product weight, class of shipping, and so on.

```
'   Calculate the shipping charges
Public Sub CalculateShipping()

'   Shipping rate table
'   $00.00 to $10.00 shipping is $5.00
'   $10.01 to $50.00 shipping is $7.50
'   $50.01 and up    shipping is $15.00

'   Check to see if the subtotal is less
'   than $10
If mvarSubTotal <= 10 Then
```

```
        '   Set the shipping
        mvarShipping = 5

End If

'  Check to see if the subtotal is less
'  than $50 and greater than $10
If mvarSubTotal > 10 And mvarSubTotal <= 50 Then

        '   Set the shipping
        mvarShipping = 7.5

End If

'  Check to see if the subtotal is greater
'  than $50
If mvarSubTotal > 50 Then

        '   Set the shipping
        mvarShipping = 15

End If

End Sub
```

The Add method of the class handles adding a new basket item to the database and assigning it to the basket. The values for the basket item are passed into the method. A new basket item class is created, and the properties are set.

Once the basket is set, the SaveBasket item method of the basket item class is called to save the new basket item to the database. Finally, the class is added to the collection of basket items for the basket.

```
'   Add a new item to the basket
Public Function Add(Quantity As Integer, idProduct As Integer, _
                dblPrice As Double, strProductName As String, _
                intSaleFlag As Integer, Optional sKey As _
                String) As clsBasketItem
```

```
' create a new object
Dim objNewMember As clsBasketItem
Set objNewMember = New clsBasketItem

'  set the properties passed into the method
objNewMember.Quantity = Quantity
objNewMember.idBasket = mvarIDBasket
objNewMember.idProduct = idProduct
objNewMember.Price = dblPrice
objNewMember.ProductName = strProductName
objNewMember.OnSale = intSaleFlag

'  Save the basket to the database
objNewMember.SaveBasketItem

'  Add to the collection with the ID of
'  the basket being the key
mCol.Add objNewMember, CStr(objNewMember.idBasketItem)

'  return the object created
Set Add = objNewMember
Set objNewMember = Nothing

End Function
```

The Item property allows us to index into the collection of basket items for the basket.

```
Public Property Get Item(vntIndexKey As Variant) As clsBasketItem
    'used when referencing an element in the collection
    'vntIndexKey contains either the Index or Key to the collection,
    'this is why it is declared as a Variant
    'Syntax: Set foo = x.Item(xyz) or Set foo = x.Item(5)
    Set Item = mCol(vntIndexKey)
End Property
```

The Count property will return the number of basket items assigned to the basket.

```
Public Property Get Count() As Long
    'used when retrieving the number of elements in the
    'collection. Syntax: Debug.Print x.Count
    Count = mCol.Count
End Property
```

The Remove method handles removing an item from the basket. Not only do we have to remove the item from the collection for the basket, we also need to remove the item from the database.

The first step is to open a database connection and remove the item from the database using the sp_DeleteBasketItem stored procedure and passing in the basket item ID. Next we remove the basket item from the collection of basket items for the basket.

```
Public Sub Remove(vntIndexKey As Variant)
    'used when removing an element from the collection
    'vntIndexKey contains either the Index or Key, which is why
    'it is declared as a Variant
    'Syntax: x.Remove(xyz)

    '   Declare our variables
    Dim dbBasket As New ADODB.Connection
    Dim rsBasket As New ADODB.Recordset
    Dim SQL As String

    '   Open our connection
    dbBasket.Open "dsn=prjShopping"

    '   Delete the basket item using the
    '   sp_DeleteBasketItem stored procedure
    SQL = "execute sp_DeleteBasketItem " & vntIndexKey

    '   Remove from the collection
    mCol.Remove CStr(vntIndexKey)

End Sub
```

The NewEnum property allows us to enumerate the basket item collection.

```
Public Property Get NewEnum() As Iunknown
    'this property allows you to enumerate
    'this collection with the For...Each syntax
    Set NewEnum = mCol.[_NewEnum]
End Property
```

When the class is initialized, we want to go ahead and insert a new basket into the database. This will initialize the shopping system to allow users to place items in their basket and shop. The SaveBasket method of the class is called. Recall that the first call to SaveBasket will insert a new basket into the database.

```
Private Sub Class_Initialize()
    'creates the collection when this class is created
    Set mCol = New Collection

    '   Ensure our basket ID is 0
    mvarIDBasket = 0

    '   Insert a new basket into the system
    SaveBasket

End Sub
```

When the class is terminated, the collection is deleted.

```
Private Sub Class_Terminate()
    'destroys collection when this class is terminated
    Set mCol = Nothing
End Sub
```

The basket class serves as our central tracking system of what the shopper is doing with regard to purchasing items. It tracks product prices, product quantities, and makes the appropriate calculations to come up with the order total. And, in this case, we have implemented the order data to also be stored as part of the order basket. When the order is submitted, the shopper is finished with the current basket.

Basket Item Class

Next we have the basket item class. This class will define each item added to the basket. As we say in the basket class, the basket item class will be assigned to a particular basket. The first section of our code defines the member property variables.

```
Option Explicit

'local variable(s) to hold property value(s)
Private mvarQuantity As Integer 'local copy
Private mvaridBasketItem As Integer 'local copy
Private mvarIDBasket As Integer 'local copy
```

```
Private mvaridProduct As Integer 'local copy
Private mvarPrice As Double 'local copy
Private mvarProductName As String 'local copy
Private mvarOnSale As Integer 'local copy
```

The OnSale property indicates whether the price of the basket item represents a sale price.

```
'   OnSale property indicates if the basket item
'   is on sale
Public Property Let OnSale(ByVal vData As Integer)
    mvarOnSale = vData
End Property

Public Property Get OnSale() As Integer
    OnSale = mvarOnSale
End Property
```

The product name from the product table is stored in the basket item table. This is done more for historical purposes. If we want to review a particular person's order at a later time, we will have a record of the product name, even if the product no longer is available.

```
'   Product name
Public Property Let ProductName(ByVal vData As String)
    mvarProductName = vData
End Property

Public Property Get ProductName() As String
    ProductName = mvarProductName
End Property
```

The Price property defines the price of the product when it was added to the basket. That price may represent the sale price, a price at a different time, or the current price.

```
'   Price (including the sale price)
Public Property Let Price(ByVal vData As Double)
    mvarPrice = vData
End Property
```

```
Public Property Get Price() As Double
    Price = mvarPrice
End Property
```

The ID of the product is stored in the basket item. This would amount to the product SKU.

```
'  ID of the product
Public Property Let idProduct(ByVal vData As Integer)
    mvaridProduct = vData
End Property

Public Property Get idProduct() As Integer
    idProduct = mvaridProduct
End Property
```

The SaveBasketItem method handles saving the basket item to the database. A check is first done to see if the basket item has been previously saved. If not, the sp_InsertBasketItem stored procedure is called to insert the basket item into the database. The ID of the basket item is then returned. If the basket item has been inserted already, the sp_UpdateBasket item stored procedure is called to update the basket item data.

```
'  Saves the basket item to the database
Public Sub SaveBasketItem()

'  Declare our variables
Dim dbBasketItem As New ADODB.Connection
Dim rsBasketItem As New ADODB.Recordset
Dim SQL As String

'  Open our connection
dbBasketItem.Open "dsn=prjShopping"

'  Check to see if an ID has been assigned to
'  the basket item yet
If mvaridBasketItem = 0 Then
```

```
       '  SQL statement that will insert the item into the
       '  basketitem table using the sp_InsertBasketItem
       '  stored procedure
       SQL = "execute sp_InsertBasketItem " & _
                   mvaridProduct & ", " & _
                   mvarQuantity & ", " & _
                   mvarIDBasket & ", " & _
                   mvarPrice

       '  Execute the SQL statement
       Set rsBasketItem = dbBasketItem.Execute(SQL)

       '  Get the ID of the basket item
       idBasketItem = rsBasketItem(0)

Else

       '  SQL statement that will update the basket item
       '  in the database using the sp_UpdateBasketItem
       '  stored procedure
       SQL = "execute sp_UpdateBasketItem " & _
             mvaridProduct & ", " & _
             mvarQuantity & ", " & _
             mvarIDBasket & ", " & _
             mvarPrice & ", " & _
             mvaridBasketItem

       '  Execute the SQL statement
       Set rsBasketItem = dbBasketItem.Execute(SQL)

End If

End Sub
```

The idBasket property indicates which basket the basket item belongs to.

```
'  ID of the basket the item is assigned to
Public Property Let idBasket(ByVal vData As Integer)
    mvarIDBasket = vData
End Property
```

```
Public Property Get idBasket() As Integer
    idBasket = mvarIDBasket
End Property
```

The ID of the basket item is returned from the insert of the basket item into the database.

```
'  ID of the basket item
Public Property Let idBasketItem(ByVal vData As Integer)
    mvaridBasketItem = vData
End Property

Public Property Get idBasketItem() As Integer
    idBasketItem = mvaridBasketItem
End Property
```

The Quantity property defines the number of items the shopper wishes to purchase.

```
'  Quantity of the item to be purchased
Public Property Let Quantity(ByVal vData As Integer)
    mvarQuantity = vData
End Property

Public Property Get Quantity() As Integer
    Quantity = mvarQuantity
End Property
```

When the class is initialized, we ensure that the ID of the basket item is 0 to indicate it has not been inserted into the database.

```
Private Sub Class_Initialize()

'  Set the ID to zero when the
'  class is initalized
mvaridBasketItem = 0

End Sub
```

INTERNET APPLICATION DEVELOPMENT

The BasketItem class will allow us to track all the items in the basket for the shopper. Each item will be stored in the database.

Shopper Class

Next we have the shopper class. This class will serve to manage our shopper data. The properties hold all the appropriate shipping and billing data as well as the password to retrieve the shopper data. The general declarations section defines the member property values.

```
Option Explicit

'local variable(s) to hold property value(s)
Private mvarShipPhone As String 'local copy
Private mvarShipEmail As String 'local copy
Private mvarShipAddress As String 'local copy
Private mvarShipCity As String 'local copy
Private mvarShipFirstName As String 'local copy
Private mvarShipLastName As String 'local copy
Private mvarShipState As String 'local copy
Private mvarShipZipCode As String 'local copy
Private mvarBillFirstName As String 'local copy
Private mvarBillLastName As String 'local copy
Private mvarBillAddress As String 'local copy
Private mvarBillCity As String 'local copy
Private mvarBillState As String 'local copy
Private mvarBillZipCode As String 'local copy
Private mvarBillPhone As String 'local copy
Private mvarBillEmail As String 'local copy
Private mvarIDShopper As Integer 'local copy
Private mvarPassword As String 'local copy
```

The Password property defines the password that will be stored in the database for this shopper data. The shopper will later be able to retrieve the shopper data by combining the email address and the password.

```
'  Password to retrieve shopper data
Public Property Let Password(ByVal vData As String)
    mvarPassword = vData
End Property

Public Property Get Password() As String
```

```
      Password = mvarPassword
End Property
```

The ID of the shopper is defined when the shopper data is inserted into the database.

```
'  ID of the shopper
Public Property Let idShopper(ByVal vData As Integer)
    mvarIDShopper = vData
End Property

Public Property Get idShopper() As Integer
    idShopper = mvarIDShopper
End Property
```

The SaveShopper method handles saving the shopper data to the database. As with the basket and basket item classes, we will check to see if the shopper data has been inserted into the Shopper SQL table. If not, the sp_InsertShopper stored procedure will be called to insert the shopper and return an ID.

If the shopper has been stored, the sp_UpdateShopper stored procedure is called to update the shopper data. Each time shoppers save their data, they have the opportunity to update their password.

```
'  Saves the shopper to the database
Public Sub SaveShopper()

'  Declare our variables
Dim dbShopper As New ADODB.Connection
Dim rsShopper As New ADODB.Recordset
Dim SQL As String

'  Open our connection
dbShopper.Open "dsn=prjShopping"

'  Check to see if the shopper has been
'  inserted into the database
If mvarIDShopper = 0 Then

    '  SQL statement that will insert the shopper
    '  into the shopper table using the
```

```
    '   sp_InsertShopper stored procedure
    SQL = "execute sp_InsertShopper"

    '   Execute the SQL statement
    Set rsShopper = dbShopper.Execute(SQL)

    '   Retrieve the ID of the shopper returned from
    '   the database
    mvarIDShopper = rsShopper(0)

Else

    '   SQL statement that will update the shopper
    '   data in the database by using the
    '   sp_UpdateShopper stored procedure
    SQL = "execute sp_UpdateShopper " & _
        mvarIDShopper & ", '" & _
        mvarShipFirstName & "', '" & _
        mvarShipLastName & "', '" & _
        mvarShipAddress & "', '" & _
        mvarShipCity & "', '" & _
        mvarShipState & "', '" & _
        mvarShipZipCode & "', '" & _
        mvarShipPhone & "', '" & _
        mvarShipEmail & "', '" & _
        mvarPassword & "', '" & _
        mvarBillFirstName & "', '" & _
        mvarBillLastName & "', '" & _
        mvarBillAddress & "', '" & _
        mvarBillCity & "', '" & _
        mvarBillState & "', '" & _
        mvarBillZipCode & "', '" & _
        mvarBillPhone & "', '" & _
        mvarBillEmail & "'"

    '   Execute the SQL statement
    Set rsShopper = dbShopper.Execute(SQL)

End If

End Sub
```

The LoadShopper method will load shopper data from the database and populate the class. The email address and password are passed into the method. The sp_RetrieveShopper stored procedure will query the database. If a record is returned, the class is updated from the data; if not, the method returns a false value indicating the data was not recalled.

Tip   *You may want to consider how much of the data is pulled from the database. If your shoppers tend to ship to the same place and use different billing methods, perhaps only the shipping data should be returned. Or if the billing data is the same and the shipping data changes, then only return the billing data. And, of course, if both are regular, then return both.*

```
'  Loads the shopper from the database by correlating
'  the billing email address and the password
Public Function LoadShopper(chrBillEmail As String, _
                chrPassword As String) As Integer

'  Declare our variables
Dim dbShopper As New ADODB.Connection
Dim rsShopper As New ADODB.Recordset
Dim SQL As String

'  Check to see if the password is blank
If Trim(chrPassword) = "" Then

    '  Indicate the shopper data was not retrieved
    LoadShopper = 0

    '  Exit the function
    Exit Function

End If

'  Open our connection
dbShopper.Open "dsn=prjShopping"

'  SQL statement that will retrieve the
'  shopper data from the database using the
'  sp_RetrieveShopper stored procedure
SQL = "execute sp_RetrieveShopper '" & _
    chrBillEmail & "', '" & _
    chrPassword & "'"
```

```
'  Execute the SQL statement
Set rsShopper = dbShopper.Execute(SQL)

'  Check to see if a record was returned
If Not rsShopper.EOF Then

    '  Load the shopper data
    mvarIDShopper = rsShopper("idshopper")
    mvarShipFirstName = rsShopper("chrShipFirstName")
    mvarShipLastName = rsShopper("chrShipLastName")
    mvarShipAddress = rsShopper("chrShipAddress")
    mvarShipCity = rsShopper("chrShipCity")
    mvarShipState = rsShopper("chrShipState")
    mvarShipZipCode = rsShopper("chrShipZipCode")
    mvarShipPhone = rsShopper("chrShipPhone")
    mvarShipEmail = rsShopper("chrShipEmail")
    mvarPassword = rsShopper("chrPassword")
    mvarBillFirstName = rsShopper("chrBillFirstName")
    mvarBillLastName = rsShopper("chrBillLastName")
    mvarBillAddress = rsShopper("chrBillAddress")
    mvarBillCity = rsShopper("chrBillCity")
    mvarBillState = rsShopper("chrBillState")
    mvarBillZipCode = rsShopper("chrBillZipCode")
    mvarBillPhone = rsShopper("chrBillPhone")
    mvarBillEmail = rsShopper("chrBillEmail")

    '  Indicate success
    LoadShopper = 1

Else

    '  Indicate no shopper was retrieved
    LoadShopper = 0

End If

End Function
```

Next we have all the properties for the shopper. To review, these were defined in Chapter 17 for both the class and the SQL database.

```
'   Billing email address
Public Property Let BillEmail(ByVal vData As String)
    mvarBillEmail = vData
End Property

Public Property Get BillEmail() As String
    BillEmail = mvarBillEmail
End Property

'   Billing phone number
Public Property Let BillPhone(ByVal vData As String)
    mvarBillPhone = vData
End Property

Public Property Get BillPhone() As String
    BillPhone = mvarBillPhone
End Property

'   Billing zip code
Public Property Let BillZipCode(ByVal vData As String)
    mvarBillZipCode = vData
End Property

Public Property Get BillZipCode() As String
    BillZipCode = mvarBillZipCode
End Property

'   Billing state
Public Property Let BillState(ByVal vData As String)
    mvarBillState = vData
End Property

Public Property Get BillState() As String
    BillState = mvarBillState
End Property

'   Billing city
Public Property Let BillCity(ByVal vData As String)
    mvarBillCity = vData
End Property

Public Property Get BillCity() As String
    BillCity = mvarBillCity
End Property
```

```
'  Billing address
Public Property Let BillAddress(ByVal vData As String)
    mvarBillAddress = vData
End Property

Public Property Get BillAddress() As String
    BillAddress = mvarBillAddress
End Property

'  Billing last name
Public Property Let BillLastName(ByVal vData As String)
    mvarBillLastName = vData
End Property

Public Property Get BillLastName() As String
    BillLastName = mvarBillLastName
End Property

'  Billing first name
Public Property Let BillFirstName(ByVal vData As String)
    mvarBillFirstName = vData
End Property

Public Property Get BillFirstName() As String
    BillFirstName = mvarBillFirstName
End Property

'  Shipping zip code
Public Property Let ShipZipCode(ByVal vData As String)
    mvarShipZipCode = vData
End Property

Public Property Get ShipZipCode() As String
    ShipZipCode = mvarShipZipCode
End Property

'  Shipping state
Public Property Let ShipState(ByVal vData As String)
    mvarShipState = vData
End Property
```

```
Public Property Get ShipState() As String
    ShipState = mvarShipState
End Property

'  shipping last name
Public Property Let ShipLastName(ByVal vData As String)
    mvarShipLastName = vData
End Property

Public Property Get ShipLastName() As String
    ShipLastName = mvarShipLastName
End Property

'  Shipping first name
Public Property Let ShipFirstName(ByVal vData As String)
    mvarShipFirstName = vData
End Property

Public Property Get ShipFirstName() As String
    ShipFirstName = mvarShipFirstName
End Property

'  Shipping city
Public Property Let ShipCity(ByVal vData As String)
    mvarShipCity = vData
End Property

Public Property Get ShipCity() As String
    ShipCity = mvarShipCity
End Property

'  Shipping address
Public Property Let ShipAddress(ByVal vData As String)
    mvarShipAddress = vData
End Property

Public Property Get ShipAddress() As String
    ShipAddress = mvarShipAddress
End Property
```

```
'   Shipping email address
Public Property Let ShipEmail(ByVal vData As String)
    mvarShipEmail = vData
End Property

Public Property Get ShipEmail() As String
    ShipEmail = mvarShipEmail
End Property

'   Shipping phone number
Public Property Let ShipPhone(ByVal vData As String)
    mvarShipPhone = vData
End Property

Public Property Get ShipPhone() As String
    ShipPhone = mvarShipPhone
End Property
```

When the class is initialized, the shopper is inserted into the database by calling the
SaveShopper method.

```
Private Sub Class_Initialize()

'   Save the shopper when the class is
'   initialized
SaveShopper

End Sub
```

The shopper table will represent the shopper-specific data in both the web class and
the database. The only shopper-specific data that is not stored directly in the shopper
table is the credit data. But, because of the volatility of that data, the decision on how
long to keep it, and privacy issues for credit data, the two should be separated.

That is it for the class code. Now we are ready to move to the "glue" of the
application—the web class.

Building the Web Class Code

The last step! We have our database defined, HTML prototype pages, object model,
and our classes built. Now let's put it all together in our web class.

In the general declarations section of the web class, we need to define several key global classes for our shopping basket system. We will have one product class, department class, and the shopper class.

For each new session of the web class, the shopper will be assigned a department that she or he is currently viewing, a shopping basket, and shopper data. Remember that the web class is set to persist state during the ASP session. So these classes will stay around while the shopper stays around.

```
'  Require all variables to be declared
Option Explicit
Option Compare Text

' Will hold the current product being worked with
Dim CurProduct As New clsProducts

'  Will hold the current basket being worked with
Dim CurBasket As New clsBasket

'  Will hold the department and products for the
'  current department being browsed
Dim CurDepartment As New clsDepartment

'  Will hold the current shopper data
Dim CurShopper As New clsShopper
```

The ValidateCredit function handles validating the credit data entered by the user. The function returns a true or false depending on the check. Each value in the request object is checked to see if the value meets the validation requirements.

Primarily, we are checking to ensure that the card name and card number fields are not empty. Also, we do a check to ensure the expiration date is not earlier than the current date.

If any of the validation requirements are not met, a string variable is set up to contain an error message. A check is then done to see if there were any errors. If there is an error, an error page is built on the fly to let the user click back to resubmit the data. If there is no error, the data is retrieved from the request variables.

Tip   *Much more extended validation could be done on the credit card data. For example, there are check sum functions that can be performed on the credit card number to ensure it meets the length and check sum requirements.*

INTERNET APPLICATION DEVELOPMENT

```vb
'  This function validates the data entered
'  into the credit screen
Private Function ValidateCredit() As Integer

'  Declare our variables
Dim strError As String

'  Check to ensure a card name was entered
If Request("CardName") = "" Then

    '  Build the error string
    strError = strError & "<li><i>You need to enter" & _
    " in the name on the credit card.<br></i>"

End If

'  Check to ensure a card number was entered
If Request("CardNumber") = "" Then

    '  Build the error string
    strError = strError & "<li><i>You need to enter " & _
    " a number for the card.<br></i>"

End If

'  Check to see if the year is the current year
If CInt(Request("CardYear")) = CInt(Year(Date)) Then
    '  Check to see if the month is less than
    '  the current month
    If CInt(Request("CardMonth")) < CInt(Month(Date)) Then

        '  Build the error string
        strError = strError & "<li><i>You need to enter " & _
        " a valid card date.<br></i>"

    End If

End If

'  Check to see if an error was set
If strError <> "" Then
```

```
'  Indicate the credit card did not validate
ValidateCredit = 0

'  Write out the page header
Response.Write "<HTML>"
Response.Write "<BODY BGCOLOR=""#ffff99"">"
Response.Write "<center><img src=""images/logo.bmp""></center>"

'  Start the list
Response.Write "<UL>"

'  Write out the error string
Response.Write strError
Response.Write "</UL>"

'  Build a link back to the credit page
Response.Write "Click <a href=""" & _
               URLFor(Credit) & _
               """>Here</a> to go to the credit" & _
               "form.<BR><BR><BR>"

'  Write out the navigation bar
Response.Write GetNavigation

'  Close the page
Response.Write "</body>"
Response.Write "</HTML>"

Else

    '  Retrieve the card name
    CurBasket.CardName = Request("CardName")

    '  Retrieve the card type (Amex, Visa, etc.)
    CurBasket.CardType = Request("CardType")

    '  Retrieve the card number
    CurBasket.CreditCardNumber = Request("CardNumber")

    '  Retrieve the expiration date which is a
    '  combination of the month and year
```

```
   CurBasket.ExpDate = Request("CardMonth") & "/" & Request("CardYear")

   '  Indicate the credit card was validated
   ValidateCredit = 1

End If

End Function
```

The ValidateAddress function handles validating the address data. In this case, we are simply checking to ensure data has been entered into each field. As with the credit card validation, we build an error string for each invalid field. The only extended checking being done is to ensure the state field is only two characters long.

Tip *You may want to ensure the password meets certain minimum requirements such as a minimum length and/or one or two non-numeric characters in addition to the alpha characters. Also, the email address could be validated to have an @ sign and an appropriate "dot" extension such as .com.*

Once the card data has been validated, we check to see if there are any error messages. If there are, then a custom error page is built to indicate the user needs to review the checkout data. If the data is valid, the function returns a true for success.

```
'  Validate the address data entered
Private Function ValidateAddress() As Integer

'  Declare our variables
Dim strError As String

' Check to ensure a shipping first name
' was entered
If Request("ShipFirstName") = "" Then

    '  Build the error string
    strError = strError & "<li><i>You need to enter " & _
    "a shipping first name.<br></i>"

End If

'  Check to ensure a shipping last name
'  was entered
If Request("ShipLastName") = "" Then
```

```
    '  Build the error string
    strError = strError & "<li><i>You need to enter " & _
    "a shipping last name.<br></i>"

End If

'  Check to ensure a shipping address
'  was entered
If Request("ShipAddress") = "" Then

    '  Build the error string
    strError = strError & "<li><i>You need to enter a " & _
    "shipping address.<br></i>"

End If

'  Check to ensure a shipping city
'  was entered
If Request("ShipCity") = "" Then

    '  Build the error string
    strError = strError & "<li><i>You need to enter a " & _
    "shipping first name.<br></i>"

End If

'  Check to ensure a shipping state
'  was entered
If Request("ShipState") = "" Then

    '  Check to ensure the length is not
    '  greater than 2
    If Len(Request("ShipState")) > 2 Then

        '  Build the error string
        strError = strError & "<li><i>You need to enter a " & _
        "valid shipping state.<br></i>"

    Else
```

```
        '  Build the error string
        strError = strError & "<li><i>You need to enter a " & _
        "shipping state.<br></i>"

    End If

End If

'  Check to ensure a shipping zip code
'  was entered
If Request("ShipZipCode") = "" Then

    '  Build the error string
    strError = strError & "<li><i>You need to enter a " & _
    "shipping zip code.<br></i>"

End If

'  Check to ensure a shipping phone number
'  was entered
If Request("ShipPhone") = "" Then

    '  Build the error string
    strError = strError & "<li><i>You need to enter a " & _
    "shipping phone number.<br></i>"

End If

'  Check to ensure a shipping email address
'  was entered
If Request("ShipEmail") = "" Then

    '  Build the error string
    strError = strError & "<li><i>You need to enter a " & _
    "shipping email address.<br></i>"

End If

'  Check to see if the user wants to copy
'  the shipping information to the billing
'  information
```

```
If Request("BillAddress") <> 1 Then

    ' Check to ensure a billing first name
    ' was entered
    If Request("BillFirstName") = "" Then

        ' Build the error string
        strError = strError & "<li><i>You need to enter a " & _
        "billing first name.<br></i>"

    End If

    ' Check to ensure a billing last name
    ' was entered
    If Request("BillLastName") = "" Then

        ' Build the error string
        strError = strError & "<li><i>You need to enter a " & _
        "billing last name.<br></i>"

    End If

    ' Check to ensure a billing address
    ' was entered
    If Request("BillAddress") = "" Then

        ' Build the error string
        strError = strError & "<li><i>You need to enter a " & _
        "billing address.<br></i>"

    End If

    ' Check to ensure a billing city
    ' was entered
    If Request("BillCity") = "" Then

        ' Build the error string
        strError = strError & "<li><i>You need to enter a " & _
        "billing first name.<br></i>"

    End If
```

```
'  Check to ensure a billing state
'  was entered
If Request("BillState") = "" Then

      '  Check to ensure the state length is
      '  not greater than two
      If Len(Request("BillState")) > 2 Then

            '  Build the error string
            strError = strError & "<li><i>You need to enter a " & _
            "valid billing state.<br></i>"

      Else

            '  Build the error string
            strError = strError & "<li><i>You need to enter a " & _
            "billing state.<br></i>"

      End If

End If

'  Check to ensure a billing zip code
'  was entered
If Request("BillZipCode") = "" Then

      '  Build the error string
      strError = strError & "<li><i>You need to enter a " & _
      "billing zip code.<br></i>"

End If

'  Check to ensure a billing phone number
'  was entered
If Request("BillPhone") = "" Then

      '  Build the error string
      strError = strError & "<li><i>You need to enter a " & _
      "billing phone number.<br></i>"
```

```
      End If

   '  Check to ensure a billing email address
   '  was entered
   If Request("BillEmail") = "" Then
       '  Build the error string
       strError = strError & "<li><i>You need to enter a " & _
       "billing email address.<br></i>"

   End If

End If

'  Check to see if an error was set
If strError <> "" Then

   '  Indicate that the address data is not
   '  valid
   ValidateAddress = 0

   '  Write out the page header
   Response.Write "<HTML>"
   Response.Write "<BODY BGCOLOR=""#ffff99"">"
   Response.Write "<center><img src=""images/logo.bmp""></center>"

   '  Start the error list
   Response.Write "<UL>"

   '  Write out the error messages
   Response.Write strError
   Response.Write "</UL>"

   '  Build a link back to the checkout page
   Response.Write "Click <a href=""" & _
               . URLFor(CheckOut) & _
               """>Here</a> to go to the " & _
               "checkout form.<BR>"

   '  Write out the navigation block
   Response.Write GetNavigation
```

```
'   Close the page
    Response.Write "</body>"
    Response.Write "</HTML>"

Else

'   Indicate the address data is valid
    ValidateAddress = 1

End If

End Function
```

The GetNavigation function will build the navigation block for our Web pages. The URLFor method is used to create links to the department, basket, checkout, and get shopper template pages. The HTML text is returned from the function.

The navigation bar for our shopping system is fairly straightforward. But there are many possibilities to provide context-sensitive navigation bars. For example, you may not want to show the navigation link to a page that is currently showing. For example, if the shopper is on the get shopper template page, you might not want to show the navigation link to it—or at least not have the link active, just the text.

```
'   Returns the navigation block for the
'   shopping basket system
Private Function GetNavigation() As String

'   Write out a horizontal divider line
GetNavigation = "<hr>"

'   Build a link to the Department page
GetNavigation = GetNavigation & "<a href=""" & _
                URLFor(Department) & _
                """>Departments</a> | "

'   Build a link to the GetShopper page
GetNavigation = GetNavigation & "<a href=""" & _
                URLFor(GetShopper) & _
                """>Lookup Shopper</a> | "
```

```
'  Build a link to the Basket page
GetNavigation = GetNavigation & "<a href=""" & _
               URLFor(Basket) & _
               """>Basket</a> | "

'  Build a link to the checkout page
GetNavigation = GetNavigation & "<a href=""" & _
               URLFor(CheckOut) & _
               """>Check Out</a>"

End Function
```

The GetDepartments function will retrieve a list of the departments from the system and build an HTML href list to each department. This is where the Meta ListDepartments function of the department class comes into play. We create a temporary department class and call the function. A collection of departments is returned. That collection is then looped through and the HTML links are built to the department. The URLFor method is used to build a custom event to the ProductList template page. The ID of the department is passed in as the custom event name.

```
'  Retrieves the departments in the system
Private Function GetDepartments() As String

'  Declare our variables
Dim Dept As clsDepartment
Dim DeptCol As Collection

'  Get the collection of departments by calling
'  the ListDepartments meta function of the
'  clsDepartments class
Set DeptCol = CurDepartment.ListDepartments

'  Start out the list
GetDepartments = "<ul>"

'  Loop through the departments
For Each Dept In DeptCol
```

INTERNET APPLICATION DEVELOPMENT

```
'   Build a link to the product list page.
'   We will pass into the userevent for
'   the product list page the ID of
'   the department
GetDepartments = GetDepartments & "<li><a href=""" & _
                    URLFor(ProductList, CStr(Dept.idDepartment)) & _
                    """>" & Dept.Description & "</a>"

Next


'   Close the list
GetDepartments = GetDepartments & "</ul>"


End Function
```

The Hyperlink1 event of the basket page manages linking to the checkout page. When the hyperlink is clicked, the next item for the web class is set to the checkout page.

```
'   The checkout hyperlink on the
'   basket page
Private Sub Basket_Hyperlink1()

'   Go to the checkout page
Set NextItem = CheckOut

End Sub
```

The Hyperlink2 event for the basket page will clear the basket of all current items. The ClearBasket method of the current shopping basket is called to delete the items from the basket. Once that is done, the user is returned to the basket, which will then indicate that there are no items in the basket.

```
'   The clear basket hyperlink on the
'   basket page
Private Sub Basket_Hyperlink2()

'   Call the clear basket method of the
'   current clsBasket class
CurBasket.ClearBasket
```

```
'  Go back to the basket
Set NextItem = Basket

End Sub
```

The ProcessTag custom event for the basket page will process all custom tags on the basket template. We have two custom web tags on the page. The first processes the basket items.

The collection of basket items in the basket is looped through to display the product code, product name, product price, quantity, and delete link. For the product price, a check is done to see if the product is on sale. If it is, the price is shown in red text to indicate a sale.

For the quantity, a text-input element is created with the value being the current quantity. Finally, the delete hyperlink will call the custom event for the basket page. The ID of the basket item is passed in as the event name.

```
'  Process the custom tags for the Basket template page
Private Sub Basket_ProcessTag(ByVal TagName As String, TagContents As _
String, SendTags As Boolean)

'  Declare our Variables
Dim intCnt As Integer

'  Process each tag name
Select Case TagName

    '  The basket items tag
    Case "wc@BASKETITEMS"
        '  Loop through the items in the basket
        For intCnt = 1 To CurBasket.Count

            '  Show the Product Code
            TagContents = TagContents & "<tr><td align=""center"">" & _
                    CurBasket.Item(intCnt).idProduct & "</td>"

            '  Show the Product Name
            TagContents = TagContents & "<td>" & _
                    CurBasket.Item(intCnt).ProductName & "</td>"
```

```
                        '  Check to see if the product is on sale
                    If CurBasket.Item(intCnt).OnSale = 1 Then

                            '  Product Price
                        TagContents = TagContents & "<td><font color=""red"">" & _

                                    FormatCurrency(CurBasket.Item(intCnt).Price, 2) & _
                                    "</font></td>"

                    Else

                            '  Sale Price
                        TagContents = TagContents & "<td>" & _
                                    FormatCurrency(CurBasket.Item(intCnt).Price, 2) & _
                                    "</td>"

                    End If

                    '  Build a quantity input box with the current
                    '  quantity displayed
                    TagContents = TagContents & _
                                "<td align=""center""><input type=""Text"" value=""" & _
                                CurBasket.Item(intCnt).Quantity & _
                                """ name=""quantity"" size=5></td>"

                    '  Create a custom delete URL to indicate which
                    '  item should be deleted from the basket.
                    '  The ID of the basket item will be passed to
                    '  the user event
                    TagContents = TagContents & "<td><a href=" & Chr(34) & _
                                URLFor(Basket,_
                                CStr(CurBasket.Item(intCnt).idBasketItem)) & Chr(34) & _
                                ">Delete</a></td></tr>"

                '  Move to the next item
                Next
            '  Build the navigation bar
        Case "wc@NAVIGATION"
                '  Call the GetNavigation method to display
                '  the navigation bar
            TagContents = GetNavigation

    End Select

End Sub
```

The Respond event of the basket page will check to see if there are any items in the basket. If there are no items in the basket, we build a custom page on the fly to indicate there are no items in the basket. If there are items in the basket, the basket page is written out to the browser.

```
'  Respond event of the basket page
Private Sub Basket_Respond()

'  Check to see if there are any items in the basket
If CurBasket.Count = 0 Then

    '  Display the page header
    Response.Write "<HTML>"
    Response.Write "<BODY BGCOLOR=""#ffff99"">"
    Response.Write "<center><img src=""images/logo.bmp""></center>"

    '  Indicate no items are in the basket and build
    '  a link to the department page
    Response.Write "<BR><BR><BR><BR>There are no items in your basket. " & _
                   "Click <a href=""" & _
                   URLFor(Department) & _
                   """>Here</a> to continue shopping.<BR><BR><BR>"

    '  Build the navigation bar
    Response.Write GetNavigation

    '  Close the page
    Response.Write "</body>"
    Response.Write "</HTML>"

Else

    '  Write out the shopping basket
    Basket.WriteTemplate

End If

End Sub
```

The UpdateBasket custom event handles updating the quantities of the items in the basket. The UpdateQuantity method of the basket is called. The quantity request value is passed into the function. Once the update is done, the basket template is set as the next item for the web class.

```
'  Update Basket form submission event
Private Sub Basket_UpdateBasket()

'  Update the quantities on the items in
'  the basket by calling the UpdateQuantity
'  method of the basket class and passing in
'  the array (comma delimited) of quantities
CurBasket.UpdateQuantity Request("quantity")

'  Return to the basket
Set NextItem = Basket

End Sub
```

The User event of the basket handles the delete functionality. The ID of the basket item is passed in as the event name argument. The Remove method of the basket class is called to remove the item from the basket, which also deletes the item from the database. Then the basket is set as the next item for the web class.

```
'  User event of the basket. Only called when an
'  item is going to be deleted
Private Sub Basket_UserEvent(ByVal EventName As String)

'  Call the remove function of the basket class
'  and pass in the ID of the item to be removed
CurBasket.Remove CInt(EventName)

'  Return to the basket
Set NextItem = Basket

End Sub
```

The CheckOut event of the checkout template page handles the processing of the shopper data the user entered. The ValidateAddress function is called to review the address data. If the result is positive, the shopper data is read into the current shopper class.

A check is done to see if the user selected the Billing Same as Shipping option. If the option is checked, the billing address data is set the same as the shipping data. Finally, the shopper data is saved, and the next web class item is set to the credit page.

```
'  Checkout form submission of the
'  Checkout page
Private Sub CheckOut_CheckOut()
```

```
'  Declare our variables
Dim intSuccess As Integer

'  Validate the address data
intSuccess = ValidateAddress

'  If the data was validated
If intSuccess = 1 Then

    '  Set the Shopper properties to the data
    '   in the form
    CurShopper.ShipAddress = Request("ShipAddress")
    CurShopper.ShipCity = Request("ShipCity")
    CurShopper.ShipEmail = Request("ShipEmail")
    CurShopper.ShipFirstName = Request("ShipFirstName")
    CurShopper.ShipLastName = Request("ShipLastName")
    CurShopper.ShipPhone = Request("ShipPhone")
    CurShopper.ShipState = Request("ShipState")
    CurShopper.ShipZipCode = Request("ShipZipCode")
    CurShopper.Password = Request("Password")

    '  Check to see if the billing data is the same
    '  as the shipping data
    If Request("BillAddress") = 1 Then

        '  Set the billing data to be the same as
        '   the shipping data
        CurShopper.BillAddress = CurShopper.ShipAddress
        CurShopper.BillCity = CurShopper.ShipCity
        CurShopper.BillEmail = CurShopper.ShipEmail
        CurShopper.BillFirstName = CurShopper.ShipFirstName
        CurShopper.BillLastName = CurShopper.ShipLastName
        CurShopper.BillPhone = CurShopper.ShipPhone
        CurShopper.BillState = CurShopper.ShipState
        CurShopper.BillZipCode = CurShopper.ShipZipCode

    Else

        '  Retrieve the billing data from the form
        '  data
        CurShopper.BillAddress = Request("BillAddress")
```

```
         CurShopper.BillCity = Request("BillCity")
         CurShopper.BillEmail = Request("BillEmail")
         CurShopper.BillFirstName = Request("BillFirstName")
         CurShopper.BillLastName = Request("BillLastName")
         CurShopper.BillPhone = Request("BillPhone")
         CurShopper.BillState = Request("BillState")
         CurShopper.BillZipCode = Request("BillZipCode")

      End If

      '  Save the shopper to the database
   CurShopper.SaveShopper

      '  Set the basket idShopper property
      '  to be the ID of the shopper
   CurBasket.idShopper = CurShopper.idShopper

      '  Set the shipping state in the basket so
      '  we can calculate tax appropriately
   CurBasket.ShipState = CurShopper.ShipState

      '  Go to the Credit page
   Set NextItem = Credit

   End If

End Sub
```

On the checkout page, we have a lot of tags to process—one for each of the inputs for the shopper data. The key is reading the current values from the shopper class and setting the default values for the text-input elements. That way, the user does not have to retype data if he or she filled it out once, decided to continue shopping, then returned.

```
'  Process the tags on the checkout page
Private Sub CheckOut_ProcessTag(ByVal TagName As String, _
TagContents As String, SendTags As Boolean)

'  Process by tag name
Select Case TagName
```

```
'  Ship to first name
Case "wc@SHIPTOFIRSTNAME"
    '  Build an input element and display the
    '  shopper shipping first name if there is one
    TagContents = "<input type=""text"" value=""" & _
                CurShopper.ShipFirstName & _
                """ name=""ShipFirstName"">"

'  Build an input element and display the
'  shopper shipping last name if there is one
Case "wc@SHIPTOLASTNAME"
    TagContents = "<input type=""text"" value=""" & _
                CurShopper.ShipLastName & _
                """ name=""ShipLastName"">"

'  Build an input element and display the
'  shopper shipping address if there is one
Case "wc@SHIPTOADDRESS"
    TagContents = "<input type=""text"" value=""" & _
                CurShopper.ShipAddress & _
                """ name=""ShipAddress"">"

'  Build an input element and display the
'  shopper shipping city if there is one
Case "wc@SHIPTOCITY"
    TagContents = "<input type=""text"" value=""" & _
                CurShopper.ShipCity & _
                """ name=""ShipCity"">"

'  Build an input element and display the
'  shopper shipping state if there is one
Case "wc@SHIPTOSTATE"
    TagContents = "<input type=""text"" value=""" & _
                CurShopper.ShipState & _
                """ name=""ShipState"" size=2>"

'  Build an input element and display the
'  shopper shipping zip code if there is one
Case "wc@SHIPTOZIPCODE"
    TagContents = "<input type=""text"" value=""" & _
                CurShopper.ShipZipCode & _
                """ name=""ShipZipCode"">"
```

```
'  Build an input element and display the
'  shopper shipping phone if there is one
Case "wc@SHIPTOPHONE"
     TagContents = "<input type=""text"" value=""" & _
                   CurShopper.ShipPhone & _
                   """ name=""ShipPhone"">"


'  Build an input element and display the
'  shopper first name if there is one
Case "wc@SHIPTOEMAIL"
     TagContents = "<input type=""text"" value=""" & _
                   CurShopper.ShipEmail & _
                   """ name=""ShipEmail"">"


'  Build an input element and display the
'  shopper password if there is one
Case "wc@PASSWORD"
     TagContents = "<input type=""password"" value=""" & _
                   CurShopper.Password & _
                   """ name=""Password"">"


'  Build an input element and display the
'  shopper billing first name if there is one
Case "wc@BILLTOFIRSTNAME"
     TagContents = "<input type=""text"" value=""" & _
                   CurShopper.BillFirstName & _
                   """ name=""BillFirstName"">"


'  Build an input element and display the
'  shopper billing last name if there is one
Case "wc@BILLTOLASTNAME"
     TagContents = "<input type=""text"" value=""" & _
                   CurShopper.BillLastName & _
                   """ name=""BillLastName"">"


'  Build an input element and display the
'  shopper billing address if there is one
Case "wc@BILLTOADDRESS"
     TagContents = "<input type=""text"" value=""" & _
                   CurShopper.BillAddress & _
                   """ name=""BillAddress"">"
```

```
'  Build an input element and display the
'  shopper billing city if there is one
Case "wc@BILLTOCITY"
    TagContents = "<input type=""text"" value=""" & _
                CurShopper.BillCity & _
                """ name=""BillCity"">"


    '  Build an input element and display the
    '  shopper billing state if there is one
Case "wc@BILLTOSTATE"
    TagContents = "<input type=""text"" value=""" & _
                CurShopper.BillState & _
                """ name=""BillState"" size=2>"

'  Build an input element and display the
'  shopper billing zip code if there is one
Case "wc@BILLTOZIPCODE"
    TagContents = "<input type=""text"" value=""" & _
                CurShopper.BillZipCode & _
                """ name=""BillZipCode"">"

'  Build an input element and display the
'  shopper billing phone if there is one
Case "wc@BILLTOPHONE"
    TagContents = "<input type=""text"" value=""" & _
                CurShopper.BillPhone & _
                """ name=""BillPhone"">"

'  Build an input element and display the
'  shopper billing email address if there is one
Case "wc@BILLTOEMAIL"
    TagContents = "<input type=""text"" value=""" & _
                CurShopper.BillEmail & _
                """ name=""BillEmail"">"

'  Process the navigation bar request
Case "wc@NAVIGATION"
    '  Get the Navigation bar HTML
    TagContents = GetNavigation
```

```
End Select

End Sub
```

The Respond event of the checkout page does a check to see if any items have been added to the basket. The user cannot be allowed to check out if there are no items in the basket. If there are not any, a page is built on the fly to indicate the user has an empty basket. Otherwise, the checkout page is written to the browser.

```
'  Respond event of the checkout page
Private Sub CheckOut_Respond()

'  Check to see if there are any items in
'  the basket. We cannot check out if there
'  is nothing to purchase
If CurBasket.Count = 0 Then

    '  Build the page header
    Response.Write "<HTML>"
    Response.Write "<BODY BGCOLOR=""#ffff99"">"
    Response.Write "<center><img src=""images/logo.bmp""></center>"

    '  Indicate there are no items in the basket
    '  and build a link for the user to the department
    '  page
    Response.Write "<BR><BR><BR><BR>There are no" & _
            "items in your basket. " & _
            "Click <a href=""" & _
            URLFor(Department) & _
            """>Here</a> to continue shopping.<BR><BR><BR>"

    '  Display the navigation bar
    Response.Write GetNavigation

    '  Close the page
    Response.Write "</body>"
    Response.Write "</HTML>"

Else
```

```
  '   Write out the checkout page
     CheckOut.WriteTemplate

End If

End Sub
```

The Credit event of the credit template page calls the ValidateCredit function. If the credit data is valid, the basket credit fields are set to the request values for the form.

Once the data is validated, we need to save the credit data to complete the order. Following that, the confirmation page is created on the fly, and the order number that was returned from the SQL database is shown. Once the basket is complete, we delete the current basket to ensure the user cannot start shopping all over again on a new basket.

```
Private Sub Credit_Credit()

'  Declare our variables
Dim intSuccess As Integer

'  Validate the credit card data
intSuccess = ValidateCredit

'  Check to see if the data is valid
If intSuccess = 1 Then

    '   Get the card name, type, number
    '   and expiration date
    CurBasket.CardName = Request("CardName")
    CurBasket.CardType = Request("CardType")
    CurBasket.CreditCardNumber = Request("CardNumber")
    CurBasket.ExpDate = Request("CardMonth") & "/" & _
    Request("CardYear")

    '   Save the credit card data
    CurBasket.SaveCreditData

    '   Write out the page header
    Response.Write "<HTML>"
    Response.Write "<BODY BGCOLOR=""#ffff99"">"
    Response.Write "<center><img src=""images/logo.bmp""></center>"
```

```
'   Display the confirmation order number
Response.Write "<BR><BR><BR><BR>Your confirmation number" & _
               "is <b>" & _
               "<font color=""red"">" & _
               CurBasket.idOrder & _
               "</font></b>"

'   Build a link to continue shopping
Response.Write "<BR><BR>Click <a href=""" & _
               URLFor(Department) & _
               """>Here</a> to continue shopping.<BR><BR><BR>"

'   Show the navigation bar
Response.Write GetNavigation

'   Close the page
Response.Write "</body>"
Response.Write "</HTML>"

'   Delete the current basket to ensure
'   the user can't purchase the same
'   basket again
Set CurBasket = Nothing

End If

End Sub
```

The ProcessTag event of the credit page handles displaying the basket subtotal, shipping, tax, and basket total. A table is built to display the data in a structured format. Note that the FormatCurrency function is used to format the amounts returned from the server.

```
'   Process the tags on the credit card page
Private Sub Credit_ProcessTag(ByVal TagName As String, TagContents _
As String, SendTags As Boolean)

'   Process by tag name
Select Case TagName
```

```
    '  Build the subtotal, tax, shipping and total
    Case "wc@SHOWTOTAL"
        '  Start the table
        TagContents = "<table cellpadding=3 cellspacing=3>"

        '  Display the subtotal
        TagContents = TagContents & "<tr><td align=""right"">SubTotal:</td>" & _
                      "<td>" & FormatCurrency(CurBasket.SubTotal, 2) & _
                      "</td></tr>"

        '  Display the Shipping amount
        TagContents = TagContents & "<tr><td align=""right"">Shipping:" & _
                      "</td>>" & _
                      "<td>" & FormatCurrency(CurBasket.Shipping, 2) & _
                      "</td></tr>"

        '  Display the tax amount
        TagContents = TagContents & "<tr><td align=""right"">Tax:</td><td>" & _
                      FormatCurrency(CurBasket.Tax, 2) & _
                      "</td></tr>"

        '  Display the total
        TagContents = TagContents & "<tr><td align=""right""><b>" & _
                      "<font size=""4"">Total:</b></font></td>>" & _
                      "<td><b><font size=""4"">" & _
                      FormatCurrency(CurBasket.Total, 2) & _
                      "</font></b></td></tr>"

        '  End the table
        TagContents = TagContents & "</table>"

    '  Process the navigation request
    Case "wc@NAVIGATION"
        '  Retrieve the Navigation bar
        TagContents = GetNavigation

End Select

End Sub
```

The Respond event of the credit page ensures that there are items in the basket. The user cannot complete the order process if there are no orders in the basket. This is important because many users will click the browser's Back button once they have completed the order. If they do, and the credit page comes back up requesting data, that may cause confusion.

```
'  Respond event of the credit card page
Private Sub Credit_Respond()

'  Check to see if there are any items in
'  the basket
If CurBasket.Count = 0 Then

    '  Build the page header
    Response.Write "<HTML>"
    Response.Write "<BODY BGCOLOR=""#ffff99"">"
    Response.Write "<center><img src=""images/logo.bmp""></center>"

    '  Indicate that no items are in the basket and
    '  build a link to the department page
    Response.Write "<BR><BR><BR><BR>There are no items in your basket. " & _
                "Click <a href=""" & _
                URLFor(Department) & _
                """>Here</a> to continue shopping.<BR><BR><BR>"

    '  Display the navigation bar
    Response.Write GetNavigation

    '  Close the page
    Response.Write "</body>"
    Response.Write "</HTML>"

Else

    '  Write out the page
    Credit.WriteTemplate

End If

End Sub
```

The ProcessTag event of the department page handles writing out the department listing. The GetDepartments function is called to build the HTML for the department list.

```
'  Process the tags for the department page
Private Sub Department_ProcessTag(ByVal TagName As String, TagContents As _
String, SendTags As Boolean)

'  Process by tag name
Select Case TagName

    '  List the departments
    Case "wc@DEPARTMENTLIST"
```

```
      '  Get the Department listing
      TagContents = GetDepartments

   '  Process the navigation request
   Case "wc@NAVIGATION"
      '  Display the navigation bar
      TagContents = GetNavigation

End Select

End Sub
```

The Respond event of the page handles writing out the template to the browser.

```
'  Respond event of the department page
Private Sub Department_Respond()

'  Write out the page
Department.WriteTemplate

End Sub
```

The GetShopper method of the get shopper template page will retrieve the email address and password entered and pass them into the LoadShopper method of the current shopper class. The method returns a true or false.

If the return is false, we write out a page on the fly indicating that the shopper data could not be found. If the return is true, the shopper's first and last names are written to a page that indicates the record was found.

Tip *One thing to consider doing is providing a way for the password to be emailed to users based on the email address they enter. That way, if they forget, they can still have it sent to them.*

```
'  The GetShopper form submission event
Private Sub GetShopper_GetShopper()

'  Declare our variables
Dim intSuccess As Integer

'  Load the shopper from the database
intSuccess = CurShopper.LoadShopper(Request("chrBillEmail"), _
                          Request("chrPassword"))
```

```
' Check to see if a shopper was successfully loaded
If intSuccess = 0 Then

    ' Build the page header
    Response.Write "<HTML>"
    Response.Write "<BODY BGCOLOR=""#ffff99"">"
    Response.Write "<center><img src=""images/logo.bmp""></center>"

    ' Indicate the shopper data could not be found
    Response.Write "<BR><BR><BR><BR>Your shopper data could not be found."

    ' Build a link back to the get shopper page
    Response.Write "<BR><BR>Click <a href=""" & _
                URLFor(GetShopper) & _
                """>Here</a> to try again.<BR><BR><BR>"

    ' Get the navigation bar
    Response.Write GetNavigation

    ' Close the page
    Response.Write "</body>"
    Response.Write "</HTML>"

Else

    ' Build the page header
    Response.Write "<HTML>"
    Response.Write "<BODY BGCOLOR=""#ffff99"">"
    Response.Write "<center><img src=""images/logo.bmp""></center>"

    ' Indicate the shopper was found. Display the
    ' user's first and last names
    Response.Write "<BR><BR><BR><BR>Thank you " & _
                CurShopper.BillFirstName & " " & _
            CurShopper.BillLastName & _
            ". Your shopper data has been retrieved."

    ' Build a link to the department page
    Response.Write "<BR><BR>Click <a href=""" & _
                URLFor(Department) & _
                """>Here</a> to continue shopping.<BR><BR><BR>"

    ' Display the navigation bar
    Response.Write GetNavigation
```

```
       '  Close the page
       Response.Write "</body>"
       Response.Write "</HTML>"

End If

End Sub
```

The ProcessTag event of the get shopper template handles writing out the navigation bar to the page.

```
'  Process the tags on the get shopper page
Private Sub GetShopper_ProcessTag(ByVal TagName As String, _
TagContents As String, SendTags As Boolean)

'  Process by tag name
Select Case TagName

    '  Process the navigation bar request
    Case "wc@NAVIGATION"
        '  Get the navigation bar
       TagContents = GetNavigation

End Select

End Sub
```

The Respond event of the get shopper page writes the page out to the browser.

```
'  Respond event of the get shopper page
Private Sub GetShopper_Respond()

'  Write out the page
GetShopper.WriteTemplate

End Sub
```

The AddToBasket method of the product template handles adding the current product to the shopping basket. A check is done to see if the product is on sale. If so, then we want to place the sale price rather than the regular price in the basket.

The Add event of the basket is called with all the appropriate data for the basket item sent into it. That will add the item to the basket. Once that is done, the user is sent to the basket page.

```vb
'  Add to basket event of the product page
Private Sub Product_AddToBasket()

'  Declare our variables
Dim dblPrice As Double
Dim intSaleFlag As Integer

'  Check to see if the product is on sale or not
If Date >= CurProduct.SaleStart And Date <= CurProduct.SaleEnd Then

    '  Get the sale price
    dblPrice = CurProduct.SalePrice

    '  Indicate the product is on sale
    intSaleFlag = 1

Else

    '  Get the standard price
    dblPrice = CurProduct.Price

    '  Indicate the product is not on sale
    intSaleFlag = 0

End If

'  Add the item to the basket
CurBasket.Add Request("quantity"), _
        CurProduct.idProduct, _
        dblPrice, _
        CurProduct.ProductName, _
        intSaleFlag

'  Go to the basket
Set NextItem = Basket

End Sub
```

The ProcessTag event of the product page will display all the different product data values. If the product is on sale, the product price is shown in red. Note, for the product image, a complete image tag is set up so the graphic will be displayed.

```
'  Process tag event of the product page
Private Sub Product_ProcessTag(ByVal TagName As String, TagContents As _
String, SendTags As Boolean)

'  Process by tag name
Select Case TagName

    '  Product name
    Case "wc@PRODUCTNAME"
        '  Display the product name
        TagContents = "<b>" & CurProduct.ProductName & "</b>"

    '  Product description
    Case "wc@PRODUCTDESC"
        '  Show the product description
        TagContents = CurProduct.Description

    '  Product price
    Case "wc@PRODUCTPRICE"
        ' Check to see if the product is on sale
        If Date >= CurProduct.SaleStart And Date <= CurProduct.SaleEnd Then

            '  Display the sale price in red
            TagContents = "<font color=""red"">Sale Price: " & _
                        FormatCurrency(CurProduct.SalePrice, 2) & _
                        "</font>"

        Else

            '  Display the standard price
            TagContents = "Price: " & _
                        FormatCurrency(CurProduct.Price, 2)

        End If

    '  Process the image request
    Case "wc@IMAGE"
        '  Build the image display tags
        TagContents = "<center><img src=""images/" & _
                    CurProduct.ProductImage & _
                    """></center>"
```

```
    ' Process the navigation request
    Case "wc@NAVIGATION"
        ' Display the navigation bar
        TagContents = GetNavigation

End Select

End Sub
```

The UserEvent of the product page is called to display a specific product. The ProductList page makes a link to the product page with the ID of the product passed in. The CurProduct global class is set to the selected product for reference.

```
' User event of the product page
' The event name is the id of the
' product
Private Sub Product_UserEvent(ByVal EventName As String)

    ' Set up our global product class to be
    ' the product selected. We will index
    ' into the collection of products for
    ' the current department
    Set CurProduct = CurDepartment.Item(EventName)

    ' Write out the page
    Product.WriteTemplate

End Sub
```

The ProcessTag event for the product list handles showing the product list for the current department. The department name and the product list are displayed.

For the product list, the collection of products for the current department is processed with a URL built for each product. The product URL will call the user event of the product page. The ID of the product will be passed in.

```
' Process tags for the Product List page
Private Sub ProductList_ProcessTag(ByVal TagName As String, TagContents As _
String, SendTags As Boolean)

    ' Declare our variables
    Dim intCnt As Integer
```

```
'  Process by tag name
Select Case TagName

    '  Department tag
    Case "wc@DEPARTMENTNAME"
        '  Display the current department
        TagName = "<b>" & CurDepartment.Description & "</b>"

    '  Product listing
    Case "wc@PRODUCTLIST"
        '  Start out the list
        TagContents = "<UL>"

        '  Loop through the products in the department
        For intCnt = 1 To CurDepartment.Count

            '  Build a listing of products. Build a link for
            '  each one to the product page by passing into the
            '  userevent the ID of the product
            TagContents = TagContents & "<li><a href=""" & _
                          URLFor(Product, _
                          CStr(CurDepartment.Item(intCnt).idProduct)) & _
                          """>" & _
                          CurDepartment.Item(intCnt).ProductName & _
                          "</a>"

        '  Loop back
        Next

        '  Close the list
        TagContents = TagContents & "</ul>"

    '  Process the navigation bar request
    Case "wc@NAVIGATION"
        '  Get the navigation bar
        TagContents = GetNavigation

End Select

End Sub
```

The Respond event of the product list page will write out the template to the browser.

```
'  Respond event of the product list page
Private Sub ProductList_Respond()

'  Write out the page
ProductList.WriteTemplate

End Sub
```

The UserEvent of the product list page will retrieve the ID of the department selected. The current global department will be deleted and a new one created for the new department. The ID of the department will be set, and the LoadProducts method of the department class is called to build the product collection for the department. Then the product list page is displayed.

```
'  User event of the product list page. The
'  event name is the department id
Private Sub ProductList_UserEvent(ByVal EventName As String)

'  Delete the current department
Set CurDepartment = Nothing

'  Create a new department
Set CurDepartment = New clsDepartment

'  Set the ID of the department to the
'  ID passed in
CurDepartment.idDepartment = CInt(EventName)

'  Load the products for the department
CurDepartment.LoadProducts

'  Write out the product list page
Set NextItem = ProductList

End Sub
```

When the web class starts up, the department page is displayed.

```
'  Start event of the web class
Private Sub WebClass_Start()
```

```
'  Go to the department page
Set NextItem = Department

End Sub
```

There is a lot of glue in the classes and the web class. But you can see how a well-defined object model and database structure provide an elegant way of managing the shopping basket environment. The IIS application capabilities provide a fluid and flexible environment for mixing the static HTML code with the interactive data-driven HTML coding. Now, let's run through the interface!

Shop Until You Drop!

The best way to cruise our shopping system is to start at the beginning and work through, page by page. Figure 18-1 shows the department page. In the figure, there are two departments listed.

 Don't forget to load your database with some test product data.

Figure 18-2 shows the product listing for the infamous Thingama Jigger product line. You have a choice of round, square, and triangle types. I would highly recommend that you select the Round Thingama Jigger (RTJ) … they make your life easier.

Figure 18-3 shows the product data. Note the product image and the rest of the product data. There is a text-input element for purchasing multiple RTJs. To order the product, click on the Submit button. Now go back to the product list page and select a product that is on sale. When you do, the product price will be in red. Figure 18-4 shows a product, Red Widgets, that is on sale.

Now let's click on the Basket hyperlink on the navigation bar. We will have our RTJ in the basket. Figure 18-5 shows the shopping basket. Note the product code, price, and quantity inputs, and the delete link to remove the item from the basket.

Figure 18-6 shows the basket with the red widget that is on sale. Note that the price is shown in red to indicate the item is on sale. You can continue to add items to the basket. One thing not implemented in the basket is the ability to aggregate multiple entries of the same product. In other words, if we added another red widget to the basket, we would have two entries. While this does nothing to hurt the system, it may be confusing for the user.

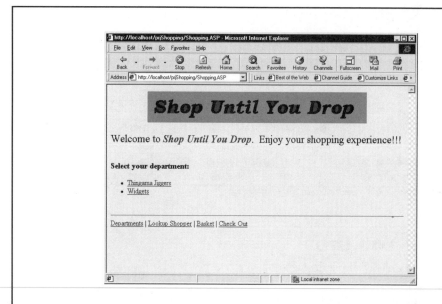

Figure 18-1. *Department page*

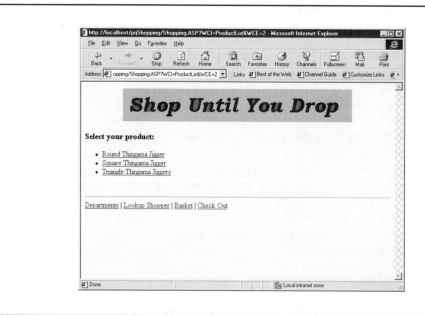

Figure 18-2. *Product listing page*

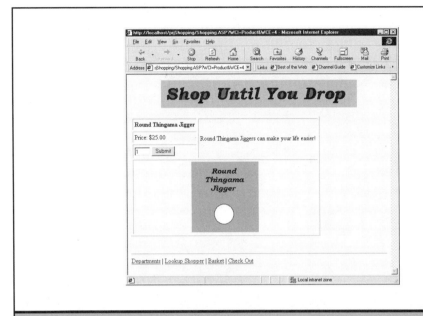

Figure 18-3.   *Nonsale item product page*

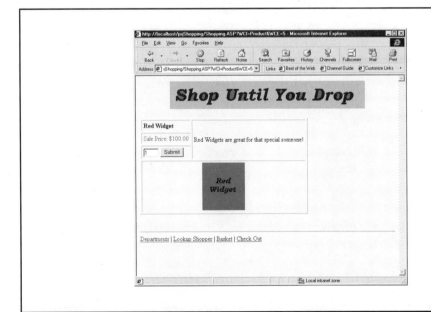

Figure 18-4.   *Sale item product page*

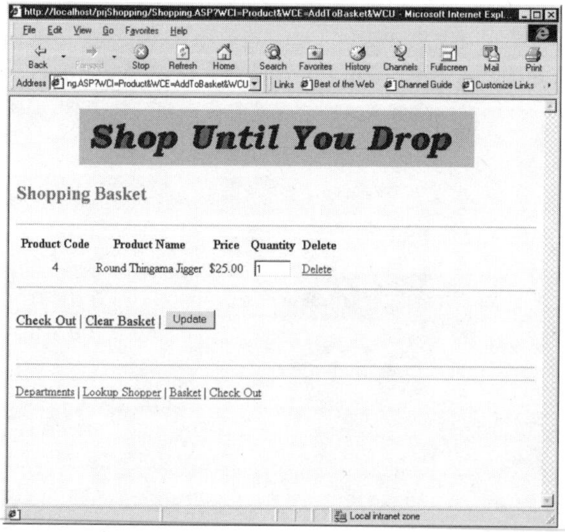

Figure 18-5. *Basket with one item*

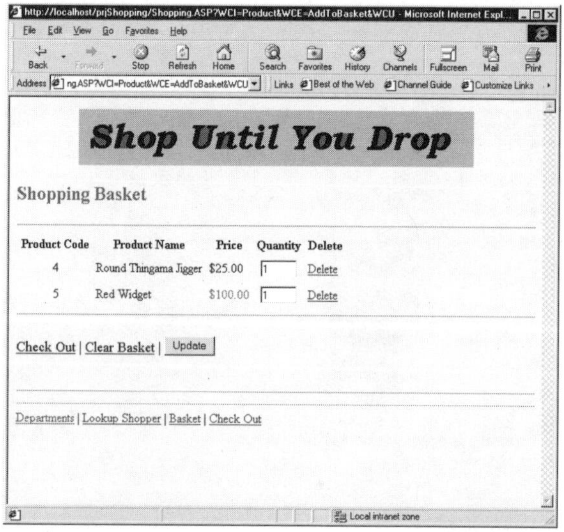

Figure 18-6. *Basket with two items*

Let's test the quantity updates. Enter **3** and **4** for the quantities of the items in the basket. Figure 18-7 shows the quantities updated once the Update button is clicked. The only thing we cannot do is set the quantities to be 0. They need to be at least 1.

Let's next test deleting a product. Figure 18-8 shows two items in our basket. To the right of each is a delete hyperlink to delete the appropriate item. A click on the delete hyperlink next to the Triangle Thingama Jigger will process the event and delete the item from the basket. Figure 18-9 shows the updated basket.

Now let's clear the basket. Click on the Clear Basket link at the bottom of the basket items. When you do, all the items will be deleted from the basket. Figure 18-10 shows the message displayed on the basket page.

Go ahead and add a few items to the basket so we can go through the checkout process. Figure 18-11 shows the blank checkout page. Note the shipping table and the tax notification. Go ahead and click on the Submit button before filling out any data. Figure 18-12 shows the error page that is generated.

Be sure you have already placed a couple of test orders and have some shopper data in the system. Now let's test pulling up that shopper data from the database. Click on the Lookup Shopper navigation bar link. That will take you to the shopper lookup page shown in Figure 18-13. Figure 18-14 shows the response page if you submit invalid data.

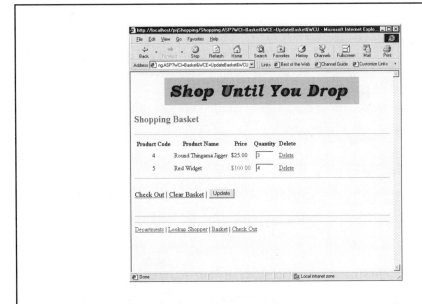

Figure 18-7. *Basket with quantity updates*

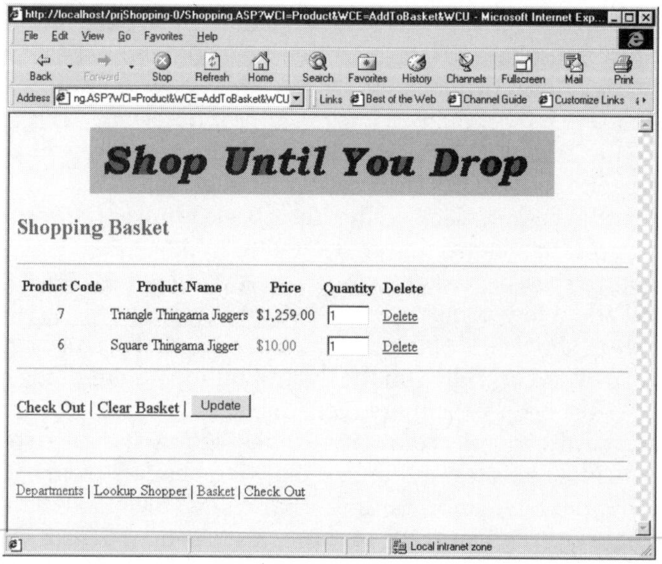

Figure 18-8. Basket before delete

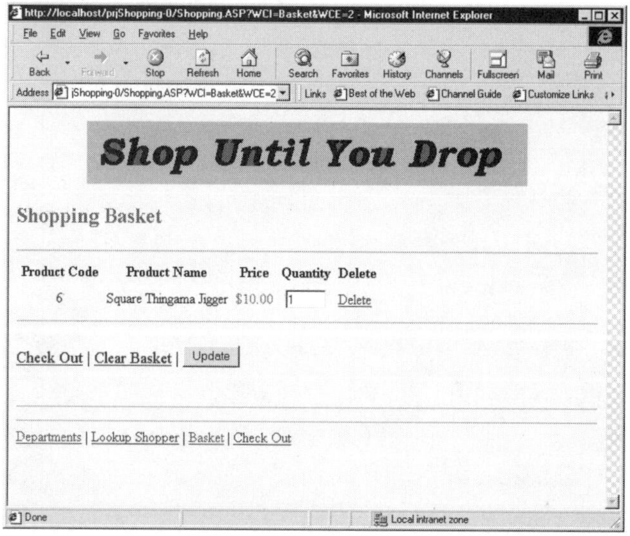

Figure 18-9. Basket after delete

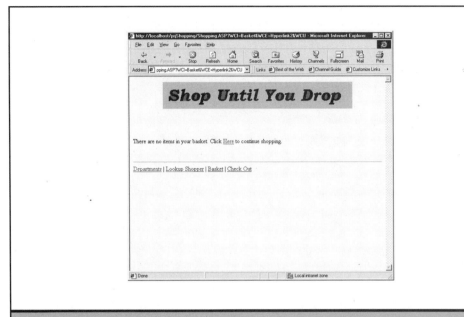

Figure 18-10.   *Basket after the clear*

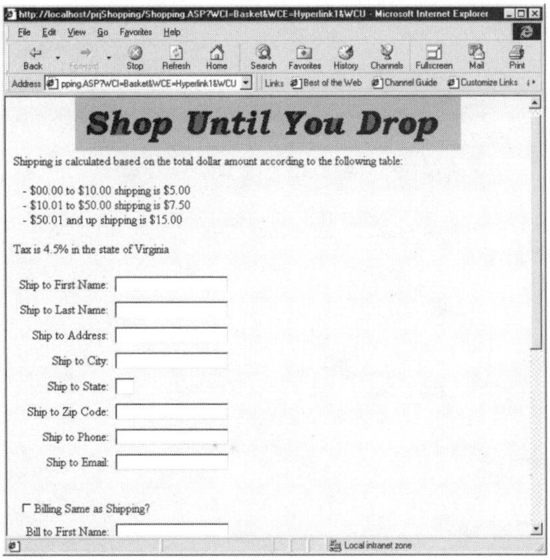

Figure 18-11.   *Blank checkout page*

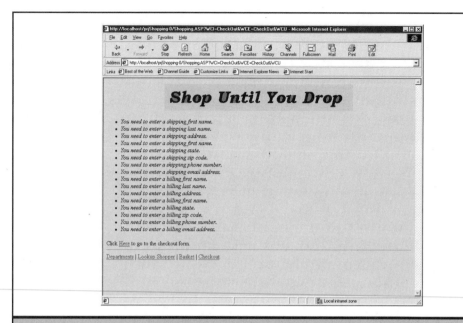

Figure 18-12. *Checkout page with an error*

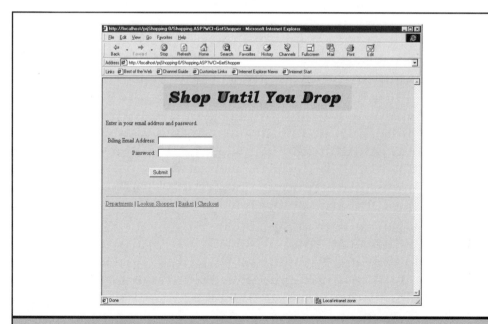

Figure 18-13. *Shopper lookup page*

Figure 18-14.   *Shopper lookup error page*

Now go back and pull up a valid record using a good billing email address and password. When you submit the form, the shopper data will be pulled from the database (see Figure 18-15). Next go to the checkout page. When you do so, the shopper data should be filled out. Figure 18-16 shows the checkout form completely filled out.

Finally, we are ready to enter our credit card data. Figure 18-17 shows the credit page. Figure 18-18 shows the page with an error if no data is entered. Go ahead and fill out the appropriate data for the credit card page. When you do so and submit the page, you will get a confirmation with the ID of the order. Figure 18-19 shows a sample page.

There are a few considerations to keep in mind when building an e-commerce system. Certainly, scalability of the application to handle a targeted number of shoppers is essential. Also, the database configuration and size may be an issue, depending on the type of traffic the store will receive.

For example, there are going to be a lot of dead baskets in the system where the user never purchased anything. You may wish to consider having an automated process to clear out old baskets that have no order ID. Also, for security reasons, you should make a decision as to how long you want to store the credit card data in the on-line database.

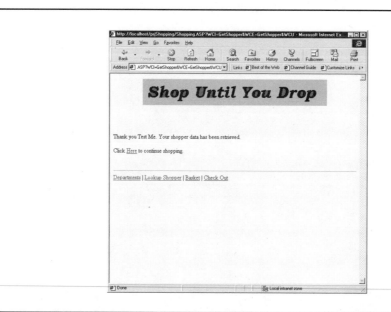

Figure 18-15. *Shopper lookup with no error*

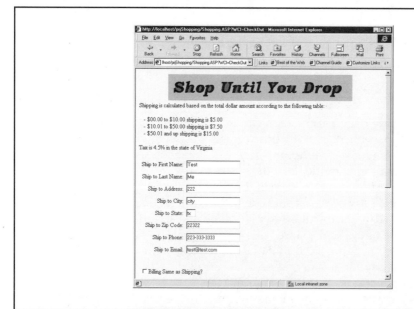

Figure 18-16. *Shopper data looked up*

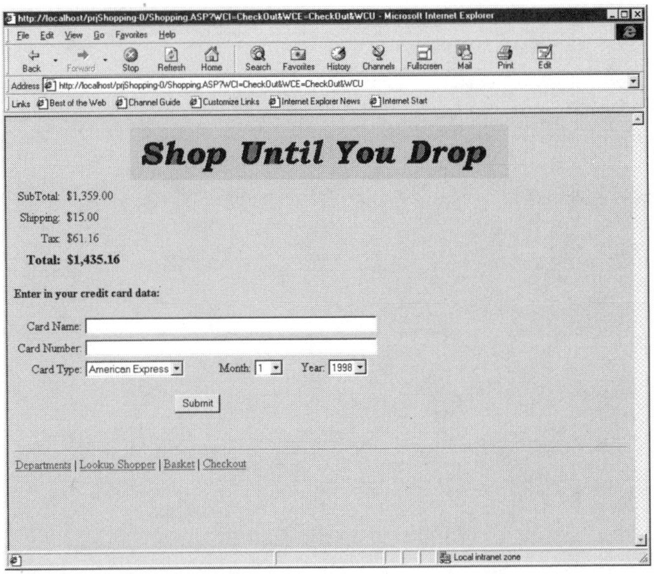

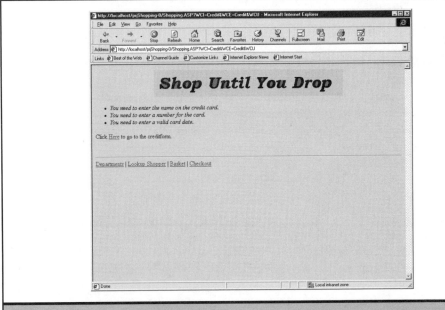

Figure 18-17.   *Credit page*

Figure 18-18.   *Credit error page*

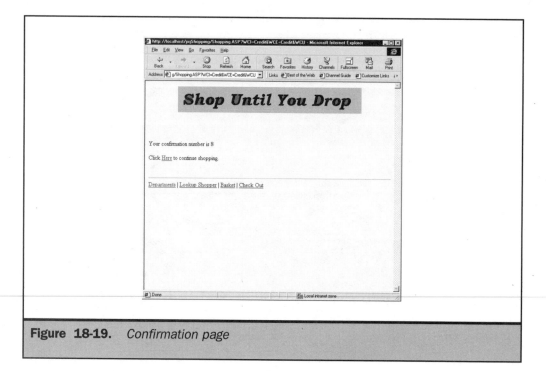

Figure 18-19.   *Confirmation page*

The number of features and options to be added to this base system is almost unlimited. You could add up-sell items, cross-sell items, product bundles, banner ads, quick pay, multiple shopping options, an on-line management system for the back end of the store, and even on-line automated credit card processing.

Also keep in mind that the browser interface provided in this example is fairly bland and will be supported by almost any browser. You can jazz up your interface with style sheets, DHTML, Java Applets, ActiveX, and much more. Have fun—the possibilities are wide open!

Summary

The e-commerce shopping system built in these final two chapters provides an excellent foundation for building a system based on an IIS application. The value of working with Visual Basic is that you have a wide range of enterprise-ready programming tools to integrate your shopping system with any existing systems you may have in place.

If you are already involved in Information Technology for retailing/selling development with Visual Basic, you have an excellent opportunity to use IIS applications to integrate that technology on-line. Visual Basic has become one of the most popular programming tools on the market today, and there is no reason why it shouldn't be your first choice when moving to the Internet as well.

What's Next

That is it! In this book we have covered everything from the simplest of VB forms to the power of e-commerce on-line. No matter what your targeted use of Visual Basic, you will find something that will meet your development requirements. And if you have been developing in VB for a while, take a close look at the many new Internet and data access features. There is no doubt that Visual Basic 6 is a powerful tool for enterprise-level development.

The Complete Reference

Visual
Basic 6

Part V

Appendixes

Appendix A

Active Server Pages Object Model and Installable Components

This appendix outlines the six built-in Active Server Pages objects available in your IIS applications or, conversely, in Active Server Pages programming. The last section describes some useful components in IIS 4.

Application

The following table describes the components of the Application object. Note that within the context of building IIS applications, you may want to consider using the web class start and terminate events as surrogates for the application OnStart and OnEnd events. You can still set application-level variables at that stage.

Collections	Description
Contents	Contains all the items that have been added to the application through script commands. This will include application variables, objects, etc.
StaticObjects	Contains all the objects added to the session with the <OBJECT> tag.
Methods	
Lock	Prevents other clients from modifying application object properties.
UnLock	Allows other clients to modify application object properties.
Events	
Application_OnEnd	Occurs when the application quits, after the Session_OnEnd event. Only the Application and Server built-in objects are available. Use this event to manage the closing of any objects when your Active Server Pages application is closing. This may include writing any cached data to a database, etc.
Application_OnStart	Occurs before the first new session is created, that is, before the Session_OnStart event. Only the Application and Server built-in objects are available. Referencing the Session, Request, or Response objects in the Application_OnStart event script causes an error. Use the OnStart event to build any application-level global variables, objects, connections, etc., when the Active Server Pages application is loading.

ObjectContext

You can use the ObjectContext object either to commit or abort a transaction, managed by Microsoft Transaction Server (MTS), that has been initiated by a script contained in an ASP page. When an ASP contains the @TRANSACTION directive, the page runs in a transaction and does not finish processing until the transaction either succeeds completely or fails.

Methods	Description
SetComplete	Declares that the script is not aware of any reason for the transaction not to complete. If all components participating in the transaction also call SetComplete, the transaction will complete.
SetAbort	Declares that the transaction initiated by the script has not completed and the resources should not be updated.

Events	
OnTransactionCommit	Occurs after a transacted script's transaction commits. When the OnTransactionCommit event occurs, IIS will process the script's OnTransactionCommit subroutine, if it exists.
OnTransactionAbort	Occurs if the transaction is aborted. When the OnTransactionAbort event occurs, IIS will process the script's OnTransactionAbort subroutine, if it exists.

Request

Throughout all of the server-side Web programming in this book, the Request object was key in interfacing with the data entered by the user. There are many collections, properties, and methods we didn't utilize that are at your disposal.

Collections	Description
ClientCertificate	The values of fields stored in the client certificate that is sent in the HTTP request.
Cookies	The values of cookies sent in the HTTP request.

Form	The values of form elements in the HTTP request body.
QueryString	The values of variables in the HTTP query string.
ServerVariables	The values of predetermined environment variables.

Properties

TotalBytes	Read-only. Specifies the total number of bytes the client is sending in the body of the request.

Methods

BinaryRead	Retrieves data sent to the server from the client as part of a POST request.

Response

The Response object was also key in building our IIS applications. It allows the developer to customize content back out to the user. For example, cookies can be set and data written to the page.

Properties	Description
Buffer	Indicates whether page output is buffered. When page output is buffered, the server does not send a response to the client until all of the server scripts on the current page have been processed, or until the Flush or End method has been called.
CacheControl	Determines whether proxy servers are able to cache the output generated by ASP.
Charset	Appends the name of the character set to the content-type header.
ContentType	Specifies the HTTP content type for the response.
Expires	Specifies the length of time before a page cached on a browser expires.
ExpiresAbsolute	Specifies the date and time on which a page cached on a browser expires.
IsClientConnected	Indicates whether the client has disconnected from the server.

Pics	Adds the value of a PICS label to the pics-label field of the response header.
Status	Contains the value of the status line returned by the server.

Methods

AddHeader	Sets the HTML header *name* to *value*.
AppendToLog	Adds a string to the end of the Web server log entry for this request.
BinaryWrite	Writes the given information to the current HTTP output without any character-set conversion.
Clear	Erases any buffered HTML output.
End	Stops processing the .asp file and returns the current result.
Flush	Sends buffered output immediately.
Redirect	Sends a redirect message to the browser, causing it to try and connect to a different URL.
Write	Writes a variable to the current HTTP output as a string.

Tip   *The Buffer property cannot be set after the server has sent output to the client. For this reason, the call to Response.Buffer should be the first line of the .asp file.*

Server

The Server object provides access to methods and properties on the server. Most of these methods and properties serve as utility functions.

Properties

ScriptTimeOut	The amount of time that a script can run before it times out.

Methods

CreateObject	Creates an instance of a server component.
HTMLEncode	Applies HTML encoding to the specified string.

MapPath	Maps the specified virtual path—either the absolute path on the current server or the path relative to the current page—into a physical path.
URLEncode	Applies URL encoding rules, including escape characters, to the string.

Session

You can use the Session object to store information needed for a particular user session. Variables stored in the Session object are not discarded when the user jumps between pages in the application; instead, these variables persist for the entire user session.

Note	*The Session object is used to retain settings of an IIS application if you have selected state to be kept between pages.*

The Web server automatically creates a Session object when a Web page from the application is requested by a user who does not already have a session. The server destroys the Session object when the session expires or is abandoned.

Collections	Description
Contents	Contains the items you have added to the session with script commands.
StaticObjects	Contains the objects created with the <OBJECT> tag and given session scope.

Properties	
CodePage	The code page that will be used for symbol mapping.
LCID	The locale identifier.
SessionID	Returns the session identification for this user.
Timeout	The duration of a time-out for the session state for this application, in minutes.

Methods	
Abandon	Destroys a Session object and releases its resources.

Events	
Session_OnEnd	Occurs when a session is abandoned or times out. Of the server built-in objects, only the Application, Server, and Session objects are available.

Session_OnStart

Occurs when the server creates a new session. The server processes this script prior to executing the requested page. The Session_OnStart event is a good time for you to set any sessionwide variables, because they will be set before any pages are accessed. All the built-in objects (Application, ObjectContext, Request, Response, Server, and Session) are available and can be referenced in the Session_OnStart event script.

IIS 4 Components

Internet Information Server 4 includes various components for building additional functionality in your applications. For example, you can use the ad rotator to implement a simple advertising system, the browser capabilities component to check out a browser, and much more. Explore each to see how you can enhance your applications.

Component	Description
Ad Rotator	Creates an AdRotator object that automatically rotates advertisements displayed on a page according to a specified schedule.
Browser Capabilities	Creates a BrowserType object that determines the capabilities, type, and version of each browser that accesses your Web site.
Database Access	Provides access to databases using ActiveX Data Objects (ADO).
Content Linking	Creates a NextLink object that creates tables of contents for Web pages and links them sequentially like pages in a book.
File Access Component	Provides access to file input and output.
Collaboration Data Objects for NTS Component	Lets you quickly and easily add the ability to send and receive messages to your Web page. This component is only available on Internet Information Server for Windows NTServer.
Tools	Creates a Tools object that provides utilities for adding sophisticated functionality to your Web pages.

APPENDIXES

Status	Creates a Status object that has properties containing server status information. Currently, this server status is only available on Personal Web Server for Macintosh.
MyInfo	Creates a MyInfo object that keeps track of personal information, such as the site administrator's name, address, and display choices.
Counters	Creates a Counters object that can create, store, increment, and retrieve any number of individual counters.
Content Rotator	Automates the rotation of HTML content strings on a Web page.
Page Counter	Counts and displays the number of times a Web page has been opened.
Permission Checker	Uses the password authentication protocols provided in Microsoft Internet Information Server (IIS) to determine whether a Web user has been granted permissions to read a file.

Appendix B

Visual Basic
Application Types

Type	Description
Standard EXE	Creates a standard executable file.
ActiveX EXE	Creates an ActiveX EXE file.
ActiveX DLL	Creates an ActiveX DLL file.
ActiveX control	Creates an ActiveX control.
VB Application wizard	Generates a new, fully functional application from which you build a more complex application. You are taken through a series of steps to create your application.
VB wizard manager	Creates a framework of steps in your wizard and helps you manage the order in which they will appear when the wizard is run. You add your code to the framework to perform the actual tasks. The resulting wizards look and operate like other wizards.
Data project	Starts a new standard EXE project with a data environment and data form loaded.
IIS application	Creates an Internet Information Server application that will run on a Web server running IIS 3/4.
Add-in	Creates a framework for building a Visual Basic add-in.
ActiveX document DLL	Creates an ActiveX document that will run in-process as a DLL file in the document manager.
ActiveX document EXE	Creates an ActiveX document that will run out of process as an EXE file.
DHTML application	Creates a Dynamic HTML project with a DHTML page designer for building client-side Internet Explorer Web applications.
VB Enterprise Edition controls	Loads all the enterprise-level controls in a new project.

Table B-1. *Visual Basic Application Types*

The Complete Reference

Visual Basic 6

Appendix C

Visual Basic ActiveX Controls

Control	Description
Animation	Handles playing of AVI video files. AVI files with sound are not supported.
Communications	Allows you to add both simple serial port communication functionality to your application and advanced functionality to create a full-featured, event-driven communications tool.
CoolBar	Allows you to create user-configurable toolbars similar to those found in Internet Explorer.
DataRepeater	Creates a data bound user control that allows the user to view one record in a database. The DataRepeater control "repeats" the user control by creating multiple instances of it in a scrolling view, allowing the user to view several records at once.
DateTimePicker	Provides a drop-down calendar to users, useful for date or time input.
FlatScrollBar	Provides an alternative to the original VscrollBar and HscrollBar controls. It features hot tracking— the scroll bar changes appearance as the cursor hovers over it.
ImageCombo	Provides functionality similar to the standard ComboBox control, with the addition of an image, so you can easily distinguish items in a list.
ImageList	Lets you manage images by adding them to the control. You can insert pictures at design time or run time and access them at run time.
Internet Transfer	Transfers files to and from a remote computer using the HTTP or FTP protocol.
ListView	Displays data as ListItem objects. Each ListItem object can have an optional icon associated with the label of the object.
MAPI	Supports the Message Application Program Interface (MAPI) to provide email applications for your customers.

Table C-1.   *Visual Basic ActiveX Controls*

Control	Description
Masked Edit	Creates mask patterns that prompt users for date, time, currency, or customized data input such as phone numbers.
MonthView	Presents a graphical representation of a calendar for easy input of dates into any application.
MSChart	Allows you to plot data in charts. You can create a chart by setting data in the control's properties page, or by retrieving data to be plotted from another source, such as an Excel spreadsheet.
Multimedia	Allows you to manage Media Control Interface (MCI) devices. These devices include sound boards, MIDI sequencers, CD-ROM drives, audio players, videodisc players, and videotape recorders and players.
PictureClip	Acts as an image resource for other Visual Basic controls by storing multiple images in a single image resource and then retrieving individual images by "clipping" specific regions.
ProgressBar	Provides progress status capabilities through different formats.
RichTextBox	Allows you to load and create Rich Text Format (RTF) data in your Visual Basic application.
Slider	Allows you to set values. Basic operation includes setting Min and Max values and allowing the user to select a range of data.
StatusBar	Lets you add Panel objects to the Panels collection, and program text and images to be displayed in the control. You can set the Style property to automatically view keyboard status, time, and date.
SysInfo	Allows you to detect system events such as desktop resizing, resolution changes, time changes, or to provide operating system platform and version information.

Table C-1.   *Visual Basic ActiveX Controls* (continued)

Control	Description
Tabbed Dialog	Provides a tabbed interface for managing multiple tab interfaces for user presentation.
TabStrip	Acts like the dividers in a notebook or the labels on a group of file folders. You can define multiple pages for the same area of a window or dialog box in your application.
ToolBar	Lets you give users quick access to frequently used operations. You can add Button objects to the control and associate images, text, and tool tips with each button. You can also allow the user to reconfigure the toolbar by setting the AllowCustomize property.
TreeView	Displays data that is hierarchical in nature, such as organization trees, the entries in an index, or the files and directories on a disk.
UpDown	Provides a pair of arrow buttons that the user can click to increment or decrement a value, such as a scroll position or a number displayed in a buddy control. The buddy control can be any other kind of control, as long as it has a property that can be updated by the UpDown control.
WinSock	Allows you to connect to a remote machine and exchange data using either the User Datagram Protocol (UDP) or the Transmission Control Protocol (TCP). Both protocols can be used to create client and server applications.

Table C-1.   *Visual Basic ActiveX Controls* (continued)

Index

F

I

P

U

About the CD

The CD included with this book contains all of the source code for the sample exercises. All of the code is in Visual Basic 6.0 format with some corresponding HTML web pages. The CD is organized by chapter and sample number. For example, to see the first sample exercise in Chapter 4, you would go to the Chapter 4 directory on the CD and go to the sample1 directory. In the book text, look for the CD Icon to indicate when the source code will be found on the CD.

Many of the sample exercises will run directly off of the CD. Some of the samples will need to have appropriate ODBC DSNs setup for database connectivity. Look for readme.txt files on the CD for other specific information regarding an exercise.

The IIS Application examples on the CD have to be copied to your local system to run since data is written out to the disk each time the application is run.

If you copy samples from the CD to your local hard drive, you will need to set the file attribute to not be 'Read Only.' To do this, right-click on the files copied from the CD and select the 'Properties' option. On the 'General' tab of the properties dialogue, uncheck the 'Read Only' attribute.

You will find a wealth of different projects on the CD. Highlights include a starter project tracking system (Chapters 12 and 13) and an e-commerce shopping basket system (Chapter 18). All of the code is fully commented with the necessary SQL Scripts and MDB for working with the associated database.

WARNING: BEFORE OPENING THE DISC PACKAGE, CAREFULLY READ THE TERMS AND CONDITIONS OF THE FOLLOWING COPYRIGHT STATEMENT AND LIMITED CD-ROM WARRANTY.

Copyright Statement

This software is protected by both United States copyright law and international copyright treaty provision. Except as noted in the contents of the CD-ROM, you must treat this software just like a book. However, you may copy it into a computer to be used and you may make archival copies of the software for the sole purpose of backing up the software and protecting your investment from loss. By saying, "just like a book," The McGraw-Hill Companies, Inc. ("Osborne/McGraw-Hill") means, for example, that this software may be used by any number of people and may be freely moved from one computer location to another, so long as there is no possibility of its being used at one location or on one computer while it is being used at another. Just as a book cannot be read by two different people in two different places at the same time, neither can the software be used by two different people in two different places at the same time.

Limited Warranty

Osborne/McGraw-Hill warrants the physical compact disc enclosed herein to be free of defects in materials and workmanship for a period of sixty days from the purchase date. If the CD included in your book has defects in materials or workmanship, please call McGraw-Hill at 1-800-217-0059, 9am to 5pm, Monday through Friday, Eastern Standard Time, and McGraw-Hill will replace the defective disc.

The entire and exclusive liability and remedy for breach of this Limited Warranty shall be limited to replacement of the defective disc, and shall not include or extend to any claim for or right to cover any other damages, including but not limited to, loss of profit, data, or use of the software, or special incidental, or consequential damages or other similar claims, even if Osborne/McGraw-Hill has been specifically advised of the possibility of such damages. In no event will Osborne/McGraw-Hill's liability for any damages to you or any other person ever exceed the lower of the suggested list price or actual price paid for the license to use the software, regardless of any form of the claim.

OSBORNE/McGRAW-HILL SPECIFICALLY DISCLAIMS ALL OTHER WARRANTIES, EXPRESS OR IMPLIED, INCLUDING BUT NOT LIMITED TO, ANY IMPLIED WARRANTY OF MERCHANTABILITY OR FITNESS FOR A PARTICULAR PURPOSE. Specifically, Osborne/McGraw-Hill makes no representation or warranty that the software is fit for any particular purpose, and any implied warranty of merchantability is limited to the sixty-day duration of the Limited Warranty covering the physical disc only (and not the software), and is otherwise expressly and specifically disclaimed.

This limited warranty gives you specific legal rights; you may have others which may vary from state to state. Some states do not allow the exclusion of incidental or consequential damages, or the limitation on how long an implied warranty lasts, so some of the above may not apply to you.

This agreement constitutes the entire agreement between the parties relating to use of the Product. The terms of any purchase order shall have no effect on the terms of this Agreement. Failure of Osborne/McGraw-Hill to insist at any time on strict compliance with this Agreement shall not constitute a waiver of any rights under this Agreement. This Agreement shall be construed and governed in accordance with the laws of New York. If any provision of this Agreement is held to be contrary to law, that provision will be enforced to the maximum extent permissible, and the remaining provisions will remain in force and effect.

NO TECHNICAL SUPPORT IS PROVIDED WITH THIS CD-ROM.